REIMAGINING APOCALYPTICISM

EARLY JUDAISM AND ITS LITERATURE

Ariel Feldman and Timothy J. Sandoval, General Editors

Editorial Board:
Randall D. Chesnutt
Atar Livneh
Daniel Machiela
Carol Newsom

Number 57

REIMAGINING APOCALYPTICISM

Apocalyptic Literature in the Dead Sea Scrolls and Related Writings

Edited by
Lorenzo DiTommaso and Matthew Goff

SBL PRESS

Atlanta

Copyright © 2023 by SBL Press

All rights reserved. No part of this work may be reproduced or transmitted in any form or by any means, electronic or mechanical, including photocopying and recording, or by means of any information storage or retrieval system, except as may be expressly permitted by the 1976 Copyright Act or in writing from the publisher. Requests for permission should be addressed in writing to the Rights and Permissions Office, SBL Press, 825 Houston Mill Road, Atlanta, GA 30329 USA.

Library of Congress Control Number: 2023940933

לאוהב אמונה אין מחיר
ואין משקל לטובתו

For a faithful friend there is no price,
And for his goodness there is no measure.

Ben Sira 6:15 (MS A II recto, line 17)
(translation based on Rey and Reymond,
Critical Edition of the Hebrew Manuscripts of Ben Sira)

For Jim Aitken, our friend

Contents

Preface xi
Abbreviations xiii

Introduction: Reimagining "Apocalypticism" and
    Rethinking "Apocalyptic"
    Lorenzo DiTommaso and Matthew Goff 1

Part 1: Apocalypse and Its Discontents: Texts, Contexts, and Retrospectives

Apocalypses in the Dead Sea Scrolls
    John J. Collins 35

"The Heavens Were Opened and I Saw Visions of God":
The Open Heaven—Four Decades On
    Christopher Rowland 61

Revealed Things in Apocalyptic Literature
    Lorenzo DiTommaso 85

Revelatory Literature, in Which a Revelation Is Mediated by an
    Otherworldly Being: Revelation in the Dead Sea Scrolls
    Stefan Beyerle 111

Qumran and the Apocalyptic
    Devorah Dimant 129

Apocalypse and Authoritative Literatures in Second
    Temple Judaism
    Armin Lange 143

The Use of Genre for Many Text Meanings:
   Apocalypse and 1 Enoch
   Alex Samely 157

   Part 2. Apocalyptic Texts and Traditions in Ancient Judaism

Aramaic as a Language of Antediluvian Wisdom:
   The Early Enoch Apocalypses, Astronomy, and the
   Deep Past in the Hellenistic Near East
   Matthew Goff 199

Daniel Traditions and the Qumran Movement?
   Reconsidering the Interface between Texts, Traditions,
   Identities, and Movements
   Andrew B. Perrin 233

It's the End of the World (as the Persians Know It)?
   Iranian Influence on Jewish Apocalypticism in Light of
   the Complete Publication of the Dead Sea Scrolls
   Jason M. Silverman 257

A New Proposal: Rereading Dreams and Visions in
   Early Jewish Literature (4Q530, 4Q544, 4Q204, and
   1 Enoch 1–36)
   Frances Flannery 281

Immersing Oneself in the Narrative World of Second
   Temple Apocalyptic Visions
   Angela Kim Harkins 297

Poor Subjects of the Hodayot: Apocalyptic Class
   Subjectivities in Practice
   G. Anthony Keddie 329

The Changing Apocalypse: Apocalyptic Literature as a
   Provisional Genre in Early Rabbinic Judaism
   Rebecca Scharbach Wollenberg 357

Part 3. The Jewish Apocalyptic Tradition and Early Christianity

Divine Kingdom: Between the Songs of the Sabbath
Sacrifice and the Synoptic Gospels
Giovanni B. Bazzana 377

Aramaica Qumranica Apocalyptica and the
Book of Revelation
Garrick V. Allen 403

Heavenly Ascent Revisited
Martha Himmelfarb 429

Apocalypses and Apocalyptic Literature in the Early Church:
Apocalypse and Apocalyptic as Rhizome
Harry O. Maier 471

The Importance of the Gnostic Apocalypses from
Nag Hammadi for the Study of Early Jewish Mysticism
Dylan M. Burns 503

Contributors 537
Ancient Sources Index 539
Modern Authors Index 567

Preface

While scholarship is often understood as the product of a solitary scholar, writing alone at a computer, the present volume is a reminder that it is frequently a collaborative enterprise. This volume collects papers presented at the International Society of Biblical Literature meeting in Berlin, 2017. The editors thank these scholars for their contributions. Several other scholars were also asked later on to include essays in this volume, which could not have been successful without their participation. We are grateful to Bob Buller and Nicole L. Tilford for helping the volume reach its final form. The insightful comments of the anonymous reader reports also improved the quality of the volume. We also acknowledge the helpful proofreading of Tommy Woodward, doctoral student at Florida State University. In addition, we thank Randy Garcia and Jordan Barr, also of Florida State University, for compiling the indices.

The work of Lorenzo DiTommaso on this project was facilitated by major research grants from the Social Sciences and Humanities Research Council of Canada (2011-16, 2018-24).

Abbreviations

1 En.	1 Enoch
2 En.	2 Enoch
2 Bar.	2 Baruch
3 Bar.	3 Baruch
3 En.	3 Enoch
AB	Anchor Bible
ABD	Freedman, David Noel, ed. *Anchor Bible Dictionary*. 6 vols. New York: Doubleday, 1992.
ABR	*Australian Biblical Review*
Ad. Const.	Hilary of Poitiers, *Ad Constantius*
ADPV	Abhandlungen des Deutschen Palästina-Vereins
AFLNW	Arbeitsgemeinschaft für Forschung des Landes Nordrhein-Westfalen
AIL	Ancient Israel and Its Literature
A.J.	Josephus, *Antiquitates judaicae*
AJEC	Ancient Judaism and Early Christianity
Allogenes	Allogenes the Stranger
An.	Iamblichus, *De anima*; Tertullian, *De anima*
ANEM	Ancient Near East Monographs
ANES	Ancient Near Eastern Studies
ANF	Roberts, Alexander, and James Donaldson, eds. *The Ante-Nicene Fathers: Translations of the Writings of the Fathers Down to A.D. 325*. 10 vols. 1885–1887.
ANRW	Temporini, Hildegard, and Wolfgang Haase, eds. *Aufstieg und Niedergang der römischen Welt: Geschichte und Kultur Roms im Spiegel der neueren Forschung*. Part 2, *Principat*. Berlin: de Gruyter, 1972–.
AOS	American Oriental Series
Apoc. Abr.	Apocalypse of Abraham
Apoc. Paul	Apocalypse of Paul

Apol.	Tertullian, *Apologeticus*
ARSHLL	Acta Regiae Societatis Humaniorum Litterarum Lundensis
AS	*Aramaic Studies*
Ascen. Isa.	Ascension of Isaiah
AYB	Anchor Yale Bible
b.	Babylonian Talmud
BA	*Biblical Archaeologist*
BAC	Biblioteca de autores cristianos
BagM.	Baghdader Mitteilungen
Barn.	Barnabas
BASOR	*Bulletin of the American Schools of Oriental Research*
BBA	Berliner Byzantinische Arbeiten
BBB	Bonner biblische Beiträge
BBR	*Bulletin for Biblical Research*
BCNH	Bibliothèque copte de Nag Hammadi
BDB	Brown, Francis, Samuel R. Driver, and Charles Briggs, *A Hebrew and English Lexicon of the Old Testament*. Peabody: Hendrickson, 1997.
BEHER	Bibliothèque de l'École des hautes études: Sciences religieuses
BeO	*Bibbia e oriente*
Ber.	Berakhot
BERG	Beiträge zur europäischen Religionsgeschicte
BETL	Bibliotheca Ephemeridum Theologicarum Lovaniensium
BEvT	Beiträge zur evangelischen Theologie
Bib	*Biblica*
Bib. hist.	Diodorus Siculus, *Bibliotheca historica*
BibInt	*Biblical Interpretation*
BIOSCS	*Bulletin of the International Organization for Septuagint and Cognate Studies*
B.J.	Josephus, *Bellum judaicum*
BJRL	*Bulletin of the John Rylands University Library of Manchester*
BJS	Brown Judaic Studies
BM	British Musuem
Bodl.	Bodleian Libraries, University of Oxford
BR	*Biblical Research*

BSJS	Brill's Series in Jewish Studies
BThS	Biblisch-Theologische Studien
BZNW	Beihefte zur Zeitschrift für die neutestamentliche Wissenschaft
Catech. Disc.	Gregory of Nyssa, *Catechetical Discourse*
CBET	Contributions to Biblical Exegesis and Theology
CBQ	*Catholic Biblical Quarterly*
CBQMS	Catholic Biblical Quarterly Monograph Series
CD	Damascus Document
CEJL	Commentaries on Early Jewish Literature
CH	*Church History*
CHANE	Culture and History of the Ancient Near East
CHJ	Cambridge History of Judaism
Chron.	Julius Africanus, *Chronographia*
Civ.	Augustine, *De civitate Dei*
Comm. Dan.	Hippolytus, *Commentarium in Danielem*; Jerome, *Commentarium in Danielem*
Comm. Jo.	Origen, *Commentarii in evangelium Joannis*
Comm. Matt.	Origen, *Commentarium in evangelium Matthaei*
Comm. Phaedr.	Damascus, *Commentary on the Phaedrus*
Comm. Rev.	Victorinus of Pettau, *Commentary on the Book of Revelation*
CQ	Church Quarterly
CRINT	Compendia Rerum Iudaicarum ad Novum Testamentum
CSCO	Corpus Scriptorum Christianorum Orientalium
CSS	Cistercian Studies Series
CT	*Cuneiform Texts from Babylonian Tablets in the British Museum*
CurBR	*Currents in Biblical Research*
DCLS	Deuterocanonical and Cognate Literature Studies
Dem. Ev.	Eusebius, *Demonstratio evangelica*
Demetr.	Cyprian, *Ad Demetrianum*
Dial.	Justin Martyr, *Dialogus cum Tryphone*; Sulpicius Severus, *Dialogues*
Did.	Didache
Div.	Cicero, *De divinatione*
DJD	Discoveries in the Judaean Desert
DSD	*Dead Sea Discoveries*

EBR	Encyclopaedia of the Bible and Its Reception
EC	*Early Christianity*
ECDSS	Eerdmans Commentaries on the Dead Sea Scrolls
Ecl. proph.	Eusebius, *Eclogae propheticae*
EDSS	Schiffman, Lawrence H., and James C. VanderKam, eds. *Encyclopedia of the Dead Sea Scrolls*. 2 vols. New York: Oxford University Press, 2000.
EIr	Yarshater, Ehsan, ed. *Encyclopaedia Iranica*. London: Routledge & Kegan Paul, 1982–.
EJL	Early Judaism and Its Literature
EJud	Neusner, Jacob, Alan J. Avery-Peck, and William Scott Green. *The Encyclopedia of Judaism*. 2nd ed. 5 vols. Leiden: Brill, 2005.
EKKNT	Evangelisch-katholischer Kommentar zum Neuen Testament
Enn.	Plotinus, *Enneades*
Ep.	*Epistle*
ETL	*Ephemerides Theologicae Lovanienses*
Exc.	Clement of Alexandria, *Excerpta ex Theodoto*
FAT	Forschungen zum Alten Testament
Fug.	Tertullian, *De fuga in persecutione*
GAP	Guides to Apocrypha and Pseudepigrapha
Gen. Apoc.	Genesis Apocrphon
Haer.	Irenaeus, *Adversus haereses*
Hag.	Hagigah
HANE/M	History of the Ancient Near East/Monographs
HBAI	*Hebrew Bible and Ancient Israel*
HdO	Handbuch der Orientalistik
Hen	*Henoch*
Herm. Mand.	Shepherd of Hermas, Mandate
Hist.	Herodotus, *Historiae*
Hist. eccl.	Eusebius, *Historia ecclesiastica*
HistTh	*History and Theory*
Hom.	Pseudo-Marcius, *Fifty Spiritual Homilies*
Hom. Lev.	Origen, *Homiliae in Leviticum*
Hom. Matt.	John Chrysostom, *Homily on Matthew*
HR	*History of Religions*
HSS	Harvard Semitic Studies
HTR	*Harvard Theological Review*

IEJ	*Israel Exploration Journal*
IELOA	Instruments pour l'étude des langues de l'Orient ancient
Inst.	Commodian, *Instructiones*; Lactantius, *Divinarum institutionum*
Int	*Interpretation*
IOS	*Israel Oriental Studies*
Is. Os.	Plutarch, *Isis and Osiris*
JAAR	*Journal of the American Academy of Religion*
JAJSup	Journal of Ancient Judaism Supplement Series
JANER	*Journal of Ancient Near Eastern Religions*
JAOC	Judaïsme ancien et origines du christianisme
JAOS	*Journal of the American Oriental Society*
JBL	*Journal of Biblical Literature*
JCP	Jewish and Christian Perspectives
JECS	*Journal of Early Christian Studies*
JHeb	*Journal of Hebrew Scriptures*
JJS	*Journal of Jewish Studies*
JJTPSup	Supplements to the Journal of Jewish Thought and Philosophy
JNES	*Journal of Near Eastern Studies*
JPS	*Journal of Persianate Studies*
JQR	*Jewish Quarterly Review*
JRS	*Journal of Roman Studies*
JS	Jüdische Studien
JSJ	*Journal for the Study of Judaism in the Persian, Hellenistic, and Roman Periods*
JSJSup	Journal for the Study of Judaism in the Persian, Hellenistic, and Roman Periods Supplement Series
JSNT	*Journal for the Study of the New Testament*
JSNTSup	Journal for the Study of the New Testament Supplement Series
JSOTSup	Journal for the Study of the Old Testament Supplement Series
JSP	*Journal for the Study of the Pseudepigrapha*
JSPSup	Journal for the Study of the Pseudepigrapha Supplement Series
JSS	*Journal of Semitic Studies*

JSSEA	*Journal of the Society for the Study of Egyptian Antiquities*
JTS	*Journal of Theological Studies*
Jub.	Jubilees
KAI	Donner, Herbert, and Wolfgang Röllig. *Kanaanäische und aramäische Inschriften*. 2nd ed. Wiesbaden: Harrassowitz, 1966–1969.
LAB	Liber antiquitatum biblicarum
Ladd. Jac.	Ladder of Jacob
LCL	Loeb Classical Library
LHBOTS	The Library of Hebrew Bible/Old Testament Studies
LNTS	The Library of New Testament Studies
LSTS	The Library of Second Temple Studies
LUÅ	Lunds Universitets Årsskrift
m.	Mishnah
Mars.	Marsanes
Meg.	Megillah
Midr. Ps.	Midrash Psalms
MnemosyneSup	Mnemosyne Supplement Series
Mort.	Lactantius, *De mortibus persecutorum*
Mos.	Gregory of Nyssa, *De Vita Moses*
MTSR	*Method and Theory in the Study of Religion*
Myst.	Iamblichus, *De mysteriis Ægyptiorum*
Nat. Rulers	Nature of the Rulers
NBS	Numen Book Series
Neot	*Neotestamentica*
NHMS	Nag Hammadi and Manichean Studies
NHS	Nag Hammadi Studies
NJPS	*Tanakh: The Holy Scriptures: The New JPS Translation according to the Traditional Hebrew Text*
NovT	*Novum Testamentum*
NovTSup	Supplements to Novum Testamentum
NTOA	Novum Testamentum et Orbis Antiquus
OLA	Orientalia Lovaniensia Analecta
Orig. World	On the Origin of the World
OTE	*Old Testament Essays*
OTM	Oxford Theological Monographs
OTP	Charlesworth, James H., ed. *The Old Testament Pseudepigrapha*. 2 vols. Garden City: Doubleday, 1983, 1985.

P. Mich.	Michigan Papyri
P. Oxy.	Oxyrhynchus Papyri
PA	Philosophia antiqua
Paenit.	John Chrysostom, *De paenitentia*
PAM	Palestine Archaeological Museum
PBA	Proceedings of the British Academy
Praep. ev.	Eusebius, *Praeparatio evangelica*
Pss. Sol.	Psalms of Solomon
PTSDSSP	Princeton Theological Seminary Dead Sea Scrolls Project
PtSt	Patristic Studies
RAC	Klauser, Theodor, et al., eds. *Reallexikon für Antike und Christentum*. Stuttgart: Hiersemann, 1950–.
RB	*Revue biblique*
REJ	*Revue des études juives*
Res.	Tertullian, *De resurrectione carnis*
ResOr	*Res Orientales*
RevQ	*Revue de Qumran*
RGRW	Religions in the Graeco-Roman World
RMP	*Rheinisches Museum für Philologie*
RS	Religion and Society
SAAS	State Archives of Assyria Studies
Sanh.	Sanhedrin
SBLSP	Society of Biblical Literature Seminar Papers
SBM	Stuttgarter biblische Monographien
SBS	Stuttgarter Bibelstudien
SC	Sources Chrétiennes
SCS	Septuagint and Cognate Studies
SECA	Studies on Early Christian Apocrypha
Sem	*Semitica*
SHR	Studies in the History of Religions
Sib. Or.	Sibylline Oracles
SJLA	Studies in Judaism in Late Antiquity
SNT	Studien zum Neuen Testament
SNTSMS	Society for New Testament Studies Monograph Series
SPNPT	Studies in Platonism, Neoplatonism, and the Platonic Tradition
SSAWL	Sitzungsberichte der sächsischen Akademie der Wissenschaften zu Leipzig

SSN	Studia Semitica Neerlandica
STAC	Studien und Texte zu Antike und Christentum
STDJ	Studies on the Texts of the Desert of Judah
Steles Seth	Three Steles of Seth
STJHC	Studies and Texts in Jewish History and Culture
StJud	Studia Judaeoslavica
StPatrSup	Studia Patristica Supplement
SVTP	Studia in Veteris Testamenti Pseudepigraphica
Symp.	Methodius of Olympus, *Symposium*
SymS	Symposium Series
T. Abr.	Testament of Abraham
T. Ash.	Testament of Asher
T. Isaac	Testament of Isaac
T. Jacob	Testament of Jacob
T. Jud.	Testament of Judah
T. Levi	Testament of Levi
T. Reu.	Testament of Reuben
T. Sim.	Testament of Simeon
TAD	Porten, Bezalel, and Ada Yardeni, eds. *Textbook of Aramaic Documents from Ancient Egypt*. 4 vols. Jerusalem: Hebrew University, Dept. of the History of the Jewish People, 1986–1999.
Three Forms	Three Forms of First Thought
TKH	Theologie–Kultur–Hermeneutik
TLZ	*Theologische Literaturzeitung*
TSAJ	Texte und Studien zum antiken Judentum
TUGAL	Texte und Untersuchungen zur Geschichte der altchristlichen Literatur
TWQ	*Theologisches Wörterbuch zu den Qumrantexten*
VC	*Vigiliae Christianae*
VCSup	Supplements to Vigiliae Christianae
Virg.	Gregory of Nyssa, *De virginitate*
Vit. Plot.	Porphyry, *Vita Plotini*
VT	*Vetus Testamentum*
VTSup	Supplements to Vetus Testamentum
WGRWSup	Writings from the Greco-Roman World Supplement Series
WUNT	Wissenschaftliche Untersuchungen zum Neuen Testament

y.	Jerusalem Talmud
Yad.	Yadayim
ZAC	*Zeitschrift für Antikes Christentum/Journal of Ancient Christianity*
ZAH	*Zeitschrift für Althebräistik*
Zost.	Zostrianos

Introduction:
Reimagining "Apocalypticism" and Rethinking "Apocalyptic"

Lorenzo DiTommaso and Matthew Goff

With the full corpus of the Dead Sea Scrolls now available, it is time to take stock of their impact on the study of early Jewish and Christian apocalyptic literature. This volume, *Reimagining Apocalypticism: Apocalypses, Apocalyptic Literature, and the Dead Sea Scrolls*, examines the ways in which the Scrolls have altered our views on apocalyptic speculation and things apocalyptic. Can the apocalyptic writings of ancient Judaism and Christianity still be examined meaningfully with reference to the genre apocalypse? How have the Scrolls caused us to reconsider the world of apocalyptic and the registers of apocalyptic rhetoric? Has the new evidence shed light on the function of apocalyptic writings and the communities and the social contexts in which these writings were produced? Has the reevaluation of the forms, contents, and settings of apocalyptic literature changed (or reinforced) how the subject is approached in contemporary scholarship? Does the adjective *apocalyptic* remain descriptively meaningful and diagnostically useful?

These and other questions are raised by the central fact that the Dead Sea Scrolls reveal the existence of an apocalyptically-minded community that antedates Christianity by perhaps a century. The self-designation *yaḥad* ("community") likely was used by several groups of traditionalist observant Jews who shared a coherent theological outlook. The core group is probably to be identified with the Essenes, who are mentioned in the Jewish and Roman sources of the era. The most plausible model suggests that the *yaḥad* was founded in the second or third quarter of the first century BCE. Its historical memory, though, reached back to the seismic events of the Maccabean Revolt of circa 167–160 BCE and the Hasmonean usurpation of the kingship and the high priesthood in the decades that followed. Whatever its origin, it is certain that the Dead Sea sect did not survive the Great Jewish Revolt of 66–73 CE, when the Scrolls were deposited in the caves near Qumran in an attempt to shelter them from the Roman legions.

Roughly 30 percent of the writings preserved in the Dead Sea Scrolls are sectarian; that is, they were composed by the members of the *yaḥad* and reflect its distinctive ideas, codes, and practices. Virtually all these works were unknown to scholarship before their discovery.[1] The remainder of the writings in the Scrolls are nonsectarian. Slightly over half consist of copies of material that accords with books of the Hebrew Scriptures, including its sole apocalypse, Daniel, which is extant in eight partial manuscripts.[2] The oldest, 4QDan^c (4Q114) and 4QDan^e (4Q116), were copied in the late second century BCE, only two generations after the final redaction of the Hebrew-Aramaic version of the book in early 164 BCE. Several other texts from Qumran were regarded as authoritative or scriptural texts. These include fragmentary copies of early Enochic writings and the book of Jubilees (in Aramaic and Hebrew, respectively).[3] Although by and large forgotten in the West until their scholarly rediscovery, the importance that Enochic writings and Jubilees once had in antiquity is retained in the Ethiopian Orthodox Church, one of the oldest forms of Christianity, in which they are books of the Old Testament. The inclusion of Enochic texts and Jubilees at Qumran, along with the fact that the scriptural texts attested at Qumran exhibit a great deal of variation and pluriformity, suggests that not only was scripture important in ancient Judaism, but also that it was regarded and transmitted with a degree of textual diversity and scribal creativity not fully conveyed by the term *bib-*

---

1. Solomon Schechter identified pages from two medieval manuscript copies of the Damascus Document in the Genizah of the Ben Ezra Synagogue in Old Cairo. After the discovery of the Dead Sea Scrolls, a partial manuscript of the Songs of the Sabbath Sacrifice was discovered at Masada.

2. Peter W. Flint, "The Daniel-Tradition at Qumran," in *The Book of Daniel: Composition and Reception*, ed. John J. Collins and Peter W. Flint, VTSup 83, 2 vols. (Leiden: Brill, 2001), 2:329–67.

3. Loren T. Stuckenbruck, "The Early Traditions Related to 1 Enoch from the Dead Sea Scrolls: An Overview and Assessment," in *The Early Enoch Literature*, ed. Gabriele Boccaccini and John J. Collins, JSJSup 121 (Leiden: Brill, 2007), 41–63; James C. VanderKam, *Jubilees: A Commentary on the Book of Jubilees Chapters 1–21*, Hermeneia (Minneapolis: Fortress, 2018), 4–8.

lical, which in our culture implies a fixed and irrevocable text. The Dead Sea Scrolls also revealed a fascinating hodgepodge of other texts, such as the Genesis Apocryphon and the Temple Scroll (reworkings, respectively, of Genesis and pentateuchal law), most of which also had been previously unknown to scholars.[4]

A significant proportion of these new texts from the Dead Sea Scrolls, both sectarian and nonsectarian, have greatly enlarged the corpus of early Jewish apocalyptic literature and expanded our ideas of apocalyptic.[5] Works such as the pesharim, the Hodayot, and 4QInstruction, have challenged assumptions regarding the literary forms and contents of apocalyptic literature. Others, including the War Rule (1QM), the Community Rule (1QS), and the Son of God text (4Q246), have stretched views about themes such as cosmic dualism, the periodization of history, and expectations for messianic figures and a final eschatological battle. In addition, many of the Aramaic revelatory-visionary writings, particularly the early Enochic material, have prompted fresh proposals about the embryonic history of apocalyptic literature and the social contexts of their production.

What the Dead Sea Scrolls do not preserve, however, are any new apocalypses. An apocalypse, according to the standard definition, is:

> a genre of revelatory literature with a narrative framework, in which a revelation is mediated by an otherworldly being to a human recipient, disclosing a transcendent reality which is both temporal, insofar as it envisions eschatological salvation, and spatial as it involves another, supernatural world.

This definition was proposed by the Apocalypse Group of the Society of Biblical Literature Genres Project, led by John J. Collins. The group investigated all the texts from 250 BCE to 250 CE that had been or could be classified as apocalypses. The results of the group's research were disseminated in 1979 in the landmark volume *Semeia* 14.[6] They were later extended to a special study of early Christian apocalypses in *Semeia* 36

---

4. Here again, a few texts (the Aramaic Levi Document is a prime example) were known to scholarship before the discovery of manuscript copies in the Dead Sea caves.

5. Lorenzo DiTommaso, "Eschatology in the Early Jewish Pseudepigrapha and the Early Christian Apocrypha," in *Eschatology in Antiquity: Forms and Functions*, ed. Hilary Marlow, Karla Pollmann, and Helen Van Noorden (New York: Routledge, 2021), 235–49.

6. John J. Collins, ed., *Apocalypse: The Morphology of a Genre*, *Semeia* 14 (1979).

(1986) and refined by Collins in his magisterial 1984 volume, *The Apocalyptic Imagination*, now in its third (2016) edition.[7]

The group identified over sixty early Jewish, Christian, gnostic, and classical examples of the genre.[8] These are divided into two types: apocalypses that do not feature an otherworldly journey (type 1), and apocalypses that do (type 2). Each type is subdivided into three categories: (1) apocalypses that include a review of history and feature an eschatological crisis and "cosmic and/or political eschatology"; (2) apocalypses that display a cosmic and/or political eschatology but lack a historical review; and (3) apocalypses that feature "personal eschatology" but lack both a historical review and cosmic transformation. Collins soon abandoned the *Semeia* 14 taxonomy in favor of a less baroque classification that features only two types of apocalypses, "historical" and "otherworldly." Historical apocalypses disclose the meaning of history and its end, while otherworldly apocalypses are interested more in cosmological speculation.

The *Semeia* 14 definition was intended to bring clarity to the scholarly usage of apocalyptic terminology. It is important to stress, as Collins does in *Semeia* 14, that the definition is etic, a modern category.[9] The group self-consciously focused on literary features and not historical contexts, the logic being that one should first identity the object of study (apocalypses) and then study them in context. Collins's *Apocalyptic Imagination* is therefore a kind of phase 2 project. It begins with the ancient Jewish texts that are identified as apocalypses in *Semeia 14* and explicates them one by one in their historical-cultural contexts.

The *Semeia* 14 definition is still widely deployed by scholars. But one should not confuse the object of investigation (what one sees) with one's methodological lens (with which one sees). Recognizing the *Semeia* definition as the latter rather than the former is particularly important with respect to the Dead Sea Scrolls. The definition, having been promulgated in the 1970s, was put forward long before many of the Dead Sea Scrolls were published. The Scrolls, even those that were available at the time,

---

7. Adela Yarbro Collins, ed., *Early Christian Apocalypticism: Genre and Social Setting*, Semeia 36 (1986); John J. Collins, *The Apocalyptic Imagination: An Introduction to the Jewish Matrix of Christianity*, 3rd ed. (Grand Rapids: Eerdmans, 2016).

8. John. J. Collins, "Introduction: Towards the Morphology of the Genre," *Semeia* 14 (1979): 13–15.

9. Collins, "Introduction," 2. It is argued in *Semeia* 14 that the ancient use of *apocalypse* as a title is not a "reliable guide" to the genre.

are not prominent in *Semeia* 14.[10] One wonders: if the Genres group were doing its work today, would it define the genre apocalypse in a way that would more robustly include Qumran texts?

This does not necessarily mean that the scholarly task should be to update or revise the genre apocalypse now that all the Qumran scrolls have been published. It is also important to assess the viability of the definition now that the corpus of Dead Sea texts is available. The issue is not simply recognizing that many texts of this horde are now available. The intellectual climate of biblical studies is very different today from what it was in the 1970s. In addition to new texts, there is also more interest in methods and approaches that are popular across the humanities. This is particularly relevant with regard to the genre apocalypse, since the issue of genre and literary classification has in recent years commanded a great deal of critical reflection.[11] The authoritative status of the *Semeia* 14 definition has centralized issues of genre and literary taxonomy with regard to the study of apocalyptic literature. This raises the issue of what other approaches and insights can be gleaned if one does not prioritize genre.

In our current academic context, then, rich in new texts and newer methods, it is not simply a matter of accepting or rejecting the *Semeia* 14 definition as a point of doctrine. Rather, one should recognize its use-value as one among many intellectual approaches that may have value for interpreters. As intended, the definition gives scholars a clear and coherent framework to analyze apocalyptic texts across a range of historical periods. At the same time, other methods and approaches are possible. The value of the *Semeia* 14 definition as a heuristic tool depends on the kinds of work the individual scholar wants to do and the questions they want to ask.

---

10. One and a quarter pages of Collins's forty-page essay ("The Jewish Apocalypses," *Semeia* 14 [1979]: 48–49) are devoted to Qumran texts.

11. See, for example, Carol A. Newsom, "Spying Out the Land: A Report from Genology," in *Seeking Out the Wisdom of the Ancients: Essays Offered to Honor Michael V. Fox on the Occasion of His Sixty-Fifth Birthday*, ed. Ronald L. Troxel, Kelvin G. Friebel, and Dennis Robert Magary (Winona Lake, IN: Eisenbrauns, 2005), 437–50; and Matthew Goff, "The Apocalypse and the Sage: Assessing the Contribution of John J. Collins to the Study of Apocalypticism," in *Apocalyptic Thinking in Early Judaism: Engaging with John Collins'* The Apocalyptic Imagination, ed. Sidnie White Crawford and Cecilia Wassén, JSJSup 182 (Leiden: Brill, 2018), 8–22. Collins has also himself addressed his earlier work in light of contemporary genre theory: see John J. Collins, "Epilogue: Genre Analysis and the Dead Sea Scrolls," *DSD* 17 (2010): 389–401.

The current volume reflects in miniature the diversity and intellectual richness in the field sketched out above with respect to the Dead Sea Scrolls, now fully published, and the study of apocalypticism. Some contributors utilize the *Semeia* 14 definition as a key departure point. Other contributors, realizing that alternative constructions of the genre apocalypse are possible, offered their own proposal, often in ways that prioritize the Dead Sea Scrolls (e.g., Lange, Dimant, Samely). Other essays have rethought their earlier usage of the definition (Himmelfarb). For still other contributors, the *Semeia* 14 approach is not rejected per se but rather utilized only minimally, if at all, as contributors concentrate rather on questions for which issues of taxonomy and genre are not central (e.g., Harkins, Flannery). Having sketched out the volume as a whole and situated it in its scholarly context, we turn now to an examination of specific issues and texts raised by contributors in this volume.

Several Dead Sea revelatory texts survive in such fragmentary condition that their genre is difficult to determine. This raises the possibility that the Qumran scrolls may have included apocalypses, going by the standard definition, but the key exempla are too poorly preserved to make the genre identification with confidence. In the first essay of part 1, "Apocalypse and Its Discontents: Texts, Contexts, and Retrospectives," Collins reviews in "Apocalypses in the Dead Sea Scrolls" evidence for Qumran texts that have been considered apocalypses but are not listed in *Semeia* 14 as such. They include the New Jerusalem text, 4QPseudo-Daniel[a-b], and the Aramaic Levi Document. These texts in general exhibit some but not all of the elements that comprise the *Semeia* 14 definition of the apocalypse. Collins also explores the fact that his definition of the genre was drawn up before the publication of most of the Qumran texts from Cave 4. The recent accessibility of this material has led some scholars to revisit the definition of the genre, including Armin Lange, Ulrike Mittmann-Richert, and Bennie H. Reynolds.[12] The full publication of the Dead Sea Scrolls does not lead Collins to reject or revise his long-authoritative definition of an apocalypse. Rather, he argues that its main value with regard to scholarly reflection on the genre is "that they remind us of the fluidity of generic boundaries, and that the networks of intertextual affinities are not exhausted by our definitions."

To this statement must be added the key realization, sketched out above, that the genre apocalypse is a heuristic category. Ancient Jewish

---

12. See Armin Lange's paper for this volume, discussed below.

Introduction 7

and Christian apocalyptic literature was composed over a span of six centuries and expresses a very great diversity of themes, symbols, expectations, genres, and social settings. The cardinal question that has animated the study of ancient apocalyptic literature since the 1970s is "What is apocalyptic?"[13] But it always freights a follow-up query, "What is the most appropriate approach to the subject?" For two generations, the generic approach has often been found to offer the best answer to both questions, largely because it explains so much of the evidence very well.

Even so, the generic approach has not been universally accepted. A major criticism is its inability to shed light on the social function of the early apocalypses.[14] Objections also have been raised regarding its methodology, as well as its fixation on the genre apocalypse as opposed to revelatory literature as a class (including oracles, divination, and prophecy).[15]

The primary alternative to the generic approach has been that which Christopher Rowland outlined in his watershed 1982 volume, *The Open Heaven*.[16] Rowland defines apocalyptic, which he uses as a noun, as the revelation of heavenly mysteries. He constrains this sprawling definition somewhat by stressing the horizontal and vertical dimensions of apocalyptic texts. Horizontal refers to the axis of time and the forward march of history to its eschatological culmination. Vertical refers to the axis of space and the literature's concern "with the world above and its mysteries as a means of explaining human existence in the present."[17]

In this volume Rowland revisits the origins of his approach in "'The Heavens Were Opened and I Saw Visions of God': *The Open Heaven—*

---

13. It should also be noted that this question did not and, for the most part, still does not animate the investigation in later eras and different cultures.

14. See the summary in David A. Aune, "The Apocalypse of John and the Problem of Genre," *Semeia* 36 (1986): 65–96.

15. Aune, "Apocalypse of John"; Newsom, "Spying Out the Land"; and Gregory L. Linton, "Reading the Apocalypse as Apocalypse: The Limits of Genre," in *The Reality of Apocalypse: Rhetoric and Politics in the Book of Revelation*, ed. David L. Barr, SymS 39 (Atlanta: Society of Biblical Literature, 2006), 9–41. Collins marshals a redoubtable defense of the generic approach in his essay, "The Genre Apocalypse Reconsidered," *ZAC* 20 (2016): 21–40. For apocalypse as opposed to revelatory literature, see, most recently, Luca Arcari, *Vedere Dio: La apocalissi giudaiche e protocristiane (iv sec a.C–ii sec. d.C.)* (Rome: Carocci, 2020).

16. Christopher Rowland, *The Open Heaven: A Study of Apocalyptic in Judaism and Christianity* (New York: Crossroad, 1982).

17. Rowland, *Open Heaven*, 2.

Four Decades On," which proceeds from two key assumptions. First, his investigation begins with the revelatory experience. Whereas Collins's approach, generally speaking, emphasizes the distinctive aspects of the genre apocalypse in relation to other forms of revelation, including prophecy, Rowland's approach, generally speaking, stresses the points of contact between apocalyptic texts and the revelatory experience. The elasticity of his approach has had a profound impact on the ways that apocalyptic has been envisioned and studied in contexts outside early Judaism. Rowland's second assumption, which has exerted an equally great gravitational effect, is that eschatology is neither the sole nor the defining component of apocalyptic literature. Apocalyptic texts, he observes, can disclose information about other subjects, especially the nature of heaven and the cosmos. Although Rowland arrived at this view independently, he acknowledges the significance of Michael E. Stone's 1976 article, "Lists of Revealed Things in the Apocalyptic Literature."[18]

Stone's article is widely credited with expanding the notion of apocalyptic revelation to include heavenly journeys and overcoming the belief that apocalyptic writings are concerned only with history and eschatology. Of course, 1 Enoch had been part of the academic study of early Jewish apocalyptic literature since the nineteenth century.[19] It is no accident that the first academic study of ancient Jewish and Christian apocalyptic literature, by Friedrich Lücke in 1832, came after the transmission of Ethiopian manuscripts of the "Book of Enoch the Prophet" (1 Enoch) to Europe in the late eighteenth century. At the time, though, it was known only in its Ethiopic translation and in fragments and citations in other languages, primarily Greek. None of these spoke to the antiquity of the book or its component parts. The recovery of ancient Dead Sea manuscripts of all but one of these parts (in their original Aramaic, as noted) catapulted them and otherworldly apocalypses in general into the scholarly spotlight. The

---

18. Michael E. Stone, "Lists of Revealed Things in the Apocalyptic Literature," in *Magnalia Dei, the Mighty Acts of God: Essays on the Bible and Archaeology in Memory of G. Ernest Wright*, ed. Frank Moore Cross, Werner E. Lemke, and Patrick D. Miller (Garden City, NY: Doubleday, 1976), 414–35.

19. Note, e.g., F. Crawford Burkitt, *Jewish and Christian Apocalypses*, Schweich Lectures 1913 (London: Humphrey Milford; Oxford University Press, 1914), and the inclusion of 1 Enoch and 2 Enoch in the two great pseudepigrapha collections of that age: Emil Kautzsch, ed., *Die Apokryphen und Pseudepigraphen des Alten Testaments*, 2 vols. (Tübingen: Mohr, 1900); and Robert H. Charles, ed. *The Apocrypha and Pseudepigrapha of the Old Testament*, 2 vols. (Oxford: Clarendon, 1913).

first major result of research was Józef T. Milik's celebrated if speculative 1976 volume, *The Books of Enoch: Aramaic Fragments from Qumrân*.[20]

Stone's article, Milik's volume, and Rowland's approach inaugurated a new chapter in the study of ancient apocalyptic literature.[21] To that point, theories on the origin and nature of apocalyptic literature had been informed almost exclusively by historical-eschatological apocalypses such as Daniel and Revelation. The discovery of the Aramaic Enoch texts among the Scrolls invited scholars to regard apocalyptic literature as more than the recrudescence of late biblical prophecy and to consider more seriously its overlaps with wisdom traditions, cosmological investigation, divinatory practices, dream interpretation, and mystical speculation.

The approach of Rowland and others has also led to the presumption that apocalyptic is *either* eschatological *or* cosmological (or "speculative"). This perspective suggests that texts which are without eschatological content can be labelled and studied as apocalyptic on the grounds that they disclose heavenly mysteries of any kind.

The presumption that apocalyptic literature can be defined without an eschatological component is critiqued in Lorenzo DiTommaso's essay, "Revealed Things in Apocalyptic Literature." Building from Collins's typology, DiTommaso shows that the categories historical and otherworldly apply not only to the formal apocalypses but to apocalyptic literature of every genre. The evidence also demonstrates that these categories are relative, not absolute. On the one hand, the revelatory content of apocalyptic texts of the historical type is predominantly but not exclusively concerned with history and eschatology. On the other hand, even though the revelatory focus of apocalyptic texts of the otherworldly type is not primarily historical, it is always oriented by an eschatological horizon. DiTommaso ends his paper with two conclusions. First, the revelatory content of apocalyptic writings is practically unlimited, extending to sub-

---

20. Józef T. Milik, *The Books of Enoch: Aramaic Fragments from Qumrân Cave 4*, with the collaboration of Matthew Black (Oxford: Clarendon, 1976). A new critical edition of these texts is now available in Henryk Drawnel, *Qumran Cave 4: The Aramaic Books of Enoch; 4Q201, 4Q202, 4Q204, 4Q205, 4Q206, 4Q207, 4Q212* (Oxford: Oxford University Press, 2019).

21. The other milestone study of the era is the collection of essays edited by David Hellholm, *Apocalypticism in the Mediterranean World and the Near East: Proceedings of the International Colloquium on Apocalypticism Uppsala, August 12–17, 1979*, 2nd ed. (Tübingen: Mohr Siebeck, 1989). On the whole, it has weathered less well over time.

jects beyond those that Stone lists in his pioneering article. Second, the eschatological horizon is integral to the apocalyptic worldview and thus definitive to all apocalyptic texts, including those of the cosmological or otherworldly type.

The eschatological dimension of early Jewish apocalypses is also the subject of Stefan Beyerle's expository paper, "Revelatory Literature, in Which a Revelation Is Mediated by an Otherworldly Being: Revelation in the Dead Sea Scrolls." Beyerle notes that, while the Scrolls do not contain any new apocalypses (with the possible exceptions of the New Jerusalem text and the Son of God text [4Q246]), sectarian works such as the Hodayot and the Community Rule evince the overall apocalyptic worldview of the sectarians and confirm Collins's definition of the genre to be relevant to the investigation of the Dead Sea Scrolls. For Beyerle, the apocalyptic worldview and the sectarian perspective find common ground in the concept of revelation, which leads him to regard the community's eschatology as apocalyptic. He further distinguishes between two types of eschatology, spatial and temporal (or the "realized" and "future"), the former most clearly apparent in the Hodayot and the Songs of the Sabbath Sacrifice.

Although the leading approaches to things apocalyptic remain those of Collins and Rowland, other scholars have quarried the evidence of the Scrolls to construct alternative ways of classifying or approaching apocalyptic literature. On the whole, the impetus for these new classifications is dissatisfaction with the generic approach rather than with Rowland's more expansive "revelation of heavenly mysteries."

Devorah Dimant's programmatic study, "Qumran and the Apocalyptic," is critical of Collins's definition on the grounds that it ignores the specific historical contexts and distinctive features of each text.[22] She advocates an alternative classification of apocalyptic writings that instead highlights the examination of thematic clusters as they appear in specific historical contexts. One cluster of texts, which includes the Apocalypse of Weeks and Dan 7, displays a pervasive interest in the nature of history. She contends that reports of cosmic travel, such as parts of the Book of the Watchers or the Astronomical Book, both booklets of 1 Enoch, are better understood as a genre that is separate from the historical apocalypses and

---

22. A similar critique is made by Annette Yoshiko Reed in *Demons, Angels, and Writing in Ancient Judaism* (Cambridge: Cambridge University Press, 2020).

should not be considered apocalypses at all. A third cluster that she examines consists of throne visions, of which the Book of Giants contains a key example (4Q530 2 II). Dimant also argues that the periodization of history exhibited in Hebrew texts written by the Dead Sea sect, such as the pesharim, betrays the influence of the older historical apocalypses. This, she suggests, provides a context to understand the formation of the extreme and totalizing dualistic perspective espoused by the *yaḥad*.

Armin Lange proposes a different methodology in his "Apocalypse and Authoritative Literatures in Second Temple Judaism." Lange concentrates on one facet of his well-known project, in collaboration with Ulrike Mittmann-Richert and Bennie H. Reynolds III, to classify the Dead Sea Scrolls according to genre. He suggests that texts which have been categorized as apocalypses should be understood as "parabiblical," or, as he now prefers, "paratextual." He defines this with respect to the deployment of exegetical techniques in a way that involves important traditional figures, such as Moses or the prophets, in the creation of new texts. (In this respect, his approach recalls Dimant's classification by thematic cluster, above). Lange lists a number of texts he considers to be apocalypses that are associated with authoritative figures, such as Enoch, Jeremiah, or Ezekiel. He also asserts that testaments are similarly paratextual, in that they are attributed to authoritative figures. The book of Jonah, he asserts, is the only prophetic book of the Hebrew Bible that is paratextual and its late date indicates a shift towards paratextuality in early Hellenism. This macro-shift is also evident in Hellenistic-era genres such as apocalypse and testament and attests a transformation of Jewish literary production that should be seen, he argues, as a response to Hellenism. This shift makes intelligible the centrality of appeal to traditional Jewish authoritative figures that Lange understands to be a core aspect of ancient Jewish paratextuality and critical to the formation of authoritative and eventually canonical scriptures.

Alex Samely outlines a highly original approach in "The Use of Genre for Many Text Meanings: Apocalypse and 1 Enoch." Samely observes that, while Collins's definition of the genre apocalypse stresses content, descriptions of other literary genres highlight different aspects, such as form. Although a contents-oriented genre such as apocalypse has useful roles, Samely argues that it can also facilitate an improper transition from literary artefact to presumptive audiences and social conditions. Such definitions also tend to erase the multiplicity of meanings/themes within a text by reducing them to a few meanings or themes. This is no small matter with a long and complicated text like 1 Enoch, where such reductions in meaning can impose a simplistic coherency. An option to the generic approach, Samely notes, is the Manchester-Durham Inventory, which "constitutes a discipline of text description, as a half-way house between the use of contents-oriented genre labels on the one hand, and the plurality of meanings as experienced at first hand on the other." The catalogue of questions that comprise the inventory inhibits selection bias and compels the scholar to consider alternatives. Read in this light, 1 Enoch becomes a far richer document. Among other things, this interpretation highlights the central theme of the future in 1 Enoch, which, as we have seen, has tended to be overlooked or even ignored in other approaches.

As important as they are, the fragmentary manuscripts of the Book of the Watchers and other portions of 1 Enoch comprise only a part of the treasure-trove of revelatory texts in Aramaic that have been recovered from the Dead Sea caves. Some, such as the Aramaic Astronomical Book and the Book of Giants, have expanded the compass of the early Enochic tradition. Others are either ascribed to different figures (notably Amram, Levi, and Daniel) or, as with the New Jerusalem text (1Q32, 2Q24, 4Q554, 4Q554a, 4Q555, 5Q15, and 11Q18) and the Four Kingdoms text (4Q552–553), are extant without ascription (if ever they had one).

These "Aramaica qumranica apocalyptica," as Florentino García Martínez describes them, have been the subject of intensive study since the 1990s.[23] None of these texts is sectarian; most appear to be relatively early in date. Whether apocalyptica remains an appropriate designation is no longer clear. "Aramaic revelatory-visionary writings" might be a better term, since it does not presume an apocalyptic character. What is clear, though, is that these revelatory-visionary writings have cast new light on the emergence of apocalyptic literature in early Judaism and the central role of the Aramaic language in this process.

---

23. Florentino García Martínez, "Aramaica qumranica apocalyptica?," in *Aramaica Qumranica: Proceedings of the Conference on the Aramaic Texts from Qumran at Aix-en-Provence, 30 June–2 July 2008*, ed. Katell Berthelot and Daniel Stökl Ben Ezra, STDJ 94 (Leiden: Brill, 2010), 435–48. See also the other papers therein and the essays in Mette Bundvad and Kasper Siegismund, ed., *Vision, Narrative, and Wisdom in the Aramaic Texts from Qumran: Essays from the Copenhagen Symposium, 14–15 August, 2017*, STDJ 131 (Leiden: Brill, 2020), as well as the editions, monographs, and studies on each of the Aramaic revelatory-visionary texts from the Dead Sea. See also Andrew B. Perrin, *The Dynamics of Dream-Vision Revelation in the Aramaic Dead Sea Scrolls*, JAJSup 19 (Göttingen: Vandenhoeck & Ruprecht, 2015).

Part 2 is entitled "Apocalyptic Texts and Traditions in Ancient Judaism." The first essay of this section is Matthew Goff's "Aramaic as a Language of Antediluvian Wisdom: The Early Enoch Apocalypses, Astronomy, and the Deep Past in the Hellenistic Near East." In this paper, Goff suggests that the production of the Book of the Watchers and the Astronomical Book of 1 Enoch "should be understood primarily as a product of this material's abiding interest in the deep past." Aramaic, he argues, had an "archaizing potential" since it was understood as the language of ancestors from long ago and as a language of Mesopotamia. Why Jewish scribes in this period exhibited an interest in the distant past is intelligible in terms of the cultural politics of the Hellenistic age. Mesopotamian culture was understood in the period as being of deep antiquity. The Qumran Aramaic literature, including the early Enochic writings, betrays a strategy of appropriating Mesopotamian knowledge and reconfiguring it as having Jewish origins. The Hellenistic age, broadly speaking, is characterized by the overthrow of ancient peoples such as the Egyptians and Babylonians by a people who are understood to be much younger—the Greeks (Macedonians). This gave subject peoples a powerful rationale to highlight their own antiquity. This, in turn, helped give rise to a vibrant Hellenistic discourse among intellectuals of these subject peoples about the origins of civilization, in which they articulated the origins of various types of knowledge (often including astronomy, a key topic of Enochic literature) in a way that gave pride of place to their own national traditions. This cultural and intellectual context helps explains why Jewish scribes in the early Hellenistic period exhibit a strong interest in the primordial past, as articulated in terms of their own traditions and why this engagement with the past was conducted in Aramaic, a language which was understood to be spoken by their ancestors from long ago.

In terms of sheer numbers, the Daniel texts take second place only to the Enochic writings among the Aramaic revelatory-visionary writings that were recovered from the Dead Sea caves. There are the eight partial manuscript copies of Daniel, which confirm the antiquity of the Hebrew-Aramaic text in its Masoretic form. The Scrolls additionally preserve the Pseudo-Daniel works (4Q243–244, 4Q245), the Prayer of Nabonidus (4Q242), the Son of God text (4Q246), and a slew of other compositions, such as the Four Kingdoms text that scholars, with varying degrees of success, have associated with Daniel or with episodes or themes reminiscent of the biblical book.

The totality of these Danielic writings is the subject of Andrew B. Perrin's exemplary essay on "Daniel Traditions and the Qumran Movement? Reconsidering the Interface between Texts, Traditions, Identities, and Movements." According to Perrin, the Dead Sea sect engaged a range of Danielic traditions and texts that should not be simplistically equated with the later book of Daniel. He examines three topics that are by turn scribal (the use of paleo-Hebrew), exegetical (utilization of Ps 106), and ideological (conceptions of election and eschatological expectation), to show forms of continuity and difference regarding the Dead Sea sect and the scribes who were responsible for 4Q243-245. For Perrin, the Dead Sea sect should not be understood as an isolated or marginalized group but rather as part of a broader and complex array of scribal networks that includes ones that produced the Aramaic Danielic material. Thus while the members of the *yaḥad* are generally regarded as not having composed apocalypses, these broader scribal movements included persons who did.

Another subject about which the discovery of the Dead Sea Scrolls has precipitated fresh ideas is the origins of apocalyptic literature. It is generally accepted that this literature emerged from a matrix of older influences including late biblical prophecy, ancient mythic traditions, Near Eastern mantic practices, wisdom writings and scribal circles, Hellenistic ideas, and Zoroastrian dualism.[24] But the lines of transmission are by no means clear. For example, Dan 7-12 and the Book of the Watchers are both apocalypses, yet their revelatory content seems to draw from disparate traditions. Did apocalyptic literature independently develop in different times and social settings? More broadly, do we understand the relationship between the first apocalypses and their sources in terms of historical evolution? If so, what is the probative value of categories such as proto-apocalyptic? Or should apocalyptic (however defined) be regarded as a radical break with tradition, to the effect that it is a new expression of the human imagination?

The chief obstacle to proposing firm answers to such questions is the poverty of evidence. A case in point is the hypothesis of Persian-era Zoroastrian influence on early Jewish apocalyptic literature. Here the issue is compounded by issues of dating. The oldest manuscripts of the core Zoroastrian texts are medieval, a full millennium removed from the time when the relevant elements of the religion purportedly had an influence on

---

24. See further, Collins, *Apocalyptic Imagination*, 28-46.

early Judaism. Moreover, much of the content of these texts resembles the character of the early medieval apocalyptic tradition that is their primary context. As a result, studies on the subject in a sense are locked into a certain view by their stance on the manuscript evidence, one way or the other.

The Dead Sea Scrolls not only have enlarged the data set of writings that might inform the issue of Zoroastrian influence, but also have suggested new ways by which it might be interrogated. Jason M. Silverman's fresh approach, "It's the End of the World (as the Persians Know It)? Iranian Influence on Jewish Apocalypticism in Light of the Complete Publication of the Dead Sea Scrolls," lays out six criteria by which one can identify the influence of one text or tradition upon another. In this, Silverman stresses the interaction of cultural and social structures and also "concentric levels of context." That is, the investigation should consider not only Persian influence on Judaism writ large, but also specific social structures, such as the imperial contexts of the Persian Empire. After delineating his method for assessing influence, Silverman proceeds to two case studies. The first involves the Aramaic New Jerusalem text and Yima's Vara, a myth in which the god Ahura Mazda commands King Yima to construct an enclosure to protect the good creatures of the earth from harsh winters. This has been understood as a template for the ending of the book of Revelation, in which the New Jerusalem motif is significant. This proposal, Silverman concludes, does not adequately meet his criteria for identifying influence. His second case study involves Persian dualism and the famous "Treatise on the Two Spirits" (1QS III, 13–IV, 26). For Silverman, the cosmological dualism of the Treatise fits all of his six criteria and thus Persian influence on the dualism of the Treatise should be considered plausible. Silverman concludes by advocating the interdisciplinary study of ancient Jewish and Persian literature with an eye toward better understanding an "apocalyptic hermeneutic" as well as an interest more broadly in forms of discourse and hermeneutics that a comparative perspective can illuminate.

An important feature of the *Semeia* 14 definition of the genre is the criterion that heavenly revelation is "mediated by an otherworldly being." Perhaps highlighting the mediated nature of the heavenly disclosure in apocalypses was meant to differentiate it from prophetic utterance.[25] Whatever the rationale, mediated revelation is observed in many religious

---

25. Cf. Collins, "Introduction," 9: "A few elements are constant in every work we have designated as an apocalypse.… There is always a narrative framework in which the manner of revelation is described. This always involves an otherworldly mediator

systems and is not distinctive to the genre apocalypse or apocalyptic literature as a class. Mediated revelation features prominently in apocalypses such as Daniel and 4 Ezra. The latter contains a revelatory dialogue that occurs between an angelic figure and the seer, while the former involves a vision that is shown to a seer and whose meaning requires interpretation by an angelic figure. In both cases, the seer is understood to remain on earth, although sometimes he places himself in a receptive state of mind or locates to a special place such as "the field that is called Ardat" (4 Ezra 9:26 NRSV). Mediated revelation appears in modified form in the heavenly-journey format that is characteristic of the Enochic writings of early Judaism and the ascent apocalypses of late-antique Christianity. There, the seer travels to otherworldly locales such as heaven but also the infernal realms and even unknown terrestrial places.

The stationary seer and the sojourning visionary hardly exhaust the means by which heavenly revelation may be communicated in apocalyptic texts. A partial roster includes: the final testaments of revered figures on their deathbeds, who straddle the threshold between this world and the next; the recovery of documents from an earlier age that record heavenly information such as the tablets of Seth; the inspired utterances of Sibyls and other oracular figures; the activity of pneumatic agencies such as the Holy Spirit; the inspired interpretation of scriptural texts, as with the pesharim; and the reflective observation of natural phenomena, the latter sometimes a feature of wisdom (or "sapiential") texts. Most of these modes find expression in the Dead Sea Scrolls. They confirm what intuition suggests: the means of heavenly revelation is not definitional to the genre apocalypse specifically or apocalyptic literature categorically.

One of the oldest typologies of revelatory mechanisms distinguishes between dreams and visions. The distinction is usually made on philological, contextual, or historical grounds and centers on the plain-sense idea that dreams are nocturnal events that occur when one is asleep while visions are diurnal and happen when one is awake ("waking dreams"). Both dreams and visions play a special role in the Aramaic revelatory-visionary writings, including the early Enochic works and the court-tales and revelatory visions of the book of Daniel.

---

and a human recipient—it is never simply a direct oracular utterance by either heavenly being or human."

Introduction 17

In "A New Proposal: Rereading Dreams and Visions in Early Jewish Literature (4Q530, 4Q544, 4Q204, and 1 Enoch 1–36)," Frances Flannery lays out an exciting new approach to the meanings of dreams and visions in early Jewish revelatory works. The default English translation of both חזה and ראה as "see" is not always warranted, given the spectrum of meanings that these words have depending on their literary contexts. Flannery details the way in which dreams and visions are imagined and reported in a range of early Aramaic Enochic writings: 4Q530 (4QEnGiants[b] ar), 4Q544 (4QVisions of Amram[b] ar) and 1 En. 1–36 and 4Q204 (4QEnoch[c] ar). She observes that in several problematic passages the experiences of having a dream are better understood as a hypnagogic state. This state, which is encountered through sleep and is sometimes equated with it, in turn facilitates a vision. A vision, by contrast, is "the totality of numinous experiences of all of the beings, sights, places, and new realities that are beheld, apprehended, felt emotionally, and understood, whether in an altered waking state, or within the container of a dream." With these explanations in hand, Flannery proposes a preliminary visionary continuum where references to dreams and visions in the literature may be slotted after careful textual and contextual analysis. At one end of the spectrum are "clear dreams in which visions are beheld during sleep," while at the other end are "clear visions beheld while awake." In between reside a range of cases in which the hypnagogic state is unclear. Here the term *vision* may be deployed whether the visionary is awake, asleep, or somewhere in between these two states.

The effect of revelatory visions in apocalyptic literature is the subject of Angela Kim Harkins's thoughtful study, "Immersing Oneself in the Narrative World of Second Temple Apocalyptic Visions." Harkins explores how apocalyptic writings make visions palpable and vivid, opening up the possibility of what she terms "an experience of presence" within the reader. To examine this, she turns to cognitive literary theorists such as Anežka Kuzmičová and Marco Caracciolo. Harkins emphasizes that apocalyptic visions have the potential to destabilize readers, thereby intensifying their immersion in the visionary experience. Vision accounts accomplish this, she argues, in part by their accumulation of counterintuitive imagery, such as the monstrous, hybrid creatures of Dan 7, that conveys a narrative world that is very different from the one in which the reader lives. Narrative reports of visions can also convey a sense of suspense that intensifies readers' immersion into the visionary experience by causing them to want to know what will happen next. This is the case for example in both Daniel and the New Testament book of Revelation. Harkins further discusses how the construction of a vision report in the first person allows the reader to enact and in a sense experience the vision. She makes a distinction between "interoceptive" and "proprioceptive" embodied experiences that vision accounts can engender. The former denotes physical experiences of the body, such as pain or hunger, while the latter involves kinesthetic activity, a body moving through space. Understanding how vision reports immerse readers in the experience of a vision, Harkins suggests, can help explain the phenomenon of pseudepigraphy, as for example in the ongoing production of new texts attributed to visionaries such as Daniel and Enoch.

Pseudonymous attribution is a common feature in the formal apocalypses of early Judaism and Christianity and other forms of stand-alone apocalyptic works. Ascribing an apocalyptic text to an authoritative figure from the past serves a variety of purposes that facilitate its social functions. But what is the function of apocalyptic literature? As we have seen, the definition of the genre proposed in *Semeia* 14 has been criticized for its lack of reference to the function of the apocalypses or their social contexts.[26] Such criticisms are misplaced, however. There is no reason to assume that literary genres necessarily must correlate to specific purposes or social settings,[27] and, in fact, all the evidence suggests otherwise. In the case of apocalyptic texts specifically, scholars have come to recognize—in no small part as a result of the Dead Sea discoveries—that they have multiple purposes and reflect a diversity of social milieux.

This is not to imply that general patterns are impossible to detect. The most obvious one is the link between eschatological-predictive apocalyptic writings and social situations of oppression, persecution, and existential threats to group identity. This correlation is manifest in the apocalyptic

---

26. The information here and the following paragraphs is drawn from Lorenzo DiTommaso, "Class Consciousness, Group Affiliation, and Apocalyptic Speculation," in *The Struggle over Class: Socioeconomic Analysis of Ancient Christian Texts*, ed. G. Anthony Keddie, Michael Flexsenhar, and Steven J. Friesen, WGRWSup 14 (Atlanta: SBL Press, 2021), 277–312.

27. The ultimate source of this assumption is probably the old, genre-critical approach towards biblical literature as developed by the *Religionsgeschichtliche Schule* and, most importantly, the work of Hermann Gunkel (1862–1932), which exerted a considerable influence on the study of apocalyptic texts. See Collins, *Apocalyptic Imagination*, 20–21; and Pieter G. R. de Villiers, "Hermann Gunkel as Innovator," *OTE* 20 (2007): 333–51.

literature across every historical era and cultural ecology; it is extremely well documented in the secondary scholarship. But too often this strong correlation has been assumed to be a universal rule.

A specific case in point is that apocalyptic speculation is rooted in economic oppression and class conflict. This thesis was first presented in a systematic fashion in Norman Cohn's classic 1957 volume, *The Pursuit of the Millennium*.[28] According to Cohn, economic upheaval generated by the dissolution of the feudal order in Western Europe in the late Middle Ages resulted in widespread social unrest among the urban poor and rural peasantry. This created an existential tension whose remedy was projected into the eschatological future, typically in the expectation for an imminent and radical social upheaval.

Cohn's thesis dovetailed well with conventional ideas about the functions and settings of the two biblical apocalypses, Daniel and Revelation, which at the time were considered representative of apocalyptic literature *tout court*. It also became a highly influential explanatory model outside the field of medieval studies.[29] For example, it was instrumental in the social-scientific study of new religious movements ("cults," pejoratively) that caught the attention of the academy and the public in the late 1960s and 1970s. It also shaped ideas about apocalyptic protest movements in areas that had been subject to European colonization, notably Latin and South America in the nineteenth and twentieth centuries.

However, medievalists (who knew the evidence first-hand) criticized Cohn's model as unbalanced.[30] While the late medieval era did record a surfeit of millennial-apocalyptic movements, many other apocalyptic texts, they pointed out, were composed by stakeholder elements in society

---

28. Norman Cohn, *The Pursuit of the Millennium* (London: Secker & Warburg, 1957). Cohn was not a Marxist, but historical and sociological scholarship in Britain during this era had a leftist orientation, and Cohn's book should be appreciated in this light. In his 1959 book, *Primitive Rebels: Studies in Archaic Forms of Social Movement in the Nineteenth and Twentieth Centuries* (Manchester: Manchester University Press), the Marxist historian Eric Hobsbawm argued that all millenarian movements are revolutionary in nature.

29. One early vector of Cohn's model of millennial speculation was the wide-ranging collection of papers edited by Sylvia L. Thrupp, *Millennial Dreams in Action: Essays in Comparative Study* (Den Haag: Mouton, 1962).

30. These and other criticisms prompted Cohn to modify and contextualize his model; see the third edition of his book *The Pursuit of the Millennium* (Oxford: Oxford University Press, 1970).

rather than by (and for) members of economically or socially disadvantaged, marginalized, or oppressed classes.[31] Moreover, these texts neither proceeded from a setting of economic disadvantage nor derived their social function from the prospect for the imminent radical upheaval of the social order.

In "Poor Subjects of the Hodayot: Apocalyptic Class Subjectivities in Practice," G. Anthony Keddie critiques the uncritical application of the thesis that apocalyptic speculation is a response to class oppression. He argues that the Dead Sea sect was neither impoverished nor ostracized from Palestinian society. An emphasis on the movement as a whole as oppressed or downtrodden hinders an appreciation of the social hierarchies promoted within the sect. The apocalyptic discourse of the *yaḥad* should be understood as a means by which structures of authority were promoted within the group, while an apocalyptic perspective also helped create worldviews and mindsets that shaped sectarian identity. The Hodayot, for example, promotes an ideology according to which the intended readership of these hymns enjoy access to esoteric, supernatural knowledge and the sect comprises poor people who endure antagonistic treatment from wealthy opponents. This language should be understood as a rhetorical means of identity construction within the sect, not as evidence that the group suffered a genuine lack of material sufficiency. This is suggested, Keddie points out, by the fact that the excavations of the Qumran site indicate that its inhabitants enjoyed a degree of material comfort.

In Judaism, the failure of three revolts against Rome, capped by the catastrophe of Bar Kokhba, quenched robust apocalyptic speculation for the next four or five centuries.[32] Despite its rich heritage of apocalyptic texts, the classical period of rabbinic Judaism (ca. second to sixth centuries) did not generate a single stand-alone apocalyptic text. More strikingly still, the corpus of rabbinic writings is devoid of explicit citations from Second Temple apocalyptic texts. While eschatological expectation did not entirely disappear in rabbinic-era Judaism, it was sublimated to other concerns that were dictated by internal and external circumstances and expressed mainly in the form of a general messianic utopianism.

---

31. See, among others, Bernard McGinn, *Visions of the End: Apocalyptic Traditions in the Middle Ages* (New York: Columbia University Press, 1979).

32. This statement requires some modification if apocalyptic is equated with mystical speculation, either directly or by means of a third category such as Rowland's "revelation of heavenly mysteries."

Or was it? In a stimulating and provocative paper, "The Changing Apocalypse: Apocalyptic Literature as a Provisional Genre in Early Rabbinic Judaism," Rebecca Scharbach Wollenberg posits that a few rabbinic texts exhibit some evidence for their engagement with apocalyptic literature. She cites passages from the eleventh chapter of the tractate Sanhedrin in the Babylonian Talmud as evidence that its authors were aware of the formal aspects of the genre apocalypse. In addition, these passages preserve "excerpts from lost Jewish literature that resembled in many respects the extant apocalyptic literature that has been preserved from earlier and later periods." Wollenberg also describes how the logical structure in other passages in tractate Sanhedrin deviates from the typical talmudic pattern. Such deviation does not seem to have been inspired by the patterns in the earlier Mishnah but are better explained with reference to apocalyptic literature. Wollenberg suggests the rabbinic thinkers had a provisional attitude to apocalyptic writings, which could be "engaged with pleasure" but also with "a certain casualness at the edges of the rabbinic literary canon." This attitude would explain the lack of reference to apocalyptic works in the rabbinic literature yet admit the possibility that rabbis did not wholly reject them.

Part 3 of the volume examines "The Jewish Apocalyptic Tradition and Early Christianity." In the first essay of this section, an incisive paper on "Divine Kingdom: Between the Songs of the Sabbath Sacrifice and the Synoptic Gospels," Giovanni B. Bazzana explores how the theme of the kingdom of God can be better understood through comparison with the Dead Sea Scrolls. Whether the kingdom should be understood in a spatial sense as a territory or in the more abstract sense of sovereignty is disputed in the study of the New Testament. There is also a lack of agreement about the extent to which the kingdom is manifest in the present time or the eschatological future. Bazzana argues that the Songs of the Sabbath Sacrifice illustrate that the kingdom of God in the New Testament should be understood as participating in a common discourse about the kingdom (*malkut, basileia*) as something that could be entered. But that does not mean that the kingdom was a static or passive entity. Rather, the term has agency and human participation is important for understanding its sovereignty. A comparison with the Songs of the Sabbath Sacrifice also suggests that the verses that mention the kingdom of God in the New Testament, some of which suggest it should be understood primarily in relation to the present and others the future, are not contradictory. Together, the Songs of the Sabbath Sacrifice and the New Testament gospels illustrate that conceptions of temporality from the period should be rethought in a way which acknowledges that the present and the future could overlap.

In terms of cultural history, the Revelation of John is the most important apocalypse and one of the most influential books ever composed. Its place as the last book of the New Testament and thus the final book in the Christian Bible closes the story of humanity that opens in its first book, Genesis. What began with God's good creation, the garden of Eden, and Adam's sin and the entry of evil into the world is brought to its apocalyptic resolution with the resurrected Christ as the new Adam, the climactic overthrow of Satan and the power of evil, and the heavenly descent of the New Jerusalem and new creation.

Yet the Revelation of John is also the anomaly of anomalies. Of all the apocalypses of the Second Temple period, Revelation is the only one that is not obviously pseudonymous.[33] Although its themes and expectations are grounded in the prophetic books and earlier apocalypses, in its form and content Revelation is unlike all the Second Temple examples of the genre, to the point of being sui generis. Other apocalypses tend toward the episodic, a result of either agglomeration (Daniel, the Book of the Watchers) or design (2 Baruch, 4 Ezra).[34] This is not to deny that these apocalypses lack common themes that link their various sections. The clearest and most theologically sophisticated expression of authorial intent in compositional form is 4 Ezra. Its overarching narrative details Ezra's gradual conversion to the apocalyptic theology of history, which links all seven sections of the apocalypse and is central to its social function.[35] But only Rev 4–22 is a "through" apocalypse, the only full-blown example of the type.[36] The

---

33. On the subject, see Garrick Allen's paper in this volume and Lorenzo DiTommaso, "Pseudonymity and the Revelation of John," in *Revealed Wisdom: Studies in Apocalyptic in Honour of Christopher Rowland*, ed. John F. Ashton, AJEC 88 (Leiden: Brill, 2014), 305–15.

34. The periodization of history that is typical to many apocalyptic texts of the period also contributes to its episodic character.

35. Michael E. Stone in his commentary, *Fourth Ezra: A Commentary on the Book of Fourth Ezra*, Hermeneia (Minneapolis: Fortress, 1990), 32, calls this the "Odyssey of Ezra's soul"; cf. Stone, "A Reconsideration of Apocalyptic Visions," *HTR* 96 (2003): 167–80.

36. The term is borrowed from classical opera. It distinguishes full-realized dramatic examples of the late nineteenth century, whose musical leitmotifs and narrative features are deeply embedded in the opera along its length and integral to its understanding and appreciation, from earlier examples whose musical and lyrical structures are more episodic.

book's themes and motifs are restated, recombined, and recapitulated, yet manage to weave together in a theological narrative that advances to its shattering climax. There is only so much that a comparison with the other Second Temple apocalypses can reveal about the Revelation of John, and it is in this context that the Dead Sea discoveries have proven enlightening.

In "Aramaica Qumranica Apocalyptica and the Book of Revelation," Garrick V. Allen skillfully interrogates the book of Revelation in relation to two Aramaic texts from Qumran, the Visions of Amram (4Q543–548) and the Son of God text (4Q246). Comparing Revelation with Visions of Amram shows how Revelation "subverts apocalyptic traditions by minimizing the seer's interpretive agency" in that it presents the figure of John as simply a scribe who records a divine vision rather than an authoritative figure from the past. Allen also details how 4Q246 and Revelation appropriate in various ways the vision of the Ancient of Days and the "one like a son of man" of Dan 7. Such dependency illustrates not only that this material was important in ancient Judaism but also that it could be interpreted in different ways. Finally, Allen reviews the identification of Revelation's genre as an apocalypse, which has long been a topic of debate. Its affinities with the older Aramaic apocalyptic texts from Qumran suggest that such compositions should be compared not solely in light of the definition of the genre but also in terms of how they utilize traditions, in particular with regard to the appropriation of scriptural texts.

The early second century was a period of great transition in Judaism and Christianity.[37] In Judaism, the failure of the Bar Kokhba Revolt (132–136 CE) signals the end of the Second Temple period and the beginning of the rabbinic era. In Christianity, the same decades witnessed the closing of the New Testament and the opening of what is often called the patristic period. At the same time, and in both Judaism and Christianity, the composition of historical-eschatological type of apocalyptic writings almost entirely disappeared. This extraordinary event, which was backlit by the much-debated parting of the ways between Judaism and Christianity, marks the dividing line between Second Temple apocalyptic speculation and late antique apocalyptic speculation.

The production of historical-predictive apocalyptic texts largely ceased in late antique Christianity, as it had in rabbinic Judaism. Unlike the rabbis,

---

37. The information here and in subsequent paragraphs is distilled from Lorenzo DiTommaso, "Il genere 'apocalisse' e l'apocalittico' nella tarda antichità," *Rivista di storia del cristianesimo* 17 (2020): 73–99.

however, the Christians of the era continued to compose apocalyptic writings, but only in the otherworldly mode. This otherworldly orientation is the hallmark characteristic of late-antique apocalyptic speculation in Christianity.[38] Its primary vehicles are the patristic works and the ascent/descent apocalypses such as the Apocalypse of Peter and the Apocalypse of Paul. Its cardinal features are (1) a far greater prominence to issues of personal eschatology and the fate of the individual soul after death than to corporate eschatology and the place of the group within the stream of history in relation to its predestined ending; and (2) an interest in protology and the explication of first causes to a degree well beyond anything in the Jewish apocalypses, except the early Enochic writings, and particularly the Book of Watchers.

It is from this perspective that the ascent/descent apocalypses, with their guided tours of the heavenly and infernal realms and detailed descriptions of their denizens, should be appreciated. For two generations of scholars, the foundational study on the subject has been Martha Himmelfarb's classic 1993 book, *Ascent to Heaven in Jewish and Christian Apocalypses*.[39] In a highly innovative and far-reaching paper for the present volume, "Heavenly Ascent Revisited," Himmelfarb sketches a picture of the ascent apocalypses that is "considerably different" from that which she offered in her book. She reexamines the trope of the otherworldly journey in the Aramaic revelatory-visionary writings, including the early Enochic works. Despite the influence of the Book of the Watchers, Himmelfarb concludes that there is surprisingly little evidence of development in the heavenly ascent writings until the late first and second centuries CE.[40] This represents a shift from her earlier position, which she admits was overly informed by *Semeia* 14 and its attention to genre and takes into account

---

38. The resurgence in historical-predictive apocalyptic speculation in the late fourth and fifth centuries marks the medieval apocalyptic tradition. See the papers in part 1 of Lorenzo DiTommaso and Colin McAllister, eds., *The Mediaeval Apocalyptic Tradition: From the Twilight of the Roman Empire to the Dawn of Early Modern Europe* (Cambridge: Cambridge University Press, forthcoming).

39. Martha Himmelfarb, *Ascent to Heaven in Jewish and Christian Apocalypses* (New York: Oxford University Press, 1993).

40. Himmelfarb also comments that the Parables of Enoch, one of only two ascent apocalypses with some claim to a pre-70 CE date, is far more eschatologically than otherworldly oriented and "shares few points of contact with the other ascent apocalypses," while 3 Baruch is likely a Christian work dating from the end of the fourth century CE rather than a Jewish work from the end of the first century CE.

the new Dead Sea texts such as the New Jerusalem text, the Aramaic Levi Document, and the Aramaic Astronomical Book. Himmelfarb locates the emergence of the ascent apocalypses during the late first and second centuries CE in a newfound interest in the heavenly realms (e.g., the idea of seven heavens) and a Christian concern with the fate of souls after death.

The central features of late-antique Christian apocalypticism—a focus on protological events rather than eschatological expectations, a concern with the origin and nature of evil, and, above all, a deep interest in issues related to ultimate personal destiny—are typical also of the Christian gnostic tractates and the Manichaean writings. They additionally find refraction in an attitude towards existence and human destiny that was conspicuous across the late-Roman world and was expressed in an enthusiasm for a variety of religious-philosophical systems and practices.

How do we explain the otherworldly inclination of apocalyptic speculation in late-antique Christianity both in itself and within its broader cultural milieux? Scholars have directed much attention to individual texts or specific bodies of literature, but only recently have come to consider the evidence holistically.[41] As we have observed, the purposes of apocalyptic literature are related to its social settings and reflected in its revelatory content. In other words, the character of late-antique apocalyptic speculation is directly related to the nature of its environment.

In his comprehensive study, "Apocalypses and Apocalyptic Literature in the Early Church: Apocalypse and Apocalyptic as Rhizome," Harry O. Maier suggests that the approaches of Collins and Rowland may be too narrowly conceived to illuminate such relationships. For Maier, the number of phenomena and the manifold and often hidden complexities of their interactions "make apocalypse and apocalyptic in the early church impossible to summarize or to codify." Borrowing a philosophical notion developed by Gilles Deleuze and Félix Guattari, Maier contends that early Christian apocalypses and apocalyptic literature are better comprehended in terms of a rhizomatic system. Maier's investigative compass is admirably wide-ranging. He is one of the few scholars who instinctively comprehend that Christian apocalyptic during these centuries must be assayed with reference to more than the stand-alone apocalypses. He investigates the means by which the patristic authors dealt with eschatology in both chiliastic and nonchiliastic modes and then the contents of the tours of

---

41. See further, DiTommaso, "Il genere 'apocalisse.'"

heaven and hell in the apocalypses. According to Maier, the great variety of interpretative strategies deployed by these early Christian writers can only be explained by a view of apocalyptic that assumes a plurality of contents, forms, messages, settings, and audiences.

As mentioned, late antique Christian apocalypticism cannot be completely understood apart from the gnostic writings of the period. Yet no firm consensus regarding their relationship has emerged. This is largely because the investigation has proceeded along a variety of paths whose direction is determined by competing conceptions of apocalyptic and gnostic. Some paths begin with the genre apocalypse. The Nag Hammadi codices and related manuscripts contain between twelve and twenty-five apocalypses, depending on the authority consulted.[42] Other scholars follow the more conventional path of phenomenological comparison. In this view, multiple correspondences in themes, functions, expectations, and messages imply a close historical connection between the apocalyptic and gnostic writings.[43] Still other scholars prefer to regard the matter with reference to Rowland's definition of apocalyptic, which permits a far broader range of material to be classified under the rubric. While the logic of his definition is questionable, the application of his approach has been salutary in many cases.

A good example of this application is the study of the overlaps between apocalyptic speculation and mysticism and the mystical experience, which in turn have clarified points about the relationship between apocalyptic and gnostic texts. This is the subject of Dylan M. Burns's insightful paper on "The Importance of the Gnostic Apocalypses from Nag Hammadi for the Study of Early Jewish Mysticism." Burns argues that the Nag Hammadi material constitutes valuable comparanda for better understanding Jewish mystical traditions from the second to the fifth centuries CE. His inquiry centers on the Nag Hammadi works that are designated "Sethian" apocalypses on account of prominence they accord to the patriarch Seth as a source of revelation and salvation. Burns highlights the trope of the

---

42. Collins, "Introduction," records twelve examples, while Dylan M. Burns, "The Gnostic Apocalypses," in *The Cambridge Companion to Apocalyptic Literature*, ed. Colin McAllister (Cambridge: Cambridge University Press, 2020), 59–78, esp. 62–65, cites twenty-five.

43. Per Bilde, "Gnosticism, Jewish Apocalypticism, and Early Christianity," in *In the Last Days: On Jewish and Christian Apocalyptic and Its Period*, ed. Knud Jeppesen, Kirsten Nielsen, and Bent Rosendal (Aarhus: Aarhus University Press, 1994), 9–32.

angelification of the seer in texts such as First Thought in Three Forms, in which the seer is transformed in the context of liturgical worship and participates with angels as they glorify God. He argues, however, that the Sethian literature is not theurgic and highlights the importance of the recitation of *nomina barbara* (unknown or nonsensical clusters of letters) as a technique of ascent. Burns contends that, despite their diversity, the Christian gnostic-Sethian writings and the Jewish Hekhalot texts rely on a common assumption that some humans possess the ability to acquire a type of divine status. Moreover, the Sethian material cautions against making a facile distinction between the *unio liturgica* (the communal joining of humans and angels in the context of worship) and the *unio mystica*, whereby people assert the experience of union with God. Although attempts to articulate the origins of gnosticism in terms of Judaism have now largely been abandoned, Burns wisely asserts that putting gnosticism and Jewish mysticism in conversation with another can still be instructive with regard to the development of traditions, particularly tropes such as angelification and heavenly ascent, which in turn are common to apocalyptic literature.

* * *

The discovery and full publication of the Dead Sea Scrolls has had a transformative effect on the study of ancient Jewish and Christian apocalyptic literature and movements. While the approaches of Collins and Rowland remain at the vanguard of scholarly investigation, the expansion of the corpus of apocalyptic literature occasioned by the Scrolls have prompted new classifications and fresh approaches. The *Semeia* 14 definition of the apocalypse genre is now one among several useful approaches to the investigation of apocalyptic and apocalyptic literature. This situation reflects the current academic climate, with renewed attention and engagement with methods and critical theory from elsewhere in the humanities and social sciences. The *Semeia* 14 definition retains its heuristic value, but in the sense that it was originally intended, as a tool that scholars can opt to use, as the case suggests—or perhaps to use in tandem with other tools in one's belt. Scholars today have more diversity in the ways they apprehend material evidence, as well as more actual ancient texts from antiquity, not simply ancient texts as mediated through centuries of scribal transmission. In the final analysis, the Dead Sea Scrolls have played a foundational role in mediating this transition, which remains ongoing.

Bibliography

Arcari, Luca. *Vedere Dio: La apocalissi giudaiche e protocristiane (iv sec a.C–ii sec. d.C.)*. Rome: Carocci, 2020.

Aune, David A. "The Apocalypse of John and the Problem of Genre." *Semeia* 36 (1986): 65–96.

Bilde, Per. "Gnosticism, Jewish Apocalypticism, and Early Christianity." Pages 9–32 In *the Last Days: On Jewish and Christian Apocalyptic and Its Period*. Edited by Knud Jeppesen, Kirsten Nielsen, and Bent Rosendal. Aarhus: Aarhus University Press, 1994.

Bundvad, Mette, and Kasper Siegismund, eds. *Vision, Narrative, and Wisdom in the Aramaic Texts from Qumran: Essays from the Copenhagen Symposium, 14–15 August, 2017*. STDJ 131. Leiden: Brill, 2020.

Burkitt, F. Crawford. *Jewish and Christian Apocalypses*. Schweich Lectures 1913. London: Humphrey Milford; Oxford University Press, 1914.

Burns, Dylan M. "The Gnostic Apocalypses." Pages 59–78 in *The Cambridge Companion to Apocalyptic Literature*. Edited by Colin McAllister. Cambridge: Cambridge University Press, 2020.

Charles, Robert H., ed. *The Apocrypha and Pseudepigrapha of the Old Testament*. 2 vols. Oxford: Clarendon, 1913.

Cohn, Norman. *The Pursuit of the Millennium*. London: Secker & Warburg, 1957. 3rd ed. Oxford University Press, 1970.

Collins, John J., ed. *Apocalypse: The Morphology of a Genre*. Semeia 14 (1979).

———. *The Apocalyptic Imagination: An Introduction to Jewish Apocalyptic Literature*. 3rd ed. Grand Rapids: Eerdmans, 2016.

———. "Epilogue: Genre Analysis and the Dead Sea Scrolls." *DSD* 17 (2010): 389–401.

———. "The Genre Apocalypse Reconsidered." *ZAC* 20 (2016): 21–40.

———. "Introduction: Towards the Morphology of a Genre." *Semeia* 14 (1979): 1–20.

———. "The Jewish Apocalypses." *Semeia* 14 (1979): 21–59.

DiTommaso, Lorenzo. "Class Consciousness, Group Affiliation, and Apocalyptic Speculation." Pages 277–312 in *The Struggle over Class: Socioeconomic Analysis of Ancient Christian Texts*. Edited by G. Anthony Keddie, Michael Flexsenhar, and Steven J. Friesen. WGRWSup 14. Atlanta: SBL Press, 2021.

———. "Eschatology in the Early Jewish Pseudepigrapha and the Early Christian Apocrypha." Pages 235–49 in *Eschatology in Antiquity:*

Forms and Functions. Edited by Hilary Marlow, Karla Pollmann, and Helen Van Noorden. New York: Routledge, 2021.

———. "Il genere 'apocalisse' e l'apocalittico' nella tarda antichità." *Rivista di storia del cristianesimo* 17 (2020): 73–99.

———. "Pseudonymity and the Revelation of John." Pages 305–15 in *Revealed Wisdom: Studies in Apocalyptic in Honour of Christopher Rowland*. Edited by John F. Ashton. AJEC 88. Leiden: Brill, 2014.

DiTommaso, Lorenzo, and Colin McAllister, eds. *The Mediaeval Apocalyptic Tradition: From the Twilight of the Roman Empire to the Dawn of Early Modern Europe*. Cambridge: Cambridge University Press, forthcoming.

Drawnel, Henryk. *Qumran Cave 4: The Aramaic Books of Enoch; 4Q201, 4Q202, 4Q204, 4Q205, 4Q206, 4Q207, 4Q212*. Oxford: Oxford University Press, 2019.

Flint, Peter W. "The Daniel-Tradition at Qumran." Pages 329–67 in vol. 2 of *The Book of Daniel: Composition and Reception*. Edited by John J. Collins and Peter W. Flint. 2 vols. VTSup 83. Leiden: Brill, 2001.

García Martínez, Florentino. "Aramaica qumranica apocalyptica?" Pages 435–48 in *Aramaica Qumranica: Proceedings of the Conference on the Aramaic Texts from Qumran at Aix-en-Provence, 30 June–2 July 2008*. Edited by Katell Berthelot and Daniel Stökl Ben Ezra. STDJ 94. Leiden: Brill, 2010.

Goff, Matthew. "The Apocalypse and the Sage: Assessing the Contribution of John J. Collins to the Study of Apocalypticism." Pages 8–22 in *Apocalyptic Thinking in Early Judaism: Engaging with John Collins' The Apocalyptic Imagination*. Edited by Sidnie White Crawford and Cecilia Wassén. JSJSup 182. Leiden: Brill, 2018.

Hellholm, David, ed. *Apocalypticism in the Mediterranean World and the Near East: Proceedings of the International Colloquium on Apocalypticism Uppsala, August 12–17, 1979*. 2nd ed. Tübingen: Mohr Siebeck, 1989.

Himmelfarb, Martha. *Ascent to Heaven in Jewish and Christian Apocalypses*. New York: Oxford University Press, 1993.

Hobsbawm, Eric. *Primitive Rebels: Studies in Archaic Forms of Social Movement in the Nineteenth and Twentieth Centuries*. Manchester: Manchester University Press, 1959.

Kautzsch, Emil, ed. *Die Apokryphen und Pseudepigraphen des Alten Testaments*. 2 vols. Tübingen: Mohr, 1900.

Linton, Gregory L. "Reading the Apocalypse as Apocalypse: The Limits of Genre." Pages 9–41 in *The Reality of Apocalypse: Rhetoric and Politics in the Book of Revelation*. Edited by David L. Barr. SymS 39. Atlanta: Society of Biblical Literature, 2006.

McGinn, Bernard. *Visions of the End: Apocalyptic Traditions in the Middle Ages*. New York: Columbia University Press, 1979.

Milik, Józef T. *The Books of Enoch: Aramaic Fragments from Qumrân Cave 4*. With the collaboration of Matthew Black. Oxford: Clarendon, 1976.

Newsom, Carol A. "Spying Out the Land: A Report from Genology." Pages 437–50 in *Seeking Out the Wisdom of the Ancients: Essays Offered to Honor Michael V. Fox on the Occasion of His Sixty-Fifth Birthday*. Edited by Ronald L. Troxel, Kelvin G. Friebel, and Dennis Robert Magary. Winona Lake, IN: Eisenbrauns, 2005.

Perrin, Andrew B. *The Dynamics of Dream-Vision Revelation in the Aramaic Dead Sea Scrolls*. JAJSup 19. Göttingen: Vandenhoeck & Ruprecht, 2015.

Reed, Annette Yoshiko. *Demons, Angels, and Writing in Ancient Judaism*. Cambridge: Cambridge University Press, 2020.

Rowland, Christopher. *The Open Heaven: A Study of Apocalyptic in Judaism and Christianity*. New York: Crossroad, 1982.

Stone, Michael E. *Fourth Ezra: A Commentary on the Book of Fourth Ezra*. Hermeneia. Minneapolis: Fortress, 1990.

———. "Lists of Revealed Things in the Apocalyptic Literature." Pages 414–35 in *Magnalia Dei, the Mighty Acts of God: Essays on the Bible and Archaeology in Memory of G. Ernest Wright*. Edited by Frank Moore Cross, Werner E. Lemke, and Patrick D. Miller. Garden City, NY: Doubleday, 1976.

———. "A Reconsideration of Apocalyptic Visions." *HTR* 96 (2003): 167–80.

Stuckenbruck, Loren T. "The Early Traditions Related to 1 Enoch from the Dead Sea Scrolls: An Overview and Assessment." Pages 41–63 in *The Early Enoch Literature*. Edited by Gabriele Boccaccini and John J. Collins. JSJSup 121. Leiden: Brill, 2007.

Thrupp, Sylvia L. *Millennial Dreams in Action: Essays in Comparative Study*. Den Haag: Mouton, 1962.

VanderKam, James C. *Jubilees: A Commentary on the Book of Jubilees Chapters 1–21*. Hermeneia. Minneapolis: Fortress, 2018.

Villiers, Pieter G. R. de. "Hermann Gunkel as Innovator." *OTE* 20 (2007): 333–51.

Yarbro Collins, Adela, ed. *Early Christian Apocalypticism: Genre and Social Setting. Semeia* 36 (1986).

Part 1
Apocalypse and Its Discontents: Texts, Contexts, and Retrospectives

Apocalypses in the Dead Sea Scrolls

John J. Collins

The definition of *apocalypse* published in *Semeia* 14 in 1979 was worked out before the publication of most of the material from Qumran Cave 4.[1] It is reasonable to ask, then, whether the material subsequently published contains works that might be classified as apocalypses or whether they might call for some adjustment of the definition of the genre. My own essay on the Jewish apocalypses in *Semeia* 14 included a very brief perusal of the Scrolls.[2] I suggested that the work that was closest to the form of an apocalypse was 4QVisions of Amram and noted 4QPseudo-Daniel and the Vision of the New Jerusalem as other possible apocalypses, but their genre was uncertain because of their fragmentary nature. I dismissed the so-called Angelic Liturgy (later known as The Songs of the Sabbath Sacrifice) and the Book of Giants as works that were clearly not in the form of apocalypses and noted that Józef T. Milik had referred to 4Q384-389 as an "Apocalypse of Ten Jubilees," which was to be published by John Strugnell but was otherwise unknown.[3] None of these works was officially published at the time.

In the same year, Hartmut Stegemann inquired into possible apocalypses in the Scrolls in his contribution to the Uppsala Colloquium on apocalypticism.[4] Stegemann noted that the main contribution of the Scrolls to the study of the genre was the evidence of the early date of the

---

1. John J. Collins, ed., *Apocalypse: The Morphology of a Genre*, Semeia 14 (1979).
2. John J. Collins, "The Jewish Apocalypes," *Semeia* 14 (1979): 48-49.
3. Józef T. Milik, *The Books of Enoch: Aramaic Fragments of Qumrân Cave 4*, with collaboration of Matthew Black (Oxford: Clarendon, 1976), 254.
4. Hartmut Stegemann, "Die Bedeutung der Qumranfunde für die Erforschung der Apokalyptik," in *Apocalypticism in the Mediterranean World and the Near East*, ed. David Hellholm, 2nd ed. (Tübingen: Mohr Siebeck, 1989), 495-530. Another survey was published in that year by Jean Carmignac, "Qu'est-ce que l'apocalyptique? Son

Enoch apocalypses, not an expansion of the corpus. He also noted the New Jerusalem text, Pseudo-Daniel, and the Visions of Amram as possible apocalypses and observed that most early apocalypses were written in Aramaic.

When the unpublished fragments from Qumran Cave 4 became available in the 1990s, the identification of apocalypses was taken up again.[5] Devorah Dimant offered a broad survey in 1994.[6] She attempted to describe "all the Qumran cave 4 fragments which, in my opinion, are closely related to the apocalyptic literature in theme, literary form, and central preoccupation."[7] She did not distinguish clearly between apocalypses and related literature. She included as a subcategory "visions and forecasts in a court setting."[8] This category included such works as the so-called Proto-Esther (4Q550) and the Prayer of Nabonidus: "Only narrative material from the two texts has survived but originally they may have also contained visions or dreams."[9] Dimant was evidently casting a wide net. The virtue of her approach was that she noticed points of contact between texts that are only loosely related, but it did not do much to address the question of genre. In a more recent essay in the Festschrift for Florentino García Martínez, she categorized the apocalyptic Aramaic compositions as "visionary compositions" and included in this category the New Jerusalem text, the Four Kingdoms text (4Q552–553), the Words of Michael

---

emploi a Qumrân," *RevQ* 10 (1979): 3–33, but it did not distinguish between apocalypses and works that were related loosely to apocalypticism.

5. Florentino García Martínez, *Qumran and Apocalyptic*, STDJ 9 (Leiden: Brill, 1992) published several studies of works broadly related to apocalyptic literature, but he did not focus on the question of genre. Likewise, his paper on "Apocalypticism in the Dead Sea Scrolls," in *The Origins of Apocalypticism in Judaism and Christianity*, vol. 1 of *The Encyclopedia of Apocalypticism*, ed. John J. Collins (New York: Continuum, 1998), 162–92, is concerned with the broader phenomenon of apocalypticism. This is also true of Lorenzo DiTommaso, "Apocalypticism and the Aramaic Texts from Qumran," in *Aramaica Qumranica: Proceedings of the Conference on the Aramaic Texts from Qumran in Aix-en-Provence 30 June–2 July 2008*, ed. Katell Berthelot and Daniel Stökl Ben Ezra, STDJ 94 (Leiden: Brill, 2010), 451–79 [and his contribution to this volume eds.].

6. Devorah Dimant, "Apocalyptic Texts at Qumran," in *The Community of the Renewed Covenant: The Notre Dame Symposium on the Dead Sea Scrolls*, ed. Eugene Ulrich and James C. VanderKam (Notre Dame: University of Notre Dame Press, 1994), 175–91.

7. Dimant, "Apocalyptic Texts at Qumran," 178.

8. Dimant, "Apocalyptic Texts at Qumran," 184–85.

9. Dimant, "Apocalyptic Texts at Qumran," 185.

(4Q529), the so-called Birth of Noah (4Q534–536), the Apocryphon of Levi (4Q540–541), and Pseudo-Daniel.[10] Dimant has written repeatedly on the Aramaic texts from Qumran, but she has also made an important contribution to the study of Hebrew material related to apocalypses by her edition of 4Q385–390 (roughly Milik's "Apocalypse of Ten Jubilees"), especially 4Q390 (Pseudo-Ezekiel and Apocryphon of Jeremiah C), which figures prominently in the recent discussion.[11]

I myself returned to the topic in 1999 in the Brill volumes celebrating the fiftieth anniversary of the discovery of the Scrolls.[12] In addition to the books of Enoch and Daniel, which are undisputed apocalypses, and Jubilees, which is a somewhat ambiguous example of the genre,[13] I considered the Book of Noah, Pseudo-Daniel, the Son of God text (or Aramaic Apocalypse, 4Q246), the Four Kingdoms, New Jerusalem, and Testament/Visions of Amram. All of these works are in Aramaic. I argued that the Book of Noah should be considered a narrative text, not an apocalypse, and I was also skeptical of the genre of the Pseudo-Daniel fragments. The Son of God text, the Four Kingdoms, the New Jerusalem, and the Testament/Visions of Amram can reasonably be regarded as apocalypses, granted the uncertainty demanded by their fragmentary state. The only plausible Hebrew apocalypses found at Qumran, other than Jubilees, are 4Q390 (the Apocryphon of Jeremiah C) and 4QPseudo-Ezekiel (4Q385, 386, 388). All of these texts are too fragmentary to allow for certainty. It is apparent that most of the texts that can

---

10. Devorah Dimant, "The Qumran Aramaic Texts and the Qumran Community," in *Flores Florentino: Dead Sea Scrolls and Other Early Jewish Studies in Honour of Florentino García Martínez*, ed. A. Hilhorst, Émile Puech, and Eibert J. C. Tigchelaar, JSJSup 122 (Leiden: Brill, 2007), 200–201. See the comments of Florentino García Martínez, "Aramaica qumranica apocalyptica," in Berthelot and Ben Ezra, *Aramaica Qumranica*, 438. García Martínez argues that a disproportionately large segment of the Aramaic writings has an apocalyptic character, even if they are not strictly apocalypses.

11. Devorah Dimant, *Qumran Cave 4.XXI. Parabiblical Texts, Part 4: Pseudo-Prophetic Texts*, DJD 30 (Oxford: Clarendon, 2000).

12. John J. Collins, "Apocalypticism and Literary Genre in the Dead Sea Scrolls," in *The Dead Sea Scrolls after Fifty Years*, ed. Peter W. Flint and James C. VanderKam (Leiden: Brill, 1999), 2:406–21.

13. See John J. Collins, "The Genre of the Book of Jubilees," in *A Teacher for All Generations: Essays in Honor of James C. VanderKam*, ed. Eric F. Mason et al., JSJSup 153 (Leiden: Brill, 2011), 2:737–55.

plausibly be identified as apocalypses are in Aramaic, and very few are in Hebrew.[14]

A new attempt to sketch out a classification was made by Armin Lange and Ulrike Mittmann-Richert in DJD 39, published in 2002, in the context of an inventory of the entire corpus of Scrolls.[15] Lange and Mittmann-Richert attempted to classify the whole corpus in a few pages and provided minimal discussion of their criteria. They rendered a service to scholarship by making a preliminary classification, but their work is a starting point rather than a complete analysis. Their schematic outline was filled out in an excellent study by Lange's student Bennie Reynolds.[16] The focus of Reynolds's work was on distinguishing between symbolic and nonsymbolic apocalypses, rather than on identifying apocalypses in the Dead Sea Scrolls, but while he was not exhaustive he discussed most of the works that Lange and Mittmann-Richert identified as apocalypses. Another brief overview was provided by Jörg Frey in 2007. Frey noted but did not follow the Lange and Mittmann-Richert classification. He began with Daniel and Enoch and related texts. He associated the Apocryphon of Jeremiah with Jubilees. He also classified as apocalyptic texts the New Jerusalem, Visions of Amram, and Words of Michael.[17]

Lange and Mittmann-Richert acknowledged a distinction between the literary genre apocalypse and apocalyptic thought, which can be expressed in various literary forms. They focused on the genre and supplemented it with a broader category of "eschatological texts." They did not state a definition, but they distinguished three kinds of apocalypses:

> Some of them use a symbolic cypher to encode their message as is already well known, for example, from the book of Daniel, while others like the Apocryphon of Jeremiah reveal their predestinarian interpreta-

---

14. [See the essay in this volume by Matthew Goff—eds.]

15. Armin Lange, with Ulrike Mittmann-Richert, "Annotated List of the Texts from the Judaean Desert Classified by Content and Genre," in *The Texts from the Judaean Desert: Indices and an Introduction to the Discoveries in the Judaean Desert Series*, ed. Emanuel Tov, DJD 39 (Oxford: Clarendon, 2002), 141–42.

16. Bennie H. Reynolds III, *Between Symbolism and Realism: The Use of Symbolic and Non-symbolic Language in Ancient Jewish Apocalypses 333–63 B.C.E.*, JAJSup 8 (Göttingen: Vandenhoeck & Ruprecht, 2011).

17. Jörg Frey, "Die Bedeutung der Qumrantexte für das Verständnis der Apokalyptik im Frühjudentum und im Urchristentum," in *Apokalyptik und Qumran*, ed. Jörg Frey and Michael Becker, Einblicke 6 (Paderborn: Bonifatius, 2007), 30–33.

tions of Israel's history and their eschatological forecasts without such a symbolic encoding.... A third type of apocalypse focuses on journeys of visionaries to a world beyond this one.[18]

It is always possible to classify texts in more than one way. My purpose here is to compare this way of classifying apocalyptic texts with the morphology published in *Semeia* 14 and consider the different implications of the two systems.

In fact, the two approaches can be easily correlated. *Semeia* 14 distinguished two main subtypes of apocalypses, one dubbed "historical apocalypses," characterized by a review of history in the guise of prophecy, and the other "cosmic" apocalypses or otherworldly journeys. Each of these subtypes was further subdivided on the basis of their eschatology. Lange and Mittman-Richert, in effect, subdivided the historical apocalypses into two types, one of which encodes the account of history in symbolic form while the other does not. But they also omitted from consideration some of the main defining characteristics of apocalypses in *Semeia* 14: the fact that the text is presented as a revelation mediated by an otherworldly being (usually an angel) to a human recipient and the fact that it envisions a final judgment that includes the judgment of the dead, while it may or may not include transformation of this world. Lange and Mittman-Richert's discussion was very brief, and I suspect that they presupposed that the texts are revelatory in some way, but the lack of explicit attention to the form of revelation and the specificity of eschatological expectations makes a difference as to which texts are classified as belonging to the genre. If the typology were to be based strictly on the type of symbolism, there would be no reason to distinguish otherworldly journeys as a separate type; they would be classified as nonsymbolic apocalypses. The distinction between symbolic and nonsymbolic apocalypses, corresponding to that between symbolic dreams and message dreams in the ancient world,[19] is certainly valid and useful. I would argue that a distinction between apocalypses that focus on the course of history and those that focus on otherworldly geography is more significant for the worldview of the texts, but the two classifications are complementary and certainly not mutually exclusive.

---

18. Lange and Mittmann-Richert, "Annotated List," 121.
19. Reynolds, *Between Symbolism and Realism*, 62, following Leo Oppenheim, *The Interpretation of Dreams in the Ancient Near East* (Philadelphia: American Philosophical Society, 1956). The distinction goes back to Artemidorus.

1. Symbolic Apocalypses

By "symbolic apocalypses," Lange and Mittman-Richert mean apocalypses that provide an overview of history cloaked in symbolism. The prototypical symbolic apocalypse is Daniel, especially chapter 7, where four kingdoms are presented as four beasts rising from the sea, and chapter 8, where the Persian and Greek kingdoms are depicted as a ram and a he-goat. The Animal Apocalypse in 1 Enoch is another clear example. Lange and Mittman-Richert suggest two other examples, 4Q246 (the Son of God text) and 4QFour Kingdoms (4Q552–553).

1.1. 4Q246

4Q246, sometimes called "the Aramaic Apocalypse," is indeed plausibly understood as the interpretation of a symbolic vision, although that classification hangs by a narrow thread ("like sparks that you saw, so will their kingdoms be"; 4QapocDan ar II, 1–2).[20] Whether the interpreter is necessarily an *angelus interpres*, as Lange and Mittman-Richert suggest, is not so clear; the interpreter could conceivably be a human being, like Daniel in Dan 2. (He seems to be explaining the king's dream.) The interpretation predicts a time when the people of God will arise and all will cease from the sword. I have argued at length elsewhere that the figure that is called "son of God" should be interpreted as a Jewish messiah.[21] While we do not have the end of the document, it would seem to be similar to Dan 7 in predicting an eternal kingdom without reference to individual afterlife or the judgment of the dead.

1.2. The Four-Kingdom Apocalypse

The situation is similar with the Four-Kingdom Apocalypse, where the kingdoms are symbolized as trees. The first tree is clearly identified as Babylon, and it is said to rule over Persia. The second tree is most prob-

---

20. See Reynolds, *Between Symbolism and Realism*, 368–69; and Andrew Perrin, *The Dynamics of Dream-Vision Revelation in the Aramaic Dead Sea Scrolls*, JAJSup 19 (Göttingen: Vandenhoeck & Ruprecht, 2015), 72–73. Unless otherwise stated, all translations are my own.

21. John J. Collins, *The Scepter and the Star: Messianism in Light of the Dead Sea Scrolls*, 2nd ed. (Grand Rapids: Eerdmans, 2010), 171–90.

ably to be identified as Greece. (The visionary looks to the west, and the kingdom rules over the harbors and the sea.)[22] The identity of the other two trees is disputed. They may have been identified as the Ptolemies and Seleucids, or perhaps as the Seleucids and Rome. It is clear that the text offers variations on the four-kingdom schema known from Dan 2 and 7, but it departs from Daniel's identification of the four kingdoms. In this case, the interpreter is very probably angelic. Again, we do not know how the vision concludes. By analogy with Dan 2 and 7, we should expect that the pagan kingdoms will pass away and the kingdom of God endure. Whether this will entail a judgment of the dead is impossible to say on the basis of the fragments, but the judgment is not attested in the extant text.

1.3. Dream Visions of Noah

The Genesis Apocryphon preserves several dream-visions of Noah.[23] These are sometimes thought to derive from a Book of Noah.[24] They are very fragmentary. The most important of these for our purposes is found in GenAp XII, 26(?) through column XV. The content is summarized as follows by Dan Machiela:

> Here Noah is portrayed as a great cedar tree and his three sons as shoots springing from it. Future events are explained through various interactions between the shoots and further offshoots of the cedar, which appear to include the travel of Shem, Ham, and Japheth's sons to their various geographic allotments.... At some point after these events Noah is told of a cataclysmic, final judgment during which the Lord is depicted as a warrior coming from the south, with fire at his side and sickle in hand.[25]

---

22. Reynolds, *Between Symbolism and Realism*, 200.

23. For the text and translation see Daniel A. Machiela, *The Dead Sea Genesis Apocryphon: A New Text and Translation with Introduction and Special Treatment of Columns 13–17*, STDJ 79 (Leiden: Brill, 2009).

24. Reynolds, *Between Symbolism and Realism*, 207–14.

25. Daniel A. Machiela, "Genesis Revealed: The Apocalyptic Apocryphon from Qumran Cave 1," in *Qumran Cave 1 Revisited: Texts from Cave 1 Sixty Years after Their Discovery; Proceedings of the Sixth Meeting of the IOQS in Ljubljana*, ed. Daniel K. Falk et al., STDJ 91 (Leiden: Brill, 2010), 216.

As Reynolds comments, this passage "unquestionably contains both a symbolic vision and an angelic interpretation."[26] It also appears to contain an overview of history with an eschatological conclusion.[27] There is no mention of resurrection or postmortem judgment in the preserved text, which is admittedly fragmentary. The correspondence with the definition of *Semeia* 14, then, is not complete but is extensive nonetheless.

2. Nonsymbolic Apocalypses

The prototypical nonsymbolic apocalypse in the classification of Lange and Mittmann-Richert is Dan 11, where the angel gives Daniel a prediction of Hellenistic history, without encoding it in symbols. The Apocalypse of Weeks in 1 Enoch would also qualify, even if the weeks are not taken literally. Lange and Mittmann-Richert classify five fragmentary texts in this category: 4QHistorical Text A (4Q248), 4QpsDan^{a-b}, 4QpsDan^c, Apocryphon of Jeremiah C, and Words of Michael (4Q529).[28]

2.1. 4QHistorical Text A

4QHistorical Text A is a short Hebrew fragment reminiscent of Dan 11.[29] The editors regard it as a source for the canonical apocalypse. It is an account in the guise of prophecy of an invasion of Egypt, possibly by Antiochus Epiphanes, although the protagonist is not named.[30] The edi-

---

26. Reynolds, *Between Symbolism and Realism*, 214.

27. Reynolds suggests that Noah is being warned of the impending flood through a symbolic vision, but he notes the problem with this interpretation: the flood has apparently taken place in the text before it is predicted in the dream (*Between Symbolism and Realism*, 214). Machiela, "Genesis Revealed," 216, and Andrew B. Perrin, "The Aramaic Imagination: Incubating Apocalyptic Thought and Genre in Dream Visions among the Qumran Aramaic Texts," in *Apocalyptic Thinking in Early Judaism: Engaging with John Collins'* The Apocalyptic Imagination, ed. Sidnie White Crawford and Cecilia Wassén, JSJSup 182 (Leiden: Brill, 2018), 126, regard the vision as eschatological.

28. Lange and Mitmann-Richert, "Annotated List," 141–42.

29. Magen Broshi and Esther Eshel, "248. 4QHistorical Text A," in *Qumran Cave 4.XXVI: Cryptic Texts and Miscellanea, Part 1*, ed. Stephen J. Pfann et al., DJD 36 (Oxford: Clarendon, 2000), 192–200.

30. Magen Broshi and Esther Eshel, "The Greek King Is Antiochus IV (4QHistorical Text = 4Q248)," *JJS* 48 (1997): 120–29.

tors read the last two lines of the fragment as an eschatological conclusion: "And when the shattering of the power of the ho[ly] people [comes to an end] [then shall] all these things [be fulfilled]. The children of [Israel] shall return."[31] They read the first phrase of the passage just cited as נפץ יד עם הק[דש], the shattering of the power of the holy people. This phrase corresponds closely to Dan 12:7: ככלות נפץ יד עם קדש. As pointed in the MT, the word נפץ is an infinitive, "shattering." Many commentators, however, follow Anthony Ashley Bevan in emending to read a participle and transposing the words נפץ and יד to read "when the power of the shatterer of the holy people comes to an end."[32] The reference then is to the death of Antiochus Epiphanes. The transposition is supported by the word order of the Old Greek. If the same Hebrew expression were found in the Qumran text, the emendation would be questionable. But the reading of the crucial Hebrew words is problematic. Only the ligature of the nun of נפץ is preserved, and the *pe* does not look like other *pes* in the text. Milik read this line בציר עם הקיץ, "the vintage with the summer fruits."[33] This reading has its own problems, since the fourth Hebrew letter seems to be a clear *daleth*, not a *resh*. It should possibly be read as בציד, "with provisions." In this case, line 9 is not an eschatological turning point but simply a continuation of the *ex eventu* prediction.[34]

It is certainly possible that this prophecy was presented as a revelation by an angel, as was Dan 11, but there is no mention of an angel in the extant fragment. Formally, the passage might equally well be compared to passages in the Sibylline Oracles. There is no clear evidence that it should be regarded as an apocalypse.[35]

---

31. Broshi and Eshel, "248. 4QHistorical Text A," 193, lines 9–10.

32. Anthony Ashley Bevan, *A Short Commentary on the Book of Daniel* (Cambridge: Cambridge University Press, 1892), 206; see John J. Collins, *Daniel: A Commentary on the Book of Daniel*, Hermeneia (Minneapolis: Fortress, 1993), 399.

33. For Milik's reading, see Ben Zion Wacholder and Martin G. Abegg, *A Preliminary Edition of the Unpublished Dead Sea Scrolls*, vol. 3 (Washington, DC: Biblical Archeology Society, 1995), 33. It is followed by Michael O. Wise, in Michael O. Wise, Martin G. Abegg, and Edward Cook, *The Dead Sea Scrolls: A New Translation* (San Francisco: Harper, 1996), 271.

34. See further John J. Collins, "New Light on the Book of Daniel from the Dead Sea Scrolls," in *Perspectives in the Study of Old Testament and Early Judaism*, ed. Florentino García Martínez and Edward Noort, VTSup 73 (Leiden: Brill, 1998), 194–95.

35. George J. Brooke, "What Makes a Text Historical?," in *Reading the Dead Sea Scrolls: Essays in Method*, ed. George J. Brooke, EJL 39 (Atlanta: Society of Biblical

2.2. The Apocryphon of Jeremiah C

In Reynolds's exposition, the primary exemplar of a nonsymbolic apocalypse is the Apocryphon of Jeremiah C.[36] This is also an overview of history in the guise of prophecy. The identification and extent of this text is a matter of ongoing controversy. As noted already, Milik had referred to an "apocalypse of ten jubilees" in 4Q384–389. It subsequently became apparent that 4Q383–391 contained fragments of prophetic texts and that more than one composition was involved. (It is not clear just which fragments Milik had in mind.) 4Q385–390 were eventually entrusted to Dimant. At first, she separated out 4Q390 as a separate work, called Pseudo-Moses.[37] In the DJD edition, however, she distinguished only two compositions, Pseudo-Ezekiel (4Q385, 385b, 385c, 386, and 388) and the Apocryphon of Jeremiah (4Q383, 385a, 387, 388a, 389, 390, 387a).[38] All the fragments of the Apocryphon of Jeremiah except 4Q383 are assigned to Apocryphon of Jeremiah C, but there are no overlaps between 4Q390 and the other fragments. Consequently, there is still debate as to whether 4Q390 is part of the same work as the other Apocryphon of Jeremiah C fragments.[39] Reynolds argues that 4Q390 is part of the Jeremianic text but not integrated with the other fragments.[40] (Compare Dan 7–12, where the different visions are formally distinct.) Kipp Davis argues that 4Q390 represents a later reinterpretation of the Apocryphon.[41]

Literature, 2013), 195, suggests that it is "an apocalyptic text of some kind" or "apocalyptic source material for the Book of Daniel." We may grant the analogy with Dan 11, but that does not in itself determine the genre of the text. The specific argument for dependence of Daniel on this text is problematic.

36. Reynolds, *Between Symbolism and Realism*, 263–325.

37. Devorah Dimant, "New Light from Qumran on the Jewish Pseudepigrapha—4Q390," in *The Madrid Qumran Congress: Proceedings of the International Congress on the Dead Sea Scrolls*, ed. Julio Trebolle Barrera and Luis Vegas Montaner, STDJ 11 (Leiden: Brill, 1991), 2:405–48.

38. Dimant, *Qumran Cave 4.XXI*.

39. Eibert J. C. Tigchelaar, "Classifications of the Collection of Dead Sea Scrolls and the Case of Apocryphon of Jeremiah C," *JSJ* 43 (2012): 540–49. Tigchelaar concludes that 4Q390 does not belong with the other Apocryphon of Jeremiah manuscripts.

40. Reynolds, *Between Symbolism and Realism*, 268.

41. C. J. Patrick Davis, "Torah-Performance and History in the Golah: Rewritten Bible or 'Re-Presentational' Authority in the Apocryphon of Jeremiah C," in *Celebrating the Dead Sea Scrolls: A Canadian Collection*, ed. Kyung S. Baek, Peter W. Flint,

On Dimant's reconstruction, the Apocryphon begins with a narrative account of a public reading in Babylon of a document sent by Jeremiah from Egypt. The document reviews history, beginning with the Exodus, and then continues to predict the history of the Second Temple period in the future tense. 4Q390 refers to a period of subjection to the sons of Aaron for seventy years, and to the rule of Belial over them.

The predictive, or *ex eventu*, part of the overview extends from the Babylonian exile to the eschaton and is evidently a revelation spoken by God to Jeremiah. It is not clear whether Jeremiah has a vision; the extant fragments report direct divine speech. The ending of the text is also lost. The main clue that it envisages eschatological salvation is a reference to "the foliage of the tree of life" (4Q385a 17 II, 2–3). Reynolds argues that this implies both resurrection and eternal life and argues that this sets the Apocryphon apart both from most prophetic texts that do not envision an eschaton and from apocalyptic texts that do not narrate it as part of a revelation.[42]

Another indication that the Apocryphon may be an apocalypse lies in the fact that it has a developed angelology and demonology. The word *mal'āk* may be used to indicate both angels and demons. The demons are more specifically called "the angels of Mastemot." This distinctive phrase is also found in 4Q390 and is one of the main reasons for associating 4Q390 with the Apocryphon. The Apocryphon also refers to "goat demons" (4Q385a 2). In the eschatological period, an evil king of the nations will arise, and Israel will be removed from being a people. The kingdom of Egypt will also be broken. The land of Israel will be abandoned into the hands of the angels of Mastemot. The text goes on to describe various other upheavals, but it is very fragmentary.

Reynolds reasonably concludes that "not enough of the text of *Apocryphon of Jeremiah C* is preserved to make a definitive statement about its genre."[43] He claims that it is "most reasonably read together with other apocalypses." In light of its fragmentary condition, however, much remains uncertain.

---

and Jean Duhaime, EJL 30 (Atlanta: Society of Biblical Literature, 2012), 468–72. See further Kipp Davis, *The Cave 4 Apocryphon of Jeremiah and the Qumran Jeremianic Traditions: Prophetic Persona and the Construction of Community Identity*, STDJ 111 (Leiden: Brill, 2014), 101.

42. Reynolds, *Between Symbolism and Realism*, 271–72.

43. Reynolds, *Between Symbolism and Realism*, 272. So also Frey, "Die Bedeutung der Qumrantexte," 30.

2.3. Pseudo-Daniel

4QpsDan^a and 4QpsDan^b recount a long review of history, recited by Daniel before Belshazzar.[44] Unlike the visions of Dan 2 and 7, the history is not encoded in symbolism. Real names are mentioned (Enoch, Nebuchadnezzar, and a Hellenistic ruler called Balakros, who has not been identified). There is mention of a kingdom in the eschatological period. It is followed by an adjective, of which only the initial letter, ק, is preserved. Milik restored קדמיתא, first, and supposed that the text spoke of four kingdoms.[45] In the DJD volume, Peter Flint and I opted for קדישתא, holy, on the assumption that the reference is to a final, eschatological kingdom. Milik read 4Q245 as part of the same composition and took the verb יקומון in 4Q245 2 as a reference to resurrection, thereby completing a classic apocalyptic overview of history. But 4Q245 is largely taken up with the names of rulers, including some Hasmoneans, and is clearly part of a different composition. Even there, it is not apparent that "arise" must refer to resurrection.

4QpsDan^{a–b} is certainly a revelatory text.[46] The fact that Daniel acts as interpreter suggests an analogy with Dan 2 rather than Dan 7 or 8, granted that the revelation is not symbolic in this case. The revelation seems to be in the form of a writing (see the references to something "written" in 4Q243 6). This could be a book, such as one of the books of Enoch, or a heavenly tablet. (It is evidently much longer than the writing on the wall in Dan 5.) Reynolds makes a strong case for heavenly tablets.[47] If this is correct, it strengthens the case for viewing Pseudo-Daniel as an apocalypse. The text does not mention angels, but one of the worst sins of Judah is the offering of child sacrifices to "the demons of error" (4Q243 13; 4Q244 12). The review of history has an eschatological conclusion, which includes the gathering of the elect. Reynolds rightly notes that the next verse relates to continuing life on earth, and so the reference is probably not to resurrec-

---

44. John J. Collins and Peter W. Flint, "Pseudo-Daniel," in *Qumran Cave 4.XVII: Parabiblical Texts, Part 3*, ed. George J. Brooke et al., DJD 22 (Oxford: Clarendon, 1996), 133–52; and Reynolds, *Between Symbolism and Realism*, 327–74.

45. Józef T. Milik, "'Prière de Nabonide' et autres écrits d'un cycle de Daniel," *RB* 63 (1956): 411–15. See Collins and Flint, "Pseudo-Daniel," 150.

46. Reynolds, *Between Symbolism and Realism*, 332.

47. Reynolds, *Between Symbolism and Realism*, 333–38.

tion of the dead.[48] Here again we may have a review of history that corresponds to that of the historical apocalypses to a great degree but does not refer explicitly to the judgment of the dead.

4QpsDan[c] (4Q245) also involves the interpretation of a writing by Daniel. It appears to contain lists of priests and kings. There is also an eschatological conclusion when wickedness will be exterminated. Some people will arise, whether in a final resurrection or in a more mundane sense.

In both cases, the similarities to the standard apocalypses are considerable, but there are also differences. One significant difference concerns the manner of revelation. Unlike Dan 7–12, where Daniel is the recipient of revelations mediated by an angel, here Daniel is the interpreter, and the revelation is given in writing of some form, whether a book or a heavenly tablet. The eschatological scenarios are uncertain because of the fragmentary nature of the texts. It is not clear that either one concludes with resurrection and judgment of individuals.

2.4. 4QWords of Michael

The final example adduced by Lange and Mittmann-Richert, and listed by Reynolds, is 4QWords of Michael ar (4Q529).[49] This very fragmentary text is different from those we have been considering, since it is not a revelation to a human recipient. Rather it is a revelation mediated by Michael to the other angels. Nonetheless, it entails a vision and a book. It was evidently concerned with human history ("a city will be built to the name of my Great One … all that is wicked will be done before my Great One," 4Q529 9–10). There is also mention of a man who will arise in a distant province, but the text is too fragmentary to tell whether there is an eschatological finale.

3. Otherworldly Journey?

The prototypical otherworldly journey is that of Enoch in the Book of the Watchers, later developed in more elaborate form in 2 Enoch.[50] Hebrew

---

48. Reynolds, *Between Symbolism and Realism*, 341.
49. Émile Puech, "Paroles de Michel ar," *Qumrân Grotte 4.XXII: Textes araméens, première partie, 4Q529–549*, ed. Émile Puech, DJD 31 (Oxford: Clarendon, 2001), 1–8.
50. See John J. Collins, "Journeys to the World beyond in Ancient Judaism," in *Apocalypse, Prophecy, and Pseudepigraphy: On Jewish Apocalyptic Literature*, ed. John J. Collins (Grand Rapids: Eerdmans, 2015), 178–97.

prophets sometimes claimed to have stood in the council of the Lord or to have seen the Lord on his heavenly throne. In the case of Enoch, however, the actual ascent is described, and he is guided on his travels by an angel. There were precedents for this kind of revelatory journey in the Mediterranean world and the Near East, dating back to Gilgamesh, but they appear as a novelty in Jewish tradition in the apocalyptic literature. The Book of the Watchers and the Astronomical Book of Enoch, both attested at Qumran, are recognized as otherworldly journeys in *Semeia* 14. Lange and Mittmann-Richert also classify the Aramaic New Jerusalem text as an otherworldly journey, but this is problematic.

3.1. The New Jerusalem Text

The New Jerusalem text is a visionary account of the New Jerusalem, in which the visionary appears to be guided by an angel.[51] The introductory section is missing, but there is no description of a journey beyond the normal realm of human experience. Lorenzo DiTommaso allows that an otherworldly journey may be implied but comments that "none of these actions necessarily demands the context of an otherworldly journey."[52] The model for the New Jerusalem text is clearly Ezek 40–48.[53] The biblical vision is located "in visions of God," not in heaven but in the land of Israel, a kind of visionary third-space, so to speak. It bears significant analogies to apocalyptic visions, but it lacks an eschatological dimension, beyond the restoration of an ideal Jerusalem. For that reason, it is usually regarded as at most protoapocalyptic. The Aramaic New Jerusalem text does include an eschatological section, unfortunately very badly preserved.[54] It out-

---

51. Fragments are preserved in 1Q32, 2Q24, 4Q554, 4Q554a, 4Q555, 5Q15, and 11Q18. See Florentino García Martínez, Eibert Tigchelaar, and A. S. van der Woude, "11QNew Jerusalem ar," in *Qumran Cave 11.II. 11Q2–18, 11Q20–31*, ed. Florentino García Martínez, et al., DJD 23 (Oxford: Clarendon, 1998), 305–55; García Martínez, "New Jerusalem," *EDSS* 2:606–10; and Lorenzo DiTommaso, *The Dead Sea New Jerusalem Text: Contents and Contexts*, TSAJ 110 (Tübingen: Mohr Siebeck, 2005).

52. DiTommaso, *Dead Sea* New Jerusalem *Text*, 110.

53. García Martínez, "New Jerusalem," 608; and Eibert J. C. Tigchelaar, "The Imaginal Context and the Visionary of the Aramaic New Jerusalem," in *Flores Florentino: Dead Sea Scrolls and Other Early Jewish Studies in Honour of Florentino García Martínez*, ed. A. Hilhorst, Émile Puech, and Eibert J. C. Tigchelaar, JSJSup 122 (Leiden: Brill, 2007), 257. Tigchelaar suggests that the implied visionary was Jacob.

54. DiTommaso, *The Dead Sea* New Jerusalem *Text*, 62.

lines a succession of kingdoms that appear one after another. The passage appears to end with the subordination of these kingdoms, presumably to the people of God (4Q554 2 III, 22). This kind of scenario is atypical of otherworldly journeys in the pre-Christian period and more typical of the historical type of apocalypse.

DiTommaso is confident that New Jerusalem "itself is almost certainly an apocalypse."[55] Even this much is in some doubt in view of the fragmentary state of the composition. The passage on the succession of kingdoms may have concluded in the manner of Dan 2 or 7, with the resolution of the earthly kingdoms but without any reference to the judgment of the dead. The Aramaic New Jerusalem text may very well be a fragmentary apocalypse. More cautiously, one could classify it as a revelatory text too fragmentary for further classification. The surviving fragments do not describe an otherworldly journey.

3.2. Aramaic Levi

Apart from the Book of the Watchers, the only account of an otherworldly journey in the Dead Sea Scrolls is found in the vision of Levi in Aramaic Levi.[56] In 4Q213a 2 15–18 we read

> Then I was shown visions [
> In the vision of visions and I saw the heaven[s
> Beneath me, high until it reached to the heaven[s
> To me the gates of heaven, and an angel ...[57]

---

55. DiTommaso, *The Dead Sea New Jerusalem Text*, 110. So also García Martínez, "New Jerusalem," 608–9; Jörg Frey, "The New Jerusalem Text in Its Historical and Traditio-Historical Context," in *The Dead Sea Scrolls Fifty Years after Their Discovery: Proceedings of the Jerusalem Congress, July 20–25, 1997*, ed. Lawrence H. Schiffman et al. (Jerusalem: Israel Exploration Society, 2000), 800–16; and Frey, "Die Bedeutung der Qumrantexte," 30.

56. Michael E. Stone and Jonas C. Greenfield, "Aramaic Levi Document," in *Qumran Cave 4.XVII: Parabiblical Texts, Part 3*, ed. George J. Brooke et al., DJD 22 (Oxford: Clarendon, 1996), 1–72; Jonas C. Greenfield, Michael E. Stone, and Esther Eshel, *The Aramaic Levi Document: Edition, Translation, Commentary*, SVTP 19 (Leiden: Brill, 2004); Perrin, *Dynamics of Dream-Vision Revelation*, 61–65.

57. Stone and Greenfield, "Aramaic Levi Document," 33.

The Greek Testament of Levi contains an account of the ascent of Levi. The heavens were opened, and an angel called on Levi to enter. In the Greek, he is shown seven heavens, but it is apparent that the cosmology has gone through a process of growth. In chapter 2, Levi sees three heavens and is promised that he will see four more. Chapter 3 speaks of seven heavens, but the highest heaven, where God resides, is mentioned fourth in the sequence.[58] The Aramaic Levi Apocryphon does not mention a numbered sequence of heavens at all, in the extant fragments, but it seems to have included at least a rudimentary heavenly journey.

4. Other Apocalypses?

The list proposed by Lange and Mittmann-Richert is not exhaustive. Eschatological texts such as the War Scroll are clearly not presented as apocalyptic revelations. The so-called Messianic Apocalypse, 4Q521, is a hymnic text rather than a revelation. The Songs of the Sabbath Sacrifice is not presented as revelation either.[59] The text that stands out as intriguingly like the apocalypses is the Aramaic Visions of Amram.[60] This is simultaneously a testament and a revelation: it is a copy of the writing of the words of the vision of Amram, son of Qahat, son of Levi. Amram relates how he saw two superhuman figures battling over him and asking him by which of them he chose to be ruled. Each had three names. One is called Melchiresha, so his counterpart is presumably Melchizedek. Plausible suggestions for the other names are Michael and Prince of Light, on the one hand, and Belial and Prince of Darkness, on the other.[61] One rules over all darkness and the other over all that is bright. By analogy with the Instruction on the Two Spirits in the Community Rule, we should expect that the conflict

---

58. The textual tradition of the Testaments is confused. See Marinus de Jonge, *The Testaments of the Twelve Patriarchs: A Critical Edition of the Greek Text* (Leiden: Brill, 1978), 24–29; and Adela Yarbro Collins, "The Seven Heavens in Jewish and Christian Apocalypses," in *Cosmology and Eschatology in Jewish and Christian Apocalypticism*, JSJSup 50 (Leiden: Brill, 1996), 26.

59. Similarly Frey, "Die Bedeutung der Qumrantexte," 31–32.

60. So also Frey, "Die Bedeutung der Qumrantexte," 31. For the text, see Puech, "Visions de 'Amram," in Puech, *Qumrân Grotte 4.XXII*, 283–405.

61. Paul J. Kobelski, *Melchizedek and Melchiresha*, CBQMS 10 (Washington, DC: Catholic Biblical Association of America, 1981), 24–36; Liora Goldman, "Dualism in the Visions of Amram," *RevQ* 95 (2010): 421–32; and Perrin, *Dynamics of Dream-Vision Revelation*, 67–69.

between Light and Darkness has an eschatological resolution. As usual with the new texts from Qumran, the attempt to classify them definitively is frustrated by the fragmentary state of preservation, but the Visions of Amram is very plausibly viewed as an apocalypse.

Another plausible apocalypse absent from Lange and Mittmann-Richert's list is Pseudo-Ezekiel (4Q385, 385b, 385c, 386, 388).[62] This Hebrew text is based on the book of Ezekiel. Much of it seems to consist of a dialogue between God and Ezekiel, but the *merkabah* vision (Ezek 1; 4Q385 6) is introduced as "the vision that Ezekiel saw." The best preserved section concerns the vision of the valley of dry bones (Ezek 37). This is represented by three copies (4Q385 2+3; 4Q386 1 I; 4Q388 7). In the biblical book, the resurrection was a metaphor for the restoration of Israel. In the text from Qumran, it seems to be taken literally. Dimant claims that "resurrection and related matters provide the exegetical axis underlying 4Q385 2+3, 4, and 6."[63] Other fragments of 4Q386 concern the future deliverance of Israel and return to the land. Dimant summarizes the sequence produced by the combination of 4Q385 and 4Q386 as follows: resurrection of the righteous; future redemption of Israel and the defeat of Egypt and Babylon; and hastening time so that Israel will inherit the land. Thus far the sequence resembles Ezek 38–39. Thereafter follows the *merkavah* vision. Dimant suggests that the placement of the *merkavah* vision may be influenced by Ezek 43:1–5, where Ezekiel has a vision like the one he had at the beginning of the book.[64]

Frey claims that this text has no formal features of an apocalypse and classifies it as a parabiblical text.[65] In view of the fragmentary state of the text, the genre of the whole is uncertain, but at least it contains an apocalypse as a constituent part. Dialogue with God or an angel is a well-attested mode of apocalyptic revelation (especially in 4 Ezra). If the resurrection is indeed understood as an eschatological event, then the sequence described by Dimant essentially corresponds to that of an historical apocalypse. Pseudo-Ezekiel would seem to be a clearer example of an apocalypse than the Apocryphon of Jeremiah.

---

62. Dimant, *Qumran Cave 4.XXI*, 7–88.
63. Dimant, *Qumran Cave 4.XXI*, 9.
64. Dimant, *Qumran Cave 4.XXI*, 10.
65. Frey, "Die Bedeutung der Qumrantexte," 32.

5. Genres and Constellations

We have then a number of texts that exhibit significant features of apocalypses, although all are fragmentary. Several of these are in Aramaic: 4Q246, Pseudo-Daniel, the Visions of Amram, the New Jerusalem, the Four Kingdoms, Aramaic Levi, 4QWords of Michael, and the Vision of Noah in the Genesis Apocryphon. The only Hebrew texts that come into consideration are Pseudo-Ezekiel and the Apocryphon of Jeremiah. Most of these texts deviate from the definition in *Semeia* 14 in some respect, at least in the preserved fragments. In some cases, the manner of revelation is unclear (Apocryphon of Jeremiah), or the interpreter is human rather than angelic (Pseudo-Daniel, 4Q246, Four Kingdoms). Several lack explicit reference to a judgment of the dead in the preserved fragments.

Recent work on genre theory has increasingly favored prototype theory, whereby works are recognized as members of a genre because of their resemblance to a prototypical example, and that resemblance can vary in degree.[66] So genres inevitably have fuzzy edges, borderline cases, and related types. Most of the texts considered in this essay lie on the fuzzy edges of the genre as defined in *Semeia* 14.

The most intriguing problem, to my mind, is posed by texts such as the Four Kingdoms text, 4Q246 (the Son of God text), and Pseudo-Daniel (4Q243-244), all of which greatly resemble the historical apocalypses in content but are mediated by a human interpreter and lack explicit mention of judgment of the dead in the preserved text. The difference between symbolic (Four Kingdoms) and nonsymbolic (Pseudo-Daniel; the symbolic character of 4Q246 hangs on a single symbol) does not seem to be especially significant. This kind of revelation has a notable precedent in Dan 2. Even Dan 7 and 8, taken apart from the rest of the book, lack explicit mention of postmortem judgment. The eschatological dream-vision in Dan 2 was left aside in the categorization of texts as apocalypses in *Semeia* 14

---

66. Carol A. Newsom, "Spying out the Land: A Report from Genology," in *Seeking Out the Wisdom of the Ancients: Essays Offered to Honor Michael V. Fox on the Occasion of His Sixty-Fifth Birthday*, ed. Ronald L. Troxel, Kelvin G. Friebel, and Dennis Robert Magary (Winona Lake, IN: Eisenbrauns, 2005), 437-50; Hindy Najman and Mladen Popović, eds., *Rethinking Genre: Essays in Honor of John J. Collins*, DSD 17 (2010); and John J. Collins, "Introduction: The Genre Apocalypse Reconsidered," in Collins, *Apocalypse, Prophecy, and Pseudepigraphy*, 1-20.

because it was exceptional. In light of the corpus of Aramaic dream visions found in the Scrolls, it does not seem exceptional any longer.

The question therefore arises, how should such texts be categorized? Should the definition of apocalypse be expanded to allow for texts that are mediated by a human interpreter, or do not mention judgment of the dead? Should such texts be regarded as a distinct subtype of the genre? Or should they be acknowledged as a distinct though closely related type? What is important, of course, is that both similarities and differences be recognized.

Andrew Perrin argues that "the saturation of dream-visions in the Aramaic corpus indicates the centrality of this divinatory medium to apocalyptic thought in general. This may give further reason to revisit the idea of the origination of the apocalypse in dream-vision literature as [Jean] Carmignac proposed initially in his contribution to the Uppsala conference in 1979."[67] But Carmignac defined apocalypse as "a literary genre that describes celestial revelations by means of symbols."[68] Consequently, he found apocalypses in every book of the Old Testament, and few if any scholars took him seriously. Dream visions are undoubtedly an important ingredient in apocalypses,[69] but they are surely not the only one. Many apocalypses can be subsumed into a broader category of symbolic dream visions.[70] This is a perfectly valid way of organizing Jewish literature in the late Second Temple period. It has the advantage of highlighting some connections and the disadvantage of downplaying others. For example, Perrin lists the Pseudo-Daniel texts as "mistakenly associated with dream-vision revelation."[71] And indeed they are not dream-visions. But they may nonetheless be validly associated with apocalypses. Apocalypse is a multi-faceted genre, and any attempt to derive it from a single root is reductionistic.

---

67. Perrin, *Dynamics of Dream-Vision Revelation*, 243, referring to Jean Carmignac, "Description du phénomène d'apocalyptique dans l'Ancien Testament," in *Apocalypticism in the Mediterranean World and the Near East*, ed. David Hellholm, 2nd ed. (Tübingen: Mohr Siebeck, 1989), 163–70.

68. Carmignac, "Description," 165, my translation.

69. Frances Flannery, "Dreams and Visions in Early Jewish and Early Christian Apocalypses and Apocalypticism," in *The Oxford Handbook of Apocalyptic Literature*, ed. John J. Collins (New York: Oxford University Press, 2014), 104–20.

70. See especially Perrin, *Dynamics of Dream-Vision Revelation*; and Frances Flannery-Dailey, *Dreamers, Scribes and Priests: Jewish Dreams in the Hellenistic and Greco-Roman Eras*, JSJSup 90 (Leiden: Brill, 2004).

71. Perrin, *Dynamics of Dream-Vision Revelation*, 83–84.

Hindy Najman has offered another way of classifying texts that are related but not necessarily members of a single genre. Following Walter Benjamin, she categorizes these texts by means of a constellation of features or elements. "Constellations depend for their legibility on our interests as readers. Still, they are objectively out there."[72] There are several component parts of apocalypses that can also be found in other genres. Think, for example, of *ex eventu* prophecy, such as we find in the Apocryphon of Jeremiah. The presence of *ex eventu* prophecy in a text unquestionably constitutes a point of affinity with apocalypses, but it does not necessarily determine the genre of the text. The authors of revelatory texts in ancient Judaism were not bound by any strict rules. They could mix and match component parts in innovative ways. There was no reason in principle why a dream interpreted by a human such as Daniel might not have similar content to a dream elsewhere interpreted by an angel.

The genre apocalypse as defined in *Semeia* 14 was always recognized to be an etic, modern analytic category, not one that is explicitly identified as such in the ancient texts. Perhaps the main contribution of the Dead Sea Scrolls to the discussion of the genre apocalypse is that they remind us of the fluidity of generic boundaries and that the networks of intertextual affinities are not exhausted by our definitions.

Bibliography

Benjamin, Walter. *The Origins of German Tragic Drama*. London: NLB, 1977.
Bevan, Anthony Ashley. *A Short Commentary on the Book of Daniel*. Cambridge: Cambridge University Press, 1892.
Brooke, George J. "What Makes a Text Historical?" Pages 193–210 in *Reading the Dead Sea Scrolls: Essays in Method*. Edited by George J. Brooke. EJL 39. Atlanta: Society of Biblical Literature, 2013.
Broshi, Magen, and Esther Eshel. "248. 4QHistorical Text A." Pages 192–200 in *Qumran Cave 4.XXVI: Cryptic Texts and Miscellanea, Part 1*. Edited by Stephen J. Pfann et al. DJD 36. Oxford: Clarendon, 2000.

---

72. Hindy Najman, "The Idea of Biblical Genre: From Discourse to Constellation," in *Prayer and Poetry in the Dead Sea Scrolls and Related Literature*, ed. Jeremy Penner et al., STDJ 98 (Leiden: Brill, 2012), 316; cf. Walter Benjamin, *The Origins of German Tragic Drama* (London: NLB, 1977).

———. "The Greek King Is Antiochus IV (4QHistorical Text = 4Q248." *JJS* 48 (1997): 120–29.
Carmignac, Jean. "Description du phénomène d'apocalyptique dans l'Ancien Testament." Pages 163–70 in *Apocalypticism in the Mediterranean World and the Near East*. Edited by David Hellholm. 2nd ed. Tübingen: Mohr Siebeck, 1989.
———. "Qu'est-ce que l'apocalyptique? Son emploi a Qumrân." *RevQ* 10 (1979): 3–33.
Collins, John J., ed. *Apocalypse: The Morphology of a Genre*. Semeia 14 (1979).
———. "Apocalypticism and Literary Genre in the Dead Sea Scrolls." Pages 403–30 in vol. 2 of *The Dead Sea Scrolls after Fifty Years*. Edited by Peter W. Flint and James C. VanderKam. Leiden: Brill, 1999.
———. *Daniel: A Commentary on the Book of Daniel*. Hermeneia. Minneapolis: Fortress, 1993.
———. "The Genre of the Book of Jubilees." Pages 737–55 in vol. 2 of *A Teacher for All Generations: Essays in Honor of James C. VanderKam*. Edited by Eric F. Mason et al. JSJSup 153. Leiden: Brill, 2011.
———. "Introduction: The Genre Apocalypse Reconsidered." Pages 1–20 in *Apocalypse, Prophecy, and Pseudepigraphy: On Jewish Apocalyptic Literature*. Edited by John J. Collins. Grand Rapids: Eerdmans, 2015.
———. "The Jewish Apocalypes," *Semeia* 14 (1979): 21–49.
———. "Journeys to the World beyond in Ancient Judaism." Pages 178–97 in *Apocalypse, Prophecy, and Pseudepigraphy: On Jewish Apocalyptic Literature*. Edited by John J. Collins. Grand Rapids: Eerdmans, 2015.
———. "New Light on the Book of Daniel from the Dead Sea Scrolls." Pages 180–96 in *Perspectives in the Study of Old Testament and Early Judaism*. Edited by Florentino García Martínez and Edward Noort. VTSup 73. Leiden: Brill, 1998.
———. *The Scepter and the Star: Messianism in Light of the Dead Sea Scrolls*. 2nd ed. Grand Rapids: Eerdmans, 2010.
Collins, John J., and Peter W. Flint. "Pseudo-Daniel." Pages 95–164 in *Qumran Cave 4.XVII: Parabiblical Texts, Part 3*. Edited by George J. Brooke et al. DJD 22. Oxford: Clarendon, 1996.
Davis, C. J. Patrick. "Torah-Performance and History in the Golah: Rewritten Bible or 'Re-Presentational' Authority in the Apocryphon of Jeremiah C." Pages 467–95 in *Celebrating the Dead Sea Scrolls: A Canadian Collection*. Edited by Kyung S. Baek, Peter W. Flint, and Jean Duhaime. EJL 30. Atlanta: Society of Biblical Literature, 2012.

Davis, Kipp. *The Cave 4 Apocryphon of Jeremiah and the Qumran Jeremianic Traditions: Prophetic Persona and the Construction of Community Identity.* STDJ 111. Leiden: Brill, 2014.

Dimant, Devorah. "Apocalyptic Texts at Qumran." Pages 175–91 in *The Community of the Renewed Covenant: The Notre Dame Symposium on the Dead Sea Scrolls.* Edited by Eugene Ulrich and James C. VanderKam. Notre Dame: University of Notre Dame Press, 1994.

———. "New Light from Qumran on the Jewish Pseudepigrapha—4Q390." Pages 405–48 in vol. 2 of *The Madrid Qumran Congress: Proceedings of the International Congress on the Dead Sea Scrolls.* Edited by Julio C. Trebolle Barrera and Luis Vegas Montaner. STDJ 11. Leiden: Brill, 1991.

———. "The Qumran Aramaic Texts and the Qumran Community." Pages 197–205 in *Flores Florentino: Dead Sea Scrolls and Other Early Jewish Studies in Honour of Florentino García Martínez.* Edited by A. Hilhorst et al. JSJSup 122. Leiden: Brill, 2007.

———. *Qumran Cave 4.XXI. Parabiblical Texts, Part 4: Pseudo-Prophetic Texts.* DJD 30. Oxford: Clarendon, 2000.

DiTommaso, Lorenzo. "Apocalypticism and the Aramaic Texts from Qumran." Pages 451–79 in *Aramaica Qumranica: Proceedings of the Conference on the Aramaic Texts from Qumran in Aix-en-Provence 30 June–2 July 2008.* Edited by Katell Berthelot and Daniel Stökl Ben Ezra. STDJ 94. Leiden: Brill, 2010.

———. *The Dead Sea New Jerusalem Text: Contents and Contexts.* TSAJ 110. Tübingen: Mohr Siebeck, 2005.

Flannery[-Dailey], Frances. "Dreams and Visions in Early Jewish and Early Christian Apocalypses and Apocalypticism." Pages 104–20 in *The Oxford Handbook of Apocalyptic Literature.* Edited by John J. Collins. New York: Oxford University Press, 2014.

———. *Dreamers, Scribes and Priests: Jewish Dreams in the Hellenistic and Greco-Roman Eras.* JSJSup 90. Leiden: Brill, 2004.

Frey, Jörg. "Die Bedeutung der Qumrantexte für das Verständnis der Apokalyptik im Frühjudentum und im Urchristentum." Pages 11–62 in *Apokalyptik und Qumran.* Edited by Jörg Frey and Michael Becker. Einblicke 6. Paderborn: Bonifatius, 2007.

———. "The New Jerusalem Text in Its Historical and Traditio-Historical Context." Pages 800–16 in *The Dead Sea Scrolls Fifty Years after Their Discovery: Proceedings of the Jerusalem Congress, July 20–25, 1997.*

Edited by Lawrence H. Schiffman et al. Jerusalem: Israel Exploration Society, 2000.

García Martínez, Florentino. "Apocalypticism in the Dead Sea Scrolls." Pages 162–92 in *The Origins of Apocalypticism in Judaism and Christianity*. Vol. 1 of *The Encyclopedia of Apocalypticism*. Edited by John J. Collins. New York: Continuum, 1998.

———. "Aramaica qumranica apocalyptica?" Pages 435–48 in *Aramaica Qumranica: Proceedings of the Conference on the Aramaic Texts from Qumran in Aix-en-Provence 30 June–2 July 2008*. Edited by Katell Berthelot and Daniel Stökl Ben Ezra. STDJ 94. Leiden: Brill, 2010.

———. "New Jerusalem." *EDSS* 2:606–10.

———. *Qumran and Apocalyptic*. STDJ 9. Leiden: Brill, 1992.

García Martínez, Florentino, Eibert Tigchelaar, and A. S. van der Woude. "11QNew Jerusalem ar." Page 305–55 in *Qumran Cave 11.II. 11Q2–18, 11Q20–31*. Edited by Florentino García Martínez et al. DJD 23. Oxford: Clarendon, 1998.

Greenfield, Jonas C., Michael E. Stone, and Esther Eshel. *The Aramaic Levi Document: Edition, Translation, Commentary*. SVTP 19. Leiden: Brill, 2004.

Goldman, Liora. "Dualism in the Visions of Amram." *RevQ* 95 (2010): 421–32.

Jonge, Marinus de. *The Testaments of the Twelve Patriarchs: A Critical Edition of the Greek Text*. Leiden: Brill, 1978.

Kobelski, Paul J. *Melchizedek and Melchiresha*. CBQMS 10. Washington, DC: Catholic Biblical Association of America, 1981.

Lange, Armin, with Ulrike Mittmann-Richert. "Annotated List of the Texts from the Judaean Desert Classified by Content and Genre." Pages 115–64 in *The Texts from the Judaean Desert: Indices and an Introduction to the Discoveries in the Judaean Desert Series*. Edited by Emanuel Tov. DJD 39. Oxford: Clarendon, 2002.

Machiela, Daniel A. *The Dead Sea Genesis Apocryphon: A New Text and Translation with Introduction and Special Treatment of Columns 13–17*. STDJ 79. Leiden: Brill, 2009.

———. "Genesis Revealed: The Apocalyptic Apocryphon from Qumran Cave 1." Pages 205–21 in *Qumran Cave 1 Revisited: Texts from Cave 1 Sixty Years after Their Discovery; Proceedings of the Sixth Meeting of the IOQS in Ljubljana*. Edited by Daniel K. Falk et al. STDJ 91. Leiden: Brill, 2010.

Milik, Józef T. *The Books of Enoch: Aramaic Fragments from Qumrân Cave 4*. With the collaboration of Matthew Black. Oxford: Clarendon, 1976.

———. "'Prière de Nabonide' et autres écrits d'un cycle de Daniel." *RB* 63 (1956): 411–15.

Najman, Hindy. "The Idea of Biblical Genre: From Discourse to Constellation." Pages 307–21 in *Prayer and Poetry in the Dead Sea Scrolls and Related Literature*. Edited by Jeremy Penner et al. STDJ 98. Leiden: Brill, 2012.

Najman, Hindy, and Mladen Popović, eds. *Rethinking Genre: Essays in Honor of John J. Collins*. DSD 17 (2010).

Newsom, Carol A. "Spying out the Land: A Report from Genology." Pages 437–50 in *Seeking Out the Wisdom of the Ancients: Essays Offered to Honor Michael V. Fox on the Occasion of His Sixty-Fifth Birthday*. Edited by Ronald L. Troxel, Kelvin G. Friebel, and Dennis Robert Magary. Winona Lake, IN: Eisenbrauns, 2005.

Oppenheim, Leo. *The Interpretation of Dreams in the Ancient Near East*. Philadelphia: American Philosophical Society, 1956.

Perrin, Andrew B. "The Aramaic Imagination: Incubating Apocalyptic Thought and Genre in Dream Visions among the Qumran Aramaic Texts." Pages 110–40 in *Apocalyptic Thinking in Early Judaism: Engaging with John Collins' The Apocalyptic Imagination*. Edited by Sidnie White Crawford and Cecilia Wassén. JSJSup 182. Leiden: Brill, 2018.

———. *The Dynamics of Dream-Vision Revelation in the Aramaic Dead Sea Scrolls*. JAJSup 19. Göttingen: Vandenhoeck & Ruprecht, 2015.

Puech, Émile. "Paroles de Michel ar." Pages 1–8 in *Qumrân Grotte 4.XXII: Textes araméens, première partie, 4Q529–549*. Edited by Émile Puech. DJD 31. Oxford: Clarendon, 2001.

———. "Visions de 'Amram." Pages 283–405 in *Qumrân Grotte 4.XXII: Textes araméens, première partie, 4Q529–549*. Edited by Émile Puech. DJD 31. Oxford: Clarendon, 2001.

Reynolds, Bennie H., III. *Between Symbolism and Realism: The Use of Symbolic and Non-symbolic Language in Ancient Jewish Apocalypses 333–63 B.C.E.* JAJSup 8. Göttingen: Vandenhoeck & Ruprecht, 2011.

Stegemann, Hartmut. "Die Bedeutung der Qumranfunde für die Erforschung der Apokalyptik." Pages 495–530 in *Apocalypticism in the Mediterranean World and the Near East*. Edited by David Hellholm. 2nd ed. Tübingen: Mohr Siebeck, 1989.

Stone, Michael E., and Jonas C. Greenfield. "Aramaic Levi Document." Pages 1–72 in *Qumran Cave 4.XVII. Parabiblical Texts, Part 3*. Edited by George J. Brooke et al. DJD 22. Oxford: Clarendon, 1996.

Tigchelaar, Eibert C. "Classifications of the Collection of Dead Sea Scrolls and the Case of Apocryphon of Jeremiah C." *JSJ* 43 (2012): 519–50.

———. "The Imaginal Context and the Visionary of the Aramaic New Jerusalem." Pages 257–70 in *Flores Florentino: Dead Sea Scrolls and Other Early Jewish Studies in Honour of Florentino García Martínez*. Edited by A. Hilhorst, Émile Puech, and Eibert J. C. Tigchelaar. JSJSup 122. Leiden: Brill, 2007.

Wise, Michael O., Martin G. Abegg, and Edward Cook. *The Dead Sea Scrolls: A New Translation*. San Francisco: Harper, 1996.

Wacholder, Ben Zion, and Martin G. Abegg. *A Preliminary Edition of the Unpublished Dead Sea Scrolls*. Vol. 3. Washington, DC: Biblical Archeology Society, 1995.

Yarbro Collins, Adela. "The Seven Heavens in Jewish and Christian Apocalypses." Pages 21–54 in *Cosmology and Eschatology in Jewish and Christian Apocalypticism*. Edited by Adela Yarbro Collins. JSJSup 50. Leiden: Brill, 1996.

"The Heavens Were Opened and I Saw Visions of God": *The Open Heaven*—Four Decades On

Christopher Rowland

This essay is a plea for the necessity of recognizing that, in the way in which we use words, we risk excluding crucial aspects of their meaning by our use of them. This is nowhere more true than in the case of *apocalypse* and *apocalyptic*, which have come to be firmly fixed in common usage as ways of speaking about cataclysm and the doom-laden scenario of the end of the world. The reasons for this are not difficult to understand, given the content of the book of Revelation. Nevertheless, the plea to bear in mind the revelatory dimension of apocalypse/apocalyptic is a necessary component of the adequate understanding of key aspects of the Bible and, indeed, Jewish and Christian history.

The essay starts with a personal journey, from the study of the possible impact of nascent mystical ideas on the New Testament and other significant challenges to a dominant understanding of apocalyptic. This is followed by a brief consideration of the early nineteenth century use of these terms and then back to a consideration of passages from the Dead Sea Scrolls and neglected apocalyptic elements in key texts in the New Testament, such as the Pauline letters and the gospel of John.

1. *The Open Heaven*—Four Decades On

My perspective on apocalyptic literature came through an unusual route, being introduced to the history of Jewish mysticism during my time as a student in Cambridge. John Bowker in the late 1960's gave an innovative course of lectures on the Jewish background to the New Testament, in the midst of which were a couple of remarkable lectures about *merkabah* mysticism and its impact on Paul.¹ During my early time as a graduate student, I read the work of Hugo Odeberg, which introduced me to the groundbreaking studies of Gershom Scholem.²

The New Testament has never seemed the same again. A thorough discussion of apocalyptic had not been part of the teaching at Cambridge. Manifesting a distaste for the approach taken by Johannes Weiss and Albert Schweitzer, the dominant ethos was to strip the Son of Man sayings in the gospels of any apocalyptic significance, however one construed the word. So my route to the study of the apocalypses, Revelation included, was through the early Jewish mystical traditions. What I found in those texts were many affinities between them, the heavenly journeys, the heavenly mysteries, and the like, whatever the differences in genre. Unsurprisingly, it was this perspective that dominated my doctoral thesis on the influence of Ezek 1 on Judaism and early Christianity and the importance of dreams, visions, and auditions in understanding the character of early Christianity, following on from what we find in the Jewish tradition.³ What it enabled me to do was to see how the subject matter of the dissertation impacted more widely on biblical study.

Out of this in 1982 emerged *The Open Heaven* and, twenty-five years later, my contribution to *The Mystery of God*.⁴ The former has a simple thesis that I would summarize as follows: it challenged the notion that apocalypse/-tic/-ticism was about the end of the world and argued that apocalypse-as-revelation better captures much of what we find in apocalyptic literature.

---

1. E.g., John W. Bowker, "Merkabah Visions and the Visions of Paul," *JSS* 16 (1971): 157–73.

2. Hugo Odeberg, *The Fourth Gospel Interpreted in Its Relation to Contemporaneous Religious Currents in Palestine and the Hellenistic-Oriental World* (Uppsala: Almqvist & Wiksell, 1929); Odeberg, *The View of the Universe in the Epistle to the Ephesians*, LUÅ 1, n.f. 29.6 (Lund: Gleerup, 1934). Initially Gershom Scholem, *Major Trends in Jewish Mysticism* (London: Thames & Hudson, 1955); Scholem, *Jewish Gnosticism, Merkabah Mysticism and Talmudic Tradition* (New York: Jewish Theological Seminary, 1960); and Scholem, *Origins of the Kabbalah* (Philadelphia: Jewish Publication Society, 1990).

3. Frances Flannery-Dailey, *Dreamers, Scribes, and Priests: Jewish Dreams in the Hellenistic and Roman Eras*, JSJSup 90 (Leiden: Brill, 2004).

4. Christopher Rowland, *The Open Heaven: A Study of Apocalyptic in Judaism and Early Christianity* (New York: Crossroad, 1982); and Christopher Rowland and Christopher R. A. Morray-Jones, *The Mystery of God: Early Jewish Mysticism and the New Testament*, CRINT 12 (Leiden: Brill, 2009).

So, apocalyptic texts were not primarily about eschatology so much as an alternative way of discerning the divine will. The opening words of Ezek 1 quoted in the title of this essay ("The heavens were opened and I saw visions of God") beautifully encapsulate the essence of apocalypticism.

The Mystery of God is more explicitly linked with the New Testament and offers an account of early Christian intellectual history from the perspective of visionary apocalypticism. So, the book's thesis is the conviction that the Jewish apocalyptic and mystical writings have much to offer the interpretation of the New Testament. My coauthor Christopher Morray-Jones and I shared a common conviction that, despite the challenges to Scholem's thesis, the roots of *merkabah* mysticism are to be found in the second temple.[5] Whether or not there was an established mystical tradition in the late second temple and early tannaitic periods is less important to me than openness to the possibility that there might have been engagement with Ezekiel's *merkabah* vision, which involved an imaginative and experiential engagement with what Ezekiel saw, which might have been linked with the attempt to elucidate some of the more mysterious aspects of the vision. An apocalypse like Revelation is, I believe, a prime testimony to such visionary appropriation. It is, of course, possible that Revelation is a text that is a deliberate attempt to exploit the apocalyptic genre in order to offer a veneer of authority. That possibility cannot be excluded; I cannot prove that Revelation's claim that it offers a visionary report is credible. But, notwithstanding the occasional evidence of reflection in the text itself (e.g., 4:5 and 17:9–14), I continue to believe that this text, which ended up in the Christian canon, offers at least one example of Ezekiel's words inspiring a later visionary appropriation, or what David Halperin (no disciple of Scholem) has characterized as follows: "When the apocalyptic visionary 'sees' something … we may assume that he is seeing the … vision as he has persuaded himself it really was, as (the prophet) would have seen it, had he been inspired wholly and not in part."[6]

A simple distinction between exegesis and visionary experience, which I presupposed when I wrote *The Open Heaven*, I now doubt. The work of Mary Carruthers on memory and rhetoric has shown me how the exercise of imagination, which included the visualization in the mind

---

5. Peter Schäfer, *The Origins of Jewish Mysticism* (Princeton: Princeton University Press, 2011).

6. David Halperin, *The Faces of the Chariot: Early Jewish Responses to Ezekiel's Vision*, TSAJ 16 (Tübingen: Mohr Siebeck, 1988).

of objects, has been an important part of the reading of scripture.[7] The emphasis upon interpreters picturing what they recall, or hear, and then using these for further thinking are a striking and continuous feature of medieval monastic hermeneutics.[8] So, ancient readers and hearers of texts could seek to visualize what they read (or heard), and that seeing or listening would frequently involve the creation of mental images. Such meditative practice was the result of a sophisticated process of memorization of scriptural texts, in which, in imitation of Ezekiel's and John's digestion of the scroll passages (often mentioned in medieval treatises on the reading and interpretation of scripture), the one meditating was able to recall and envision.

The preceding account explains both the genesis of my understanding of apocalyptic and also why it is that the important study by Michael E. Stone, which appeared six years before *The Open Heaven* was published, does not loom larger in that book.[9] It was not long after I had completed *The Open Heaven,* in the summer of 1976, that I discovered Stone's article, which so convincingly and eruditely underpinned my hunches and thoughts about the nature of apocalypticism. That article and a welter of his other publications have substantiated the position that both he and I hold.

Stone's article was a landmark contribution to the debate in the discussion of apocalypticism.[10] The apocalyptic writings had to be seen not simply in a stream of tradition that flowed from the prophets; they also bore some of the characteristics of Jewish wisdom literature. Stone argued that, if we take the opening chapters of 1 Enoch seriously, and particularly the introductory miscellany preceding the story of the seduction of the

---

7. Mary Carruthers, *The Book of Memory: A Study of Memory in Medieval Culture* (Cambridge: Cambridge University Press, 1990); Carruthers, *The Craft of Thought: Meditation, Rhetoric, and the Making of Images, 400–1200* (Cambridge: Cambridge University Press, 1998); and Carruthers, *The Medieval Craft of Memory* (Philadelphia: University of Pennsylvania Press, 2002).

8. Carruthers, *Craft of Thought,* 304.

9. Michael E. Stone, "Lists of Revealed Things in the Apocalyptic Literature," in *Magnalia Dei, the Mighty Acts of God: Essays on the Bible and Archaeology in Memory of G. Ernest Wright,* ed. Frank Moore Cross, Werner E. Lemke, and Patrick D. Miller (Garden City, NY: Doubleday, 1976), 414–35.

10. George W. E. Nickelsburg, "The Study of Apocalypticism from H. H. Rowley to the Society of Biblical Literature" (1979): https://www.sbl-site.org/assets/pdfs/Nickelsburg_Study.pdf.

women by the Watchers, the wisdom elements parallel lists of revealed things in other apocalyptic texts. The legends and the cosmography, which we also find in the opening chapters of 1 Enoch, might give us pause for thought before we emphasize eschatology as the interpretative key of apocalyptic.

Stone discussed lists of revealed things found in 1 Enoch, 2 Baruch, and 4 Ezra and traced them back to similar lists in the sapiential literature. He drew on the newly published Qumran Enoch fragments as well, and, opposing the critical consensus, Stone dated large parts of 1 Enoch prior to the book of Daniel.[11] So his definition of apocalyptic began not with Daniel, but with 1 Enoch. That is, so-called apocalyptic eschatology and its prophetic roots could no longer be privileged in discussions and definitions of apocalypticism.[12] Cosmology, for example, had to be incorporated into the discussion. The discovery of the Aramaic fragments of parts of 1 Enoch in Cave 4 and of Jubilees (a text which is apocalypse-like in its genre) underlines the importance of recognizing the variegated character of the material in the Enochic corpus, some of which is eschatological, but by no means all, suggesting that we consider them less as eschatological tracts but as a revelation of divine secrets whose unveiling will enable a different perspective on the present situation. In many respects, this is true also of other examples of Jewish apocalyptic literature, which have come down to us in translation, such as 4 Ezra, 2 Baruch, and the Apocalypse of Abraham. These are less certainly dated. But with the early dating of parts of 1 Enoch, one had to completely rethink the shape of Jewish religious and intellectual life in the third century BCE.[13]

The quest for a succinct summary of the nature of apocalypticism had gathered speed mid-century, as is exemplified by the International Colloquium on Apocalypticism, which was organized by David Hellholm and its proceedings published as *Apocalypticism in the Mediterranean World*

---

11. Michael E. Stone, *Scriptures, Sects, and Visions: A Profile of Judaism from Ezra to the Jewish Revolts* (Oxford: Blackwell, 1980).

12. E.g., Otto Plöger, *Theocracy and Eschatology*, 2nd ed., trans. by S. Rudman (Oxford: Blackwell, 1968); and Paul D. Hanson, *The Dawn of Apocalyptic: The Historical and Sociological Roots of Jewish Apocalyptic Eschatology*, rev. ed. (Philadelphia: Fortress, 1979).

13. Michael E. Stone, ed., *Jewish Writings of the Second Temple Period: Apocrypha, Pseudepigrapha, Qumran, Sectarian Writings, Philo, Josephus*, CRINT 2.1 (Assen: Van Gorcum; Minneapolis: Fortress, 1984).

and the Near East.[14] More successful, and subsequently influential, has been the definition offered by John J. Collins in volume 14 of the journal *Semeia*, subtitled "Apocalypse: The Morphology of a Genre."[15] The volume is a report of the Apocalypse Group of the Society of Biblical Literature Genres Project. With references to apocalypses in antiquity, which included works of Jewish, early Christian, gnostic, Greek and Latin, rabbinic and mystical, and Persian origin, it attempted a master paradigm within which one could view the literary shape, and to some extent, the content of these works. It defined apocalypse as follows:

> "Apocalypse" is a genre of revelatory literature with a narrative framework, in which a revelation is mediated by an otherworldly being to a human recipient, disclosing a transcendent reality which is both temporal, insofar as it envisages eschatological salvation, and spatial insofar as it involves another, supernatural world.[16]

The emphasis in this definition starts not from eschatology but revelation. The eschatological aspect of it only comes to the fore in the context of the mystery of eschatological salvation, which is such an important component of many apocalypses. Not all revelations are mediated. Those found in 4 Ezra and occasionally Daniel, where an otherworldly agent communicates information, are not normative. An ordinary human being, however unusual, whether it be Enoch, Abraham, or Isaiah, and preeminently the prophet John in his visions on the island of Patmos, see the mysteries of God, angels, the past, the present, and the future for themselves and are instructed to share these after their return to everyday life. The temporality of eschatological salvation (for example, the descent of the New Jerusalem from heaven to earth, or the appearance of the messiah, and even his descent through the heavenly world in the Ascension of Isaiah) is seen by the respective visionary seers in anticipation. They are disclosures, apocalypses. At the time of the vision, they are transcendent realities to be realized on earth in the messianic age.

---

14. David Hellholm, ed., *Apocalypticism in the Mediterranean World and the Near East: Proceedings of the International Colloquium on Apocalypticism Uppsala, August 12–17, 1979*, 2nd ed. (Tübingen: Mohr Siebeck, 1989).

15. John J. Collins, ed., *Apocalypse: Morphology of a Genre*, Semeia 14 (1979).

16. John J. Collins, "Introduction: Towards the Morphology of a Genre," *Semeia* 14 (1979): 9.

In some cases, the transcendent realities will be revealed on earth in the course of implementation of divine judgement in history, for example, in the case of John's vision of Babylon mounted on the seven-headed Beast. In sum, this definition is the basis for those working on apocalypticism.

2. Contrasting Perspectives on Apocalyptic: A Historical Perspective on Etymology and Use

Apocalyptic was taken up and used to describe a particular development of prophetic eschatology at the beginning of the nineteenth century. As Johann M. Schmidt shows in his invaluable study, Friedrich Lücke's survey of apocalyptic writings first published in 1832 made a strong case for the continuity between prophetic and apocalyptic texts, but he used the word *Apokalyptik* as a means of designating the peculiar form of eschatology that he found in the apocalyptic texts.[17] Lücke saw Revelation as "the revelations of the end of all things" and offered an outline of the content of *Apokalyptik* based on this that has pervaded scholarly, and indeed popular, understanding ever since. In some ways, it is strange that the eschatological should have dominated Lücke's discussion as, since a decade before his study, Richard Laurence's English translation of the Ethiopic Apocalypse of Enoch had been published.[18] Lücke made much of the difference that the discovery of this text would have on the study of the origins of apocalyptic ideas as *Apokalyptik*, a pattern of *eschatological* religion. This religious perspective was characterized by the following: imminent expectation, radical contrast between present and future, the hope for another world breaking into and overtaking this world, the doctrines of angels and demons, as well as complex visionary imagery succinctly summarized in Philipp Vielhauer's 1965 essay:

> a contrast between the present age, which is perishable and temporary, and a new age, which is still to come, and which is imperishable and eternal; a belief that the new age is of a transcendent kind, which breaks in

---

17. Friedrich Lücke, *Versuch einer vollständigen Einleitung in der Offenbarung Johannis und in die gesammelte apokalyptische Literatur* (Bonn: Weber, 1832). See Johann M. Schmidt, *Die jüdische Apokalyptik: Die Geschichte ihrer Erforschung von den Anfängen bis zu den Textfunden von Qumran* (Neukirchen: Neukirchener Verlag, 1969).

18. Richard Laurence, *The Book of Enoch* (Oxford: Parker, 1821). The German translation of August Dillmann did not appear until three decades later, however: *Das Buch Henoch: Übersetzt und erklärt* (Leipzig: Vogel, 1851).

from beyond through divine intervention and without human activity; a wider concern than merely the destiny of Israel; an interest in the totality of world history; the belief that God has foreordained everything and that the history of the world has been divided into epochs; and finally, an imminent expectation that the present unsatisfactory state of affairs will only be short lived.[19]

As Stone and others have reminded us, when we cast our net wider in the literature of antiquity, we find an emphasis on a revelatory idea of wisdom, which embraces eschatology as well as protology, and much else. It is what Martin Hengel termed "higher wisdom through revelation."[20]

Another key witness to the early interpretation of the term apocalyptic is the poet and critic Samuel Taylor Coleridge (1772–1834), who wrote a decade or so before Lücke published his book. Coleridge assessed the writings of the artist and poet William Blake and judged that they were produced by a man who was both "apocalyptic" and "mystic":

> A man of Genius—and I apprehend, a Swedenborgian certainly, a mystic emphatically. You perhaps smile at my calling another Poet, a Mystic, but verily I am in the very mire of commonplace common-sense compared with Mr. Blake, apo-, or rather ana-, calyptic Poet, and Painter![21]

Coleridge suggests that Blake was a Swedenborgian, following in the footsteps of Emanuel Swedenborg (1688–1772), the Swedish visionary writer. Blake regarded Swedenborg as a "divine teacher" and formally approved of his theological writings. This is further explained by regarding him as

---

19. Philipp Vielhauer, "Apocalyptic in Early Christianity," in *Writings Relating to the Apostles, Apocalypses, and Related Subjects*, vol. 2 of *New Testament Apocrypha*, ed. Edgar Hennecke and Wilhelm Schneemelcher, trans. by R. McLean Wilson (Philadelphia: Westminster, 1965), 608–42.

20. Martin Hengel, *Judaism and Hellenism: Studies in Their Encounter in Palestine during the Early Hellenistic Period* (London: SCM, 1974), 210, 217; see also Grant Macaskill, *Revealed Wisdom and Inaugurated Eschatology in Ancient Judaism and Early Christianity*, JSJSup 115 (Leiden: Brill, 2007).

21. Samuel Taylor Coleridge, *Collected Letters*, ed. Earl Leslie Griggs (Oxford: Oxford University Press, 1956), 4:833–34. On this, see Michael Ferber, "Coleridge's 'Anacalyptic' Blake: An Exegesis," *Modern Philology* 76 (1978): 189–93; and Christopher Rowland, *Blake and the Bible* (London: Yale University Press, 2011), 240–41. On Blake's links with Swedenborgianism, see G. E. Bentley Jr., *The Stranger from Paradise: A Biography of William Blake* (New Haven: Yale University Press, 2001), 126–29.

a mystic and finally an "apo-, or rather ana-, calyptic Poet, and Painter" (in the quotation above). He was "apo-/ana- calyptic" in the sense that his mind was unclouded and able to discern things that other poets or painters could not see, so that his words and images enabled those who engaged with them themselves to have that anacalyptic experience, in which the veil is removed (2 Cor 3:14; 18) from the mind to discern the deep things of God (1 Cor 2:10). This is very much what Blake envisioned when he wrote "if the doors of perception were cleansed everything would appear to man as it is, infinite."[22]

Coleridge also spent a year in Germany and acquainted himself with emerging biblical criticism, becoming an important intermediary of the insights of German scholars to British theology. His elucidation of Martin Luther's famous dream manifests a similar understanding:

> I see nothing improbable, that in some of those momentary Slumbers, into which the suspension of all Thought in the perplexity of intense thinking so often passes; Luther should have had a full view of the Room in which he was sitting, of his writing Table and all the implements of Study, as they really existed, and at the same time a brain-image of the Devil, vivid enough to have acquired *Outness*, and a distance regulated by the proportion of its distinctness to that of the objects really impressed on the outward senses.[23]

Here Coleridge, the author of "Kubla Khan," goes on to offer a meditation on "this Law of imagination" and to identify with "the heroic Student, in his Chamber in the Warteburg," and the way in which the apparitions insert themselves into his life. In this passage, we may grasp not only the extraordinary insight but also the peculiar fecundity of the poet and mystic impinging on historical interpretation. Coleridge allows the poet's genius to fructify his biblical interpretation, which takes the discussion to extraordinary levels of insight, as he does his reproach of Johann Gottfried Eichhorn for his lack of understanding of Ezekiel's *merkabah* vision. His critique of Eichhorn's discussion of Ezekiel's visionary experience deserves mention because it complements what is contained in this book and encapsulates the essence of Coleridge's best work. That Ezekiel's

---

22. William Blake, *The Marriage of Heaven and Hell* (Boston: Luce, 1906), 26.
23. In Anthony J. Harding, *Coleridge on the Bible*, vol. 2 of *Coleridge's Responses* (London: Continuum, 2007), 79.

call vision is mere poetic decoration, which needs to be explained and deciphered, represents for Coleridge a fundamental misunderstanding of the nature of the experience, which the prophet struggles to articulate and which Coleridge understands so well:

> It perplexes me to understand how a Man of Eichhorn's sense, learning and acquaintance with psychology could form or attach belief to so cold blooded an hypothesis. That in Ezekiel's vision ideas or spiritual entities are presented in visual symbols, I never doubted; but as little can I doubt, that such symbols did present themselves to Ezekiel in visions—and by a law so closely connected with, if not contained, in that by which sensations are organized into images and mental sounds in our ordinary sleep.[24]

There is much to learn from Coleridge's approach to visionary texts. It draws on Coleridge's own experience, doubtless, but also that subtle mix of historical enquiry and reverence for the text, the former impelling him to understand better its peculiarity. As many Christian scholars from the Middle Ages on have realized, there are aspects of the Jewish mystical and cabbalistic tradition that have many affinities with Christianity, and this is something that Coleridge himself appreciated.

What we find in the use of apocalyptic in these passages from Coleridge and Lücke is that they pick up on different aspects of the book of Revelation, Coleridge stressing the visionary and revelatory, Lücke the cataclysmic and eschatological. It is worth adding that both these approaches to the book of Revelation have been intertwined in its reception history down the centuries.

3. Apocalypse/Apocalyptic/Mysticism: Etymology and Usage

If we ask whether genre criticism has any contribution to make to the categorization of texts, the answer to that question may rest as much on the nature of the question itself as the object of study. Can we ascertain whether the Dead Sea Scrolls have shed new light on the function of apocalyptic writings or on apocalyptic communities and the social con-

---

24. Samuel Taylor Coleridge, *Marginalia*, ed. George Whalley (Princeton: Princeton University Press 1979), 2:410; see also Elinor S. Shaffer, *"Kubla Khan" and the Fall of Jerusalem: The Mythological School in Biblical Criticism and Secular Literature 1770–1880* (Cambridge: Cambridge University Press, 1979), 89.

texts in which these writings were produced, and whether it has led to a reevaluation of the forms, contents, and settings of apocalyptic literature and changed, or reinforced, how the subject is approached in contemporary scholarship?

Such questions reflect the widespread assumption that the adjective apocalyptic is perspicuous. To readers of newspapers on 12 September 2001, the banner headline "APOCALYPSE" over a picture of Manhattan in flames needed no explaining. This was what most people think of as an apocalyptic event. The function of epithets is exegetical; they explain the meaning of words. The problem with the word apocalyptic is that its usage and its etymology do not overlap. So, apocalyptic has become, to say the least, an ambiguous epithet, requiring careful definition of what we mean by it.

The term apocalypse has its origins in the opening words of Revelation, a book full of visions, which disclose divine mysteries, principally eschatological mysteries, but not only these, but also the Mystery of the Woman and the beast that carries her (Rev 17:7). Its closest analogy in the Hebrew Bible is the book of Daniel, though other books, such as Isaiah, Ezekiel (in particular), Amos, and Zechariah contain visionary reports that in some ways anticipate the genre of Revelation and may be seen as analogues of John's visionary experience and indeed provide the language of many of the visions.

It is understandable why apocalyptic is used as a generic term evoking the book of Revelation. First, and most common, it is the contents of the book of Revelation, the cataclysmic upheavals, the terrifying irruptions evident in John's visionary world, and the contrast between this world and the world to come that resonate with people, just as they did with the newspaper headlines. In addition, there is the form of Revelation, encapsulated by the opening word of the book, apocalypse, in the sense of revelation, unveiling, or disclosure, where the mysteries of past, present, and future are laid bare in John's case through a divinely inspired vision. This dimension of the book, which is key to its genre, is all too easily forgotten, and it is a reminder that while usage should take precedence in understanding the meaning of words, etymology should never be neglected.

There is clearly a problem of the use of labels such as apocalyptic and mysticism. In *The Mystery of God*, I understood the latter as something along the lines of the Oxford English Dictionary's definition as a "belief in or devotion to the spiritual apprehension of truths inaccessible to the intellect." I would still stand by that rough and ready working definition, though complemented by that offered by Bernard McGinn, which arises out of a detailed historical study not only of the texts but also the terminological discussion that he summarizes under three headings: "a part or element of religion ... a process or way of life ... an attempt to express a direct consciousness of the presence of God."[25] McGinn rightly argues that mysticism should not be hived off into a separate category but should be part and parcel of the fabric of religion, a particular dimension of its theological claim, which is encapsulated by his words "direct consciousness of the presence of God by whatever means, vision, a sense of being caught up into the divine or some other immediate apprehension of divinity."[26]

4. Apocalypticism and the Dead Sea Scrolls

The discovery of the Dead Sea Scrolls has certainly expanded the corpus of early Jewish literature. But in what ways can the Scrolls be said to be apocalyptic? Whether it can be said to have extended our horizons with regard to core apocalyptic themes is an open question. Yes, the prescriptions for an eschatological warfare have certainly done that. Also, there is the apocalyptic in the sense of revelatory character of texts, which are themselves very different from the hitherto extant apocalyptic literature, like 1 Enoch, are evident. So, other writings, including the pesharim, the Hodayot, and 4QInstruction, have broadened our ideas regarding the forms and contents of apocalyptic literature. Similarly, many nonsectarian texts discovered at Qumran, notably those composed in Aramaic, have reshaped our views on the origin and early history of apocalyptic speculation. And, of course, the Scrolls present us with a second well-documented example, along with early Christianity, of an ancient apocalyptic movement.

John Ashton helpfully contrasts between accessible and revealed wisdom and suggests that the Dead Sea Scrolls enable us to see that both accessible revelation, mediated in the law of Moses, and hidden wisdom stand alongside each other, which suggests we should be careful about the radical polarization between the two.[27] Wisdom and understanding

---

25. Bernard McGinn, *The Foundations of Mysticism* (London: SCM, 1992), 1:xv–xvi.

26. McGinn, *Foundations of Mysticism*, xv–xvi.

27. John Ashton, "'Mystery' in the Dead Sea Scrolls and the Fourth Gospel,"

are identified with the law.[28] Whereas "the things that are revealed belong to us and to our children forever," the secret things belong to God (Deut 29:29; cf. 30:11–14). Similarly, it is accessible wisdom which is commended, whereas "hidden wisdom and unseen treasure" has nothing to offer (Sir 20:30; cf. 18:4–6). By contrast, texts that give special importance to an extra revelation, above and outside the law, testify to the importance of access to the hidden things reserved for God,[29] so reminiscent of that which is apocalyptic:

> For the truth of God is the rock of my steps, and his might the support of my right hand. From the spring of his justice is my judgement and from the wonderful mystery is the light in my heart. My eyes have observed what always is, wisdom that has been hidden from mankind, knowledge and prudent understanding (hidden) from the sons of men, fount of justice and well of strength and spring of glory (hidden from the assembly of flesh. To those whom God has selected he has given them as everlasting possession; and he has given them an inheritance in the lot of the holy ones. He unites their assembly to the sons of the heavens in order to form the council of the Community and a foundation of the building of holiness to be an everlasting plantation throughout all future ages. (1QS XI, 5–9)[30]

The claim to have observed what always is, wisdom that has been hidden from humanity, knowledge and prudent understanding (hidden) from the "sons of men" (1QS XI, 5–7) is apocalyptic insofar as it refers to the revelation of hidden wisdom. In the biblical exegesis of the Pesher on Habakkuk, the Teacher of Righteousness (like John of Patmos) wrote all that God had made known to him, namely, "all the mysteries of the words of his servants the Prophets" (1QpHab VII, 1–5). Indeed, the words of

---

in *John, Qumran, and the Dead Sea Scrolls: Sixty Years of Discovery and Debate*, ed. Mary L. Coloe and Tom Thatcher, EJL 32 (Atlanta: Society of Biblical Literature, 2011), 53–68.

28. Ashton, "'Mystery' in the Dead Sea Scrolls," 58–60. Note the rabbinic proscription regarding mystical matters to "neither seek what is too difficult for you, nor investigate what is beyond your power. Reflect upon what you have been commanded, for what is hidden is not your concern. Do not meddle in matters that are beyond you, for more than you can understand has been shown you" (quoted in b. Hag.13a).

29. Ashton, "'Mystery' in the Dead Sea Scrolls," 59.

30. Translation from Florentino García Martínez and Eibert J. C. Tigchelaar, *The Dead Sea Scrolls Study Edition*, 2 vols. (Leiden: Brill 1997), 1:97.

the Teacher of Righteousness are "from the mouth of God" (1QpHab II, 2). But elsewhere we find instruction in wonderful mysteries, which are more immediate revelations (1QH^a XII, 27–28). Knowledge of the truth depends upon the revelation of such divine mysteries, and in the Hodayot the writer declares that he has been made "a knowledgeable mediator of secret wonders" (1QH^a X, 13) in the manner of Enoch, and "you have taught me your truth, you have made me know your wonderful mysteries, enlightened me through thy truth" (1QH^a XV, 26–27).

In 4QInstruction alongside what Ashton calls *accessible* wisdom observations on the pragmatics of life, is set *remote/hidden* wisdom that can be accessed, if at all, only through a special revelation originating in God. Relevant here are two more texts from the Scrolls. The first, from 4QInstruction, concerns the one who will walk "in the correctness of understanding" and to whom

> are made known the secrets of his thought [cf. 1 Cor 2:10], while one walks perfectly in all one's deeds. Be constantly intent on these things, and understand all their effects. And then you will know eternal glory with his wonderful mysteries and his mighty deeds. (4Q417 1 I, 11–13)[31]

None of the writings composed by the Qumran sectarians themselves is strictly speaking an apocalypse, at least in the literary form which we have in texts like Revelation and 1 Enoch, since visionary reports and heavenly journeys among the sectarian texts are missing. But the number of manuscripts of 1 Enoch and Jubilees, plus a quantity of hitherto unknown Aramaic texts that were also found, testifies to their appreciation of heavenly revelation, and also how their own writings are suffused with their sense that they are the privileged recipients of a special revelation unavailable to ordinary mortals. This does not mean that they reject the torah; the presence among the scrolls of various halakhic texts, especially 4QMMT, shows how seriously they took its interpretation. But because of the value they attach to their own revealed mysteries, the torah may be said to be no more significant to them than this new truth.

---

31. García Martínez and Tigchelaar, *The Dead Sea Scrolls Study Edition*, 2:859.

5. The Apocalyptic Dimension in the Pauline Letters and the Gospel of John

The points just made highlight the contrast between accessible and hidden wisdom, the last of which the apocalyptic claims to offer. Still, the evidence from the Dead Sea Scrolls suggests that both forms of wisdom coexisted and may have determined the common life of the community, which lived according to this material. It thus provides an illuminating analogy to the New Testament sources.

Paul's extant writings do not include an apocalypse. Rather what we have is a mix of the pragmatic, the rhetorical, and the apologetic along with flashes of claims to apocalyptic insight into divine mysteries and ecstatic experiences. With regard to Paul and apocalyptic and mystical matters, the emphasis will depend on the understanding of apocalyptic, but, if it is apocalyptic as access to hidden mysteries, passages like 2 Cor 12:2-4; the references to divine mysteries to which Paul has access (Rom 11:25; 16:25; 1 Cor 2:1, 7; 4:1; 13:2; 15:51), and the language about knowledge of the depths of God (1 Cor 2:10) are all relevant to the revelation of divine mysteries.[32] First Corinthians is arguably, at least in part, about the management of the claims to the mystical. Whatever we make of the remarkable section in 1 Cor 2, where Paul talks about access to the depths of God, something which not only Paul and his companions but also the Corinthians might enjoy, by the time he is writing this letter he was seeking to challenge a form of piety that may be mystically sublime but not ethical enough. Paul offers himself as a role model, in a way like the stories that are offered in rabbinic texts.[33] That learning is rooted in the ancestral tra-

---

32. Alan F. Segal, *Paul the Convert: The Apostolate and Apostasy of Saul the Pharisee* (New Haven: Yale University Press, 1990); Ulrich Luz, "Paul as a Mystic," in *The Holy Spirit and Christian Origins: Essays in Honor of James D. G. Dunn*, ed. Graham N. Stanton, Bruce W. Longenecker, and Stephen C. Barton (Grand Rapids: Eerdmans, 2004), 131-43; John Ashton, *The Religion of Paul the Apostle* (New Haven: Yale University Press, 2000); Colleen Shantz, *Paul in Ecstasy: The Neurobiology of the Apostle's Life and Thought* (Cambridge: Cambridge University Press, 2009); and Christopher Rowland, "Paul as Apocalyptist," in *The Jewish Apocalyptic Tradition and the Shaping of the New Testament*, ed. Benjamin E. Reynolds and Loren T. Stuckenbruck (Minneapolis: Fortress, 2017), 173-204.

33. Such as those in the Talmuds, where Yohanan ben Zakkai gives his seal of approval to Eleazar ben Arak (cf. the problem with the Corinthians), teaching that, to paraphrase the encomium of Eleazar ben Arak, exposition and fulfillment do not

ditions derived from the authoritative teacher. High-flown angelic words, for example, are not matched by deeds: what is needed is following the example of the apostle/teacher who imitates Christ, accepting his authority and the halakhah-like instructions he offered. For Paul, the community is a holy temple (1 Cor 3:16; 6:19; 2 Cor 6:14–7:1)—a purified space, an extension of the temple in Jerusalem—in the Corinthian community. Paul lays down the level of holiness expected of those who had access to the divine world in their midst and the measures needed to ensure that this holiness was not compromised. Peter Tomson's words accurately sum up the Paul of 1 Corinthians: "truly Jewish and Pharisaic, Paul's apocalyptic faith is consummated in active life."[34] First Corinthians is a letter that is distinguished by its ethical demand and is peppered with Paul's appeals to tradition (e.g., 7:10; 11:2; 14:37), his role as a steward of divine mysteries (4:1; 2:1, 6), his apostolic authoritative pronouncements (7:6, 8, 12; 11:33; 16:1) and examples in his own life (4:16; 9:1–23; 11:1).

In 2 Cor 3–4, Paul gives us a glimpse of beliefs about the present transformation. This takes place not through heavenly ascent to the angelic realm but through identification with the pattern of Christ whose path to glory involved affliction and death. Such themes are at the heart of Paul's theology. The mystery that has been hidden from before the foundation of the world is one that is now revealed, but this apocalypse is of the crucified Christ, a stumbling block to many. The divine is revealed in the world of flesh, not through heavenly ascent but in the cross of Christ and the lives of his followers, especially his apostle, whose path involves affliction and death. But the revelation remains a mystery to those on the way to perdition (2 Cor 2:16).

The Gospel of John stands in contrast with the Pauline letters. Ashton is probably right that

> Unlike Enoch and the Qumran community, the Gospel of John abandons the Law completely: the Law is not just superseded, but cancelled … (John 1:17), and it is Jesus, so he himself asserts, to whom the scrip-

---

coincide. See the allusive m. Hag. 2:1, where learning is a basis for understanding of one's own knowledge, a maturity that later tradition based on knowledge of rabbinic learning, is a prerequisite for the sage who would embark on the interpretation of passages such as the first chapter of Ezekiel.

34. Peter J. Tomson, *Paul and the Jewish Law: Halakha in the Letters of Paul*, CRINT 1.3 (Assen: Van Gorcum; Minneapolis: Fortress, 1990), 80.

tures bear witness (5:39). He has both succeeded the Law as the object of revelation and replaced it as the object of revelation.[35]

Not all will agree with his judgement, but it encapsulates the rather more clear-cut prioritization of hidden revelation over accessible revelation. Better put, the hidden revelation itself is deemed to be accessible and so replaces the torah, and so immediate access to God is found in him, Jesus ("He who has seen me has seen the Father" [John 14:9]). The God who appeared to Ezekiel on the throne chariot appears now in Jesus, who reveals God's glory to humans.[36] The Fourth Gospel locates revelation in the person of Jesus, though it does hint that Jesus has privileged access to information from God as well as sight of the divine. Jesus proclaims himself as the revelation of the hidden God (1:18; 14:8). The highest wisdom of all, the knowledge of God, comes not through the information disclosed in visions and revelations but through the Word become flesh, Jesus of Nazareth, whose authority relies on the communication he has received from his father. The goal of the apocalyptic seer, the glimpse of God enthroned in glory (1 En. 14), is to be found in Jesus (1:18; 6:46; 12:41; 14:9), and, to borrow from the letter to the Colossians, he it is "in whom are hid all the treasures of wisdom and knowledge" (Col 2:3). He is the goal of the angels' search for the divine mysteries (1:51; cf. 1 Pet 1:11–12).

But there is even more going on in the Gospel of John, which brings it close to the poles of accessible and hidden/remote wisdom that we have discussed. Like the Teacher of Righteousness, the Johannine Jesus prioritizes immediate revelation, which he has received from the Father. The Johannine Jesus is impelled by a higher call than obedience to the law of Moses and its tradition of interpretation, and this appeal is the basis for his action. Jesus has seen God and heard God's words. Here John recalls Isa 6:1, 5, who "saw his glory and spoke of him" (John 12:41, 49–50). In Isa 6, Isaiah both saw and was sent, two themes which are central to the Gospel of John. Isaiah was remembered as faithful in his vision, who showed

---

35. Ashton, "'Mystery' in the Dead Sea Scrolls," 64.
36. Jey Kanagaraj, *"Mysticism" in the Gospel of John: An Inquiry into the Background of John in Jewish Mysticism*, JSNTSup 158 (Sheffield: Sheffield Academic, 1998). See also John A. Ashton, *Understanding the Fourth Gospel*, 2nd ed. (Oxford: Oxford University Press, 2007); Catrin H. Williams and Christopher Rowland, *John's Gospel and Intimations of Apocalyptic* (London: Bloomsbury, 2013); and John A. Ashton, *The Gospel of John and Christian Origins* (Minneapolis: Fortress, 2014).

hidden things before they happened (Sir 48:22, 25). In a similar vein, the early chapters of the Ascension of Isaiah suggest Isaiah's reputation as a visionary prophet who saw the Lord. Isaiah retreats from Jerusalem to the desert and along with the faithful prophets who believed in the ascension to heaven and lived on wild herbs (Ascen. Isa. 2.7–11). The charge against Isaiah was that he had contradicted Moses and asserted that he had seen God and lived. So he was called a false prophet (3.6–10).

Jesus, too, is depicted in the Gospel of John as a visionary prophet who sees God and reports what he has seen and heard and is sent by the Father. The Johannine Jesus is impelled by divine impulse. But in the Gospel of John there is more, as Jesus claims to offer revelation of God in his person (e.g., 14:9). Comparing the Pauline texts with the Gospel of John, there is a mix of accessible and remote wisdom in the Pauline letters, less so in the Gospel of John where Jesus comes as the revealer of remote wisdom, which turns out to be the clue to the divine purposes, and thus superseding the law of Moses (cf. John 1:17).

6. Conclusion

When I wrote *The Open Heaven*, part of what I wanted to achieve was to bring together all that I had learnt from Scholem about Jewish mysticism in the discussion of apocalypticism. I still remain convinced that the eschatological elements in apocalyptic texts, whether transcendent or otherwise, are not the determining feature of what constitutes apocalyptic. Nevertheless, for reasons I have sketched, I do understand that if apocalyptic is used as a generic term, it is because of the character of the *contents* of the book of Revelation. But that needs to be complemented by an understanding that attends to the revelatory *form* of apocalyptic literature and any visionary experience to which it bears witness. As I indicated, I do think that the Society of Biblical Literature definition in large part does embrace both.

It was part of the exegetical culture in which I was raised to want to illuminate the Bible by being able to relate documents and individual verses to particular parallel texts. This was the motor behind the method I learned. So, it mattered greatly to demonstrate that, for example, later rabbinic mystical texts reflect earlier ideas, which could have influenced the New Testament. When I wrote *The Open Heaven*, and at the start of writing *The Mystery of God*, I was more interested in being able to trace genealogical relationships between ancient Jewish and Christian texts, even if, as is the case with many Jewish texts, these came from centuries later than the Christian texts. I do not want to turn my back on this method. Indeed, I am still convinced that there was a visionary-experiential practice in parts of Second Temple Judaism that might have made an impact on early Christianity, particularly evident in the book of Revelation.

But I am now as interested in the reception history task of Ezek 1 in Christianity as well as Judaism. My interest has moved to a different kind of diachronic perspective, which concentrates less on antecedents and more on effects. Strangely, this has taken me back to where I started as a graduate student, when I was interested to explore how far early Christian texts were a part of the *Wirkungsgeschichte* of the *merkabah*, though I did not at that time see it in those terms! This story, as Michael Lieb has shown, from the Apocalypse via Dante to Boehme and Blake, is in its way every bit as fascinating as elucidating the history of *merkabah* mysticism.[37]

The history of the study of apocalyptic and of mysticism deserves elucidation. A more thorough and systematic analysis than I have offered here would reveal a more nuanced picture. Hans-Georg Gadamer wrote in his foreword to the second edition of *Truth and Method*, that our interpretation is "not what we do or what we ought to do, but what happens to us over and above our wanting and doing."[38] Far from standing outside history, we are firmly within history. Gadamer emphasizes the crucial role of the interpretative subject in the hermeneutical process:

> In fact history does not belong to us; we belong to it. Long before we understand ourselves through the process of self-examination, we understand ourselves in a self-evident way in the family, society, and state in which we live. The focus of subjectivity is a distorting mirror. The self-awareness of the individual is only a flickering in the closed circuits of historical life. *That is why the prejudices of the individual, far more than his judgements, constitute the historical reality of his being.*[39]

The hermeneutical task involves recognizing the extent to which traditions of historical scholarship are themselves bound by their diachronic

---

37. Michael Lieb, *The Visionary Mode: Biblical Prophecy, Hermeneutics and Cultural Change* (Ithaca, NY: Cornell University Press, 1991).
38. Hans-Georg Gadamer, *Truth and Method*, 2nd ed. (London: Sheed & Ward, 1989), xxvi; on which see Mark Knight, "*Wirkungsgeschichte*, Reception History, Reception Theory," *JSNT* 33 (2010): 137–46.
39. Gadamer, *Truth and Method*, 276–77, emphasis original.

determinants. The task of each generation is not so much to be free of them but to be aware of the pervasiveness of their influence.

Bibliography

Ashton, John. *The Gospel of John and Christian Origins*. Minneapolis: Fortress, 2014.

———. "'Mystery' in the Dead Sea Scrolls and the Fourth Gospel." Pages 53–68 in *John, Qumran, and the Dead Sea Scrolls: Sixty Years of Discovery and Debate*. Edited by Mary L. Coloe and Tom Thatcher. EJL 32. Atlanta: Society of Biblical Literature, 2011.

———. *The Religion of Paul the Apostle*. New Haven: Yale, 2000.

———. *Understanding the Fourth Gospel*. 2nd ed. Oxford: Oxford University Press, 2007.

Bentley, G. E., Jr. *The Stranger from Paradise: A Biography of William Blake*. New Haven: Yale University Press, 2001.

Blake, William. *The Marriage of Heaven and Hell*. Boston: Luce, 1906.

Bowker, John W. "Merkabah Visions and the Visions of Paul." *JSS* 16 (1971): 157–73.

Carruthers, Mary. *The Book of Memory: A Study of Memory in Medieval Culture*. Cambridge: Cambridge University Press, 1990.

———. *The Craft of Thought: Meditation, Rhetoric, and the Making of Images, 400–1200*. Cambridge: Cambridge University Press, 1998.

———. *The Medieval Craft of Memory*. Philadelphia: University of Pennsylvania Press, 2002.

Coleridge, Samuel Taylor. *Collected Letters*. Edited by Earl Leslie Griggs. Oxford: Oxford University Press, 1956.

———. *Marginalia*. Edited by George Whalley. Princeton: Princeton University Press 1979.

Collins, John J., ed. *Apocalypse: The Morphology of a Genre*. Semeia 14 (1979).

———. "Introduction: Towards the Morphology of a Genre." *Semeia* 14 (1979): 1–20.

Dillmann, August. *Das Buch Henoch: Übersetzt und erklärt*. Leipzig: Vogel, 1851.

Ferber, Michael. "Coleridge's 'Anacalyptic' Blake: An Exegesis." *Modern Philology* 76 (1978): 189–93.

Flannery-Dailey, Frances. *Dreamers, Scribes, and Priests: Jewish Dreams in the Hellenistic and Roman Eras*. JSJSup 90. Leiden: Brill, 2004.

Gadamer, Hans-Georg. *Truth and Method*. 2nd ed. London: Sheed & Ward, 1989.
García Martínez, Florentino, and Eibert J. C. Tigchelaar. *The Dead Sea Scrolls Study Edition*. 2 vols. Leiden: Brill, 1997.
Halperin, David. *The Faces of the Chariot: Early Jewish Responses to Ezekiel's Vision*. TSAJ 16. Tübingen: Mohr Siebeck, 1988.
Hanson, Paul D. *The Dawn of Apocalyptic: The Historical and Sociological Roots of Jewish Apocalyptic Eschatology*. Rev. ed. Philadelphia: Fortress, 1979.
Harding, Anthony J. *Coleridge on the Bible*. Vol. 2 of *Coleridge's Responses*. London: Continuum, 2007.
Hellholm, David, ed. *Apocalypticism in the Mediterranean World and the Near East: Proceedings of the International Colloquium on Apocalypticism Uppsala, August 12–17, 1979*. 2nd ed. Tübingen: Mohr Siebeck, 1989.
Hengel, Martin. *Judaism and Hellenism: Studies in Their Encounter in Palestine during the Early Hellenistic Period*. London: SCM, 1974.
Kanagaraj, Jey. *'Mysticism' in the Gospel of John: An Inquiry into the Background of John in Jewish Mysticism*. JSNTSup 158. Sheffield: Sheffield Academic, 1998.
Knight, Mark. "*Wirkungsgeschichte*, Reception History, Reception Theory." *JSNT* (2010): 137–46.
Laurence, Richard. *The Book of Enoch*. Oxford: Parker, 1821.
Lieb, Michael. *The Visionary Mode: Biblical Prophecy, Hermeneutics and Cultural Change*. Ithaca, NY: Cornell University Press, 1991.
Lücke, Friedrich. *Versuch einer vollständigen Einleitung in der Offenbarung Johannis und in die gesammelte apokalyptische Literatur*. Bonn: Weber, 1832.
Luz, Ulrich. "Paul as a Mystic." Pages 131–43 in *The Holy Spirit and Christian Origins: Essays in Honor of James D. G. Dunn*. Edited by Graham N. Stanton, Bruce W. Longenecker, and Stephen C. Barton. Grand Rapids: Eerdmans, 2004.
Macaskill, Grant. *Revealed Wisdom and Inaugurated Eschatology in Ancient Judaism and Early Christianity*. JSJSup 115. Leiden: Brill, 2007.
McGinn, Bernard. *The Foundations of Mysticism*. London: SCM, 1992.
Nickelsburg, George W. E. "The Study of Apocalypticism from H. H. Rowley to the Society of Biblical Literature." 1979. https://www.sbl-site.org/assets/pdfs/Nickelsburg_Study.pdf

Odeberg, Hugo. *The Fourth Gospel Interpreted in Its Relation to Contemporaneous Religious Currents in Palestine and the Hellenistic-Oriental World.* Uppsala: Almqvist & Wiksell, 1929.

———. *The View of the Universe in the Epistle to the Ephesians.* LUÅ 1, n.f. 29.6. Lund: Gleerup, 1934.

Plöger, Otto. *Theocracy and Eschatology.* 2nd German ed. Translated by S. Rudman. Oxford: Blackwell, 1968.

Rowland, Christopher. *Blake and the Bible.* London: Yale University Press, 2011.

———. *The Open Heaven: A Study of Apocalyptic in Judaism and Early Christianity.* New York: Crossroad, 1982.

———. "Paul as Apocalyptist." Pages 173–204 in *Jewish Apocalyptic Tradition and the Shaping of New Testament Thought.* Edited by Benjamin Reynolds and Loren T. Stuckenbruck. Minneapolis: Fortress, 2017.

Rowland, Christopher, and Christopher R. A. Morray-Jones. *The Mystery of God: Early Jewish Mysticism and the New Testament.* CRINT 12. Leiden: Brill, 2009.

Schäfer, Peter. *The Origins of Jewish Mysticism.* Princeton: Princeton University Press, 2011.

Schmidt, Johann M. *Die jüdische Apokalyptik: Die Geschichte ihrer Erforschung von den Anfängen bis zu den Textfunden von Qumran.* Neukirchen: Neukirchener Verlag, 1969.

Scholem, Gershom. *Jewish Gnosticism, Merkabah Mysticism and Talmudic Tradition.* New York: Jewish Theological Seminary, 1960.

———. *Major Trends in Jewish Mysticism.* London: Thames & Hudson, 1955.

———. *Origins of the Kabbalah.* Philadelphia: Jewish Publication Society, 1990.

Segal, Alan F. *Paul the Convert: The Apostolate and Apostasy of Saul the Pharisee.* New Haven: Yale University Press, 1990.

Shaffer, Elinor S. *'Kubla Khan' and the Fall of Jerusalem: The Mythological School in Biblical Criticism and Secular Literature 1770–1880.* Cambridge: Cambridge University Press, 1979.

Shantz, Colleen. *Paul in Ecstasy: The Neurobiology of the Apostle's Life and Thought.* Cambridge: Cambridge University Press, 2009.

Stone, Michael E. "Lists of Revealed Things in the Apocalyptic Literature." Pages 414–52 in *Magnalia Dei, the Mighty Acts of God: Essays on the Bible and Archaeology in Memory of G. Ernest Wright.* Edited by Frank

Moore Cross, Werner E. Lemke, and Patrick D. Miller. Garden City, NY: Doubleday, 1976.

———, ed. *Jewish Writings of the Second Temple Period: Apocrypha, Pseudepigrapha, Qumran, Sectarian Writings, Philo, Josephus.* CRINT 2.1. Assen: Van Gorcum; Minneapolis: Fortress, 1984.

———. *Scriptures, Sects, and Visions: A Profile of Judaism from Ezra to the Jewish Revolts.* Oxford: Blackwell, 1980.

Tomson, Peter J. *Paul and the Jewish Law: Halakha in the Letters of Paul.* CRINT 1.3. Minneapolis: Fortress, 1990.

Vielhauer, Phillip. "Apocalyptic in Early Christianity." Pages 608–42 in *Writings Related to the Apostles; Apocalypses and Related Subjects.* Vol. 2 of *New Testament Apocrypha.* Edited by Edgar Hennecke and Wilhelm Schneemelcher. Translated by R. McLean Wilson. Philadelphia: Westminster, 1965.

Williams, Catrin, and Christopher Rowland. *John's Gospel and Intimations of Apocalyptic.* London: Bloomsbury, 2013.

Revealed Things in Apocalyptic Literature

Lorenzo DiTommaso

Michael E. Stone's 1976 article, "Lists of Revealed Things," is one of the landmark studies on apocalyptic literature.[1] Prior to its publication, *apocalyptic* was construed primarily with reference to the biblical books of Daniel and the Revelation of John, on which tradition and theology had bestowed a unique status.[2] These books were regarded as the paradigmatic apocalypses, and their historical and eschatological content were thought to be characteristic of apocalyptic revelation.[3]

Stone, however, pointed out that the early Jewish apocalypses attributed to the antediluvian figure of Enoch disclose information about matters other than history and its expected end. These apocalypses reveal the motion of celestial bodies, the location of the winds, the workings of the

---

Alexander Kulik kindly reviewed an early version of this paper. Research for this paper has been supported by 2011-16 and 2018-24 grants from the Social Sciences and Humanities Research Council of Canada.

1. Michael E. Stone, "Lists of Revealed Things in the Apocalyptic Literature," in *Magnalia Dei, the Mighty Acts of God: Essays on the Bible and Archaeology in Memory of G. Ernest Wright*, ed. Frank Moore Cross, Werner E. Lemke, and Patrick D. Miller (Garden City, NY: Doubleday, 1976), 414–35. Stone submitted his article in 1971, but publication issues compounded by Wright's death in 1974 resulted in the volume's delay (personal correspondence with Stone).

2. The other apocalyptic writings that scholars of that era regularly studied, 4 Ezra (= 2 Esdr 3–14) and the Sibylline Oracles, also are historical-eschatological in tenor and so reinforced the paradigm established by Daniel and Revelation.

3. Indeed, a common title of Revelation in the older scholarship is *"the* Apocalypse," i.e., the *ne plus ultra* specimen of the type, for which a qualifying adjective is unnecessary. Cf. the corresponding titles in German ("Die Apokalypse"), French ("L'Apocalypse"), Italian ("L'Apocalisse"), and Spanish ("El Apocalipsis"), and their standard abbreviations, which persist to the present day. The distinction between an object and its category can blur when brand names (so to speak) become generic.

natural world, and the nature of the heavenly realm itself. In addition, many of the same topics are recorded in lists of revealed things in historical apocalypses such as 4 Ezra and 2 Baruch.[4]

In overturning the conviction that early Jewish apocalyptic writings are concerned solely with history and eschatology, Stone's article also called into question conventional views about their origin. If apocalypses disclose the secrets of heaven as well as those of history, they must be rooted in other ancient sources besides late biblical prophecy, such as the neo-Babylonian astrological tradition or the psalms and wisdom books. Likewise, the attention of these early apocalypses to topics other than eschatological salvation challenged assumptions, again based on Daniel and Revelation, that apocalypses are oppression literature and that their natural audience is the small, persecuted religious group or "conventicle" whose members anticipated divine deliverance from hostile foreign rule.[5]

Stone's article surveyed the early Jewish apocalypses and the relatively few Dead Sea Scrolls that were known to scholars at the time. This paper revisits the subject of revealed things in apocalyptic literature in view of the full corpus of the Scrolls and other Jewish apocalyptic texts of the Second Temple period. What kinds of things are revealed in apocalyptic literature? Can they be classified into meaningful heuristic categories? Is eschatology an essential or a secondary component of apocalyptic speculation?

1. Approaches to Apocalyptic and the Issue of Apocalyptic Content

The answers to these questions depend in part on the definition of *apocalyptic*, which varies from field to field. For medievalists, apocalyptic—and hence revelatory content—is understood primarily in terms of Christian eschatology and its social functions.[6] In contemporary popular culture, as

---

4. Stone, "Lists of Revealed Things," 414.

5. See, e.g., Philipp Vielhauer, "Apokalypsen und Verwandtes," in *Neutestamentliche Apokryphen in deutscher Übersetzung*, 3rd ed. (Tübingen: Mohr Siebeck, 1964), 2:405–27. This assumption owed much to the pioneering volume of Norman Cohn, *The Pursuit of the Millennium* (London: Secker & Warburg, 1957), on the apocalyptic-millennial groups of late medieval Europe.

6. Although some late medieval apocalyptic texts include astrology and alchemy, these subjects are unparalleled in the early Jewish apocalyptic literature.

well as for those who study it, apocalyptic is equated with the end of the world, which translates to many different things.[7]

In biblical studies, apocalyptic is often mediated by scholarly approaches to the subject. These function like models or, better still, maps. It is often said that "map is not territory,"[8] but it is also the case that different kinds of maps model the same terrain in different ways. This is true with approaches to apocalyptic, the most influential of which are those of Christopher Rowland and John J. Collins. Each model proceeds from a bedrock definition and makes claims about the nature of revealed things.

Christopher Rowland defines apocalyptic as "the revelation of heavenly mysteries," as proposed in his 1982 book, *The Open Heaven*.[9] He argues that apocalyptic texts disclose two types of material, "eschatological" and "cosmological," which he describes in terms of the horizontal and the vertical axes of apocalyptic speculation. Rowland's approach is popular among scholars who study the New Testament, which contains only one formal apocalypse but much in the way of apocalyptic speculation.[10] The weakness of the approach is that heavenly revelation is not unique to apocalyptic speculation. By this definition, the prophetic books of the Hebrew Bible are apocalyptic, since they also reveal God's will to Israel.[11] So also

---

7. Lorenzo DiTommaso, "Apocalypticism and Popular Culture," in *The Oxford Handbook of Apocalyptic Literature*, ed. John J. Collins (New York: Oxford University Press, 2014), 473–509.

8. Alfred Korzybski, *Science and Sanity: An Introduction to Non-Aristotelian Systems and General Semantics* (Institute of General Semantics, 1994), 58. The concept was introduced to scholars of religion in Jonathan Z. Smith's book, *Map Is Not Territory: Studies in the History of Religions* (Chicago: University of Chicago Press, 1975).

9. Christopher Rowland, *The Open Heaven: A Study of Apocalyptic in Judaism and Christianity* (New York: Crossroad, 1982), 14: "To speak of apocalyptic, therefore, is to concentrate on the theme of the direct communication of the heavenly mysteries in all their diversity." See also 1–5, 351–57 and passim; and Rowland, "Apocalyptic: The Disclosure of Heavenly Knowledge," in *The Early Roman Period*, ed. William Horbury, W. D. Davies, and John Sturdy, CHJ 3 (Cambridge: Cambridge University Press, 1999), 776–97, 1172–76.

10. See, most recently, Benjamin E. Reynolds and Loren T. Stuckenbruck, eds., *The Jewish Apocalyptic Tradition and the Shaping of the New Testament* (Minneapolis: Fortress, 2017). Rowland's attention to the cosmological or vertical dimension of apocalyptic revelation has also proven attractive to scholars of mysticism and Gnosticism.

11. By the same criterion, the revelatory utterings of the Sibylline oracle of Cumaea, the Pythian oracle at Delphi, and the Nechung oracle in Tibet are also apocalyptic.

are the interpretation of Pharaoh's dreams (Gen 41) and the handwriting on the wall (Dan 5), since in both cases a heavenly mystery is revealed.[12]

John J. Collins's approach rests on the definition of the literary genre apocalypse that was developed by the Society of Biblical Literature Genres Project and later promulgated in his 1984 volume, *The Apocalyptic Imagination*.[13] Based on their content, Collins identifies two types of apocalypses, "historical" and "otherworldly."[14] Historical apocalypses disclose the meaning of history and its end, while otherworldly apocalypses are interested more in cosmological speculation. Over the past forty years, Collins's approach and the Society of Biblical Literature definition have profoundly shaped the study of apocalyptic literature both inside and outside biblical studies.[15] The weakness of the generic approach is the nature of the evidence. Formal apocalypses make up only a small percentage of the corpus of early Jewish apocalyptic writings, which include the early Aramaic writings from the Dead Sea, Hebrew works such as the revelatory visions of Dan 8–12 and the apocalyptic texts of the Qumran sectarians, and Greek works in the New Testament and elsewhere.

A third leading approach to apocalyptic is the phenomenological. There are many variations on the theme,[16] and it is only in comparison

---

12. "And the doubling of Pharaoh's dream means that the thing is fixed by God, and God will shortly bring it about" (Gen 41:32 NRSV).

13. John J. Collins, ed., *Apocalypse: The Morphology of a Genre*, Semeia 14 (1979); and esp. Collins, "Introduction: Towards the Morphology of the Genre," *Semeia* 14 (1979): 1–20. An apocalypse is "a genre of revelatory literature with a narrative framework, in which a revelation is mediated by an otherworldly being to a human recipient, disclosing a transcendent reality which is both temporal, insofar as it envisions eschatological salvation, and spatial as it involves another, supernatural world." See also John J. Collins, *The Apocalyptic Imagination: An Introduction to Jewish Apocalyptic Literature* (New York: Crossroad, 1984). Subsequent references to this volume are to its third edition (2016).

14. Collins, *Apocalyptic Imagination*, 7. The initial taxonomy proposed in *Semeia* 14 (Collins, "Introduction," 13–15) was more complicated and soon abandoned by Collins. A vestige survives in the three-fold classification of otherworldly apocalypses in Collins, *Apocalyptic Imagination*, 8.

15. In my experience, if a study of medieval or modern apocalypticism cites something from biblical studies, that source is usually Collins's *Apocalyptic Imagination*.

16. See, among others, Jean Carmignac, "Description du phénomène de l'Apocalyptique dans l'Ancien Testament," in *Apocalypticism in the Mediterranean World and the Near East*, ed. David Hellholm, 2nd ed. (Tübingen: Mohr Siebeck, 1989), 163–70, and Per Bilde, "Gnosticism, Jewish Apocalypticism, and Early Christianity," in

with the work of Rowland and Collins that a family resemblance emerges. The assumption among all expressions of the type is that apocalyptic is defined as the sum of its characteristic features. These typically include descriptions of the content of the revelation. Greg Carey's 2005 volume, *Ultimate Things*, exemplifies the methodology.[17] Carey's interpretative lens is "apocalyptic discourse," which he defines as the aggregate of eleven "characteristic topics."[18] The primary advantage of this approach is its adaptability. The category of apocalyptic discourse transcends form and so can shed as much light on contemporary media as on ancient texts. The disadvantage of phenomenological approaches is that they are based on a suite of features rather than a bedrock category that can anchor the taxonomy and define all its expressions. As a result, every model that defines or describes apocalyptic ends up mirroring the characteristics of its suite of features, which is a tautology: input determines output.

These three approaches to apocalyptic have exerted a tremendous gravitational pull on the study of ancient apocalyptic literature, albeit in different directions. Each makes claims about the nature of apocalyptic that scholars employ as a diagnostic model of the first order. In this, then, each approach functions like an interpretative lens. As time passes, however, the way that the evidence is perceived through such lenses comes to be regarded as normal, as anyone who wears corrective glasses knows. With the approaches of Rowland and Collins in particular, they have become so much a part of the way that scholars construe apocalyptic that they are often taken at face value. This *amnesia of definitions*, where useful heuristic models become habituated over time, is common to all fields of research. It causes the conceptual articulation of the evidence to be confused for the evidence itself. Or, put another way, the map is mistaken for the territory.

This blurring of map and territory has affected the way that scholars have come to view apocalyptic content. Even though their approaches

---

In the Last Days: On Jewish and Christian Apocalyptic and Its Period, ed. Knud Jeppesen, Kirsten Nielsen, and Bent Rosendal (Aarhus: Aarhus University Press, 1994), 9–32.

17. Greg Carey, *Ultimate Things: An Introduction to Jewish and Christian Apocalyptic Literature* (St. Louis: Chalice, 2005), 3 ("characteristic topics") and 6–10 (their enumeration, cf. next note).

18. These are: (1) an interest in alternative worlds in both space and time; (2) heavenly visions or auditions; (3) heavenly intermediaries; (4) intense symbolism; (5) pseudonymous attribution; (6) the expectation of cosmic catastrophe; (7) dualism; (8) determinism; (9) a concern about final judgment and the afterlife; (10) ex euentu prophecy; and (11) cosmic speculation.

begin at different points and endorse contradictory notions about the nature of apocalyptic, Collins and Rowland recognize the same two types of apocalyptic literature based on its revelatory content: (1) historical-eschatological and (2) otherworldly-cosmological. This correspondence, which occurs on the diagnostic level, has led to the conviction that eschatological content is present solely in apocalyptic texts of the historical type, that is, apocalyptic speculation is *either* historical-eschatological *or* otherworldly-cosmological. The weak form of this position is the view that the label apocalyptic may be applied to texts where an eschatological dimension is absent. The strong form is the view that eschatology is not integral to apocalyptic literature.

The absolute distinction between two types of apocalyptic literature is implicit in Collins's approach and explicit in Rowland's. Although Collins has repeatedly underscored its etic quality, the Society of Biblical Literature definition is deployed as an emic category, as if the ancient authors were familiar with a modern literary genre.[19] This is perhaps the result of the schematic chart that appears in all three editions of Collins's *Apocalyptic Imagination*.[20] It divides the early Jewish apocalypses into two groups. In one group are the otherworldly journeys of the Apocalypse of Zephaniah, the Testament of Abraham, 3 Baruch, T. Levi 2–5, 2 Enoch, the Similitudes of Enoch, the Astronomical Book, and 1 En. 1–36. The other group contains the historical apocalypses of 2 Baruch, 4 Ezra, Jubilees, the Apocalypse of Weeks, the Animal Apocalypse, and Daniel. In between them is the Apocalypse of Abraham.

---

19. John J. Collins, "The Genre Apocalypse Reconsidered," *ZAC* 20 (2016): 21–40; Collins, "The Genre of Fourth Ezra," *Rivista di storia del cristianesimo* 17 (2020): 59. For the deployment as an emic category, see, e.g., Todd Hanneken, *The Subversion of the Apocalypses in the Book of Jubilees*, EJL 34 (Atlanta: Society of Biblical Literature, 2012). The question as to whether the ancient authors were familiar with a literary genre ἀποκάλυψις (Rev 1:1 NA[27]; parr. Syriac, Coptic, and Latin) should not be confused with whether they were familiar with the genre according to its *Semeia* 14 definition. Alexander Kulik proposes that the ancient authors deployed the idea of *gilayon* ("revealed book") in a generic sense; see Alexander Kulik, "Genre without a Name: Was There a Hebrew Term for 'Apocalypse'?," *JSJ* 40 (2009): 540–50. See also Michelle Fletcher, "Apocalypse Noir: Rereading Genre through Pastiche," in *Reading Revelation as Pastiche: Imitating the Past*, LNTS 571 (New York: Bloomsbury, 2017), 182–213.

20. Collins, *Apocalyptic Imagination*, 7.

Rowland defends the absolute distinction between the two types and advocates the strong form of the position. On the one hand, apocalyptic texts of the eschatological type disclose the heavenly mysteries of the past, present, and future. On the other hand, texts of the cosmological type are concerned with the "mysteries of God, the Angels and astronomy."[21] On the unconditional segregation of eschatological texts from the larger category of apocalyptic Rowland is clear: "In our attempt to ascertain the essence of apocalyptic *no place was found for eschatology* in our definition."[22]

Rowland's distinction between eschatological and noneschatological types of apocalyptic literature is reflected in many studies, particularly those that focus on New Testament apocalyptic. In his *Revelation and Mystery in Ancient Judaism and Pauline Christianity*, Marcus Bockmuehl differentiates between "eschatological" and "cosmological" kinds of apocalyptic mysteries.[23] Likewise, in their introduction to their fine edited volume, *The Jewish Apocalyptic Tradition and the Shaping of the New Testament*, Benjamin E. Reynolds and Loren T. Stuckenbruck contrast the revealed mysteries of temporal transcendence ("eschatology") with those of spatial transcendence ("cosmos and wisdom").[24] These are but a few examples among many.[25]

---

21. Rowland, *Open Heaven*, 78–103 (the quotation is the title of chapter 4).

22. Rowland, *Open Heaven*, 26; see also 48: "a dominant feature of the mysteries revealed to the apocalypticists is the secret of the future, particularly with regard to Israel. To say that, however, is not the same as saying that eschatology is a constitutive feature of apocalyptic. An apocalypse often does contain much eschatological material, *but it need not*" (emphasis added).

23. Marcus Bockmuehl, *Revelation and Mystery in Ancient Judaism and Pauline Christianity*, WUNT 2/36 (Tübingen: Mohr Siebeck, 1990), 33–36.

24. Benjamin E. Reynolds and Loren T. Stuckenbruck, introduction to *Jewish Apocalyptic Tradition and the Shaping of the New Testament*, 6–7: "An evenly focused understanding of 'apocalyptic' as revelation of temporal *and* spatial transcendence," they write, "opens the possibility for considering the disclosure of the cosmos and of wisdom as 'apocalyptic'" (italics original). In Reynolds's contribution to the same volume, he asserts that "the Jewish apocalypses have more to do with the revelation of hidden mysteries than with the expectation of the end, even though the resolution of time is sometimes the content of what is revealed" ("Apocalyptic Revelation in the Gospel of John: Revealed Cosmology, the Vision of God, and Visionary Showing," in Reynolds and Stuckenbruck, *Jewish Apocalyptic Tradition and the Shaping of the New Testament*, 109).

25. Cf., e.g., Philip J. Alexander, "From Son of Adam to Second God: Transformations of the Biblical Enoch," in *Biblical Figures outside the Bible*, ed. Michael E. Stone and Theodore A. Bergren (Harrisburg, PA: Trinity Press International, 1998), 89: "In

2. Revealed Things in Apocalyptic Literature

A survey of the early Jewish apocalyptic texts reveals a literary terrain that contains much of the information in the older maps yet presents a different perspective. The survey demonstrates that the two types of apocalyptic literature are relative categories, not absolute ones, and that an eschatological horizon is present in every example.

2.1. The Eschatological Dimension of Apocalyptic Writings of the Otherworldly Type

The sample of Jewish and Christian writings below is divided into three groups: (1) two early Enochic apocalypses (the Book of Watchers and the Astronomical Book); (2) two Second-Temple works that exhibit broad generic diversity and derive from different social milieus (the Dead Sea Hodayot, the Parables of Enoch); and (3) two ascent apocalypses of late-antique Christianity (the Apocalypse of Peter and the Apocalypse of Paul). Each highlights a different issue relevant to the typology of apocalyptic literature.

2.1.1. Early Enochic Writings

The Book of Watchers (1 En. 1–36) and the Astronomical Book (1 En. 72–82), also called the Book of the Luminaries, are among the earliest

---

terms of its content *1 Enoch* is an apocalypse: a revelation of secrets and mysteries"; Crispin T. Fletcher-Louis, "Jewish Apocalyptic and Apocalypticism," in *Handbook for the Study of the Historical Jesus*, ed. Tom Holmén and Stanley E. Porter (Leiden: Brill, 2011), 4:1588: "no distinctively eschatological content is required by the word [apocalypse]"; Fletcher-Louis, "*2 Enoch* and the New Perspective on Apocalyptic," in *New Perspectives on 2 Enoch: No Longer Slavonic Only*, ed. Andrei Orlov and Gabriele Boccaccini, StJud 4 (Leiden: Brill, 2012), 125–48, as well as several of the essays in Catrin H. Williams and Christopher Rowland, eds., *John's Gospel and Intimations of Apocalyptic* (London: Bloomsbury, 2013); and Garrick V. Allen, ed., *The Book of Revelation: Currents in British Research on the Apocalypse*, WUNT 411 (Tübingen: Mohr Siebeck, 2015). The abiding persistence of Rowland's approach is also reflected in the conclusion of James P. Davies's critical review of *Apocalyptic Literature in the New Testament*, by Greg Carey, *CBQ* 79 (2017): 518: "[Carey's] definition of apocalyptic is overly restrictive *in its emphasis on eschatology and suppression of other revealed mysteries*, which leads to the relegation of some texts that might otherwise have been given more attention" (emphasis added).

known apocalyptic texts.[26] Each includes much cosmological material, which is presented in revelatory format. For this reason, these two compositions are most frequently highlighted by scholars who presume an absolute categorical distinction between two types of apocalyptic literature.[27]

The discovery of the Dead Sea Scrolls confirmed the great antiquity of the Book of Watchers in its original language, Aramaic. The Scrolls also preserve fragmentary manuscript copies of related writings such as the Book of Giants and the Aramaic Astronomical Book.[28] The composition history of the Book of Watchers is convoluted and remains only partly understood. In its present form, it describes a series of otherworldly tours that are undertaken by Enoch, including his ascent to heaven, where God commissions him to announce the divine judgment against the Watchers. This event is recounted thrice (1 En. 13.7–10; 14.1–7; 14.8–16.4). The third time it is accompanied by a detailed description of the heavenly throne and the divine presence, a hallmark feature of cosmological speculation in Second Temple Jewish apocalyptic literature. The final section of the Book

---

26. George W. E. Nickelsburg, *1 Enoch 1: A Commentary on the Book of 1 Enoch, Chapters 1–36; 81–108*, Hermeneia (Minneapolis: Fortress, 2001), esp. 25–26 and 169–72; and James C. VanderKam, "1 Enoch 72–82: The Book of the Luminaries," in *1 Enoch 2: A Commentary on the Book of Enoch Chapters 37–82*, ed. George W. E. Nickelsburg and James C. VanderKam, Hermeneia (Minneapolis: Fortress, 2012), 339–40. VanderKam, though, cautions against the presumption of such an early date of composition.

27. The evidence strongly suggests that the present versions of the Book of Watchers and the Astronomical Book are the result of a long and complicated editorial process that began in the third or even fourth centuries BCE. The main hypotheses are presented and discussed in Nickelsburg, *1 Enoch 1*, and Nickelsburg and VanderKam, *1 Enoch 2*. There are two possibilities regarding the eschatological component in the Book of Watchers and/or the Astronomical Book: it was present in the embryonic states of one text or the other, or it was added later. A stronger formulation of the second possibility is that the Book of Watchers and the Astronomical Book acquired their present apocalyptic valence at the same time as the composition of Dan 7–12 and the Animal Apocalypse and in response to the same social conditions. The latter is my own position, which I will unpack in a forthcoming book.

28. See Józef T. Milik, with the collaboration of Matthew Black, *The Books of Enoch: Aramaic Fragments from Qumrân Cave 4* (Oxford: Clarendon, 1976); Loren T. Stuckenbruck, "The Early Traditions Related to 1 Enoch from the Dead Sea Scrolls: An Overview and Assessment," in *The Early Enoch Literature*, ed. Gabriele Boccaccini and John J. Collins, JSJSup 121 (Leiden: Brill, 2007), 41–63; and now, especially, Henryk Drawnel, *Qumran Cave 4: The Aramaic Books of Enoch; 4Q201, 4Q202, 4Q204, 4Q205, 4Q206, 4Q207, 4Q212* (Oxford: Oxford University Press, 2019).

of Watchers, corresponding to 1 En. 17–36, consists of Enoch's journeys to locations on earth such as Jerusalem (26) and the four corners of the world (33–36), which contain the gates of heaven through which the celestial bodies and winds pass (cf. also 18). In his travels, Enoch is also told the names of the archangels (20).

Yet even though the Book of Watchers is an otherworldly apocalypse—for many authorities, the hallmark specimen of the type—its revelatory content is oriented throughout by an eschatological horizon. As George W. E. Nickelsburg notes, the "focal point" of 1 En. 1–5, which prefaces the story of the Watchers and its explanation for the entry of evil into the world, is the expectation of eschatological judgment (cf. esp. 5.6–7).[29] This expectation is reiterated in 1 En. 10.11–15 and again in chapter 22, this time along with that of their human wives and impious humans more generally. The place of their punishment is specified in 1 En. 21, mentioned again in 27.1–4, and contrasted with the paradise of righteous humans in 32.3–6.

The Astronomical Book is unprecedented in early Judaism in its lengthy technical descriptions of meteorological phenomena, the phases of the moon, and the motion of the stars in relation to the seasons of the year. It also represents the earliest Jewish evidence for a solar calendar of 364 days.[30] All this information is presented as a revelation of heavenly mysteries.[31]

The revelation is oriented, however, by an eschatological horizon: "The entire book about [the motion of the heavenly luminaries], he showed me and how every year of the world will be forever, until a new creation lasting

---

29. Nickelsburg, *1 Enoch 1*, 37. See further Nickelsburg, *Resurrection, Immortality, and Eternal Life in Intertestamental Judaism and Early Christianity*, exp. ed., HTS 56 (Cambridge: Harvard University Press, 2006), *passim*; Casey D. Elledge, *Resurrection of the Dead in Early Judaism 200 BCE–CE 200* (New York: Oxford University Press, 2017), 130–49; and Jan A. Sigvartsen, *Afterlife and Resurrection Beliefs in the Apocrypha and Apocalyptic Literature*, Jewish and Christian Texts in Contexts and Related Studies 29 (New York: Bloomsbury, 2019), 98–110.

30. The basics of calendrical calculation, then and now, is a function of the apparent movement of celestial bodies ("heavenly luminaries") as observed from the surface of the earth.

31. Henryk Drawnel argues that the revelatory showing and seeing in the Book of the Luminaries should be understood not as elements of a heavenly tour but rather as the interchange between teacher and student: the teacher "shows" or explains a calculation and the students "sees" or understands the calculation. See Henryk Drawnel, *The Aramaic Astronomical Book (4Q208–4Q211) from Qumran: Text, Translation, and Commentary* (Oxford: Clarendon, 2011), 36–37.

forever is made" (1 En. 72.1).[32] As the angel Uriel later explains to Enoch, the corruption of the divine order by the entry of evil into the world has necessitated the coming new creation (82.2–8). The eschatological character of the Astronomical Book is also implied in its position as a constituent part of Ethiopic Enoch, where its cosmological content is informed by its two historical apocalypses, the Animal Apocalypse and the Apocalypse of Weeks (1 En. 93.1–10 + 91.11–17), and the end-time expectations of the Book of Watchers.

To sum up: the Book of Watchers and Astronomical Book are remarkable for their long sections of cosmological data as well as information about a host of other subjects. In both cases, however, the revelation is oriented by the eschatological horizon that is part of the heavenly revelation of each apocalypse in their present forms. As with the revelatory visions of Daniel and the Animal Apocalypse, with which they stand at the dawn of apocalyptic, the apocalyptic character of the Book of Watchers and the Astronomical Book is rudimentary yet still exhibits all the essential features, including an eschatological dimension.

2.1.2. The Hodayot and the Parables of Enoch

This subsection surveys two primarily otherworldly (or perhaps mixed-type) apocalyptic writings from the Second Temple era: the Dead Sea Hodayot and the Parables of Enoch. Neither is usually regarded as a historical-type text, but both include the revelation of historical-eschatological information. The limitations of space permit only a brief accounting of each work.

The Hodayot

The Hodayot is a collection of thanksgiving hymns (or psalms) that was discovered among the Dead Sea Scrolls. Seven manuscripts are extant, including 1QH[a], the only one that does not consist solely of small fragments. The textual relationship among the manuscripts is sufficiently distant to suggest that they preserve different states of the collection. Some hymns reflect the solitary voice of an authoritative Teacher; others the collective voice of the *yaḥad*. All are brimming with the distinctive religious

---

32. VanderKam, "1 Enoch 72–82," 409.

ideas and vocabulary of the *yaḥad*, including its basic apocalyptic outlook on the nature of the cosmos, time, and human existence in a world sundered by the conflict between good and evil. As with the biblical psalms, the psalmist of the Hodayot confesses his humble humanity. He recounts his sufferings and tribulations at the hands of his enemies and how he has been delivered from these tribulations and the pitfalls of the evil world by God's gracious assistance.

The apocalyptic worldview of the Hodayot is explicit in its eschatological language of resurrection. The hymns express the conviction that the members of the *yaḥad* enjoyed a corporate, antemortem exalted status among the angels (1QH[a] XI, 19–23; XII, 6–XIII, 6; XIX, 10–14). This is one of the most distinctive aspects of the eschatology of the *yaḥad*.[33] It is also accompanied by several passages that can be read in terms of the expectation for the traditional postmortem resurrection of individuals (XIV, 32–37).

The Parables of Enoch

The origin and authorship of the Parables (or Similitudes) of Enoch have been the subject of much debate. The *communis opinio* inclines to a date in the late Second-Temple period, likely in the first century CE. The Parables feature a series of eight vision reports by Enoch, including a divine theophany (1 En. 46). Collins classifies the text as an apocalypse of the otherworldly type.

Despite its otherworldly framework, the Parables of Enoch contain much historical-eschatological content. A suite of passages, for example, relate the history of the Noah and the flood (54.7–55.2; 60.1–25; 65.1–67.3). Most prominent, though, is the series of statements that describe the enthronement of the Son of Man and expectations concerning the coming judgment (48.2–10; 50.1–51.5b; 63.1–12). One of the many striking aspects of these eschatological passages (50.1–5) is what appears to be an early version of the tripartite anthropology that appears in later Manichean texts and, in another form, would later contribute to the development of the Christian notion of purgatory.[34]

---

33. Elledge, *Resurrection of the Dead*, 153–57, Collins, *Apocalyptic Imagination*, 217.

34. Manichean anthropology admits three types of humans—the elect, the catechumens, and the damned. The middle category is one of potentiality, with the future hope of salvation, rather than the certainty of the elect. See Iain Gardner and Samuel

2.1.3. The Ascent Apocalypses of Late-Antique Christianity

The Apocalypse of Peter dates from the early middle of the second century CE, perhaps around the time of Bar Kokhba Revolt (132–136 CE).[35] Two versions of the work are known: the Greek original, which is fragmentarily preserved, and the Ethiopic (Akhmim). Although significant differences exist between them, both versions relate Peter's guided tours of the infernal and the celestial realms. The Apocalypse of Paul was composed in Greek around 250 years later, in the last quarter of the fourth century.[36] It features Paul's tours of hell and heaven and drew on traditions in the Apocalypse of Peter among other sources.[37] The Apocalypse of Paul is preserved in many languages and multiple versions and is the most significant apocalyptic text to appear between the Revelation of John and the *Revelationes* of Pseudo-Methodius. It established a good part of the conceptual framework for later western Christian views on the fate of the soul after death.[38]

Although both the Apocalypse of Peter and the Apocalypse of Paul are otherworldly apocalypses in the pattern of the Book of Watchers, their primary concern is not the revelation of cosmological mysteries or other kinds of otherworldly information. Rather, they are focused on the judgment and

---

Nan-Chiang Lieu, *Manichaean Texts from the Roman Empire* (Cambridge: Cambridge University Press, 2004), 19. *Tripartite* here refers to a present-day state rather than an eschatological one. The members of the others, the third category, have the chance to change their ways and be included among the elect at the time of the end, when there are only two destinations. See the discussions in Nickelsburg and VanderKam, *1 Enoch 2*, 182–83, and Sigvartsen, *Afterlife and Resurrection Beliefs*, 112–15.

35. Richard Bauckham, "The *Apocalypse of Peter*: A Jewish Christian Apocalypse from the Time of Bar Kokhba," *Apocrypha* 5 (1994): 7–8. This dating is generally but not universally accepted.

36. Kristi B. Copeland suggests a time after the year 388. See Kristi B. Copeland, "Thinking with Oceans: Muthos, Revelation, and the *Apocalypse of Paul*," in *The Visio Pauli and the Gnostic Apocalypse of Paul*, ed. Jan N. Bremmer and István Czachesz, SECA 9 (Leuven: Peeters, 2007), 77–78 n. 1. Note also Pierluigi Piovanelli, "Les origines de l'*Apocalypse de Paul* reconsiderées," *Apocrypha* 4 (1993): 25–64. The original Greek text is lost, although an epitomized form is extant; the best complete version is the Latin *Visio sancti Pauli*.

37. Anthony Hilhorst, "The *Apocalypse of Paul*: Previous History and Afterlife," in Bremmer and Czachesz, *Visio Pauli and the Gnostic Apocalypse of Paul*, 1–22, esp. 21.

38. Claude Carozzi, *Le Voyage de l'âme dans l'au-delà d'après la littérature latine (V^e–XIIIe siècle)*, Collections de l'École française de Rome 189 (Rome: Publications de l'École française de Rome, 1994).

fate of the individual soul after death and thus, by implication, the road by which salvation or damnation is attained.[39] Their cosmological geography is important, but only as a vehicle for connecting an individual's eschatological state with his or her present-day behavior. The mechanism by which the connection is made is a baroque elaboration of the apocalyptic theory of justice, where postmortem punishment fits the antemortem sin. Although this echoes the Roman legal concept of *lex talionis* ("an eye for an eye"), it reflects a developing conception of the harmonious and righteous justice of the overall system that is witnessed in the increasingly expansive descriptions of the multiple heavenly and infernal levels that characterize late-antique apocalyptic speculation. The punishments are validated by God, who asks the damned soul begging for mercy whether he showed any mercy on earth when alive (Apoc. Paul 17, etc.). In both apocalypses, the message is oriented by the eschatological horizon, which informs present-day behavior on the part of individuals: to remain steadfast to the good/God and to abhor evil/Satan.[40]

2.1.4. Observations

Despite their fixation on subjects other than the meaning of history and its end, apocalyptic texts of the otherworldly type *always have an eschatological dimension*. Even texts that are typically held up as exemplars of the absolute distinction between the two types of apocalyptic literature have an eschatological component.

2.2. Noneschatological Revelatory Content in Apocalyptic Writings of the Historical Type

Apocalyptic texts that disclose the meaning of history and its end are well-represented in every era except late antiquity (mid-second to fifth

---

39. The description of the judgment of the dead in the Apocalypse of Paul in particular presents some interesting aspects whose discussion resides beyond the scope of this paper. See Meghan Henning, "Eternal Punishment as Paideia: The Ekphrasis of Hell in the *Apocalypse of Peter* and the *Apocalypse of Paul*," BR 58 (2013): 29–48, and Emiliano Fiori, "Death and Judgment in the *Apocalypse of Paul*: Old Imagery and Monastic Reinvention," ZAC 20 (2016): 92–108.

40. A classic illustration is in the Apocalypse of Peter (§25, Akhmim), where murderers and their accessories are cast into a gorge and tormented by worms and venomous reptiles, while the souls of those whom they had murdered stand nearby, saying, "O God, righteous is thy judgment."

centuries CE).[41] In most periods they are extraordinarily predominant. During the medieval millennium (fifth to fifteenth-sixteenth centuries), Christians, Jews, and Muslims produced well over a thousand examples of the historical type in virtually every conceivable literary genre—and comparatively few examples of the otherworldly type.[42]

The argument in this section is this: although historical apocalyptic texts are typically and overwhelmingly concerned with history and eschatology, even the most robust specimens of the type include revelatory information about a variety of other, noneschatological topics. A small sample of ancient texts illustrates what is a universal point: Dan 7–12, the Animal Apocalypse, Jubilees, the New Jerusalem text, the Jewish Sibylline Oracles, 4 Ezra, and the Revelation of John.

2.2.1. Daniel 7–12

As noted, the four revelatory visions of MT Dan 7–12 are among the earliest apocalyptic writings.[43] The visions of Dan 7, 8, and 10–12 present what soon became the classic apocalyptic combination of *ex euentu* historical review and eschatological forecast, while that of Dan 9 is more of a revelatory dialogue between Daniel the seer and Gabriel the angel, albeit also on history and its meaning in light of the end.

Each of the four visions, however, also discloses small packets of information about subjects other than history or its ending. Most obvious is the otherworldly theophany of Dan 7:9–14, with its description of the Ancient One and the one "like a son of man," which much resembles what one finds in the Enochic writings of a similar vintage. Another example is Daniel's prayer in 9:4b–19, which recounts Israel's covenantal transgressions that have led to its present state of exile. Likewise, the long historical review in the final revelation of Dan 10–12 forecasts the actions of the final king (Antiochus IV Epiphanes) and highlights ostentatious wealth and improper land redistribution (Dan 11:39; cf. 11:43 and the Revelation of John, below).

---

41. Lorenzo DiTommaso, "Il genere 'apocalisse' e l'apocalittico' nella tarda antichità," *Rivista di storia del cristianesimo* 17.1 (2020): 73–99.

42. This might come as a surprise to scholars of early Judaism, who are used to balancing the Enochic writings against Daniel, 4 Ezra, and Revelation. Yet, the fact is that otherworldly texts represent only a small fraction of the apocalyptic literature in other historical eras and cultural settings.

43. I refer here to the visions in their present form as a constituent part of MT Daniel.

These snippets of information, embedded as they are in historical reviews, are neither random nor casual but speak to authorial concerns and audience realities. A parade example is the way that the visions advocate a quietist response to the excesses of Antiochus IV, assuring their audience that God will soon deliver his faithful and that divine justice is imminent.

2.2.2. The Animal Apocalypse

The Animal Apocalypse (1 En. 85–90) derives from the same Maccabean-era setting of the revelatory visions of Daniel.[44] It consists of a long and highly selective *ex euentu* retelling of the history of Israel with an eschatological climax. Most strikingly, the text presents humans as animals, while good angelic figures appear as white humanoids and disobedient ones as falling stars. It is a remarkable text by any standard.

Yet even though the Animal Apocalypse focuses squarely on historical events and eschatological judgment, one of its central functions is to explain the presence of evil in the world in view of a good and just God (cf. 4 Ezra below).[45] To this end, its revelatory content also includes information about the antediluvian history of Israel (85.1–89.8), which is typical of the early Enochic texts overall. In addition, the Animal Apocalypse contains information about morality and ethics, such as the apostasy of the two kingdoms of Israel and Judah (89.51–58), echoing the concern of Dan 9. Again, these little bits of information are an important part in the text's paraenetic message to its intended audience: stay the ethical/moral course, and deliverance will surely come soon and justice will be served.

2.2.3. Jubilees

The book of Jubilees dates from the generation or two after the Maccabean revolt.[46] It recounts the history of the world and Israel from creation to the giving of the law, selectively covering the events in Genesis and the first part

---

44. As with all the component parts of 1 Enoch, the date of the Animal Apocalypse has elicited a range of suggestions. According to Nickelsburg, the text's internal data correlates well to a date of 165–163 BCE (*1 Enoch 1*, 355).

45. Dan 9 is an exception in this regard, with its presentation of the apocalyptic theology of history.

46. James C. VanderKam, *Jubilees: A Commentary on the Book of Jubilees Chapters 1–21*, Hermeneia (Minneapolis: Fortress, 2018), esp. 37–38.

of Exodus. This story is framed as a revelation that is received by Moses on Sinai and structured in divisions of forty-nine years each (or "jubilees"). Fragments of fourteen manuscript copies of Jubilees were discovered among the Dead Sea Scrolls,[47] along with those of several Pseudo-Jubilees texts.

Whether Jubilees is an apocalypse is unimportant to our argument. Collins calls the book a "borderline case" but also classifies it as a historical apocalypse.[48] What is important is that Jubilees is an apocalyptic text with an *ex euentu* historical framework and eschatological horizon (1.29; 5.13; and esp. ch. 23) that is replete with other kinds of revelatory information. A few examples suffice to make the point. As with the Astronomical Book, Jubilees contains much calendrical information (6.32–38, etc.), although it is presented in the form of a divine revelation to the seer rather than as the record of the seer's tour through the cosmos. In addition, the book is intensely interested in the world of angels and demons and their place in the universe and action in history and daily life. The revelatory content of Jubilees also extends to morals and ethics, particularly in the matter of apostate behavior and the requirement to observe the correct festival times. Jubilees is an apocalyptic book whose revelatory content is primarily geared to halakhic matters that are intended to regulate a pious-traditionalist mode of Jewish life.[49]

2.2.4. The New Jerusalem Text

The New Jerusalem text was unknown before the discovery of the Dead Sea Scrolls. This Jewish apocalypse is composed in Aramaic and survives in seven fragmentary and partially overlapping manuscript copies.[50] Its literary genre, language of composition, and contents suggest that it was written in or around Jerusalem in the mid-second century BCE, possibly during the reign of Antiochus IV.[51] The text describes the walls and interior structures of a monumental city. Although the city is not named, it

---

47. VanderKam, *Jubilees*, 5.
48. Collins, *Apocalyptic Imagination*, 8, 104.
49. See further, Michael Segal, *The Book of Jubilees: Rewritten Bible, Redaction, Ideology and Theology*, JSJSup 117 (Leiden: Brill, 2007).
50. 1Q32 (1QNJ ar), 2Q24 (2QNJ ar), 4Q554 (4QNJ^a ar), 4Q554a (4QNJ^b ar), 4Q555 (4QNJ^c ar), 5Q15 (5QNJ ar), and 11Q18 (11QNJ ar).
51. Lorenzo DiTommaso, *The Dead Sea New Jerusalem Text: Contents and Contexts*, TSAJ 110 (Tübingen: Mohr Siebeck, 2005).

is the eschatological "New Jerusalem," a common expectation in the late prophetic and early apocalyptic writings, notably Ezek 40–48. The eschatological horizon of the New Jerusalem text is confirmed by other features, including a version of the four-kingdom schema that is known elsewhere in Dan 2 and 7 and the Jewish Sibylline Oracles.

Most of the New Jerusalem text contains noneschatological content, even though its context is eschatological. One lengthy, if fragmentary, section of the text outlines the offerings, rituals, and implements of the new temple. But most obvious is the detailed description of the New Jerusalem itself, which proceeds inward from city's massive walls and gates to its broad boulevards and open spaces and down to its individual urban structures. As we have seen, the revelation of otherworldly geography is paralleled in early Jewish apocalyptic works, including Enoch's tour of faraway lands and other places in 1 En. 17–36.

2.2.5. The Jewish Sibylline Oracles

The Sibylline Oracles comprise twelve books of apocalyptic oracles that are written in Greek epic hexameters and attributed to an unnamed Sibyl, one of the famed prophetesses of classical antiquity. Most books are compilations of older oracles, the earliest of which were composed by Egyptian Jews during the late Second Temple period (ca. 165 BCE to 135 CE).[52] The overall tenor of the Sibylline Oracles is among the most resolutely historical-eschatological of all ancient apocalyptic writings. The revelatory content of the early Jewish oracles stresses the doings and happenings of rulers, kingdoms, politics, and war, which are regularly interspersed with predictions of natural disasters, cosmic catastrophes, and future woe against foreign and hostile enemy nations (especially Rome).

Even so, the Sibylline Oracles additionally contain multiple exhortations against idolatry (Sib. Or. 3.8–45; 4.6–24; 8.359–428) and moral behavior (3.762–766; 4.24–39; 8.17–36). Unlike the small snippets of extra information in Daniel and the Animal Apocalypse, the ethical exhortations of the Sibylline Oracles are lengthy and commonplace, and their function is patent. Their inclusion reflects the origin of the oracles in the Egyptian diaspora, where the principal concern was to maintain Jewish identity in a foreign land. Repeated injunctions against improper behav-

---

52. See John J. Collins, "Sibylline Oracles," *OTP* 1:319–472.

ior, backed by the authority of heavenly revelation, reinforced the firewalls against apostasy and conversion that were necessary to preserve group cohesion and survival.

2.2.6. Fourth Ezra

The book of 4 Ezra (= 2 Esdr 3–14) is one of four historical-type apocalypses that were composed in the aftermath of the failure of the Great Jewish Revolt against Rome (66–73 CE) and the destruction of the Jerusalem temple.[53] Fourth Ezra comprises seven visions, each of which has a clear eschatological dimension. The final three visions consist of Danielic-style reviews of history with an eschatological climax, which are divulged to Ezra the seer and interpreted by the angel Uriel.

The first three visions, however, are revelatory dialogues between Ezra and Uriel, whose conversations include information on multiple subjects besides eschatological. Indeed, their range of interest extends well beyond the limited contents of the lists of revealed things that are highlighted by Stone,[54] including: the limitations of the human imagination (4.1–12; 5.33–40); the nature of the created world (6.38–53); issues of theodicy and the goodness of God (3.3–27; 6.55–59); the state of the dead before the final judgment (7.75–101); and the efficacy of prayer (7.102–115). None of this content is any less revelatory than that which is transmitted in the visions shown to Ezra later in the book. In both the dialogues and the visions that follow, the information is a product of heavenly disclosure that is oriented by an eschatological horizon.

2.2.7. The Revelation of John

As with 4 Ezra, the Revelation of John was composed around the end of the first century CE, though slightly earlier, during the reign of the emperor

---

53. The others are 2 Baruch, the lost original of the Apocalypse of Abraham, and the Revelation of John. On 4 Ezra, see Michael E. Stone, *Fourth Ezra: A Commentary on the Book of Fourth Ezra*, Hermeneia (Minneapolis: Fortress, 1990), and Lorenzo DiTommaso, "Who Is the 'I' of *4 Ezra*?," in Fourth Ezra *and* Second Baruch: *Reconstruction after the Fall*, ed. Matthias Henze and Gabriele Boccaccini, JSJSup164 (Leiden: Brill, 2013), 119–33.

54. The same may be said of 2 Baruch, which on several points exhibits a close affiliation with 4 Ezra.

Domitian (81–96 CE). No other ancient apocalyptic text dilates more on eschatological events than Revelation. Its vivid images and super-charged vocabulary became the blueprint for Christian end-time speculation for the next two thousand years.

That said, the book also contains revelatory content of a noneschatological nature. Prime examples are the letters to the seven congregations of Asia in chapters 2–3.[55] Although their messages are oriented by an eschatological horizon, they are concerned with morality and the present-day behavior of the members of each congregation. These letters are not a secondary addition to the book but an integral part of its claim to be a revelation from Jesus Christ. They are prefixed by the announcement of John's revelation (Rev 1:1), are addressed to each congregation in a revelatory format, and include vocabulary and themes that are integral to the rest of the book. Revelation also has a strong economic message that spoke to its audience in its present-day situation.[56] Rome is described as the great whore (17:1–9). She has given herself over to all the sumptuary excesses possible, including the traffic in human lives, sold herself to the nations, kings, and merchants, who have "grown rich from the power of her luxury" (18:3). The wealth, greed, and corruption of the sprawling world empire represent earthly antitheses of heavenly values to which the faithful aspired. Its punishment will be swift, total, and inescapable.

3. Conclusions

This paper opened with three questions. Although this survey focuses on the apocalyptic texts of ancient Judaism and Christianity, the following answers to these questions apply to apocalyptic speculation globally:

---

55. As Craig R. Koester, in *Revelation*, AYB 38A (New Haven: Yale University Press, 2014), 231, writes, "In this first cycle, John sees a vision of the exalted Christ, who directs him to write to seven congregations about the challenges they face, while warning them of judgment and offering hope."

56. The information in the rest of this paragraph (with secondary sources) is drawn from Lorenzo DiTommaso, "Class Consciousness, Group Affiliation, and Apocalyptic Speculation," in *The Struggle over Class: Socioeconomic Analysis of Ancient Jewish and Christian Texts*, ed. G. Anthony Keddie, Michael Flexsenhar, and Steven J. Friesen, WGRWSup 14 (Atlanta: SBL Press, 2021), 277–312.

3.1. What kinds of things are revealed in apocalyptic literature?

The short answer is *virtually anything*.[57] The revelatory content of the apocalyptic texts of early Judaism and Christianity extends to history, eschatology, protology, cosmology, geography, meteorology, physiognomy, economics, ethics, morals, rituals, theodicy, calendrical issues, and more. In the medieval and modern apocalyptic texts, the compass of revealed things in apocalyptic literature is even more expansive, ranging across the full spectrum of knowledge from astrology to zoology.

3.2. Can these revealed things be classified into meaningful heuristic categories?

Despite their exceptionally wide range of revelatory content, apocalyptic writings may still be classified into two types, historical and otherworldly, based on their revelatory content. This is the binary classification of Collins but with a critical modification. It does not presume the priority of the genre apocalypse, which is a heuristically weak category. Instead, the classification into historical and otherworldly types reflects the disposition of apocalyptic literature *tout court*, that is, apocalyptic writings (1) of every literary genre (and not just formal apocalypses) and (2) throughout history (and not just its early Jewish exemplars).

The label cosmological very poorly describes the broad range of content of the second type of apocalyptic texts and is also misleading. If one presumes an absolute distinction between eschatological and noneschatological apocalyptic writing and if the second type is equated with cosmological, the result is that any revelatory text with cosmological content may be designated apocalyptic. For this reason, I suggest a moratorium on the word when it is used to describe a type of apocalyptic writings. Otherworldly is not a perfect substitute, but it is a much better alternative.[58]

---

57. This is not an exaggeration. Theoretically, apocalyptic speculation can include any topic except those that are contradicted by the axioms of the underlying worldview (e.g., a cyclical notion of time or the expectation of personal reincarnation). Practically, the subject matter is more restricted.

58. Among other things, the label otherworldly covers revelatory travel to places beyond the usual meaning of cosmological, including locations on Earth outside the

The classification of apocalyptic literature into historical and otherworldly types is overwhelmingly well-represented in the sources, making it an excellent diagnostic tool. Indeed, the relative distribution of the types in different historical eras and cultural settings over the past twenty-two centuries is the principal means by which the history of apocalyptic speculation may be written.

3.3. Is an eschatological horizon an essential or a secondary component of apocalyptic revelation?

An eschatological horizon is intrinsic to early Jewish apocalyptic literature as well as apocalyptic speculation more broadly. Almost without exception, apocalyptic writings of the historical-eschatological type contain revelatory information of a noneschatological character. Without exception, apocalyptic writings of the otherworldly type contain revelatory information of an eschatological character, often quite a bit of it.

In the final analysis, every apocalyptic text has an eschatological dimension. No type, kind, or category of apocalyptic writing is without an eschatological component. Any heuristic approach to apocalyptic that presumes an absolute distinction between eschatological and noneschatological texts is contradicted by the literary evidence, including the early Jewish apocalyptic texts that are held to be exemplary of such approaches. Apocalyptic speculation can include many things besides eschatology, but it is never anything less than eschatological.[59]

Bibliography

Alexander, Philip J. "From Son of Adam to Second God: Transformations of the Biblical Enoch." Pages 87–122 in *Biblical Figures outside the*

---

pale of human knowledge of the time and thus, literally *other* worldly. Late-medieval Christian journeys to purgatory are a long-removed descendant of this type of travel.

59. But what is apocalyptic eschatology? For my preliminary thoughts, see Lorenzo DiTommaso, "The Apocrypha and Apocalypticism," in *The Oxford Handbook of the Apocrypha*, ed. Gerbern S. Oegema (New York: Oxford University Press, 2021), 219–52; and DiTommaso, "Eschatology in the Early Jewish Pseudepigrapha and the Early Christian Apocrypha," in *Eschatology in Antiquity: Forms and Functions*, ed. Hilary Marlow, Karla Pollmann, and Helen Van Noorden (New York: Routledge, 2021), 235–49.

Bible. Edited by Michael E. Stone and Theodore A. Bergren. Harrisburg, PA: Trinity Press International, 1998.

Allen, Garrick V., ed. *The Book of Revelation: Currents in British Research on the Apocalypse*. WUNT 411. Tübingen: Mohr Siebeck, 2015.

Bauckham, Richard. "The *Apocalypse of Peter*: A Jewish Christian Apocalypse from the Time of Bar Kokhba." *Apocrypha* 5 (1994): 7–111.

Bockmuehl, Marcus. *Revelation and Mystery in Ancient Judaism and Pauline Christianity*. WUNT 2/36. Tübingen: Mohr Siebeck, 1990.

Bilde, Per. "Gnosticism, Jewish Apocalypticism, and Early Christianity." Pages 9–32 in *In the Last Days: On Jewish and Christian Apocalyptic and Its Period*. Edited by Knud Jeppesen, Kirsten Nielsen, and Bent Rosendal. Aarhus: Aarhus University Press, 1994.

Carey, Greg. *Ultimate Things: An Introduction to Jewish and Christian Apocalyptic Literature*. St. Louis: Chalice, 2005.

Carmignac, Jean. "Description du phénomène de l'Apocalyptique dans l'Ancien Testament." Pages 163–70 in *Apocalypticism in the Mediterranean World and the Near East*. Edited by David Hellholm. 2nd ed. Tübingen: Mohr Siebeck, 1983.

Carozzi, Claude. *Le Voyage de l'âme dans l'au-delà d'après la littérature latine (V^e–XIIIe siècle)*. Collections de l'École française de Rome 189. Rome: Publications de l'École française de Rome, 1994.

Cohn, Norman. *The Pursuit of the Millennium*. London: Secker & Warburg, 1957.

Collins, John J., ed. *Apocalypse: The Morphology of a Genre*. Semeia 14 (1979).

———. *The Apocalyptic Imagination: An Introduction to Jewish Apocalyptic Literature*. 3rd ed. Grand Rapids: Eerdmans, 2016.

———. "The Genre Apocalypse Reconsidered." *ZAC* 20 (2016): 21–40.

———. "The Genre of Fourth Ezra." *Rivista di storia del cristianesimo* 17.1 (2020): 59–71.

———. "Introduction: Towards the Morphology of a Genre." *Semeia* 14 (1979): 1–20.

———. "Sibylline Oracles." *OTP* 1:319–472.

Copeland, Kristi B. "Thinking with Oceans: Muthos, Revelation, and the *Apocalypse of Paul*." Pages 74–104 in *The Visio Pauli and the Gnostic Apocalypse of Paul*. Edited by Jan N. Bremmer and István Czachesz. SECA 9. Leuven: Peeters, 2007.

Davies, James P. Review of *Apocalyptic Literature in the New Testament*, Greg Carey, *CBQ* 79 (2017): 516–18.

DiTommaso, Lorenzo. "The Apocrypha and Apocalypticism." Pages 219–52 in *The Oxford Handbook of the Apocrypha*. Edited by Gerbern S. Oegema. New York: Oxford University Press, 2021.

———. "Apocalypticism and Popular Culture." Pages 473–509 in *The Oxford Handbook of Apocalyptic Literature*. Edited by John J. Collins. New York: Oxford University Press, 2014.

———. "Class Consciousness, Group Affiliation, and Apocalyptic Speculation." Pages 277–312 in *The Struggle over Class: Socioeconomic Analysis of Ancient Christian Texts*. Edited by G. Anthony Keddie, Michael Flexsenhar, and Steven J. Friesen. WGRWSup 14. Atlanta: SBL Press, 2021.

———. *The Dead Sea New Jerusalem Text: Contents and Contexts*. TSAJ 110. Tübingen: Mohr Siebeck, 2005.

———. "Eschatology in the Early Jewish Pseudepigrapha and the Early Christian Apocrypha." Pages 235–49 in *Eschatology in Antiquity: Forms and Functions*. Edited by Hilary Marlow, Karla Pollmann, and Helen Van Noorden. New York: Routledge, 2021.

———. "Il genere 'apocalisse' e 'apocalittico' nella tarda antichità." *Rivista di storia del cristianesimo* 17 (2020): 73–99.

———. "Who Is the 'I' of *4 Ezra*?" Pages 119–33 in Fourth Ezra *and* Second Baruch: *Reconstruction after the Fall*. Edited by Matthias Henze and Gabriele Boccaccini. JSJSup164. Leiden: Brill, 2013.

Drawnel, Henryk. *The Aramaic Astronomical Book (4Q208–4Q211) from Qumran: Text, Translation, and Commentary*. Oxford: Clarendon, 2011.

———. *Qumran Cave 4: The Aramaic Books of Enoch; 4Q201, 4Q202, 4Q204, 4Q205, 4Q206, 4Q207, 4Q212*. Oxford: Oxford University Press, 2019.

Elledge, Casey D. *Resurrection of the Dead in Early Judaism 200 BCE–CE 200*. New York: Oxford University Press, 2017.

Fiori, Emiliano. "Death and Judgment in the Apocalypse of Paul: Old Imagery and Monastic Reinvention." *ZAC* 20 (2016): 92–108.

Fletcher, Michelle. "Apocalypse Noir: Rereading Genre through Pastiche." Pages 182–213 in *Reading Revelation as Pastiche: Imitating the Past*. LNTS 571. New York: Bloomsbury, 2017.

Fletcher-Louis, Crispin T. "*2 Enoch* and the New Perspective on Apocalyptic." Pages 125–48 in *New Perspectives on 2 Enoch: No Longer Slavonic Only*. Edited by Andrei A. Orlov and Gabriele Boccaccini. StJud 4. Leiden: Brill, 2012.

———. "Jewish Apocalyptic and Apocalypticism." Pages 1569–607 in vol.

4 of *Handbook for the Study of the Historical Jesus*. Edited by Tom Holmén and Stanley E. Porter. Leiden: Brill, 2011.
Hanneken, Todd. *The Subversion of the Apocalypses in the Book of Jubilees*. EJL 34. Atlanta: Society of Biblical Literature, 2012.
Henning, Meghan. "Eternal Punishment as Paideia: The Ekphrasis of Hell in the *Apocalypse of Peter* and the *Apocalypse of Paul*." BR 58 (2013): 29–48.
Hilhorst, Anthony. "The *Apocalypse of Paul*: Previous History and Afterlife." Pages 1–22 in *The Visio Pauli and the Gnostic Apocalypse of Paul*. Edited by Jan N. Bremmer and István Czachesz. SECA 9. Leuven: Peeters, 2007.
Gardner, Iain, and Samuel Nan-Chiang Lieu. *Manichaean Texts from the Roman Empire*. Cambridge: Cambridge University Press, 2004.
Koester, Craig R. *Revelation*. AYB 38A. New Haven: Yale University Press, 2014.
Korzybski, Alfred. *Science and Sanity: An Introduction to Non-Aristotelian Systems and General Semantics*. Brooklyn: Institute of General Semantics, 1994.
Kulik, Alexander. "Genre without a Name: Was There a Hebrew Term for 'Apocalypse'?" *JSJ* 40 (2009): 540–50.
Milik, Jósef T. *The Books of Enoch: Aramaic Fragments of Qumrân Cave 4*. With the collaboration of Matthew Black. Oxford: Clarendon, 1976.
Nickelsburg, George W. E. *1 Enoch 1: A Commentary on the Book of 1 Enoch, Chapters 1–36; 81–108*. Hermeneia. Minneapolis: Fortress, 2001.
———. *Resurrection, Immortality, and Eternal Life in Intertestamental Judaism and Early Christianity*. Exp. ed. HTS 56. Cambridge: Harvard University Press, 2006.
Piovanelli, Pierluigi. "Les origines de l'*Apocalypse de Paul* reconsidérées." *Apocrypha* 4 (1993): 25–64.
Reynolds, Benjamin E. "Apocalyptic Revelation in the Gospel of John: Revealed Cosmology, the Vision of God, and Visionary Showing." Pages 109–28 in *The Jewish Apocalyptic Tradition and the Shaping of the New Testament*. Edited by Benjamin E. Reynolds and Loren T. Stuckenbruck. Minneapolis: Fortress, 2017.
Reynolds, Benjamin E., and Loren T. Stuckenbruck. Introduction to *The Jewish Apocalyptic Tradition and the Shaping of the New Testament*. Edited by Benjamin E. Reynolds and Loren T. Stuckenbruck. Minneapolis: Fortress, 2017.

———, eds. *The Jewish Apocalyptic Tradition and the Shaping of the New Testament*. Edited by Benjamin E. Reynolds and Loren T. Stuckenbruck. Minneapolis: Fortress, 2017.

Rowland, Christopher. "Apocalyptic: The Disclosure of Heavenly Knowledge." Pages 776–97 and 1172–76 in *The Early Roman Period*. Edited by William Horbury, W. D. Davies, and John Sturdy. CHJ 3. Cambridge: Cambridge University Press, 1999.

———. *The Open Heaven: A Study of Apocalyptic in Judaism and Early Christianity*. New York: Crossroad, 1982.

Segal, Michael. *The Book of Jubilees: Rewritten Bible, Redaction, Ideology and Theology*. JSJSup 117. Leiden: Brill, 2007.

Sigvartsen, Jan A. *Afterlife and Resurrection Beliefs in the Apocrypha and Apocalyptic Literature*. Jewish and Christian Texts in Contexts and Related Studies 29. New York: Bloomsbury, 2019.

Smith, Jonathan Z. *Map Is Not Territory: Studies in the History of Religions*. Chicago: University of Chicago Press, 1975.

Stone, Michael E. *Fourth Ezra: A Commentary on the Book of Fourth Ezra*. Hermeneia. Minneapolis: Fortress, 1990.

———. "Lists of Revealed Things in the Apocalyptic Literature." Pages 414–35 in *Magnalia Dei, the Mighty Acts of God: Essays on the Bible and Archaeology in Memory of G. Ernest Wright*. Edited by Frank Moore Cross, Werner E. Lemke, and Patrick D. Miller. Garden City, NY: Doubleday, 1976.

Stuckenbruck, Loren T. "The Early Traditions Related to 1 Enoch from the Dead Sea Scrolls: An Overview and Assessment." Pages 41–63 in *The Early Enoch Literature*. Edited by Gabriele Boccaccini and John J. Collins. JSJSup 121. Leiden: Brill, 2007.

VanderKam, James C. "1 Enoch 72–82: The Book of the Luminaries." Pages 333–569 in *1 Enoch 2: A Commentary on the Book of 1 Enoch; Chapters 37–82*. Edited by George W. E. Nickelsburg and James C. VanderKam. Hermeneia. Minneapolis: Fortress, 2012.

———. *Jubilees 1: A Commentary on the Book of Jubilees Chapters 1–21*. Hermeneia. Minneapolis: Fortress, 2018.

Vielhauer, Philipp. "Apokalypsen und Verwandtes." Pages 405–27 in vol. 2 of *Neutestamentliche Apokryphen in deutscher Übersetzung*. 3rd ed. Tübingen: Mohr Siebeck, 1964.

Williams, Catrin, and Christopher Rowland, eds. *John's Gospel and Intimations of Apocalyptic*. London: Bloomsbury, 2013.

Revelatory Literature, in Which a Revelation Is Mediated by an Otherworldly Being: Revelation in the Dead Sea Scrolls

Stefan Beyerle

1. The Definition of a Literary Genre Apocalypse

Considering that the quest for a literary genre apocalypse deserves a synchronic approach, while the investigation of an apocalyptic tradition or an apocalyptic worldview demands diachronic and historical methods,[1] the examination of apocalypticism in the Dead Sea Scrolls requires a bifocal assessment in terms of methods. With this bifocal assessment in mind, a problem arises when scrutinizing the sources among the Dead Sea Scrolls. One of the main reasons for these problems becomes apparent when the often extremely fragmentary character of these manuscripts is considered.[2] As a consequence, the preserved fragments among the Dead Sea Scrolls do not attest a composition that could be called an apocalypse in due consideration of the definition of the genre as proposed by John J. Collins (see below), even though texts like 1QMilḥamah, the War Scroll(s), or the composition called New Jerusalem clearly include an apocalyptic worldview. As

---

1. Matthew Goff, "The Apocalypse and the Sage: Assessing the Contribution of John J. Collins to the Study of Apocalypticism," in *Apocalyptic Thinking in Early Judaism: Engaging with John Collins' The Apocalyptic Imagination*, ed. Sidnie White Crawford and Cecilia Wassén, JSJSup 182 (Leiden: Brill, 2018), 9–11, who calls the genre apocalypse an etic term. On the *apocalyptic worldview* in early Judaism, see now Lorenzo DiTommaso, "The Apocrypha and Apocalypticism," in *The Oxford Handbook of the Apocrypha*, ed. Gerbern S. Oegema (New York: Oxford University Press, 2021), 219–52.

2. E.g., Goff, "Apocalypse and the Sage," 12, suggests that the Aramaic Son of God text (4Q246) and the Four Kingdoms fragments may have constituted a genre apocalypse in their—once upon a time—original form.

Bennie Reynolds emphasized most recently in a footnote: "The Qumran community and others like it may not have produced any literary apocalypses, but it is abundantly clear that they *read* literary apocalypses and derived significant aspects of their worldview from those texts."[3]

Nevertheless, the textual evidence from the Dead Sea Scrolls lacks any source that relate topics, motifs, and traditions of an apocalyptic worldview to a Qumran *apocalypse*, following the authoritative, etic definition of Collins. Consequently, every investigation of the Dead Sea Scrolls that looks for an apocalyptic worldview or apocalyptic thought, and apocalypticism in general, actually lacks every matrix of an apocalypse—apart from those fragments that attest apocalypses, known from evidence beyond the Dead Sea Scrolls, like manuscripts of the book of Daniel, Jubilees, or 1 Enoch.[4]

In his influential article in *Semeia* 14 (1979), Collins proposes a *definition*, not a *description*,[5] of the literary genre apocalypse. He states that an apocalypse is

> a genre of revelatory literature with a narrative framework, in which a revelation is mediated by an otherworldly being to a human recipient, disclosing a transcendent reality which is both temporal, insofar as it envisages eschatological salvation, and spatial insofar as it involves another, supernatural world.[6]

Although Collins's definition has garnered broad consensus,[7] it has not escaped criticism, particularly in its generic classification and methodological

---

3. Bennie H. Reynolds III, "A Dwelling Place of Demons: Demonology and Apocalypticism in the Dead Sea Scrolls," in Crawford and Wassén, *Apocalyptic Thinking in Early Judaism*, 24 n. 4 (emphasis original) and 41–42.

4. John J. Collins, *The Apocalyptic Imagination: An Introduction to Jewish Apocalyptic Literature*, 3rd ed. (Grand Rapids: Eerdmans, 2016), 179, states: "The fact that the books of Daniel, *Enoch*, and *Jubilees* are all found in multiple copies at Qumran, and seem to be regarded as authoritative writings, already bespeaks an interest in apocalyptic revelations."

5. For differences concerning the typology and definition of a literary genre and a simple taxonomy, see most recently Christoph Markschies, "Editorial/Einleitung," *ZAC* 20 (2016): 15–16.

6. John J. Collins, "Introduction: Towards the Morphology of a Genre," *Semeia* 14 (1979): 9.

7. Cf. Lorenzo DiTommaso, "Apocalypses and Apocalypticism III. Judaism," *EBR* 2 (2009): 325–26; and Frederick James Murphy, *Apocalypticism in the Bible and Its World: A Comprehensive Introduction* (Grand Rapids: Baker Academic, 2012), 4–8.

implications.[8] Carol Newsom emphasizes that the genre-specific "classificatory schemes are by their very nature static, whereas genres are dynamic."[9] She correctly highlights and explains the common implications of the genre apocalypse whose function is to relate the sources to one another: "transcendence, linking the manner of revelation, the existence of a heavenly world, the nature of its beings, and the function of apocalyptic eschatology."[10] Consequently, apocalypses embrace an intrinsic relation between revelation and a form of eschatology that leads to salvation.

The inclusion of eschatology in the definition is also a focus of critical queries. Eschatology associates a primarily Christian perspective with apocalypses. As Marvin Sweeney asks, "Is eschatology a defining feature of Jewish apocalyptic literature or does the introduction of such a concern give precedence to an element of Christian theological expectation found, for example, in the book of Revelation?"[11] The quotation refers to the larger problem of Christian stereotypes, which occur frequently when the term *eschatology* is applied to religious, especially Jewish, sources from the Hellenistic-Roman era. With a view to particular Christian concepts of eschatology, this application becomes all the more clear: especially in Lutheran exegesis, one finds a division into axiological and teleological eschatology that reminds one to some extent of the way in which Collins speaks of "a transcendent reality which is both temporal ... and spatial."[12]

However, eschatology, including references to its temporal and spatial dimensions, is not exclusively Christian. To give just one example: in his

---

8. Carol A. Newsom, "Spying Out the Land: A Report from Genology," in *Seeking out the Wisdom of the Ancients: Essays Offered to Honor Michael V. Fox on the Occasion of His Sixty-Fifth Birthday*, ed. Ronald L. Troxel, Kelvin G. Friebel, and Dennis Robert Magary (Winona Lake, IN: Eisenbrauns, 2005), 437–50. Newsom did not mean to criticize the *Semeia* 14 approach overall (p. 438).

9. Newsom, "Spying out the Land," 439.

10. Newsom, "Spying out the Land," 444.

11. Marvin A. Sweeney, review of *The Apocalyptic Imagination: An Introduction to Jewish Apocalyptic Literature*, John J. Collins, *RBL* (2017): https://www.sblcentral.org/home/bookDetails/11304.

12. For a division into axiological and teleological eschatology, see Paul Althaus, a German Lutheran—and anti-Semitic—theologian from Rostock and Erlangen, who explained the difference in the early editions of his book *Die letzten Dinge* that appeared in 1922. See Sigurd Hjelde, *Das Eschaton und die Eschata: Eine Studie über Sprachgebrauch und Sprachverwirrung in protestantischer Theologie von der Orthodoxie bis zur Gegenwart*, BEvT 102 (München: Kaiser Verlag, 1987), 380–90.

"Jewish Theology," Michael Fishbane refers to spatial and temporal aspects by using qualifications like "axial," "transcendent," or "infinity."[13] While Fishbane understands the axiological or axial aspect in terms of moral ethics, which is similar to how Lutheran theology articulates axiological eschatology, his intention is not to explain an *eschatological* existence but rather the life of Israel or of all humans.

2. Apocalyptic Eschatology in the Dead Sea Scrolls

The inclusion of eschatology in the definition of the literary genre apocalypse prompts additional questions when we consider the evidence of the Dead Sea Scrolls. After Frank Moore Cross described the Essenes as an apocalyptic community, a lively scholarly discussion, spanning several years, questioned whether the genre apocalypse could be found among the Dead Sea Scrolls.[14] At the same time, Cross's theory must be criticized in two ways: first and most recently, Qumran scholars are involved in an ongoing debate about the group's identity and whether the label Essenes is appropriate for characterizing even parts of the community or communities, as they are described in the sectarian scrolls.[15] Second, most scholars agree that the sectarian texts among the Dead Sea Scrolls, which are available to the public, do not preserve a literary apocalypse.[16] Even so, several motifs and literary conventions in the Dead Sea Scrolls, as they

---

13. Michael Fishbane, *Sacred Attunement: A Jewish Theology* (Chicago: University of Chicago Press, 2008), 176–205. See also Michael E. Stone, *Ancient Judaism: New Visions and Views* (Grand Rapids: Eerdmans, 2011), 77–79.

14. Frank Moore Cross, *The Ancient Library of Qumran and Modern Biblical Studies*, The Haskell Lectures 1956–1957 (London: Duckworth, 1958), 68–69: "Each of these characteristics of the sect's doctrine and practice, especially the appearance of prophecy among its members, points directly to its apocalyptic structure." See also 73–74, 77, 79, 107, 147–53, 173–84. For an updated version see Cross, *The Ancient Library of Qumran and Modern Biblical Studies*, 3rd ed. (Minneapolis: Fortress, 1995).

15. Collins, who favors the Essene-Hypothesis, also agrees with this; see his *Apocalyptic Imagination*, 179–219. For a critical reevaluation, note Nicole Rupschus, *Frauen in Qumran*, WUNT 2/457 (Tübingen: Mohr Siebeck, 2017), 213–61.

16. See above and, e.g., John J. Collins, *Apocalypticism in the Dead Sea Scrolls* (London: Routledge, 1997), 10, 150–51; and Collins, "Apocalypticism and Literary Genre in the Dead Sea Scrolls," in *The Dead Sea Scrolls after Fifty Years: A Comprehensive Assessment*, ed. Peter W. Flint and James C. VanderKam (Leiden: Brill, 1999), 2:403–30.

are used in sectarian and nonsectarian texts, attest to the existence of an apocalyptic worldview.[17]

That being said, modern scholarship has labeled some Qumran compositions as apocalypses. Most of these sources were written in Aramaic, and some of them are older than the Qumran community. Here I refer only to the Messianic Apocalypse (4Q521), the Aramaic Apocalypse or Son of God text (4Q246; see also Pseudo-Daniel: 4Q243–245), the Testament or Visions of Amram (4Q543–548), the New Jerusalem Text (1Q32; 2Q24; 4Q554–555; 5Q15; 11Q18) or 4QPseudo-Ezekiel (4Q385, 386, 388). Fragments of the book of Jubilees, 1 Enoch, and the book of Daniel also belong to this category. Most scholars agree that these sources were copied, not composed, by members of the communities; these communities are instead primarily defined with respect to sectarian texts like the Serek Ha-Yaḥad and the Cairo Damascus Document(s). Nevertheless, the fact that these apocalyptic compositions were found among the Dead Sea Scrolls supports the thesis that the worldview of this ancient Jewish sect should indeed be called apocalyptic.[18]

In sum, the Dead Sea Scrolls, including the sectarian sources, refer to an eschatological or, what is more, an apocalyptic worldview.[19] This worldview can be described more closely with a view to a passage from the Hodayot. In 1QH[a] XI, 20–23 one reads:

20 I thank you, Lord, that you have redeemed [פדה, in the "perfect" tense: פדיתה] my life [נפש] from the pit [שחת], and that from Sheol-Abaddon

---

17. Cecilia Wassén, "End Time Temples in the Dead Sea Scrolls: Expectations and Conflicts," in Crawford and Wassén, *Apocalyptic Thinking in Early Judaism*, 55–87.

18. James C. VanderKam, "Apocalyptic Tradition in the Dead Sea Scrolls and the Religion of Qumran," in *Religion in the Dead Sea Scrolls*, ed. John J. Collins and Robert A. Kugler (Grand Rapids: Eerdmans, 2000), 113–16. For an examination and listings of Aramaic apocalypses found among the Dead Sea Scrolls, see Daniel A. Machiela, "The Aramaic Dead Sea Scrolls and the Historical Development of Jewish Apocalyptic Literature," in *The Seleucid and Hasmonean Periods and the Apocalyptic Worldview: The First Enoch Seminar Nangeroni Meeting, Villa Cagnola, Gazzada (June 25–28, 2012)*, ed. Lester L. Grabbe, Gabriele Boccaccini, and Jason Zurawski, LSTS 88 (London: Bloomsbury T&T Clark, 2016), 147–56. For a discussion of most of the nonsectarian apocalyptic texts, see Stefan Beyerle, "Qumran und die Apokalyptik," in *Qumran aktuell: Texte und Themen der Schriften vom Toten Meer*, ed. Stefan Beyerle and Jörg Frey, BThS 120 (Neukirchen-Vluyn: Neukirchener Verlag, 2011), 159–223.

19. Louis F. Hartman, "Eschatology," *EJ* 6:489–500; and DiTommaso, "Apocrypha and Apocalypticism."

²¹you have lifted me up [עלה, "perfect" tense: העליתני] to an eternal height [רום עולם], so that I walk about on a limitless plain. I know that there is hope for one whom ²²you have formed from the dust for an eternal council [סוד עולם]. And a perverted spirit you have purified from great sin that it might take its place with ²³the host of the holy ones [צבא קדושים] and enter into the community [יחד] with the congregation [עדה] of the children of heaven [בני שמים].²⁰

The beginning of the hymn emphasizes the successful rescue of the praying "I." The Hebrew phrase "eternal height" (רום עולם) is also mentioned in Benedictions (1QSb V, 21–23), in which God raises the community to an "eternal height." Also, the expressions "its place with the host of the holy ones [צבא קדושים]" and the "congregation of the children of heaven" (עדת בני שמים) resonate with other sectarian passages from the Hodayot (e.g., 1QHᵃ XVIII, 35). Furthermore, the Community Rule declares that God had placed his "chosen ones" among the "lot of the holy ones" and that he had provided companionship for them with the "children of heaven" (cf. 1QS XI, 7–9).

All these references highlight that the passage from 1QHᵃ XI uses terminology that is well known from the sectarian texts of the Dead Sea Scrolls. Moreover, 1QHᵃ XI expresses an eschatology that is already reflected in the perspective of the hymnist (cf. also 1QHᵃ XIX, 13–16). Collins explains that the "hymnist uses the perfect tense for salvation that is assured, even if it is still in the future. But it is also possible that the hymnist is claiming to experience this salvation already in the present."²¹ He calls this subtype of an apocalyptic eschatology "realized eschatology," using a term from Charles Harold Dodd, albeit there referring to specific *Christian* contexts.²² Nevertheless, to some extent, the Hodayot attest to

---

20. For text and translation, see Hartmut Stegemann, with Eileen Schuller and Carol Newsom, *1QHodayotᵃ: With Incorporation of 1QHodayotᵇ and 4QHodayotᵃ⁻ᶠ*, DJD 40 (Oxford: Clarendon, 2009), 145, 155.

21. So John J. Collins, "Metaphor and Eschatology: Life beyond Death in the Hodayot," in *Is There a Text in this Cave? Studies in the Textuality of the Dead Sea Scrolls in Honour of George J. Brooke*, ed. Ariel Feldman, Charlotte Hempel, and Maria Cioată, STDJ 119 (Leiden: Brill, 2017), 416.

22. See Collins, *Apocalypticism in the Dead Sea Scrolls*, 111–28 and 148–49, and the discussion in Beyerle, "Qumran und die Apokalyptik." For the theory of a "realized eschatology" see, e.g., Charles Harold Dodd, *The Parables of the Kingdom* (London: Collins Fontana, 1961), 36–41 and 151. Heinz-Wolfgang Kuhn and Émile Puech discuss whether the Hodayot include a "realized" (Heinz-Wolfgang Kuhn, *Enderwartung und gegenwärtiges Heil: Untersuchungen zu den Gemeindeliedern von Qumran mit*

an "apocalyptic eschatology" within the genre of hymns and thanksgiving prayers. This specific eschatology understands the this-worldly life of the prayers as connected to an angelic or heavenly existence or realm.[23]

Another work, the liturgical Songs of the Sabbath Sacrifice, also refers to this type of eschatology. Devorah Dimant even goes so far as to identify the angelic life, or communion with the angels, as the core of the self-image of the Qumranites.[24] Sometimes integrated in a realized eschatology, sectarian compositions of the Dead Sea Scrolls also include a temporal or future eschatology, as seen in the War Scroll and in messianic expectations.[25] However, the realized eschatology in the sectarian compositions in particular testifies to differences regarding the sources from Qumran when they are compared with eschatological concepts from later prophetic writings in the Tanak.[26]

---

einem Anhang über Eschatologie und Gegenwart in der Verkündigung Jesu, SUNT 4 [Göttingen: Vandenhoeck & Ruprecht, 1966], 11, 20–21, 61: "Heilsperfekta") or "future eschatology" (Émile Puech, "Messianism, Resurrection, and Eschatology at Qumran and in the New Testament," in *The Community of the Renewed Covenant: The Notre Dame Symposium on the Dead Sea Scrolls*, ed. Eugene Ulrich and James C. VanderKam, Christianity and Judaism in Antiquity 10 [Notre Dame: University of Notre Dame Press, 1994], 250–51). The former makes his argument on the basis of grammatical insights into the functions of different verbal modes and tenses, while the latter draws on observations on the structure of the Hodayot. See Ken M. Penner, *The Verbal System of the Dead Sea Scrolls: Tense, Aspect, and Modality in Qumran Hebrew Texts*, SSN 64 (Leiden: Brill, 2015), 161–71.

23. For a multidimensional apocalyptic eschatology in 1 Enoch, see Loren Stuckenbruck, "Eschatology and Time in 1 Enoch," in Crawford and Wassén, *Apocalyptic Thinking in Early Judaism*, 160–80.

24. Devorah Dimant, "Men as Angels: The Self-Image of the Qumran Community," in *History, Ideology and Bible Interpretation in the Dead Sea Scrolls: Collected Studies*, FAT 90 (Tübingen: Mohr Siebeck, 2014), 465–72, especially 470–71 and 471 n. 42. But the question as to whether the composition of Songs of the Sabbath Sacrifice includes sectarian language and ideas is highly disputed.

25. Michael A. Knibb, "Eschatology and Messianism in the Dead Sea Scrolls," in *Essays on the Book of Enoch and Other Early Jewish Texts and Traditions*, SVTP 22 (Leiden: Brill, 2009), 327–48.

26. See the discussion in John J. Collins, "Eschatology," *EDSS* 1:256–61. See also Géza Xeravits, "Eschatology III. Judaism," *EBR* 7:1161: "It seems that the Qumranites thought that they were living in an exceptional period of history, presaged by the HB/OT authors, which would culminate in the visitation of God: this is an eschatology that had begun to be realized." The key difference between late prophetic and apocalyptic eschatology is that the latter refers to a transcendent world, as the angelic realm,

3. Revelation in the Dead Sea Scrolls

These two types of eschatology, spatial and temporal (or the realized and future), are initiated by an act that the *Semeia* definition calls "revelation." Collins's definition, again: "a revelation is mediated, disclosing a transcendent reality which is both temporal and spatial."[27] Recent discussion on the subject of genre points to an epistemological paradigm called prototype theory and rejects the family resemblance model as proposed by the philosopher Ludwig Wittgenstein. Although Wittgenstein did not refer to literary genres per se, literary critics frequently use his arguments to reject a definition of genre in general, because not every resemblance shared by members within a set is significant. By contrast, Newsom and Collins prefer prototype theory.[28] Collins emphasizes:

> The main difference is that prototype theory would refuse to establish a strict boundary between texts that are members of the genre and those that are not. It rather distinguishes between texts that are highly typical and those that are less typical. And this, I think, is an improvement that might have saved us some agonizing about boundary cases.[29]

Already back in the nineteenth century, the book of Revelation, and to some extent the motif of revelation as such, was taken as prototypical to identify other Second Temple apocalypses by means of comparison.[30]

---

a hope for resurrection and the like (see also Collins, *Apocalyptic Imagination*, 15; DiTommaso, "Apocalypses and Apocalypticism III," 333–34).

27. Among these apocalypses, we find Dan 7–12; most of the Enoch material, Jubilees (esp. ch. 23), 2 Baruch, 3 Baruch, 4 Ezra or Apocalypse of Zephaniah: see, most recently, Collins, *Apocalyptic Imagination*, 5–11. In her instructive essay, Rebecca Raphael, "Metacritical Thoughts on 'Transcendence' and the Definition of Apocalypse," in *Sibyls, Scriptures, and Scrolls: John Collins at Seventy*, ed. Joel Baden, Hindy Najman, and Eibert J. C. Tigchelaar, JSJSup 175 (Leiden: Brill, 2017), 2:1096–109, endorses the inductive and etic approach of *Semeia* 14 but questions the use and function of transcendence or transcendent reality.

28. See Newsom, "Spying out the Land," 443; and John J. Collins, "Introduction: The Genre Apocalypse Reconsidered," in *Apocalypse, Prophecy, and Pseudepigraphy: On Jewish Apocalyptic Literature* (Grand Rapids: Eerdmans, 2015), 9–13.

29. Collins, "Introduction: The Genre Apocalypse Reconsidered," 13. The boundary cases are also significant for the family resemblance theory.

30. For prototype theory, see also John J. Collins, "Epilogue: Genre Analysis and the Dead Sea Scrolls," *DSD* 17 (2010): 394–96; Collins, "The Genre Apocalypse Recon-

The emphasis here is squarely on the aspect of revelation. Within the scholarly debate, some established apocalypticists suggest minimizing the importance of revelation when it comes to a definition of the genre apocalypse.[31] The use of the term *revelation* as a title in superscriptions only dates back to the literature of the Common Era.[32] Also, the search for a Semitic equivalent of ἀποκάλυψις and ἀποκαλύπτω, like גלה, גלי, or גליון, is contested, although Alexander Kulik argues that apocalyptic imagery should be connected to Semitic terminology.[33] However, there is no denying an intrinsic or text-immanent and more or less constant link between apocalypses, apocalyptic texts, and the topic of revelation.[34]

Broadly speaking, revelation pertains to the mighty acts of God as they are conceptualized in epiphanies, visions, or auditions.[35] Here the use of the Hebrew and Aramaic root גלי/גלה provides orientation within the text corpus of the Dead Sea Scrolls.[36] With a view to the sectarian texts, the concept of revelation does occur in rather specific ways that do not always relate to an apocalyptic worldview. At some points, religious

---

sidered," ZAC 20 (2016): 32–33. For the most elaborate discussion of the genre apocalypse within the contexts of method and epistemology, see Collins, "Introduction: The Genre Apocalypse Reconsidered," 1–20.

31. Hartmut Stegemann, "Die Bedeutung der Qumranfunde für die Erforschung der Apokalyptik," in *Apocalypticism in the Mediterranean World and the Near East: Proceedings of the International Colloquium on Apocalypticism Uppsala, August 12–17, 1979*, ed. David Hellholm, 2nd ed. (Tübingen: Mohr Siebeck, 1989), 523–24; see also, from a methodological perspective, Raphael, "Metacritical Thoughts," 1098–108.

32. DiTommaso, "Apocalypses and Apocalypticism III," 325; and Collins, *Apocalyptic Imagination*, 3.

33. Alexander Kulik, "Genre without a Name: Was There a Hebrew Term for 'Apocalypse'?," *JSJ* 40 (2009): 540–50.

34. See e.g., the following description of apocalyptic texts by George W. E. Nickelsburg, "Apocalyptic Texts," *EDSS* 1:29: "Writings that are governed by a worldview in which the revelation of divine secrets is constitutive of salvation from an alien or threatening world are referred to as apocalyptic." See also DiTommaso, "Apocrypha and Apocalypticism."

35. See Stefan Beyerle, *Die Gottesvorstellungen in der antik-jüdischen Apokalyptik*, JSJSup 103 (Leiden: Brill, 2005); George W. E. Nickelsburg, "Revelation," *EDSS* 2:770–72.

36. For the semantic structure and range of the root גלה in Hebrew and other Semitic languages, note Frank A. Gosling, "An Open Question Relating to the Hebrew Root *glh*," *ZAH* 11 (1998): 125–32.

knowledge was revealed that belongs to the core of the sectarian belief systems in general.[37]

In many respects, the concept of revelation combines sectarian belief systems and an apocalyptic worldview. Among the sectarian texts, the Serek Ha-Yaḥad compositions represent a rigid belief system that endorses a temple-like self-image of the *yaḥad* (cf. 1QS VI, 1–6; VIII, 4–8).[38] As a congregation that strictly obeys purity rules (cf. 1QS II, 26–III, 6) and refers to a dualistic ideology (see 1QM; cf. also 1QS III, 13–IV, 26), its members fervently held to a form of interpretation of the torah guided by divine revelation. In 4QMMT, one finds the reference to the torah situated within an eschatological setting: in C 21, the final section of 4QMMT moves from halakhic instruction to a description of Belial's power that should be overcome by the addressees "at the end of days."[39] If Cecilia Wassén is correct, the halakhic impurity is only a first step within an apocalyptic scenario, which is followed by an accusation of moral defilement, also attested in the Book of Dreams (1 En. 83–90), Dan 9, and Jub. 23 (v. 21), which leads the latter community towards a total separation.[40] All of this is conceptualized with respect to a realized eschatology (see above).[41]

Another aspect of apocalyptic eschatology in the sectarian writings emerges in references to the end-time battle. In the War Scroll, the officers prepare the chosen people for the end battle (1QM X, 8–11):

⁸ [...] Who is like you, O God of Israel, in the hea[ve]ns or on earth, to act according to your great works ⁹and your mighty strength? Who is like your people Israel whom you have chosen for yourself among all

---

37. As the rule texts, such as the Serek Ha-Yaḥad and the Cairo Damascus Document, include different approaches to religious belief, the plural "belief systems" seems appropriate: see John J. Collins, *Beyond the Qumran Community: The Sectarian Movement of the Dead Sea Scrolls* (Grand Rapids: Eerdmans, 2010), 12–87.

38. Cf. Stefan Beyerle, "Kriterien jüdischer Identitäten: Am Beispiel von 'Propaganda' und 'Apokalyptik,'" in *Die Erfindung des Menschen: Person und Persönlichkeit in ihren lebensweltlichen Kontexten*, ed. Stefan Beyerle, TKH 21 (Leipzig: Evangelische Verlagsanstalt, 2016), 115–21.

39. Wassén, "End Time Temples in the Dead Sea Scrolls," 74, who concludes that the outlook of the halakhic letter in 4QMMT is apocalyptic.

40. Wassén, "End Time Temples in the Dead Sea Scrolls," 81–83.

41. See the recent overview and discussion in Daniel Stökl Ben Ezra, *Qumran: Die Texte vom Toten Meer und das antike Judentum*, JS 3 (Tübingen: Mohr Siebeck, 2016), 283–392.

the peoples of the lands [מכול עמי הארצות], [10] the holy people of the covenant [עם קדושי ברית], learned in the statute, taught in discern[ment ...], hearers of the glorious voice, seers of [11]the holy angels [רואי מלאכי קודש], open of ear [מגולי אוזן], (and) hearers of deep things?[42]

The passage combines divine power, expressed as God's incomparability, with Israel's election. The people are prepared for the battle in the eschaton, because they hear the glorious voice, with revelation in their ears and the holy angels in front of them. To a certain extent, the text in 1QM combines spatial and temporal aspects of eschatology.

One of the most prolific protagonists of the community, the Teacher of Righteousness, was pursued by the Wicked Priest, after the Spouter of the Lie had misdirected many; after that knowledge was revealed to members of the sect (Hebrew: ואחר תגלה להם הדעת; 1QpHab X, 9–XI, 2).[43] Earlier in the pesher, the Teacher of Righteousness (Hebrew: מורה הצדק) is defined as the only person "to whom God made known all the mysteries of the words of his servants the prophets" (Hebrew: הודיעו אל את כול רזי דברי עבדיו הנבאים; 1QpHab VII, 4–5). Here, in the Pesher of Habakkuk, the revealed divine word is based on the earlier prophetic revelation to the prophet Habakkuk. Consequently, the revelation to the Teacher can be seen as secondary.

Furthermore, explicit reference is made between the torah and eschatology, as the "observance of the torah" (Hebrew: עושי התורה) is connected to the events of the "last period" (Hebrew: הקץ האחרון) and the "judgment" (cf. 1QpHab VII, 10–12; VIII, 1–3).[44] As regards the end time, Alex Jassen emphasizes that the "end of days envisioned in *Pesher Habakkuk* and throughout the *Pesharim* is not some distant eschatological age. These

---

42. For text and translation, see Jean Duhaime, "War Scroll (1QM; 1Q33; 4Q491–496 = 4QM1–6; 4Q497)," in *Damascus Document, War Scroll, and Related Documents*, vol. 2 of *The Dead Sea Scrolls: Hebrew, Aramaic, and Greek Texts with English Translations*, ed. James H. Charlesworth, PTSDSSP 2 (Tübingen: Mohr Siebeck; Louisville: Westminster John Knox, 1995), 116–17.

43. For text and translation, cf. Mauyra P. Horgan, "Habakkuk Pesher," in *Pesharim, Other Commentaries, and Related Documents*, vol. 6B of *The Dead Sea Scrolls: Hebrew, Aramaic, and Greek Texts with English Translations*, ed. James H. Charlesworth, PTSDSSP 6B (Tübingen: Mohr Siebeck; Louisville: Westminster John Knox, 2002), 178–81.

44. See Nickelsburg, "Revelation," 772. For text and translation, see Horgan, "Habakkuk Pesher," 172–75.

texts bear evidence that the sectarian community envisioned the unfolding of the eschatological age in its own age."[45] The observance of torah, the imminence of judgment, and the imminent salvation conceptualize a religious amalgamation that combines "covenantal nomism" with "eschatological salvation."[46]

The latter combination is also apparent in another thanksgiving hymn, which explicitly mentions torah and salvation. In 1QH[a] XIII, the hymnist thanks God that he did not judge the speaker according to his guilt (lines 7–8). The hymnist confesses: "And you delivered my life from the pit" (line 8: ותעזור משחת חיי). Furthermore, God established the one praying for judgment and "closed the mouth of the young lions whose teeth are like a sword and whose jaw teeth are like a pointed spear" (lines 11–12). The young lions are a metaphor for the enemies of the hymnist and the community he represented. The elaborate manner in which the hymn refers to lions resembles the story of Daniel and the lion's den (Dan 6).[47] In 1QH[a] XIII, 13–15, one reads:

> [13][...] For you, O my God, have sheltered me against mortals [בני אדם], and your law you have hidden in [me] until the time [14]when your salvation is revealed to me [עֹד קץ הגלות ישעכה לי)ב(חבתה ותורתכה]. For you have not abandoned me in the distress of my soul, you have heard my cry for help in the bitterness of my soul, [15] and the outcry of my misery you have recognized in my groaning. You rescued the life of the poor one in the dwelling of the lions [ותצל נפש עני במעון אריות] that whet their tongue like a sword.[48]

The torah is hidden until divine salvation is revealed to the hymnist. The context, especially the metaphorical speech about the enemies as young lions, clearly raises the issue of judgment.[49] The speaker of the hymn appears to be a receiver of revealed knowledge that pertains to salvation. Prior to

---

45. So Alex P. Jassen, "Survival at the End of Days: Aspects of Soteriology in the Dead Sea Scrolls *Pesharim*," in *The World and the World to Come: Soteriology in Early Judaism*, ed. Daniel M. Gurtner, LSTS 74 (London: T&T Clark, 2011), 194. See also Collins, *Apocalypticism in the Dead Sea Scrolls*, 64–66.

46. See Jassen, "Survival at the End of Days," 204–8, who also refers to 4QMMT on this.

47. Cf. Angela Kim Harkins, *Reading with an 'I' to the Heavens: Looking at the Qumran Hodayot through the Lens of Visionary Traditions*, Ekstasis 3 (Berlin: de Gruyter, 2012), 148–51.

48. For text and translation, see Stegemann (with Schuller and Newsom), *1QHodayot[a]*, 167, 179.

49. Daniel A. Machiela, "גָּלָה *gālāh*," *TWQ* 1:609.

the revelation of salvation, the knowledge of torah is hidden. The hidden and secret revelation reminds one of apocalyptic hermeneutics. Moreover, the hymnist's mediation recalls the pattern of "a prophet like Moses" (cf. Deut 18:9–22) and consequently also testifies to the covenantal concept.[50]

4. Summary

Revelation is one of the core motifs for a definition of the genre apocalypse. It denotes not only the starting point in the *Semeia* definition, but also functions as a key term to describe an apocalypse. The insight that revelation is a key concept of the genre apocalypse and, at the same time, of the apocalyptic worldview, has been conceded even by those scholars whose definitions and descriptions refer rather critically to the *Semeia* definition.[51]

In general, the Dead Sea Scrolls have greatly enriched our knowledge about apocalyptic literature, although most of the new texts and compositions from that corpus, especially the sectarian ones, do not attest the genre. Even though they should not be counted as sectarian compositions, the fragments of the Son of God text or the New Jerusalem composition, in their original state, may have once been part of an apocalypse.[52] Collins agrees with Cross's theory that the Dead Sea Scrolls collect writings of an apocalyptic community that has never written an apocalypse.[53] But, Collins further emphasizes the apocalyptic perspective of both the apocalypses and many of the sectarian Dead Sea texts. Also, in some of the sectarian sources, revelation combines an apocalyptic worldview, especially if it concerns realized eschatology, with covenantal nomism. The latter points to a core element of the religious ideology of the Dead Sea sect.

---

50. Trine B. Hasselbalch, *Meaning and Context in the Thanksgiving Hymns: Linguistic and Rhetorical Perspectives on a Collection of Prayers from Qumran*, EJL 42 (Atlanta: SBL Press, 2015), 208–9.

51. E.g., Michael Wolter, "Apokalyptik als Redeform im Neuen Testament," in *Theologie und Ethos im Frühen Christentum: Studien zu Jesus, Paulus und Lukas*, WUNT 236 (Tübingen: Mohr Siebeck, 2009), 429–52.

52. Both texts were written in Aramaic, as with many other apocalypses that were preserved in the scrolls (cf. 1 Enoch, the Book of Giants, or probably the Visions of Amram or the Four Kingdoms text), but represent copies, not authentic scriptures of the group or groups.

53. See also Collins, *Apocalypticism in the Dead Sea Scrolls*, 10–11.

Bibliography

Beyerle, Stefan. *Die Gottesvorstellungen in der antik-jüdischen Apokalyptik.* JSJSup 103. Leiden: Brill, 2005.

———. "Kriterien jüdischer Identitäten: Am Beispiel von 'Propaganda' und 'Apokalyptik.'" Pages 97–134 in *Die Erfindung des Menschen: Person und Persönlichkeit in ihren lebensweltlichen Kontexten.* Edited by Stefan Beyerle. TKH 21. Leipzig: Evangelische Verlagsanstalt, 2016.

———. "Qumran und die Apokalyptik." Pages 159–223 in *Qumran aktuell: Texte und Themen der Schriften vom Toten Meer.* Edited by Stefan Beyerle and Jörg Frey. BThS 120. Neukirchen-Vluyn: Neukirchener Verlag, 2011.

Collins, John J. *The Apocalyptic Imagination: An Introduction to Jewish Apocalyptic Literature.* 3rd ed. Grand Rapids: Eerdmans, 2016.

———. "Apocalypticism and Literary Genre in the Dead Sea Scrolls." Pages 403–30 in vol. 2 of *The Dead Sea Scrolls after Fifty Years: A Comprehensive Assessment.* Edited by Peter W. Flint and James C. VanderKam. 2 vols. Leiden: Brill, 1999.

———. *Apocalypticism in the Dead Sea Scrolls.* London: Routledge, 1997.

———. *Beyond the Qumran Community: The Sectarian Movement of the Dead Sea Scrolls.* Grand Rapids: Eerdmans, 2010.

———. "Epilogue: Genre Analysis and the Dead Sea Scrolls." *DSD* 17 (2010): 389–401.

———. "Eschatology." *EDSS* 1:256–61.

———. "The Genre Apocalypse Reconsidered." *ZAC* 20 (2016): 21–40.

———. "Introduction: The Genre Apocalypse Reconsidered." Pages 1–20 in *Apocalypse, Prophecy, and Pseudepigraphy: On Jewish Apocalyptic Literature.* Edited by John J. Collins. Grand Rapids: Eerdmans, 2015.

———. "Introduction: Towards the Morphology of a Genre." *Semeia* 14 (1979): 1–19.

———. "Metaphor and Eschatology: Life beyond Death in the Hodayot." Pages 407–22 in *Is There a Text in This Cave? Studies in the Textuality of the Dead Sea Scrolls in Honour of George J. Brooke.* Edited by Ariel Feldman, Charlotte Hempel, and Maria Cioată. STDJ 119. Leiden: Brill, 2017.

Cross, Frank Moore. *The Ancient Library of Qumran and Modern Biblical Studies.* The Haskell Lectures 1956–1957. London: Duckworth, 1958.

———. *The Ancient Library of Qumran and Modern Biblical Studies.* 3rd ed. Minneapolis: Fortress, 1995.

Dimant, Devorah. "Men as Angels: The Self-Image of the Qumran Community." Pages 465–72 in *History, Ideology and Bible Interpretation in the Dead Sea Scrolls: Collected Studies*. FAT 90. Tübingen: Mohr Siebeck, 2014.

DiTommaso, Lorenzo. "Apocalypses and Apocalypticism III. Judaism." *EBR* 2:325–37.

———. "The Apocrypha and Apocalypticism." Pages 219–52 in *The Oxford Handbook of the Apocrypha*. Edited by Gerbern S. Oegema. New York: Oxford University Press, 2021.

Dodd, Charles Harold. *The Parables of the Kingdom*. London: Collins Fontana, 1961.

Duhaime, Jean. "War Scroll (1QM; 1Q33; 4Q491–496 = 4QM1–6; 4Q497)." Pages 80–203 in *Damascus Document, War Scroll, and Related Documents*. Vol. 2 of *The Dead Sea Scrolls: Hebrew, Aramaic, and Greek Texts with English Translations*. Edited by James H. Charlesworth. PTSDSSP 2. Tübingen: Mohr Siebeck; Louisville: Westminster John Knox Press, 1995.

Fishbane, Michael. *Sacred Attunement: A Jewish Theology*. Chicago: University of Chicago Press, 2008.

Goff, Matthew. "The Apocalypse and the Sage: Assessing the Contribution of John J. Collins to the Study of Apocalypticism." Pages 8–22 in *Apocalyptic Thinking in Early Judaism: Engaging with John Collins' The Apocalyptic Imagination*. Edited by Sidnie White Crawford and Cecilia Wassén. JSJSup 182. Leiden: Brill, 2018.

Gosling, Frank A. "An Open Question Relating to the Hebrew Root *glh*." *ZAH* 11 (1998): 125–32.

Harkins, Angela Kim. *Reading with an "I" to the Heavens: Looking at the Qumran Hodayot through the Lens of Visionary Traditions*. Ekstasis 3. Berlin: de Gruyter, 2012.

Hartman, Louis F. "Eschatology." *EJud* 6:489–500.

Hasselbalch, Trine B. *Meaning and Context in the Thanksgiving Hymns: Linguistic and Rhetorical Perspectives on a Collection of Prayers from Qumran*. EJL 42. Atlanta: SBL Press, 2015.

Hjelde, Sigurd. *Das Eschaton und die Eschata: Eine Studie über Sprachgebrauch und Sprachverwirrung in protestantischer Theologie von der Orthodoxie bis zur Gegenwart*. BEvT 102. München: Kaiser Verlag, 1987.

Horgan, Maurya P. "Habakkuk Pesher." Pages 157–85 in *Pesharim, Other Commentaries, and Related Documents*. Vol. 6B of *The Dead Sea*

Scrolls: Hebrew, Aramaic, and Greek Texts with English Translations. Edited by James H. Charlesworth. PTSDSSP 6B. Tübingen: Mohr Siebeck; Louisville: Westminster John Knox, 2002.

Jassen, Alex P. "Survival at the End of Days: Aspects of Soteriology in the Dead Sea Scrolls *Pesharim*." Pages 193–210 in *The World and the World to Come: Soteriology in Early Judaism*. Edited by Daniel M. Gurtner. LSTS 74. London: T&T Clark, 2011.

Knibb, Michael A. "Eschatology and Messianism in the Dead Sea Scrolls." Pages 327–48 in *Essays on the Book of Enoch and Other Early Jewish Texts and Traditions*. SVTP 22. Leiden: Brill, 2009.

Kuhn, Heinz-Wolfgang. *Enderwartung und gegenwärtiges Heil: Untersuchungen zu den Gemeindeliedern von Qumran mit einem Anhang über Eschatologie und Gegenwart in der Verkündigung Jesu*. SUNT 4. Göttingen: Vandenhoeck & Ruprecht, 1966.

Kulik, Alexander. "Genre without a Name: Was There a Hebrew Term for 'Apocalypse'?" *JSJ* 40 (2009): 540–50.

Machiela, Daniel A. "גָּלָה *gālāh*." *TWQ* 1:605–12.

———. "The Aramaic Dead Sea Scrolls and the Historical Development of Jewish Apocalyptic Literature." Pages 147–56 in *The Seleucid and Hasmonean Periods and the Apocalyptic Worldview: The First Enoch Seminar Nangeroni Meeting, Villa Cagnola, Gazzada (June 25-28, 2012)*. Edited by Lester L. Grabbe, Gabriele Boccaccini, and Jason Zurawski. LSTS 88. London: Bloomsbury T&T Clark, 2016.

Markschies, Christoph. "Editorial/Einleitung." *ZAC* 20 (2016): 1–20.

Murphy, Frederick James. *Apocalypticism in the Bible and Its World: A Comprehensive Introduction*. Grand Rapids: Baker Academic, 2012.

Newsom, Carol A. "Spying out the Land: A Report from Genology." Pages 437–50 in *Seeking out the Wisdom of the Ancients: Essays Offered to Honor Michael V. Fox on the Occasion of His Sixty-Fifth Birthday*. Edited by Ronald L. Troxel, Kelvin G. Friebel, and Dennis Robert Magary. Winona Lake, IN: Eisenbrauns, 2005.

Nickelsburg, George W. E. "Apocalyptic Texts." *EDSS* 1:29–35.

———. "Revelation." *EDSS* 2:770–72.

Penner, Ken M. *The Verbal System of the Dead Sea Scrolls: Tense, Aspect, and Modality in Qumran Hebrew Texts*. SSN 64. Leiden: Brill, 2015.

Puech, Émile. "Messianism, Resurrection, and Eschatology at Qumran and in the New Testament." Pages 235–56 in *The Community of the Renewed Covenant: The Notre Dame Symposium on the Dead Sea Scrolls*. Edited by Eugene Ulrich and James C. VanderKam. Christianity and Judaism in Antiquity 10. Notre Dame: University of Notre Dame Press, 1994.

Raphael, Rebecca. "Metacritical Thoughts on 'Transcendence' and the Definition of Apocalypse." Pages 1096–109 in vol. 2 of *Sibyls, Scriptures, and Scrolls: John Collins at Seventy*. Edited by Joel S. Baden, Hindy Najman, and Eibert J. C. Tigchelaar. JSJSup 175. Leiden: Brill, 2017.

Reynolds III, Bennie H. "A Dwelling Place of Demons: Demonology and Apocalypticism in the Dead Sea Scrolls." Pages 23–54 in *Apocalyptic Thinking in Early Judaism: Engaging with John Collins' The Apocalyptic Imagination*. Edited by Sidnie White Crawford and Cecilia Wassén. JSJSup 182. Leiden: Brill, 2018.

Rupschus, Nicole. *Frauen in Qumran*. WUNT 2/457. Tübingen: Mohr Siebeck, 2017.

Stegemann, Hartmut. "Die Bedeutung der Qumranfunde für die Erforschung der Apokalyptik." Pages 495–530 in *Apocalypticism in the Mediterranean World and the Near East: Proceedings of the International Colloquium on Apocalypticism Uppsala, August 12–17, 1979*. Edited by David Hellholm. 2nd ed. Tübingen: Mohr Siebeck, 1989.

Stegemann, Hartmut, with Eileen Schuller and Carol Newsom. *1QHodayot^a: With Incorporation of 1QHodayot^b and 4QHodayot^{a-f}*. DJD 40. Oxford: Clarendon, 2009.

Stökl Ben Ezra, Daniel. *Qumran: Die Texte vom Toten Meer und das antike Judentum*. JS 3. Tübingen: Mohr Siebeck, 2016.

Stone, Michael E. *Ancient Judaism: New Visions and Views*. Grand Rapids: Eerdmans, 2011.

Stuckenbruck, Loren T. "Eschatology and Time in 1 Enoch." Pages 160–80 in *Apocalyptic Thinking in Early Judaism: Engaging with John Collins' The Apocalyptic Imagination*. Edited by Sidnie White Crawford and Cecilia Wassén. JSJSup 182. Boston: Brill, 2018.

Sweeney, Marvin A. Review of *The Apocalyptic Imagination: An Introduction to Jewish Apocalyptic Literature*, by John J. Collins. *RBL* (2017): https://www.sblcentral.org/home/bookDetails/11304.

VanderKam, James C. "Apocalyptic Tradition in the Dead Sea Scrolls and the Religion of Qumran." Pages 113–34 in *Religion in the Dead Sea Scrolls*. Edited by John J. Collins and Robert A. Kugler. Grand Rapids: Eerdmans, 2000.

Wassén, Cecilia. "End Time Temples in the Dead Sea Scrolls: Expectations and Conflicts." Pages 55–87 in *Apocalyptic Thinking in Early Judaism: Engaging with John Collins' The Apocalyptic Imagination*. Edited by

Sidnie White Crawford and Cecilia Wassén. JSJSup 182. Leiden: Brill, 2018.

Wolter, Michael. "Apokalyptik als Redeform im Neuen Testament." Pages 429–52 in *Theologie und Ethos im Frühen Christentum: Studien zu Jesus, Paulus und Lukas*. WUNT 236. Tübingen: Mohr Siebeck, 2009.

Xeravits, Géza. "Eschatology III. Judaism." *EBR* 7:1160–64.

Qumran and the Apocalyptic

Devorah Dimant

Jewish apocalyptic and the Qumran library have preoccupied the research on the Dead Sea Scrolls from its inception. Frank Moore Cross, who wrote one of the first and most influential surveys of the Qumran findings, viewed the authors of the Scrolls as "an apocalyptic community" and labeled them "priestly apocalypticists."[1] But his characterization is marked by its early date and displays the terminological fuzziness that is typical of previous as well as recent treatments of the subject. In part, this has been due to the debate on the meaning of the terms *apocalyptic* and *apocalypticism*. Some scholars restrict the adjective apocalyptic to literary apocalypses alone.[2] Others judge that Qumran sectarian texts share ideas with apocalypses and that a distinction should be made between the literary genre apocalypse and the core ideas that they share with texts that are not apocalypses.[3] The latter view, still held by many scholars, indeed accounts

---

A version of this paper was delivered at the 2017 International Meeting of the Society of Biblical Literature in Berlin, in a session organized by the editors of this volume.

1. See Frank M. Cross, *The Ancient Library of Qumran and Modern Biblical Studies*, rev. ed. (Garden City, NY: Anchor Books, 1961), 78. In the third edition of the book, published some thirty years later, Cross still held the view that the community was "profoundly rooted in older Judaism, specifically in the priestly laws of purity coupled with a thoroughgoing apocalypticism" (*The Ancient Library of Qumran*, 3rd ed. [Minneapolis: Fortress, 1995], 68).

2. See Jean Carmignac, "Qu'est-ce que l'apocalyptique? Son emploi à Qumrân," *RevQ* 10 (1979): 7–15; and Hartmut Stegemann, "Die Bedeutung der Qumranfunde für die Erforschung der Apokalyptik," in *Apocalypticism in the Mediterranean World and the Near East: Proceedings of the International Colloquium on Apocalypticism Uppsala, August 12-17, 1979*, ed. David Hellholm, 2nd ed. (Tübingen: Mohr Siebeck, 1989), 495–530.

3. See John J. Collins, "Genre, Ideology, and Social Movements in Jewish Apocalyp-

for the undeniable affinity between central notions that are characteristic of apocalypses and specific ideas expressed by the Qumran texts. However, while plausible, this view rests on vague generalities and all-inclusive definitions that obscure the particularities.

These faults are particularly conspicuous in the influential typological definition of the literary genre apocalypse proposed by John Collins and a group of collaborators.[4] Based on a wide range of individual Jewish, Christian, Greco-Roman, and Persian apocalypses, Collins's definition blurs the specifics of particular historical-thematic contexts, a fault that becomes apparent especially when applied to early Jewish apocalypses attested at Qumran. For instance, his definition includes both revelations mediated by otherworldly beings and what are labeled "otherworldly travels" as features characteristic of the apocalypse genre. However, most of the early apocalypses found among the Dead Sea Scrolls can be categorized as historical surveys and lack such otherworldly travels.

The discussions of apocalypses and apocalyptic notions at Qumran have been further hampered by other misconceptions. For instance, they have often treated the Qumran collection en bloc, without regarding its multifaceted character. The nonbiblical texts from Qumran consist of three distinct groups, each relating to apocalypse and the apocalyptic in a different manner: sectarian works, Aramaic compositions, and nonsectar-

---

ticism," in *Mysteries and Revelations: Apocalyptic Studies since the Uppsala Colloquium*, ed. John J. Collins and James H. Charlesworth, JSPSup 9 (Sheffield: Sheffield Academic, 1991), 11. Earlier, James Barr wrote in a similar vein: "It seems to me reasonable to use the word apocalypse for the literary genre ... but (for) many aspects of the content and ideas (that) may be found also in books that in form are not apocalypses ... we can conveniently use the term apocalyptic." See his "Jewish Apocalyptic in Recent Scholarly Study," *BJRL* 58 (1975–1976): 15–16.

4. Cf. John J. Collins, "Introduction: Towards the Morphology of a Genre," *Semeia* 14 (1979): 1–20. The definition and its adjacent typological paradigm are used by Collins in other surveys. See Collins, *The Apocalyptic Imagination: An Introduction to the Jewish Matrix of Christianity*, 3rd ed. (Grand Rapids: Eerdmans, 2016), 4–5; and Collins, *Apocalypticism in the Dead Sea Scrolls* (London: Routledge, 1997), 3. In his response to the lecture version of this article (above), Matthew Goff noted that Collins limited his proposed definition to the literary features of the apocalypses (cf. Collins, "Introduction," 4–5). While this is true, it does not dismiss or validate the weaknesses and the distortions created by such an encompassing literary definition. The following analysis is intended to serve as a necessary corrective to this already established definition, given the influence it has exercised and its frequent use in scholarly discussions.

ian parabiblical writings.[5] In a recent analysis of this complex of ideas in the Qumran scrolls, I proposed amending these deficiencies by replacing the traditional linear development of apocalyptic and apocalypses with thematic clusters appearing in specific historical circumstances.[6] Let me summarize the arguments introduced therein in order to advance the discussion on these topics.

If one defines the genre apocalypse as a revelation of hidden things, temporal or spatial, the Dead Sea Scrolls yield only the following works that may be labeled properly as apocalypses: the Dream Visions of 1 En. 83–90; the so-called Apocalypse of Weeks embedded in the Epistle of Enoch of 1 En. 93.1–10; 91.12–17; and the vision reported in Dan 7. The most salient feature of these apocalypses is their preoccupation with the meaning and progress of history. Themes that are usually considered apocalyptic, such as eschatology and interest in the final events of the course of history, are, in fact, aspects of this fundamental notion of history, whether stated explicitly or just implied.[7] The cohesion of this group is apparent in its shared major characteristics. All three describe history as a sequence of periods, the Enochic examples being computed in heptadic chronology, namely, a calculation in terms of seven years and jubilees. This implies the view that the historical sequence is final, and its total length can be calculated with the aid of the jubilees system. In all of the above-listed apocalypses, the information regarding history is divulged to a seer through visions or dream-visions, explained to him by angels or via other supernatural means.

All these specimens are written in Aramaic and are attested among the Qumran documents, dated to the second century BCE or even somewhat earlier. Sharing such important characteristics, these texts may be assigned to a single cluster of themes. To this cluster may be added the

---

5. For the tripartite division of the Qumran texts, see the classification of Devorah Dimant, "The Qumran Manuscripts: Contents and Significance," in *History, Ideology and Bible Interpretation in the Dead Sea Scrolls: Collected Studies*, FAT 90 (Tübingen: Mohr Siebeck, 2014), 27–56.

6. For details of these arguments, see Devorah Dimant, "Apocalyptic and the Qumran Library," in *From Enoch to Tobit: Collected Studies in Ancient Jewish Literature*, FAT 114 (Tübingen: Mohr Siebeck, 2017), 31–54.

7. On history and apocalyptic, see Lorenzo DiTommaso, "Time and History in Ancient Jewish and Christian Apocalyptic Writings," in *Dreams, Visions, Imaginations: Jewish, Christian and Gnostic Views of the World to Come*, ed. Jens Schröter, Tobias Nicklas, and Armand Puig i Tàrrech, BZNW 247 (Berlin: de Gruyter, 2021), 53–87.

following Aramaic texts that contain historical reviews, although their fragmentary state does not permit a more precise categorization: Four Kingdoms (4Q552, 4Q553, 4Q552a), the Apocryphon of Daniel (4Q246), and Pseudo-Daniel (4Q243, 4Q244, 4Q245). The Aramaic language of the exemplars of this cluster suggests a specific background, perhaps Iranian, related to an interest in history.

Hebrew exemplars of historical apocalypses were also found at Qumran, namely, Jub. 1 and 23, Dan 8–12, and the Qumranic Apocryphon of Jeremiah C. They originated somewhat later than the Aramaic exemplars. Although dated to around 100 CE, 4 Ezra and 2 Baruch may also be attached to this cluster, for they contain historical visions and display numerous contacts with the Qumran writings.

Incorporating two historical apocalypses, the anthology of 1 Enoch has been central in all discussion related to apocalypses, as it is in the present analysis. However, the practice of including 1 Enoch in its entirety in the lists of apocalypses is misleading. Not all the Enochic works included in the collocation of writings that is 1 Enoch may be defined as apocalypses. Thus, no part of the Book of Watchers of 1 En. 1–36 or the Astronomical Book of 1 En. 72–82 contains an apocalypse, going by the understanding of the genre adopted here, namely, that it is a genre primarily occupied with surveys of history. Instead, the two booklets report on the cosmic travels of Enoch in the company of the angels. Collins includes such travels in his definition of the genre. Yet historical apocalypses and cosmic travels display significant differences, which indicate that they belong to different genres and have different origins. Although historical apocalypses contain symbolic representations of history, which are experienced in dream-visions, Enoch embarks on his cosmic travels while awake and observes concrete physical sites. Though mysterious and remote, lying beyond the reach of ordinary humans, the locations visited during these travels are situated within the earthly realm. Moreover, the early literature associates such cosmic tours only with Enoch, probably due to the Babylonian background of this ancient sage. No other seer who features in early apocalypses has similar experiences. Notably, none of the Enochic historical apocalypses, namely, the Animal Apocalypse and the Apocalypse of Weeks, contain cosmic tours. The reverse is also true. Works depicting Enoch's cosmic travels do not include apocalypses. These particular traits designate the Enochic cosmic tours as a distinct cluster of themes belonging to a genre different from that of the early historical apocalypses.

Surveys of apocalypses also consider the throne vision of Enoch, reported in the Book of Watchers (1 En. 14–16), to be a characteristic feature of apocalypses. Collins takes it to be part of the otherworldly journeys.[8] However, Enoch's throne vision differs from both cosmic journeys and historical apocalypses in important respects. First, it occurs in a dream (1 En. 14.1–2) and not in a state of wakefulness as do the cosmic travels. Second, in this dream, Enoch ascends upwards beyond the realm of the earthly world and crosses the vaulted heaven (1 En. 14.8) into the heavenly temple, situated beyond the skies. It is thus clearly different from Enoch's cosmic travels, which were conducted within the earthly sphere and in the company of angels. The differences between heaven and earth and wakefulness and sleep reflect the different levels of reality and consciousness in which each experience took place. So, the two accounts depict different types of journeys that are experienced in different ways and belong to separate genres. In addition, Enoch's throne vision is not part of an apocalypse, and therefore it must be differentiated from the historical apocalypses.

That Enoch's throne vision differs from his cosmic travels is also suggested by its distinct literary provenance. Unlike the cosmic travels, which are attributed solely to Enoch, his throne vision has two counterparts: the throne vision in Dan 7:9–10 and a throne vision recorded in the Book of Giants (4Q530 2 II). In Dan 7, the seer experiences the vision in a dream, which he later records in writing. In the Book of Giants, the giant Ohaya has a dream in which he witnesses a throne scene similar to that depicted in Dan 7 (4Q530 2 II, 16–20). The dream-visions of Enoch, Daniel, and Ohaya share not only the same topic but also specific details.[9] All recount judgment scenes and display striking linguistic agreements in descriptions of the throne. Most importantly, all three are composed in Aramaic. Though these visions diverge in some details, their common theme and major similarities suggest that they drew on the same tradition, but each adapted it to its own individual context and purpose. A fourth throne vision is, perhaps, to be included in this cluster, namely, that depicted in the Aramaic Levi Document, as suggested by 4Q213a 2

---

8. Collins, "Introduction," 15.
9. For details, see Ryan E. Stokes, "The Throne Visions of Daniel 7, *1 Enoch* 14, and the Qumran *Book of Giants* (4Q530)," *DSD* 15 (2008): 340–58; and Jonathan R. Trotter, "The Tradition of the Throne Vision in the Second Temple Period: Daniel 7:9–10, *1 Enoch* 14:18–23, and the *Book of Giants* (4Q530)," *RevQ* 25 (2012): 451–66.

14–18. However, the fragmentary state of this evidence does not permit a fuller evaluation.

It is thus evident that the Qumran documents evince three distinct clusters of themes that differ in content, literary form, and probably provenance: historical apocalypses, cosmic travels, and throne visions. The dominance of Aramaic in these three clusters merits further consideration, but it is reserved for another occasion. Here, I will only note that this feature points to a distinct origin that differs from the Hebrew sectarian and nonsectarian texts found at Qumran.

Indeed, none of the historical apocalypses, cosmic travels, or throne visions contains sectarian terminology or style, or any of the organizational patterns specific to the Qumran *yaḥad*. Therefore, they do not belong to the Hebrew literature authored by this community. This observation tallies with the fact that all the available texts with explicit sectarian features are composed in Hebrew, suggesting that the Qumranites did not create texts in Aramaic.

However, Hebrew apocalypses were also found among the Scrolls. Chapters 1 and 23 of Jubilees, a work written originally in Hebrew, may be defined as apocalypses; various Hebrew pieces that are too fragmentary for any meaningful consideration seem to produce passages from forecasts, visions, and historical reviews. While their details and general framework are obscure, they show the vigor and productivity of this kind of literary form even in Hebrew.

Of particular interest are two Hebrew writings related to biblical prophets, Pseudo-Ezekiel and Apocryphon of Jeremiah C, which have survived in relatively substantial fragments. As noted above, Apocryphon of Jeremiah C may be defined as a historical apocalypse. It contains a historical survey revealed to Jeremiah (4Q385a 18 I, 2), includes a sequence of historical periods based on the heptadic principle (e.g., 4Q387 2 II, 3–4; 4Q390 1 7), and expresses eschatological hopes (4Q387 3 9). It is, therefore, the first example of a historical apocalypse attributed to a biblical prophet.

Interestingly, the case of Pseudo-Ezekiel is significantly different. Advancing notions that feature in other apocalypses (e.g., resurrection and the hastening of time in order to speed the final recompense), Pseudo-Ezekiel nevertheless lacks historical sequence in periods, at least in the extant fragments, but it offers a most intriguing instance of the rewriting of passages from a biblical prophet. It has yet to be studied as an example of the evolution from prophecy to its later apocalyptic interpretation.

While written in Hebrew, these works do not display the distinctive style and terminology characteristic of the sectarian texts, so they too may not be assigned to its literature.

These Hebrew texts and the three Aramaic clusters outlined above were read and perhaps copied in part by the owners of the Qumran library. Thus, members of the *yaḥad* were the custodians of the various apocalypses and related texts but were not their authors.

The defining of the distinct character of the three thematic clusters in question sheds fresh light on the apocalyptic stratum embedded in some of the Qumran documents. Within the Qumran collection as a whole, cosmic tours and throne visions stand apart. They have no counterparts in Hebrew sectarian or nonsectarian compositions. Though described in the Hebrew Songs of the Sabbath Sacrifice, the celestial temple and the throne are nevertheless inaccessible to humans and may be invoked only in prayer. For this reason, throne visions and cosmic tours remained outside the sectarian orbit, belonging as they did to the primordial and biblical spheres.

The case of the early historical apocalypses is strikingly different. Without composing apocalypses themselves, the Qumranites nevertheless adopted the major apocalyptic concept of history consisting of a string of periods. In the sectarian literature, this notion is not presented in vision form but is indicated by a specific set of terms. The chief term that conveys this concept is the plural of the word קץ ("period"), that is, קצים ("periods"). The singular means "end, completion," but the contemporaneous Dan 9:26 and 12:6 already use the singular in the sense of "period, time span." The plural form found in the Scrolls clearly indicates that the meaning of "end" is not intended but rather "temporal units." The condensed character of the term and its frequent use in a variety of sectarian contexts suggest that it is a known concept. The Pesher of the Periods explains in detail the nature of the historical periods: "Pesher concerning the periods made by God, [each] period in order to complete [all that is] and all that will be. Before he created them he set up [their] activi[ties to the exact meaning of their periods] one period after another" (4Q180 1 1-4).[10] The term *periods* marks cosmic time (1QM X, 15), as well as the chronology of human history (1QS X, 1, 5; 1QH[a]

---

10. On the pesher, see Devorah Dimant, "The *Pesher on the Periods* (4Q180) and 4Q181," in *History, Ideology and Bible Interpretation*, 385–404; and Chanan Ariel, Alexey (Eliyahu) Yuditsky, and Elisha Qimron, "The Pesher on the Period

XX, 11). In the sectarian view, the sequence of periods is predetermined by the divine blueprint for the created world, an idea also intimated by the expressions קיצי אל ("periods of God"; 1QpHab VII, 13), and קצי נצח (1QHª IX, 26), קצי עולם (1QHª V, 26), and קצי עד (1QM X, 15), all three meaning "eternal periods." Other terms reflect the dualistic aspects of the temporal flow. Beside "periods of peace" (קצי שלום; 1QHª XXI, 16) stands the contrastive "periods of wrath" (קצי חרון; 4Q266 11 19; 4Q270 7 II, 13; 1QHª XXII, 9; 4Q166 I, 12 [Pesher of Hosea]), marking the alternation between punishment and peace in human history. The phrases קץ הרשע (CD VI, 10, 14; XV, 7; 4Q269 8 II, 5; 4Q271 2 12) and קץ הרשעה (CD XII, 23; 1QpHab V, 7-8), both meaning "the period of wickedness," indicate the rule of wickedness prevalent in the Qumran community's own times.[11] Another term that serves as a vehicle for expressing the idea of the periods in history is עת, "time, age." In cases where it is used in the plural (עתים), it obviously refers to this notion (4Q217 2 1; 4Q228 1 I, 2; CD XVI, 3).[12]

That the sectarians were also familiar with the heptadic system of calculating periods is imparted by scattered references in the sectarian works. Such allusions fit into their broader concern, namely, their interest in time and time measurement. Such an interest is evident in their preoccupation with the calendar and chronologies of years and jubilees, evinced by numerous calendrical texts. Notably, the members of the *yaḥad* did not produce depictions that trace the entire string of the historical periods, as do the historical apocalypses. For such information, they probably turned to the apocalypses they stored so carefully in their library. But they clearly built on the materials provided by these apocalypses, embracing their basic notion of historical periods. In fact, the rigorous regularity of calendrical time as well as of periodical history espoused by the *yaḥad* constitutes an expression of the preordained divine laws imprinted on the universe (see, e.g., 1QS IX, 26–X, 8; 1QH XX, 8-14).[13] The idea of the sequence of

---

A-B (4Q180-181): Editing, Language and Interpretation" [Hebrew], *Meghillot* 11-12 (2015): 3-39.

11. See Devorah Dimant, "The Vocabulary of the Qumran Sectarian Texts," in *History, Ideology and Bible Interpretation*, 84-85.

12. See Devorah Dimant, "What Is the 'Book of the Divisions of the Times'?," in *History, Ideology and Bible Interpretation*, 369-83.

13. See Devorah Dimant, "Election and Laws of History in the Apocalyptic Literature," in *From Enoch to Tobit*, 19-30.

historical periods formed part of their general concept of measured time, governed by strict predetermined laws.

While the view of history as a sequence of periods, espoused by the literature of the Qumran community, may have drawn from or at least been influenced by the historical apocalypses, its additional aspects were probably taken from other sources. Central in this respect is the idea that the temporal sequence of periods is "measured and weighed," a concept not found in the early historical apocalypses but elaborated in later ones, especially in 4 Ezra (see, e.g., 4 Ezra 4.37-38).[14] The idea that creation came into being "in measure and weight" is adopted already by later biblical books (Isa 40:12-13; Job 28:25), but in the thinking of the *yaḥad* it was developed further and applied to the sequence of periods.[15]

Thus the sectarian sapiential work Instruction states that the world was created by measure and weight: "[for] with a measure of truth and a weight of justice has God established all" (4Q418 126 II, 3; similarly 4Q418 127 5-6). The implications of this view are spelled out in the practical instructions laid down for the Maśkil, the person versed in the learning and teaching of the community who instructs his fellow-members in these matters. In this context, the Community Rule concludes its exposition as follows:

> These are the laws for the Maśkil by which he shall conduct himself toward every living being, according to the measure[16] of every age [עת]

---

14. See the discussion in Devorah Dimant, "*4 Ezra* and *2 Baruch* in Light of the Qumran Literature," in *From Enoch to Tobit*, 280-81.

15. See the collection of sources on weight and measure in Second Temple literature assembled and discussed by Menahem Kister, "Physical and Metaphysical Measurements Ordained by God in the Literature of the Second Temple Period," in *Reworking the Bible: Apocryphal and Related Texts at Qumran*, ed. Esther G. Chazon, Devorah Dimant, and Ruth Clements, STDJ 58 (Leiden: Brill, 2005), 153-76. In the present context, I discuss these themes only in connection with the sectarian notions of the course of time.

16. The expression "according to the measure" translates here the original Hebrew לתכון. On the meaning of the verb תכן and derived nouns in the Qumran literature, see Menachem Kister, "Commentary to 4Q298," *JQR* (1994): 241; and Eibert J. C. Tigchelaar, *To Increase Learning for the Understanding Ones: Reading and Reconstructing the Fragmentary Early Jewish Sapiential Text 4QInstruction*, STDJ 44 (Leiden: Brill, 2001), 242-44. Nili Shupak detects in these notions the influence of Egyptian ideas on the weighing of a person's heart and deeds after death. See her "Weighing in the Scales: How an Egyptian Concept Made Its Way into Biblical and Postbiblical Literature," in *From Author to Copyist: Essays on the Composition, Redaction, and Transmission of the*

and the weight of every man; to do the will of God according to everything which has been revealed from age to age, and measure all the understanding which has been found according to the ages, and the law of the age. (1QS IX, 12–14)[17]

This statement affirms that every age reveals a particular understanding and specific laws. The same dynamic perception of time is evoked by the Damascus Document: "These are the laws for the Maśkil to conduct himself towards every living being according to the regulation of every age" (CD XII, 20–21). In consequence, each period involves different rules of behavior and entails a different understanding. This dynamic perception of time permitted the *yaḥad* to apply it to their exegetical activity of interpreting the Torah or the Prophets.[18] According to their view, an unraveling of the inner meaning of each period, especially their own, depended on an understanding of the inner logic and sense of the entire temporal sequence. Certain sectarian texts, such as the calendrical text 4Q320, even evince the notion that time "exists independently of natural phenomena,"[19] a level of abstraction not attained by the apocalypses themselves. The preoccupation of the *yaḥad* with time in its daily and year-chronology manifestations accounts for the Qumranites' need to keep the precise calculation of time in their calendar, yearly festivals, and temporal chronology of jubilees.[20]

Embracing the notion of historical periods, the Qumranites also adopted a wide range of ideas that went with it, such as predestination,

---

Hebrew Bible in Honor of Zipi Talshir, ed. Cana Werman (Winona Lake, IN: Eisenbrauns, 2015), 249–58.

17. The translation, with some alterations of my own, is that of Elisha Qimron and James H. Charlesworth, "Rule of the Community," in *Rule of the Community and Related Documents*, ed. James H. Charlesworth et al., PTSDDSP 1 (Tübingen: Mohr Siebeck; Louisville: Westminster John Knox, 1994), 41. See also the comments of Menahem Kister, "Wisdom Literature at Qumran" [Hebrew], in *The Qumran Scrolls and Their World*, ed. Menahem Kister (Jerusalem: Yad Ben-Zvi, 2009), 1.299–319 at 306–7.

18. See my analysis in "Time, Torah and Prophecy at Qumran," and "Exegesis and Time in the Pesharim from Qumran," in *History, Ideology and Bible Interpretation*, 301–14 and 315–32. See also the observations of Jonathan Ben-Dov, "Apocalyptic Temporality: The Force of Here and Now," *HBAI* 5 (2016): 296.

19. Thus Ben-Dov, "Apocalyptic Temporality," 292.

20. On this theme, see the detailed comments of Carol A. Newsom, *The Self as Symbolic Space: Constructing Identity and Community at Qumran*, STDJ 52 (Leiden: Brill, 2004), 117–81.

the prominence of evil during the closing stages of history, and the final judgment. But they developed this cluster of ideas in their own way to serve their own purposes. Thus, a special emphasis was placed on historical events of their own times, taking the dualistic principle to the extreme. Even though, at a certain point, the Animal Apocalypse introduces demonic angels who play a part in some of the events (1 En. 89.59–90.25),[21] no all-embracing battle between good and evil of the type evinced by the sectarian literature is expressed there. As for the Book of Watchers, it usually speaks of the Watchers and their giant offspring as primordial sinners (1 En. 6–11; 19.1) as do other Enochic writings (86.6; 106.13–15), rather than as representatives of the evil powers. The tradition developed in 1 En. 12–16 regarding the spirits of the dead giants becoming demons that pester humans on earth (15.9–16.1) is the exception. For most of the Enochic literature, the story of the Watchers is one of sin and punishment rather than an explanation of the origins of evil as so often claimed. It is therefore worthwhile reflecting on the real origin and background of the far-reaching dualism espoused by the Qumran sectarian texts. The early apocalypses, which furnish only a pale reflection of it, cannot be the source of the sectarian dualism.

Espousing such a constant battle between good and evil, the notion of historical periods, deployed through a logical, well-organized, finite sequence, provided the sectaries with an overall theoretic framework for this idea. It permitted them to attribute purpose, order, and divine origin to unfolding historical events, and their finality allowed hope for the approaching end and its positive conclusion. So, within this ideological framework, the meaning invested in the historical process through the idea of a specific string of periods gave purpose and meaning to what took place around and within them.

In summary, the worldview of the Qumran *yaḥad* advanced the apocalyptic teaching about the sequence of history in significant respects, some of which have been taken up and elaborated by later apocalypses such as 4 Ezra and 2 Baruch.

The foregoing survey provides the necessary background for understanding why apocalypses were collected and studied by the members of the *yaḥad*. Evidently, they were a source of inspiration and an object of

---

21. Cf. Devorah Dimant, "Ideology and History in the *Animal Apocalypse* (*1 Enoch* 85–90)," in *From Enoch to Tobit: Collected Studies*, 107–13.

meditation for the community. Thus, a careful sorting out and defining of the distinct literary strands present within the Qumran library offers a clearer perception of their individual characters as well as their position and purpose within the Qumran collection as a whole.

Bibliography

Ariel, Chanan, Alexey (Eliyahu) Yuditsky, and Elisha Qimron. "The Pesher on the Period A–B (4Q180–181): Editing, Language and Interpretation" [Hebrew]. *Meghillot* 11–12 (2015): 3–39.

Barr, James. "Jewish Apocalyptic in Recent Scholarly Study." *BJRL* 58 (1975–1976): 9–35.

Ben-Dov, Jonathan. "Apocalyptic Temporality: The Force of Here and Now." *HBAI* 5 (2016): 289–303.

Carmignac, Jean. "Qu'est-ce que l'apocalyptique? Son emploi à Qumrân." *RevQ* 10 (1979): 3–33.

Collins, John J. *The Apocalyptic Imagination: An Introduction to the Jewish Matrix of Christianity*. 3rd ed. Grand Rapids: Eerdmans, 2016.

———. "Genre, Ideology, and Social Movements in Jewish Apocalypticism." Pages 11–32 in *Mysteries and Revelations: Apocalyptic Studies since the Uppsala Colloquium*. Edited by John J. Collins and James H. Charlesworth. JSPSup 9. Sheffield: Sheffield Academic, 1991.

———. "Introduction: Towards the Morphology of a Genre." *Semeia* 14 (1979): 1–20.

Cross, Frank Moore. *The Ancient Library of Qumran and Modern Biblical Studies*. Rev. ed. Garden City, NY: Anchor Books, 1961. 3rd ed. Minneapolis: Fortress, 1995.

Dimant, Devorah. "*4 Ezra* and *2 Baruch* in Light of the Qumran Literature." Pages 269–94 in *From Enoch to Tobit: Collected Studies in Ancient Jewish Literature*. FAT 114. Tübingen: Mohr Siebeck, 2017.

———. "Apocalyptic and the Qumran Library." Pages 31–54 in *From Enoch to Tobit: Collected Studies in Ancient Jewish Literature*. FAT 114. Tübingen: Mohr Siebeck, 2017.

———. "Election and Laws of History in the Apocalyptic Literature." Pages 19–30 in *From Enoch to Tobit: Collected Studies in Ancient Jewish Literature*. FAT 114. Tübingen: Mohr Siebeck, 2017.

———. "Exegesis and Time in the Pesharim from Qumran." Pages 315–32 in *From Enoch to Tobit: Collected Studies in Ancient Jewish Literature*. FAT 114. Tübingen: Mohr Siebeck, 2017.

———. "Ideology and History in the *Animal Apocalypse* (*1 Enoch* 85–90)." Pages 91–118 in *From Enoch to Tobit: Collected Studies in Ancient Jewish Literature*. FAT 114. Tübingen: Mohr Siebeck, 2017.

———. "The *Pesher on the Periods* (4Q180) and 4Q181." Pages 385–404 in *History, Ideology and Bible Interpretation in the Dead Sea Scrolls: Collected Studies*. FAT 90. Tübingen: Mohr Siebeck, 2014.

———. "The Qumran Manuscripts: Contents and Significance." Pages 27–56 in *History, Ideology and Bible Interpretation in the Dead Sea Scrolls: Collected Studies*. FAT 90. Tübingen: Mohr Siebeck, 2014.

———. "Time, Torah and Prophecy at Qumran." Pages 301–14 in *History, Ideology and Bible Interpretation in the Dead Sea Scrolls: Collected Studies*. FAT 90. Tübingen: Mohr Siebeck, 2014.

———. "The Vocabulary of the Qumran Sectarian Texts." Pages 57–100 in *History, Ideology and Bible Interpretation in the Dead Sea Scrolls: Collected Studies*. FAT 90. Tübingen: Mohr Siebeck, 2014.

———. "What Is the 'Book of the Divisions of the Times'?" Pages 369–83 in *History, Ideology and Bible Interpretation in the Dead Sea Scrolls: Collected Studies*. FAT 90. Tübingen: Mohr Siebeck, 2014.

DiTommaso, Lorenzo. "Time and History in Ancient Jewish and Christian Apocalyptic Writings." Pages 53–87 in *Dreams, Visions, Imaginations: Jewish, Christian and Gnostic Views of the World to Come*. Edited by Jens Schröter, Tobias Nicklas, and Armand Puig i Tàrrech. BZNW 247. Berlin: de Gruyter, 2021.

Kister, Menachem. "Commentary to 4Q298." *JQR* (1994): 237–49.

———. "Physical and Metaphysical Measurements Ordained by God in the Literature of the Second Temple Period." Pages 153–76 in *Reworking the Bible: Apocryphal and Related Texts at Qumran*. Edited by Esther G. Chazon, Devorah Dimant, and Ruth Clements. STDJ 58. Leiden: Brill, 2005.

———. "Wisdom Literature at Qumran" [Hebrew]. Pages 299–319 in *The Qumran Scrolls and Their World*. Edited by Menahem Kister. 2 vols. Jerusalem: Yad Ben-Zvi, 2009.

Newsom, Carol A. *The Self as Symbolic Space: Constructing Identity and Community at Qumran*. STDJ 52. Leiden: Brill, 2004.

Qimron, Elisha, and James H. Charlesworth. "Rule of the Community." Pages 1–51 in *Rule of the Community and Related Documents*. Edited by James H. Charlesworth et al. PTSDSSP 1. Tübingen: Mohr Siebeck; Louisville: Westminster John Knox, 1994.

Shupak, Nili. "Weighing in the Scales: How an Egyptian Concept Made Its Way into Biblical and Postbiblical Literature." Pages 249–58 in *From Author to Copyist: Essays on the Composition, Redaction, and Transmission of the Hebrew Bible in Honor of Zipi Talshir*. Edited by Cana Werman. Winona Lake, IN: Eisenbrauns, 2015.

Stegemann, Hartmut. "Die Bedeutung der Qumranfunde für die Erforschung der Apokalyptik." Pages 495–530 in *Apocalypticism in the Mediterranean World and the Near East: Proceedings of the International Colloquium on Apocalypticism Uppsala, August 12–17, 1979*. Edited by David Hellholm. 2nd ed. Tübingen: Mohr Siebeck, 1989.

Stokes, Ryan E. "The Throne Visions of Daniel 7, 1 Enoch 14, and the Qumran *Book of Giants* (4Q530)." *DSD* 15 (2008): 340–58.

Tigchelaar, Eibert J. C. *To Increase Learning for the Understanding Ones: Reading and Reconstructing the Fragmentary Early Jewish Sapiential Text 4QInstruction*. STDJ 44. Leiden: Brill, 2001.

Trotter, Jonathan R. "The Tradition of the Throne Vision in the Second Temple Period: Daniel 7:9–10, 1 Enoch 14:18–23, and the *Book of Giants* (4Q530)." *RevQ* 25 (2012): 451–66.

Apocalypse and Authoritative Literatures in Second Temple Judaism

Armin Lange

The definition of what is an apocalypse (below, §1.1) is as much a matter of extensive debate in scholarly literature as is the distinction between different forms of apocalypses. Together with Ulrike Mittmann-Richert, I compiled a list classifying the ancient Jewish literature attested by the Dead Sea Scrolls according to genre.[1] In that list, I distinguished between symbolic and nonsymbolic apocalypses—an idea that was later on developed by my student, Bennie H. Reynolds III.[2] I was asked by the editors of this volume to elaborate further on my ideas about the genre of apocalypse as expressed in the index volume to the series Discoveries in the Judaean Desert (DJD). Instead of repeating the more detailed arguments of Reynolds, I would like to use this opportunity to focus on a different aspect of the genre apocalypse, which I have also highlighted in the list of DJD 39, namely, its relation to authoritative literature. The "Annotated List" that Mittmann-Richert and I have compiled argues that almost all apocalypses belong to a category of texts that are described in the DJD series as parabiblical and that I would prefer to call "paratextual" instead (below, §1.2): "Most apocalypses are parabiblical in character and thus exhibit the basic exegetical orientation of apocalyptic writing."[3]

---

1. Armin Lange and Ulrike Mittmann-Richert, "Annotated List of the Texts from the Judaean Desert Classified by Content and Genre," in *The Texts from the Judaean Desert: Indices and an Introduction to the Discoveries in the Judaean Desert Series*, ed. Emanuel Tov, DJD 39 (Oxford: Oxford University Press, 2002), 115–64.

2. Bennie H. Reynolds III, *Between Symbolism and Realism: The Use of Symbolic and Non-symbolic Language in Ancient Jewish Apocalypses 333–63 B.C.E.*, JAJSup 8 (Göttingen: Vandenhoeck & Ruprecht, 2011).

3. Lange and Mittmann-Richert, "Annotated List," 121.

For this purpose, I will discuss apocalypses and other ancient Jewish texts that were authored until the destruction of the Herodian temple in the year 70 CE, that is, in the latter half of the Second Temple period. After briefly discussing terminological issues, I will compare the ancient Jewish apocalypses with ancient Jewish testaments, on the one hand, and with the prophetic books of the Hebrew Bible and ancient Jewish sapiential literature, on the other hand. Afterwards, I will ask about the motivation of apocalyptic paratextuality and draw some conclusions.

1. Terminology

1.1. The Genre of Apocalypse

The definition of the genre of apocalypse was the subject of a long and extensive scholarly discourse that, before the discovery of the Dead Sea Scrolls, was mainly guided by the biblical books of Daniel and Revelation. The genre was first described by Friedrich Lücke in 1832.[4] More than 150 years later, a scholarly consensus was reached that is marked by the definition of John J. Collins, who describes an apocalypse as

> a genre of revelatory literature with a narrative framework, in which a revelation is mediated by an otherworldly being to a human recipient, disclosing a transcendent reality which is both temporal, insofar as it envisages eschatological salvation, and spatial insofar as it involves another, supernatural world.[5]

Collins's definition provides also the basis for the present brief study.

1.2. Paratextuality

Literature in the second degree, that is, texts that are written based on earlier (authoritative) compositions, are widespread in the ancient, medieval, and modern worlds.[6] In ancient Judaism, such literature was composed mainly

---

4. Friedrich Lücke, *Einleitung in die Offenbarung Johannis*, vol. 4.1 of *Commentar über die Schriften des Evangelisten Johannes* (Bonn: Eduard Weber, 1832), esp. 23–26.
5. John J. Collins, "Introduction: Towards the Morphology of a Genre," *Semeia* 14 (1979): 9.
6. For the phrase literature "in the second degree" to describe transtextual relationships, see Gérard Genette, *Palimpsests: Literature in the Second Degree*, trans.

based on texts that at the end of the Second Temple period became part of the Jewish Bible. Other ancient cultures composed similar literary works based on the writings of Homer or other highly regarded books. Traditionally, in the context of ancient Jewish literature, such works are described as pseudepigraphic, rewritten Bible, parabiblical, or parascriptural.[7] Exceptions notwithstanding, literature in the second degree neither wanted to wrongly claim authorship by one of the famous literati of the past nor in many cases intended to simply retell an authoritative narrative, making the terms pseudepigraphic and rewriting problematic. Because literature in the second degree occurred in Judaism long before the biblical canon was closed and because literature in the second degree was not restricted to Judaism but was widespread in the ancient cultures, the terms parabiblical and parascriptural seem also to be problematic as a characterization of this type of literature. In his famous book *Palimpsests: Literature in the Second Degree*, Gérard Genette uses the term *hypertextual* instead.[8] To allow for an association with the ancient Jewish metagenre formerly identified as parabiblical or parascriptural, I have suggested that ancient Jewish literature that is in the second degree be described instead as *paratextual*. As a definition of paratextual literature I have proposed the following:

> On the basis of authoritative texts or themes, the authors of paratextual literature employ exegetical techniques to provide answers to questions of their own time, phrased, for example, as answers by God through Moses or the prophets. The result of their exegetical efforts is communicated in the form of a new literary work.[9]

Channa Newman and Claude Doubinsky, Stages 8 (Lincoln: University of Nebraska Press, 1997).

7. For a discussion of the scholarly discourse regarding literature in the second degree and a more detailed argumentation of my own positions, see Armin Lange, "In the Second Degree: Ancient Jewish Paratextual Literature in the Context of Graeco-Roman and Ancient Near Eastern Literature," in *In the Second Degree: Paratextual Literature in Ancient Near Eastern and Ancient Mediterranean Cultures and Its Reflections in Medieval Literature*, ed. Philip S. Alexander, Armin Lange, and Renate Pillinger (Leiden: Brill, 2010), 3–40. The definition of paratext given above differs from that of Gérard Genette. See his *Paratexts: Thresholds of Interpretation*, trans. Jane E. Lewin (Cambridge: Cambridge University Press, 1997). Note also Molly M. Zahn, *Genres of Rewriting in Second Temple Judaism: Scribal Composition and Transmission* (Cambridge: Cambridge University Press, 2020).

8. Genette, *Palimpsests*, 5.

9. Lange, "In the Second Degree."

2. Paratextual Visions:
The Apocalypses of Second Temple Jewish Literature

One of the most interesting aspects of ancient Jewish apocalypses surfaced when the publication of the Dead Sea Scrolls was finalized in the first decade of the new millennium. The Dead Sea Scrolls have added a significant amount of previously unknown texts to the list of ancient Jewish apocalypses. The picture that emerges shows that most if not all apocalypses from the Second Temple period affiliate themselves with literary figures from the authoritative literature of Judaism from that period, such as Enoch, Jeremiah, Ezekiel, Daniel, and Zephaniah. Only two apocalypses from Second Temple Judaism are not clearly affiliated with an authoritative figure: 4QHistorical Text A (4Q248) and Words of Michael (4QWords of Michael ar [4Q529], 6QpapUnclassified frags. ar [6Q23]). Both compositions were found in the caves close to the Qumran. However, the textual damages of these Qumran manuscripts are so extensive that an affiliation with an authoritative Jewish literary figure cannot be ruled out for either. The evidence summarized in the lists below leaves no doubt that ancient Jewish apocalypses were predominantly, if not exclusively, paratextual in nature.[10]

2.1. Ancient Jewish Apocalypses Affiliated with Literary Figures from Jewish Authoritative Literature

Enoch (Gen 5:21–24)
- Astronomical Book of Enoch (1 En. 72–82; 4QEnastr^{a-d} ar [4Q208–211])
- Book of the Watchers (1 En. 1–36; 4QEn^{a-b} ar [4Q201–202]; 4QEn^c ar [4Q204] 1 I–XIII; 4QEn^d ar [4Q205] 1 XI–XII; 4QEn^e ar [4Q206] 1 XX–XXII, XXVI–XXVIII)
- Book of Dreams (1 En. 83–91; 4QEn^c ar [4Q204] 4; 4QEn^d ar [4Q205] 2 I–III; 4QEn^e ar [4Q206] 4 I–III; 4QEn^f ar [4Q207] 4; 4QEn^g ar [4Q212] 1 I, 1–II, 21);
- Similitudes of Enoch (1 En. 37–71)

---

10. Why I regard these texts from Qumran as apocalypses is argued in more detail in Lange and Mittmann-Richert, "Annotated List." The same is true for how I group the manuscripts listed below. Apocalypses that are part of works of another literary genre like Jub. 23.8–31 remain unrecognized in the below list, as it is uncertain if they ever existed on their own.

- Apocalypse of Weeks (1 En. 91.12–17; 93.1–10)

Jeremiah
- Apocryphon of Jeremiah (4QapocrJer A [4Q383]; 4Qpap apocrJer B? [4Q384]; 4QapocrJer C^{a-f} [4Q385a, 387, 388a, 389–390, 387a])

Ezekiel
- New Jerusalem (1QNJ ar [1Q32]; 2QNJ ar [2Q24]; 4QNJ^{a-b} ar [4Q554–555]; 5QNJ ar [5Q15]; 11QNJ ar [11Q18])

Daniel (Ezek 14:14, 20; 28:3)
- book of Daniel
- 4QpsDan^{a-b} ar (4Q243–244)
- 4QpsDan^c ar (4Q245)
- 4QapocrDan ar (4Q246)
- 4QFour Kingdoms^{a-b} ar (4Q552–553)

Zephaniah
- Apocalypse of Zephaniah

2.2. Ancient Jewish Apocalypses for which an Affiliation with Literary Figures from Jewish Authoritative Literature Remains Uncertain

- 4QHistorical Text A (4Q248)
- 4QWords of Michael ar (4Q529)
- 6QpapUnclassified frags. ar (Words of Michael? [6Q23])

3. Paratextual Inheritance: The Testaments of Second Temple Jewish Literature

It has to be asked whether this paratextual affiliation with literary figures from authoritative literature is a unique characteristic of ancient Jewish apocalypses or if it was more widespread in Jewish literature of the second half of the Second Temple period. To answer this question, I will compare the evidence of ancient Jewish apocalypses with ancient Jewish testaments from the same period.

As with all other genres of ancient Jewish literature, the discourse about the formal characteristics of testaments is extensive.[11] As space constraints prohibit a detailed discussion of this discourse, my below deliberations of ancient Jewish testaments are guided by Collins's description:[12]

> The most fundamental defining characteristic of a testament is that it is a discourse delivered in anticipation of imminent death. Typically the speaker is a father addressing his sons, or a leader addressing his people, or his successor. The testament begins by describing in the third person the situation in which the discourse is delivered, and ends with an account of the speaker's death. The actual discourse, however, is delivered in the first person.... In short, the form of a testament is constituted by the narrative framework; the contents cannot be said to follow a fixed pattern.

Testaments are ideally suited for a comparison with Jewish apocalypses from the Second Temple period, as they have many similarities with apocalypses but belong nevertheless to a distinct literary genre. Like apocalypses, testaments often have an interest in eschatology. Like apocalypses, they are clearly paratextual in nature because they are all attributed to literary figures from authoritative Jewish literature. Like apocalypses, in Judaism, testaments are known only from the Hellenistic period onwards. Finally, just like apocalypses, testaments were poorly attested in Second Temple Jewish literature before the publication of the Dead Sea Scrolls.

The list below leaves no doubt that all testaments extant from the Second Temple period are paratextual in nature:[13]

- Abraham: Testament of Abraham
- Jacob: 4QTJacob? ar (4Q537)

---

11. For a more extensive discussion of the testaments in the Qumran library, see Jörg Frey, "On the Origins of the Genre of the 'Literary Testament': Farewell Discourses in the Qumran Library and Their Relevance for the History of the Genre," in *Aramaica Qumranica: Proceedings of the Conference on the Aramaic Texts from Qumran in Aix-en-Provence 30 June–2 July 2008*, ed. Katell Berthelot and Daniel Stökl Ben Ezra, STDJ 94 (Leiden: Brill, 2010), 345–72.

12. John J. Collins, "Testaments," in *Jewish Writings of the Second Temple Period: Apocrypha, Pseudepigrapha, Qumran Sectarian Writings, Philo, Josephus*, ed. Michael E. Stone, CRINT 2.2 (Assen: Van Gorcum; Minneapolis: Fortress, 1984), 325.

13. My reasons for regarding these texts from Qumran as testaments are argued in more detail in Lange and Mittmann-Richert, "Annotated List." The same is true for how I group the manuscripts listed below.

- Levi: 4QapocrLevi^{a-b}? ar (4Q540–541)
- Judah: 3QTJud? (3Q7) and 4QpapTJud? (4Q484)
- Benjamin: 4QTJud ar (4Q538)
- Amram: 4QVisions of Amram$^{a-g?}$ ar (4Q543–549)
- Testaments of the Twelve Patriarchs[14]
- Moses: Testament of Moses
- Job: Testament of Job

That not only apocalypses but also testaments and other Jewish genres are composed based on earlier authoritative literary works leaves little doubt that the apocalypses of Second Temple Judaism participate in an overall reorientation of ancient Jewish literature.[15]

4. The Prophets in Pre- and Postexilic Jewish Literature

The distinctive nature of the change in the literary creativity of ancient Judaism in early Hellenistic times is illustrated by a comparison of the apocalypses of the second half of the Second Temple period with the prophetic books that were composed and reworked between the eighth and fourth centuries BCE.

With the exception of the book of Jonah, all of these prophetic books were attributed to prophets who were not previously mentioned in Jewish/Israelite literature, that is, Amos, Deutero-Isaiah, Ezekiel, Habakkuk, Haggai, Hosea, Isaiah, Jeremiah, Joel, Malachi, Micah, Nahum, Obadiah, Zechariah, and Zephaniah. Until the end of Persian and the beginning of Hellenistic times, these prophetic books were reworked in the shape of various redactions—Deuteronomistic and otherwise—and variant literary editions. But no new books were composed about any of these prophets, except for the relevant texts mentioned above.

The only exception to this rule is the book of Jonah. Dating from the fourth or third century BCE,[16] the book of Jonah is quite comparable to

---

14. For the debate about the Jewish origin and Christian reworking of the Testaments of the Twelve Patriarchs, see Robert A. Kugler, *The Testaments of the Twelve Patriarchs*, GAP 10 (Sheffield: Sheffield Academic, 2001).

15. For a survey of the paratextual literature among the Dead Sea Scrolls, see Lange and Mittmann-Richert, "Annotated List."

16. For a fourth or third century BCE date of Jonah, see Erich Zenger et al., *Einleitung in das Alte Testament*, 5th ed. (Stuttgart: Kohlhammer, 2004), 551.

paratextual literature like the Astronomical Book of Enoch (1 En. 72–82) or the Book of Watchers (1 En. 1–36). The book of Jonah elaborates on the brief remark about the prophet Jonah ben Amitai in 2 Kgs 14:25.

> He [Jeroboam II] restored the border of Israel from Lebo-hamath to the Seas of the Arabah, according to the word of YHWH, god of Israel, which he had spoken through his servant Jonah ben Amitai, the prophet from Gath-Hepher.

By way of using additional authoritative reference texts,[17] the author of the book of Jonah spins a story about how Jonah was sent to Nineveh to prophesy the city's downfall, how Jonah opposed God's decree to go Nineveh, and how God forgave the repenting city. The book of Jonah is thus the only prophetic book in the Hebrew Bible that was composed in a paratextual way.[18] Given its late date, it marks the shift toward the preference for paratextual literature in Judaism in the late Persian or early Hellenistic period. That prophetic literature participated in the general move toward paratextuality in ancient Jewish literature is confirmed by later texts like the Apocryphon of Ezekiel or the Lives of the Prophets.

My comparison of apocalypses with both ancient Jewish testaments and the prophetic literature of Iron Age and Persian time Judaism could leave the impression that the paratextual nature of most if not all ancient Jewish apocalypses is due to a general reorientation of Jewish literary creativity toward paratextuality. If this were true, the paratextual nature of Jewish apocalypses should not be regarded as a formal characteristic of the genre apocalypse but as a general tendency in the literature of Hellenistic Judaism. Before drawing such a conclusion, it needs to be asked though if all genres of ancient Jewish literature participated in that reorientation and if there are indicators in the text of ancient Jewish apocalypses what motivated their paratextuality.

---

17. Jonah 3:9 // Joel 2:14; Jonah 4:2 // Joel 2:13; cf. also Jonah 2:2–10 // Pss 18:7; 22:26; 30:4; 31:7, 23; 40:3; 42:8; 69:2–3; 116:17–18; and 130:1.

18. For more details, see Armin Lange, "The Pre-Maccabean Literature from the Qumran Library and the Hebrew Bible," *DSD* 13 (2006): 296–300.

5. The Lack of Paratextuality in Jewish Wisdom Literature of the Second Temple Period

As apocalypses unite in their content both prophetic and sapiential ideas,[19] the sapiential literature of the second half of the Second Temple period provides further comparanda for apocalypses, illuminating apocalyptic paratextuality further.

With regard to the paratextuality of wisdom literature in the second half of the Second Temple period, a different picture emerges. Only three compositions of this sapiential corpus can be described as paratextual. Two of them are attributed to Solomon, thus resembling apocalypses and testaments in their pseudonymous attribution. One Jewish wisdom text from that period is attributed, though to the Greek gnomic philosopher Phocylides. This represents a cultural fusion of the authoritative literature of ancient Judaism with Hellenism by way of a paratextual attribution to a Greek philosopher.

Solomon
- Qoheleth
- Wisdom of Solomon

Phocylides
- Sentences of Pseudo-Phocylides

Compared to these three paratextual wisdom texts, a total of eighteen sapiential compositions are either not paratextual in nature or are too fragmentary to determine a paratextual relation toward earlier authoritative literature:

---

19. For the complicated relationship between ancient Jewish wisdom literature and apocalypses, see, e.g., James C. VanderKam, "The Prophetic-Sapiential Origins of Apocalyptic Thought," in *A Word in Season: Essays in Honor of William McKane*, ed. James D. Martin and Philip R. Davies, JSOTSup 42 (Sheffield: Sheffield Academic, 1986), 163–76; and the contributions to Benjamin G. Wright and Lawrence M. Wills, ed., *Conflicted Boundaries in Wisdom and Apocalypticism*, SymS 35 (Atlanta: Society of Biblical Literature, 2005).

Sapiential Instructions
- Instruction (Musar l[e]-Mevîn; 1QInstruction [1Q26]; 4QInstruction[a-e] [4Q415–418, 418a]; 4QInstruction[f]? [4Q418c]; 4QInstruction[g] [4Q423])
- Book of Mysteries (1QMyst [1Q27]; 4QMyst[a-b] [4Q299–300]; 4QMyst[c]? [4Q301])
- Ben Sira (2QSir [2Q18]; MasSir [Mas1h])
- 4QSapiential-Didactic Work A (4Q412)
- 4QSapiential-Hymnic Work A (4Q426)
- 4QBeatitudes (4Q525)

Collections of Proverbs
- 4QInstruction-like Composition B (4Q424)

Didactic Speeches
- Treatise of the Two Spirits (1QS III, 13–IV, 26 par 4QpapS[c] [4Q257] v–vi)
- 4QSapiential Work (4Q185)
- 4QcryptA Words of the Maskil to All Sons of Dawn (4Q298)

Sapiential Poetic Text
- 4QSapiential Hymn (4Q411)

Sapiential Texts Too Fragmentary for Classification
- 4QWiles of the Wicked Woman (4Q184)
- 4QpapAdmonitory Parable (4Q302)
- 4QMeditation on Creation A (4Q303)
- 4QMeditation on Creation C (4Q305)
- 4QComposition Concerning Divine Providence (4Q413)
- 4QSapiential-Didactic Work B (4Q425)
- 4QThe Two Ways (4Q473)

The wisdom texts of Hellenistic and Roman times demonstrate thus that, despite a reorientation toward paratextuality in Jewish literary creativity, a whole genre of literature could remain more or less unaffected. Despite the widespread paratextuality in Jewish literature of the second half of the Second Temple period, the paratextual orientation of the literary genre of apocalypse should thus be regarded as one of its formal characteristics.

6. Why Do Jewish Apocalypses Attribute Their Visions to Heroes of the Past?

The texts of Jewish apocalypses from the late Second Temple period indicate what motivated their paratextuality. One aspect of apocalyptic paratextuality is clearly the authorization of apocalyptic visions by way of attribution to heroes of Israel's past. Apocalyptic authors chose not only famous prophets such as Jeremiah or Ezekiel but also relatively unknown literary figures such as Enoch (Gen 5:21-24) or Daniel (Ezek 14:14, 20; 28:3), to whom no prophetic books were dedicated. That such marginal figures occurred only in brief passages of Israel's authoritative literature could imply that the paratextuality of Jewish apocalypses was only interested in their authorization. This idea seems to be confirmed by apocalyptic visions such as Dan 7-8, which do not include a single allusion to or quotation of Jewish authoritative literature.

Other passages of Second Temple Jewish apocalypses are characterized though by extensive intertextuality with and interpretation of Jewish authoritative literature.[20] Two examples need to suffice as cases in point. The description of the heavenly temple and Enoch's encounter with God in the Book of Watchers (1 En. 14.10-15.1) employs the books of Exodus, Isaiah, and Ezekiel to describe, on the one hand, the heavenly sanctuary and, on the other hand, how God interacted with Enoch as a human being inside this sanctuary.

1 En. 14.18 (4QEn^c ar [4Q204])	Isa 6:1
1 En. 14.18-20 (4QEn^c ar [4Q204])	Ezek 1:26-28
1 En. 14.18 (4QEn^c ar [4Q204])	Ezek 1:16
1 En. 14.19 (4QEn^c ar [4Q204])	Exod 33:20
1 En. 14.21	Exod 33:20
1 En. 14.24-15.1	Ezek 1:28-2:2

---

20. The lists of quotations and allusions in these tables are drawn from Armin Lange and Matthias Weigold, *Biblical Quotations and Allusions in Second Temple Jewish Literature*, JSJSup 5 (Göttingen: Vandenhoeck & Ruprecht, 2011).

In Dan 9, the interpretation of the "seventy years" of desolation from Jer 25:11–12 as "seventy weeks of years" is developed by reference to a whole range of texts from Jewish authoritative literature.

Dan 9:2	Jer 25:11–12
Dan 9:4	Neh 1:5
Dan 9:4	Deut 10:17
Dan 9:5	1 Kgs 8:47 // 2 Chr 6:37
Dan 9:6	Neh 9:32
Dan 9:7	Ezra 9:7
Dan 9:7	Jer 16:15
Dan 9:7	Jer 23:3
Dan 9:7	Jer 23:8
Dan 9:7	Jer 32(39):37
Dan 9:8	Neh 9:34
Dan 9:10	Deut 28:15
Dan 9:11	Lev 26:14–39
Dan 9:11	Deut 28:15–69
Dan 9:14	Neh 9:33
Dan 9:15	Jer 32(39):20–21
Dan 9:18	2 Kgs 19:16 par. Isa 37:17

These two examples show that the apocalyptic authors had an exegetical interest. Their visions were not always but at least sometimes developed out of earlier authoritative Jewish literature. Given this exegetical interest, the paratextuality of ancient Jewish apocalypses goes beyond merely the desire on the part of their authors to authorize their visions through pseudonymous attribution. It should be seen as an expression of the appreciation in which various apocalyptic milieus held Jewish authoritative literature.

7. Conclusions

My deliberations about the paratextual nature of Second Temple Jewish apocalypses have two important implications for the description of the genre apocalypse as well as for the canonical history of the Jewish Bible.

Importance for the genre apocalypse: apocalypses and testaments document two new genres of Jewish literature that evolved after the conquests of Alexander the Great. Both genres should thus be seen as literary responses to the increased pressure of Hellenization that occurred after Alexander's conquests. With its paratextuality, the genre of apocalypse seems thus to participate in a general reorientation in Jewish literary creativity responding to Hellenism. As apocalypses are heavily dependent on authoritative Jewish literature not only for the authorization of their visions but also to develop their understanding of the otherworld and of Jewish history, their paratextual nature should become part of the definition of this genre in scholarship.

Importance for canonical history of the Jewish Bible: beginning with the third century BCE, apocalypses document a significant impact of authoritative literature on Jewish literary creativity. While not yet forming an exclusive canon of holy books, authoritative literature had developed such a significance that even whole literary genres like apocalypses and testaments could to a huge extent be phrased in dependence of authoritative texts, that is, in a paratextual way. My observations regarding the paratextual nature of Second Temple apocalypses emphasize thus the increasingly dominant role that Jewish authoritative literature developed in response to the impact of Hellenism. To support Jewish heritage against the impact of Hellenistic culture, authoritative literature became so dominant that it became increasingly difficult if not impossible to express visions about the otherworld or the history of Israel disconnected from it.

Bibliography

Collins, John J. "Introduction: Towards the Morphology of a Genre." *Semeia* 14 (1979): 1–20.

———. "Testaments." Pages 325–55 in *Jewish Writings of the Second Temple Period: Apocrypha, Pseudepigrapha, Qumran Sectarian Writings, Philo, Josephus*. Edited by Michael E. Stone. CRINT 2.2. Assen: Van Gorcum; Minneapolis: Fortress, 1984.

Frey, Jörg. "On the Origins of the Genre of the 'Literary Testament': Farewell Discourses in the Qumran Library and Their Relevance for the History of the Genre." Pages 345–72 in *Aramaica Qumranica: Proceedings of the Conference on the Aramaic Texts from Qumran in Aix-en-Provence 30 June–2 July 2008*. Edited by Katell Berthelot and Daniel Stökl Ben Ezra. STDJ 94. Leiden: Brill, 2010.

Genette, Gérard. *Palimpsests: Literature in the Second Degree*. Translated by Channa Newman and Claude Doubinsky. Stages 8. Lincoln: University of Nebraska Press, 1997.

———. *Paratexts: Thresholds of Interpretation*. Translated by Jane E. Lewin. Cambridge: Cambridge University Press, 1997.

Kugler, Robert A. *The Testaments of the Twelve Patriarchs*. GAP 10. Sheffield: Sheffield Academic, 2001.

Lange, Armin. "In the Second Degree: Ancient Jewish Paratextual Literature in the Context of Graeco-Roman and Ancient Near Eastern Literature." Pages 3–40 in *In the Second Degree: Paratextual Literature in Ancient Near Eastern and Ancient Mediterranean Cultures and Its Reflections in Medieval Literature*. Edited by Philip S. Alexander, Armin Lange, and Renate Pillinger. Leiden: Brill, 2010.

———. "The Pre-Maccabean Literature from the Qumran Library and the Hebrew Bible." *DSD* 13 (2006): 276–305.

Lange, Armin, and Ulrike Mittmann-Richert. "Annotated List of the Texts from the Judaean Desert Classified by Content and Genre." Pages 115–64 in *The Texts from the Judaean Desert: Indices and an Introduction to the Discoveries in the Judaean Desert Series*. Edited by Emanuel Tov. DJD 39. Oxford: Oxford University Press, 2002.

Lange, Armin, and Matthias Weigold. *Biblical Quotations and Allusions in Second Temple Jewish Literature*. JSJSup 5. Göttingen: Vandenhoeck & Ruprecht, 2011.

Lücke, Friedrich. *Einleitung in die Offenbarung Johannis*. Vol. 4.1. of *Commentar über die Schriften des Evangelisten Johannes*. Bonn: Eduard Weber, 1832.

Reynolds, Bennie H., III. *Between Symbolism and Realism: The Use of Symbolic and Non-symbolic Language in Ancient Jewish Apocalypses 333–63 B.C.E.* JAJSup 8. Göttingen: Vandenhoeck & Ruprecht, 2011.

VanderKam, James C. "The Prophetic-Sapiential Origins of Apocalyptic Thought." Pages 163–76 in *A Word in Season: Essays in Honor of William McKane*. Edited by James D. Martin and Philip R. Davies. JSOTSup 42. Sheffield: Sheffield Academic, 1986.

Wright, Benjamin G., and Lawrence M. Wills, ed. *Conflicted Boundaries in Wisdom and Apocalypticism*. SymS 35. Atlanta: Society of Biblical Literature, 2005.

Zahn, Molly M. *Genres of Rewriting in Second Temple Judaism: Scribal Composition and Transmission*. Cambridge: Cambridge University Press, 2020.

Zenger, Erich, et al. *Einleitung in das Alte Testament*. 5th ed. Stuttgart: Kohlhammer, 2004.

The Use of Genre for Many Text Meanings: Apocalypse and 1 Enoch

Alex Samely

In this paper, I will try to make an argument concerning the use of genre labels in historical research. I will distinguish types of genre labels and will interpret one group of them, of which apocalypse is a key example, as being *summaries of the academic's experience* when reading texts such as 1 Enoch, Daniel, and Revelation.

I will claim that apocalypse and similar genre labels are oriented strongly but selectively toward the contents of the text. Because of this orientation, they appear to facilitate academic inferences from the text to historical events and social groups, an exceedingly common move in the scholarship on ancient Judaism. I will question if transitions from text to history can, in fact, be reliably supported by genre classifications. I will claim that such genre labels reduce the internal diversity of themes and meanings that one experiences firsthand when reading any text, by selecting an emphasis among those meanings. I will present an alternative approach to describing single texts, namely, an inventory of textual features. This inventory occupies a middle ground between, on the one hand, reproducing the full meaning complexities of a unique text (for which there exists no known procedure) and, on the other, selecting one main content under a genre label. In order to show what is at stake here, I will examine afresh 1 Enoch, in the inclusive overall shape it has in the Ethiopic manuscripts.

1. The Argument

Let me begin by addressing the definition of apocalypse. It was John J. Collins who, in 1979, proposed what has been the most consistently influential and durable definition of this genre. I choose this case for exploring how the use of genre labels can mislead and limit our understanding, even when the characteristics they ascribe to the texts are impeccably crafted in their own right, as Collins's *apocalypse* was. Collins first collected recurring textual elements that might be associated with the notion of apocalypse in ancient Jewish texts. Identifying a common core of those, he then provided the following definition:

> This common core of constant elements permits us, then, to formulate a comprehensive definition of the genre: "Apocalypse" is a genre of revelatory literature with a narrative framework, in which a revelation is mediated by an otherworldly being to a human recipient, disclosing a transcendent reality which is both temporal, insofar as it envisages eschatological salvation, and spatial insofar as it involves another, supernatural world.[1]

This definition makes reference to the form as well as the contents of texts, but it is much more detailed about the contents. The discussion of how the genre of apocalypse should be defined has, in fact, largely pivoted around contents. Scholars have asked questions such as: Should eschatology be stressed? How central is a belief in individual resurrection? Are accounts of heavenly journeys also essential to the genre?[2] What about the astronomical content of 1 Enoch?[3] What are the wisdom contents of such texts? These are questions of emphasis; they address the relative importance and exclusivity of themes in a text. As such, they frame how contents-oriented genre terms do their text-descriptive work and provide a focus not only on scholarly contestations of such genres but also on the manner in which the sources themselves are read.

---

1. John J. Collins, "Introduction: Towards the Morphology of a Genre," *Semeia* 14 (1979): 9. See further, Collins, "Introduction: The Genre Apocalypse Reconsidered," in *Apocalypse, Prophecy, and Pseudepigraphy: On Jewish Apocalyptic Literature*, ed. John J. Collins (Grand Rapids: Eerdmans, 2015), 1–20.

2. See the summary of Adela Yarbro Collins, "Apocalypse Now: The State of Apocalyptic Studies near the End of the First Decade of the Twenty-First Century," *HTR* 104 (2011): 447–51.

3. See the diachronic-anthological approach of Annette Yoshiko Reed, "Categorization, Collection, and the Construction of Continuity: *1 Enoch* and *3 Enoch* in and beyond 'Apocalypticism' and 'Mysticism,'" *MTSR* 29 (2017): 281–82.

Genre terms are of different kinds and are used in diverse ways in various academic disciplines, subject areas, and even specialisms within the same discipline. *Apocalypse* is closely allied to perceptions of a text's contents and to some extent its form, and the same goes for *wisdom* and *law*, as used in the study of ancient Judaism. But other genre labels select other dimensions of a text. For instance, the expressions rewritten Scripture and rewritten Bible (the latter called a "quasi-genre" by Collins)[4] stress the exegetical dependency on an earlier, authoritative text.

Genre terms used in literary and historical studies other than ancient Jewish literature can emphasize the form of a text much more than the term apocalypse does. In literary studies the most important instances are terms that emphasize a certain form-content combination, fixed conventionally as part of a particular literary tradition. Thus, terms such as *sonnet* or *novel* denote formal features but link them to certain types of contents, even if these contents can change between periods and places, and thus require historical qualifiers, such as *early modern* European novel or *Petrarchan* sonnet.

The concept of sonnet illustrates another tendency. In addition to a highly specific combination of content and form, it indicates the perpetuation of the genre as a self-conscious literary tradition in a particular cultural context. Certain poets produced sonnets in deliberate and highly self-aware responses to models. This self-conscious continuity is part of the meaning of such genre terms, so much so that, if someone were to compose an octave rhyming abbaabba followed by a mood-changing sestet rhyming cdecde[5] in total ignorance of the literary tradition, that is, by *accidental* similarity to other poems, the resulting poem could only with difficulty be classified as a sonnet. This shows that the way the label sonnet works in the academic discourse is quite different from apocalypse, for which few scholars would claim that a deliberate, self-conscious responsiveness to specific form-content requirements is decisive. The emulation of textual

---

4. Collins, "The Genre Apocalypse Reconsidered," 18, 17.

5. John Anthony Cuddon, "Sonnet," in *Dictionary of Literary Terms and Literary Theory*, rev. Claire E. Preston (London: Penguin, 1999), 844. Here is an example of the form-content interaction: "The Petrarchan sonnet sequence is a series of fourteen-line sonnets ... exploring the contrary states of feeling a lover experiences as he desires and idolizes an unattainable lady." See "The Sixteenth Century, 1485–1603," in *The Norton Anthology of English Literature*, ed. Meyer Howard Abrams et al., vol. 1, 6th ed. (New York: Norton, 1993), 407.

features of existing models does indeed play a role in the discussion of ancient Jewish literary production, but it is conceptualized as pseudepigraphy, rewriting of Scripture, and the like. These notions conceptualize emulation as arising from the reception of certain messages in the earlier texts as authoritative, rather than from a reception a particular form-contents combination as a value within a literary practice.

Modern literary studies speak of genres in still another sense, namely, when using the terms epic, dramatic, and lyrical. These have often been considered to be genres in the strongest sense. They appear to have a wide scope, divide the field in a seemingly exhaustive manner, have been used in the Western discourse on texts for a long time, and have been applied in a variety of scholarly fields. Yet they are quite atypical, as genre terms go. Gérard Genette has emphasized that the distinction that ultimately underpins these terms is one of "modes of enunciation." Taking them as modes of enunciation and simplifying matters somewhat, *drama* is constituted when only the voices of the text's characters are heard; *lyrical poetry*, when only the voice of the poet is heard; and *epic*, when both types of voice are heard in the text. Genette points out that these concepts therefore belong to what we today call linguistic pragmatics more than to literary studies.[6]

Within this wider landscape of types and uses of genres, then, apocalypse can be seen as being a term that draws attention to certain types of themes, presented in a text with a basic formal constitution as narrative (as in Collins's definition). Furthermore, when using this term, scholars do not usually foreground the ancient writers' embrace of a *literary* tradition as a value in itself, in the same way as for the sonnet. Rather, scholars of ancient Judaism tend to highlight the text's ideological contents as urgently important to its authors and readers. Indeed, many scholars are interested in the texts and their classification largely as clues to extra-textual historical realities, in terms of the worldviews and ideologies of social groups.

There are good reasons for this. For students of ancient Judaism, the bulk of the historical evidence consists of texts such as 1 Enoch, Daniel, or Jubilees, that is, literary texts in contrast to documentary texts or records. These Jewish literary texts do not survive alongside a contemporary

---

6. Gérard Genette, "The Architext," in *The Lyric Theory Reader: A Critical Anthology*, ed. Virginia Jackson and Yopie Prins, trans. Jane E. Lewin (Baltimore: Johns Hopkins University Press, 2014), 17–30; cf. John Frow, *Genre* (Abingdon: Routledge, 2006), 63–65.

corpus of other sources, such as documents of record, chronicles, correspondences, narrative accounts by historians, and so on.[7] In other words, the types of sources that allow, say, a historian of Rome to write a history of the public, political, social, religious, military, and everyday realities of Rome at key periods are not available. With the exception of events close to or contemporaneous with Josephus, the literary texts are almost all we have when it comes to writing the history of any period and place of Jewish antiquity. So our need to read 1 Enoch for clues to history is incomparably more pressing than a Roman historian's need to read Virgil's *Aeneid* for such clues. When we read nondocumentary sources such as 1 Enoch, Daniel, and Jubilees, by contrast, we often attempt thereby to ascertain the most basic historical information.

In this endeavor, a genre concept like apocalypse, with its orientation towards the contents of texts, plays a helpful, occasionally pivotal, role, because it facilitates the transition from text meaning to historical protagonists. Through this use of the idea of genre, the people who composed and received 1 Enoch can become the members of an apocalyptic movement, which is an extratextual historical reality. The procedure is basically this: we read the text's contents as theologically or otherwise ideologically determinative (the genre term apocalypse does precisely that), then assign this theology, ideology, or worldview to a group defined on that basis,[8] and finally infer from the undeniable existence of the text the hypothetical existence of such a group. In presenting the work of Benjamin G. Wright III, Lorenzo DiTommaso illustrates clearly how contents-oriented genres (here, wisdom) can be used to fuse the literary and the historical:

> Wright posits that while Sirach, 1 Enoch and Aramaic Levi shared multiple interests and a scribal/priestly setting, they represent competing ideas of wisdom and groups or communities "who know about each other, who do not really like each other, and who actively polemicize against each other although not necessarily directly."[9]

---

7. Some of the terms I use here reflect Arthur Marwick, *The Nature of History*, 3rd ed. (London: Macmillan, 1989), 208-10.

8. See, as one example of many, Gabriele Boccaccini's heavy emphasis on ideology in "From a Movement of Dissent to a Distinct Form of Judaism: The Heavenly Tablets in Jubilees as a Foundation of a Competing Halakah," in *Enoch and the Mosaic Torah: The Evidence of Jubilees*, ed. Gabriele Boccaccini and Giovanni Ibba (Grand Rapids: Eerdmans, 2009), 197.

9. Lorenzo DiTommaso, "Apocalypses and Apocalypticism in Antiquity, Part II,"

One of the concepts that accomplish the leverage of historical reality here is to polemicize, in particular the indirect or even *tacit* polemic. Modern scholars assume, partly because many extant works of ancient Judaism are narrative and not explicitly discursive, that the presentation of a worldview in these works can be polemical without containing rhetorical or literary signals that concede even the existence of a counter-position. This means that scholars can, if they so wish, assign to any passage, regardless how formed, a theological or ideological position as tacit polemic. This opens up unlimited possibilities for defining relationships between texts in terms of relationships between real-life groups. The term polemic, which can denote a genre in its own right in other contexts, can be seen as supporting the formation of a group identity through conscious differentiation from other groups and thus constitutes one avenue for the transition from text to wider historical reality.[10] The polemical text is capable of leveraging the historical reality of not just one, but two or more social groups. In this context it is interesting to note that Gabriele Boccaccini sees key aspects of the worldview of Enochic Judaism as arising from resentment against other groups:

> The problem was not the Mosaic Torah.... The concern of the Enochians was rather their own victimization, which they took as a paradigm of the victimization of all of humankind. A group of priests who felt excluded from, or marginalized within, the Zadokite priesthood gave cosmic dimension to their exclusion ... *the early Enochians were not competing with Moses, they were merely complaining.*[11]

This reconstruction ultimately requires reading the contents of 1 Enoch (and strands of other texts, such as Jubilees) as polemic, but largely tacitly. Feeling victimized, excluding people—these historical realities have no direct sources for the group here called "Enochian." Rather, it is the

---

CurBR 5 (2007): 378, with reference to Benjamin G. Wright III, "Putting the Puzzle Together: Some Suggestions Concerning the Social Location of the Wisdom of Ben Sira," in *Conflicted Boundaries in Wisdom and Apocalypticism*, ed. Benjamin G. Wright III and Lawrence M. Wills, SymS 35 (Atlanta: Society of Biblical Literature, 2005), 108.

10. The dialogical dynamic across group boundaries is clearly formulated and assumed as a universal rule of culture in Carol A. Newsom, *The Self as Symbolic Space: Constructing Identity and Community at Qumran* (Leiden: Brill, 2004), 3, 4–11. She is not relying on a genre label, and see her caveats on pp. 48–49.

11. Boccaccini, "From a Movement of Dissent," 201–2, emphasis original.

contents of 1 Enoch (and others) that give rise to the existence of Enochic Judaism in the first place. In other words, the argument is, in a very fundamental way yet not necessarily visible in every detail, circular. In any case, evidence for the existence of a social group must be considered weak if it rests on a license to assign the function of polemic to any of the themes and positions by which the contents of individual texts may routinely differ from each other. There are innumerable thematic differences between texts that have no polemical function whatsoever but are indistinguishable on internal evidence from tacit polemics.

More generally speaking, the study of ancient Judaism offers a number of ready-made scholarly agendas for the transfer of themes from text to historical reality, depending on the period and style of scholarship about which we are talking. Such an agenda might include, for instance, Jewish attitudes to the Jerusalem temple; views on divine election; attitudes to Persian, Greek and Roman overlords; views on non-Jewish neighbors and ignorant Jews; moral dualism and predestination; attitudes to resurrection; acceptance/rejection of the traditions and practices of the fathers; the structure of the calendar; and the shape of a biblical canon. Depending on specialism and approach, the list will look different. New themes are constantly added to existing scholarly agendas, as earlier ones go out of fashion; this is partly how scholars or scholarly generations assert their original contribution to the field. We are capable of focusing on one particular topic within a text, naming that topic in a certain way (on the role of modern names, see below), assigning to it two or three ideologically differentiating positions, and treating them as historically relevant to a particular period, geographical setting, and set of sources. We accomplish the latter by postulating the existence of rival groups whose boundaries are defined precisely by those postulated ideological differences.

It is furthermore common for modern critical readings to detect mutually inconsistent views or contradictions within ancient Jewish works. In such cases, text criticism is capable of providing further ammunition for the derivation of history from text structures. Diachronic explanations of the final form of the text postulate, as deduced from the very fact of internal inconsistencies, the existence of different authors or redactors with different outlooks, who in turn can be seen as representing competing worldviews and groups. Thus Loren T. Stuckenbruck postulates for 1 Enoch "a web of traditions in which the work of at least 19 originally discrete literary outputs with perhaps the authorial involvement of as many hands have at various stages been brought together."[12] Alternatively, a book's diachronically distinguishable parts can be taken to indicate a measure of continuity across generations. Reflecting on the lateness of the Book of Parables within 1 Enoch, Collins cautiously allows for the problematic longevity of the overall social group:

> Even the Similitudes of Enoch, which are later in date than any other part of 1 Enoch by at least a century, seem to envision the righteous as a community. It is not unreasonable, then, to suppose that these books of Enoch were composed within a movement of some sort, although continuity becomes problematic in the case of the Similitudes.[13]

The academic discussion surrounding 1 Enoch illustrates particularly well the trends I have just outlined. Certainly, the practice of leveraging social-ideological groups from the text can be seen at work in research on 1 Enoch and often through the very prism of the labels apocalypse and wisdom,[14] as the work's alternative or combined genres. First Enoch has prompted the postulate of the existence of a whole separate type of Judaism, namely, Enochic, as opposed to Mosaic, Judaism. A very significant group of scholars consider the existence of 1 Enoch, alongside certain other texts, as proving the existence of such a group or movement of thought. For Boccaccini, 1 Enoch is "the core of a distinct variety of second temple Judaism that played an essential role in Qumran (and Christian) origins."[15] In the wake of research by Boccaccini and Paolo Sacchi, 1 Enoch's "Enochic Judaism" is contrasted with the ideology of another entity, "Mosaic Juda-

---

12. Loren T. Stuckenbruck, "The Epistle of Enoch: Genre and Authorial Presentation," *DSD* 17 (2010): 391.

13. John J. Collins, "How Distinctive Was Enochic Judaism?," *Meghillot* 5–6 (2008): 18; also Collins, "Enochic Judaism: An Assessment," in Collins, *Apocalypse, Prophecy, and Pseudepigraphy*, 75. For an example of the move from text to social group, see Collins, "Pseudepigraphy and Group Formation in Second Temple Judaism," in *Pseudepigraphic Perspectives: The Apocrypha and Pseudepigrapha in Light of the Dead Sea Scrolls*, ed. Esther G. Chazon and Michael Stone, STDJ 31 (Leiden: Brill, 1999), 44–48.

14. As far as explicit themes are concerned, the single most important passage in 1 Enoch on wisdom specifically appears to be 1 En. 42.1–3. Otherwise, the topic is rare, while the themes of knowing and understanding in general are prominent throughout. See below.

15. Gabriele Boccaccini, *Beyond the Essene Hypothesis: The Parting of the Ways between Qumran and Enochic Judaism* (Grand Rapids: Eerdmans, 1998), 195.

ism," which is taken to be represented by books in due course accepted as canonical and by rabbinic Judaism later. In arguing for or against the existence of Enochic (and Mosaic) Judaism, the question of what the work 1 Enoch is really *about* plays an important role, and one guiding answer is: it is an apocalypse, alongside other apocalypses. Boccaccini's ideas have been criticized. But most of his critics are happy to subscribe to the procedure of leverage itself. Thus David Carr speaks of "Enochic traditions"— that is, specific themes and positions found in 1 Enoch and elsewhere— as providing clues to which groups existed.[16] The notion of traditions is capable of immediately adding to any text an extratextual dimension. To ascribe traditions to a text is to conceptualize that text as being merely a crystallization of views that existed independently of it socially, indeed as the views of an intergenerationally continuous collective. This is often an automatic extension of the assumption that written texts derived from preexisting oral entities.

In 1992, Collins sounded a note of caution: "We should beware of inferring social movements too readily from literary evidence." In the case of 4 Ezra, he was content to allow that texts can be the products of isolated individuals rather than historically effective groups.[17] But the existence of texts is nevertheless in principle widely accepted as an indicator of the existence, not of mere individual authors with possibly quite idiosyncratic interests, but of groups. The basic move is put very clearly, once more, by Collins:

> But the people who produced the Enoch literature did represent a distinctive form of Judaism.... The distinguishing marks of this form of Judaism were not only the explanation of the origin of evil by the myth of the Watchers, but the invocation of the pre-diluvian Enoch rather than Moses as the revealer of essential wisdom, and the view that angelic life was the ultimate ideal for humanity. Whether the authors of this literature were dissident priests is not so clear.[18]

---

16. David M. Carr, *Writing on the Tablet of the Heart: Origins of Scripture and Literature* (Oxford: Oxford University Press, 2005), 204.

17. John J. Collins, "Apocalypses and Apocalypticism: Early Jewish Apocalypticism," *ABD* 1:284.

18. Collins, "How Distinctive Was Enochic Judaism?," *34, *33. See also Collins, "Enochic Judaism," 80, and his statement, "There is no real doubt that the 'chosen righteous from the chosen plant of righteousness,' or the elect group envisioned in 1 Enoch, constituted a Jewish sect" (78).

Collins clearly explains that the contours of the particular social group whose existence is being postulated depend on the presence of and an emphasis on certain themes in certain texts, such as 1 Enoch, partly viewed in contrast to or comparison with selected other themes appearing in other texts. The distinguishing marks of the social group are postulated by saying that these groups consider important certain topics which the modern reader finds treated in the texts (like 1 Enoch), and since those texts also contain many other topics, certain themes need to be emphasized over others before they can emerge as pointing to social groups.

These topics also require a certain way of being summarized: for instance, the myth of the Watchers as explanation of the origin of evil; Enoch, rather than Moses, as revealer and as revealer of essential wisdom; seeing angelic life as the ultimate ideal for humanity. These themes, thus formulated, constitute and determine selections from a much larger pool of themes that a reader will find in 1 Enoch and thus help in discovering or imposing certain emphases and hierarchies between themes. The themes are named and thus also selected through the lens of modern concepts that are abstract, theological, ideological, and the like and belong to a modern academic (meta)language, whether that is English, Hebrew, Ethiopic, or any other. As summaries of and abstractions from many details in the narrative and in the reported speeches of 1 Enoch, they act as lenses for rereading and create unifying perspectives.[19]

Scholarly work with a limited number of extant Second Temple Jewish texts has produced a bewildering array of hypothetical historical groups and milieus[20] and many permutations, fusions, and splits among them. They all share having been postulated and defined on the basis of specific ideologies ascribed to texts (or text parts), and those ideologies are effectively textual emphases. But getting the emphasis of a text right is notoriously difficult, and most difficult when one is not part of the text's historical context. Readers always have to choose from many possible themes. Yet contents-oriented genre labels, such as apocalypse, wisdom, and law, name

---

19. Cf. Reed, "Categorization, Collection," 300–2.

20. The *apocalyptic milieu* is another term used in the leveraging of historical reality; see, e.g., Armin Lange, "Dream Visions and the Apocalyptic Milieus," in *Enoch and Qumran Origins: New Light on a Forgotten Connection*, ed. Gabriele Boccaccini (Grand Rapids: Eerdmans, 2005), 27–34. See also Lorenzo DiTommaso's use of apocalypticism as an overarching, sense-defining worldview, in "Apocalyptic Historiography," *EC* 10 (2019): 435–60 [and in his contribution to this volume—eds.].

fixed super-emphases for texts, selected emphases of selected emphases. They can influence the scholarly discussion very efficiently because they are ready-made, constant focal points for whole texts and groups of texts.

The ease with which the genre term apocalypse can be used to leverage history from text has troubled researchers. Even as scholars have agreed with the principle of leverage, some have for this reason introduced terminological barriers that were meant to separate the label for a text type from the label for a social group or ideologies. Thus Paul D. Hanson suggested using the term *apocalypse* exclusively for a text type; the term *apocalypticism*, for the worldview tied to that text type; and the expression *apocalyptic movement* for the corresponding social groups.[21] The genre label apocalypse is here viewed as a victim of its own success: the slippage from text to history and back was so easy that it produced chaos in the scholarly discourse or, as Michael Stone put it, "a semantic confusion of the first order."[22] Lester Grabbe made the distinction bluntly clear: "There is no necessary connection between apocalypses and apocalyptic communities."[23] But the problem is not the genre label as such. It is rather its use, and indeed any procedure is problematical which dramatically reduces the productive multiplicity of themes in a complex text to a few, insofar as this reduction claims validity across all scholarly occasions of reading that text.

2. The Many Meanings of a Text—Experienced and Reduced

How does the use of the contents-oriented genre label help achieve and, crucially, maintain across diverse interpretative contexts, choices of

---

21. James C. VanderKam, *Enoch and the Growth of an Apocalyptic Tradition*, CBQMS 16 (Washington, DC: Catholic Bible Association of America, 1984), 2–3; Robert L. Webb, "'Apocalyptic': Observations on a Slippery Term," *JNES* 49 (1990): 115–26; and Paul D. Hanson, "Apocalypses and Apocalypticism: Introductory Overview," *ABD* 1:280.

22. Michael E. Stone, "Lists of Revealed Things in the Apocalyptic Literature," in *Magnalia Dei: the Mighty Acts of God; Essays on the Bible and Archaeology in Memory of G. Ernest Wright*, ed. Frank Moore Cross et al. (Garden City: Doubleday, 1976), 439.

23. Lester L. Grabbe, "The Social Setting of Early Jewish Apocalypticism," *JSP* 4 (1989): 29; for Grabbe's working method, see, e.g., Grabbe, "The Parables of Enoch in Second Temple Jewish Society," in *Enoch and the Messiah Son of Man: Revisiting the Book of Parables*, ed. Gabriele Boccaccini (Grand Rapids: Eerdmans, 2007), 386–402. See also Jeff S. Anderson, "From 'Communities of Texts' to Religious Communities: Problems and Pitfalls," in Boccaccini, *Enoch and Qumran Origins*, 351–55.

emphasis that leverage history from textuality? It does so by reducing the complexity of the text's meanings, as experienced firsthand. The reduction makes it possible to use a single idea to summarize the essence (or historically effective essence) of the text. It thereby produces a summary that allows postulating the existence of a single entity of the past, particularly a reality that can be described in one collocation, such as apocalyptic movement, priestly group, scribal/wisdom tradition, monastic community, rabbis, or messianic group.

When scholars have worried about genre labels, this tended to concern the inappropriate subordination of uniquely different texts under a single class term. There have been, in particular with regard to Second Temple texts, discussions on how best to resolve such issues. Is classification under a superordinate to be complemented by a list of features, some of which are optional, others mandatory? That was the approach of the famous *Semeia* 14 volume on the genre apocalypse edited by Collins, which is the source of the above-cited definition of apocalypse. Or would it be best to abandon the idea of a classification altogether and move to a Wittgensteinian concept of family resemblance, as received in some literary studies? Such a notion of family resemblance was adopted and developed further by Eleanor Rosch in empirical psychological research into how contemporary language users classify objects. Her prototype theory has been welcomed as helpful by a number of scholars of ancient Jewish texts, including Carol Newsom and Collins.[24]

---

24. For family resemblance, see Collins, "Genre Apocalypse Reconsidered," 9–11, giving consideration to Alastair Fowler, *Kinds of Literature: An Introduction to the Theory of Genres and Modes* (Oxford: Clarendon, 1982), 40–43. The discussion has tended not to engage with Wittgenstein's overall point, which appears to me to be that no classification of objects can be judged other than by the context in which it is used (i.e., usually from *within* a shared context). Rosch's approach is welcomed by Collins ("Genre Apocalypse Reconsidered," 13), and Carol A. Newsom, "Spying Out the Land: A Report from Genology," in *Seeking Out the Wisdom of the Ancients: Essays Offered to Honor Michael V. Fox on the Occasion of His Sixty-Fifth Birthday*, ed. Ronald L. Troxel et al. (Winona Lake, IN: Eisenbrauns, 2005), 445. Again there is a tendency for scholars in literary and historical studies to ignore the antiessentialist and context-bound thrust of Rosch's work; for such a thrust in a postmodern garb, see Jacques Derrida, "The Law of Genre," in *Acts of Literature*, ed. Derek Attridge, trans. Avital Ronell (New York: Routledge, 1992), 221–52, partly responding critically to the work of Genette cited above. There is also another issue. Members of a linguistic group may recognize objects of perception (e.g., a starling) as falling under a general term (e.g., "bird") by

My criticism of certain uses of contents-oriented genre labels here is different. I am not concerned at the moment with the fact that genre labels erase important differences between whole separate texts, but that they erase the multiplicity of meanings/themes within the *single* text by reducing them to one or a handful of meanings and themes. Contents-oriented genre labels unify the individual text across itself—apocalypse is meant to *sum up* something essential about 1 Enoch—and they tend to do so in uncontrolled ways. Let me illustrate. The opening lines of the *Iliad* appear to announce that the book is concerned with the rage of Achilles. But many other themes are treated in the *Iliad* alongside the rage of Achilles, and, in fact, his rage is not necessarily what the book is about. Or at least, readers make up their own mind about this by reading the whole. This is what reading means: encountering, in a way that is not reduced in advance to one theme, every theme of every sentence (or of every poetic line, or whatever other provisionally self-contained unit of meaning the reader initially takes for granted) and gaining from that a sense of the meaning/s of the text. This sense of the text is transitory: the reader remakes it whenever they have occasion to recollect, reread, reflect upon, and articulate it. The occasion of reflection matters for this remaking, and the resulting sense of the text.

The plurality of meanings and themes encountered in reading tens or hundreds of sentences (or other meaning-units) that make up a single text is not a trivial matter. Its effect is that any longer text has many different themes, each of which could potentially be selected for emphasis, be selected as the lens through which all or some of the other themes should be viewed, or to which they should be subordinated. The intuitions by which we create governing emphases for texts are often shared among scholars of a certain period; however, this may well be not because they reflect universal reading practices but because those scholars share a cultural background, training, purpose, and so on, which are aspects of the occasion of interpretation. Scholars share with each other what they by definition never share with the original producers and readers of historical texts: the context and occasions of reading. The confluence of a text's multi-

---

quite different mechanisms from the way they recognize a text (e.g., 1 Enoch) as falling under a general term (e.g., "prophecy"). For texts are themselves verbal entities and as such have the potential of interfering with the verbal terms of their classification. That interference is a central theme of Derrida's paper (228–31 and passim), which considers it as constitutive for the very workings of genres.

ple sentence themes in *one* theme, or in a handful of themes, is never obvious in advance of reading the text. Nor is such a confluence obvious while one reads the text's individual sentences/units, or rereads them. A confluence of meanings, or an emphasis among them, may become compelling with hindsight, but it depends on the purpose of the hindsight and the occasion of reflection, recollection, or articulation. What needs are being served by me here and now thinking about, rereading, or remembering the text? Alternatively, such a confluence may never come about for me at all. I do not have to seek it in order to read the text or in order to have read it.

The text we call 1 Enoch has some 14,000 words in the Ethiopic, according to my own estimate, based on an average of the number of words per column in Manchester, John Rylands University Library 23, which is the manuscript that Michael Knibb used as the basis for his edition.[25] Its chapters contain 1,062 verses, and each of these will consist of usually at least one sentence and often more than one. The sentence is here considered merely as the most common example of a meaning unit which a reader may take initially for granted as being provisionally self-contained, so that they wish to understand its meaning before moving on to the next unit.

Thus there are, at a conservative estimate, two thousand or more discrete sentence meanings in 1 Enoch. Each has prima facie its own theme, subject matter, propositional content, or message. The reader understands them one by one but builds up in the process an implicit and fluid sense of the text as a larger meaning entity. This build-up stays to a considerable extent under the radar of consciousness and attention, although some of it can be selectively addressed in reflective hindsight, by way of thematic comparisons, syntheses, links due to word echoes, recognitions of continuity, surprises, anticipations, and similar process-like dynamics.[26] Depending on the circumstances of reading, the experience of these sentence meanings creates a sense of the themes of the text, which may well remain vague or fluid until there is a specific occasion on which readers

---

25. Michael Knibb, *The Ethiopic Book of Enoch*, 2 vols. (Oxford: Clarendon, 1978); Knibb mentions the number of verses on pp. 12 and 20 in vol. 2.

26. See Alexander Samely, *Reading and Experience*, forthcoming; Samely, "How Coherence Works: Reading, Re-reading and Inner-Biblical Exegesis," *HeBAI* 9 (2020) 130–82; see also Samely, "Jewish Studies and Reading," in *'Let the Wise Listen and Add to Their Learning': Festschrift for Günter Stemberger on the Occasion of His Seventy-Fifth Birthday*, ed. Constanza Cordoni and Gerhard Langer (Berlin: de Gruyter, 2016), 757–89.

selectively reflect on or articulate them. So that sense of the themes of the text will be responsive to some extent to the reasons for articulating it, to the occasion itself. Sometimes, and in particular in the scholarly pursuit of knowledge, there will be an attempt to recollect not just some particularly relevant meaning, but to decide on an *overall* meaning or set of meanings. But this too will shift with—in this case, scholarly—occasions of articulation, unless marooned to a rigid, precommitted, summary as expressed in a contents-oriented genre label or in some other manner.

Just considered for the plurality of themes explicitly addressed in its sentences and the many possible relationships of priority or subordination between and across them, a text as complex and long as 1 Enoch will throw up any number of potential candidates for overall meaning/s and theme/s. That the reader is academically trained and disciplined does not mean that they select the overall meaning/s without scholarly and other prompts arising from the occasion of selection. To my mind it is questionable that one can find an overall confluence of meanings whose scholarly validity exceeds the occasion in which it renders a service: but such a validity is precisely the implicit or explicit claim of a contents-oriented genre label, as in the case of apocalypse.

Thus a contents-oriented genre label for a substantial text claims to recognize some overarching emphasis, theme, or meaning in, or impose in some legitimate fashion upon, many individual unit/sentence meanings. This must mean the recognition or imposition also of textual coherence, for example, by deemphasizing (or even diachronically bracketing) certain text parts and by combining the meaning of passages to make up a coherent whole theme.[27] So recognizing or imposing an emphasis is related to reading a text's coherence and providing a contents-oriented genre label amounts to unifying the contents. In this context, it is interesting to note that intellectual historian Quentin Skinner has warned his colleagues against making works of early modern political theory *too coherent*:

> It may be (and indeed it very often happens) that a given classic writer is not altogether consistent, or even that he fails altogether to give any systematic account of his beliefs. If the basic paradigm for the conduct of

---

27. The link between selective emphasis and unification is brought out clearly in Annette Yoshiko Reed's critique of Boccaccini's reading of 1 Enoch in "Interrogating Enochic Judaism: *1 Enoch* as a Source for Intellectual History, Social Realities, and Literary Tradition," in Boccaccini, *Enoch and Qumran Origins*, 341–42.

the historical investigation has been conceived as the elaboration of each classic writer's doctrines on each of the themes most characteristic of the subject, it will become dangerously easy for the historian to conceive it as his task to supply or find in each of these texts the coherence which they may appear to lack.[28]

If we replace mention of a classic writer in the above observation with the author/s of 1 Enoch, we can see that Skinner is interested in a problem similar to that of the contents-oriented genre label. This is the case even though Skinner speaks of texts that were undoubtedly written by single authors. Yet, even for Hooker, Hobbes, and Hume, Skinner sees modern scholars produce a "mythology of coherence," a problem, he says, exacerbated by what he aptly calls "the notorious difficulty of preserving the proper emphasis and tone of a work in paraphrasing it."[29] And what is a contents-oriented genre label, such as apocalypse, if not an attempt to preserve and paraphrase the proper emphasis of a text, indeed of a whole group of texts? If 1 Enoch is classed as an apocalypse, then, in the further definition offered by Collins, its proper emphasis and tone is "revelation … disclosing a transcendent reality" (as cited above).

The implicit claim of such genre labels is to be able to reduce once and for all the complexity of experiencing the meanings in a text by distilling from that multiplicity the unity of a theme or of a coordinated set of themes. But on the basis of their firsthand reading experience, readers very commonly remain uncertain of whether they are indeed distilling such a unity or rather imposing it on the multiplicity. Trust in genre labels reduces this healthy, critical ambiguity. By the time I take for granted that a text as complex as 1 Enoch can be summed up for scholarly purposes by the term apocalypse, the plurality of meaning experiences that produced an understanding of 1 Enoch for me when I read it may become sidelined in favor of a summary that is suited to doing a job at a particular occasion of articulation: for example, the scholarly job of leveraging sociopolitical history from a text. There is a good chance that the term comes to guide, in the sense of limiting at least temporarily, my

---

28. Quentin Skinner, "Meaning and Understanding in the History of Ideas," *HistTh* 8 (1969): 16. See also L. A. Selby-Bigge's preface to David Hume, *Enquiries Concerning Human Understanding and Concerning the Principles of Morals*, ed. Lewis Amherst Selby-Bigge, rev. by Peter H. Nidditch, 3rd ed. (Oxford: Clarendon, 1975), vii.

29. Skinner, "Meaning and Understanding in the History of Ideas," 16.

recollection of my own firsthand, complex, experience with the book. If one believes in the accuracy of a label before starting to read the text thoroughly, a very common situation when graduate students train as future researchers, then it is even possible that the genre term's meaning impoverishes the trainee reader's own firsthand experience. The opposite may also happen, in particular for readers at the other end of the spectrum, experienced researchers. They can treat a genre label as richly informative because they inject into the label's meaning, as they are using it, some of the vagueness, complexity, and multiplicity of their recollection of their own reading experiences. If they then employ the label in that intended rich, multi-faceted meaning, as *tacit* shorthand for their complex experiences, a kind of semantic confusion arises that is quite common in disagreements over genre terms.

Scholarly occasions of articulation, within which awareness of genre labels is a factor, can differ by historical and situational context, goal, agenda, research question, and other aspects of the situation. Yet contents-oriented genre labels are not responsive to this variety of contexts and uses. There will be scholarly occasions on which a term like apocalypse, say in Collins's definition cited above, will do justice splendidly to 1 Enoch. But there will be other occasions when it does not.

In the critical argument I have made so far, a concept such as apocalypse emerges as making an intricate but often crucial contribution to the way scholarly attention is directed, and research results are shaped. Summing up its features and the discourse moves often connected to it, one might say, with the exaggeration that is inherent in all neatness, that the contents-oriented genre label:

1. is oriented prominently toward the text's *contents*,
2. sums up the modern scholarly reader's firsthand *experience* of the contents
3. does so by *selecting* some themes from a large pool of text themes,
4. (*re-*)*defines* the themes so selected by expressing their sense in a modern language and scholarly vocabulary,
5. can be used to see the selected themes as components of *worldviews*, and
6. to employ these components to define the boundaries of *postulated* social groups, and

7. to support this postulate by other postulates, such as traditions and tacit polemics, and by checking the text's contents against conscious or unconscious lists of themes assumed to have divided ideological groups in a particular historical time and place (in this case, Jewish antiquity).

A substantial number of researchers may feel that a whole network of indirect but mutually related pieces of evidence makes the existence of text themes and historical groups plausible and thereby supports these steps. I do not deny that. I merely draw attention to the fact that if one unravels this network of reconstructive historical coherence at any point, it is capable of falling apart or of being reconfigured in quite a different way. This is because it relies on hypothetical—not random, but also not directly attested—assumptions (which often differ from scholar to scholar) on who wrote the text, when it was written, where and why. Given this situation, it does not appear helpful that nowadays the main effect of a contents-oriented genre label is to make less visible the *many* meanings of a text that the reader experiences firsthand. Such a reduction of textual complexity is clearly legitimate for certain scholarly purposes but not if it becomes forgotten that this *is* a reduction, and a radical one at that. Yet it is precisely such a forgetting that has allowed certain procedures in the scholarship on ancient Judaism to become dominant, indeed practically automated.

3. The Manchester-Durham Inventory: A Repository of Many Possible Emphases

It will have become clear that I do not believe that we have a methodology that could accurately select certain themes from large, complex historical sources as defining their meaning or that would allow us to assign to a text a fixed unity of theme/s or meaning/s. Such scholarly acts of identification and assignation are occasioned: they have a live and, at the moment they are made, unexamined link to the reader's purposes and horizons of understanding. In order to be rendered generally valid, they would require an articulation of the occasion's purpose and context, beyond it being scholarly. But when it comes to the business of reflecting on occasions, that is, the invisible filters which contingent contextual factors may impose on us as readers of historical sources, from gender to economic situation, intellectual landscape, geography, race, and other factors, we remain forever beginners.

If, as academic readers, we ought to cherish and enhance our ability to recall the complexity of our temporally dispersed but firsthand experience of reading the text, what are the alternatives to contents-oriented genre labels? Such alternatives would have to preserve more of our experience with the many-sided meaningfulness of a text, while allowing us to articulate different or contested emphases on different occasions of articulation with a certain amount of transparency and comparability.

There now exists an approach that might meet these needs, developed at Manchester and Durham Universities between 2007 and 2012. It constitutes a discipline of text description, as a half-way house between the use of contents-oriented genre labels, on the one hand, and the plurality of meanings as experienced at firsthand, on the other. It consists of a catalogue of questions that can be asked of any text whatsoever, although it was empirically built up from features actually found in ancient Jewish literature. The questions are explicitly coordinated with each other. Answering them one by one with a particular text in mind—and a copy of it to hand—allows producing a profile of features for that text. The catalogue of questions, called the "Inventory,"[30] lists and defines generically some five hundred features that texts may have. A particular text's profile—referred to as its "Profile"—often consists of about one hundred of those features contained in the Inventory, as actually applying to that particular text. All the others do not apply to this particular text but are attested in other texts, which provides a basis for comparison and contrast.

Once the discipline of description demanded by working through a particular source by way of the Inventory has been met, a very comprehensive list of features exists for a given text—the aforementioned Profile. Readers of the text can use this Profile as a starting point for all manner of research connected to this and other sources, but also to help them in selecting certain emphases appropriate to particular scholarly occasions. But behind every selection of a particular emphasis, the Profile as a whole

---

30. First published as Alexander Samely, Philip Alexander, Rocco Bernasconi, and Robert Hayward, "Inventory of Structurally Important Literary Features in the Anonymous and Pseudepigraphic Jewish Literature of Antiquity," *AS* 9 (2011): 199–246; explained and illustrated in Samely, Alexander, Bernasconi, and Hayward, *Profiling Jewish Literature in Antiquity: An Inventory, from Second Temple Texts to the Talmuds* (Oxford: Oxford University Press, 2013); available online at: http://www.otherliteratures.co.uk/inventory/1.html. The project was funded by the AHRC (grant AH/E009085/1).

will continue to document the existence of many other potential emphases for the same text. The Profile is effectively a protocol, manifestation, and transformation of a researcher's firsthand reading experience, preserving some of that experience's temporal dispersion and unavailability to synopsis. Having to decide on each Inventory option constitutes a discipline that structures and interprets the reader's firsthand reading experiences and produces a record of many decisions of interpretation taken by a reader, for later consideration by that reader or other readers of the same text.

The same discipline produces *comparability* of interpretations across texts. Searchable in a database, hundreds of ancient Jewish works have already been profiled and thus become accessible to quite direct comparison and contrast, albeit as mediated through the individually distinct firsthand reader experiences that stand behind each Profile (and in future, rival Profiles for the same text that may be published). The database is publicly and freely available online, alongside the Inventory that provides its structuring.[31] The Inventory itself and the idea of such a tool of scholarship undeniably also reflect a particular cultural-scholarly occasion and a historical and cultural junction; the confluence of certain personal, cultural, intellectual, and academic strands in an early twenty-first century setting.

Why think of the Inventory as a discipline of description? Because, if one wishes to describe a text, the catalogue of questions that make up the Inventory obliges one to consider aspects of the text that one may find intuitively not important, aspects that do not answer a question felt in one's particular situation of description. The catalogue of questions thereby requires one to go beyond one's current needs and to decide some of the many ambiguities that one would be happy to leave unaddressed or unnoted or that one would not notice as being ambiguous, were it not for the prompt of a particular Inventory question. Yet these text features, once addressed, may well modify one's view of the aspects one is currently interested in. The Inventory is thus a mechanism for very slow and comprehensive reading of the primary sources and for leaving a record of hundreds of reading decisions according to a generic agenda, an agenda not immediately beholden to current purposes or to

---

31. Alexander Samely, Rocco Bernasconi, Philip Alexander, and Robert Hayward, eds., *Database for the Analysis of Anonymous and Pseudepigraphic Jewish Texts of Antiquity*, http://literarydatabase.humanities.manchester.ac.uk/ListAllBooks.aspx

specialists' concerns, such as a canon of themes that we *know* must have mattered to Jews in antiquity.

4. Possible Emphases when Reading 1 Enoch through the Inventory

I will now use 1 Enoch to show how the Inventory can assist in further discussions about what might constitute the "proper emphasis and tone" (Skinner) of a particular text. An attempt to produce a Profile of 1 Enoch according to the Manchester-Durham inventory is available online (see n. 31). Having created the basics of this Profile recently, I will now revisit my experiences as a reader of 1 Enoch and use the profiled features to assist me in formulating certain emphases of meaning which appear to me appropriate at the moment. I will also connect them selectively to topics that have been discussed in the scholarship. Where relevant, I will indicate by a number in brackets the feature of the Inventory upon which my discussion of 1 Enoch touches and on which the corresponding entry in my Profile of the text in the Database will be found to elaborate.

4.1. Narrative

In my view, 1 Enoch is, in its most comprehensive literary manifestation, the Ethiopic one, a narrative, fitting in with Collins's definition of apocalypse cited above. It is a narrative of speech acts by the character Enoch, most of them consisting of an extended speech, rather than a short utterance. It is thus an episodic narrative of lengthy speech events (matching Inventory feature 5.1), and the speeches are anchored, with some exceptions, in the life story of Enoch. The occasions of speech remain mostly vague. Their physical setting is sometimes identified (in particular when in heaven or when defined by what he sees), but mostly not. Their temporal distance from each other is left unclear, although a basically chronological order appears to be suggested by the order of the text parts (matching Inventory feature 5.1.2).[32] A key structure related to the occasions of speech is a year's sojourn on earth that separates two heavenly sojourns. The speeches are implicitly and approximately situated in that gap between heavenly sojourns: they presuppose at least the first heavenly sojourn and

---

32. Cf. Devorah Dimant, "The Biography of Enoch and the Books of Enoch," *VT* 33 (1983): 14-29.

appear mostly[33] to predate the second heavenly sojourn. The purpose of Enoch's year on earth is spelled out, namely, to transmit to his family the knowledge acquired during his first period in heaven.

> We will leave you with your son for one year until you again give your (last) command, to teach your children, write for them, and testify to all your children. (1 En. 81.5)[34]

There is little doubt in my mind that this double sojourn in heaven matches a double mention of Enoch's "walking with God" in Gen 5:21–24:

> [21]When Enoch had lived 65 years, he begot Methuselah. [22]After the birth of Methuselah, Enoch walked with God 300 years; and he begot sons and daughters. [23]All the days of Enoch came to 365 years. [24]Enoch walked with God: then he was no more, for God took him. (NJPS)

It is therefore likely that this important narrative structure has, or originally had, a scripture-interpretative function (matching Inventory feature 7.1.2.1.2).[35] Additionally, *'elohim* in these verses may have been read as "angels."[36]

---

33. In 1 En. 106.1a, Enoch speaks in the first person; if verse 1b is still in his voice (and his voice is, in fact, confirmed in verse 8), he tells *as in the past* an event that only happened after his (second) raising to heaven, namely, the birth of Noah; he locates himself "at the ends of the earth" at that point in the narrative, the phrase perhaps an attempt to defuse the chronological or spatial paradox.

34. Unless otherwise indicated, translations are from George W. E. Nickelsburg and James C. VanderKam, *1 Enoch: A New Translation; Based on the Hermeneia Commentary* (Minneapolis: Fortress, 2004).

35. VanderKam, *Enoch and the Growth*, 43, seems to understand the biblical text itself as speaking of two sojourns. Ithamar Gruenwald by contrast sees the biblical wording as "inspiring" the idea of Enoch's two heavenly sojourns; see his *Apocalyptic and Merkavah Mysticism*, AGAJU 90 (Leiden: Brill, 2014), 81 n. 58. On reading redundancy in rabbinic hermeneutics, see Alexander Samely, *Rabbinic Interpretation of Scripture in the Mishnah* (Oxford: Oxford University Press, 2002), 328–42.

36. Cp. James C. VanderKam, *Enoch: A Man for All Generations* (Columbia: University of South Carolina Press, 1995), 13 and 19; and Loren T. Stuckenbruck, *1 Enoch 91–108*, CEJL (Berlin: de Gruyter, 2007), 83 n. 162. See John J. Collins, "Pseudepigraphy and Group Formation," in *Apocalypse, Prophecy, and Pseudepigraphy*, 221, on the role which "walking with" might have played in the development of the Book of the Watchers.

4.2. Voices, Types of Contents, Types of Speech Act

An anonymous voice repeatedly introduces or reintroduces Enoch as speaking. Thus, one hears Enoch speaking in the first person for much of the text of 1 Enoch as a whole. But there are two sizeable segments that are not in his voice, nor mediated by his voice: an extended narrative of events surrounding the Watchers told by an anonymous voice (1 En. 6.1–12.2);[37] and a section that has Noah speaking directly without being quoted by Enoch (1 En. 65.2b–69.25; compare Inventory point 2.3).

Within passages that present Enoch's reported speech, four main types of speech act, and thus of contents, may be distinguished. First, a tale or tales of what happened to Enoch by himself, recounting what he did, saw, heard, read, wrote, and said. Second, descriptions of the realities Enoch could perceive in various corners of the universe and the heavens and a description of the laws that govern regular occurrences in nature or the heavens that he learned about. Third, predictions of what events will take place in the future and what will be the fate of various groups, defined mostly in moral terms. And, fourth, exhortations addressed to various groups defined in moral terms, regarding what they need to understand, what they need to expect, and how they should behave and feel, including blessings or exclamations of woe regarding them. The last three types of contents, which are not narrative as such, often consist of Enoch quoting verbatim speeches which he heard angels and God utter. The four main types of contents—narrative, description, prediction, and exhortation—are not evenly distributed across the work 1 Enoch. Tentatively speaking, as they are not mutually exclusive, these contents occur as presented in table 1:

---

37. Relating effectively to Gen 6:1–4. The scope of this section is: 1 En. 6.1–8; 7.1–6; 8.1–4; 9.1–11 (direct speech of the angels presenting—effectively recapitulating for the reader—what has been happening on earth and galvanizing God into action); 10.1–22; 11.1–2 (direct speech of God giving instruction to each of the archangels and laying out the future); in 12.1–2, there is a flashback: "Before these things, Enoch was taken and no human being knew where he had been taken." Enoch's first-person speech abruptly resumes at 12.3 ("I, Enoch, was standing, blessing the Lord of the majesty, the King of the ages. And look, the watchers of the Great Holy One called me, Enoch the scribe, and said to me"). Stuckenbruck ("Epistle of Enoch," 396) rightly stresses that this key part (6.1–12.2) is not in the voice of Enoch.

Table 1. Distribution of Voices, Types of Contents, and Types of Speech Act in 1 Enoch

Voices Heard or Reported as Speaking in the Narrative	Tentative List of Passages of Description (Mostly Visual; cp. Inventory feature 8.1.16)	Tentative List of Passages of Prediction (cp. Inventory feature 8.1.18)	Tentative List of Passages of Exhortation (cp. Inventory feature 2.6.3)	The Scholarly Names of Books in 1 Enoch
anonymous: 1.1				Watchers (1–36)
Enoch: 1.2b–5.9	2.1–5.3	1.2b–9; 5.5–9	5.4	
anonymous: 6.1–12.2		10.17–19;		
Enoch: 12.3–(64.2)	14.8–25; 17–36	14.4–7; 24.5–6; 27.2–4		
Enoch: (12.3–)64.2	39.4–7; 40.1–7; 41.3–44; 46.1; 47.3–48.1; 49.1–3; 53.1–2a; 54.1–56.8; 60.1–2; 60.11–23	38.1–39.1; 45.3–6 (or 45.2–6); 46.4–47.2; 48.4–5; 48.8–10; 49.4; 50.1–51.5; 52.1–9; 53.2b–10; 55.3–56.8; 58.2–6; 60.6; 61.3–5; 61.8–12; 62.3–6; 62.8–63.11	58.2	Parables (37–71)
Noah: 65.2b–69.25	65.7–8; 69.2–15; 69.16–21, 25	65.11–12; 66.1–2; 67.1–13		
Enoch: 69.26–(105.2)	71.1–17	69.27b–29		
Enoch: (69.26)–105.2	72.2–79.6; 82.6–12; 82.13–20	80.2–8; 81.7–9; 82.2–5	(82.4)	Luminaries (72–82)
Enoch: (69.26)–105.2		(Meant as prediction: 83.1–90.38)		Dream Visions (83–90) (85–90 = "Animal Apocalypse")

Enoch: (69.26)–105.2		91.5–10; 91.11–17; 93.4–10; 95.2; 96; 97.1–100.11; 102.2–3; 104.10–105.2	91.3–4; 91.18–92.2; 93.11–14; 94.1–5; 98.7; 101.1; 102.4–104.9; 105.1b, 105.2b	Epistle of Enoch (91–105) (93.1–10/91.11–17 = "Apocalypse of Weeks")
Enoch: 106.1–107.2				Birth of Noah (106–107)
Enoch: 108.2–15	108.6–9	108.3; 108.11–15	108.2	Another Book by Enoch (108)

The narrative contents that the text offers are not separately represented in this table but are largely what remains if one deducts from the verse ranges in column 1 the verses and verse ranges indicated in columns 2, 3, and 4. In 1 En. 6.1–12.2, the narrative themes are foregrounded in a sustained manner, told by an anonymous voice. In the other sections, narrative mostly serves to locate and frame conversations and speeches of characters, that is, those of Enoch, those of characters whose words Enoch cites *verbatim*, and the speech of Noah. It is the speeches that carry the nonnarrative themes description, prediction, and exhortation. The exception to this is some brief narrated conversations, in particular 1 En. 106.8–107.3.[38] Whether one thinks of the linear progression of the text in its Ethiopic overall shape as a conglomerate of independent books placed in their sequence by some comparatively superficial principle or as the result of a deliberate process of anthologizing, sequencing and curating,[39] the preponderance of types of contents/speech acts changes as the text progresses: from that of narrative (mostly *not* presented by Enoch's voice), to that of description partly combined with prediction in the Book of Parables and the Book of the Luminaries, to prediction in the Dream Visions/Animal Apocalypse, to prediction together with exhortation in

---

38. 1 En. 91.2–3a constitutes a report on a speech situation (Enoch's account having reached the present in 91.2) and a reintroduction of Enoch's voice by an anonymous narrator, "And he spoke (of) righteousness to all his sons and he said." From here on several dialogue situations are reported by the anonymous voice, by Enoch himself, or by an oscillation between these two voices.

39. See Reed, "Categorization, Collection," 280–83, who speaks of "anthological logic" (283).

the so-called Epistle.[40] Considered in the abstract, this overall sequence of preponderances could be understood as constituting a rhetorical arc: from describing the reality of the past and of the present (e.g., nature, the heavens, etc.), to prediction of what will happen, to exhortation on how to behave when it happens, in other words, the practical consequences that Enoch's implied readers must draw from all this information. In practice, however, the same arc and related ways to interconnect these types of contents are found in many individual sections, paragraphs or complex sentences of the book. The overall development of contents is still noteworthy, though; and while the Birth of Noah section provides narrative information, the last part (108.2–15), a divine speech quoted by Enoch, returns to a pattern that interlinks description, prediction, and exhortation.

The speeches are shot through with reaffirmations of the speaking situation, vague as it is, testifying to a certain degree of interest, on the side of the authors of 1 Enoch, in a narrative or chronological anchoring of the speaking Enoch. There is a shift throughout the book from Enoch delivering speeches outside any specific situation of speaking and audience, to a more defined setting that resembles the death-bed situation of testaments (e.g., a family gathered around),[41] and finally to the situation of a dialogue between Enoch and Methuselah. One can hear an anonymous voice that is unlikely to be Enoch's (because it refers to him in the third person) at certain points in the text.[42] The main purpose of most, but not all, of these passages is to introduce or reintroduce, albeit often by breaking into, Enoch's own first-person speech. Frequently the switch between the anonymous and Enoch's voice is left unmarked and unexplained (matching Inventory feature 2.3), a fact sometimes effectively masked by the supply of quotation marks in the modern translations. But scholars also use some of these switch points as diachronic or synchronic points of text division.

Much of the substance of the speeches of 1 Enoch consists of Enoch quoting other speakers, more authoritative than himself, in particular

---

40. For examples of one particular way to combine these two types of contents in the Epistle, see Stuckenbruck, *1 Enoch 91–108*, 199–200.

41. On this, see Stuckenbruck, "Epistle of Enoch," 397. In Enoch's speech at 1 En. 91.1, the narrative has caught up with the diegetic time of speaking. Jubilees has a somewhat similar structure at Jub. 50.6; see Alexander Samely, "Profile Jubilees," in Samely et al., Database, Feature 1.7.

42. 1 En. 1.1–2a; 6.1–12.2; 37.1; 39.1–2 (or 2); 65.1–2; 70.1–2; 84.2a; 91.2–3a; 92.1a; 93.1; 93.3a; 107.3; and 108.1 ("book").

where events in the future are concerned. The sources are usually God or angels or texts written by God or angels. With regard to this epistemic perspective, the dream visions are functionally equivalent to utterances attributed to other speakers. Visions as much as speech by others make Enoch the mere transmission point, rather than the origin, of the information. But symbolic visions differ from quoted speeches in that they do not ascribe the responsibility for the very words to angels or God. A passage like 1 En. 14.2 draws attention to this: "In this vision I saw in my dream what I now speak with a human tongue and with the breath of my mouth, which the Great One has given to humans, to speak with them and to understand their heart." The voice describing what there was to be seen is Enoch's, and therefore the verbal choices are also ascribed to him for those particular contents.

4.3. The Theme of Knowledge

Let me now set some thematic emphases as a reader who has interrogated 1 Enoch with the help of the Inventory. Perhaps the single most important message of the text is hidden in the relentless use of verb forms that indicate the future, together with the high degree of repetition of the verb "to see" and its variations, of which there are several hundred occurrences.[43] Enoch only occasionally asks an angel to explain what it is that he sees, perhaps as a mere nod in the direction of literary markers of certain types of prophecy. But almost all of what he sees and hears (and quotes *verbatim*) he actually presents as if it was self-explanatory to him, and at times he explicitly characterizes it as such ("and I understand what I saw," 1 En. 1.2). The most enigmatic contents, that of the Animal Apocalypse, are left without otherworldly mediation or any other explanation. In any case, seeing expresses the height of certainty. What you see is indisputable, even if you still need to understand its significance. What strikes me most about the text in this regard is, first, the consistency with which it refers to the future and the future as fixed in the present; and, second, combined with that, the text's insistence on the certainty of knowledge that is conveyed by seeing something with your own eyes or opening your eyes and seeing what is in

---

43. Counting the verb "to see" in Charles's English version (available digitized) yields ca. three hundred occurrences (though not all with Enoch as the subject). See Robert H. Charles, *The Book of Enoch* (London: SPCK, 1917); https://www.sacred-texts.com/bib/boe/.

front of you. The way I make sense of this to myself, and connect it with topics in 1 Enoch scholarship, is by saying that one key message of the text is that the future of the world is certain and known already to those who read this text. A number of passages in 1 Enoch link the certainty of its information to writing (matching Inventory feature 2.4.1.6).[44] The idea of "tablets," let alone "heavenly tablets," also draws a link from writing to certainty.[45] This is additionally important for the self-presentation of 1 Enoch as a written text. Although the work's format is dominated by long, reported direct speeches and thus claims an ultimate, albeit clearly distant oral origin for substantial parts of the written text of 1 Enoch in its overall Ethiopic form, the work does not mask its own existence as a written text, nor does it appear to have been transmitted through oral performance. So passages that link the reliability of information to writing promote trust in the medium of writing, the medium in which the text is likely to have reached its historical audiences.[46] This is reinforced by its contents deriving to some extent from Enoch having read in the heavenly writings. Writing also plays a role on the level of the narrative action, in that it is mentioned as the medium of forensic testimony before God: the record of the evil deeds will be used to condemn the sinners, and Enoch the scribe is one of those contributing to a full record by means of which no misdeed is forgotten (e.g., 1 En. 89.62–63; 103.7). First Enoch 108.15 states that sinners "will depart to where the days and times are written for them."

---

44. These include: *1 En.* 14.7; 33.4 (Uriel writing down for Enoch "everything"); 69.8; 90.14/17; 92.1; and 100:6, making a self-reference to "this" text (መጽሐፍ, book/epistle/writing), with another self-reference perhaps in 108.10 ("and all their blessings I have recounted in the books"); mentions of "book" occur in: 14.1, 7 ("writing" in Nickelsburg and VanderKam); 39.2; 47.3; 68.1; 72.1; 81.2, 4; 82.1; 89.68–71, 76; 90.17, 20; 93.1, 3 ("discourse"); 100.6 ("this epistle"); 103.2 ("writing"); 104.10 (writing as object of falsification); 104.12; and 108.1, 3, 10; for tablets, see: 81.1–2 (መጽሐፈ ህጸፋጸ ሰማይ, the writing/book of the tablets of heaven, Knibb, *Ethiopic Book of Enoch*, 1:266, 2:186); 93.2; 103.2; and 106.19.

45. VanderKam, *Enoch and the Growth*, 150–51, speaks of the tablet image as "implying a kind of pre-determination." See also Leslie Baynes, *The Heavenly Book Motif in Judeo-Christian Apocalypses 200 B.C.E.–200 C.E.*, JSJSup 152 (Leiden: Brill, 2012), 93–96 et passim.

46. Though acceptance of writing is prominent throughout 1 Enoch, there are passages that complicate its evaluation. The gift of writing is ascribed to Penemue in 1 En. 69.8 and of the evil effects of this gift it is said: "For humans were not born for this purpose, to confirm their trustworthiness [or faith, Knibb] through pen and ink"; see also 104.10.

4.4. The Theme of the Future

Certainty of knowledge also plays a role in other aspects of 1 Enoch, in particular the reliability of knowledge of the future. First Enoch strongly indicates certainty about future events. Knowledge of the future is effectively identified as being the same as knowledge of God's will in the present. This is stressed at numerous points throughout, as for instance, "Let not your spirit be troubled because of the times; for the Great Holy One has appointed days for everything" (1 En. 92.2). Such passages chime with the fact that one could read 1 Enoch overall as making an argument. This would run as follows: the will of God is what determines the future. That will is fully determined in the now, at the moment when Enoch speaks with God. What guarantees reliable knowledge of future events therefore is that God's will is constant, that it will not change after God reveals it to Enoch.[47]

God's constancy with regard to the future can be demonstrated in two ways. First, with hindsight, much of what is future for Enoch will be past for the implied reader of 1 Enoch and can thus be verified by them, starting with the flood. The implied reader is here conceptualized as living at the impending point of cataclysmic judgment. Through the story-world's family of Enoch, all who are deserving of the message in future generations are included in this implied readership. But key events are still in the future even for the implied reader of 1 Enoch and so cannot be directly observed as conforming to the predictions: these are the cataclysmic events themselves.

The second kind of manifestation of God's constancy of will, which guarantees Enoch's knowledge of the future as reliable, is directly and readily observable in the present. They are the regularities of the visible world,[48] including the heavenly bodies. Natural phenomena and the luminaries in the sky show the constancy of God's will through their regular changes and movements, through law-governed, predictable repetition (what law here means requires further unpacking). There are, however, also statements in 1 Enoch that see the world's order as being disrupted by moral

---

47. For instance, 1 En. 39.11: "He knew before the age was created what would be forever, and for all the generations that will be."

48. I avoid using the term *nature* here, because it is capable of importing into ancient texts a whole raft of tacit contemporary assumptions. See, for instance, Francesca Rochberg, *Before Nature: Cuneiform Knowledge and the History of Science* (Chicago: University of Chicago Press, 2016).

corruption and expect the final restoration of the moral balance by way of a renewal of nature. These passages link moral with natural corruption and moral with natural restitution,[49] and a similar link is implied wherever the rebellious angels are identified with the stars of heaven in a number of passages across 1 Enoch. Nature's regularity—and thus God's power—is depicted as having indeed been disrupted by immoral forces in the past, and God's restorative actions in the past as well as the future also can have a disruptive effect on nature. Nevertheless, when it comes to certainty about the future, 1 Enoch emphasizes by extended descriptions the regularity of the observable world prominently. This links the certainty of knowledge, in my reading, to the other themes of the book, that is, prediction of the future and exhortation, by the implicit argument indicated above.

That argument's final step is as follows. If the known will of God determines the future reliably because of its constancy, then readers can satisfy themselves of that constancy every day, every month, every season, and every year through direct observation of the regularities of the visible world, the seasons and the sky, as captured in the correct calendar.[50] In other words, the correctness of the calendar allows perceiving in the visible world the same reliability with which God will mete out justice and judgment in due course. First Enoch claims that constancy of the divine will at several points in the text. But mostly the text makes the argument in its detailed descriptions of directly observable regularities and of order, in the sense of: this is how God wants and has ordained it. That explains the prominence and some of the overall functions of description as a category presented in table 1 above (column 2).[51] It also means that there is a functional transition or equivalence between natural phenomena and the, at times, very detailed descriptions of the current universe, on the one hand, and the prophetic and moral contents, on the other, as unfolded in prediction, exhortation, prescription, reward, and punishment. It appears to me that the two are functionally related in the way just described. The

---

49. The list of passages where that happens or is presupposed includes: 1 En. 15.6–10 (cf. 19.1); 57.2; 60.1, 4; 80.2–7; 83.3–5, 7, 11; 91.11; and 102.2.

50. See 1 En. 83.5 on erring in matters of the calendar despite its eternal fixedness.

51. Consider also the exhortation, "Contemplate all (his) works … how they do not alter their paths" (1 En. 2.1 and subsequent lines to 5.3). Later expressions of the appreciation of order cover rivers (5.3), winds (e.g., 18.1–5; 59.12), lightning and thunder (e.g., 41.3; 59.13–15) and the sun, moon and stars (e.g., 41.5, also 72.1–78.17, alongside the seasons, gates/windows of heaven/sun's chariot, winds and stores; 82.9–20).

relationship has sometimes been raised as problematic, but if one considers it on the level of specific contents and does not allocate opposing genre labels to them (e.g., wisdom and apocalypse), then the overall argument explained here emerges arguably quite clearly. In this view, 1 Enoch creates a perspective on phenomena of the observable world that makes them an expression of God's will, while presenting ultimate punishments and rewards at the end of history as an expression of the very same divine will.

4.5. The Observable World and Language

I would like to suggest that this is a profoundly different perspective on natural phenomena from that of certain strands of Judaism that are contemporaneous with 1 Enoch and gain more strength later. For one thing, it means that specific commandments as ascribed to God in the Pentateuch do not really figure as pivotal in 1 Enoch.[52] Hand in hand with this difference goes a particular stance regarding the role of language. In 1 Enoch, written texts are presented as recording what was said. The text of 1 Enoch itself is also presented as a record of speech and of the verbalization of events or visions, in the sense of putting them into words in a reliable manner. Language is once even mentioned as a means of creation, as when oaths uttered by certain angels are said to provide the foundation of the earth (1 En. 69.13–22), echoing perhaps divine creation by the word in Gen 1 or theurgic powers wielded through magical formulae. Yet despite all this, language is not presented in 1 Enoch as affording special access to the real significance of what is reported to have happened or to have been said. The language contained in 1 Enoch is not signaled or treated as being a repository of signs whose ultimate meaning has yet to be deciphered in the first place. That, however, is precisely how the language contained in the Torah came to be considered in rabbinic Judaism and apparently began to be considered well before the rabbinic period, so perhaps contemporaneously with the production of 1 Enoch. Already younger layers of the Hebrew Bible itself rephrase what they see as the real message of the words used in preexisting sources. In other words, they treat language in those layers as having a false bottom, as it were—an attitude that will later pervade midrashic practice. (In all likelihood this goes hand in hand with

---

52. For a nuanced summary of some of the accents that distinguish 1 Enoch, Daniel, 2 Baruch, and 4 Ezra from texts that take into view what is anachronistically called halakhah (as a dimension of *torah*), see Newsom, *Self as Symbolic Space*, 47.

considering the formulations as authoritative.) I can find no evidence in the text that 1 Enoch considers the language of the speeches it contains, or any part of itself, in this light. This arguably gives the observation of the visible world a larger role in indicating to humankind the presence and meaning of God's will than it mostly had in rabbinic discourse, where the language of the Torah diverts, as it were, some of the power of natural phenomena to reveal God. (Rabbinic liturgy is a somewhat different matter, as it often adopts a perspective on the world that reflects biblical wording or attitudes, which are closer to that of 1 Enoch.) The stance of 1 Enoch therefore also implies that the people of Israel as recipients of the Torah are not especially privileged as observers,[53] because the regularities of the world are patent and require no special ways of reading them. So, relying on some modern abstractions, one might tentatively draw the following contrast, questionably broad as it is, between language, natural phenomena, and history in 1 Enoch (top) and in much of rabbinic discourse (bottom):

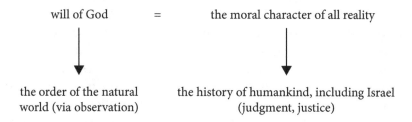

In 1 Enoch, language is not indicated as affording a special, unique access to reality. It is, however, so indicated in much of rabbinic literature:

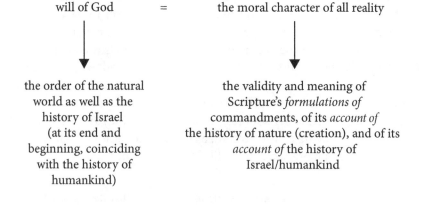

---

53. As pointed out by Collins, "Enochic Judaism," 79.

The Use of Genre for Many Text Meanings 189

In many rabbinic passages, and perhaps implicitly in the hermeneutic endeavor of rabbinic Judaism as such, meaning in language is seen as a privileged manifestation of the will of God (qua commandments, among other things) *as well as* of the character of the natural world: the view of that world is mediated to a great extent by Scripture's way of speaking of it. Direct observation of it is not probative in itself, that is, in isolation from the way the language of Scripture describes it.

This concludes my attempt to reflect on how one might preserve the proper emphasis and tone of 1 Enoch by paraphrasing it, after having interpreted my reading experiences by way of the questions set by the Manchester-Durham Inventory.

5. Conclusion

My argument in this paper has been that contents-oriented genre labels, which play an important role in the research on ancient Judaism, unify or reduce more than is appropriate in many contexts the complexity of plural meanings that are necessarily experienced by the academic (or any other) reader of individual texts, such as 1 Enoch. I am happy to concede that the individual text's complexity has a way of reasserting itself and bubbling up again in the critical scholarly reception and contestation of such labels. But if so, that happens despite them: for their inherent intention is to codify in a single expression an insight about the texts once and for all. They could be seen as pitting one-sided scholarly positions against each other, rather than inviting more organic views of the texts. One might thus look for alternative scholarly techniques which address more directly, while nevertheless simplifying, the complexity of reader experiences with a text. I presented the Manchester-Durham Inventory as one such technique. Using 1 Enoch, I demonstrated that, despite profiling a text with regard to many more discrete aspects than any genre label or ad hoc list of features could do, the Inventory nevertheless allows selecting certain emphases and producing comprehensive interpretations. It does so, however, while keeping other dimensions of the experience of the text present and open, dimensions that are available to be selected for particular emphasis on other occasions.

The results have turned out to be both similar and significantly different from Collins's famous definition of apocalypse if taken to classify 1 Enoch. I have dwelled on knowledge (but not a genre wisdom) and the certainty of future events as key themes in 1 Enoch, alongside seeing and observing the manifest world. I have ascribed to the text a pervasive concern with the underlying divine moral order in both history and nature, so that its description and narration are tied to its prediction and exhortation. One can quite easily read the *Semeia* definition of apocalypse in light of these themes, and vice versa, although one is comparing a particular text's interpretation with a generic definition of a text type, so not like with like. But there are important differences in conceptualization and perspectivization. My emphases do not include otherworldly mediation, although I have acknowledged its limited role. I have implicitly deemphasized certain themes that are definitely substantially present in 1 Enoch but that become marginalized in my provisional project of seeking overarching emphases. These marginalized themes include localities (geography) and angels and their names, among others. I would not see them currently as credible candidates for overarching emphases of the totality of 1 Enoch, as in the Ethiopic transmission.

The terms of my paraphrase are different from the *Semeia* 14 definition of apocalypse even where I refer to the same 1 Enoch contents, although they are similarly abstract and modern. I do not conceptualize the contents by transcendence, salvation, eschatology, and the supernatural but by knowledge, certainty, and (moral) order.[54] There are also important differences that concern the formal features of the text. My analysis was interested in disentangling which voice one hears at which point in the text, how the anonymous voice interacts with the voices of Enoch and Noah, how the text works as a narrative of speech events (Inventory feature 5.1), and how types of contents are connected with types of narrated speech acts—all topics unsurprisingly absent from the generic definition.

Not all the differences between my sketch of 1 Enoch and the *Semeia* description of apocalypse flow directly from any advantages that an open inventory approach may have over a narrow genre approach. Some of them reflect instead diverse intellectual climates, different scholarly and personal agendas, and forty years' worth of general historical change. But I have tried to make the two approaches directly comparable by conceding

---

54. Collins, "Towards the Morphology of a Genre," 9. I am thus in sympathy with Carol Newsom's choice of two key topics of apocalyptic literature, "(1) knowledge, hidden and revealed; and (2) patterns of order, which are the primary objects of that knowledge," although I am unconvinced by her particular emphasis on mystery, at least for 1 Enoch, for the reasons explained above. See Carol Newsom, "The Rhetoric of Jewish Apocalyptic Literature," in *The Oxford Handbook of Apocalyptic Literature*, ed. John J. Collins (Oxford: Oxford University Press, 2014), 209.

that it can make scholarly sense to seek out some overarching configuration of themes from the multiplicity of meanings that make up the text, or at least, to see what obstacles one encounters when trying to do that.

The search for overarching configurations of meaning requires the synthesis of many part-meanings, regardless what textual shape of 1 Enoch one considers. It applies to the whole of 1 Enoch in the Ethiopic transmission and also to its individual parts insofar modern scholarship tends to treat them separately as preexisting sources/books. For the *nature* of this endeavor, which underlies all genre classification by contents, it makes not much difference whether one seeks out a thematic emphasis within these sources or across their combination, although it does, of course, make a difference for the resulting emphasis. Each of the books already consists of many meanings, and, on the other hand, finding unity in each whole is always likely to be successful on some level, regardless how haphazard the process of growth of a text, if one tries hard enough.[55] So, I have attempted to show that one can use the inventory approach to unify the contents of a text, even though this is a goal which its modular catalogue of questions does not inherently embody or presuppose. And if one does use it for that purpose, then new candidates for thematic emphases emerge or become strengthened, for example, by the consistent integration of formal features. Thus the Inventory is a way of generating interpretations of individual works of Jewish antiquity that can usefully complement existing and dominant perspectives.

But the Inventory can equally serve a number of other scholarly agendas. Among these are open-ended and flexible, yet unusually comprehensive, accounts of a text's features.[56] The Inventory mandates the scholarly reader to hang on to, and preserve an echo of, the crucial plurality of

---

55. On this, see Alexander Samely, *Forms of Rabbinic Literature and Thought: An Introduction* (Oxford: Oxford University Press, 2007), 16–19; Samely, "Literary Structures and Historical Reconstruction: The Example of an Amoraic Midrash," in *Rabbinic Texts and the History of Late-Roman Palestine*, ed. Martin Goodman and Philip S. Alexander, PBA 165 (Oxford: Oxford University Press for the British Academy, 2010), 185–216; and Samely et al., *Profiling Jewish Literature in Antiquity*, 16–18.

56. See, e.g., the papers in *AS* 9 (2011); Alexander Samely, "Observations on the Structure and Literary Fabric of the Temple Scroll," in *The Temple in Text and Tradition: A Festschrift in Honour of Robert Hayward*, ed. Timothy McLay (London: T&T Clark, 2015), 233–77; Rocco Bernasconi, "A Literary Analysis of the *Sefer Yetsirah*," in *La mystique théorétique et théurgique dans l'Antiquité gréco-romaine: Judaïsmes et christianismes*, ed. Simon C. Mimouni and Madeleine Scopello, JAOC 6 (Turnhout:

meaning experiences they have undergone. This provides a reorientation of research results towards the features of the primary evidence in their as-yet unconceptualized multiplicity. Although this complicates the procedure by which we infer historical realities from textual themes, it may also free our historical imagination from some of the consequences of an over-determined approach to the sources.[57]

Bibliography

Anderson, Jeff S. "From 'Communities of Texts' to Religious Communities: Problems and Pitfalls." Pages 351–55 in *Enoch and Qumran Origins: New Light on a Forgotten Connection*. Edited by Gabriele Boccaccini. Grand Rapids: Eerdmans, 2005.

Baynes, Leslie. *The Heavenly Book Motif in Judeo-Christian Apocalypses 200 B.C.E.–200 C.E.* JSJSup 152. Leiden: Brill, 2012.

Bernasconi, Rocco. "A Literary Analysis of the *Sefer Yetsirah*." Pages 145–57 in *La mystique théorétique et théurgique dans l'Antiquité gréco-romaine: Judaïsmes et christianismes*. Edited by Simon C. Mimouni and Madeleine Scopello. JAOC 6. Turnhout: Brepols, 2016.

Boccaccini, Gabriele. *Beyond the Essene Hypothesis. The Parting of the Ways between Qumran and Enochic Judaism*. Grand Rapids: Eerdmans, 1998.

———. "From a Movement of Dissent to a Distinct Form of Judaism: The Heavenly Tablets in Jubilees as a Foundation of a Competing Halakah." Pages 193–210 in *Enoch and the Mosaic Torah: The Evidence of Jubilees*. Edited by Gabriele Boccaccini and Giovanni Ibba. Grand Rapids: Eerdmans, 2009.

Carr, David M. *Writing on the Tablet of the Heart: Origins of Scripture and Literature*. Oxford: Oxford University Press, 2005.

Charles, Robert H., trans. *The Book of Enoch*. London: SPCK, 1917. https://www.sacred-texts.com/bib/boe/.

Collins, Adela Yarbro. "Apocalypse Now: The State of Apocalyptic Studies

---

Brepols, 2016), 145–57; and Katharina E. Keim, *Pirqei deRabbi Eliezer: Structure, Coherence, Intertextuality* (Leiden: Brill, 2016).

57. I am in broad agreement with the plea by Annette Yoshiko Reed for a critical distance to whatever modern concepts we have to use to prefigure how we see the ancient Jewish past ("Categorization, Collection," 301–4).

near the End of the First Decade of the Twenty-First Century." *HTR* 104 (2011): 447–57.
Collins, John J. "Apocalypses and Apocalypticism: Early Jewish Apocalypticism." *ABD* 1:282–88.
———. "Enochic Judaism: An Assessment." Pages 73–88 in *Apocalypse, Prophecy, and Pseudepigraphy: On Jewish Apocalyptic Literature*. Grand Rapids: Eerdmans, 2015.
———. "How Distinctive Was Enochic Judaism?" *Meghillot* 5–6 (2008): *17–*34.
———. "Introduction: The Genre Apocalypse Reconsidered." Pages 1–20 in *Apocalypse, Prophecy, and Pseudepigraphy: On Jewish Apocalyptic Literature*. Edited by John J. Collins. Grand Rapids: Eerdmans, 2015.
———. "Introduction: Towards the Morphology of a Genre." *Semeia* 14 (1979): 1–20.
———. "Pseudepigraphy and Group Formation." Pages 219–34 in *Apocalypse, Prophecy, and Pseudepigraphy: On Jewish Apocalyptic Literature*. Grand Rapids: Eerdmans, 2015.
———. "Pseudepigraphy and Group Formation in Second Temple Judaism." Pages 43–58 in *Pseudepigraphic Perspectives: The Apocrypha and Pseudepigrapha in Light of the Dead Sea Scrolls*. Edited by Esther G. Chazon and Michael E. Stone. STDJ 31. Leiden: Brill, 1999.
Cuddon, John Anthony. "Sonnet." Pages 843–48 in *Dictionary of Literary Terms and Literary Theory*. Revised by Claire E. Preston. London: Penguin, 1999.
Derrida, Jacques. "The Law of Genre." Pages 221–52 in *Acts of Literature*. Edited by Derek Attridge. Translated by Avital Ronell. New York: Routledge, 1992.
Dimant, Devorah. "The Biography of Enoch and the Books of Enoch." *VT* 33 (1983): 14–29.
DiTommaso, Lorenzo. "Apocalypses and Apocalypticism in Antiquity, Part II." *CurBR* 5 (2007): 367–432.
———. "Apocalyptic Historiography." *EC* 10 (2019): 435-60.
Fowler, Alastair. *Kinds of Literature. An Introduction to the Theory of Genres and Modes*. Oxford: Clarendon, 1982.
Frow, John. *Genre*. London: Routledge, 2006.
Genette, Gérard. "The Architext." Pages 17–30 in *The Lyric Theory Reader: A Critical Anthology*. Edited by Virginia Jackson and Yopie Prins. Translated by Jane E. Lewin. Baltimore: Johns Hopkins University Press, 2014.

Grabbe, Lester L. "The Parables of Enoch in Second Temple Jewish Society." Pages 386–402 in *Enoch and the Messiah Son of Man: Revisiting the Book of Parables*. Edited by Gabriele Boccaccini. Grand Rapids: Eerdmans, 2007.

———. "The Social Setting of Early Jewish Apocalypticism." *JSP* 4 (1989): 27–47.

Gruenwald, Ithamar. *Apocalyptic and Merkavah Mysticism*. 2nd ed. Leiden: Brill, 2014.

Hanson, Paul D. "Apocalypses and Apocalypticism: Introductory Overview." *ABD* 1:280–82.

Hume, David. *Enquiries Concerning Human Understanding and Concerning the Principles of Morals*. Edited by L. A. Selby-Bigge. Revised by P. H. Nidditch. 3rd ed. Oxford: Clarendon, 1975.

Keim, Katharina E. *Pirqei deRabbi Eliezer: Structure, Coherence, Intertextuality*. Leiden: Brill, 2016.

Knibb, Michael A. *The Ethiopic Book of Enoch*. 2 vols. Oxford: Clarendon, 1978.

Lange, Armin. "Dream Visions and the Apocalyptic Milieus." Pages 27–34 in *Enoch and Qumran Origins: New Light on a Forgotten Connection*. Edited by Gabriele Boccaccini. Grand Rapids: Eerdmans, 2005.

Marwick, Arthur. *The Nature of History*. 3rd ed. London: Macmillan, 1989.

Newsom, Carol A. "The Rhetoric of Jewish Apocalyptic Literature." Pages 201–17 in *The Oxford Handbook of Apocalyptic Literature*. Edited by John J. Collins. Oxford: Oxford University Press, 2014.

———. *The Self as Symbolic Space: Constructing Identity and Community at Qumran*. Leiden: Brill, 2004.

———. "Spying Out the Land: A Report from Genology." Pages 437–50 in *Seeking Out the Wisdom of the Ancients: Essays Offered to Honor Michael V. Fox on the Occasion of His Sixty-Fifth Birthday*. Edited by Ronald L. Troxel, Kelvin G. Friebel, and Dennis Robert Magary. Winona Lake, IN: Eisenbrauns, 2005.

Nickelsburg, George W. E., and James C. VanderKam. *1 Enoch: A New Translation; Based on the Hermeneia Commentary*. Minneapolis: Fortress, 2004.

Reed, Annette Yoshiko. "Categorization, Collection, and the Construction of Continuity: *1 Enoch* and *3 Enoch* in and beyond 'Apocalypticism' and 'Mysticism.'" *MTSR* 29 (2017): 268–311.

———. "Interrogating Enochic Judaism: *1 Enoch* as a Source for Intellectual History, Social Realities, and Literary Tradition." Pages 336–44 in *Enoch and Qumran Origins: New Light on a Forgotten Connection*. Edited by Gabriele Boccaccini. Grand Rapids: Eerdmans, 2005.

Rochberg, Francesca. *Before Nature: Cuneiform Knowledge and the History of Science*. Chicago: University of Chicago Press, 2016.

Samely, Alexander. *Forms of Rabbinic Literature and Thought: An Introduction*. Oxford: Oxford University Press, 2007.

———. "How Coherence Works: Reading, Re-reading and Inner-Biblical Exegesis." *HBAI* 9 (2020): 130–82.

———. "Jewish Studies and Reading." Pages 757–89 in *'Let the Wise Listen and Add to Their Learning': Festschrift for Günter Stemberger on the Occasion of His Seventy-Fifth Birthday*. Edited by Constanza Cordoni and Gerhard Langer. Berlin: de Gruyter, 2016.

———. "Literary Structures and Historical Reconstruction: The Example of an Amoraic Midrash." Pages 185–216 in *Rabbinic Texts and the History of Late-Roman Palestine*. Edited by Martin Goodman and Philip S. Alexander. PBA 165. Oxford: Oxford University Press for the British Academy, 2010.

———. *Reading and Experience*. Forthcoming.

———. "Observations on the Structure and Literary Fabric of the Temple Scroll." Pages 233–77 in *The Temple in Text and Tradition: A Festschrift in Honour of Robert Hayward*. Edited by R. Timothy McLay. London: Bloomsbury T& T Clark, 2015.

———. "Profile 1 Enoch." Database for the Analysis of Anonymous and Pseudepigraphic Jewish Texts of Antiquity. 2013. http://literarydatabase.humanities.manchester.ac.uk/ListAllBooks.aspx.

———. "Profile Jubilees." Database for the Analysis of Anonymous and Pseudepigraphic Jewish Texts of Antiquity. 2013. http://literarydatabase.humanities.manchester.ac.uk/ListAllBooks.aspx.

———. *Rabbinic Interpretation of Scripture in the Mishnah*. Oxford: Oxford University Press, 2002.

Samely, Alexander, Philip Alexander, Rocco Bernasconi, and Robert Hayward. *Database for the Analysis of Anonymous and Pseudepigraphic Jewish Texts of Antiquity*. 2013. http://literarydatabase.humanities.manchester.ac.uk/ListAllBooks.aspx.

———, eds. "Inventory of Structurally Important Literary Features in the Anonymous and Pseudepigraphic Jewish Literature of Antiquity." *AS* 9 (2011): 199–246.

———. *Profiling Jewish Literature in Antiquity: An Inventory, from Second Temple Texts to the Talmuds*. Oxford: Oxford University Press, 2013.

"The Sixteenth Century, 1485–1603." Pages 395–413 in vol. 1 of *The Norton Anthology of English Literature*. Edited by Meyer Howard Abrams et al. 6th ed. New York: Norton, 1993.

Skinner, Quentin. "Meaning and Understanding in the History of Ideas." *HistTh* 8 (1969): 3–53.

Stone, Michael E. "Lists of Revealed Things in the Apocalyptic Literature." Pages 414–52 in *Magnalia Dei: The Mighty Acts of God; Essays on the Bible and Archaeology in Memory of G. Ernest Wright*. Edited by Frank Moore Cross, Werner E. Lemke, and Patrick D. Miller. Garden City, NY: Doubleday, 1976.

Stuckenbruck, Loren T. *1 Enoch 91–108*. CEJL. Berlin: de Gruyter, 2007.

———. "The Epistle of Enoch: Genre and Authorial Presentation." *DSD* 17 (2010): 387–417.

VanderKam, James C. *Enoch and the Growth of an Apocalyptic Tradition*. CBQMS 16. Washington, DC: Catholic Bible Association of America, 1984.

———. *Enoch: A Man for All Generations*. Columbia: University of South Carolina Press, 1995.

Webb, Robert L. "'Apocalyptic': Observations on a Slippery Term." *JNES* 49 (1990): 115–26.

Wright III, Benjamin G. "Putting the Puzzle Together: Some Suggestions Concerning the Social Location of the Wisdom of Ben Sira." Pages 89–112 in *Conflicted Boundaries in Wisdom and Apocalypticism*. Edited by Benjamin G. Wright and Lawrence M. Wills. SymS 35. Atlanta: Society of Biblical Literature, 2005.

Part 2
Apocalyptic Texts and Traditions in Ancient Judaism

Aramaic as a Language of Antediluvian Wisdom: The Early Enoch Apocalypses, Astronomy, and the Deep Past in the Hellenistic Near East

Matthew Goff

1. Introduction

The Dead Sea Scrolls include fragments of approximately 129 Aramaic texts, comprising roughly 13 percent of the Qumran corpus.[1] Two DJD volumes are devoted to this material, volumes 31 and 37. A range of studies on these texts have appeared, with recent scholarship produced in particular by Daniel Machiela and Andrew Perrin.[2] There is an extensive proceedings

---

I thank Giancarlo Angulo and Blake Jurgens for their comments on this essay.

1. For a comprehensive list of the Qumran Aramaic texts, see Eibert J. C. Tigchelaar, "Aramaic Texts from Qumran and the Authoritativeness of Hebrew Scriptures: Preliminary Observations," in *Authoritative Scriptures in Ancient Judaism*, ed. Mladen Popović, JSJSup 141 (Leiden: Brill, 2010), 158–59; Andrew B. Perrin, *The Dynamics of Dream-Vision Revelation in the Aramaic Dead Sea Scrolls*, JAJSup 19 (Göttingen: Vandenhoeck & Ruprecht, 2015), 24. Note also Klaus Beyer, *Die aramäischen Texte vom Toten Meer*, 2 vols. (Göttingen: Vandenhoeck & Ruprecht, 1984); Beyer, *Die aramäischen Texte vom Toten Meer; Ergänzungsband* (Göttingen: Vandenhoeck & Ruprecht, 1994); and Jonathan Ben-Dov, "Hebrew and Aramaic Writing in the Pseudepigrapha and the Qumran Scrolls: The Ancient Near Eastern Background and the Quest for a Written Authority" [Hebrew], *Tarbiz* 78 (2009): 27. See also now Daniel Machiela, *A Handbook of the Aramaic Scrolls from the Qumran Caves: Manuscripts, Language, and Scribal Practices*, STDJ 140 (Leiden: Brill, 2022).

2. See, for example, Daniel Machiela, "Situating the Aramaic Texts from Qumran: Reconsidering Their Language and Socio-historical Settings," in *Apocalyptic Thinking in Early Judaism: Engaging with John Collins' The Apocalyptic Imagination*, ed. Sidnie White Crawford and Cecilia Wassén, JSJSup 182 (Leiden: Brill, 2018), 88–109, and, in

volume dedicated to this corpus.[3] Philological aids have been published, including two grammars and a dictionary.[4] The study of Qumran Aramaic texts has become a leading issue in the study of the Dead Sea Scrolls.

Much of the current scholarship on this material follows an approach laid out by Devorah Dimant.[5] She calls for the study of the Qumran Aramaic texts as a distinct corpus and to this end identifies six subclusters of material within this unit: (1) works about the period of the flood; (2) works dealing with the history of the patriarchs; (3) visionary compositions; (4) legendary narratives and court-tales; (5) astronomy and magic; and 6) varia.[6] Eibert J. C. Tigchelaar organizes the material into two categories: texts attributed to pre-Mosaic figures and compositions that have a setting in the eastern diaspora.[7] Putting aside the question of which texts should go into which of Dimant's categories, her theme-based taxonomy, along with renewed scholarly interest in the material, has helped clarify four key issues about the Qumran Aramaic texts.[8] (1) While dating this material is difficult, it seems that many of these writings are early, composed in

---

the same volume, Andrew B. Perrin, "The Aramaic Imagination: Apocalyptic Thought and Genre in Dream-Visions among the Qumran Aramaic Texts," 110–40.

3. Katell Berthelot and Daniel Stökl Ben Ezra, eds., *Aramaica Qumranica: Proceedings of the Conference on the Aramaic Texts from Qumran in Aix-en-Provence, 30 June–2 July 2008*, STDJ 94 (Leiden: Brill, 2010).

4. Ursula Schattner-Rieser, *L'araméen des manuscrits de la mer Morte. 1, Grammaire*, IELOA 5 (Prahins: Éditions du Zèbre, 2004); Takamitsu Muraoka, *A Grammar of Qumran Aramaic*, ANES 38 (Leuven: Peeters, 2011); and Edward M. Cook, *Dictionary of Qumran Aramaic* (Winona Lake, IN: Eisenbrauns, 2015).

5. Devorah Dimant, "The Qumran Aramaic Texts and the Qumran Community," in *Flores Florentino: Dead Sea Scrolls and Other Early Jewish Studies in Honour of Florentino García Martínez*, ed. A. Hilhorst, Émile Puech, and Eibert J. C. Tigchelaar, JSJSup 122 (Leiden: Brill, 2007), 197–205. For an earlier effort at classifying the Qumran Aramaic texts, see Ben Zion Wacholder, "The Ancient Judaeo-Aramaic Literature (500–164 B.C.E.): A Classification of Pre-Qumran Texts," in *Archaeology and History in the Dead Sea Scrolls: The New York University Conference in Memory of Yigael Yadin*, ed. Lawrence H. Schiffman, JSPSup 8 (Sheffield: JSOT Press, 1990), 257–81.

6. Dimant, "Qumran Aramaic Texts," 198, 200–1. See also Machiela, "Situating the Aramaic Texts from Qumran," 89.

7. Tigchelaar, "Aramaic Texts from Qumran," 261. See further Florentino García Martínez, "Aramaica qumranica apocalyptica?," in Berthelot and Ben Ezra, *Aramaica Qumranica*, 436.

8. García Martínez, "Aramaica qumranica apocalyptica?," 435–36.

the third or early second centuries BCE, thus providing an impression of concerns and attitudes that predate a Hasmonean-era wave of nationalism that encouraged literary production in Hebrew.[9] (2) None of the corpus contains an obvious allusion to the *yaḥad*, such as a reference to the Teacher of Righteousness or any of the community regulations delineated in the Hebrew rulebooks, the Damascus Document and the Community Rule. Relatedly, the Aramaic texts in general show little interest in halakah. (3) Pseudepigraphy is a notable trait, found in material placed in several of Dimant's clusters (e.g., the Aramaic Levi Document, the Genesis Apocryphon, the Visions of Amram). (4) Relatedly, the Aramaic texts are often set in the deep past, as formulated in Jewish tradition—in the antediluvian period, as in, for example, the Book of the Watchers, the Astronomical Book, and the Book of Giants.

This essay focuses on the fact that our earliest examples of the genre apocalypse, the Astronomical Book and the Book of the Watchers, were composed in Aramaic.[10] Key apocalyptic material from Daniel (e.g., ch. 7) is also in Aramaic. The earliest manuscript evidence for Jewish apocalypses, 4Q201 and 4Q208 (the Book of the Watchers and the Astronomical Book, respectively), dates to roughly the first half of the second century BCE. It is reasonable to posit, as is commonly acknowledged, that the textual formation of our earliest extant apocalypses began in the third century.[11]

Two recent contributions to the issue of apocalypticism vis-à-vis Aramaic are by Machiela and Perrin. Perrin identifies the dream-vision as a

---

9. William M. Schniedewind, *A Social History of Hebrew: Its Origins through the Rabbinic Period* (New Haven: Yale University Press, 2013), 164–90; and Daniel Machiela, "The Aramaic Dead Sea Scrolls and the Historical Development of Jewish Apocalyptic Literature," in *The Seleucid and Hasmonean Periods and the Apocalyptic Worldview: The First Enoch Seminar Nangeroni Meeting, Villa Cagnola, Gazzada (June 25–28, 2012)*, ed. Lester L. Grabbe, Gabriele Boccaccini, and Jason Zurawski, LSTS 88 (London: T&T Clark, 2016), 150.

10. Józef T. Milik, *The Books of Enoch: Aramaic Fragments of Qumrân Cave 4*, with the collaboration of Matthew Black (Oxford: Clarendon, 1976). See also now Henryk Drawnel, *Qumran Cave 4: The Aramaic Books of Enoch; 4Q201, 4Q202, 4Q204, 4Q205, 4Q206, 4Q207, 4Q212* (Oxford: Oxford University Press, 2019).

11. Michael E. Stone, "The Book of Enoch and Judaism in the Third Century BCE," *CBQ* 40 (1978): 486, 489; John J. Collins, "Jewish Apocalypticism against its Hellenistic Near Eastern Environment," in *Seers, Sibyls, and Sages in Hellenistic-Roman Judaism* (Leiden: Brill, 2001), 59–74; and Collins, *The Apocalyptic Imagination: An Introduction to Jewish Apocalyptic Literature*, 3rd ed. (Grand Rapids: Eerdmans, 2016), 41–45.

major theme in the Qumran Aramaic corpus—in texts conventionally classified as apocalypses and those that are not. He suggests that dream-visions in this corpus may provide a window into a critical early stage of the development of the genre.[12] He also observes that key exempla of the Aramaic dream-visions, in texts such as the Aramaic Levi Document and the Visions of Amram, convey priestly themes and perspectives.[13] It follows, he argues, that the Aramaic material shines a light on a point not stressed in the classic articulation of the genre apocalypse in *Semeia* 14— that visionary accounts within a priestly milieu are an important context for understanding the development of the genre.[14]

Perrin's recent study also illustrates the limits of the approach advocated by Dimant. Her key methodological move, as mentioned above, is to define the Qumran Aramaic corpus as an object of study. Perrin shows awareness of the arbitrary nature of this delimitation, which is determined by the exigencies of what Aramaic texts survived at Qumran.[15] This problematizes the conclusion that themes that are prominent in the extant writings of this corpus were in fact prominent in the third and second centuries BCE. Moreover, articulating the Qumran Aramaic texts as an object of study à la Dimant can lead to the consideration of Aramaic primarily as a delimiting taxon, a criterion used to define the boundaries within which reflection takes place, rather than an object of scrutiny itself.

Machiela's recent contributions to the study of Qumran Aramaic texts attempt to do just that. He situates this material within a broader understanding of Aramaic in the Hellenistic Near East.[16] He understands the

---

12. Perrin, "Aramaic Imagination," 123; and Perrin, *Dynamics of Dream-Vision Revelation*, 233–47. For earlier investigations of this topic, see, for example, Florentino García Martínez, *Qumran and Apocalyptic*, STDJ 9 (Leiden: Brill, 1992).

13. Perrin, "Aramaic Imagination," 129.

14. Perrin, "Aramaic Imagination," 132. It should be noted that *Semeia* 14 identifies apocalypses primarily on the basis of literary or formal features without emphasizing whatever language in which these elements are articulated.

15. Perrin, "Aramaic Imagination," 114; and Perrin, *The Dynamics of Dream-Vision Revelation*, 24–26.

16. Machiela, "Situating the Aramaic Texts from Qumran"; Machiela, "Aramaic Dead Sea Scrolls"; Machiela, "Aramaic Writings of the Second Temple Period and the Growth of Apocalyptic Thought: Another Survey of the Texts," *Judaïsme Ancien* 2 (2014): 113–34; and Machiela, "The Compositional Setting and Implied Audience of Some Aramaic Texts from Qumran: A Working Hypothesis," in *Vision, Narrative, and Wisdom in the Aramaic Texts from Qumran: Essays from the Copenhagen Symposium,*

Qumran Aramaic material as the product of priestly scribes who wrote texts for hortatory, pedagogical purposes: stories in which righteousness is eventually rewarded and wickedness punished, to promote a message of hope that encourages Jews to remain committed to their ancestral traditions amidst the cultural diversity of the Hellenistic age.[17] That the articulation of this message was conducted in Aramaic, Machiela argues, is less of an ideological decision and more of a practical one—by using a lingua franca of the period, they could reach more people.

My goal in this essay is not to argue that the apocalypse in its original form should be redefined as an Aramaic genre. Our priority should not be to provide additional criteria by which to define an etic literary category but rather to better understand the evidence that we have. I would like to argue for a position, similar to those of Jonathan Ben-Dov and Annette Yoshiko Reed, that the fact that our earliest Jewish apocalypses are in Aramaic should be understood primarily as a product of this material's abiding interest in the deep past. This language was regarded in this period as an appropriate medium for knowledge and tales from the days before the flood. Those who produced and transmitted this material should be understood as custodians of an ancient heritage, valorizing Judaism and construing themselves as the ones able to disclose the archaic legacy of Judaism.[18] Aramaic had an archaizing potency, an ability to evoke the distant past, which these texts utilize.[19] The fact that Aramaic was a language widely understood is clearly a factor, and Machiela is certainly correct that it was a lingua franca at the time and that these texts were written by people who wanted others to understand them—Jews who could learn about their heritage as articulated in these writings. This, however, is not the only factor as to why these texts are in Aramaic. Emphasizing the archaizing potential of Aramaic helps explain

---

14-15 August, 2017, ed. Mette Bundvad and Kasper Siegismund, STDJ 131 (Leiden: Brill, 2019), 168-202.

17. Machiela, "Situating the Aramaic Texts from Qumran," 105-6.

18. Annette Yoshiko Reed, "Writing Jewish Astronomy in the Early Hellenistic Age: The Enochic Astronomical Book as Aramaic Wisdom and Archival Impulse," *DSD* 24 (2017): 36.

19. Ben-Dov, "Hebrew and Aramaic Writing," 30. Machiela, "Situating the Aramaic Texts from Qumran," 99-100, argues against the view Aramaic had an archaizing aspect in this period on the grounds that "there is virtually no evidence before the rabbinic period that Jews believed the patriarchs to be associated with Aramaic." As explicated in this essay, Aramaic is crucial for the figure of Enoch and the earliest apocalypses.

a key cultural program of many early Qumran Aramaic texts, including the early Enoch apocalypses: to engage and appropriate Mesopotamian *Kulturgut*, a topic of great interest in recent scholarship. Understanding why these apocalypses and other early Qumran Aramaic texts have such an overarching interest in the distant past should not be engaged simply vis-à-vis Mesopotamian tradition but also as a Hellenistic issue. In this era, intellectuals across the Near East strove to present their own culture as the oldest and their own culture-heroes as developing knowledge critical for the development of civilization and thus of benefit to all humankind. Aramaic is a vehicle of transmission between Judah and Mesopotamia for technical, scientific information, as Seth L. Sanders has stressed.[20] It should also be understood in terms of the cultural politics of knowledge of the early Hellenistic age.

2. Aramaic: Context and Background

The written record for the Aramaic language extends for approximately three thousand years—a claim one can make about very few languages of the world.[21] Our earliest extant evidence for Aramaic is the Tel Fekheriye inscription (*KAI* 309), a bilingual inscription also in Akkadian dated to the ninth century BCE from northeastern Syria.[22] Forms of Aramaic are still in use today, as the liturgical language (Syriac) of several eastern church traditions, such as the Chaldean Catholic church. While its use waned after the rise of Islam and the spread of Arabic, it is still the language of daily communication in several villages in the Middle East, such as Maaloula (Syria), in the form of dialects that are now mutually

---

20. Seth L. Sanders, *From Adapa to Enoch: Scribal Culture and Religious Vision in Judea and Babylon*, TSAJ 167 (Tübingen: Mohr Siebeck, 2017), 129–52. See also Jonathan Ben-Dov, "Scientific Writings in Aramaic and Hebrew at Qumran: Translation and Concealment," in Berthelot and Ben Ezra, *Aramaica Qumranica*, 379–99; and Dimant, "Qumran Aramaic Texts," 203.

21. For a comprehensive review of the language, upon which this section is quite reliant, see Holger Gzella, *A Cultural History of Aramaic: From the Beginnings to the Advent of Islam*, HdO 111 (Leiden: Brill, 2015). See also Klaus Beyer, *The Aramaic Language: Its Distribution and Subdivisions* (Göttingen: Vandenhoeck & Ruprecht, 1986); and Holger Gzella and Margaretha L. Folmer, eds., *Aramaic in Its Historical and Linguistic Setting* (Wiesbaden: Harrassowitz, 2008).

22. Gzella, *Cultural History of Aramaic*, 63–67; and Sanders, *From Adapa to Enoch*, 167–68.

unintelligible.[23] The chronological breadth for Aramaic is also matched by its geographical scope, with ancient evidence for the language ranging from the Indus River region to Hadrian's Wall in Britain.[24] The diversity of the evidence suggests Aramaic should be understood as an umbrella term encompassing a range of alphabetic dialects and vernaculars, whose changes over time in various regions can be traced and related to one another.[25] The long survival and vast geographical range of the evidence for Aramaic is a complex issue but should doubtlessly be related to the fact that it was the chancellery language of three consecutive empires in the ancient Near East—the Assyrian, the Babylonian, and the Persian.[26]

With the rise to power of the Neo-Assyrian and then the Babylonian Empires, the use of Aramaic developed as a supraregional language in the provinces under their control. Aramaic often served as a language of royal administration and commerce, indicating its use on both the elite and popular levels. There is preexilic evidence, such as the Neo-Assyrian Assur ostracon (*KAI* 233; seventh century BCE), for a type of a cuneiform-Aramaic bilingualism among scribes.[27] The Neo-Assyrian and Babylonian

---

23. Geoffrey Khan and Lidia Napiorkowska, eds., *Neo-Aramaic and Its Linguistic Context* (Piscataway, NJ; Gorgias, 2015); Beyer, *Aramaic Language*, 53–55.

24. Ashoka, an emperor of the Maurya Dynasty in India (third century BCE) and generally remembered as an important early convert to Buddhism, had several edicts produced, some of which are in a form of Aramaic. They include one in Taxila (*KAI* 273), which is near Islamabad, and a bilingual Greek-Aramaic one in Kandahar (*KAI* 279). The British example comes from a second-century CE epitaph, in Latin and Aramaic, near Hadrian's Wall. A Syrian man by the name of Barates from Palmyra wrote it for his wife Regina, who was from the Celtic Catuvellaunian tribe. He may have been in northern England as a merchant or through some association with the Roman army. See Beyer, *Aramaic Language*, 17; Gzella, *Cultural History of Aramaic*, 200–1; Namita Sugandhi, "Context, Content, and Composition: Questions of Intended Meaning and the Aśokan Edicts," *South Asia* 42 (2003): 224–46; and Mary Beard, *SPQR: A History of Ancient Rome* (New York: Liverlight, 2015), 509–10.

25. Gzella, *Cultural History of Aramaic*, 51.

26. Gzella, *Cultural History of Aramaic*, 37, 105; and Ben-Dov, "Hebrew and Aramaic Writing," 30.

27. The Assur ostracon is an Aramaic epistolary text between individuals known from contemporary sources as officials in the empire and who thus would have in their professions worked in cuneiform. Also note that, in an Akkadian document from the time of Sargon II, one official reminds his colleagues that they should write in cuneiform, not Aramaic. See Frederick Mario Fales, "New Light on Assyro-Aramaic Interference: The Assur Ostracon," in *CAMSEMUD 2007: Proceedings of the 13th Italian*

periods attest Aramaic letters on bricks, a format presumably used to organize them in their proper order during construction, suggesting at least a rudimentary knowledge of Aramaic among these laborers.[28] Aramaic, being an alphabetic script, was poorly suited to clay tablets, the classic medium of cuneiform. This led to the production of Aramaic texts on parchment and similar writing materials that were more perishable than clay tablets.[29] This suggests that the preponderance of our cuneiform evidence in Mesopotamia, which far outnumbers that for Aramaic, can be understood as a sort of false positive that does not convey an adequate impression of the importance of Aramaic in the region from the Neo-Assyrian period onward.

The importance of Aramaic in Mesopotamia is also evident from the presence of *sēpiru* ("alphabet scribes"), who were paired with and distinct from *ṭupšarru* ("cuneiform scribes").[30] While earlier the *sēpiru* were primarily important in royal administration, with scribal activity in temples conducted in cuneiform, by the Persian period Aramaic-writing scribes were fully part of the temple scribal establishment.[31] This suggests that, in

---

Meeting of Afro-Asiatic Linguistics, Held in Udine, May 21st–24th, 2007, ed. Frederick Mario Fales and Giulia Francesca Grassi, HANE/M 10 (Padova: S.A.R.G.O.N., 2010), 189–204; Manfried Dietrich, *The Babylonian Correspondence of Sargon and Sennacherib*, SAAS 17 (Helsinki: Helsinki University Press, 2003), 5 (text 2 [CT 54 10], given the modern title "You May Not Write Your Messages in Aramaic"); Gzella, *Cultural History of Aramaic*, 110, 142; and Sanders, *From Adapa to Enoch*, 181–83.

28. Gzella, *Cultural History of Aramaic*, 138 (also 107).

29. Sanders, *From Adapa to Enoch*, 188–96.

30. L. E. Pearce, "Sepīru and ᴸᵘ́A.BA: Scribes of the Late First Millennium," in *Languages and Cultures in Contact: At the Crossroads of Civilizations in the Syro-Mesopotamian Realm*, ed. Karel van Lerberghe and Gabriela Voet, OLA 96 (Leuven: Peeters, 2000), 355–68; Henryk Drawnel, "Between Akkadian *tupšarrūtu* and Aramaic ספר: Some Notes on the Social Context of the Early Enoch Literature," *RevQ* 24/95 (2010): 374; and Matthew Neujahr, "Babylonian Scribalism and the Production of Apocalypses and Related Early Jewish Texts," *HBAI* 5 (2016): 226. For iconography of the two kinds of scribes, with the cuneiform scribe writing on a tablet and the alphabet scribe on a type of parchment or leather, see the frontispiece of Mikko Luukko, Saana Svärd, and Raija Mattila, eds., *Of God(s), Trees, Kings, and Scholars: Neo-Assyrian and Related Studies in Honour of Simo Parpola* (Helsinki: Finnish Oriental Society, 2009) (British Museum, ME 118882). Consult also Dietrich, *Babylonian Correspondence*, 5.

31. Michael Jursa, "Ein Beamter flucht auf Aramäisch: Alphabetschreiber in der spätbabylonischen Epistolographie und die Rolle des Aramäischen in der babylonischen Verwaltung des sechsten Jahrhunderts v. Chr.," in *Leggo! Studies Presented*

this era, Aramaic could function as a medium for the transmission of Mesopotamian culture. In this period, one can discern "the Aramaization of Babylonia," alongside with the continuation of cuneiform scribal culture.[32] By the beginning of Persian rule, Aramaic may have already become the key lingua franca of the ancient Near East and perhaps even more dominant than Akkadian in Babylon as a spoken language by the fifth or fourth century BCE.[33]

For this reason, the Persian Empire adapted Aramaic rather than imposed an Iranian language throughout its far-reaching domain. The role of Aramaic as the language of the Persian state is presupposed by the correspondence with the Persian officials in Ezra, for which the book switches to Aramaic (4:7–6:18; 7:12–26). The Persians under Darius I standardized Aramaic, adopting a form of the language already in use in Babylonia, as the chancellery language, which can be called Achaemenid Official Aramaic.[34] The reputation of Aramaic as the language of state for the Persian Empire is evident from Thucydides (fifth century BCE). He writes that Athenians captured correspondence between the Persian king and the Lacedaemonians, which they translated "from Assyrian letters" (ἐκ τῶν Ἀσσυρίων γραμμάτων; 4.50; cf. Herodotus, *Hist.* 4.87).[35]

The success of the Persian standardization of a form of Aramaic is evident in the fact that the same style of Aramaic is found in the fourth century in disparate regions of its empire. The Wadi Daliyeh papyri of Samaria, which include documents regarding the sale of slaves, and the recently published Khalili collection, which preserves official correspondence in Aramaic from the court of the satrap of Bactria, in the region of what is today Afghanistan and Pakistan, both attest this form of Aramaic.[36] This

---

to *Frederick Mario Fales on the Occasion of His Sixty-Fifth Birthday*, ed. Giovanni B. Lanfranchi et al. (Wiesbaden: Harrassowitz, 2012), 379–97; and Sanders, *From Adapa to Enoch*, 183.

32. Drawnel, "Between Akkadian *tupšarrūtu* and Aramaic ספר," 374; and Gzella, *Cultural History of Aramaic*, 144.

33. Gzella, *Cultural History of Aramaic*, 154.

34. I adopt here the terminology of Gzella, *Cultural History of Aramaic*, 159. He demonstrates that this is a better label than Reichsaramäisch, which covers the Aramaic of all three empires.

35. Arnaldo Momigliano, *Alien Wisdom: The Limits of Hellenization* (Cambridge: Cambridge University Press, 1975), 9.

36. Jan Dušek, *Les manuscrits araméens du Wadi Daliyeh et la Samarie vers 450–332 av. J.-C.*, CHANE 30 (Leiden: Brill, 2007); and Joseph Naveh and Shaul Shaked,

is also the case with the Elephantine texts (fifth to fourth century BCE), discovered at a military colony of soldiers from Judah stationed in Upper Egypt as part of the Persian occupation of the country. Aramaic could be used at the time not simply for commercial or administrative purposes but also as a medium for literary texts, such as Ahiqar, that articulate Jewish cultural traditions. The breadth and geographical scope of Achaemenid chancellery Aramaic suggests that it could be understood in this era as a language that held a type of prestige. This may explain why texts such as Ahiqar are written in Aramaic.

3. Aramaic as an Ancient and Jewish Language during the Hellenistic Age

The deep entrenchment of Achaemenid chancellery Aramaic is critical for understanding this language in the Hellenistic period. This base form of the language continued even after the Persian Empire was defeated. For example, the Khalili Bactrian texts were written between 353 and 324 BCE, a period covering Alexander the Great's conquest of the region, but this change in leadership was not accompanied by any corresponding transformation in the form or style of the documents.[37] Increased evidence for regional variation becomes easier to discern in the evidence during the Hellenistic era. One can begin to discern core markers that help distinguish Western and Eastern types of Aramaic that fully emerge later, such as ית as a direct object marker in the former and -ל having this function in the latter.[38]

Aramaic Documents from Ancient Bactria (Fourth Century BCE) from the Khalili Collections (London: The Khalili Family Trust, 2012). Consult also https://www.khalilicollections.org/all-collections/aramaic-documents/. These documents do not appear to be provenanced (Naveh and Shaked, *Aramaic Documents from Ancient Bactria*, ix). See also Gzella, *Cultural History of Aramaic*, 198–200.

37. Gzella, *Cultural History of Aramaic*, 199.

38. This emerging regionalization of modes of Aramaic problematizes Fitzmyer's influential designation of "Middle Aramaic" for the Aramaic of the period 200 BCE to 200 CE, as recognized by Gzella, *Cultural History of Aramaic*, 218. See Beyer, *Aramaic Language*, 30–42; Joseph A. Fitzmyer, "The Phases of the Aramaic Language," in *A Wandering Aramean: Collected Aramaic Essays* (Grand Rapids: Eerdmans, 1997), 61–62; and Steven E. Fassberg, "Salient Features of the Verbal System in the Aramaic Dead Sea Scrolls," in Berthelot and Ben Ezra, *Aramaica Qumranica*, 66–67, 81.

Aramaic is broadly attested in Palestine in the Persian and Hellenistic eras. The epigraphic evidence in Palestine for the fifth and fourth centuries is primarily in Aramaic.[39] Key factors doubtlessly include the fact that after the Neo-Babylonian conquest of Palestine Aramaic speakers from Mesopotamia were settled there and that the returnees had extensive exposure to Aramaic when they were there. Important evidence for Aramaic in Palestine in the Hellenistic period, in addition to the Dead Sea Scrolls, includes ostraca from Idumea and inscriptions from Mount Gerizim.[40] The former includes epigraphic evidence that indicates that Aramaic was used in spheres of daily life, such as a marriage contract and inscriptions that pertain to wages and agriculture.[41] The latter corpus includes almost four hundred votive inscriptions excavated from the Gerizim temple, estimated to have been produced in the third and second centuries BCE (some earlier), demonstrating that Aramaic was used in Palestine during this period in a cultic context. While Aramaic develops at this time into a Palestinian vernacular, with presumably some degree of regional variation, it appears that our core Aramaic texts from the period, the Qumran evidence and the books of Ezra and Daniel, corpora often distinguished respectively as Qumran Aramaic and Biblical Aramaic, attest what has been called Early Jewish Literary Aramaic.[42] It is a register of Aramaic that many people

---

39. Schniedewind, *Social History of Hebrew*, 142.

40. Bezalel Porten and Ada Yardeni, *Textbook of Aramaic Ostraca from Idumea*, 3 vols. (University Park, PA: Eisenbrauns, 2014–2018); and Yitzhak Magen, Haggai Misgav, and Levana Tsfania, *The Aramaic, Hebrew and Samaritan Inscriptions*, vol. 1 of *Mount Gerizim Excavations* (Jerusalem: Israel Antiquities Authority, 2004), 14, 49–253. The Gerizim finds include a small number of contemporary Hebrew inscriptions (pp. 253–61). See also Jan Dušek, *Aramaic and Hebrew Inscriptions from Mt. Gerizim and Samaria between Antiochus III and Antiochus IV Epiphanes*, CHANE 54 (Leiden: Brill, 2012).

41. Esther Eshel, "An Aramaic Ostracon of an Edomite Marriage Contract from Maresha, dated 176 BCE," *IEJ* 46 (1996): 1–22; and Esther Eshel, Amos Kloner, and Émile Puech, "Aramaic Scribal Exercises of the Hellenistic Period from Maresha: Bowls A and B," *BASOR* 345 (2007): 39–62.

42. For this phrasing, see Daniel Machiela, "The Aramaic Language of the Dead Sea Scrolls: Why It Matters and What Lies Ahead," *Ancient Jew Review*, 10 April 2017, https://tinyurl.com/SBL3551b. This adapts Greenfield's terminology; he argued for the existence of "Standard Literary Aramaic." See Jonas C. Greenfield, "Standard Literary Aramaic," in *'Al Kanfei Yonah: Collected Studies of Jonas C. Greenfield on Semitic Philology*, ed. Shalom M. Paul et al. (Jerusalem: Magnes; Leiden: Brill, 2001), 1:111–20; Aaron Koller, "Four Dimensions of Linguistic Variation: Aramaic Dialects in and

could presumably understand, which was deployed by scribal intellectuals to present legends about ancestral figures such as Enoch, Abraham, and Levi. Such literary productions helped articulate modes of Jewish identity, by virtue of the fact that members of this group were understood to share a common past, defined to a large extent by stories about these patriarchs (more on this below). This process predates the Hasmonean revival of Hebrew but also continues during this era and afterwards.[43]

In Hellenistic Palestine, Aramaic had several types of ideological value. It could be understood as a language that evoked the empires of bygone days, in particular eastern empires.[44] This is evident from Ezra and extensive court tales in Aramaic, such as Ahiqar, Dan 3–6, or Jews at the Persian Court (4Q550).[45] The fact that Daniel is presented as a court intellectual in Babylon and a composer of Aramaic texts (Dan 7:1) suggests that, in the second century, there was a type of cultural memory that associated Aramaic with regnant empires of the past. The production of these tales in a literary form of Aramaic likely gave them for some readers a degree of historical verisimilitude.

This raises another way that Aramaic could be understood—as the language of the early ancestors of Israel. A long-standing association between Aramaic and Mesopotamia is thematized in Jewish tradition as the locale where the ancestors of Israel lived until God told Abraham to leave (Gen 12). Aramaic is not prominent in the Pentateuch. But it appears there as the language of Haran, of Jacob's uncle Laban (11:32; 12:4–5; cf. Jud 8:26). Haran is an ancient city in Upper Mesopotamia; the presentation of Aramaic as the language spoken by its inhabitants is consistent with the historical fact that in this region we find early evidence for the

---

around Qumran," in *The Dead Sea Scrolls in Context: Integrating the Dead Sea Scrolls in the Study of Ancient Texts, Languages, and Cultures*, ed. Armin Lange, Emanuel Tov, and Matthias Weigold, VTSup 140 (Leiden: Brill, 2011), 2:207–8; and Fassberg, "Salient Features of the Verbal System," 67–78.

43. One manuscript of the Aramaic text Birth of Noah (4Q536), for example, has been dated to the Herodian period. See Émile Puech, *Qumrân Grotte 4.XXII: Textes araméens, première partie, 4Q529–549*, DJD 31 (Oxford: Clarendon, 2001), 162; and Ben-Dov, "Hebrew and Aramaic Writing," 33.

44. Anathea Portier-Young, "Languages of Identity and Obligation: Daniel as Bilingual Book," *VT* 60 (2010): 98–115.

45. Devorah Dimant, "Themes and Genres in the Aramaic Texts from Qumran," in Berthelot and Ben Ezra, *Aramaica Qumranica*, 36.

Aramaic language.⁴⁶ Aramaic explicitly enters the Torah only in Gen 31:47. The pillar raised by Jacob to mark a border of separation between him and Laban is the "mound of witness," a heap of stones that is named in two languages, in Hebrew by the former as גלעד and in Aramaic by the latter, יגר שהדותא.⁴⁷ The mound has a clear function in Gen 31. It is not simply a geographical marker but also a chronological one—on one side is Jacob and his family life in Canaan (associated with Hebrew), and on the other is Laban and his family (associated with Aramaic), who at this point disappear from the narrative. One can infer that Abraham and his family spoke Aramaic before they arrived in Haran. This is not explicit, presumably, out of deference to the view that Hebrew, which flourished in the Hasmonean period, is the fitting medium for recounting the ancestral traditions of Israel.⁴⁸ Also, the well-known line from Deut 26:5 ("A wandering Aramean [ארמי] was my father") may have been shaped by the cultural memory that the early ancestors of Israel were Aramaic speakers. The conception that ancestors of an earlier age spoke Aramaic is also evident in the book of Tobit. The book, often dated to the third century BCE, is set earlier, in the eighth century, during the dominance of the Neo-Assyrian Empire, not unlike Aramaic Ahiqar. The book of Tobit was likely composed in Aramaic and in antiquity translated into Hebrew, in the context of the Hasmonean revival of this language.⁴⁹

The presentation of early ancestors as speakers of Aramaic appears prominently in the Aramaic Dead Sea Scrolls. This trope is deployed in various ways. Several texts, like the Book of the Watchers or columns II–XI of

---

46. Ronald Hendel, "Cultural Memory," in *Reading Genesis: Ten Methods*, ed. Ronald Hendel (Cambridge: Cambridge University Press, 2010), 40–41.

47. The articulation of this episode in Jubilees does not mention the Aramaic name of the pillar, in keeping with the composition's exclusive focus on Hebrew (Jub. 29.5–9).

48. Even in Jubilees, which prioritizes Hebrew, Abraham only learns this language when an angel teaches it to him when he is a young adult (Jub. 12.25). The composition does not state, in what is reasonably considered another instance of the text avoiding a reference to Aramaic, what his main spoken language was prior to this important event.

49. The Qumran evidence for Tobit includes Hebrew and Aramaic manuscripts (4Q196–200; 4Q196–199 are in Aramaic; 4Q200 is in Hebrew). See Carey A. Moore, *Tobit*, AB 40A (New York: Doubleday, 1996), 39; and Joseph A. Fitzmyer, *Tobit*, CEJL (Berlin: de Gruyter, 2003), 18–28. Consult also Ben-Dov, "Hebrew and Aramaic Writing," 30.

the Genesis Apocryphon, focus on the antediluvian period. Others, such as the Visions of Amram (4Q543–549) and the Testament of Qahat (4Q542), represent a much later but still early period. These two latter texts are attributed, respectively, to the father and grandfather of Moses (Exod 6:18–20; cf. Num 3:19; 26:58–59). Many of the Qumran Aramaic texts include first person narratives about such early figures, as Genesis Apocryphon does for example with regard to Noah and Abraham. This has been observed in scholarship and reasonably understood as a pseudepigraphic technique that helps endow a particular text with the authority of the particular ancestor.[50] This narrative technique construes major patriarchs as writers of Aramaic. This trope is evident not only in the early Enochic literature but also in the Book of Giants and the Visions of Amram, both of which purport to preserve a "copy" (פרשגן) of written texts produced, respectively, by Enoch and Amram (4Q203 8 3; 4Q543 1a–c 1).[51] These texts present themselves as transmitting genuine copies of actual writings by key patriarchs, creating a scribal link between the production of these Qumran manuscripts and the distant past.[52] Writing in literary Aramaic functions in this material as an archaizing technique, with the language understood by the compilers of these texts as an appropriate medium for conveying stories about the early ancestors of Israel.[53] The view that Aramaic was the early, pre-Sinai language of the ancestors of Israel is also preserved in Talmudic literature, as in the description of Adam in b. Sanh. 38b: "The first man spoke Aramaic."[54]

---

50. Loren T. Stuckenbruck, "Pseudepigraphy and First Person Discourse in the Dead Sea Documents: From the Aramaic Texts to Writing of the Yaḥad," in *The Dead Sea Scrolls and Contemporary Culture: Proceedings of the International Conference Held at the Israel Museum, Jerusalem (July 6–8, 2008)*, ed. Adolfo Daniel Roitman, Lawrence H. Schiffman, and Shani Tzoref, STDJ 93 (Leiden: Brill, 2011), 295–326.

51. Mladen Popović, "Pseudepigraphy and a Scribal Sense of the Past in the Ancient Mediterranean: A Copy of the Book of the Words of the Vision of Amram," in *Is There a Text in This Cave? Studies in the Textuality of the Dead Sea Scrolls in Honour of George J. Brooke*, ed. Ariel Feldman, Charlotte Hempel, and Maria Cioată, STDJ 119 (Leiden: Brill, 2017), 308–18.

52. Reed, "Writing Jewish Astronomy," 31.

53. Machiela, "Situating the Aramaic Texts from Qumran," 99, disputes the archaizing potential of Aramaic in this period, on the grounds that not all texts employ Aramaic to reflect the distant past. But this fact should not obscure the fact that in some texts, such as those under discussion here, use of this language can evoke a long-gone era.

54. Jonathan Ben-Dov, "The Choice of Aramaic and Hebrew: Ideological Considerations," *Ancient Jew Review*, 3 April 2017, https://tinyurl.com/SBL3551a.

It is also possible that some Qumran Aramaic compositions attest archaic grammatical features. But this is a disputed point.[55]

Another way Aramaic could be conceptualized in Hellenistic Judah, which cannot be neatly separated from the trope discussed just above, is that the language could be envisioned as a fitting form in which to convey Mesopotamian knowledge. As is well-known, some core features in the Aramaic Qumran texts draw directly from Mesopotamian prototypes.[56] The core mathematico-astronomical schema of the Aramaic Astronomical Book, which involves a sequence of fractions denoting the changing portion of the disc of the moon that is visible during the course of a month—celestial knowledge that is poorly preserved in later Ethiopic recensions of the composition—has striking parallels with cuneiform compositions, such as

---

55. At issue is identifying cases in which a text employs forms of words that reflect not contemporary usage of a language but rather forms that hearken back to how it was used at an earlier time. Establishing what constitutes archaic forms of a language hinges on the problem of understanding a language diachronically as an entity that evolves in stages. It is a static formulation of linguistic change. While it is fully possible for a text to attest archaizing forms, it is difficult for us to recognize them, once one acknowledges diversifying features of a language, such as regional and dialectal variation, and the stylistic choices of individual scribes. The relative pronoun זי, a form common in Old Aramaic, in later Aramaic is replaced by די/-ד. The presence of זי in the Animal Apocalypse, Giants, and other Aramaic texts at Qumran (e.g., 4Q206 4 II, 13; 4Q213a 3 15; 4Q530 2 II, 1) is thus often understood as an archaism, a conclusion that surely relies on the fact that Biblical Aramaic never attests זי, whereas די is common. But the historical transition from זי to די is not a smooth, linear one. Thus, it is not clear that זי is consciously used in the Enoch apocalypses as an archaism. In two different manuscripts that attest the same verse (1 En. 89.12), 4Q206 4 II, 13 reads זי but 4Q205 2 I, 25 has די, suggesting that the scribes who produced this material did not see a significant difference between the two forms. Also, in 4Q212 זי was corrected to די (1 III, 25 [1 En. 93.4]; 1 V, 17 [v. 11]), suggesting that at least the correcting scribe saw little value in זי, archaic or otherwise. The form מנו ("who?") instead of מן in 4Q212 1 V, 17, 20, and 22 (1 En. 93.11, 13, 14) may be an archaism (cf. Akkadian *mannu*). See Milik, *Books of Enoch*, 264, 269–70; Michael Sokoloff, "Notes on the Aramaic Fragments of Enoch from Cave 4," *Maarav* 1 (1978–1979): 203, 223; Edward M. Cook, "The Aramaic of the Dead Sea Scrolls," in *The Dead Sea Scrolls after Fifty Years: A Comprehensive Assessment*, ed. Peter W. Flint and James C. VanderKam (Leiden: Brill, 1998–1999), 2:368; Holger Gzella, "Dating the Aramaic Texts from Qumran: Possibilities and Limits," *RevQ* 24/93 (2009): 75; Koller, "Four Dimensions of Linguistic Variation," 206; and Machiela, "Aramaic Language of the Dead Sea Scrolls."

56. Ben-Dov, "Hebrew and Aramaic Writing," 34–35.

Enūma Anu Enlil.[57] As Henryk Drawnel recognizes, lines 32a–47 of the Aramaic Levi Document, following his reconstruction of the document, attest a sequence of numbers that comprise part of a priestly description of a meal offering.[58] Part of it mentions fractions of the talent, a unit of weight that comprises sixty minas in the sexagesimal Babylonian mathematical system. The same sequence of fractions in the Aramaic Levi Document is found in the same order in lists copied by Babylonian scribes. These parallels attest engagement with Mesopotamian learning in an Aramaic medium by Hellenistic Jewish authors. In both the Enochic Astronomical Book and the Aramaic Levi Document (see ll. 11–61), technical forms of knowledge that derive from Mesopotamia are not specifically coded as Babylonian; rather they are transmitted, respectively, by Enoch, who acquired this knowledge via supernatural revelation, and Isaac, who acquired this learning through his father Abraham (an issue discussed further below).[59]

The issue of appropriation of Babylonian traditions is not restricted to mathematical or astronomical knowledge. It has long been recognized that there are deep and extended parallels with Mesopotamian myth in the Enochic Book of the Watchers. The composition's presentation of the figure of Enoch himself resonates with Enmeduranki and Adapa.[60] Enmeduranki is a legendary king of Sippar who in some Sumerian king lists is seventh (not unlike Enoch in Genesis). He also travels to heaven and is given esoteric knowledge; Adapa is a primordial sage.[61] It is also widely

---

57. Henryk Drawnel, *The Aramaic Astronomical Book (4Q208–4Q211) from Qumran: Text, Translation, and Commentary* (Oxford: Clarendon, 2011), 302–11; and Matthew Goff and Dennis Duke, "The Astronomy of the Qumran Fragments 4Q208 and 4Q209," *DSD* 21 (2014): 176–210.

58. Henryk Drawnel, *An Aramaic Wisdom Text from Qumran: A New Interpretation of the Levi Document*, JSJSup 86 (Leiden: Brill, 2004), 280–93; Drawnel, "Priestly Education in the 'Aramaic Levi Document (Visions of Levi)' and 'Aramaic Astronomical Book' (4Q208–211)," *RevQ* 22/88 (2006): 554, 569; Neujahr, "Babylonian Scribalism," 223–24; and Sanders, *From Adapa to Enoch*, 158.

59. See Drawnel, "Priestly Education," 549, 559; and Drawnel, *An Aramaic Wisdom Text*, 360–65.

60. The parallels between Enoch and Enmeduranki have long been known in the field. For a review of Enmeduranki in Mesopotamian tradition, see Helge S. Kvanvig, *Primeval History: Babylonian, Biblical, and Enochic; An Intertextual Reading*, JSJSup 149 (Leiden: Brill, 2012), 99–106. Sanders, *From Adapa to Enoch*, 10–26, 228–29, has argued for prioritizing comparing Enoch with Adapa over Enmeduranki. See also Ben-Dov, "Hebrew and Aramaic Writing," 37.

61. For more on the figure of Adapa, see Sanders, *From Adapa to Enoch*, 38–70.

recognized that the angels who provide illicit knowledge are strikingly similar to the *apkallus*, who provide knowledge critical to human civilization.[62] Since the knowledge provided by the watchers, which involves the forging of metal weapons and innovations in female ornamentation, is coded as negative, the Book of the Watchers is often understood as mocking or disparaging the *apkallu* tradition. Similarly, the Aramaic Book of Giants, which was likely a product of the second century BCE, remarkably includes a direct reference to Mesopotamian epic lore, with one of the giants—one of the sons of the angels who descended—named Gilgamesh.[63] Qumran Aramaic texts from the Hellenistic period attest appropriation of scholarly knowledge and mythic traditions of Mesopotamia.

4. Fetishizing the Deep Past and the Origins of Knowledge in the Hellenistic Near East

Assessing the relationship between texts written in Judah during the early Hellenistic period and Mesopotamian traditions has been the subject of much recent scholarship. Sanders has stressed, and quite rightly, that the development of an Aramaic-based scribal culture in Mesopotamia, above all represented by the *sēpiru* scribes, provides a context in which Mesopotamian scholarship and myths could be appropriated and reemerge in Qumran Aramaic texts.[64] Ben Dov has emphasized that Aramaic is a fitting language for Mesopotamian scientific, astronomical knowledge.[65] Reed has contextualized the early Aramaic Qumran texts in their Hellenistic milieu, highlighting that the influence of Greek *paideia* across the region led to an increased focus on textuality and that the emphasis of the Qumran Aramaic texts on the primordial past and the cosmos should

---

62. They can also be related to Adapa. For an overview of the *apkallu* tradition, see Kvanvig, *Primeval History*, 117–58.

63. Matthew Goff, "Gilgamesh the Giant: The Qumran Book of Giants' Appropriation of *Gilgamesh* Motifs," *DSD* 16 (2009): 221–53.

64. Sanders, *From Adapa to Enoch*, 153–96. See also Neujahr, "Babylonian Scribalism," 221–30.

65. Ben-Dov, "Scientific Writings in Aramaic and Hebrew at Qumran." See also Mladen Popović, "The Emergence of Aramaic and Hebrew Scholarly Texts: Transmission and Translation of Alien Wisdom," in *The Dead Sea Scrolls: Transmission of Traditions and Production of Texts*, ed. Sarianna Metso, Hindy Najman, and Eileen Schuller, STDJ 92 (Leiden: Brill, 2010), 81–114.

be likewise contextualized against the "totalizing and encircling claims of Greek *paideia*," in which astronomy was an important topic.[66]

Following Reed, it is important to stress that the function of Aramaic as a medium in which Mesopotamian knowledge could be appropriated should be understood in its Hellenistic context. Exploring this issue can help explain a crucial element lying underneath much of the discussion— *why* Jewish authors display in the early Hellenistic period a pronounced interest in Mesopotamian lore.

Biblical scholars often characterize the Hellenistic period in terms of state-sanctioned violence. Consistent with this emphasis is the view that apocalyptic literature originates as a type of resistance literature.[67] This approach privileges 1–2 Maccabees and Daniel. There is pre-Maccabean political violence, the third century BCE Syrian wars comprising a key example. It is possible to understand the Book of the Watchers and its vivid depiction of antediluvian violence (1 En. 7) as a projection of contemporary upheaval onto the deep past.[68] But this perspective, with its focus on imperial violence, is poorly equipped to explain the prominence of technical knowledge in the Aramaic Astronomical Book or why this text, the Book of the Watchers, or other Qumran Aramaic texts would show any interest in Mesopotamian knowledge. At the very least, state violence should not be considered the sole factor when articulating the context in which early Hellenistic Aramaic texts were produced.

While much scholarship has interpreted the early Enoch apocalypses against the backdrop of political violence, exploration of cultural factors deserves more consideration.[69] It can be described as a crisis of wisdom.[70] Grand or maximalizing narratives about the Hellenistic world should be avoided, as they can inhibit appreciation of local variation and regional networks throughout this vast region.[71] Nevertheless, similar cultural

---

66. Reed, "Writing Jewish Astronomy," 37.

67. Anathea Portier-Young, *Apocalypse against Empire: Theologies of Resistance in Early Judaism* (Grand Rapids: Eerdmans, 2011).

68. George W. E. Nickelsburg, *1 Enoch 1: A Commentary on the Book of 1 Enoch, Chapters 1–36, 81–108*, Hermeneia (Minneapolis: Fortress, 2001), 170.

69. Reed, "Writing Jewish Astronomy," 6, calls for scholarship that goes in this direction.

70. Kyle Roark, "A Crisis of Wisdom: The Early Enoch Apocalypses and the Cultural Politics of Knowledge in the Hellenistic Age" (PhD diss., Florida State University, 2018).

71. Philip S. Alexander, "Hellenism and Hellenization as Problematic Histo-

shifts happened in various Near Eastern locales because of a widespread political fact—the overthrow of peoples who understood themselves as ancient—the Babylonians, the Egyptians, the Iranians, the Phoenicians, and the Jews—by a group perceived to be much, much younger—the Greeks. This produced a cultural climate in which subject peoples had a compelling interest to stress their own antiquity. This backdrop helped spark a vibrant discourse in the Hellenistic era about the origins of civilization. A major topic of speculation was which legendary figures of old were the first to develop various types of knowledge (πρῶτος εὑρετής), such as writing, astronomy, and mathematics, and which people can lay claim to such culture-heroes.[72] While intellectual query of this sort did not originate in the Hellenistic era, it takes on a new significance in this period, as is evident from the writings by intellectuals in the Near East, such as Berossus and Manetho, who were priests in Babylon and Egypt, respectively, in the third century BCE, and also the Phoenician Philo of Byblos.[73] Often in these works the topic of astronomy is particularly important, not because of its scientific value but because of its cultural import as a byword for antiquity.[74]

The respective claims to deep antiquity proffered by native elites throughout the Hellenistic world engendered a type of cultural competition. Berossus, for example, according to excerpts from Alexander Polyhistor (first century BCE) preserved in Eusebius and Syncellus, describes how a large monster, a fish-human hybrid called Oannes (Sumerian Uan) who

---

riographical Categories," in *Paul beyond the Judaism/Hellenism Divide*, ed. Troels Engberg-Pedersen (Louisville: Westminster John Knox, 2001), 63–80; Reed, "Writing Jewish Astronomy," 1–5.

72. For a comprehensive treatment of this topic, see Klaus Thraede, "Erfinder II (geistesgeschichtlich)," *RAC* 5 (1962): 1191–278; Thraede, "Das Lob des Erfinders: Bemerkungen zur Analyse der Heuremata-Kataloge," *RMP* 105 (1962): 160; and William F. McCants, *Founding Gods, Inventing Nations: Conquest and Culture Myths from Antiquity to Islam* (Princeton: Princeton University Press, 2012).

73. Johannes Haubold et al., eds., *The World of Berossos: Proceedings of the 4th International Colloquium on "The Ancient Near East between Classical and Ancient Oriental Traditions," Hatfield College, Durham 7th–9th July 2010*, Classica et Orientalia 5 (Wiesbaden: Harrassowitz, 2013); and John D. Dillery, *Clio's Other Sons: Berossus and Manetho* (Ann Arbor: University of Michigan Press, 2015).

74. Annette Yoshiko Reed, "Abraham as Chaldean Scientist and Father of the Jews: Josephus, *Ant.* 1.154–168, and the Greco-Roman Discourse about Astronomy/Astrology," *JSJ* 35 (2004): 142.

long ago gave to humankind knowledge critical to civilization, including the construction of cities and the invention of writing and agriculture (frag. 1).[75] Berossus, writing for the Seleucid royal court, articulated in Greek a Babylo-centric account of the origins of civilization, knowledge that is critical to all of humankind, including the Greeks.[76] In such accounts, it is implicit that they are not only a younger people but also passive receptors of forms of knowledge that originated in Babylon. In antiquity, Babylonia was well-known for its deep antiquity, a view very much associated with their association with astronomy. In the Hellenistic period, "Chaldean" becomes a synonym for astronomer. Pushing back against the view that the Babylonians are an incredibly old people, Cicero, writing in the first century BCE, disputed what he presents as the commonly held opinion that the culture of the Babylonians goes back 470,000 years (*Div.* 1.19).[77]

Egyptian intellectuals likewise sought to portray their own culture as the oldest and the cradle of human civilization. They thus took a polemical stance towards etiologies of human culture that privilege the Babylonians. Charaemon, an Egyptian Stoic philosopher who wrote in the first century CE, disparaged the veracity of Oannes, claiming that the only historicity behind this Babylonian myth is that a man once dressed up like a fish, and that, in fact, that person's lineage can be traced back to Hermes and Apollo (frag. 2).[78] Hermes, reflecting a synthesis between this Greek god and Thoth, the Egyptian god of writing, was important in Egypto-centric theories about the origins of civilization in the Hellenistic period. Texts attributed to Nechepso (a legendary king of Egypt) and Petosiris produced in the second century BCE assert that astronomical knowledge was first revealed to Hermes. The first century BCE historian Diodorus Siculus articulates an Egypto-centric presentation of human history. He credits Hermes with the inventions of both astronomy and writing (*Bib. hist.* 1.16.1; cf. 1.81.6).[79] He also gives an Egyptian twist to the *uralt* origins

---

75. Gerald P. Verbrugghe and John M. Wickersham, *Berossos and Manetho, Introduced and Translated* (Ann Arbor: University of Michigan Press, 1996), 44. See also Matthew Goff, "A Blessed Rage for Order: Apocalypticism, Esoteric Revelation, and the Cultural Politics of Knowledge in the Hellenistic Age," *HBAI* 5 (2016): 207.

76. Reed, "Writing Jewish Astronomy," 34.

77. Pieter van der Horst, "Antediluvian Knowledge," in *Japheth in the Tents of Shem: Studies on Jewish Hellenism in* Antiquity, CBET 32 (Leuven: Peeters, 2002), 140.

78. Pieter van der Horst, *Chaeremon: Egyptian Priest and Stoic Philosopher* (Leiden: Brill, 1987), 10–11.

79. Reed, "Abraham as Chaldean Scientist," 141; Iris Sulimani, *Diodorus' Mythis-*

of Mesopotamian civilization. It is actually the product of an even older campaign by Egypt to colonize and develop Babylonia (1.28.1–3); this is part of a broader effort of settling areas, Diodorus writes, resulting in the formation of other peoples, including the Jews. Egypt, hailed as the origin point of astronomical knowledge, relocated to Babylon its *own* astronomers. The prioritization of Babylonian astronomy is here not disputed but reconfigured to suit an Egyptian cultural agenda.

This is a brief sketch of a complex set of cultural dynamics in the Hellenistic period, but it brings to the fore two themes that are critical for understanding the early Enochic apocalypses and other texts of the Qumran Aramaic corpus—(1) in the Hellenistic period there was a robust interest in the deep past as a site that could be utilized by authors as a way to give pride of place to their own cultures, and (2) astronomy often played a critical role in these etiologies of knowledge critical to human civilization.

5. Aramaic as a Medium for Antediluvian Wisdom in Pre-Maccabean Apocalypses

Writers of Jewish lineage were also engaged in the cultural politics of knowledge sketched out above. Artapanus, for example, writing in a Hellenistic Egyptian context (third or second century BCE), asserts that Egyptian priests honored Moses by calling him Hermes (*apud* Eusebius, *Praep. ev.* 9.27.6). The praise accorded to Hermes in Egypt (sketched out above) is reprogrammed to demonstrate Moses's extensive contribution to Egyptian culture. The text attributes to him a range of forms of knowledge critical to Egypt, such as hieroglyphics and the ability to construct monuments in stone (9.27.4–5). The grandeur and antiquity of Egyptian culture, so articulated, testifies to the importance and antiquity of Jewish tradition.

By at least the second century BCE, Enoch had become an important figure in Jewish discourse about the origins of human culture. Jubilees, generally understood today as produced in the Hasmonean period, proclaims that Enoch was the inventor of writing and the first person to write down astronomical knowledge in a book (4.17–19). This is presumably an early reference to the Aramaic Astronomical Book. Jubilees presents

---

tory and the Pagan Mission: Historiography and Culture-Heroes in the First Pentad of the Bibliotheke, MnemosyneSupp 331 (Leiden: Brill, 2011); and Charles Muntz, *Diodorus Siculus and the World of the Late Roman Republic* (New York: Oxford University Press, 2017).

Enoch as the originator of the same types of knowledge roughly contemporary texts from other cultures are attributing to major early figures in their own mythic traditions, in particular Hermes-Thoth. Pseudo-Eupolemus, another Hellenistic Jewish text preserved by Eusebius (often dated to the second century BCE), asserts that Enoch "first discovered astrology" and pointedly adds "not the Egyptians" (*Prep. ev.* 9.17.8). The text likewise asserts, showing awareness of the Greek tradition that the Titan Atlas was the originator of astronomical knowledge, that Atlas and Enoch are one and the same figure. This text reworks a Greek etiological tradition, not unlike Artapanus's identification of Moses with Hermes, so that it legitimates the antiquity and prestige of a Jewish culture-hero (9.17.9). Pseudo-Eupolemus, drawing on the tradition that Abraham journeyed from Mesopotamia to Canaan then Egypt (Gen 12), depicts him as teaching astronomy to other peoples during his journey, first the Phoenicians and then the Egyptians.[80] Given Abraham's origin in Babylon, it is clear that he acquired this knowledge there (*Prep. ev.* 9.17.8). Since Pseudo-Eupolemus attributes the astronomical knowledge Abraham disseminated to Enoch, it can be inferred that, within the narrative logic of this text, Enoch's acquisition of astronomical knowledge occurred *in Babylon*. The composition appropriates the trope that Babylon is the locus in which primordial astronomical knowledge first originated to valorize the lineage of Israel, in the form of the ancestors Abraham and Enoch.

Jewish participation in Hellenistic discourse about the origins of civilization, in which a focus on the deep past and astronomy is dominant, is important for the interpretation of the Book of the Watchers and the Aramaic Astronomical Book. Neither of these texts explicitly claims in the manner of Jubilees that Enoch is the inventor or originator of key types of knowledge, and neither refutes the claims that another *ethnos*, such as the Egyptians, first developed such knowledge. But both points are implicit in the early Enoch apocalypses, suggested by the deep antiquity of Enoch and his reception of divine revelation. Understanding the early Enoch literature against the backdrop of Hellenistic debate about the origins of human civilization can help us better understand three key data points about our earliest apocalypses: (1) why they both center on Enoch; (2) why they

---

80. For more about the tradition of associating astronomical knowledge with Abraham, see Reed, "Abraham as Chaldean Scientist."

depict him as a recipient of astronomical knowledge through revelation; and (3) why they are both in Aramaic.

The emergence of the deep past as a site of cultural contention in the Hellenistic Near East helps explain why, in the third century BCE, a pronounced interest emerges in Enoch as an extolled early ancestor of Israel situated in the antediluvian age. This Hellenistic-era interest in the deep past also helps explain why there is great exegetical interest in the stories preserved in Genesis throughout Second Temple literature, whereas the books of the Hebrew Bible in general show no or at best highly limited interest in the traditions preserved in that book. The figure of Enoch is valorized in the Second Temple period as a primordial sage in a way, it is generally agreed, that constitutes appropriation of Mesopotamian tradition. The desire to adapt features of a legendary figure such as Enmeduranki or Adapa reflects an interest in Mesopotamian conceptions of the deep past in order to reconfigure them to promote a culture hero of Israelite tradition as the originator of knowledge that benefits humankind. One of the most important types of knowledge that was often regarded as profoundly ancient, and Mesopotamian, as we have discussed, was astronomy. This helps explain why astronomy is thematized in the early Enoch literature as knowledge Enoch acquired through revelation before the flood. The revelation of astronomy to Enoch is not only a central trope in the Aramaic Astronomical Book but also in the Book of the Watchers as well (1 En. 33). The parallels between the Aramaic Astronomical Book and older Mesopotamian astronomical texts such as Enūma Anu Enlil suggest that the compilers of this early Enochic text were not simply interested in astronomy as technical knowledge but because this topic was understood as *uralt* Mesopotamian knowledge.

The fact that both of our early Enoch apocalypses were composed in Aramaic fit well within the context of early Hellenistic discourse about the origins of astronomy. As discussed above, Sanders in his discussion of Aramaic scribal culture in Judah and Mesopotamia stresses that Aramaic could function as a medium in which knowledge that was long part of Mesopotamian scholarly tradition could emerge in Palestine.[81] His understanding of Aramaic in this period focuses on the fact that, in the Hellenistic era, it is a supraregional language and no longer directly used by a particular state for the valorization of its kings, as in the Old Ara-

---

81. Sanders, *From Adapa to Enoch*, 193–94.

maic inscriptions, such as the victory stele found at Tel Dan (*KAI* 310). For Sanders "Aramaic was a scribal culture whose power resided precisely in the fact that it did not seem like a culture at all."[82] In this way, he argues, Babylonian knowledge, once taken out of cuneiform and into Aramaic, was no longer marked as such—it is "now simply scholarship," the "unmarked universal heritage" that any scribe, such as the compilers of the Aramaic Astronomical Book, could freely adapt and appropriate.

While the production of scholarly literature in Aramaic in Babylon allows us to understand the liberation of knowledge from its traditional cuneiform context, understanding the appeal of Aramaic in early Hellenistic Judah requires appreciating its cache, long associated with both Mesopotamia and the early ancestors of Israel. The semantic potential of Aramaic to evoke the early lineage of Israel fits very well with the presumption in the early Enoch literature that it is an appropriate language in which to portray an ancestor who is a sage of antediluvian wisdom. It gives the texts a type of "historical mimesis" that reflects how Hellenistic Jewish authors imagined the deep past and their ancestral legacy.[83] One can understand Babylonian astronomical knowledge with Sanders as part of the universal heritage of humankind. But the Babylonianness of the specific types of knowledge in Qumran Aramaic texts that can, as we have seen, be traced back to Mesopotamian sources should not be regarded as wholly erased because astronomy was itself often regarded as a Mesopotamian topic. As discussed above, in the Hellenistic period, non-Babylonian authors did not simply refute the deep antiquity of Mesopotamia (as did Cicero); they could also develop strategies of appropriation (as did Diodorus), by which Mesopotamia's prestige as the locus of the origins of astronomy could be reconfigured to boost the claims of other cultures regarding their own antiquity. There is something similar at work in some of the Qumran Aramaic texts. In the early Enoch apocalypses, astronomy, widely understood as having Mesopotamian origins, has instead its origins in the venerable lineage of Israel, first disclosed to Enoch. The implicit Babylonianness of the knowledge helps signify its deep antiquity, making it something that Jewish scribal intellectuals would want to reconfigure for their own cultural agenda. Moreover, since the early ancestors of Israel are understood to have resided in Babylon (most famously Abraham), it

---

82. Sanders, *From Adapa to Enoch*, 196.
83. Ben-Dov, "Hebrew and Aramaic Writing," 38–49.

would have been reasonable for Jews in this period to understand Enoch, an ancestor who preceded Abraham, as a figure who lived in Babylon and that his reception of knowledge occurred there, as appears to be the case in Pseudo-Eupolemus. Since this language could be easily associated in Palestine during the Hellenistic period with both early ancestors who resided in Mesopotamia (such as Laban) and the broader cultural heritage of this region, the fact that the Astronomical Book is in Aramaic should be understood as a key strategy that helps achieve the book's larger goal of reconfiguring Babylonian knowledge as Israelite. The fact that the composition presents this knowledge as information Enoch himself wrote in a book prioritizes writing as a way to link the access to this knowledge in the present to the archaic past in which it originated.[84]

It should also be stressed that the Book of the Watchers and the Aramaic Astronomical Book thematize Mesopotamian lore differently. As mentioned above, the watchers who provide illicit revelation are reasonably and widely regarded as an appropriation of the *apkallu* tradition, a trope that makes no appearance in the Aramaic Astronomical Book. While this composition presents Enoch as the source of astronomical knowledge originally derived in Mesopotamia he acquires through divine revelation, the Book of the Watchers by contrast takes Mesopotamian etiologies of knowledge and inverts or even parodies them. The knowledge the sinful watchers provide in the early history of the world involves the production of metal weapons and advances in female adornment. These disclosures do not improve the human condition but makes it worse, leading to an increase in violence and sexual iniquity that necessitates the flood. After their revelations, which include astronomical information (1 En. 8.3), Enoch is given legitimate astronomical knowledge (33.1–3). Enoch, however, never receives revelation regarding metallurgy or cosmetics. Astronomy is understood as a better type of knowledge than the others revealed by the watchers. Astronomy is valorized in both the Book of the Watchers and the Astronomical Book, but only in the former is Enoch depicted as receiving divine knowledge that is a corrective to an older, illegitimate revelation. The Book of the Watchers, it appears, shows awareness of the trope that astronomy originates in Mesopotamia and adapted this trope into the milieu of Israelite tradition, with the *apkallus* reconfigured as sinful angels. The antiquity of Mesopotamian knowledge is not so much

---

84. Reed, "Writing Jewish Astronomy," 34.

disputed as maligned—the knowledge possessed by the watchers is older than anything learned by Enoch. But their knowledge was to the detriment rather than the benefit of humankind. The first genuine revelation of astronomical knowledge was disclosed to Enoch.

6. Conclusion

That our earliest extant Jewish apocalypses are in Aramaic should not simply be understood as practical issue, a consequence of the fact that Aramaic was a language many people in Palestine understood in the Hellenistic era. The Book of the Watchers and the Astronomical Book illustrate that Aramaic could be deployed to evoke a much earlier time, the antediluvian age. It could serve this purpose in part because it was understood as the language spoken by the early ancestors of Israel. The cultural politics in the Hellenistic age regarding the origins of knowledge critical for human civilization, a theme triggered by the subjugation of ancient peoples by the upstart Greeks, helped foment an interest in the deep past, which became a contested space to which Near Eastern intellectuals tried to lay claim, to give pride of place to their own *ethnos*. This cultural context makes intelligible why the early Enochic apocalypses have an extensive interest in astronomy, why they express this theme in Aramaic, and why the writings contain information that can be traced back to Mesopotamian lore. All three issues reflect Jewish interest in the deep past. Attention to the ability of Aramaic in the early Hellenistic period to evoke the days before the flood helps us better understand the earliest Jewish apocalypses.

Bibliography

Alexander, Philip S. "Hellenism and Hellenization as Problematic Historiographical Categories." Pages 63–80 in *Paul beyond the Judaism/Hellenism Divide*. Edited by Troels Engberg-Pedersen. Louisville: Westminster John Knox, 2001.

Beard, Mary. *SPQR: A History of Ancient Rome*. New York: Liverlight, 2015.

Ben-Dov, Jonathan. "The Choice of Aramaic and Hebrew: Ideological Considerations." *Ancient Jew Review*. 3 April 2017. https://tinyurl.com/SBL3551a.

———. "Hebrew and Aramaic Writing in the Pseudepigrapha and the Qumran Scrolls: The Ancient Near Eastern Background and the Quest for a Written Authority" [Hebrew]. *Tarbiz* 78 (2009): 27–60.

———. "Scientific Writings in Aramaic and Hebrew at Qumran: Translation and Concealment." Pages 379–99 in *Aramaica Qumranica: Proceedings of the Conference on the Aramaic Texts from Qumran in Aix-en-Provence 30 June–2 July 2008*. Edited by Katell Berthelot and Daniel Stökl Ben Ezra. STDJ 94. Leiden: Brill, 2010.

Berthelot, Katell, and Daniel Stökl Ben Ezra, eds. *Aramaica Qumranica: Proceedings of the Conference on the Aramaic Texts from Qumran in Aix-en-Provence, 30 June–2 July 2008*. STDJ 94. Leiden: Brill, 2010.

Beyer, Klaus. *The Aramaic Language: Its Distribution and Subdivisions*. Göttingen: Vandenhoeck & Ruprecht, 1986.

———. *Die aramäischen Texte vom Toten Meer*. 2 vols. Göttingen: Vandenhoeck & Ruprecht, 1984.

———. *Die aramäischen Texte vom Toten Meer, Ergänzungsband*. Göttingen: Vandenhoeck & Ruprecht, 1994.

Collins, John J. *The Apocalyptic Imagination: An Introduction to Jewish Apocalyptic Literature*. 3rd ed. Grand Rapids: Eerdmans, 2016.

———. "Jewish Apocalypticism against Its Hellenistic Near Eastern Environment." Pages 59–74 in *Seers, Sibyls, and Sages in Hellenistic-Roman Judaism*. Edited by John J. Collins. Leiden: Brill, 2001.

Cook, Edward M. "The Aramaic of the Dead Sea Scrolls." Pages 359–78 in vol. 1 of *The Dead Sea Scrolls after Fifty Years: A Comprehensive Assessment*. Edited by Peter W. Flint and James C. VanderKam. 2 vols. Leiden: Brill, 1998–1999.

———. *Dictionary of Qumran Aramaic*. Winona Lake, IN: Eisenbrauns, 2015.

Dietrich, Manfried. *The Babylonian Correspondence of Sargon and Sennacherib*. SAAS 17. Helsinki: Helsinki University Press, 2003.

Dillery, John D. *Clio's Other Sons: Berossus and Manetho*. Ann Arbor: University of Michigan Press, 2015.

Dimant, Devorah. "The Qumran Aramaic Texts and the Qumran Community." Pages 197–205 in *Flores Florentino: Dead Sea Scrolls and Other Early Jewish Studies in Honour of Florentino García Martínez*. Edited by A. Hilhorst, Émile Puech, and Eibert J. C. Tigchelaar. JSJSup 122. Leiden: Brill, 2007.

———. "Themes and Genres in the Aramaic Texts from Qumran." Pages 15–45 in *Aramaica Qumranica: Proceedings of the Conference on the Aramaic Texts from Qumran in Aix-en-Provence 30 June–2 July 2008*. Edited by Katell Berthelot and Daniel Stökl Ben Ezra. STDJ 94. Leiden: Brill, 2010.

Drawnel, Henryk. *The Aramaic Astronomical Book (4Q208–4Q211) from Qumran: Text, Translation, and Commentary.* Oxford: Clarendon, 2011.

———. *An Aramaic Wisdom Text from Qumran: A New Interpretation of the Levi Document.* JSJSup 86. Leiden: Brill, 2004.

———. "Between Akkadian *tupšarrūtu* and Aramaic ספר: Some Notes on the Social Context of the Early Enoch Literature." *RevQ* 24/95 (2010): 373–403.

———. "Priestly Education in the 'Aramaic Levi Document (Visions of Levi)' and 'Aramaic Astronomical Book' (4Q208–211)." *RevQ* 22/88 (2006): 547–74.

———. *Qumran Cave 4: The Aramaic Books of Enoch; 4Q201, 4Q202, 4Q204, 4Q205, 4Q206, 4Q207, 4Q212.* Oxford: Oxford University Press, 2019.

Dušek, Jan. *Aramaic and Hebrew Inscriptions from Mt. Gerizim and Samaria between Antiochus III and Antiochus IV Epiphanes.* CHANE 54. Leiden: Brill, 2012.

———. *Les manuscrits araméens du Wadi Daliyeh et la Samarie vers 450–332 av. J.-C.* CHANE 30. Leiden: Brill, 2007.

Eshel, Esther. "An Aramaic Ostracon of an Edomite Marriage Contract from Maresha, Dated 176 BCE." *IEJ* 46 (1996): 1–22.

Eshel, Esther, Amos Kloner, and Émile Puech. "Aramaic Scribal Exercises of the Hellenistic Period from Maresha: Bowls A and B." *BASOR* 345 (2007): 39–62.

Fales, Frederick Mario. "New Light on Assyro-Aramaic Interference: The Assur Ostracon." Pages 189–204 in *CAMSEMUD 2007: Proceedings of the 13th Italian Meeting of Afro-Asiatic Linguistics, Held in Udine, May 21st–24th, 2007.* Edited by Frederick Mario Fales and Giulia Francesca Grassi. HANE/M 10. Padova: S.A.R.G.O.N., 2010.

Fassberg, Steven E. "Salient Features of the Verbal System in the Aramaic Dead Sea Scrolls." Pages 65–81 in *Aramaica Qumranica: Proceedings of the Conference on the Aramaic Texts from Qumran in Aix-en-Provence 30 June–2 July 2008.* Edited by Katell Berthelot and Daniel Stökl Ben Ezra. STDJ 94. Leiden: Brill, 2010.

Fitzmyer, Joseph A. "The Phases of the Aramaic Language." Pages 57–74 in *A Wandering Aramean: Collected Aramaic Essays.* Grand Rapids: Eerdmans, 1997.

———. *Tobit.* CEJL. Berlin: de Gruyter, 2003.

García Martínez, Florentino. "Aramaica qumranica apocalyptica?" Pages 435–48 in *Aramaica Qumranica: Proceedings of the Conference on the Aramaic Texts from Qumran in Aix-en-Provence 30 June–2 July 2008*. Edited by Katell Berthelot and Daniel Stökl Ben Ezra. STDJ 94. Leiden: Brill, 2010.

———. *Qumran and Apocalyptic*. STDJ 9. Leiden: Brill, 1992.

Goff, Matthew. "A Blessed Rage for Order: Apocalypticism, Esoteric Revelation, and the Cultural Politics of Knowledge in the Hellenistic Age." *HBAI* 5 (2016): 193–211.

———. "Gilgamesh the Giant: The Qumran Book of Giants' Appropriation of *Gilgamesh* Motifs." *DSD* 16 (2009): 221–53.

Goff, Matthew, and Dennis Duke. "The Astronomy of the Qumran Fragments 4Q208 and 4Q209." *DSD* 21 (2014): 176–210.

Greenfield, Jonas C. "Standard Literary Aramaic." Pages 111–20 in vol. 1 of '*Al Kanfei Yonah: Collected Studies of Jonas C. Greenfield on Semitic Philology*. Edited by Shalom M. Paul, Michael E. Stone, and Avital Pinnick. Jerusalem: Magnes; Leiden: Brill, 2001.

Gzella, Holger. *A Cultural History of Aramaic: From the Beginnings to the Advent of Islam*. HdO 111. Leiden: Brill, 2015.

———. "Dating the Aramaic Texts from Qumran: Possibilities and Limits." *RevQ* 24/93 (2009): 61–78.

Gzella, Holger, and Margaretha L. Folmer, eds. *Aramaic in Its Historical and Linguistic Setting*. Wiesbaden: Harrassowitz, 2008.

Haubold, Johannes, Giovanni B. Lanfranchi, Robert Rollinger, and John M. Steele, eds. *The World of Berossos: Proceedings of the 4th International Colloquium on "The Ancient Near East between Classical and Ancient Oriental Traditions," Hatfield College, Durham 7th–9th July 2010*. Classica e Orientalia 5. Wiesbaden: Harrassowitz, 2013.

Hendel, Ronald. "Cultural Memory." Pages 28–46 in *Reading Genesis: Ten Methods*. Edited by Ronald Hendel. Cambridge: Cambridge University Press, 2010.

Horst, Pieter van der. "Antediluvian Knowledge." Pages 139–58 in *Japheth in the Tents of Shem: Studies on Jewish Hellenism in Antiquity*. CBET 32. Leuven: Peeters, 2002.

———. *Chaeremon: Egyptian Priest and Stoic Philosopher*. Leiden: Brill, 1987.

Jursa, Michael. "Ein Beamter flucht auf Aramäisch: Alphabetschreiber in der spätbabylonischen Epistolographie und die Rolle des Aramäischen in der babylonischen Verwaltung des sechsten Jahrhunderts v. Chr."

Pages 379–97 in *Leggo! Studies Presented to Frederick Mario Fales on the Occasion of His Sixty-Fifth Birthday*. Edited by Giovanni B. Lanfranchi, Daniele Morandi Bonacossi, Cinzia Pappi, and Simonetta Ponchia. Wiesbaden: Harrassowitz, 2012.

Khan, Geoffrey, and Lidia Napiorkowska, eds. *Neo-Aramaic and Its Linguistic Context*. Piscataway, NJ: Gorgias, 2015.

Koller, Aaron. "Four Dimensions of Linguistic Variation: Aramaic Dialects in and around Qumran." Pages 199–213 in vol. 1 of *The Dead Sea Scrolls in Context: Integrating the Dead Sea Scrolls in the Study of Ancient Texts, Languages, and Cultures*. Edited by Armin Lange, Emanuel Tov, and Matthias Weigold. VTSup 140. 2 vols. Leiden: Brill, 2011.

Kvanvig, Helge S. *Primeval History: Babylonian, Biblical, and Enochic; An Intertextual Reading*. JSJSup 149. Leiden: Brill, 2012.

Luukko, Mikko, Saana Svärd, and Raija Mattila, eds. *Of God(s), Trees, Kings, and Scholars: Neo-Assyrian and Related Studies in Honour of Simo Parpola*. Helsinki: Finnish Oriental Society, 2009.

Machiela, Daniel. "The Aramaic Dead Sea Scrolls and the Historical Development of Jewish Apocalyptic Literature." Pages 147–56 in *The Seleucid and Hasmonean Periods and the Apocalyptic Worldview: The First Enoch Seminar Nangeroni Meeting, Villa Cagnola, Gazzada (June 25–28, 2012)*. Edited by Lester L. Grabbe, Gabriele Boccaccini, and Jason Zurawski. LSTS 88. London: T&T Clark, 2016.

———. "The Aramaic Language of the Dead Sea Scrolls: Why It Matters and What Lies Ahead." *Ancient Jew Review*. 10 April 2017. https://tinyurl.com/SBL3551b.

———. "Aramaic Writings of the Second Temple Period and the Growth of Apocalyptic Thought: Another Survey of the Texts." *Judaïsme Ancien* 2 (2014): 113–34.

———. "The Compositional Setting and Implied Audience of Some Aramaic Texts from Qumran: A Working Hypothesis." Pages 168–202 in *Vision, Narrative, and Wisdom in the Aramaic Texts from Qumran: Essays from the Copenhagen Symposium, 14–15 August, 2017*. Edited by Mette Bundvad and Kasper Siegismund. STDJ 131. Leiden: Brill, 2019.

———. *A Handbook of the Aramaic Scrolls from the Qumran Caves: Manuscripts, Language, and Scribal Practices*. STDJ 140. Leiden: Brill, 2022.

———. "Situating the Aramaic Texts from Qumran: Reconsidering Their Language and Socio-historical Settings." Pages 88–109 in *Apocalyptic*

Thinking in Early Judaism: Engaging with John Collins' The Apocalyptic Imagination. Edited by Sidnie White Crawford and Cecilia Wassén. JSJSup 182. Leiden: Brill, 2018.

Magen, Yitzhak, Haggai Misgav, and Levana Tsfania. *The Aramaic, Hebrew and Samaritan Inscriptions.* Vol. 1 of *Mount Gerizim Excavations.* Jerusalem: Israel Antiquities Authority, 2004.

McCants, William F. *Founding Gods, Inventing Nations: Conquest and Culture Myths from Antiquity to Islam.* Princeton: Princeton University Press, 2012.

Milik, Józef T. *The Books of Enoch: Aramaic Fragments of Qumrân Cave 4.* With the collaboration of Matthew Black. Oxford: Clarendon, 1976.

Momigliano, Arnaldo. *Alien Wisdom: The Limits of Hellenization.* Cambridge: Cambridge University Press, 1975.

Moore, Carey A. *Tobit.* AB 40A. New York: Doubleday, 1996.

Muntz, Charles. *Diodorus Siculus and the World of the Late Roman Republic.* New York: Oxford University Press, 2017.

Muraoka, Takamitsu. *A Grammar of Qumran Aramaic.* ANES 38. Leuven: Peeters, 2011.

Naveh, Joseph, and Shaul Shaked. *Aramaic Documents from Ancient Bactria (Fourth Century BCE) from the Khalili Collections.* London: The Khalili Family Trust, 2012.

Neujahr, Matthew. "Babylonian Scribalism and the Production of Apocalypses and Related Early Jewish Texts." *HBAI* 5 (2016): 212–32.

Nickelsburg, George W. E. *1 Enoch 1: A Commentary on the Book of 1 Enoch, Chapters 1–36, 81–108.* Hermeneia. Minneapolis: Fortress, 2001.

Pearce, L. E. "Sepīru and ᴸᵘ́A.BA: Scribes of the Late First Millennium." Pages 355–68 in *Languages and Cultures in Contact: At the Crossroads of Civilizations in the Syro-Mesopotamian Realm.* Edited by Karel van Lerberghe and Gabriela Voet. OLA 96. Leuven: Peeters, 2000.

Perrin, Andrew B. "The Aramaic Imagination: Apocalyptic Thought and Genre in Dream-Visions among the Qumran Aramaic Texts." Pages 110–40 in *Apocalyptic Thinking in Early Judaism: Engaging with John Collins'* The Apocalyptic Imagination. Edited by Sidnie White Crawford and Cecilia Wassén. JSJSup 182. Leiden: Brill, 2018.

———. *The Dynamics of Dream-Vision Revelation in the Aramaic Dead Sea Scrolls.* JAJSup 19. Göttingen: Vandenhoeck & Ruprecht, 2015.

Popović, Mladen. "The Emergence of Aramaic and Hebrew Scholarly Texts: Transmission and Translation of Alien Wisdom." Pages 81–114 in *The Dead Sea Scrolls: Transmission of Traditions and Production of Texts.* Edited by Sarianna Metso, Hindy Najman, and Eileen Schuller. STDJ 92. Leiden: Brill, 2010.

———. "Pseudepigraphy and a Scribal Sense of the Past in the Ancient Mediterranean: A Copy of the Book of the Words of the Vision of Amram." Pages 308–18 in *Is There a Text in This Cave? Studies in the Textuality of the Dead Sea Scrolls in Honour of George J. Brooke.* Edited by Ariel Feldman, Charlotte Hempel, and Maria Cioată. STDJ 119. Leiden: Brill, 2017.

Porten, Bezalel, and Ada Yardeni. *Textbook of Aramaic Ostraca from Idumea.* 3 vols. University Park, PA: Eisenbrauns, 2014–2018.

Portier-Young, Anathea. *Apocalypse against Empire: Theologies of Resistance in Early Judaism.* Grand Rapids: Eerdmans, 2011.

———. "Languages of Identity and Obligation: Daniel as Bilingual Book." *VT* 60 (2010): 98–115.

Puech, Émile, ed. *Qumrân Grotte 4.XXII: Textes araméens, première partie, 4Q529–549.* DJD 31. Oxford: Clarendon, 2001.

Reed, Annette Yoshiko. "Abraham as Chaldean Scientist and Father of the Jews: Josephus, *Ant.* 1.154–168, and the Greco-Roman Discourse about Astronomy/Astrology." *JSJ* 35 (2004): 119–58.

———. "Writing Jewish Astronomy in the Early Hellenistic Age: The Enochic Astronomical Book as Aramaic Wisdom and Archival Impulse." *DSD* 24 (2017): 1–37.

Roark, Kyle. "A Crisis of Wisdom: The Early Enoch Apocalypses and the Cultural Politics of Knowledge in the Hellenistic Age." PhD diss. Florida State University, 2018.

Sanders, Seth L. *From Adapa to Enoch: Scribal Culture and Religious Vision in Judea and Babylon.* TSAJ 167. Tübingen: Mohr Siebeck, 2017.

Schattner-Rieser, Ursula. *L'araméen des manuscrits de la mer Morte. 1, Grammaire.* IELOA 5. Prahins: Éditions du Zèbre, 2004.

Schniedewind, William M. *A Social History of Hebrew: Its Origins through the Rabbinic Period.* New Haven: Yale University Press, 2013.

Sokoloff, Michael. "Notes on the Aramaic Fragments of Enoch from Cave 4." *Maarav* 1 (1978–1979): 197–224.

Stone, Michael E. "The Book of Enoch and Judaism in the Third Century BCE." *CBQ* 40 (1978): 479–92.

Stuckenbruck, Loren T. "Pseudepigraphy and First Person Discourse in the Dead Sea Documents: From the Aramaic Texts to Writing of the Yaḥad." Pages 295–326 in *The Dead Sea Scrolls and Contemporary*

Culture: Proceedings of the International Conference Held at the Israel Museum, Jerusalem (July 6-8, 2008). Edited by Adolfo Daniel Roitman, Lawrence H. Schiffman, and Shani Tzoref. STDJ 93. Leiden: Brill, 2011.

Sugandhi, Namita. "Context, Content, and Composition: Questions of Intended Meaning and the Aśokan Edicts." *South Asia* 42 (2003): 224-46.

Sulimani, Iris. *Diodorus' Mythistory and the Pagan Mission: Historiography and Culture-Heroes in the First Pentad of the* Bibliotheke. MnemosyneSup 331. Leiden: Brill, 2011.

Thraede, Klaus. "Das Lob des Erfinders: Bemerkungen zur Analyse der Heuremata-Katalogue." *RMP* 105 (1962): 158-86.

———. "Erfinder II (geistesgeschichtlich)." *RAC* 5 (1962): 1191-278.

Tigchelaar, Eibert J. C. "Aramaic Texts from Qumran and the Authoritativeness of Hebrew Scriptures: Preliminary Observations." Pages 155-71 in *Authoritative Scriptures in Ancient Judaism*. Edited by Mladen Popović. JSJSup 141. Leiden: Brill, 2010.

Verbrugghe, Gerald P., and John M. Wickersham. *Berossos and Manetho, Introduced and Translated*. Ann Arbor: University of Michigan Press, 1996.

Wacholder, Ben Zion. "The Ancient Judaeo-Aramaic Literature (500-164 B.C.E.): A Classification of Pre-Qumran Texts." Pages 257-81 in *Archaeology and History in the Dead Sea Scrolls: The New York University Conference in Memory of Yigael Yadin*. Edited by Lawrence H. Schiffman. JSPSup 8. Sheffield: JSOT Press, 1990.

Daniel Traditions and the Qumran Movement? Reconsidering the Interface between Texts, Traditions, Identities, and Movements

Andrew B. Perrin

1. Reopening the Question of Daniel and Qumran Beginnings

Daniel's influence on Qumran origins and outlooks has been explored at intervals. However, most discussions of this sort equate Daniel with the canonical work of his namesake and isolate the Qumranites as a solo sectarian group awaiting the eschaton off the saline beaches of the Dead Sea. One implication of this comparative approach is that the connections or parallels identified are largely terminological (e.g., alleged shared references to Maskilim, *raz*, or Kittim) or of a generic, theological sort (e.g., a broadly defined common interest in eschatology and apocalypticism). For example, John C. Trever argued twelve points that, on his read of the texts, pointed to the authorship of the biblical book by none other than the Teacher of Righteousness.[1] Frederick F. Bruce, while aware of a few other Aramaic texts such as Prayer of Nabonidus and Pseudo-Daniel, argued a somewhat more nuanced case for the interaction, even influence, of the book of Daniel on the Qumran group.[2]

---

1. John C. Trever, "The Book of Daniel and the Origin of the Qumran Community," *BA* 48 (1985): 89–102.
2. Frederick F. Bruce, "The Book of Daniel and the Qumran Community," in *Neotestamentica et Semitica: Studies in Honour of Matthew Black*, ed. E. Earle Ellis and Max E. Wilcox (Edinburgh: T&T Clark, 1969), 221–35. The main problem with Bruce's article is the motivation for the comparative study, which has little to do with an interest in either Daniel or Qumran; rather, the implications described by article's end are to illumine a certain type of New Testament exegesis affirming "the foundations of Christian theology" (235).

Most recently, and with greater methodological awareness, Charlotte Hempel advanced the discussion in a more helpful direction. While not understating the importance of similar terms and topics in the book of Daniel and select Hebrew sectarian writings, Hempel's study took note of the literary diversity of Danielic tradition and social multiplicity of the author(s)/editor(s)/group(s) behind the writings discovered in the Judean Desert.[3]

In this paper, I take a similar tack by adopting the following dual premise as a departure point. First, the Dead Sea Scrolls attest to the rapid development of a broader set of Aramaic Danielic traditions in antiquity—the eventual biblical book of Daniel is but one representation of that tradition in the mid-Second Temple period.[4] Second, the variety of views on ancient Essene life, thought, and practice in the classical sources, insights from the archaeology of Qumran, and literary finds associated closely with the so-called sectarian group that lived there, suggest that the Qumranites were likely but one expression of a larger movement in this era.[5]

Using the Aramaic Pseudo-Daniel (4Q243-244; 4Q245) materials as a case study, I will reconsider three key aspects of the fragments that may suggest they originated in a scribal or communal setting that reflects this broader socioreligious diversity. These are: (1) scribal features (particularly, the use of paleo-Hebrew for penning divine epithets or the avoidance of the Tetragrammaton); (2) approaches for extending scriptural traditions (including shared exegetical developments of the Psalms for historiographical purposes); and (3) conceptual categories or motifs of mutual interest to insider groups (for example, the emergence of an eschatological elect). While the Pseudo-Daniel texts are not sectarian in

---

3. Charlotte Hempel, "The Community Rule and the Book of Daniel," in *The Qumran Rule Texts in Context: Collected Studies*, TSAJ 154 (Tübingen: Mohr Siebeck, 2013), 231–52. Hempel's study also extends into other areas relevant to social comparative study, such as bilingual linguistic cultures and learned scribal contexts.

4. Peter W. Flint, "The Daniel Tradition at Qumran," in *The Book of Daniel: Composition and Reception*, ed. John J. Collins and Peter W. Flint, 2 vols., VTSup 83 (Leiden: Brill, 2001), 2:329–67; and Loren T. Stuckenbruck, "The Formation and Reformation of Daniel in the Dead Sea Scrolls," in *Scripture and the Scrolls*, vol. 1 of *The Bible and the Dead Sea Scrolls*, ed. James H. Charlesworth (Waco, TX: Baylor University Press, 2006), 101–30.

5. John J. Collins, *Beyond the Qumran Community: The Sectarian Movement of the Dead Sea Scrolls* (Grand Rapids: Eerdmans, 2010).

the traditional sense, they provide a space for rethinking the way complex literary traditions were informed by, or formed within, communities that may reflect some aspects of Qumran identity and thought.[6] Before delving into these details, however, I will introduce the texts collected under the modern title, Pseudo-Daniel.

2. Survey of the Aramaic Pseudo-Daniel Materials

Most modern readers know the figure of Daniel as a sage, courtier, dream interpreter, and lion tamer. This impressive resume, of course, is established in the Aramaic-Hebrew hybrid book that turns up in the Hebrew scriptures. In ancient Judaism, however, Daniel's profile extended beyond the tales told in that collection. The so-called Additions to Daniel in the Greek scriptures, for example, cast Daniel in new roles and episodes that are both entertaining and edifying for the reader. He slays a dragon with a giant hairball, offers eloquent praise and prayers at length, receives a delivery order of late-night food from Habakkuk during his overnighter in the lion's den, and rushes to the aid of a Jewish woman falsely accused by lusting voyeurs. While the Aramaic Dead Sea Scrolls do not offer up versions of these tales, they do reveal a still broader set of previously unknown works that attest to the robust Danielic imagination of ancient Jewish scribes.

Arguably, the most important manuscripts to cast Daniel in new settings are 4Q243-244 and 4Q245. Generally referred to as Pseudo-Daniel, these scrolls likely represent two separate compositions. All the fragmentary texts are associated with the figure of Daniel, merge historical reviews from the distant past with eschatological outlooks, and seem to critique aspects of the religious and political life of the mid-Second Temple period. Their historical reflections and forecasts, however, adopt a tighter focus on Israelite history than the biblical book, which has a greater interest

---

6. To date, the potential sectarian quality of 4Q243-244 has been painted only in broad strokes. John J. Collins and Peter W. Flint suggest that the relation of these manuscripts to the "Dead Sea sect may be analogous to that of *Jubilees* or the Enoch literature. It is sectarian in a broad sense, insofar as it culminates in the emergence of an elect group, but it does not refer explicitly to the Qumran *yaḥad*"; see their "Pseudo-Daniel," in *Qumran Cave 4.XVII: Parabiblical Texts, Part 3*, ed. George Brooke et al., DJD 22 (Oxford: Clarendon, 1996), 137; see also James C. VanderKam, "Apocalyptic Tradition in the Dead Sea Scrolls and the Religion of Qumran," in *Religion in the Dead Sea Scrolls*, ed. John J. Collins and Robert A. Kugler (Grand Rapids: Eerdmans, 2000), 118.

in the happenings on the world stage in view of power shifts of ancient Near Eastern and Mediterranean empires. In this way, the newly recovered Pseudo-Daniel texts may provide soundbites of lost conversations within and between ancient Jewish groups regarding the relationship between the nation's ancestral, monarchic, and priestly past; their tumultuous present experience under Jewish leadership and imperial oversight; and expectations of an imminent eschaton.

2.1. Discovery and Publication

The modern story of the Pseudo-Daniel scrolls begins with the discovery of the trove of Qumran Cave 4. By 1956, Józef T. Milik published key fragments of all three of the Pseudo-Daniel manuscripts.[7] His presentation became foundational for a number of editions and studies, most of which entailed only modest tweaks to his original transcription.[8] As Michael O. Wise observed, the Palestine Archaeological Museum (PAM) image plates taken between 1956 and 1957 indicate Milik's increasing identification and organization of fragments at an early time.[9] The full scope of the texts, however, remained unknown for decades.

The availability of microfiche images in the early 1990s resulted in some new presentations of Pseudo-Daniel, including a then-unknown fragment in the controversial edition by Robert Eisenman and Wise.[10]

---

7. For Milik's presentation and discussions, see his "Priére de Nabonide et autres écrits d'un cycle de Daniel," *RB* 63 (1956): 411–15.

8. Rudolf Meyer, *Das Gebet des Nabonid: Eine in den Qumran-Handschriften wiederentdeckte Weisheitserzählung*, SSAWL 107 (Berlin: Akademie Verlag, 1962), 85–94; Alfred Mertens, *Das Buch Daniel im Lichte der Texte vom Toten Meer*, SBM 12 (Echter: KBW Verlag, 1971), 42–50; Joseph A. Fitzmyer and Daniel J. Harrington, *A Manual of Palestinian Aramaic Texts* (Rome: Pontifical Biblical Institute, 1978), 4–9; Florentino García Martínez, *Qumran and Apocalyptic*, STDJ 9 (Leiden: Brill, 1992), 137–61; and Florentino García Martínez and Eibert J. C. Tigchelaar, *The Dead Sea Scrolls Study Edition* (Leiden: Brill, 1997), 1:488–93. See also Klaus Beyer, *Die aramäischen Texte vom Toten Meer*, 2 vols. (Göttingen: Vandenhoeck & Ruprecht, 1984), 1:224–25, 2:139–42; and Beyer, *Die aramäischen Texte vom Toten Meer; Ergänzungsband* (Göttingen: Vandenhoeck & Ruprecht, 1994), 105–7.

9. Michael O. Wise, "4Q245 (psDan^c ar) and the High Priesthood of Judas Maccabaeus," *DSD* 12 (2005): 313–62.

10. Michael O. Wise and Robert Eisenman, *The Dead Sea Scrolls Uncovered* (New York: Penguin, 1993), 68.

Eventually, John J. Collins and Peter W. Flint published the fragments of all three manuscripts in DJD 22.[11] The latest contribution to the publication history of the Pseudo-Daniel texts are found in the open-access collection of the Leon Levy Dead Sea Scrolls Digital Library, which includes the scanned PAM plates as well as new digital infrared and full spectrum color images taken between August 2012 and June 2013.

2.2. Manuscript Profiles, Text Identifications, and Compositional Dating

Traditionally, the Pseudo-Daniel fragments were studied as a single work due to their common association with the figure of Daniel. On its own, however, this association confirms only a shared tradition oriented around a figure. The modest overlap between 4Q243 13 and 4Q244 12, and potential overlap between 4Q243 2 and 4Q244 1, indicates that this pair of manuscripts constitute copies of the same work. Collins and Flint underscored that since there are no certain overlaps between 4Q243–244 and 4Q245, the latter likely attests to a different Aramaic Daniel composition.[12] It is possible, however, that references to priestly forefathers in 4Q243 28 relate to the list of priestly figures in 4Q245 1 I, yet the materials are highly fragmentary at these points. In view of this, Collins and Flint allow that if minor reconstructions of both fragments are accepted there is "possible evidence for a relationship between 4Q243 and 4Q245."[13] At most, this parallel reveals a shared thematic interest in priestly history in the two works represented by 4Q243–244 and 4Q245.

The content and quality of the individual Pseudo-Daniel manuscripts varies. The scribal hands of all three texts suggest their production in the early first century CE.[14] In order to arrive at an approximate date of the original composition of the Pseudo-Daniel texts, we must balance insights from the material quality of the manuscripts with references to historical individuals and eras within the texts.[15] In view of this, Collins and Flint

---

11. Collins and Flint, "Pseudo-Daniel," 97–164 + pl. vii–x. Following this, Beyer also revised aspects of his translation in *Die aramäischen Texte vom Toten Meer*, 2:140.

12. Collins and Flint, "Pseudo-Daniel," 154–55.

13. Collins and Flint, "Pseudo-Daniel," 116.

14. Collins and Flint, "Pseudo-Daniel," 97.

15. Regarding 4Q243–244, Lorenzo DiTommaso, *The Book of Daniel and the Apocryphal Daniel Literature*, SVTP 20 (Leiden: Brill, 2005), 207, proposed that "the original composition is at least a century older [than the palaeographic dates of the

proposed that the range of the original composition of Pseudo-Daniel is "somewhere between the beginning of the second century BCE and the coming of Pompey" (ca. mid-second century BCE to 63 BCE).[16] Several factors suggest that this is a plausible compositional date.

The inclusion of Hellenistic names, such as "Balakros" (בלכרוס) (4Q243 21 2), suggests the historical review of 4Q243–244 extended into the days of Alexander the Great's conquest. The latest figure included in the genealogy of 4Q245 is the Hasmonean High Priest Simon (142–134 BCE), suggesting that at least this work comes from no earlier than the mid- to late-first century BCE. The awareness of Enochic lore as well as the shared exegetical approach with the Damascus Document (see below) suggests the scribes behind these texts are conversant in Second Temple period traditions. As Collins and Flint observed, "none of these [i.e., 1 Enoch and CD] is older than the second century BCE."[17]

2.3. Themes and Genre

The narrative of 4Q243–244 is set in a foreign court context. In the technical sense, the work is not pseudepigraphic: it is associated with Daniel, but not attributed to him in a first-person voice.[18] It is likely that at least part of the work featured Daniel in dialogue with, or in the service of, the Babylonian ruler "Belshazzar" (4Q243 2; cf. 4Q243 1; 3; 4Q244 1–3; 4). At one point, Daniel accesses a "writing" (4Q243 6), which is likely the source of his privileged knowledge of the past, present, and future. It is unknown if this document was presented to Daniel in a revelation or if it is a volume of ancestral traditions forecasting the future.

While the exact order of the fragments of the work represented by 4Q243–244 is not certain, its progression likely flowed chronologically through eras and episodes from the antediluvian age and ancestral past, through the exile, into the imperial age of the Hellenistic period, and

---

manuscripts]." For 4Q245, he commented that the work "may be dated to the early first century CE." As described in the commentary below, it seems the genealogies of these texts culminate in the early days of the Hasmonean dynasty. While I am less convinced of such a late date for 4Q245, DiTommaso's proposal does open up the question of the continued transmission of the text in the Herodian period.

16. Collins and Flint, "Pseudo-Daniel," 137–38.
17. Collins and Flint, "Pseudo-Daniel," 137.
18. DiTommaso, *Book of Daniel*, 207.

ending with an outlook toward the eschaton.[19] While Milik was incorrect about the presence of a four kingdoms scheme in this narrative, the historical timeline of 4Q243–244 does feature some temporal markers. These include: eras clocked in durations of "years" (4Q243 12 1; 16 1; 20 2); at least one mention of a jubilee period (4Q243 12); as well as both generic references to kings (4Q243 14 2; 20 2; 24) and specific rulers (4Q243 13 3; 21 2). Since this historical retrospect and prospect are anchored in a writing, 4Q243–244 engages in *ex eventu* prophecy. The work both reviews and previews history through the ages, which claims greater credibility for the predictions of events in the author and audience's own day.

The reliable record of the past and prediction of the present is an essential foundation for the work's speculation of the close-at-hand future. The full details of the eschatological outlook of 4Q243–244, however, are unknown. Scattered among them are mentions of the deliverance of the people and likely arrival of a "holy kingdom" (4Q243 16), inklings of the decimation of foes perhaps after an eschatological war (4Q243 25), and references to the emergence of an elect group juxtaposed with those who are blind and wayward (4Q243 24). Because of this selective and strategic historical review, *ex eventu* forecast of events, and portrayal of the imminent end of the age, the composition attested in 4Q243–244 certainly has an apocalyptic tone and may have been a formal apocalypse in its original complete form.[20]

Since the relationship between 4Q245 and the composition represented by 4Q243–244 is not as clear as once thought, the fragments of these two works should not be used to reconstruct a single composition.[21] There are also important thematic differences that caution against this integration. For example, the historiographical technique of 4Q245

---

19. For a general structure along these lines, see Collins and Flint, "Pseudo-Daniel," 138–51.

20. The fragmentary nature of the evidence, of course, limits our ability to say with confidence whether the work was a formal apocalypse. For a full bibliography and analysis of scholarly characterizations of the Pseudo-Daniel texts as either apocalyptic or apocalypses, see Andrew B. Perrin, *The Dynamics of Dream-Vision Revelation in the Aramaic Dead Sea Scrolls*, JAJSup 19 (Göttingen: Vandenhoeck & Ruprecht, 2015), 240–44.

21. Several earlier editions and studies attempt integrative reconstructions, seemingly influenced heavily by the proposed outline of Milik. Compare, for example, Milik, "Prière de Nabonide," 412–15; Fitzmyer and Harrington, *Manual of Palestinian Aramaic Texts*, 4–8; Beyer, *Die aramäischen Texte vom Toten Meer*,

is largely genealogical and focused on Israel's kingdom and cult, whereas 4Q243-244 adopts an episodic approach when reflecting on the times, people, and places of Israel's former days.

While 4Q243-244 and 4Q245 are unrelated textually, the two works do exhibit some formal and thematic similarities. Both articulate a view of Israelite history that accounts for the past, present, and future. Both likely present Daniel as a privileged sage, reader, or revealer of booklore. Both seem to culminate with eschatological content. In the case of 4Q245, the emergence of two juxtaposed groups—one blind and wayward, the other holy and elect—is an essential part of the comment on the present and speculation about the future (4Q245 2). On these counts, 4Q245 is also certainly apocalyptic in its orientation and may have been part of another previously unknown Danielic apocalypse.

If the date range proposed above is correct, and in view of these preliminary observations on key ideological and literary themes, the Aramaic Pseudo-Daniel texts attest to the rapid development of the Danielic traditions starting in the mid-Second Temple period, provide a space for rethinking the evolution of apocalyptic thinking, include new insights into the theological speculation on Israel's past, present and future, and spark fresh questions of the social and scribal worlds of groups potentially related to the Qumran movement.

3. The Orientation of 4Q243-244 to Qumran's Scribal Culture and Conceptual Framework

As is clear from the overview of the Aramaic Pseudo-Daniel fragments, these materials and the compositions they represent are at once complex and fragmentary. There remain many questions about the orientation and overlap of fragments, the possibility of compositional reconstructions, their scribal origins, and the circumstances of their reception at Qumran. While our understanding of the Aramaic Dead Sea Scrolls corpus is still developing and our conception of the Qumran movement evolving, in what follows I will begin to explore some of the ways the Pseudo-Daniel materials may provide a departure point for exploring the interface between the traditions and scribal cultures of Qumran with those that

---

1:224-25, 2:139-42; Beyer, *Ergänzungsband*, 105-7; Wise and Eisenman, *Dead Sea Scrolls Uncovered*, 64-68; and García Martínez, *Qumran and Apocalyptic*, 138-40.

created the Pseudo-Daniel materials. As a conversation starter, I will consider three aspects of 4Q243–244 that relate to scribal practices, exegetical approaches, and eschatological speculations.

3.1. An Analogous Scribal Approach: Paleo-Hebrew and a Divine Epithet in 4Q243 1 2

The discovery of the Dead Sea Scrolls not only provided access to a yet-unknown trove of manuscripts for literatures received or written in the mid-Second Temple period. They also opened up a new view of the scribal culture and communities that cultivated and transmitted such writings. Prior to these finds, our knowledge of manuscript preparation and scribal culture leading up to the Common Era was largely inferential. The Scrolls, however, provided primary sources to study the process and products of scribal settings.

There are many aspects of the scribal execution of the Pseudo-Daniel texts we might consider. One feature, however, stands out as particularly intriguing for the present topic: the use of a paleo-Hebrew script to pen a divine name in 4Q243 1 2. Unfortunately, there is not much context for this fragment. The few words and phrases that survive suggest a third-person narrative in which Daniel is likely conversing with another figure in the narrative, presumably a monarch in the court setting.[22] The text and translation of this small fragment are as follows.[23]

1 שאיל דניאל לממר בד[י]ל [ ]
2 אלהך וֹמנׄןׄ]ׄ[ ]ל[ ]
3 יצלה ינׄ[ ]
4 עׄ[ ]

1. he asked Daniel, saying, "Be[ca]use [...]
2. your God and from where ... [...] ... [...]

---

22. The verb שאל ("to ask") directed at Daniel indicates dialogue that would fit within a court tale context. Milik, "Prière de Nabonide," 412, infers that the question posed to Daniel here resulted in the sage's review of history that follows. Note that a king addresses Daniel with a question on three occasions in the biblical book (Dan 2:26; 5:13; 6:20).

23. All Aramaic texts for Pseudo-Daniel are adapted from Collins and Flint, "Pseudo-Daniel," with slight revisions mostly pertaining to a reduction of theorized textual reconstructions. Translations are my own.

3. he will pray ... [...]
4. ... [...]

Several scholars have noted that Jewish writers and scribes after the third century BCE exhibit a calculated avoidance of the Tetragrammaton.[24] In many instances, the Qumran texts reflect this patterned avoidance as well as a diversity of strategies for encoding or representing the Tetragrammaton in both copied and compositional materials. One such approach, of course, was the use of paleo-Hebrew. Emanuel Tov observed that this scribal technique is concentrated in writings "mainly of a nonbiblical, sectarian nature," which led him to conclude there is "a special link between the writing of the divine names in paleo-Hebrew characters and the Qumran community."[25] Since his discussion and conclusion focused on the avoidance or handling of the tetragrammaton in Hebrew materials, Tov made no mention of the Qumran Aramaic texts. Florentino García Martínez extended in this direction and undertook a comparative study of the scribal practices reflected in the Aramaic Dead Sea Scrolls with the Hebrew materials in the collection. He concluded that, "there are no differences in the scribal practices among the two sorts of texts."[26] I would argue, however, that both the social connection proposed by Tov and the scribal consistency deduced by García Martínez need revision in view of the form in 4Q243 1 2.

---

24. Hartmut Stegemann, "Religionsgeschichtliche Erwägungen zu den Gottesbezeichnungen in der Qumrantexten," in *Qumrân: Sa piété, sa théologie et son milieu*, ed. Mathias Delcor, BETL 46 (Leuven: Leuven University Press, 1978), 195–217; Patrick Skehan, "The Divine Name at Qumran, in the Masada Scroll, and in the Septuagint," *BIOSCS* 13 (1980): 14–44; and Carol A. Newsom, "'Sectually Explicit' Literature from Qumran," in *The Hebrew Bible and Its Interpreters*, ed. William H. Propp, Baruch Halpern, and David Noel Freedman (Winona Lake, IN: Eisenbrauns, 1990), 167–87.

25. Taking together the observations on Emanuel Tov, *Scribal Practices and Approaches Reflected in the Texts Found in the Judean Desert*, STDJ 54 (Leiden: Brill, 2004), 238, 243. Tov also allows that, "when writing the diving names in paleo-Hebrew characters, the Qumran scribes may have followed the practice of an earlier generation of scribes or, alternatively, each scribe may have initiated this practice in accord with his own beliefs" (243).

26. Florentino García Martínez, "Scribal Practices in the Aramaic Literary Texts from Qumran," in *Myths, Martyrs, and Modernity: Studies in the History of Religions in Honour of Jan N. Bremmer*, ed. Jitse H. F. Dijkstra, Justin Kroesen, and Yme Kuiper, SHR 127 (Leiden: Brill, 2010), 330.

This line features a suffixed form of the divine epithet אלֹהא ("God") written in paleo-Hebrew. The scribe's familiarity with the paleo-Hebrew alphabet, however, is questionable: the medial *kaf* is neither square nor paleo-script. Apparently out of his depth, the scribe deferred to yet a third hand, which Milik rightly characterized as closer to a Samaritan script.[27] Regardless of the peculiarity of this suffix, the scribe is quite clearly plying a practice akin to what we find in the Hebrew texts. Yet there are some important distinctions.

4Q243 1 2 is the sole place in the Dead Sea Scrolls where paleo-Hebrew is used to encode a divine epithet *other* than the Tetragrammaton. With a tighter focus on the Qumran Aramaic texts, it is also the only fragment known to deploy paleo-Hebrew in this fashion.[28] Daniel Machiela demonstrated that, in light of the use of four dots to represent the form אלהא in an Aramaic Tobit manuscript (4Q196 17 I, 5; 18 1) and rendering of יהוה as אלהא in the Cave 11 Job translation (Job 42:10; 11QtgJob 38 3–4), the use of paleo-Hebrew for the form אלהכא in 4Q243 1 2 likely signals a broader appreciation of the sanctity of the epithet אלהא within some Aramaic scribal settings.[29] In view of this, we might say that the scribe of 4Q243 exhibits a similar sensitivity and solution to what has been observed in the Hebrew materials for handling the tetragrammaton yet does so for an epithet that was the common or closest equivalent in Aramaic.

With such fleeting fragmentary evidence, it is hard to know how much to make of this peculiar yet particular scribal feature in 4Q243. Since the feature is a way of encoding the epithet, it must be understood as an element that originates in the transmission process of the work. That is, the script of a work is not an inherent, compositional feature in the traditional sense. It is a scribal expression. In this case, however, the shift to a paleo-Hebrew script is no mere preference or convention. Rather, it is rooted

---

27. Cited in Collins and Flint, "Pseudo-Daniel," 98. As Alan D. Crown notes, of the three scripts typical of Samaritan manuscripts, the majuscule hand "is a developed form of the palaeo-Hebrew script"; see his *Samaritan Scribes and Manuscripts*, TSAJ 80 (Tübingen: Mohr Siebeck, 2001), 204. While the abecedaries of Samaritan texts he presents postdate the Qumran finds by a millennium at minimum, the general correspondence between the medial *kaf* in 4Q243 and many Samaritan scripts is clear (189–97, 235–42).

28. 4Q244 5 II, 5 includes the form אֱלוֹה[ין in a square script, not a paleo-Hebrew hand, as in 4Q243 1 2. It is possible that the word here is referring to "gods."

29. Daniel A. Machiela, "Lord or God? Tobit and the Tetragrammaton," *CBQ* 75 (2013): 463–72.

in social, cultural, and ideological realities. In this way, we may surmise *why* this change was made (i.e., the name was viewed as sacrosanct and deserving of a particular script). Discerning *when* this scribal interaction with the Aramaic Pseudo-Daniel tradition occurred is more difficult. As noted above, the palaeographical dating of the text provides a *terminus ante quem* in the first century CE. It is also entirely possible that the form at 4Q243 1 2 was carried over from the scribes' *Vorlage*. This leads us to the question of *where* this scribal feature fits in the known or theorized social landscape of the mid-Second Temple period. The answer it seems might point in two directions.

Option one: 4Q243 may be a copy of an outside composition that bears the marks of an insider scribal culture of Qumran. It is generally thought that the Aramaic Dead Sea Scrolls were written before and beyond the Qumran community. If Tov is correct in perceiving a close connection between the sect and the practice of ciphering divine epithets with paleo-Hebrew, then the feature of 4Q243 1 2 might reflect the receiving scribal culture's sensitivities and preferences. On this explanation, then, the feature at 4Q243 1 2 would represent both an adaptation of the traditional approach reserved for the tetragrammaton and serve as one of our clearest examples of Qumran scribal interpretation of a received Aramaic tradition. It would also open up the question of if, or how, an outsider text might *become* sectarian through use, transmission, or representation by an insider community.

Option two: perhaps 4Q243 was brought to Qumran as is and includes features that reflect the scribal culture of a group with similar proclivities to that of the Qumran community. Admittedly, our understanding of the larger movement of which the Qumran community was a part exists only in outline. However, is it possible that some Aramaic writings, such as the Pseudo-Daniel texts, betray features that help us work toward a better understanding of this broader movement? On this explanation, then, the use of paleo-Hebrew to cipher a divine epithet in an Aramaic text may suggest that this practice was not a defining feature of the Qumran community but one of a larger scribal movement that left some of its fingerprints on works written elsewhere but received at Qumran.

What is common to both of these potential explanations is that, in different ways, they reveal an interface between the thought, culture, and practice of the group that lived at Qumran with that of the group(s) that created and cultivated the Aramaic texts. It is possible that we might extend this observation further by considering overlapping approaches to interpreting and extending authoritative Hebrew traditions.

3.2. A Shared Exegetical Tradition: Interpreting the "Nations" of Ps 106:41 as "Nebuchadnezzar" in Damascus Document and 4Q243

Jewish literature of the Second Temple period is undeniably indebted to the ideas taking shape in the emerging collections of Israel's ancestral heritage. Scribes of the day were both conversant in and conversing with these developing traditions, often evolving them by the very same interpretive mechanisms that shaped Hebrew scriptural traditions. It is correct to underscore that the Bible did not yet exist in this world. The media culture was nigh, the concept of a canon was at best nascent, and the vitality of scripture at Qumran and in the Greek scriptures attest to fluidity rather than fixity. Yet it is problematic to overlook the pervasive and formative influence of emerging Hebrew scriptures on the literature, thought, and culture of the period. Andrew Teeter commented that "the majority of the literature of Second Temple Judaism would be inconceivable apart from the generative force of a corpus of compositions at its center roughly comparable in shape and scope to the received Hebrew Bible."[30] As Eibert J. C. Tigchelaar observed in a preliminary study, the Aramaic Dead Sea Scrolls are no exception.[31]

For the present topic, there are two tiers of the question to consider for a comparative study between the so-called sectarian Hebrew writings and the Aramaic Dead Sea Scrolls. First, we could gauge what authoritative traditions are used, alluded to, or embedded in the discourses of these materials. Second, and arguably more instructive, we could explore similarities and differences in how the scribes of both collections engaged and extended their antecedent traditions. Our first tier, then, is concerned with the types or range of traditions used, the second, with the scribal tactics deployed

---

30. Andrew Teeter, "The Hebrew Bible and/as Second Temple Period Literature," *DSD* 20 (2013): 354.

31. Eibert J. C. Tigchelaar, "Aramaic Texts from Qumran and the Authoritativeness of Hebrew Scriptures: Preliminary Observations," in *Authoritative Scriptures in Ancient Judaism*, ed. Mladen Popović, JSJSup 141 (Leiden: Brill, 2010), 155–71. For a preliminary tabulation, see the lists of Armin Lange and Matthias Weigold, *Biblical Quotations and Allusions in Second Temple Jewish Literature*, JAJSup 5 (Göttingen: Vandenhoeck & Ruprecht, 2011).

when incorporating those traditions in new literary contexts or interpretive frameworks. While I will not undertake a comprehensive analysis of this in the present study, the handling and extension of a cluster of Psalms allusions in some Pseudo-Daniel fragments deserve special attention due to similarities with Qumran scribal culture and interpretive approaches.

The relevant Aramaic text for this comparison is found in the overlapping materials of 4Q243 13 and 4Q244 12, which I present here in combined fashion based on Collins and Flint's reconstruction in DJD 22. Underlines indicate overlaps between the fragments, which reveal no variant readings.

1 [ ] א[סֹחֹרו בני ישראל אנפיהון מן]‏[32]
2 [דב]חין לבניהון לשידי טעותא ורגז עליהון אלוהין וא[מר] למנתן
3 אנון ביד נֹב[33][כדנצר מלך ב]בל ולאחרבא ארעהון מנהון מן די ש]
4 [ ]○○אשֹתֹאֹ[○] [○ בני גלותא ○]

1. [...] the Israelites [t]urned their face away from [...]
2. [... sac]rificing their children to demons of error. So God became angry at them and he sa[id] to give

---

32. The initial verb is better preserved in 4Q244 12 1 than in 4Q243 13 1. Milik's preliminary edition reads בחרו ("they chose") (Milik, "Prière de Nabonide," 413; so also Fitzmyer and Harrington, *Manual of Palestinian Aramaic Texts*, 6; García Martínez, *Qumran and Apocalyptic*, 141; and García Martínez and Tigchelaar, *Dead Sea Scrolls Study Edition*, 1:488). Beyer, *Ergänzungsband*, 106, reads the verb as סתרו ("to be hidden"). In the DJD edition, Collins and Flint ("Pseudo-Daniel," 107) follow Milik, and Beyer, *Die aramäischen Texte vom Toten Meer*, 2:140, subsequently deferred to this reading. While neither of these options seems correct, they share elements of the best reading. The ink traces remaining for the first character on 4Q244 12 1 are commensurate with a *samek* (so Beyer) and the second character evident in both 4Q243 13 1 and 4Q244 1 is certainly a *ḥet* (so Milik, Collins and Flint). Edward M. Cook, *Dictionary of Qumran Aramaic* (Winona Lake, IN: Eisenbrauns, 2015), 32, 168, correctly deduced the verb סחר here and proposes the reconstruction of an *Aphel* verb א]סֹחֹרו, "to turn away," which is accepted and included above.

33. Remains for the reading נֹב[כדנצר in 4Q243 13 2 are limited. However, the name is likely here given the reference to ב[בל in the continuing text of 4Q244 12 3. Following Milik, "Prière de Nabonide," 413, most subsequent editions restore the title מלך ("king") here, which, though not extant in 4Q244 12, seems plausible and is reflected in the above rendering; see Fitzmyer and Harrington, *Manual of Palestinian Aramaic Texts*, 6; García Martínez, *Qumran and Apocalyptic*, 141; Collins and Flint, "Pseudo-Daniel," 107; and García Martínez and Tigchelaar, *Dead Sea Scrolls Study Edition*, 1:488.

3. [...] them into the hand of Nebu[chadnezzar king of Ba]bylon that their land be laid waste before them because ... [

4. [...] ... [...] the exiles ...

This combined content includes a cluster of allusions to Psalms traditions. The scribe of this text used these materials to emphasize how religious waywardness, here epitomized as child sacrifice, was the pinnacle reason for the exile.[34] In this way, the theological reflection on the past here is distinctly different from the later Hebrew section of the book of Daniel, which specifies torah transgression as the cause of exile (Dan 9:11).[35]

The first allusion to Ps 106:37 is in line 2. The Aramaic Pseudo-Daniel fragments share key terms with this base text as well as adapt it new ways. For example, the text indicates that sacrifices were made to "demons of error" (שׁידי טעותא) (cf. 4Q243 13 2).[36] Here we have a creative contribution by the addition of malevolent beings. In the next allusion, to Ps 106:40 in the latter half of line 2, however, we have the omission of the divine name! Whereas the Psalms passage reads, "Then the anger of the LORD was kindled against his people" (ויחר־אף יהוה בעמו), the Qumran Aramaic text streamlines this to "So God became angry at them" (ורגז עליהון אלוהין). What happened to the Tetragrammaton in this reflection on divine anger at child sacrifice? Anthony Meyer's recent dissertation concluded that, despite additional syntactical rearrangements to the scriptural base text, the scribe of 4Q244 has clearly

---

34. For identification of these allusions, see Beyer, *Die aramäischen Texte vom Toten meer*, 1:224; García Martínez, *Qumran and Apocalyptic*, 142; Michael O. Wise, Martin G. Abegg, and Edward M. Cook, *The Dead Sea Scrolls: A New Translation* (New York: HarperSanFrancisco, 2005), 343; and Lange and Weigold, *Biblical Quotations and Allusions*, 305.

35. Loren T. Stuckenbruck, "Daniel and Early Enoch Traditions," in Collins and Flint, *Book of Daniel*, 2:368–86.

36. García Martínez, *Qumran and Apocalyptic*, 142, observes that the nearest known Aramaic expression to this is found in Targum Neofiti to Deut 32:17, which states "they sacrificed before the idols of the demons" (דבחו קדם טעוות שדיה). Tigchelaar, "Aramaic Texts from Qumran," 165, n. 37, notes that the analogous Greek phrase, "demons of error" (δαίμονες πλάνης), occurs in T. Jud. 23.1. In the Hebrew scriptures, the term שד ("demon") occurs only in Deut 32:17 and Ps 106:37, and it is only the Psalms text that pairs this with child sacrifice. Tigchelaar also notes that Jub. 1.11 likewise draws together elements of Ps 106:37 and Deut 32:17, which may have also informed the formulation in Pseudo-Daniel.

avoided the divine name in the citation.[37] When taken together with the use of paleo-Hebrew to pen אלהא in 4Q243 1 2, the avoidance of the divine name in the Psalms citation of 4Q244 takes on new significance. In this instance, the social and religious sensitivities of the scribe of 4Q244 not only impacted the execution of the manuscript, they also affected the presentation of the tradition alluded to. In short, there is an intersection between scribal practice and scribal intervention here.

As the text continues, the nature of scribal intervention entails an important interpretive extension. Line 3 of the reconstructed text includes a modified citation of Ps 106:41. The most significant departure from the base text in the Aramaic material is the exchange of the generic mention of handing the Israelites over to the "nations" (גוים) for the particular reference to deliverance into the hand of "Nebu[chadnezzar king of Ba]bylon" (נב[וכדנצר מלך ב]בל), which, though highly reconstructed, seems plausible. This variation is not likely textual from a variant in a lemma; rather, it is almost certainly exegetical and historiographical. It draws a connection between the apostasy and idolatry described in the preceding lines with the Babylonian exile. The scribe of the Damascus Document used a similar turn of phrase as a temporal marker for connecting the insider group's reflection on their history with that of Israel. This text reads, "In the era of wrath—three hundred and ninety years at the time *He handed them over to the hand of Nebuchadnezzar king of Babylon* [לתיתו אותם ביד נבוכדנאצר מלך בבל]" (CD I, 5–6).[38]

---

37. See Anthony Meyer, "The Divine Name in Early Judaism: Use and Non-use in Aramaic, Hebrew, and Greek" (PhD diss., McMaster University, 2017), 104. Donald W. Parry observes that a similar side-stepping of the divine name in scriptural citations is evident in some Qumran legal materials (i.e., CD, 1QS, 4QMMT), which avoid the Tetragrammaton through omission, paraphrase, exchange for pronouns, or substitution of other titles; see his "Notes on Divine Name Avoidance in Scriptural Units of the Legal Texts of Qumran," in *Legal Texts and Legal Issues: Proceedings of the Second Meeting of the International Organization for Qumran Studies, Cambridge, 1995: Published in Honour of Joseph M. Baumgarten*, ed. Moshe J. Bernstein, Florentino García Martínez, and John Kampen, STDJ 23 (Leiden: Brill, 1997), 437–49. Jonathan Ben-Dov concludes that the avoidance, substitution, or augmentation of the Tetragrammaton is generally localized to nonbiblical scrolls penned in Qumranic practice; see his "The Elohistic Psalter and the Writing of Divine Names at Qumran," in *The Dead Sea Scrolls and Contemporary Culture: Proceedings of the International Conference Held at the Israel Museum, Jerusalem (July 6–8, 2008)*, ed. Adolfo Daniel Roitman, Lawrence H. Schiffman, and Shani Tzoref, STDJ 93 (Leiden: Brill, 2011), 79–104.

38. Translation from Wise, Abegg, and Cook, *Dead Sea Scrolls*, 343.

So what can we say about these approaches to, and development of, psalmic material in view of the scribal practices and interpretive cultures of Qumran and the Aramaic Dead Sea Scrolls? The avoidance of the divine name in the citation of Ps 106:40 in 4Q244 may indicate that this copy originated in the same social setting as that of 4Q243. In different ways, the scribes of these manuscripts exhibit parallel sensitivities to divine epithets. They are avoided in cited material or encoded in compositional materials. I suggest that the two interpretive explanations for understanding the social location of 4Q243 proposed above apply also to 4Q244.

What can we make of the parallel development of Ps 106:41 in 4Q243–244 and Damascus Document? The scribes behind both Pseudo-Daniel and the Damascus Document are simultaneously receiving and redeploying Ps 106:41. On the surface, they did so using analogous terms that front the Babylonian king Nebuchadnezzar as the agent of exile. The tradition is no longer generic. The nations are narrowed to one empire and a single ruler. This interaction with the tradition, therefore, cultivates a certain memory of exile. This memory is also historiographical. Pseudo-Daniel developed the tradition to offer a particular explanation of exile. Damascus Document adopted a narrower focus for a group who remembered their origins in relation to a timeline of exilic experience. In this way, there is a similarity as well as a critical difference. The content of the scribal addition is very similar, yet the outcome and application of the material extends in different directions for exegetical purposes and identity formation. There is no indication that the scribes of either tradition used or were influenced by the other—both concepts are often blunt instruments for the complex formation of ancient Jewish literature. Rather, what we most likely have in this case is the result of two works contributing to, or interacting with, a shared exegetical tradition relating to the memory of exile in the mid-Second Temple period.

Our final sample of Pseudo-Daniel does not deal with a reflection on the past but with an expectation for the future.

3.3. A Parallel in Eschatological Outlooks: The Emergence of an Elect in 4Q243 24

Where the two previously discussed aspects of Pseudo-Daniel pertained to scribal practice and the formation or reuse of tradition, the final aspect of this preliminary study deals with an area of conceptual or ideological overlap. While the content, structure, and genre of the Pseudo-Daniel materials is technically unknown, as mentioned in the introduction to the texts above, there is a strong indication that 4Q243–244 was either a formal apocalypse or bears the marks of apocalyptic thought. One of the clearest places we see this is in the work's eschatological outlook. Here again, the terms of reference bear resemblance to topics and themes of other traditions in the Qumran collection.

The first such instance relates to the content of 4Q243 24. This fragment seems to include an eschatological outlook anticipating a definitive day that includes the gathering of an elect group. The text and transcription are as follows:

1 [ ]עֹ[39אֹטעו] [
2 [ ]דֹנה יתכנשון קריאי[ן [
3 [ ]עַממיא ולהוה מן יום] [
4 [ ]שֹין ומלכי עממיא[ ] [
5 [ ]עֹבדין עד יומא[ ] [

1. […] … will go astray […]
2. […] this, those who are calle[d] will be assembled […]
3. […] the peoples and there will be from (that) day […]
4. […] … and kings of the peoples […]
5. […] servants/doing until the day […]

The content of this fragment is admittedly limited and its context unknown. However, Milik's suggestion that 4Q243 24 fits in some eschatological section of the work seems reasonable.[40] While the text of lines 1–2 is fragmentary, the terms used here seem to juxtapose two groups. One is "called" (קריאי[ן]) the other has gone "astray" (אֹטעו). In view of the reference to "the day" (יומא) in line 5, it seems these groups are forecasted in the future.

The verb קרי is used widely in the Qumran Aramaic texts. However, the occurrence here is the only instance where it expresses the idea of

---

39. Milik, "Prière de Nabonide," 414, reads the beginning of the line as רש[א]עֹ. Collins and Flint, "Pseudo-Daniel," 114, extend the reconstruction and rendered "the sons of ev]il (בני רש[עֹא)." Both are correct in recovering an *ayin* from the meager ink traces at the top of the fragment. However, the proposed reconstructions extend beyond what the physical evidence allows.

40. Milik, "Prière de Nabonide," 414.

election.[41] Incidentally, the Hebrew Dead Sea Scrolls abound in this specialized use. Verbal and adjectival forms from the root קרא are found in both reflections on past election as well as that expected in the eschatological future. Compare for example, the following: CD II, 11; 4Q266 2 II, 11; 1QM III, 2; IV, 10–11; 4Q275 1 I, 2; 4Q385 3a–c 3; 4Q418 81 + 81a 12; 4Q491 19 4; 4Q496 8 9; 4Q504 1–2 II, recto 12. In this way, the idiom of Pseudo-Daniel's outlook may fit a paradigm of eschatological expectation involving the singling out of a cross-section of Jewish society in a way that resembles aspects of the apocalyptic thought of select Qumran Hebrew texts.[42]

4. Closing Thoughts

As Carol Newsom reflected, "There is a fairly widely accepted description of the Qumran sect as an apocalyptic community that did not write apocalypses."[43] In view of ongoing research on the origins and development

---

41. Reflecting on the relationship between this outlook and those of the Hebrew scriptures, DiTommaso comments that "it is safe to conclude that 4Q243/244's review of history is likely meant to highlight the special nature of the righteous elect in the larger context of the message that God controls history in a traditional, Deuteronomic sin-punishment dynamic"; see "4QPseudo-Daniel[a–b] (4Q243–4Q244) and the Book of Daniel," *DSD* 12 (2005): 119.

42. Eschatological expectations involving the emergence of an elect group is one of the clearest discernable items of conceptual overlap between the fragments of 4Q243–244 and 4Q245. The content of 4Q245 2 seems to also carve out a space for the emergence of juxtaposed groups at a future time. The first group is characterised in line 3 as existing in "blindness" (עור) and is said to "have gone astray" (טעו). In lines 4–5, the second group is said "to arise" (קום) and "to return" (תוב). The usage of these terms as descriptors for groups in Second Temple period literature is diverse. See, for example, the following: CD I, 9; II, 13; 4Q204 4 7–8 (1 En. 89.35); 4Q246 1 II, 4; 4Q541 9 I, 7; and Dan 12:2. Perhaps most significantly is the reference to the "rising up" (קום) or a reform movement in 4Q245 2 (for this interpretation, see Collins and Flint, "Pseudo-Daniel," 163; and John J. Collins, "Apocalypticism and Literary Genre in the Dead Sea Scrolls," in *The Dead Sea Scrolls after Fifty Years: A Comprehensive Assessment*, ed. Peter W. Flint and James C. VanderKam (Leiden: Brill, 1999), 403–30. Hempel, "Community Rule and the Book of Daniel," 235, suggests it may be a "missing link" in understanding the exilic roots of the community reflected in CD with respect to Danielic tradition.

43. Carol A. Newsom, "Apocalyptic and the Discourse of the Qumran Community," *JNES* 29 (1990): 135.

of the genre the apocalypse, the features of apocalypticism as a worldview, the nature of the Qumran community and its relation to other expressions of Judaism, as well as the literary, ideological, and social settings of the Aramaic Dead Sea Scrolls, this formulation should remain open-ended.

In general terms, the Aramaic materials among the Dead Sea Scrolls are essential for rethinking the bounds and definition of the apocalypse in ancient Judaism. They are also some of our earliest materials to observe the formation of apocalyptic thought in Jewish scribal settings. Since our understanding of the origins of these writings is still in process—and they need not all originate from a single location—it is difficult to identify exactly where these writings map onto the social landscape and conceptual worlds of mid-Second Temple Judaism.[44] At a minimum, the presence of the Aramaic texts in the caves of the Judean Desert indicates that the Qumran community may not have been in the business of writing apocalypses, but they were avid receivers and readers of them.[45] In this way, the Aramaic Dead Sea Scrolls provide important new data for exploring how the worldview of this one known apocalyptic community was shaped by the ideas of apocalypses penned by other groups beyond their immediate home in the wilderness.[46]

In the particular case of Pseudo-Daniel, the sampling of three scribal, exegetical, and ideological features shared between 4Q243–244 and some Hebrew writings among the Dead Sea Scrolls, not least the Damascus Document, may point the way forward for theorizing about apocalyptic groups that were part of the same movement as the Qumranites but *did* write formal apocalypses. In this sense, working toward a more nuanced

---

44. Daniel Machiela, "The Compositional Setting and Implied Audience of Some Aramaic Texts from Qumran: A Working Hypothesis," in *Vision, Narrative, and Wisdom in the Aramaic Texts from Qumran: Essays from the Copenhagen Symposium, 14–15 August, 2017*, ed. Mette Bundvad and Kasper Siegismund, STDJ 131 (Leiden: Brill, 2019), 168–202.

45. James C. VanderKam allows that "it preserved and apparently made copies of older apocalyptic works but did not compose new ones"; see "Apocalyptic Tradition in the Dead Sea Scrolls," 114.

46. Daniel Machiela recently noted that the influence of the Aramaic texts on "Essene sectarian communities" pertained mostly to the "conceptual construct within which the communities understood themselves and read their authoritative scriptures" ("The Aramaic Dead Sea Scrolls: Coherence and Context in the Library of Qumran," in *The Dead Sea Scrolls at Qumran and the Concept of a Library*, ed. Sidnie White Crawford and Cecilia Wassén, STDJ 116 [Leiden: Brill, 2016], 255).

understanding of the social histories of the communities behind the literature studied here demands broadening the scope of our question and enlarging our terms of reference. Qumran is a key part of this movement and biblical Daniel is an important representative of the Danielic tradition. Yet these are not the only variables. We are talking about a complex movement, not a cell group at a single site. We are also dealing with a larger Danielic tradition, no longer only a single book.

Bibliography

Ben-Dov, Jonathan. "The Elohistic Psalter and the Writing of Divine Names at Qumran." Pages 79–104 in *The Dead Sea Scrolls and Contemporary Culture: Proceedings of the International Conference Held at the Israel Museum, Jerusalem (July 6–8, 2008)*. Edited by Adolfo Daniel Roitman, Lawrence H. Schiffman, and Shani Tzoref. STDJ 93. Leiden: Brill, 2011.

Beyer, Klaus. *Die aramäischen Texte vom Toten Meer.* 2 vols. Göttingen: Vandenhoeck & Ruprecht, 1984.

———. *Die aramäischen Texte vom Toten Meer; Ergänzungsband.* Göttingen: Vandenhoeck & Ruprecht, 1994.

Bruce, Frederick F. "The Book of Daniel and the Qumran Community." Pages 221–35 in *Neotestamentica et Semitica: Studies in Honour of Matthew Black.* Edited by E. Earle Ellis and Max E. Wilcox. Edinburgh: T&T Clark, 1969.

Collins, John J. "Apocalypticism and Literary Genre in the Dead Sea Scrolls." Pages 403–30 in *The Dead Sea Scrolls after Fifty Years.* Edited by Peter W. Flint and James C. VanderKam. Leiden: Brill, 1999.

———. *Beyond the Qumran Community: The Sectarian Movement of the Dead Sea Scrolls.* Grand Rapids: Eerdmans, 2010.

Collins, John J., and Peter W. Flint, eds. "Pseudo-Daniel." Pages 95–164 in *Qumran Cave 4.XVII: Parabiblical Texts, Part 3.* Edited by George Brooke et al. DJD 22. Oxford: Clarendon, 1996.

Cook, Edward M. *Dictionary of Qumran Aramaic.* Winona Lake, IN: Eisenbrauns, 2015.

Crown, Alan D. *Samaritan Scribes and Manuscripts.* TSAJ 80. Tübingen: Mohr Siebeck, 2001.

DiTommaso, Lorenzo. "4QPseudo-Daniel[a–b] (4Q243–4Q244) and the Book of Daniel." *DSD* 12 (2005): 101–33.

———. *The Book of Daniel and the Apocryphal Daniel Literature.* SVTP 20. Leiden: Brill, 2005.
Fitzmyer Joseph A., and Daniel J. Harrington. *A Manual of Palestinian Aramaic Texts.* Rome: Pontifical Biblical Institute, 1978.
Flint, Peter W. "The Daniel Tradition at Qumran." Pages 329–67 in vol. 2 of *The Book of Daniel: Composition and Reception.* Edited by John J. Collins and Peter W. Flint. VTSup 83. 2 vols. Leiden: Brill, 2001.
García Martínez, Florentino. *Qumran and Apocalyptic.* STDJ 9. Leiden: Brill, 1992.
———. "Scribal Practices in the Aramaic Literary Texts from Qumran." Pages 329–41 in *Myths, Martyrs, and Modernity: Studies in the History of Religions in Honour of Jan N. Bremmer.* Edited by Jitse H. F. Dijkstra, Justin Kroesen, and Yme Kuiper. SHR 127. Leiden: Brill, 2010.
García Martínez, Florentino, and Eibert J. C. Tigchelaar. *The Dead Sea Scrolls Study Edition.* 2 vols. Leiden: Brill, 1997.
Hempel, Charlotte. "The Community Rule and the Book of Daniel." Pages 231–52 in *The Qumran Rule Texts in Context: Collected Studies.* TSAJ 154. Tübingen: Mohr Siebeck, 2013.
Lange, Armin, and Matthias Weigold. *Biblical Quotations and Allusions in Second Temple Jewish Literature.* JAJSup 5. Göttingen: Vandenhoeck & Ruprecht, 2011.
Machiela, Daniel A. "The Aramaic Dead Sea Scrolls: Coherence and Context in the Library of Qumran." Pages 244–58 in *The Dead Sea Scrolls at Qumran and the Concept of a Library.* Edited by Sidnie White Crawford and Cecilia Wassén. STDJ 116. Leiden: Brill, 2016.
———. "The Compositional Setting and Implied Audience of Some Aramaic Texts from Qumran: A Working Hypothesis." Pages 168–202 in *Vision, Narrative, and Wisdom in the Aramaic Texts from Qumran: Essays from the Copenhagen Symposium, 14–15 August, 2017.* Edited by Mette Bundvad and Kasper Siegismund. STDJ 131. Leiden: Brill, 2019.
———. "Lord or God? Tobit and the Tetragrammaton." *CBQ* 75 (2013): 463–72.
Mertens, Alfred. *Das Buch Daniel im Lichte der Texte vom Toten Meer.* SBM 12. Echter: KBW Verlag, 1971.
Meyer, Anthony. "The Divine Name in Early Judaism: Use and Non-use in Aramaic, Hebrew, and Greek." PhD diss., McMaster University, 2017.

Meyer, Rudolf. *Das Gebet des Nabonid: Eine in den Qumran-Handschriften wiederentdeckte Weisheitserzählung*. SSAWL 107. Berlin: Akademie Verlag, 1962.

Milik, Józef T. "Priére de Nabonide et autres écrits d'un cycle de Daniel." *RB* 63 (1956): 407–15.

Newsom, Carol A. "Apocalyptic and the Discourse of the Qumran Community." *JNES* 29 (1990): 135–44.

———. "'Sectually Explicit' Literature from Qumran." Pages 167–87 in *The Hebrew Bible and Its Interpreters*. Edited by William H. Propp, Baruch Halpern, and David Noel Freedman. Winona Lake, IN: Eisenbrauns, 1990.

Parry, Donald W. "Notes on Divine Name Avoidance in Scriptural Units of the Legal Texts of Qumran." Pages 437–49 in *Legal Texts and Legal Issues: Proceedings of the Second Meeting of the International Organization for Qumran Studies, Cambridge, 1995: Published in Honour of Joseph M. Baumgarten*. Edited by Moshe J. Bernstein, Florentino García Martínez, and John Kampen. STDJ 23. Leiden: Brill, 1997.

Perrin, Andrew. *The Dynamics of Dream-Vision Revelation in the Aramaic Dead Sea Scrolls*. JAJSup 19. Göttingen: Vandenhoeck & Ruprecht, 2015.

Skehan, Patrick. "The Divine Name at Qumran, in the Masada Scroll, and in the Septuagint." *BIOSCS* 13 (1980): 14–44.

Stegemann, Hartmut. "Religionsgeschichtliche Erwägungen zu den Gottesbezeichnungen in der Qumrantexten." Pages 195–217 in *Qumrân: Sa piété, sa théologie et son milieu*. Edited by Mathias Delcor. BETL 46. Leuven: Leuven University Press, 1978.

Stuckenbruck, Loren T. "Daniel and Early Enoch Traditions." Pages 368–86 in vol. 2 of *The Book of Daniel: Composition and Reception*. Edited by John J. Collins and Peter W. Flint. VTSup 83. 2 vols. Leiden: Brill, 2001.

———. "The Formation and Reformation of Daniel in the Dead Sea Scrolls." Pages 101–30 in *Scripture and the Scrolls*. Vol. 1 of *The Bible and the Dead Sea Scrolls*. Edited by James H. Charlesworth. Waco, TX: Baylor University Press, 2006.

Teeter, Andrew. "The Hebrew Bible and/as Second Temple Period Literature." *DSD* 20 (2013): 349–77.

Tigchelaar, Eibert J. C. "Aramaic Texts from Qumran and the Authoritativeness of Hebrew Scriptures: Preliminary Observations." Pages

155–71 in *Authoritative Scriptures in Ancient Judaism*. Edited by Mladen Popović. JSJSup 141. Leiden: Brill, 2010.

Tov, Emanuel. *Scribal Practices and Approaches Reflected in the Texts Found in the Judean Desert*. STDJ 54. Leiden: Brill, 2004.

Trever, John C. "The Book of Daniel and the Origin of the Qumran Community." *BA* 48 (1985): 89–102.

VanderKam, James C. "Apocalyptic Tradition in the Dead Sea Scrolls and the Religion of Qumran." Pages 113–34 in *Religion in the Dead Sea Scrolls*. Edited by John J. Collins and Robert A. Kugler. Grand Rapids: Eerdmans, 2000.

Wise, Michael O. "4Q245 (psDan^c ar) and the High Priesthood of Judas Maccabaeus." *DSD* 12 (2005): 313–62.

Wise, Michael O., Martin G. Abegg, and Edward M. Cook. *The Dead Sea Scrolls: A New Translation*. New York: HarperSanFrancisco, 2005.

Wise, Michael O., and Robert Eisenman. *The Dead Sea Scrolls Uncovered*. New York: Penguin, 1993.

It's the End of the World (as the Persians Know It)? Iranian Influence on Jewish Apocalypticism in Light of the Complete Publication of the Dead Sea Scrolls

Jason M. Silverman

The idea of Persian influence on Judaism has been of perennial interest to scholarship since the rediscovery of the Avesta in the west.[1] Scholars have often connected the topic with discussions of apocalyptic literature and, since the discovery of the Dead Sea Scrolls, with the sectarian documents

---

This paper was written as part of the Academy of Finland Centre of Excellence in Ancient Near Eastern Empires, University of Helsinki (P.I. Saana Svärd) as well as the Centre of Excellence in Changes in Sacred Texts and Traditions (P.I. Martti Nissinen). The author is grateful to the editors of this volume for their invitation to contribute to this topic and to Jutta Jokiranta for discussing with me the current state of Qumranic scholarship.

1. In general terms, I prefer to speak of *Iranian influence*, with *Persian influence* merely one subset of that. *Persia*, strictly speaking, refers to the modern province of Fars, in southwest Iran. *Iranian* refers to the groups that spoke Iranian languages, of which Old Persian was merely one. They lived and live in an area much larger than the modern state of Iran. Copies of the Avesta were first brought to the west by Abraham-Hyacinthe Anquetil-Duperron in 1771; see his *Zend-Avesta, ouvrage de Zoroastre, contenant les idées théologiques, physiques & morales de ce législateur, les cérémonies du culte religieux qu'il a établi, & plusieurs traits importans relatifs à l'ancienne histoire des Perses* (Paris: Tillard, 1771). For a lucid discussion of the context, content, and controversy around Anquetil, see Nora Kathleen Firby, *European Travellers and Their Perceptions of Zoroastrians in the Seventeenth and Eighteenth Centuries*, Archäologische Mitteilungen aus Iran Ergänzungsband 14 (Berlin: Reimer, 1988), 155–78. Others often trace scholarship to the slightly earlier work of Thomas Hyde, *Historia religionis veterum Persarum* (Oxford: Sheldonian Theatre, 1700). For a contextualization of the study of Persian influence in a broader context of central European scholarship, see Suzanne L. Marchand, *German Orientalism in the Age of Empire: Race, Religion, and Scholarship* (Cambridge: Cambridge University Press, 2009), esp. 17–20 and 279–83.

among them.[2] With a recent uptick in scholarly interest in the topic[3] and the now complete publication of the Dead Sea Scrolls, it is an opportune moment to reassess how one could better approach the potential relevance of Iranian traditions for the corpus.

In my opinion, the keys to a more nuanced approach to the issue than sometimes prevails in the discussion are threefold: (1) understanding influence as a "comparative perspective on hermeneutics"; (2) a careful analysis of relevant systemic structures; and (3) analysis within concentric levels of contexts.[4] First, I will briefly explain how I understand influence, systemic structures, and concentric levels of contexts. Second, I will expand on two relevant contexts, the Achaemenid and Parthian Empires. Finally, I will conclude with two contrasting case studies: the concept of the New Jerusalem in a number of Qumranic and apocalyptic texts, and the issue of dualism in the Treatise of the Two Spirits.

---

2. E.g., Shaul Shaked, "Zoroastrianism and Judaism," in *A Zoroastrian Tapestry: Art, Religion, and Culture*, ed. Pheroza J. Godrej and Firoza P. Mistree (Ahmedabad: Mapin, 2002), 206.

3. Most recently, see Jason M. Silverman, "From Remembering to Expecting the 'Messiah': Achaemenid Kingship as (Re)Formulating Apocalyptic Expectations of David," in *Political Memory in and after the Persian Empire*, ed. Jason M. Silverman and Caroline Waerzeggers, ANEM 13 (Atlanta: SBL Press, 2015), 419–46; Domenico Agostini, "On Iranian and Jewish Apocalyptics, Again," *JAOS* 136 (2016): 495–505; Lucas L. Schulte, *My Shepherd, Though You Do Not Know Me: The Persian Royal Propaganda Model in the Nehemiah Memoir*, CBET 78 (Leuven: Peeters, 2016); David Janzen, "Yahwistic Appropriation of Achaemenid Ideology and the Function of Nehemiah 9 in Ezra-Nehemiah," *JBL* 136 (2017): 839–56; Yishai Kiel, "Reinventing Mosaic Torah in Ezra-Nehemiah in the Light of the Law (*Dāta*) of Ahura Mazda and Zarathustra," *JBL* 136 (2017): 323–45; Konrad Schmid, "Taming Egypt: The Impact of Persian Imperial Ideology and Politics on the Biblical Exodus Account," in *Jewish Cultural Encounters in the Ancient Mediterranean and Near Eastern World*, ed. Mladen Popović, Myles Schoonover, and Marijn Vandenberghe, JSJSup 178 (Leiden: Brill, 2017), 13–29; Jason M. Silverman, "Achaemenid Creation and Second Isaiah," *JPS* 10 (2017): 26–48; and Mark Whitters, "The Persianized Liturgy of Nehemiah 8:1–8," *JBL* 136 (2017): 63–84.

4. This explanation broadly follows the arguments in Jason M. Silverman, *Persepolis and Jerusalem*, LHBOTS 558 (London: T&T Clark, 2012), especially 29–38, 206–27, although with much more emphasis on social structures and the overlapping or concentric nature of relevant contexts. The phrase "comparative perspective on hermeneutics" derives from a popularizing summary of the same book (Jason M. Silverman, "Iranian Influence on Judaism," *Bible and Interpretation* [2011]: https://tinyurl.com/SBL3551c).

1. Influence

Part of the difficulty in studying the phenomena of intercultural interaction and influence is the wide range of senses in which these and similar terms are used. On the one hand, some scholars are content to discuss vague familial similarities, while on the other some insist on evidence of textual borrowing or quotation. In my view, neither approach is adequate to the task. Nor is it helpful to abandon all consideration of the phenomenon.[5] Rather, I argue it is most fruitful to treat the issue as a "comparative perspective on hermeneutics" or the "reshaping, selection, and/or interpretation of ideas ... due to interaction with another culture."[6] The reason for making (re)interpretation the focus of influence is to take seriously the fact that all cultures and cultural systems undergo continual change—influence is merely *one mechanism among others* that facilitates this change. By focusing on this hermeneutical aspect, one is immediately forced to ask not just what changed but how and why it changed—and one is freed from anxiety over differences between the source and the recipient. Further, one need not be troubled by pluriform influences, since hermeneutics by its very nature interrelates multiple things. Also, one is forced to investigate the structures in which the change was operating and whether or not the structures themselves were undergoing change. When one begins to place the how and why into a bigger structural context, phenomena such as explicit textual borrowing only become one piece of a larger hermeneutical puzzle.

To put this perspective into practice on a practical, analytical level for specific texts, I have argued for the following six criteria:[7] (1) the influencer must predate the proposed interaction; (2) there must be a plausible historical situation in which interaction could occur; (3) the proposed idea must make more structural sense in the influencer's tradition than in

---

5. As argued, e.g., by Michael L. Satlow, "Beyond Influence: Toward a New Historiographic Paradigm," in *Jewish Literatures and Cultures: Context and Intertext*, ed. Anita Norich and Yaron Z. Eliav, BJS 349 (Providence, RI: Brown Judaic Studies, 2008), 37–53.

6. First quotation from Silverman, "Iranian Influence on Judaism," second from Silverman, *Persepolis and Jerusalem*, 34.

7. My definition of influence is meant to take into account interaction as a broader social phenomenon, though these six criteria were developed for use with textual evidence. They are paraphrased from Silverman, *Persepolis and Jerusalem*, 35–37.

the influenced tradition; (4) there must be a way for the influenced tradition to incorporate the new element; (5) there must be demonstrable elements that betray the origin; and (6) there must be interpretative and/or structural change(s) as a result of the influence. While criteria 1, 2, and 5 are often appealed to in studies of influence, 3, 4, and 6 receive less attention. Nevertheless, in my view, these are the elements that truly illuminate the how and why of influence.

To illustrate the importance of criteria 3, 4, and 6, we can briefly take an example related to this essay's later test cases: the problem of evil and of its logical solutions (ontological dualism).[8] The problem of evil is an inherent aspect of the structure of Second Temple Jewish apocalypticism (a sole deity). When one takes evil seriously, as the apocalypses do, then theodical solutions must be found. This is criterion 4. The solution one chooses to solve this problem will have major ramifications for one's understanding of the world. This is criterion 6. Many potential solutions exist. One of these is ontological dualism, which fits better into various Iranian systems than it does into Judean ones (criterion 3). One must remember, however, that whether a Judean adopts a theodicy that is dualistic or not, the issue of influence is still relevant—influence can be both positive and negative.[9] This is an issue where broader contexts come into play, to which we will return below.

2. Relevant Structural Systems

The issue of structure was mentioned several times above. Two types of structure are meant here: cultural (including religious) structure and social structure. By the former, I mean understanding traditions along the lines of what Timothy Light has called "cognitive entities": symbols, categories that arrange symbols, and rules governing their interaction, and what Hendrik M. Vroom has called a hierarchy of importance (for example, see below).[10] These are relevant for understanding the dynamics of collectivities, as well

---

8. Silverman, *Persepolis and Jerusalem*, 221–22.

9. As pointed out by John R. Hinnells, "Zoroastrian Influence on the Judeo-Christian Tradition," *Journal of the K.R. Cama Oriental Institute* 45 (1976): 1–23, and followed by Silverman, *Persepolis and Jerusalem*, 30.

10. Timothy Light, "Orthosyncretism: An Account of Melding in Religion," *MTSR* 12 (2000): 162–85; and Hendrik M. Vroom, "Syncretism and Dialogue: A Philosophical Analysis," in *Syncretism in Religion: A Reader*, ed. Anita M. Leopold and

as small and large groups. Analysis requires a good grasp of the relevant tradition(s). It is this sort of cultural structure that criteria 3 and 4 above had in view (rather than structuralism). Without an understanding of this sort of structure, one cannot properly assess the logic behind interpretative changes or their significance. Relative structures also are a way of understanding how superficially similar symbols can function in very different ways in two different systems. To use the same example as previously mentioned, a structural rule of much Second Temple Judaism is that the category of divinity only contains one element ("symbol" in Light's terminology). This is high on the hierarchy of importance ("rules governing interaction") and thus more resistant to change than other supernatural entities (such as angels). This structural rule is not the same, for example, in Roman religion, in which divinity is more open. A corollary to this is that evil does not pose the same sort of difficulty in the two traditions.

The second structure of importance is social structure. This element is left out of explicit consideration in the above six criteria, but it needs to be integrated into consideration of influence. The way one imagines the social structure of the relevant societies behind textual evidence strongly shapes the kinds of social interaction one is able to envision (and, thus, it is part of a more adequate assessment of criterion 2, above). In my current view, the understanding of Second Temple Judaism still requires a more thorough assessment of the social positions of scribes and elites in the various empires of the ancient Near East.[11] For example, scribes have been called everything from "elites" to "retainer class" to "middle class."[12] In addition to relative social structure, a distinction between social status and social

---

Jeppe Sinding Jensen (London: Equinox, 2004), 103–12. See Silverman, *Persepolis and Jerusalem*, 31–32.

11. I have started to ponder the meaning of *elites* and *scribes* through the Second Temple period, but my thinking is still very much in development.

12. John H. Kautsky, *The Politics of Aristocratic Empires* (Chapel Hill: University of North Carolina Press, 1982), 191, calls them "derivative leisure class"; James L. Crenshaw, "Education in Ancient Israel," *JBL* 104 (1985): 608, calls them "poor aristocrats"; while Karel van der Toorn, *Scribal Culture and the Making of the Hebrew Bible* (Cambridge: Harvard University Press, 2007), 105, calls them "upper middle class." Ehud Ben Zvi prefers to speak of "literati" in "The Yehudite Collection of Prophetic Books and Imperial Contexts: Some Observations," in *Divination, Politics, and Ancient Near Eastern Empires*, ed. Alan Lenzi and Jonathan Stökl, ANEM 7 (Atlanta: Society of Biblical Literature, 2014), 145–69. Seth L. Sanders has recently emphasized that not all scribal cultures in the ancient Near East can be assumed to have been

hierarchy remains to be assessed. The same is true, *mutatis mutandis*, for those who wrote and copied the Dead Sea Scrolls.

The consideration of social structure is so important for the issue of (Persian) influence on the apocalypses and the Dead Sea Scrolls because it provides clues to the kinds of social interactions needing investigation within the empires. The interaction of elites with other elites is likely to follow different patterns from that of artisans with other artisans.[13] Thus, mere presumption of priestly or schismatic authorship is insufficient to take on board the social structure that informed the Dead Sea Scrolls and its network of influences: one needs an idea how different groups interrelated with other groups within Second Temple Judaism. It also informs whether interactions are likely to have been primarily local or more wide-ranging (for some discussion of these wider contexts, see below). I think it is very unlikely that any potential interactions or influences would have been the same between different social groups and classes within Second Temple Judaism, and it should not be assumed that they were. Therefore, in my view, assessment of influence involves assessment of two types of structure as part of the historical context. For the Dead Sea Scrolls, this means assessing these structures for both the complete corpus of scrolls, as well as the corpus in relation to Second Temple Judaism more broadly.

3. Importance of Concentric Levels of Context

This leads into what I call, for lack of a more eloquent phrase, concentric levels of context. The insistence on the import of sociohistorical context for understanding Judean literature is a mainstay of historical-critical approaches to the literature of Second Temple Judaism. The point I wish to make is not a banal insistence for context, but that the assessment of influence involves understanding *interlacing levels* of context. It means that evidence that could be potentially indicative of influence must be analyzed not only in terms of its immediate and broader literary context, but also within its media contexts, social contexts, tradition contexts, and imperial contexts. Only by relating all of these contexts together will it be possible to assess the ways hermeneutics were operating in real social situations

---

uniform; see his *From Adapa to Enoch: Scribal Culture and Religious Vision in Judea and Babylon*, TSAJ 167 (Tübingen: Mohr Siebeck, 2017), 3.

13. If one takes scribes to be merely artisans rather than elites. This is beyond the present scope to assess.

and thus the potential significance of influence within that process. As the case studies at the end of this essay will attempt to show, this means that assessing something suspected of Persian influence in a manuscript from the Dead Sea means more than just comparing two systems of thought (though, as argued above, that is important). It means the relevant systems of thought must be interrelated in their own contexts, as well as in any posited wider (imperial) settings. It is in this interrelation of contexts that reshaping, selection, and reinterpretation can be understood as a social phenomenon and not just a literary epiphenomenon.

4. Imperial Contexts: The Achaemenid and Parthian Empires

For obvious reasons, studies both of the Dead Sea Scrolls and of Second Temple apocalypses take the importance of the Seleucid and Roman Empires for granted. However, when considering Iranian influence on Second Temple Judaism, two Iranian empires must also be taken into account: the (Teispid and) Achaemenid Empire (ca. 550–330 BCE) and the Arsacid or Parthian Empire (ca. 248 BCE–226 CE).

4.1. The Achaemenid Empire

I have already argued at length for the importance of the empire founded by Cyrus for the study of Iranian influence.[14] In short, all Judeans (and Samarians) lived within its boundaries for roughly two hundred years. One would need rather significant evidence to assume that somehow all Judean communities remained isolated from their social and political context, and, in fact, there is no reason to make this assumption. As Shaul Shaked has already argued, the question really is not whether the Judeans were influenced by having lived within the Achaemenid Empire but in what ways and how significant the influence was.[15] Moreover, Iranian colonists and their descendants continued to live outside Iran past the fall of this empire, up to at least the Byzantine Empire, particularly in Anatolia. This means that knowledge of, and interaction with, Iranians and Iranian

---

14. See, primarily, Silverman, *Persepolis and Jerusalem*, 39–97.
15. Shaul Shaked, "Iranian Influence on Judaism: First Century B.C.E to Second Century C.E.," in *Introduction: The Persian Period*, ed. W. D. Davies and Louis Finkelstein, CHJ 1 (Cambridge: Cambridge University Press, 1984), 309, 324.

ideas derived from an Achaemenid context cannot be assumed to have come merely via Greek mediation, even in the Hellenistic era.[16]

4.2. The Parthian Empire

A consideration of Parthia in relation to various Judean traditions remains rather sparse, despite the important but neglected work of Geo Widengren in the middle of the last century in the context of Semitic studies generally and that of Albert de Jong roughly a decade ago for Qumran studies specifically.[17] There are at least three different ways in which the Parthians are a relevant context for Judean communities. The first is the fact that they ruled directly and indirectly over a number of Judean communities in Babylonia, Iran, Adiabene, and the Caucasus at various periods of time.[18] Second, they were an arch-enemy of the Seleucids and thus an important element of late Seleucid strategy and diplomacy.[19] After the fall of the Seleucids, they rivalled Rome in the Near East.[20] Third, the Parthians invaded Palestine

---

16. Often a way to dismiss the Achaemenids' relevance, e.g., James Barr, "The Question of Religious Influence: The Case of Zoroastrianism, Judaism, and Christianity," *JAAR* 53 (1985): 219; and Paul Niskanen, *The Human and the Divine in History: Herodotus and the Book of Daniel*, JSOTSup 396 (London: T&T Clark, 2004), 41 n. 59.

17. See Geo Widengren, *Iranisch-semitische Kulturbegegnung in parthischer Zeit*, AFLNW 70 (Cologne: Westdeutscher Verlag, 1960); Widengren, "Iran and Israel in Parthian Times with Special Regard to the Ethiopic Book of Enoch," *Temenos* 2 (1966): 139–77; and Albert de Jong, "Iranian Connections in the Dead Sea Scrolls," in *The Oxford Handbook of the Dead Sea Scrolls*, ed. Timothy H. Lim and John J. Collins (Oxford: Oxford University Press, 2010), 486–87, 496. For more recent studies, see Jacob Neusner, "Judeo-Persian Communities of Iran iii. the Parthian and Sasanian Periods," *EIr* 15 (2009): 96–103; and Ted M. Erho, "The Ahistorical Nature of *1 Enoch* 56:5-8 and Its Ramifications upon the *Opinio Communis* on the Dating of the *Similitudes of Enoch*," *JSJ* 40 (2009): 23–54.

18. See, e.g., Neusner, "Judeo-Persian Communities of Iran," 97.

19. For an introduction to some of the issues, see Richard N. Frye, *The Heritage of Central Asia: From Antiquity to the Turkish Expansion* (Princeton: Markus Wiener, 1998), 111–18; and Susan Sherwin-White and Amélie Kuhrt, *From Samarkhand to Sardis: A New Approach to the Seleucid Empire* (London: Duckworth, 1993), 223–29. For discussion of some Seleucid-Parthian strife, see Jeffrey D. Lerner, *The Impact of Seleucid Decline on the Eastern Iranian Plateau: The Foundations of Arsacid Parthia and Graeco-Bactria*, Historia Einzelschriften 123 (Stuttgart: Steiner, 1999), 33–62.

20. For some recent discussions of the import of this for the early Roman period, see J. Andrew Overman, "Between Rome and Parthia: Galilee and the Implications of Empire," in *A Wandering Galilean: Essays in Honour of Seán Freyne*, ed. Zuleika Rodgers, Margaret

in 40 BCE. Investigation of the significance of Parthia for various Judean groups during this era remains an important desideratum.

5. Case Study 1: The New Jerusalem and Yima's *Vara*[21]

Two of the new texts found near the Dead Sea contain a tradition of a heavenly Jerusalem: the New Jerusalem Scroll and the Temple Scroll. The motif also appears in other Second Temple-era literature and some apocalypses (including Ezek 40–48; Isa 60 and 65; Rev 21–22; as well as 1 and 2 Enoch, Jubilees, 4 Ezra 7 and 10, Sib. Or. 5, 2 Bar. 4).[22] None of these texts presents a singular vision of this New Jerusalem; what they share is the use of the motif as a way for the authors to argue for what they see as the essence of Judean tradition in terms of sin and salvation.[23]

Marc Philonenko has argued that the form of this tradition that appears in the Revelation of John is based on a template provided by the Iranian myth of Yima's *vara*, or "enclosure."[24] The myth of Yima's enclosure is a complicated set of traditions primarily based in the rescue of good creatures from a disastrous winter.[25] In the myth as attested in the Vidēvdāt, Ahura Mazda predicts catastrophic winters, and he orders King Yima to build an enclosure to protect specimens of all good creatures. The enclosure is built like a miniature, perfect earth. Philonenko largely bases

---

Daly-Denton, and Anne Fitzpatrick-McKinley, JSJSup 132 (Leiden: Brill, 2009), 279–300; and Jason M. Schlude and J. Andrew Overman, "Herod the Great: A Near Eastern Caste Study in Roman-Parthian Politics," in *Arsacids, Romans and Local Elites : Cross-Cultural Interactions of the Parthian Empire*, ed. Jason M. Schlude and Benjamin B. Rubin (Oxford: Oxbow, 2017), 93–110.

21. Argument here first put forth in Jason M. Silverman, "It's a Craft! It's a Cavern! It's a Castle! Yima's Vara, Iranian Flood Myths, and Jewish Apocalyptic Traditions," in *Opening Heaven's Floodgates*, ed. Jason M. Silverman (Piscataway, NJ: Gorgias, 2013), 191–230. A number of scholars have suggested parallels with Yima's Vara, starting as early as Ernst Böklen, *Die Verwandtschaft der jüdisch-christlichen mit der parsischen Eschatologie* (Göttingen: Vandenhoeck & Ruprecht, 1902), 136–44.

22. Lorenzo DiTommaso, *The Dead Sea New Jerusalem Text: Contents and Contexts*, TSAJ 110 (Tübingen: Mohr Siebeck, 2005).

23. Silverman, "It's a Craft!," 216–28.

24. Marc Philonenko, "La nouvelle Jérusalem et le Vara de Yima," in *La cité de Dieu/Die Stadt Gottes. 3. Symposium Strasbourg, Tübingen, Uppsala 19.–23. September 1998 in Tübingen*, ed. Martin Hengel, Siegfried Mittmann, and Anna Maria Schwemer, WUNT 129 (Tübingen: Mohr Siebeck, 2000), 139–46.

25. See the discussion in Silverman, "It's a Craft!," 194–211.

his argument on the disappearance of night in Rev 21:25 and 22:5, a minor motif that appears in some versions of this myth; this is what is called criterion 5 above. He sees this as an unbiblical element that contrasts with the vision of the New Jerusalem in Isaiah. For him, the solution is to see the passage in Revelation as based on an anthology of biblical literature modeled on the myth of Yima.[26] If his thesis were accepted, it would be an example of selection and adaptation as a form of influence. He also attempts to posit a historical situation for the posited anthology (Iranian Jews, criterion 2). However, apart from any reservations one may have for the presently nonextant anthology that served as a template, Philonenko does not adequately deal with the structural issues (criteria 3 and 4), nor deal with interpretive change (criterion 6). Thus even if one felt the motif of the elimination of night were itself compelling, I would argue that on its own it is not sufficient to count as an instance of influence.

To assess this particular suggestion along the lines argued above, several more steps would be required.[27] The place of Revelation within both Second Temple apocalyptic literature and the use of the New Jerusalem motif would require further study. This should have included the Qumranic texts in addition to the canonical ones. This would provide a more adequate basis for determining both criteria 4 and 6. The role of the *vara* in Iranian traditions would also need a more thorough assessment (3). The significance of the use of the disappearance of night might then be analyzed for the way it re-interprets the New Jerusalem, thus helping to determine if its use in Iranian traditions is similar. (In my opinion, it is not similar.) This example shows how discrete elements that superficially appear similar are not in themselves sufficient grounds for a meaningful instance of influence.

6. Case Study 2: Dualism and Treatise of the Two Spirits

The so-called Treatise of the Two Spirits within 1QS has long garnered attention for apparent affinities with Iran.[28] The difficulties of assessing

---

26. Philonenko, "La Nouvelle Jérusalem et le Vara de Yima," 144.
27. E.g., see the analysis in Silverman, "It's a Craft!"
28. E.g., discussed in David Winston, "The Iranian Component in the Bible, Apocrypha, and Qumran," *HR* 5 (1966): 200–5; Marc Philonenko, "La doctrine qoumrânienne des deux Esprits," in *Apocalyptique iranienne et dualisme qoumranien*, ed. Geo Widengren, Anders Hultgård, and Marc Philonenko (Paris: Maisonneuve, 1995),

this question have thus been rehearsed many times—particularly the place of the Treatise within the broader corpus as well as the meaning of dualism, not to mention the interpretation of the text itself and whether or not it was originally independent of its 1QS context.[29] A full assessment of influence on this text deserves a monograph. This section will attempt to demonstrate how the methodological considerations above are necessary for a more fully satisfactory answer to the problem.

As De Jong has already sketched, the Treatise contains quite a few detailed parallels to Zoroastrian cosmology, and indeed, Collins sees them to be sufficiently strong to describe them as straightforwardly derived from Zoroastrianism.[30] For present purposes a list of some of these parallels will suffice:[31] the importance of knowledge for the ultimate divinity (1QS III, 15 // Theopompus *apud* Plutarch, *Is. Os.* 369e); divine appointment of

---

163–211; Florentino García Martínez, "Iranian Influences in Qumran?," in *Qumranica Minora I: Qumran Origins and Apocalypticism*, STDJ 63 (Leiden: Brill, 2007), 233–37; De Jong, "Iranian Connections in the Dead Sea Scrolls," 490–95; Paul Heger, "Another Look at Dualism in Qumran Writings," in *Dualism in Qumran*, ed. Géza G. Xeravits, LSTS 76 (London: T&T Clark, 2010), 46–51; Jörg Frey, "Apocalyptic Dualism," in *The Oxford Handbook of Apocalyptic Literature*, ed. John J. Collins (Oxford: Oxford University Press, 2014), esp. 279–84; John J. Collins, *The Apocalyptic Imagination*, 3rd ed. (Grand Rapids: Eerdmans, 2016), 190–93; and Mladen Popović, "Anthropology, Pneumatology, and Demonology in Early Judaism," in *Sibyls, Scriptures, and Scrolls: John Collins at Seventy*, ed. Joel Baden, Hindy Najman, and Eibert J. C. Tigchelaar, JSJSup 175 (Leiden: Brill, 2017), 2:1061–64.

29. See, e.g., Charlotte Hempel, "The Treatise on the Two Spirits and the Literary History of the Rule of the Community," in Xeravits, *Dualism in Qumran*, 102–20; and Gwynned de Looijer, *The Qumran Paradigm: Critical Evaluation of Some Foundational Hypotheses in the Construction of the Qumran Sect*, EJL 43 (Atlanta: SBL Press, 2015), 192–201.

30. De Jong, "Iranian Connections in the Dead Sea Scrolls," especially 491–95; Collins, *Apocalyptic Imagination*, 191.

31. These are all also noted by De Jong, "Iranian Connections in the Dead Sea Scrolls," 491–95, though in a different manner. For convenience, the parentheses contain first a reference to 1QS, then a reference to one plausibly Achaemenid period source for Iranian religious ideas, Theopompus as preserved in Plutarch's *Isis et Osiris*. For a commentary on the usefulness of this text for Iranian religion, see Albert de Jong, *Traditions of the Magi*, RGRW 133 (Leiden: Brill, 1997), 157–204. Native Iranian sources for each of these parallels also exist but present space does not permit their elaboration. Note: the connection between 1QS III, 15 and Plutarch, *Is. Os.* 369e is implied only negatively (as Areimanius is said to be ignorance in contrast to Oromazes).

the end (IV, 18 // 370b); two opposing spirits, associated respectively with truth and light, on one hand, and deceit and darkness, on the other (III, 18–20 // 369e); hierarchy of spirits, with marked hostility between the two groups (III, 20–25; IV, 2–14, 15–17 // 370a); an understanding of these spirits as both ontological entities as well as psychological aspects internal to humans (especially IV, 2–6 and 9–11 // 369e); differential eschatological resolution for the spirits and associated humans (IV, 6–8, 11–14, 18–26 || 370b–c); an understanding of the eschaton as involving elimination of imperfections (IV, 20–23 || 370b); and an acknowledgement of present mixture (III, 21–24; IV, 20–22, 23–26 || 370b). These parallels are specific and numerous enough to fulfill criterion 5. What of the other five criteria?

6.1. Criterion 1: Relative Dating

Without taking a position on the independence of the Treatise from 1QS, the manuscript provides a *terminus ante quem* in the early first century BCE.[32] A *post quem* is more difficult to establish, though one might presume a Hellenistic date.

The source used for comparison above was Plutarch's *Isis et Osiris*, dating to the early second century CE.[33] However, it is generally accepted that his information derives from Theopompus of Chios in the fourth century BCE, thus giving a comfortably Achaemenid era dating to the information quite apart from the other Iranian sources.[34] Thus, despite frequent protests that the best-known Iranian religious texts are attested in late manuscripts, it is clear that the parallel ideas appear in Iran before they appear in the Treatise.

6.2. Criterion 2: Historical Situation

A proper description of the historical situation must deal with the Treatise in terms of its relation to Khirbet Qumran, the Essenes and/or other

---

32. Philip S. Alexander and Géza Vermes, *Qumran Cave 4.XIX: Serekh Ha-Yaḥad and Two Related Texts*, DJD 26 (Oxford: Clarendon, 1998), 20, date 1QS to 100–75 BCE on paleographical grounds.

33. According to Glen W. Bowersock, "Some Persons in Plutarch's *Moralia*," *CQ* 15 (1965): 267.

34. Gordon S. Shrimpton, *Theopompus the Historian* (Montréal: McGill-Queen's University Press, 1991). For a discussion of Iranian sources and their dating, see Silverman, *Persepolis and Jerusalem*, 39–75.

sectarians, and/or the Hasmoneans, as well as whether the finds represent a library, libraries, or something else. These are questions on which there is no consensus, to my knowledge. However, we can sketch in very broad terms the likelihood that Hellenistic period literature continued traditions that were shaped during the Persian Empire, thus providing a set of circumstances into which the specific historical context that gave rise to the Treatise and/or its incorporation into 1QS can be placed. To do this I wish to highlight in passing three things: (1) Persian administration and its continuation; (2) Aramaic and Achaemenid local elites; and (3) Enoch and Aramaic scholarship.

6.2.1. Persian Administration

Judeans and Samarians are attested within Persian administration at various locales and in a variety of roles.[35] Despite the fact that scholars such as James Barr and Paul Heger bracket out administration from the phenomenon, it is in fact an excellent location for social interaction, adoption of new practices, and ideological influence.[36] Since many elements of Achaemenid rule were adopted by Alexander and his heirs, this is one useful context for seeing the significance of Iran on the development of the Second Temple period.

6.2.2. Aramaic and Local Elites

Imperial Aramaic formed an administrative language and elite *koine* throughout the Achaemenid Empire. The language was both a practical necessity for local elites within the empire, as well as one method for local elite competition.[37] Though the exact relations of Hebrew and

---

35. E.g., Ḥanniah in Darius II's Elephantine, and Gedaliah ben Banna-Ea in Darius I's Babylon; for the former, see *TAD* C 3.28; and Bezalel Porten and Ada Yardeni, ed., *Textbook of Aramaic Documents from Ancient Egypt* (Winona Lake, IN: Eisenbrauns, 1993), 3:260, 266–67; for the latter, see Matthew W. Stolper, "The Governor of Babylon and Across-the-River in 486 B.C.," *JNES* 48 (1989): 286.

36. *Contra* Barr, "Question of Religious Influence," 210–12; Heger, "Another Look at Dualism in Qumran Writings," 42–43.

37. For a stimulating foray into these areas, see Anne Fitzpatrick-McKinley, *Empire, Power and Indigenous Elites*, JSJSup 169 (Leiden: Brill, 2015). For a look at some economic elements within these processes, see Ian S. Moyer, "Golden Fetters and Economies of Cultural Exchange," *JANER* 6 (2006): 225–56.

Aramaic remain uncertain and contested, there is no doubt that Aramaic, including the imperial variety, was important for literate Judeans and Samarians. A significant number of the manuscripts of the Dead Sea Scrolls are written in Aramaic, some of which were in the imperial variety.[38] This implies at least some continuity in educational tradition, and education always involves values and ideas in addition to any practical elements.

6.2.3. Enoch and Aramaic Scholarship

I have previously argued elsewhere that the Enochic tradition contains under-appreciated Iranian elements, including some modeling of YHWH's heavens on the Achaemenid Empire.[39] More importantly, the Enochic and Aramaic scholarly tradition generally points to the political and social reality that the Persian period Levant was administered in close conjunction with Mesopotamia: first as part of the same satrapy and later with Babylonian satraps.[40] The educational and scholarly milieu can therefore be expected to have both Mesopotamian and Persian ties.[41]

Though these points remain on a fairly nonspecific level, they still demonstrate that there were numerous ways in which scribal practices and traditions were shaped by the Achaemenid and post-Achaemenid realities.

---

38. On the spread of Aramaic in general, see Holger Gzella, "Verbreitung, Entwicklung, und Gebrauch aramäischer Dialekte in Palästina in der ersten Hälfte des 1. Jahrtausends v. Chr.," in *Sprachen im Palästina im 2. und 1. Jahrtausend v. Chr.*, ed. Ulrich Hübner and Herbert Niehr, ADPV 43 (Wiesbaden: Harrassowitz, 2017), 231–64.

39. See Silverman, *Persepolis and Jerusalem*, 130–74; and Silverman, "Vetting the Priest in Zech 3: The Satan between Divine and Achaemenid Administrations," *JHebS* 14 (2014): 1–27. See also Philip F. Esler, *God's Court and Courtiers in the Book of the Watchers* (Eugene: Cascade, 2017).

40. E.g., Matthew W. Stolper, "Belšunu the Satrap," in *Language, Literature, and History: Philological and Historical Studies Presented to Erica Reiner*, ed. Francesca Rochberg-Halton, AOS 67 (New Haven: American Oriental Society, 1987), 389–402; and Stolper, "Governor of Babylon," 283–305.

41. For an appeal to Aramaic transmission of Mesopotamian knowledge, but from an entirely different focus and basis, see Sanders, *From Adapa to Enoch*, 153–96; cf. Mark Leuchter, *The Levites and the Boundaries of Israelite Identity* (Oxford: Oxford University Press, 2017), 222–29.

6.3. Criterion 3: Source Logic

Both Shaked and De Jong have already eloquently argued that Iranian cosmological dualism is much more coherent in its native context than in monistic ones.[42] In the Zoroastrian system, Ahura Mazda is wholly good, and thus no evil can be imparted to him. He creates the world in order to defeat his evil rival, creating a battleground in which human ethical and ritual action makes the decisive eschatological victory possible.[43] This is not to say there were no developments or inconsistencies in Iran.[44] However, it does present an answer to the problem of evil that is more or less coherent; this is in fact why Plutarch claims to cite Zoroaster's teaching (*Is. Os.* 369e).

6.4. Criterion 4: Receiving Gap

One element of the space in which a Judean in the Second Temple period could make for dualism was raised at the beginning of this essay: the problem of evil and the need for a theodicy created by YHWH's omnipotence. Received biblical traditions explicitly derive both good and evil from YHWH, and thus it is no surprise to find the Treatise doing the same. Nevertheless, this creates a theological difficulty, one so profound that it continues to vex monotheistic traditions to the present day. The problem of theodicy is one that admits a variety of solutions. The solution taken within the Treatise is merely one of these potential solutions.

---

42. Shaul Shaked, "The Notions *Mēnog* and *Gētīg* in the Pahlavi Texts and Their Relation to Eschatology," in *From Zoroastrian Iran to Islam: Studies in Religious History and Intercultural Contacts* (Aldershot: Variorum, 1995), 87 n. 88; cf. Shaked, "Eschatology I: In Zoroastrianism and Zoroastrian Influence," *EIr* 9 (1999): https://tinyurl.com/SBL3551d; and De Jong, "Iranian Connections in the Dead Sea Scrolls," 493.

43. For in-depth discussions, see James W. Boyd and Donald A. Crosby, "Is Zoroastrianism Dualistic or Monotheistic?," *JAAR* 47 (1979): 557–88; Mary Boyce, "Apocalyptic (That Which Has Been Revealed) i. In Zoroastrianism," *EIr* 2 (1986): 154–57; and Silverman, *Persepolis and Jerusalem*, 39–45.

44. Most prominent in relation to 1QS are the variations in understanding the exact relationship between Ahura Mazda (and Spenta Mainyu) and Angra Mainyu, speculations over Zurvan, and different visions of whether the *eschaton* annihilated evil or merely contained it, not to mention triplication of the scheme and varying degrees of determinism. For some of these issues, see De Jong, *Traditions of the Magi*; and Shaul Shaked, *Dualism in Transformation: Varieties of Religion in Sasanian Iran*, Jordan Lectures 1991 (London: School of Oriental and African Studies, 1994).

6.5. Criterion 5: Interpretive Change

As often noted, the Treatise departs from the typical Zoroastrian conceptions in two fundamental ways.[45] First, both good and evil are attributed to God himself (1QS III, 15–16, 25–26). Second, there is an insistence on strict "double predestination," to use an anachronistic term (III, 15–16, 25). However, reinterpretations of this kind are to be expected for the phenomenon of influence. In order for a Judean to make use of a cosmological dualism, *the dualism would have to be adapted* to the sole divinity of YHWH. The Treatise maintains the tradition of YHWH being responsible for both good and evil, but the latter is managed by increasing his transcendence and by his favoritism toward one side. Moreover, the strongly deterministic element to this vision was one reinterpretation that various Zoroastrian scholars also indulged in from time to time. This is quite understandable within teleological eschatology: if the end is purposeful and predetermined, one can do as the Treatise does and argue the same for the intervening time.[46] Inherited traditions of YHWH's choice of Israel can easily be read deterministically, much more so than the Zoroastrian insistence on individual choice. Therefore, this element is another clear sign of interpretative change on the part of the Treatise.

7. Structures

As the last three sections made clear, the structural rules of Iranian religion and Second Temple Judaism were different. This means that the moving of an idea from one to the other would involve reinterpretation, as well as likely have different importance to each system. In fact, both are clearly the case here. For the Treatise, the dualism has become second order. Moreover, while it clearly helps to fill a need (theodicy), it does not

---

45. Considered as "incompatible" by Heger, "Another Look at Dualism in Qumran Writings," 46, but due to an unproductive understanding of the phenomenon of influence, whereby something must only derive from one or another source. He makes little allowance for a more complicated human development. Similarly, De Looijer, *Qumran Paradigm*, 230–31, is too strict in her application of dualism, confusing emphasis with structure and expecting systematic coherency where that is an unreasonable expectation.

46. Not to mention Mesopotamian deterministic speculations, particularly concerning the Great Year, which influenced Iranian scholars as well; see, e.g., Mary Boyce, "Further on the Calendar of Zoroastrian Feasts," *Iran* 43 (2005): 10.

displace more central elements in the Judaic system. The understanding of human choice is impacted, but as the function is compatible with a sectarian self-understanding, it is easily adaptable to less thoroughly dualistic oppositions (as seems to be the case with its integration into and presence in 1QS). It is also clearly within a tradition that has accepted apocalypticism, with eschatological expectations structuring its view of the cosmos.[47]

A broader set of intellectual structures should also be considered for the Achaemenid and Seleucid periods. One should reckon with a more cosmopolitan intellectual horizon for the highly educated than is sometimes considered. Not only had Aramaic been a lingua franca for many years, but the Seleucids and Hasmoneans interacted with Hellenistic Greek education and scholarship. Within this setting, there were multiple avenues for Iranian ideas and traditions to be part of the intellectual discourse. Whether inherited from educational practices developed during the Achaemenid era, communities in touch with Parthian or expatriate Iranian communities, and/or Greek mediation, Iran should be considered as much a part of this mix as Greek, Egyptian, and Mesopotamian traditions are.

Sadly, this essay does not have the space to assess the place of the scribes of the manuscripts found near Qumran within the social structure of Second Temple Judaism. While it would be highly unlikely that such literate and educated individuals were peasants, their social status and relations with the local aristocracy deserve further investigation. For present purposes it is worth stating that understanding this social status is not confined to the question of whether or not some or all of the scrolls derive from a sect,[48] just as the sociological understanding of apocalypses is not confined to millenarianism. Rather, very basic questions of the relationships between scribes, priests, landowners, and artisans in Yehud and Samaria remain to be elucidated in more depth. It would be potentially helpful to know how those with interest in and/or with knowledge of Iranian ideas might be engaged in discourse with these various collectivities.

---

47. In my view, eschatology only refers to the decisive end, not just vague future hopes.

48. On Qumran sectarianism, see the useful discussion in Jutta Jokiranta, "Sociological Approaches to Qumran Sectarianism," in Lim and Collins, *Oxford Handbook of the Dead Sea Scrolls*, 200–31.

8. Imperial Contexts

One important imperial context for the Dead Sea Scrolls is the Hasmonean Dynasty's interaction with the Seleucids. While this dynamic is typically considered in terms of Hellenism, it involved struggles over the roles and definitions of key leadership positions: priests and kings. Both of these terms and roles begin their Second Temple journey under Achaemenid rule.[49] The heritage and memory of the Persian Empire is thus an important part even of the (presumed) Seleucid context of the Treatise. While this alone does not provide a very precise context for the writing of the Treatise, it does mean it is part of a broader intellectual heritage in which Iranian elements should not appear too surprising.

Overall, the use of cosmological dualism within the Treatise appears to fulfill all six criteria for Iranian influence. It also has some general structural reasons for understanding the necessary interaction as plausible. Although the lack of a more precise context for the writing of the Treatise means that finer-grained answers for why the author chose to formulate the text in the extant manner or whether the influence was conscious or unconscious are unclear, these do not detract from the basic plausibility.

9. The Corpus of the Dead Sea Scrolls, Apocalypticism, and Iran: A Way Forward

The above discussion affirmed one instance of proposed Iranian influence and rejected another. However, a proper assessment of the question cannot and should not end there. Nor should the question merely be posed for endless individual case studies. Rather, the complete publication of the Dead Sea Scrolls should be a spur towards more sophisticated, structural considerations of individual manuscripts, their relations to the various caves and potential libraries, the entire corpus, and the relation to Second Temple Judaism. These kinds of investigations will make clearer the lines of discourse and hermeneutics involved in the development of the various Judean sects, parties, and literate elites, whether apocalyptic or not. It was within these lines that the various extant authors were able to use, modify, or reject ideas that modern scholars can recognize as deriving from Iran.

---

49. E.g., Silverman, "From Remembering to Expecting the 'Messiah,'" 419–46. See also Rolf Strootman and Miguel John Versluys, eds., *Persianism in Antiquity* (Stuttgart: Steiner, 2017), especially parts 2 and 3.

This is just as true for apocalyptic elements of Second Temple Judaism as it is for those that were not. Thus I would argue that the corpus provides an opportunity not only to flesh out the "apocalyptic hermeneutic"[50] but a broader set of hermeneutics.

Moreover, in addition to taking a broad view of the relevant corpus, I think assessment of questions of influence must begin to integrate a longer-term view of imperial dynamics as well as a more sophisticated understanding of Judean social structures. It is not sufficient to speak merely of resistance to empire as the only way Judean apocalypticists (not to say scribes!) could and did interact with empires. Beyond simply recognizing the existence of positive and negative, conscious and unconscious forms of influence, the social dynamics of scribes were likely more complex than merely supporting or resisting contemporaneous regimes. A look at the complete corpus should be of help in nuancing such questions by demonstrating the multiplicity of voices and interpretations visible. Some of these interpretations were not only internal Judean developments but were part of Judean interactions with a broader world. These interactions were naturally of many kinds, and some of these we can profitably understand as influence—from Iran and beyond.

Bibliography

Agostini, Domenico. "On Iranian and Jewish Apocalyptics, Again." *JOAS* 136 (2016): 495–505.

Alexander, Philip S., and Géza Vermes. *Qumran Cave 4.XIX: Serekh ha-Yaḥad and Two Related Texts*. DJD 26. Oxford: Clarendon, 1998.

Anquetil-Duperron, Abraham-Hyacinthe. *Zend-Avesta, ouvrage de Zoroastre, contenant les idées théologiques, physiques & morales de ce législateur, les cérémonies du culte religieux qu'il a établi, & plusieurs traits importans relatifs à l'ancienne histoire des Perses*. Paris: Tillard, 1771.

Barr, James. "The Question of Religious Influence: The Case of Zoroastrianism, Judaism, and Christianity." *JAAR* 53 (1985): 201–35.

Ben Zvi, Ehud. "The Yehudite Collection of Prophetic Books and Imperial Contexts: Some Observations." Pages 145–69 in *Divination, Politics, and Ancient Near Eastern Empires*. Edited by Alan Lenzi and Jonathan Stökl. ANEM 7. Atlanta: Society of Biblical Literature, 2014.

---

50. Silverman, *Persepolis and Jerusalem*, 206–27.

Böklen, Ernst. *Die Verwandtschaft der jüdisch-christlichen mit der parsischen Eschatologie.* Göttingen: Vandenhoeck & Ruprecht, 1902.
Bowersock, Glen W. "Some Persons in Plutarch's *Moralia.*" *CQ* 15 (1965): 267–70.
Boyce, Mary. "Apocalyptic (That Which Has Been Revealed) i. In Zoroastrianism." *EIr* 2 (1986): 154–57.
———. "Further on the Calendar of Zoroastrian Feasts." *Iran* 43 (2005): 1–38.
Boyd, James W., and Donald A. Crosby. "Is Zoroastrianism Dualistic or Monotheistic?" *JAAR* 47 (1979): 557–88.
Collins, John J. *The Apocalyptic Imagination.* 3rd ed. Grand Rapids: Eerdmans, 2016.
Crenshaw, James L. "Education in Ancient Israel." *JBL* 104 (1985): 601–15.
DiTommaso, Lorenzo. *The Dead Sea* New Jerusalem *Text: Contents and Contexts.* TSAJ 110. Tübingen: Mohr Siebeck, 2005.
Erho, Ted M. "The Ahistorical Nature of *1 Enoch* 56:5–8 and Its Ramifications upon the *Opinio Communis* on the Dating of the *Similitudes of Enoch.*" *JSJ* 40 (2009): 23–54.
Esler, Philip F. *God's Court and Courtiers in the Book of the Watchers: Reinterpreting Heaven in 1 Enoch 1–36.* Eugene: Cascade, 2017.
Firby, Nora Kathleen. *European Travellers and Their Perceptions of Zoroastrians in the Seventeenth and Eighteenth Centuries.* Archäologische Mitteilungen aus Iran Ergänzungsband 14. Berlin: Reimer, 1988.
Fitzpatrick-McKinley, Anne. *Empire, Power and Indigenous Elites: A Case Study of the Nehemiah Memoir.* JSJSup 169. Leiden: Brill, 2015.
Frey, Jörg. "Apocalyptic Dualism." Pages 271–94 in *The Oxford Handbook of Apocalyptic Literature.* Edited by John J. Collins. Oxford: Oxford University Press, 2014.
Frye, Richard N. *The Heritage of Central Asia: From Antiquity to the Turkish Expansion.* Second printing. Princeton: Markus Wiener, 1998.
García Martínez, Florentino. "Iranian Influences in Qumran?" Pages 227–41 in *Qumranica Minora I: Qumran Origins and Apocalypticism.* STDJ 63. Leiden: Brill, 2007.
Gzella, Holger. "Verbreitung, Entwicklung, und Gebrauch aramäischer Dialekte in Palästina in der ersten Hälfte des 1. Jahrtausends v. Chr." Pages 231–64 in *Sprachen im Palästina im 2. und 1. Jahrtausend v. Chr.* Edited by Ulrich Hübner and Herbert Niehr. ADPV 43. Wiesbaden: Harrassowitz, 2017.

Heger, Paul. "Another Look at Dualism in Qumran Writings." Pages 39–101 in *Dualism in Qumran*. Edited by Géza G. Xeravits. LSTS 76. London: T&T Clark, 2010.

Hempel, Charlotte. "The Treatise on the Two Spirits and the Literary History of the Rule of the Community." Pages 102–20 in *Dualism in Qumran*. Edited by Géza G. Xeravits. LSTS 76. London: T&T Clark, 2010.

Hinnells, John R. "Zoroastrian Influence on the Judeo-Christian Tradition." *Journal of the K. R. Cama Oriental Institute* 45 (1976): 1–23.

Hyde, Thomas. *Historia religionis veterum Persarum*. Oxford: Sheldonian Theatre, 1700.

Janzen, David. "Yahwistic Appropriation of Achaemenid Ideology and the Function of Nehemiah 9 in Ezra-Nehemiah." *JBL* 136 (2017): 839–56.

Jokiranta, Jutta. "Sociological Approaches to Qumran Sectarianism." Pages 200–31 in *The Oxford Handbook of the Dead Sea Scrolls*. Edited by Timothy H. Lim and John J. Collins. Oxford: Oxford University Press, 2010.

Jong, Albert de. "Iranian Connections in the Dead Sea Scrolls." Pages 479–500 in *The Oxford Handbook of the Dead Sea Scrolls*. Edited by Timothy H. Lim and John J. Collins. Oxford: Oxford University Press, 2010.

———. *Traditions of the Magi: Zoroastrianism in Greek and Latin Literature*. RGRW 133. Leiden: Brill, 1997.

Kautsky, John H. *The Politics of Aristocratic Empires*. Chapel Hill: University of North Carolina Press, 1982.

Kiel, Yishai. "Reinventing Mosaic Torah in Ezra-Nehemiah in the Light of the Law (*Dāta*) of Ahura Mazda and Zarathustra." *JBL* 136 (2017): 323–45.

Lerner, Jeffrey D. *The Impact of Seleucid Decline on the Eastern Iranian Plateau: The Foundations of Arsacid Parthia and Graeco-Bactria*. Historia Einzelschriften 123. Stuttgart: Steiner, 1999.

Leuchter, Mark. *The Levites and the Boundaries of Israelite Identity*. Oxford: Oxford University Press, 2017.

Light, Timothy H. "Orthosyncretism: An Account of Melding in Religion." *MTSR* 12 (2000): 162–85.

Looijer, Gwynned de. *The Qumran Paradigm: Critical Evaluation of Some Foundational Hypotheses in the Construction of the Qumran Sect*. EJL 43. Atlanta: SBL Press, 2015.

Marchand, Suzanne L. *German Orientalism in the Age of Empire: Race, Religion, and Scholarship*. Cambridge: Cambridge University Press, 2009.

Moyer, Ian S. "Golden Fetters and Economies of Cultural Exchange." *JANER* 6 (2006): 225–56.

Neusner, Jacob. "Judeo-Persian Communities of Iran iii. The Parthian and Sasanian Periods." *EIr* 15 (2009): 96–103.

Niskanen, Paul. *The Human and the Divine in History: Herodotus and the Book of Daniel*. JSOTSup 396. London: T&T Clark, 2004.

Overman, J. Andrew. "Between Rome and Parthia: Galilee and the Implications of Empire." Pages 279–300 in *A Wandering Galilean: Essays in Honour of Seán Freyne*. Edited by Zuleika Rodgers, Margaret Daly-Denton, and Anne Fitzpatrick-McKinley. JSJSup 132. Leiden: Brill, 2009.

Philonenko, Marc. "La Doctrine qoumrânienne des deux Esprits." Pages 163–211 in *Apocalyptique iranienne et dualisme qoumranien*. Edited by Geo Widengren, Anders Hultgård, and Marc Philonenko. Paris: Maisonneuve, 1995.

———. "La Nouvelle Jérusalem et le Vara de Yima." Pages 139–46 in *La Cité de Dieu/Die Stadt Gottes. 3. Symposium Strasbourg, Tübingen, Uppsala 19.–23. September 1998 in Tübingen*. Edited by Martin Hengel, Siegfried Mittmann, and Anna Maria Schwemer. WUNT 129. Tübingen: Mohr Siebeck, 2000.

Porten, Belazel, and Ada Yardeni, eds. *Textbook of Aramaic Documents from Ancient Egypt*. 4 vols. Winona Lake, IN: Eisenbrauns, 1986–1999.

Popović, Mladen. "Anthropology, Pneumatology, and Demonology in Early Judaism: The Two Spirits Treatise (1QS 3:13–4:26) and Other Texts from the Dead Sea Scrolls." Pages 1029–67 in vol. 2 of *Sibyls, Scriptures, and Scrolls: John Collins at Seventy*. Edited by Joel Baden, Hindy Najman, and Eibert J. C. Tigchelaar. JSJSup 175.2. Leiden: Brill, 2017.

Sanders, Seth L. *From Adapa to Enoch: Scribal Culture and Religious Vision in Judea and Babylon*. TSAJ 167. Tübingen: Mohr Siebeck, 2017.

Satlow, Michael L. "Beyond Influence: Toward a New Historiographic Paradigm." Pages 37–53 in *Jewish Literatures and Cultures: Context and Intertext*. Edited by Anita Norich and Yaron Z. Eliav. BJS 349. Providence, RI: Brown Judaic Studies, 2008.

Schlude, Jason M., and J. Andrew Overman. "Herod the Great: A Near Eastern Caste Study in Roman-Parthian Politics." Pages 93–110 in

Arsacids, Romans and Local Elites: Cross-Cultural Interactions of the Parthian Empire. Edited by Jason M. Schlude and Benjamin B. Rubin. Oxford: Oxbow, 2017.

Schmid, Konrad. "Taming Egypt: The Impact of Persian Imperial Ideology and Politics on the Biblical Exodus Account." Pages 13–29 in *Jewish Cultural Encounters in the Ancient Mediterranean and Near Eastern World*. Edited by Mladen Popović, Myles Schoonover, and Marijn Vandenberghe. JSJSup 178. Leiden: Brill, 2017.

Schulte, Lucas L. *My Shepherd, Though You Do Not Know Me: The Persian Royal Propaganda Model in the Nehemiah Memoir*. CBET 78. Leuven: Peeters, 2016.

Shaked, Shaul. *Dualism in Transformation: Varieties of Religion in Sasanian Iran*. Jordan Lectures 1991. London: School of Oriental and African Studies, 1994.

———. "Eschatology I: In Zoroastrianism and Zoroastrian Influence." *EIr* 9 (1999): https://tinyurl.com/SBL3551d.

———. "Iranian Influence on Judaism: First Century B.C.E. to Second Century C.E." Pages 308–25 in *Introduction: The Persian Period*. Edited by W. D. Davies and Louis Finkelstein. CHJ 1. Cambridge: Cambridge University Press, 1984.

———. "The Notions *Mēnog* and *Gētīg* in the Pahlavi Texts and Their Relation to Eschatology." Pages 59–107 in *From Zoroastrian Iran to Islam: Studies in Religious History and Intercultural Contacts*. Aldershot: Variorum, 1995.

———. "Zoroastrianism and Judaism." Pages 198–209 in *A Zoroastrian Tapestry: Art, Religion, and Culture*. Edited by Pheroza J. Godrej and Firoza Punthakey Mistree. Ahmedabad: Mapin, 2002.

Sherwin-White, Susan, and Amélie Kuhrt. *From Samarkhand to Sardis: A New Approach to the Seleucid Empire*. London: Duckworth, 1993.

Shrimpton, Gordon S. *Theopompus the Historian*. Montréal: McGill-Queen's University Press, 1991.

Silverman, Jason M. "Achaemenid Creation and Second Isaiah." *JPS* 10 (2017): 26–48.

———. "From Remembering to Expecting the 'Messiah': Achaemenid Kingship as (Re)Formulating Apocalyptic Expectations of David." Pages 419–46 in *Political Memory in and after the Persian Empire*. Edited by Jason M. Silverman and Caroline Waerzeggers. ANEM 13. Atlanta: SBL Press, 2015.

———. "Iranian Influence on Judaism." *Bible and Interpretation* (2011): https://tinyurl.com/SBL3551c.

———. "It's a Craft! It's a Cavern! It's a Castle! Yima's *Vara*, Iranian Flood Myths, and Jewish Apocalyptic Traditions." Pages 191–230 in *Opening Heaven's Floodgates: The Genesis Flood Narrative, Its Contexts and Reception*. Edited by Jason M. Silverman. Piscataway, NJ: Gorgias, 2013.

———. *Persepolis and Jerusalem: Iranian Influence on the Apocalyptic Hermeneutic*. LHBOTS 558. London: T&T Clark, 2012.

———. "Vetting the Priest in Zech 3: The Satan between Divine and Achaemenid Administrations." *JHebS* 14 (2014): 1–27.

Stolper, Matthew W. "Belšunu the Satrap." Pages 389–402 in *Language, Literature, and History: Philological and Historical Studies Presented to Erica Reiner*. Edited by Francesca Rochberg-Halton. AOS 67. New Haven: American Oriental Society, 1987.

———. "The Governor of Babylon and Across-the-River in 486 B.C." *JNES* 48 (1989): 283–305.

Strootman, Rolf, and Miguel John Versluys, eds. *Persianism in Antiquity*. Stuttgart: Steiner, 2017.

Toorn, Karel van der. *Scribal Culture and the Making of the Hebrew Bible*. Cambridge: Harvard University Press, 2007.

Vroom, Hendrik M. "Syncretism and Dialogue: A Philosophical Analysis." Pages 103–12 in *Syncretism in Religion: A Reader*. Edited by Anita M. Leopold and Jeppe Sinding Jensen. London: Equinox, 2004.

Whitters, Mark. "The Persianized Liturgy of Nehemiah 8:1–18." *JBL* 136 (2017): 63–84.

Widengren, Geo. "Iran and Israel in Parthian Times with Special Regard to the Ethiopic Book of Enoch." *Temenos* 2 (1966): 139–77.

———. *Iranisch-semitische Kulturbegegnung in parthischer Zeit*. AFLNW 70. Cologne: Westdeutscher Verlag, 1960.

Winston, David. "The Iranian Component in the Bible, Apocrypha, and Qumran: A Review of the Evidence." *HR* 5 (1966): 183–216.

A New Proposal: Rereading Dreams and Visions in Early Jewish Literature (4Q530, 4Q544, 4Q204, and 1 Enoch 1–36)

Frances Flannery

Traditional English translations have obscured the way that many early Jewish texts from the Hellenistic and Roman eras understand the conceptual relationship between a "dream" (חלם, חלמא) and a "vision" (חזון, חזות, חזיון, חזוא, חזוה), as well as how persons would experience these phenomena. In an adjustment to earlier ways of categorizing dreams and visions, including my own,[1] I argue that some early Jewish texts understand a dream as a hypnagogic state induced by sleep, while a vision is the totality of the experiences of numinous realities accessed either within that state or in a waking state. That is, a vision is the whole sensorial, perceptual, sapiential, emotional, and numinous experience that special persons are granted by the divine, whether in a sleeping dream or in a waking state. Since the act of seeing a dream or vision therefore does not entail normal sight with the eyes, the use of the English term "see" to translate חזה, the typical verb used for experiencing dreams and visions, unintentionally limits the early Jewish understanding of what these phenomena entailed and how they were experienced.

1. Terminological and Categorical Confusion and a Proposed Solution

Throughout the various regions of Near Eastern and Mediterranean antiquity, texts describe divinely sent dreams in ways that are fairly consistent cross-culturally. As Leo A. Oppenheim pointed out, in Akkadian

---

1. Frances Flannery-Dailey, *Dreamers, Scribes, and Priests: Jewish Dreams in the Hellenistic and Roman Eras*, JSJSup 90 (Leiden: Brill, 2004), 117.

dreams are normally "seen" (*amāru, naṭālu,* and rarely *naplusu*) but then "only when the deity is introduced as causing the dream, *šubrû*."[2] In rare instances, he notes, a dream is "brought" or "carried," using the passive form of *abālu*.[3] Certainly, visual imagery predominates as the mode of experiencing dreams, but English translations that revert simply to "see" often obscure subtle distinctions. As Irene J. Winter notes, "there was a well-developed vocabulary for seeing and looking in both Sumerian and Akkadian.… A plethora of verbs … cover as many nuanced aspects as one could find in modern English: to see, behold … to regard, look at, observe, inspect; to survey, explore, examine; to stare."[4] These differences are lost when translations reduce the range of terms to seeing dreams and visions.

Most translations of early Jewish dream texts preserved in Semitic languages retain this tradition, translating the verbs by which dreams and visions are experienced as "see." A person sometimes "dreams" (חלם, Hebrew and Aramaic) but more often "sees" (חזה or ראה) a "dream" (חלום, Hebrew; חלמא, Aramaic). A person also "sees" (חזה or ראה) a "vision" (חזיון, חזות, Hebrew; חזו, חזוא, חזות, Aramaic). Translations of Syriac texts follow suit. In Syriac, ܚܠܡ denotes dreaming while the nominal forms ܚܠܡ and ܚܠܡܐ are translated as a dream. Typically the dream is paired with the verb ܚܙܐ, as in Hebrew and Aramaic. Thus, ܚܙܘܐ is a vision, usually translated "I saw a vision," ܚܙܝܬ ܚܙܘܐ (cf. 4 Ezra 11.1).[5]

However, the default translation of חזה and ראה both as "see," as well as ܚܙܐ as "see," may be misleading. The terms חזה or ܚܙܐ do not indicate any normal mode of seeing. Certainly, a dream is not seen with the eyes, and there are nuances to how early Jewish authors conveyed the experience of a dream or a vision. Moreover, this usage obscures when seeing might actually be the best translation, for example, in the case of verbs such as ראה (Zech 1:8) or εἶδον (1 En. 14.2) or in the rare cases when a dream is called a מראה, as in 4QVisSam (4Q160 1 3) and 4QPseudo-Ezekiel[a] (4Q385).

---

2. Leo A. Oppenheim, *The Interpretation of Dreams in the Ancient Near East* (Philadelphia: American Philosophical Society, 1956), 226.

3. Oppenheim, *Interpretation of Dreams*, 226.

4. Irene J. Winter, "The Eyes Have It: Votive Statuary, Gilgamesh's Axe, and Cathected Viewing in the Ancient Near East," in *Visuality before and beyond the Renaissance*, ed. Robert S. Nelson (Cambridge: Cambridge University Press, 2000), 22–44.

5. Flannery-Dailey, *Dreamers, Scribes, and Priests*, 129–32.

Early Jewish texts draw on a longstanding and widespread ancient Near Eastern and ancient Mediterranean tradition that understands a dream as a perception that occurs in a special kind of sleep. Beginning with ancient Sumer, the terms ᵈMA-MÚ or ᵈMA-MÙ mean either "dream" or "sleep." As Oppenheim noted, this state forms a kind of "cushion" for encountering extraordinary realities, whether a messenger, an otherworldly tour, or a set of symbols that relays a message when interpreted.[6] In whatever form it occurs, the substance of what dreamers encounter in this state is considered to be real. For instance, many ancient Near Eastern accounts portray deities who arrive in a dream and commence their message to the dreamer by asking, "are you asleep, NN?"[7] By arriving in a dream and meeting the dreamer first in a hypnagogic state, the dreamer is somehow better able to endure the full bracing effect of encountering a divine messenger.

Similarly, early Jewish texts approach the phenomenon of dreams as a way to soften the impact caused by encountering extraordinary realities. For instance, Ezra explains he had a dream of the angel Uriel, which scared him greatly: "Then I awoke, and my body shuddered violently, and my soul was so troubled that it fainted." He continues however, by saying, "But the angel who had come and talked with me [inside my dream earlier] held me and strengthened me" (4 Ezra 5.14).[8] The dream state was necessary for Ezra to first encounter the angel, but now he is used to Uriel, who is a comfort to him outside his dream. Thus, the dream content—meeting Uriel and having conversations—was always entirely real.[9] This sentiment is relayed quite vividly in the late antique Ladder of Jacob, when Jacob states, "But I was not afraid of [the angel's] glance, for the face *I had seen in my dream was more terrifying than this*; and I was not afraid of the angel's glance" (Ladd. Jac. 3.2–3).[10] Dreams are necessary preparations for subsequent numinous encounters, whether these occur inside or outside of the dream.

---

6. Oppenheim, *Interpretation of Dreams*, 226.

7. Oppenheim, *Interpretation of Dreams*, 189; and Flannery-Dailey, *Dreamers, Scribes, and Priests*, 20–24.

8. All English translations of 4 Ezra are from the composite manuscript established by Michael E. Stone, *Fourth Ezra: A Commentary on the Book of Fourth Ezra*, Hermeneia (Minneapolis: Fortress, 1990).

9. Flannery-Dailey, *Dreamers, Scribes, and Priests*, 215–17.

10. A. Pennington, "Ladder of Jacob," in *The Apocryphal Old Testament*, ed. H. F. D. Sparks (Oxford: Clarendon, 1984), 453–64.

The idea of a dream as a special hypnagogic state in which one may perceive extraordinary realities is conveyed clearly in the Egyptian (and Coptic) term for dream, *rswt*, which Oppenheim translated as "to see a dream" or "to see something in a dream." This term stems from the root "to awaken" and is written with the determinative or ideogram of an open eye.[11] To see in a dream is a special kind of seeing, for, the ancients believed, in this way we can encounter in some way *real* beings, events, places, and realities that we ordinarily could not physically see. Even in the case of symbolic dreams, the symbol is a version of an actual reality. We have a record of this understanding of dreams in an early second millennium BCE in the Old Babylonian fragment of Epic of Gilgamesh. The hero tells his dream to his mother, saying he *saw* a wonderful axe: "I saw it, and I felt joy; I loved it as (one would) a woman" (*āmuršuma ahtadu anāku arāmšuma kīma aššatim*; 2.32–34). Then he caressed the axe and called it his brother.[12] This dream symbol prepares him for and predicts the coming of his real weapon / friend / brother Enkidu, and encountering it in the dream evokes deep emotion.

Hence, using the English term "see" as a default translation for the experiencing of dreams and visions could be unintentionally misleading, particularly as "see" is associated primarily with eyesight or cognitive apprehension. Readers of such a translation would thus require constant reminding of the full range of the sensory, cognitive, emotional, numinous, and sapiential experiences conveyed in dreams. It would be more accurate to translate the verb חזה more literally as "visioning," since it is the verbal form of חזיון or ܚܙܘܐ, a vision. I am not against this translation. However, in English this could lead to untenable confusion, since the present tense of "visioning" would be "visions," the same form as the plural noun (i.e., it is not much improvement to say "he visions visions" or "I vision a vision").

The English verb "envision," while better than "see," is also inadequate, for it carries the implication in modern English of an inward, imaginative, fictional process. This too is misleading in ancient contexts, which considered the objects of a vision to be ultimately more real than the waking world that visionaries encountered. I propose that if we found a word meaning "accessing numinous realities in a hypnagogic state that were

---

11. Oppenheim, *Interpretation of Dreams*, 226.
12. Winter, "Eyes Have It," 24.

previously imperceptible," we would come much closer to conveying the oneiric, visionary experience the texts posit.

Until a better solution is found, a possible a suitable translation is already available in Brown, Driver, and Briggs, which offers not only "see" as a translation of חזה, but also "behold."[13] The term "behold," although archaic sounding, better captures the sensorial, perceptual, numinous, emotional, and sapiential impressions made on the visionary or dreamer during the experience of a phenomenon that is remarkable. The awe-inspiring quality is adequately conveyed by "he beheld a dream."

2. Rereading Dreams and Visions in Early Jewish Texts

The proper translation and interpretation of several passages in early Jewish texts is made difficult not only by the challenge of aptly translating הזה, but also because of the close association of the terms "dream" and "vision," which are often juxtaposed, for example: "Daniel [*beheld a dream*] [חלם חזה], *and visions of his head* [וחזוי ראשה]" (Dan 7:1). Some scholars of early Jewish texts see little distinction between dreams and visions and have opted for the elided term "dream-vision" to denote the broad range of episodes to which the terms are applied.[14] I too have stated that the terms appear at times to be used "interchangeably," but this is not quite right.[15]

Some ancient texts *do* clearly distinguish between sleeping and waking states of numinous perception. The oldest known visionary tour of the underworld, the seventh-century BCE text known as The Underworld Vision of an Assyrian Crown Prince, contains both a *šuttu*, a dream, and a *tabrītu*, a vision. Seth L. Sanders explains: "While a *šuttu* is simply a dream, *tabrītu* appears frequently in the vocabulary of Sennacherib and Essarhaddon to describe building projects—actually existing physical objects. It refers to awe-inspiring things seen with the eye."[16] I suggest

---

13. BDB, s.v. "חזה."
14. John S. Hanson, "Dreams and Visions in the Graeco-Roman World and Early Christianity," in *ANRW* 2.23.2:1395–427; and Andrew B. Perrin, *The Dynamics of Dream-Vision Revelation in the Aramaic Dead Sea Scrolls*, JAJSup 19 (Gottingen: Vandenhoeck & Ruprecht, 2015), 92–94.
15. Flannery-Dailey, *Dreamers, Scribes, and Priests*, 132.
16. Seth L. Sanders, "The First Tour of Hell: From Neo-Assyrian Propaganda to Early Jewish Revelation," *JANER* 9 (2009): 158.

that a similar distinction is to be made in the case of early Jewish dreams and visions.

Despite cultural differences, most of us have the same nightly experience, in which we dream with our eyes closed, open our eyes as we wake up, and then get up. In fact, it is the case that most mammals do.[17] Similarly, throughout the ancient Near Eastern and Greco-Roman worlds, divinely sent dreams were associated with sleeping, night, beds, and other settings that correlate with the hypnagogic state familiar to all mammals who slumber nightly. Hence, "Daniel *beheld a dream* [חזה חלם] and *visions of his head* [וחזוי ראשה] *on his bed* [על־משכבה]" (Dan 7:1). Dreams and visions are not the same phenomena, although they may be related and overlapping, as I now show is the case for several texts from Qumran.

2.1. 4Q530 (4QEnGiants[b] ar)

A dream episode[18] in 4Q530 (4QEnGiants[b] ar) offers a typical condensed report of a dream episode, save for the fact that the dreamers are two giants:

באדין חלמו תריהון חלמין ונדת שנת עיניהון וק[מו {שנת עיניהון מנהון וקמו} ופ]תחו עיניהון

---

17. While it has now been shown that all mammals (even the echidna, platypuses, and other monotremes) do dream, not all species shut their eyes to do so. Dolphins, for instance, dream in one hemisphere of the brain while they open the opposite eye, then switch. The active hemisphere allows them to continue breathing and swimming.

18. According to Stuckenbruck's proposed outline for the Book of Giants, this fragment may be the second pair of dreams that the giants Hahyah and Ohyah experience. See Loren T. Stuckenbruck, "The *Book of Giants* among the Dead Sea Scrolls: Considerations of Method and a New Proposal on the Reconstruction of 4Q530," in *Ancient Tales of Giants from Qumran and Turfan: Contexts, Traditions, and Influences*, ed. Matthew Goff, Loren T. Stuckenbruck, and Enrico Morano, WUNT 360 (Tübingen: Mohr Siebeck, 2016), 129–44.

19. מנהון appears in the editions of Milik, Puech, and Stuckenbruck but is missing in that of García Martínez and Tigchelaar. See Jósef T. Milik, *The Books of Enoch: Aramaic Fragments of Qumrân Cave 4*, with the collaboration of Matthew Black (Oxford: Clarendon, 1976); Émile Puech, *Qumrân Grotte 4.XXII: Textes araméens, première partie, 4Q529–549*, DJD 31 (Oxford: Clarendon, 2001), 28; Florentino García Martínez and Eibert J. C. Tigchelaar, eds., *The Dead Sea Scrolls Study Edition*, 2 vols. (Leiden: Brill, 1997–1998), 2:1062–64; and Loren T. Stuckenbruck, *The Book of Giants from Qumran: Texts, Translation, and Commentary*, TSAJ 63 (Tübingen: Mohr Siebeck, 1997), 119.

Then two of them dreamed their dreams, and the sleep of their eyes fled from them and they ar[ose ...], {and the sleep of their eyes from them and they arose}. (4Q530 2 II, 4)[20]

Émile Puech as well as Florentino García Martínez and Eibert J. C. Tigchelaar follow this with a fragment that reads "they opened their eyes" (פתחו עיניהון), which Loren T. Stuckenbruck omits.[21]

It is important to look carefully at the precise terms used in the Book of the Giants to explain this phenomenon. Dreams are *dreamed* (חלמו חלמין) (4Q530 2 II, 3), and the giants' eyes were filled with sleep when this occurred. Next, "the sleep of their eyes fled from them" (ונדת שנת עיניהון מנהון) (4Q530 2 II, 4).[22] A scribal error repeating most of this phrase then occurs (Puech marks it as *letter superflue* with brackets), which resonates with the phrase "sleep fled from him" in Dan 6:19 (שנתה נדת עלוהי). This action is equated with waking up, and it leads to the concluding verb, קמו, which means "to arise," "stand up," or "get up." The act of standing up (קמו) is a typical conclusion to dreams in other Jewish literature, indicating that someone is no longer asleep and lying down (e.g., 4 Ezra 5.14; 6.13; 7.1; cf. Dan 8:27). After this action, according to the reconstruction of Puech, "they opened their eyes": פתחו עיניהון. If this construction of fragments is correct, perhaps the actions occur in quick succession: the giants wake from a dream and jump to their feet before they can fully take in the waking world around them.

Thus the parameters of the setting in which the dream state is achieved are demarcated quite clearly:

Beginning: Their eyes are closed. Their eyes have sleep in them.
Middle: They dreamed a dream (the content is related later).
Conclusion: Sleep fled their eyes. They stood up. They opened their eyes.

---

20. Aramaic and English translation from García Martínez and Tigchelaar, *Dead Sea Scrolls Study Edition*, 2:1062.

21. Puech, *Qumrân Grotte 4.XXII*, 28; García Martínez and Tigchelaar, *Dead Sea Scrolls Study Edition*, 2:1062–64; Stuckenbruck, *Book of Giants*, 109; the earlier version by Milik, *Books of Enoch*, 304, differs too much for helpful comparison.

22. The remainder of the Aramaic follows Puech, *Qumrân Grotte 4.XXII*, 28, unless otherwise noted.

While common sense tells us that the text is phrasing this experience within the setting of sleep we all experience nightly, this careful textual attention to the closing and opening of the giants' eyes, and whether sleep filled their eyes, otherwise proves confusing if we were to translate their telling of the dream content merely as something they saw.

This telling occurs when one of the giants, Hahyah, decides to tell his dream to the assembly of the Nephilim. Afterwards, he states: [ב]חלמי הוית חזא בליליא דן (4Q530 2 II, 6–7). Following tradition, García Martínez and Tigchelaar translate this "[in] my dream I have *seen* [חזא] in this night."[23] Similarly, Puech translates this as, "[dans] mon songe j'ai *vue* cette nuit."[24] Yet as I have argued, both "see" and "vue" for חזא are too limiting as translations for an experience that the text painstakingly explains is perceived *with closed eyes full of sleep* and that vanishes when the sleep *leaves their eyes and their eyes are opened.*

Recognizing the multifaceted experience that Hahyah the giant describes allows us to grasp that he is not merely explaining what he saw. The thing his dream is is גברוא. Puech chooses to translate this "Une chose extraordinaire," which aptly captures the emphatic state of "the strong."[25] Hahyah then proceeds to relate the experience, repeating "I beheld" twice (חזא הוית; 4Q530 2 II, 9, 10). Similarly, 'Ohyah commences his dream report to the other giants by saying: "I beheld [חזית] in my dream in this night the mighty thing":

אנה חזית בחלמי בליליא דן גברוא (4Q530 2 II,16)

After each brother giant relays his dream report to the rest of the giants and the Nephilim, the text reads: "Here is the end of the dream" (עד כא סוף חלמא; 4Q530 2 II,12, 20). Both times the phrase is followed in the manuscript with a *vacat*, but the phrase clearly marks a conceptual ending and cognitive transition for the reader/hearer.

The two giants recognize that the dreams carry extraordinary sapiential knowledge, and they began immediately searching for someone who would interpret them, which is the purpose of telling their dream accounts to the Nephilim and giants. After 'Ohyah tells his dream, all the giants

---

23. García Martínez and Tigchelaar, *Dead Sea Scrolls Study Edition*, 2:1062–64.
24. Puech, *Qumrân Grotte 4.XXII*, 30.
25. Puech, *Qumrân Grotte 4.XXII*, 30.

(and the Nephilim, according to reconstructions) experience an emotion: they are fearful (דחלו) (4Q530 2 II, 20).

When no one from the assembly can decipher the dream, they then summon a giant named Mahawai and beg him to go to Enoch so that he may interpret the dream.[26] In 4Q531 22 9 (4QEnGiants[c]), 'Ohyah references a dream and states that "my dream has oppressed me" (חלמי אנסנ[י]) (compare Dan 8:27 and 4 Ezra 5.14). All of these dimensions of the dream experience—the sensorial, perceptual, sapiential, numinous, and emotional—are conveyed by the verb חזא. While I am not wedded to the translation "beheld," something more awe-inspiring than "see" is certainly warranted here.

2.2. 4Q544 (4QVisions of Amram[b] ar)

Early Jewish texts contain instances of visions that are perceived either while asleep or while awake, that is, while the eyes are open. Fourth Ezra is an illustrative case, because it contains both cases. Ezra first beholds several dreams, as is evident from the setting that establishes the onset of sleep, "I was troubled as I lay on my bed" (3.3), and the end of the dream, "And I awoke" (5.14). After three such dream episodes (3.3–5.20; 5.21–6.34; and 6.35–9.25), Ezra has another dream in which a woman births the city of Zion.[27] He wakes when the angel Uriel, who appears first in the dream, stands him up: "he grasped my right hand and strengthened me and *set me on my feet*" (10.29).

At this point, Ezra exclaims, "I saw, and still see, what I am unable to explain!"[28] (10.32–36). As Michael E. Stone notes, the implication of "and still see" "implies that the built city has not disappeared, that the vision was not a passing experience."[29] For this reason Ezra continues, "Or is my mind deceived, and my soul dreaming?" (v. 36). Ezra beheld something

---

26. García Martínez and Tigchelaar, *Dead Sea Scrolls Study Edition*, 2:1062–64.

27. For this interpretation see Frances Flannery, "'Go, Ask a Woman's Womb': Birth and the Maternal Body as Sources of Revelation and Wisdom in *4 Ezra*," *JSP* 21 (2012): 243–58.

28. The Syriac text of 4 Ezra is based on Milano, Biblioteca Ambrosiana, B 21 Inf., fols. 267r–276v (*siglum* 7a1), from R. J. Bidawid, ed., "4 Esdras," in *The Old Testament in Syriac according to the Peshitta Version*, part 4.3 (Leiden: Brill, 1973).

29. Stone, *Fourth Ezra*, 331.

in his dream state that he continues to behold after being fully awake and looking with his eyes.[30]

The understanding that visions are sometimes experienced in dreams and sometimes while awake sheds light on a difficult phrase from the Visions of Amram: בחזוי חזוה די חלמא, "in my vision, the vision of my dream" (4Q544 1 10).[31] Amram is referring to something that was experienced in his vision. Which vision was it? The one that Amram accessed through his dream. This suggests he may have had others, some while awake. Similarly, in Geʿez, which James C. VanderKam argues was based on a Greek translation of a Hebrew original, Jub. 4.10 reads: "In his sleep, he saw in a vision."[32] Eugène Tisserant's publication of Syriac fragments of Jubilees (in the *Chronicon ad annum Christi 1234 pertinens*) substitutes: "In his dream, he saw in a vision."[33] That which is beheld exists in a dative relationship to a vision, which is in a genitive relationship to a dream.

An additional linguistic quirk has sometimes muddled our understanding of early Jewish texts' descriptions of the relationship of dreams and visions. Since a dream is so thoroughly associated with sleep, a shorthand develops in early Jewish texts in which simply mentioning a portion of the typical setting associated with a dream implies that there is a dream, without explicitly using the vocabulary for a dream. Ancient texts may establish that a dream state ensues by simply referring to sleep, or lying down, or a bed, or night. Read this way, several early Jewish texts appear to presume that after sleep or lying down or being in bed or at night, a dream occurs (although they need not mention it), through which a vision is perceived. Put another way: lying down, bed, sleep, or night = dream > vision.

Consider how this understanding clarifies these passages, even in Geʿez and Syriac:

sekub konku ba-bēta Malālʾēl ʾemḥoweya reʾīku ba-rāʾey

---

30. Flannery-Dailey, *Dreamers, Scribes, and Priests*, 214–18.
31. Puech, *Qumrân Grotte 4.XXII*, 322.
32. VanderKam translates this "while he was sleeping" instead of the more literal "in his sleep." James C. VanderKam, *Jubilees: A Commentary on the Book of Jubilees, Chapters 1–21*, Hermeneia (Minneapolis: Fortress, 2018), 235, 237.
33. VanderKam notes that the Syriac World Chronicle substitutes "in his dream" for "in his sleep" but also notes that no Syriac manuscript of Jubilees has been found. For these Syriac fragments, see Eugène Tisserant, "Fragments syriaques du Livre des Jubilés," *RB* 30 (1921): 55–86, 206–32; and J. B. Chabot, ed. *Chronicon ad annum Christi 1234 pertinens*, CSCO 81, Scriptores Syri 36 (Louvain: Durbecq, 1953).

I was lying down in the house of Mala'el, my grandfather; I saw in a vision (1 En. 83.3)

re'iku ba-rā'eya meskābeya wa-nāhu
I saw in my vision in my bed and behold (1 En. 85.3)[34]

ܪܐܝܬ ܒܠܠܝܐ ܚܙܘܐ ܒܗ ܘܕܡܟܬ
I slept at that place and beheld in the night a vision (2 Bar. 36.1)[35]

Thus the fairly common expression "a vision of the night" (e.g., 4 Ezra 13.1; LAB 9.10; Dan 7:2) can be rightly understood as having the same meaning as "a vision of the dream," the idea conveyed in Vis. Amram[b] ar (4Q544 1 10).

2.3. 1 En. 1-36 and 4Q204 (4QEnoch[c] ar)

With this understanding, it becomes clear that a number of passages in 1 En. 1-36 and the Enochic text in 4Q204 describe a dream as a kind of portal or state through which eschatological visions are perceived. The visions are the observations, cognitive apprehensions, numinous experiences, perceptions, encounters, emotions, and so forth that the dreamer experiences. The visions thus include the sapiential knowledge accrued, which could be eschatological, cosmological, or midrashic, et cetera, as well as any visual elements.

In 1 En. 1-36, Enoch recites the memorandum of the Watchers until he falls asleep (1 En. 13.7). Immediately, the text states:

> I fell asleep. And look, *dreams came upon me, and visions fell upon me.* And I saw visions of wrath, and there came a voice, saying, "Speak to the son of heaven to reprimand them." And when I had awakened, I went to them.... And I recited in their presence *all the visions that I had seen in the dream.* (1 En. 13.7-8)[36]

---

34. All Syriac and Ethiopic text and English translations from 1 En. 1-36 and 83-85 are taken from George W. E. Nickelsburg, *1 Enoch 1: A Commentary on the Book of 1 Enoch, Chapters 1-36; 81-108*, Hermeneia (Minneapolis: Fortress, 2001).

35. The Syriac of 2 Baruch is taken from S. Dedering, "Apocalypse of Baruch," in Bidawid, *Old Testament in Syriac according to the Peshitta Version*. English translation mine.

36. Nickelsburg, *1 Enoch 1*, 251.

Previously I understood "dreams came upon me, and visions fell upon me" to be a Hellenic Semitism, a parallel repetition of the same phrase (i.e., Jesus rode in "on a colt, on a donkey"). However, understanding a dream as an altered state that facilitates a vision suggests instead that the syntactical order indicates a sequence of events, yielding "dreams came upon me, *then* visions fell upon me."

This kind of temporal sequencing of dreams and then visions is clearest in the Greek text of 1 En. 13.8, which clearly refers to "all the visions that I had seen *in the dream* [κατὰ τοὺς ὕπνου]." Here, ὕπνου (from ὕπνος), can be translated either as dream or sleep, which I have argued are often thought of as equivalent. The ὕπνος is the altered state in which the visions occur. This same idea is apparent in Daniel: "Daniel *beheld a dream* [חלם חזה], [*then*] *visions of his head* [וחזוי ראשה]" (Dan 7:1). I know of no text that mentions that someone saw "visions and [then] dreams"; rather "dreams and visions" is common.

This understanding of what constitutes a dream seems to be consistent with both 4Q204 and 1 En. 14. Jósef T. Milik's reconstruction of 4QEn[c] 1 VI, 10 reads:[37]

בחלמא די אנה]חלמת ובחזיתא דא חזית אנה בחלמי

That is, Enoch refers to God's command, a command that is "in my dream I dreamt, in the vision I beheld [חזית] in my dream." George W. E. Nickelsburg surmises that an Aramaic original lay in the background of the extant Greek manuscripts of 1 Enoch, which were in turn translated into Ethiopic.[38] Therefore he follows 4Q204 to complete the larger passage:

> THE BOOK OF THE WORDS OF TRUTH AND THE REPRIMAND OF THE WATCHERS WHO WERE FROM ETERNITY, according to the command of the Great Holy One *in the dream that <I dreamt>. In this vision I saw* [חזית] *in my dream* what I now speak with a tongue of flesh and with the breath of my mouth. (1 En. 14.1–2)

The pseudonymous narrator, Enoch, provides important clues about how the dream experience was understood: "*In this vision* [בחזיתא דא] *I saw in my dream* [חזית אנה בחלמי] what I now speak with a tongue of flesh and

---

37. Milik, *Books of Enoch*, 193.
38. Nickelsburg, *1 Enoch 1*, 20.

with the breath of my mouth." In the dream, the dreamer retains an ego-identity, an "I," but the "body"—the tongue and mouth—are not like those of a normal body. After the event, the narrator refers to the telling of the experience as "what I now speak with a tongue of flesh and with the breath of my mouth" (1 En. 14.2). That is, *before*, in the dream, Enoch spoke in his visions—but not with his regular tongue, mouth, or physical breath.

The fact that the narrator distinguishes between sensory perception in the vision while in the dream state, on the one hand, and perception after the vision while out of the dream state, on the other, once again suggests strongly that we should avoid translating the verb חזא as just "seeing" or "looking." This is no ordinary seeing, although sometimes in a vision one does "see" (ראה), just as one hears, tastes, or touches.

3. Conclusion

This is a preliminary study, and an exhaustive examination of the usage of the terms for dream and vision in early Jewish texts is still needed. However, I find enough evidence already to propose that some early Jewish texts have been misread—including by me—due to an overemphasis on the visual aspect of the verb חזה. While sensorial frames of reference may be suggested by the verb, חזה also conveys many other dimensions of experience, including perceptual, sapiential, emotional, and numinous aspects. Translating both ראה and חזה with the term "see" has caused us to miss nuances in the texts, which do understand dreams and visions partially through reference to the language of sight, but also in terms of a much wider access to extraordinary realities.

In an earlier monograph I argued that, in Hellenistic and Roman Judaism, dreams were thought to exist on a continuum with visions, such that some dreams were clearly at one end of the spectrum, cast in terms of the nightly experience of sleeping while dreaming.[39] This assertion requires a slight but important correction. As I have shown, several difficult passages in early Jewish texts are more coherent if we think of a dream as a hypnagogic state, encountered through sleep and thus sometimes equated with sleep, which facilitates a vision. A vision, then, is the totality of numinous experiences of all of the beings, sights, places, and new realities that are beheld, apprehended, felt emotionally, and understood, whether in an

---

39. Flannery-Dailey, *Dreamers, Scribes, and Priests*, 117.

altered waking state, or within the container of a dream. Thus, texts must be analyzed carefully for their precise vocabulary to see where on the visionary continuum they fall. On the one end are clear dreams in which visions are beheld during sleep; on the other end are clear visions beheld while awake. In between, in texts such as Zech 1–6 and Ezek 1–3, are muddled cases in which the nature of the hypnagogic state is puzzling—perhaps in the mind of the author or even to an original experient (we may think of Paul's autobiographical statement in 1 Cor 5:12, "whether out of the body or in the body I do not know"). The term *vision* functions in those cases to cover the range of experiences, whether the visionary is asleep, awake, or straddled somewhere in between.

Bibliography

Bidawid, R. J., ed. *The Old Testament in Syriac according to the Peshitta Version*. Part 4.3. Leiden: Brill, 1973.

Chabot, J. B., ed. *Chronicon ad annum Christi 1234 pertinens*. CSCO 81. Scriptores Syri 36. Louvain: Durbecq, 1953.

Dedering, S. "Apocalypse of Baruch." Pages 1–50 in *The Old Testament in Syriac according to the Peshitta Version*. Edited by R. J. Bidawid. Part 4.3. Leiden: Brill, 1973.

Flannery[-Dailey], Frances. *Dreamers, Scribes, and Priests: Jewish Dreams in the Hellenistic and Roman Eras*. JSJSup 90. Leiden: Brill, 2004.

———. "'Go, Ask a Woman's Womb': Birth and the Maternal Body as Sources of Revelation and Wisdom in 4 Ezra." *JSP* 21 (2012): 243–58.

García Martínez, Florentino, and Eibert J. C. Tigchelaar, eds. *The Dead Sea Scrolls Study Edition*. 2 vols. Leiden: Brill, 1997–1998.

Hanson, John S. "Dreams and Visions in the Graeco-Roman World and Early Christianity." *ANRW* 2.23.2:1395–427.

Milik, Jósef T. *The Books of Enoch: Aramaic Fragments of Qumrân Cave 4*. With the collaboration of Matthew Black. Oxford: Clarendon, 1976.

Nickelsburg, George W. E. *1 Enoch 1: A Commentary on the Book of 1 Enoch, Chapters 1–36; 81–108*. Hermeneia. Minneapolis: Fortress, 2001.

Oppenheim, Leo A. *The Interpretation of Dreams in the Ancient Near East*. Philadelphia: American Philosophical Society, 1956.

Pennington, A. "Ladder of Jacob." Pages 453–64 in *The Apocryphal Old Testament*. Edited by H. F. D. Sparks. Oxford: Clarendon, 1984.

Perrin, Andrew B. *The Dynamics of Dream-Vision Revelation in the Aramaic Dead Sea Scrolls.* JAJSup 19. Gottingen: Vandenhoeck & Ruprecht, 2015.

Puech, Émile. *Qumrân Grotte 4.XXII: Textes araméens, première partie, 4Q529–549.* DJD 31. Oxford: Clarendon, 2001.

Sanders, Seth L. "The First Tour of Hell: From Neo-Assyrian Propaganda to Early Jewish Revelation." *JANER* 9 (2009): 151–69.

Stone, Michael E. *Fourth Ezra: A Commentary on the Book of Fourth Ezra.* Hermeneia. Minneapolis: Fortress, 1990.

Stuckenbruck, Loren T. "The *Book of Giants* among the Dead Sea Scrolls: Considerations of Method and a New Proposal on the Reconstruction of 4Q530." Pages 129–44 in *Ancient Tales of Giants from Qumran and Turfan: Contexts, Traditions, and Influences.* Edited by Matthew Goff, Loren T. Stuckenbruck, and Enrico Morano. WUNT 360. Tübingen: Mohr Siebeck, 2016.

———. *The Book of Giants from Qumran: Texts, Translation, and Commentary.* TSAJ 63. Tübingen: Mohr Siebeck, 1997.

Tisserant, Eugène. "Fragments syriaques du Livre des Jubilés." *RB* 30 (1921): 55–86, 206–32.

VanderKam, James C. *Jubilees: A Commentary on the Book of Jubilees, Chapters 1–21.* Hermeneia. Minneapolis: Fortress, 2018.

Winter, Irene J. "The Eyes Have It: Votive Statuary, Gilgamesh's Axe, and Cathected Viewing in the Ancient Near East." Pages 22–44 in *Visuality before and beyond the Renaissance.* Edited by Robert S. Nelson. Cambridge: Cambridge University Press, 2000.

Immersing Oneself in the Narrative World of Second Temple Apocalyptic Visions

Angela Kim Harkins

Modern scholars of Second Temple apocalypses have labored long and hard on the meaning and interpretations of the strange visions of otherworldly realia found in these texts. Ultimately, they have been successful at identifying how these visions might correspond to specific historical moments and political regimes. The most recent studies on this topic have rightly challenged long-standing views that overdetermined apocalypses as writings generated by communities experiencing social and political crises, raising important questions about how these writings came to be.[1] We cannot say definitively that apocalypses originate from a specific type of milieu, but we can explore what gives apocalypses their lasting appeal for readers in subsequent generations.

So we turn to the question, what is it that apocalypses do to the readers who read them?[2] Our own haste to understand what these bizarre visions mean points suggestively to our own unsettling experience of reading these

---

1. While the sociological context of social and political crises may indeed be a characteristic feature of some apocalypses, it is not a necessary one. Seth Schwartz notes well that the oldest apocalypse known as the Book of the Watchers, which is dated to the third century BCE, shows no signs of Hellenistic influence or opposition. See Schwartz, *Imperialism and Jewish Society: 200 B.C.E. to 640 C.E.* (Princeton: Princeton University Press, 2001), 29–32. More recently, see the work of Paul Kosmin, who has shown well that the commonplace understanding that apocalypses are resistance literature has overdetermined these writings: *Time and Its Adversaries in the Seleucid Empire* (Cambridge: Harvard University Press, 2018), 139.

2. David Hellholm, "The Problem of Apocalyptic Genre," *Semeia* 36 (1986): 26; and John J. Collins, "Introduction: The Genre Apocalypse Reconsidered," in *Apocalypse, Prophecy, and Pseudepigraphy: On Jewish Apocalyptic Literature* (Grand Rapids: Eerdmans, 2015), 13–14.

visions and our deep-seated desire for resolution. As readers, we might say that it is our own palpable experience of confusion that precisely places us in the shoes of the seer himself who seeks to understand what is happening: "I approached one of those who were standing by and began asking him the exact meaning of all this" (Dan 7:16, all translations are mine unless otherwise noted). Perhaps modern readers rush to interpret or to find meaning in these bizarre visions when they should be lingering to savor the visionary experience itself. This essay proposes that apocalypses seek to make revelatory experiences accessible with firsthand vividness, what we might call an experience of presence. *Presence* is a cognitive state in which a reader gains awareness of being in a particular narrative world, an otherworldly space.[3] The first-person voice is the mechanism by which a reader could gain access to an immersive experience of the narrative world of the apocalypse, thus experiencing in part the things that the seer sees and the awe and wonder of these visions with the vividness of presence.

How might a reader become lost in a visionary landscape? Relevant aspects of cognitive literary theory will be used to consider how apocalyptic visions describe otherworldly experiences in such a way as to allow for the phenomenon of immersive reading. We will rely on observations that literary theorists have made for the writing of fiction and fantasy literature, both of which seek to create compelling narrative worlds in which readers can get lost.

Our discussion will begin by examining two features of apocalypses that encourage rumination and intensify cognitive and emotional engagement with the text. The first of these is the destabilizing effect that bizarre and counterintuitive elements might have on a reader. The second is the role of suspense in heightening a reader's watchfulness for what will happen next. Both of these features are common in apocalypses and effectively draw a reader more deeply into the narrative world. The second part of this study considers how the first-person reporting by the seer allows a reader to enact the experiences of being in a particular place and also to perceive the embodied experiences in that narrative world. These embodied experiences will be discussed as either interoceptive experi-

---

3. Anežka Kuzmičová, "Presence in the Reading of Literary Narrative: A Case for Motor Enactment," *Semiotica* 189 (2012): 23–48; and Marie-Laure Ryan, "The Text as World: Theories of Immersion," in *Revisiting Immersion and Interactivity in Literature and Electronic Media*, vol. 2 of *Narrative as Virtual Reality* (Baltimore: Johns Hopkins University Press, 2015), 61–84.

ences (bodily experiences associated with the viscera, including pain, hunger, temperature, and also emotions) or proprioceptive experiences, which presume an extended body moving through space (movement, balance, and any kind of kinesthetic action). The first-person narration that is characteristic of apocalypses provides many details about the interoceptive and proprioceptive experiences of the seer, thus giving access to what it is like to experience the visionary world.

1. How Do Apocalypses Generate Experiences of Presence?

Apocalypses are visionary texts that often include encounters with angelic beings. Such texts regularly employ funerary rituals that encourage the onset of grief in which the seer naturally experiences a state of intense longing or rumination. In a previous study of Dan 9, I discussed how the funerary practices associated with inculcating states of self-diminishment and liminality function in Second Temple narrative prayers.[4] Similar visionary practices are commonly used in apocalypses like 4 Ezra and 2 Baruch.[5] Ritual mourning practices of weeping, sitting in ashes, or lying prostrate generate liminality and decentering that replicate the natural pattern of problem-solving or transformation.[6] When joined with first-person prayers of petitioning and confession of sin, funerary practices can heighten an individual's receptivity to experience grief and rumination. In the case of mourning over the death of a loved one, rumination is the ongoing cognitive state of longing in which a deceased person is continually imagined in the mind. This repetitive and on-going contemplation of the deceased is often not intentionally enacted, but the bereft may experience unexpected moments of presence or a sense of continuing bonds. Rumination is a cognitive state that naturally creates an experience of presence from absence, in part through the repetitive thinking about the deceased.[7]

---

4. Angela Kim Harkins, "Ritual Mourning in Daniel's Interpretation of Jeremiah's Prophecy," *The Journal of Cognitive Historiography* 2 (2015): 14–33.

5. Daniel Merkur, "The Visionary Practices of Jewish Apocalypticists," in *Essays in Honor of Paul Parin*, ed. L. Bryce Boyer and Simon A. Gronick, The Psychoanalytic Study of Society 14 (New York: Routledge, 1989), 119–48.

6. Patrick McNamara, *The Neuroscience of Religious Experience* (Cambridge: Cambridge University Press, 2009). See also Leonard L. Martin and Abraham Tesser, "Clarifying our Thoughts," in *Ruminative Thoughts*, ed. Robert S. Wyer Jr., Advances in Social Cognition 9 (Mahwah, NJ: Erlbaum, 1996), 189–208.

7. The natural effects of mourning and rumination are applied to visionary expe-

In the context of Second Temple prayers, the ritual enactment of funerary practices and the performance of prayers that enact petitioning and the confession of sins can also cultivate self-diminishment, which effectively optimizes the naturally occurring state of rumination and heightens receptivity to an experience of presence. Penitential prayers that also enact funerary practices are frequently associated with covenant remaking experiences, perhaps because they simulate the self-diminishment that would naturally otherwise occur in the experience of encounter with the deity.[8]

In the case of apocalypses, rumination—the naturally occurring cognitive state that makes presence from absence—is cultivated within the reader by additional strategies. The first of these that we will examine is the use of bizarre or counterintuitive elements in the narrative world of the apocalypse that slow down the pace of reading, leading to a deeper contemplation of the narrative world. The second literary feature is the element of surprise, which may also lead the reader to anticipate or to heighten watchfulness for what might happen next. Both counterintuitive details and the element of surprise draw the reader more deeply into the otherworld and play a strategic role in the immersive quality of apocalypses.

1.1. Counterintuitive Aspects of Otherworldly Spaces

Apocalyptic visions often include strange and counterintuitive details about the otherworldly space itself or the bizarre otherworldly beings encountered therein, ranging from the monsters in Daniel's nighttime vision by the sea to the myriad of angels in the heavenly throne room in Dan 7. These visions effect an emotional response in the reader and heighten natural curiosity by their use of bizarre elements. In the case of the visions in Daniel, spatial details are presented to the reader in ways that appeal to our naturally occurring experiences of our own environment, while clearly preserving counterintuitive elements that remind readers and hearers that this is not the world as we know it.

---

riences in Harkins, "Ritual Mourning in Daniel's Interpretation," 14–32; and Harkins, "The Function of Prayers of Ritual Mourning in the Second Temple Period," in *Functions of Psalms and Prayers in the Late Second Temple Period*, ed. Mika S. Pajunen and Jeremy Penner, BZAW 486 (Berlin: de Gruyter, 2017), 80–101.

8. Angela Kim Harkins, "The Emotional Re-experiencing of the Hortatory Narratives Found in the Admonition of the Damascus Document," *DSD* 22 (2015): 285–307.

Spaces in apocalypses serve as more than just a literary backdrop for events and activities that take place in the foreground. Detailed descriptions of spaces alone are inadequate for creating immersive experiences; it is the description of those spaces as they are experienced by the figures in the text that make them compelling. Narrative worlds, sometimes referred to as "possible and fictional worlds" by critical literary theorists, are described as experientially fluid spaces that are generated in part by the text and in part by the reader's imaginative experiencing of the text through enactive processes.[9] When we read texts immersively, spatial metaphors readily come to mind: we get lost in a book, or we speak of a plot's twists and turns. Texts provide only a glimpse of a narrative world that readers must then extend and complete in their imaginations. An example of this is the *New York Times*: "Just as you don't need to download, say, the entire *New York Times* to be able to read it on your desktop, so you don't need to construct a representation of all the details of the scene in front of you to have a sense of its detailed presence."[10] So, too, the otherworld of the apocalypse is extended and completed when it is enacted by the reader's imagination, perhaps allowing them to add further details about what the heavenly space is like. It is this vivid imagining of the first-person report of the seer's experiences that is generative of later interpretations and writings that could then be pseudepigraphically attributed to the seer's name.

Spaces in apocalypses describe the seer's environment, details about the geography and architectural structures, and any nonhuman beings that are encountered within them. Descriptions of spaces optimize features of the environment that are fitting to the cultural and historical periods. For example, comparative studies of otherworldly spaces like paradise note the similarity between the general features of the landscape and how it differs from everyday spaces in specific counter-intuitive ways to remind the reader that this is not the world as we know it.[11] These spaces include counterintuitive elements such as divine inhabitants, talking ani-

---

9. Helpful is the discussion by Marco Caracciolo, "Ungrounding Fictional Worlds: An Enactivist Perspective on the 'Worldlikeness' of Fiction," in *Possible Worlds Theory and Contemporary Narratology*, ed. Alice Bell and Marie-Laure Ryan (Lincoln: University of Nebraska Press, 2019), 113–31.

10. Caracciolo, "Ungrounding Fictional Worlds," 127; which repeats an example from Alva Noë, *Action in Perception* (Cambridge: MIT Press, 2004), 50.

11. Jani Närhi, "Beautiful Reflections: The Cognitive and Evolutionary Foundations of Paradise Representations," *MTSR* 20 (2008): 339–65.

mals, and a lack of conflict, disease, or perishability to remind readers that this is another world.[12] In the case of Dan 7, the otherworld includes the churning sea and the heavenly throne room, but just as significant is how the strange inhabitants of those realms move, interact, and respond to the events in those spaces.[13]

In the case of the book of Daniel, the vast sea in Daniel's vision of the four beasts (ch. 7) takes on a quality of solidity when we visualize the effects of the invisible winds battering its surface, swirling the waters into towering waves. Imagining the effects of the winds on the surface of the waters transforms it from a still two-dimensional background into a watery space with depth and solidity.[14] In other words, the depth and density of the waters are realized when we imagine the *effects* of the blustery wind as it churns the sea water into thick white foamy waves. The four monstrous beasts that make their appearance from the waters perhaps are not unlike the shapes that are formed suddenly by towering and crashing waves. The first three beasts embody fierce predators from the natural world: the lion, the bear, and the four-headed leopard. These creatures are presented with multiple features in a monstrous composite, with the first and third having wings, and the third one having four leopard heads. Such details remind

---

12. On the counterintuitiveness of religious concepts, see Pascal Boyer, *The Naturalness of Religious Ideas: A Cognitive Theory of Religion* (Berkeley: University of California Press, 1994); Boyer, *Religion Explained: The Evolutionary Origins of Religious Thought* (New York: Basic Books, 2001); Boyer and Charles Ramble, "Cognitive Templates for Religious Concepts: Cross-Cultural Evidence for Recall of Counter-Intuitive representations," *Cognitive Science* 25 (2001): 535–64; and Ilkka Pyysiäinen, Marjaana Lindeman, and Timo Honkela, "Counterintuitiveness as the Hallmark of Religiosity," *Religion* 33 (2003): 341–55.

13. Nancy Easterlin gives the example of a preschool in her explanation of what is meant by "environment." When she speaks of a bad or a good environment for a small child, she is not referring to just the condition of the furniture or toys in a classroom or where they may be located. She is thinking comprehensively about an overall experience of the child in that environment, one that includes the relationships had with the people in those environments and the events that took place there. Easterlin gives the example of being bitten by another child and the child's own emotional responses to those events. See Nancy Easterlin, "'Loving Ourselves Best of All': Ecocriticism and the Adapted Mind," *Mosaic* 37 (2004): 8–9.

14. Elaine Scarry illustrates this quality of narrative description in her example of light passing over a two-dimensional wall in "On Vivacity: The Difference between Daydreaming and Imagining-under-Authorial-Instruction," *Representations* 52 (1995): 6.

the reader that these beasts are otherworldly. Daniel's vision of the four beasts capitalizes on what is already known about these large predatory animals from our own lived experience—they are unpredictable, violent, and dangerous. The first three beasts call to mind the three animals in Hos 13:7–8, which signify the foreign powers that enact YHWH's larger cosmic plan. The fourth beast, however, is not described in the same way; instead, the reader must somehow imagine its "ten horns" with "another one growing; and still other horns being taken away"—a challenge to visualize, although artists have tried. The description continues to say that one of these horns had eyes and also a mouth that spoke arrogantly. The fourth beast results in a monstrosity whose features epitomize the dangers of a fierce predator: menacing horns that eviscerate, sinister eyes that watch closely, and a large mouth that emits terrifying sounds, yet nothing is said about what kind of animalian shape it is—that is left to the imagination. The four-fold pattern of the beasts in the nighttime vision calls to mind the fourfold composite statue from Nebuchadnezzar's dream in chapter 2 and transfers the natural terror of the predatory animals onto the scenario of being subjugated by these four fierce foreign empires. The four beasts that emerge from the sea in Dan 7 also correspond to the vision of the single terrifying beast in Rev 13.

As readers, we naturally rely on our own lived experiences of this world when we imagine Daniel's nighttime vision of the beasts that emerge from the dark waters, one after the other. The first beast is a lion with the wings of an eagle, a creature that is thought to correspond with the reign of Babylon (7:17). The dream world of Daniel becomes more solid in our imaginations when we imagine the beasts moving or engaging with their environment: the lion with eagles' wings is made to stand on its hind legs (7:4), with its back feet pressing down on the soft earth. The monsters that appear here, and also in other apocalypses, suggest the usefulness of cognitive literary theory's study of fantasy literature, which highlights the way narratives about counterintuitive details seek to disturb and unsettle the reader.[15] Laura Feldt notes the way that bizarre and counterintuitive details in religious narratives destabilize readers by generating a confusion

---

15. See Renata Lachmann, *Erzählte Phantastik: Zu Phantasiegeschichte und Semantik phantastischer Texte* (Frankfurt am Main: Suhrkamp, 2002), which Laura Feldt has successfully applied to descriptions of the fantastic in the book of Exodus; see Laura Feldt, "Religious Narrative and the Literary Fantastic: Ambiguity and Uncertainty in Ex. 1–18," *Religion* 41 (2011): 251–83.

that ultimately leads to greater cognitive engagement.[16] Texts that include fantastic elements effectively seize a reader's attention and slow down the pace of reading as the mind struggles to visualize these bewildering counterintuitive elements.

1.2. Suspense

Apocalypses strategically use literary devices to build narrative suspense. Theoretical approaches to fantasy literature are especially relevant for the study of apocalypses since both literary genres rely on the use of bizarre and counterintuitive elements. Such writings have a greater chance of generating cognitive processes that seek understanding, without overdetermining that readers will have any particular response. Feldt writes, "Religious narrative does not encourage a resolution of tensions in the gap it opens between two worlds, a mundane, everyday world, and an extraordinary, divine world. Instead, it encourages a fascination with the movement between the worlds."[17] The strategic aim of such details commonly found in apocalypses is to cultivate the cognitive state of rumination over the visions seen in the narrative world.

One notable effect of the foreboding scene of monsters that emerge from the dark water, one by one, is the seizing of the reader's attention. The cultivation of the reader's natural watchfulness for what will happen next effectively prepares the reader for the heavenly throne room experience that follows. In the case of Dan 7, the vision of the Ancient of Days being ministered to by a myriad of heavenly beings (7:9–10) then returns quickly to the terrifying beasts which opened the vision. The mysterious fourth beast is suddenly destroyed and then burned in fire in a violent judgment scene (7:11). So too, after the bizarre vision of the Ram and the Goat, Daniel reports that he pondered what he saw: "While I, Daniel, was seeing the vision and endeavoring to understand it, suddenly, there appeared before me one who looked like a man" (‏ויהי בראתי אני דניאל את־‎ ‏החזון ואבקשה בינה והנה עמד לנגדי כמראה־גבר‎; Dan 8:15). Like Daniel, the reader also takes a good long look at the bizarre beasts in Daniel's nighttime vision. The first beast, a winged lion, undergoes a transformation that keeps the viewer in watchful suspense: its wings are "plucked off," its

---

16. Feldt, "Religious Narrative and the Literary Fantastic," 272–73.
17. Feldt, "Religious Narrative and the Literary Fantastic," 272.

body is made to stand upright and it is given the "heart of a human being" within it (7:4). Shortly thereafter, in Dan 7:8, the seer tells us, "While I was gazing upon these horns, a new little horn sprouted up among them." The retelling of the nighttime visions has a dynamic quality with the beasts changing before the seer's eyes. The beasts emerge, each one more terrifying than the one before it. In the course of this redirection of the reader's attention, the environment suddenly shifts from a marine view to firm land upon which the first beast is said to stand on its hind legs. After the beasts, Daniel's vision report then shifts quickly to the heavenly throne room with very little advance warning.

Suspense is created by Daniel's nighttime vision, which cultivates a keen watchfulness in a reader who becomes acutely aware of the predatory beasts that have now emerged from the dark waters one by one. The fourth and final beast is infinitely more terrifying and described solely in terms of its menacing traits—horns for gouging, eye for stalking, and a mouth for ferocious roars and, of course, mauling victims. The description resembles the experience of being stalked by an animal under the cover of night in which the terrifying jaws or horns of the predator that is pursuing becomes disproportionately magnified in the imagination. The building of narrative expectation is also a key structural feature of the book of Revelation whose series of seven seals (6:1–8:5), seven trumpets (8:6–9:21), and seven bowls (15:1–16:21) similarly cultivates the reader's attention and watchful eye. The series of events that are enumerated effectively creates a dramatic tension that is artfully built up from one to four, dissipated, and then built up again. The effect of such literary strategies is to train the reader to be watchful as the visions progress.

Surprising details can lead a reader to ruminate on the text and may lead a reader to return and reread the apocalypse with even greater attention, as one might return to reread a novel that resolves a mystery in an unexpected way. One example of the underappreciated role of surprise in apocalypses is the Book of Parables, which culminates with the surprising revelation that Enoch himself is the Son of Man (1 En. 71.14).[18] Some tra-

---

18. James C. VanderKam, "Righteous One, Messiah, Chosen One, and Son of Man in 1 Enoch 37–71," in *Enoch and the Messiah Son of Man*, ed. Gabriele Boccaccini (Grand Rapids: Eerdmans, 2007), 169–91. Here I wish to acknowledge the discussions that arose in my Apocalypses course in spring 2019 at Boston College School of Theology and Ministry, in which we examined the element of surprise as it appears throughout a range of ancient apocalypses.

ditional historical-critical and literary approaches have argued that chapters 70–71 of the Parables are secondary because of their repetitive quality and also the tension that this information has with earlier statements about the preexistence of the Son of Man.[19] John Collins, for example, highlights how extraordinarily unusual it is for the seer to see a vision of himself in ancient apocalypses and not to recognize himself.[20] After all, Enoch, like the reader, shows no awareness of who the Son of Man is in earlier sections of the Parables. Careful readers may look to 1 En. 37.1 as a possible hint to what will be revealed in 1 En. 71.14, but this subtlety may only be recognized by a careful reader who, knowing the surprising revelation, has then gone back to reread the entirety of the apocalypse.[21] Traditional historical-critical studies tend to approach apocalypses as a linear narrative and often do not consider how the readerly experience of surprise may, in fact, be a strategic aim of the apocalypse. Apocalypses often have surprising endings, like the identification of Enoch as the Son of Man or the climactic seventh vision at the end of 4 Ezra in which Ezra is given a fiery drink and then utters revelations that fill ninety-four books of scripture, all of which stimulate a deep cognitive engagement with the text.[22] The unexpectedness of the identification of Enoch as the Son of Man could even compel a reader to go back and reread the Parables more closely and with greater attention or to ponder this information in his or her imagination.

Second Temple apocalypses use the emotional responses of the seer to draw readers immersively into the text. Prayers that are embedded in late Second Temple apocalypses (e.g., Dan 9; 4 Ezra 8.19–36) construct vivid

---

19. VanderKam, "Righteous One, Messiah, Chosen One," 177. Other studies that have sought to reconcile chapters 70 and 71 with the earlier references to the preexistence of the Son of Man include Erik Sjöberg, *Der Menschensohn im äthiopischen Henochbuch*, ARSHLL 41 (Lund: Lund University Press, 1946), 159–67; Ulrich B. Müller, *Messias und Menschensohn in jüdischen Apokalypsen und in der Offenbarung des Johannes*, SNT 6 (Gütersloh: Gütersloh Verlagshaus, 1972), 54–60; and John J. Collins, "The Heavenly Representative: The 'Son of Man' in the Similitudes of Enoch," in *Ideal Figures in Ancient Judaism*, ed. George W. E. Nickelsburg and John J. Collins, SCS 12 (Chico, CA: Scholars Press, 1980), 122–24.

20. Collins, "Heavenly Representative," 122.

21. VanderKam, "Righteous One, Messiah, Chosen One," 182.

22. Isolde Andrews makes a similar point about the limitations of traditional historical-critical approaches to understanding apocalypses; see "Being Open to the Vision: A Study from Fourth Ezra," *Literature and Theology* 12 (1998): 231–41.

images that are emotionally engaging and, in effect, assist in enscripting those emotions of longing and desire to know with a firsthand intensity. These ways of experiencing prayers, especially prayers that may use vivid emotional language from foundational narratives in Israel's past, do not rely on a text's historicity for enactive perceptions to occur. While these experiences of simultaneity are not predetermined, they can be possible under the right conditions of heightened receptivity. Particularly after the exile, foundational narratives were retold first and foremost to inculcate a common memory of a shared past and also to script the appropriate dispositions that are needed for the ritual moment.

Narratives that include disorienting and counterintuitive elements slow down the cognitive process of reading and function to allow readers to engage the text more deeply. It encourages the reader to go back and reread and ruminate over the visions. Counterintuitive elements and the role of suspense slow down and invite deeper thinking about a passage.

2. Enactive Processes Provide Access to the Seer's Embodied Experiences

Critical literary theory as it is applied to narrative spaces is an integrative approach that emerged in the late twentieth century.[23] It draws attention to the complexity of the reader's embodied mind during the experience of reading and considers how immersive experiences of narrative worlds could be understood through cognitive processes like enactive reading and enactive perception, which are ways of imaging experiences through the perspective of the first-person voice. Such emerging approaches take into account the possible effects of reading visionary texts on the

---

23. Stephen Kaplan, "Environmental Preference in a Knowledge-Seeking, Knowledge-Using Organism," in *The Adapted Mind: Evolutionary Psychology and the Generation of Culture*, ed. Jerome Barkow, Leda Cosmides, and John Tooby (New York: Oxford University Press, 1992), 581–98; Glen A. Love, "Ecocriticism and Science: Toward Consilience?," *New Literary History* 30 (1999): 661–76; Easterlin, "Loving Ourselves Best of All," 1–18; Easterlin, *A Biocultural Approach to Literary Theory and Interpretation* (Baltimore: Johns Hopkins University Press, 2012); the essays in Lisa Zunshine, ed., *Introduction to Cognitive Cultural Studies* (Baltimore: Johns Hopkins University Press, 2010); Karin Kukkonen and Marco Caracciolo, "Introduction: What Is the 'Second Generation'?," *Style* 48 (2014): 261–74; Marco Caracciolo, *The Experientiality of Narrative: An Enactivist Approach* (Berlin: de Gruyter, 2014); and Caracciolo, "Cognitive Literary Studies and the Status of Interpretation: An Attempt at Conceptual Mapping," *New Literary History* 47 (2016): 187–207.

people who read, heard, and transmitted them, taking into account their embodied (biological) and cultural contexts.[24] In this section, we will use relevant aspects of cognitive literary approaches to theorize how descriptions of otherworldly spaces may have influenced readers of Jewish apocalypses.

Apocalypses often make reference to the body and specify body parts and speak about sensory experiences all in the first-person voice. Yet, how we modern people conceptualize the body and its processes today differs from premodern conceptions. For example, figures such as Enoch, Daniel, Ezra, and John of Patmos speak about what is seen or describe details that are expressly visual. For the modern world, seeing is understood as a process that is governed by the eyes; in fact, if we have trouble seeing, we would immediately go and visit an eye surgeon or some eye specialist who would localize and identify our problem by closely examining the organs that we call our eyes. But the ancient imagination understood seeing holistically, with the entire body in mind. In the ancient imagination, according to Yael Avrahami's book on the senses in the Hebrew Bible, the visual and the kinesthetic are conflated perceptions—together, both express the idea of understanding gained by investigation.[25] So, while our modern mind tends to segregate and isolate the body and its sensory functions, the ancient mind understood the body's perceptions holistically as integrated operations. A reader's sensory perception can also be heightened by the concrete descriptions of the speaker's bodily movement toward the object being viewed. Seeing is assisted by the body's ability to pick up and inspect an object so as to view it more closely. Thus, descriptions of an individual's locomotion and movement through space are natural ways in which the embodied mind can imagine the act of seeing and thus knowing through the senses. Aldo Tagliabue refers to this process as a text's ability to simulate bodily perceptions, or "enactive perception, according to which perceiving is a way of acting as the world makes itself available to the perceiver through his [sic] physical movement and interaction with a given

---

24. Armin W. Geertz, "Religious Bodies, Minds and Places: A Cognitive Science of Religion Perspective," in *Spazi e luoghi sacri: Espressioni ed esperienze di vissuto religioso*, ed. Laura Carnevale (Santo Spirito [Bari]: Edipuglia, 2017), 35–52, for an updated discussion of integrative approaches to the study of religion, like cognitive science of religion.

25. Yael Avrahami, *The Senses of Scripture: Sensory Experience in the Hebrew Bible* (New York: T&T Clark, 2012).

object in a precise environment."[26] The spatial details in apocalypses are important ways in which the prayer constructs a perceptible virtual reality in which the reader can immerse himself/herself. The most recent theorizing about the body that comes from cognitive science argues that human perception is not based on "abstract, propositional representations"[27] but shaped by the interaction of body and mind, including different senses and emotions.

Language about the sensory experiences of the seer can be enacted by a reader, thus making a two-dimensional literary environment into a three-dimensional immersive experience. This cognitive process of enactive reading can heighten a reader's ability of having an immersive experience of the text. Cognitive literary theorists like Anežka Kuzmičová and Marco Caracciolo argue that the phenomenon of immersive reading, that is, achieving an experience of presence in a narrative world, relies on first-person narration that divulges details about interoceptive, proprioceptive, and kinesthetic experiences to a reader.[28] The first-person voice can intensify a reader's experience of the text because it gives access to the elements that we associate with our own experiences and with the real people whom we encounter who possess a consciousness, interior emotional experiences, and an extended body. According to Caracciolo, vivid language about a character's bodily and emotional experiences allows us to construct an idea of that character's consciousness.[29] When readers are able to imagine Jewish apocalyptic seers as figures with a fully extended physical body and with the complexities of an interior consciousness, they heighten their own experience of deeply empathizing with the figure in the text.[30] Enactivism is a way of speaking phenomenologically about the

---

26. Aldo Tagliabue, "An Embodied Reading of Epiphanies in Aelius Aristides' *Sacred Tales*," *Ramus* 45 (2016): 214.

27. Kukkonen and Caracciolo, "What Is the 'Second Generation'?," 261.

28. Kuzmičová, "Presence in the Reading of Literary Narrative"; Marco Caracciolo, "Fictional Consciousnesses: A Reader's Manual," *Style* 46 (2012): 42–65; and Caracciolo, "Ungrounding Fictional Worlds," 113–31.

29. Caracciolo, "Fictional Consciousnesses," 43, writes, "Readers experience the fictional world through the consciousness of a character…. Readers can enact a fictional consciousness, they can perform it on the basis of textual cues."

30. Caracciolo, "Fictional Consciousnesses," 43; Jenefer Robinson, *Deeper than Reason: Emotion and Its Role in Literature, Music, and Art* (Oxford: Clarendon, 2007); and David S. Miall, "Emotions and the Structuring of Narrative Responses," *Poetics Today* 32 (2011): 323–48. See, too, the thesis of Angela Kim Harkins, *Reading with an*

mental imagery that occurs in varying degrees during the activity of reading.[31] The cognitive processing areas of the mind are engaged by language about the sensory experiences of the body, which can be described as proprioception (which includes kinesthetic and movement related experiences) and interoception.[32]

2.1. Proprioception

Proprioception includes the embodied sensations of moving through space that are often reported in apocalypses that detail otherworldly journeying. For example, in the heavenly journey of Perpetua and Saturus that is recounted at the beginning of book 4 of the Martyrdom of Perpetua and Felicity, the reader is told exactly how their bodies ascend up to heaven: they are not supine as they go up, and their bodies are pitched at a slight angle.[33] Proprioception can refer both to conscious or unconscious actions and to active or passive sensations of the body moving through space, like a loss of balance or the sensation of falling. In general, it refers to the embodied self as it moves and experiences the environment around it.

In the Book of the Watchers, Enoch's ascent and vision of the heavenly throne room specifies various physical sensations that help the reader to construct the seer's proprioceptive sense as Enoch moves into this new environment:

> [8] And in (the) vision it was shown to me thus:
> Behold, clouds in the vision were summoning me,
> and mists were crying out to me;

"I" to the Heavens: Looking at the Qumran Hodayot through the Lens of Visionary Traditions, Ekstasis 3 (Berlin: de Gruyter, 2012), that the first-person voice allows readers to emotionally reenact the experiences of the text.

31. Nicole K. Speer et al., "Reading Stories Activates Neural Representations of Visual and Motor Experiences," *Psychological Science* 20 (2009): 289–99; Kuzmičová, "Presence in the Reading of Literary Narrative," 23–48; and Kuzmičová, "Mental Imagery: A View from Embodied Cognition," *Style* 48 (2014): 275–76.

32. Kuzmičová, "Mental Imagery," 275–76.

33. The newest edition of the Martyrdom of Perpetua and Felicity by Thomas J. Heffernan offers the following translation of the text: "But we were moving, not on our backs facing upwards, but as if we were climbing a gentle hill" (11.3; *ibamus autem non supine sursum uersi, sed quasi mollem cliuum ascendentes*). See Thomas J. Heffernan, *The Passion of Perpetua and Felicity* (Oxford: Oxford University Press, 2011).

and shooting stars and lightning flashes
were *hastening* me and *speeding* me along,
and winds in my vision *made me fly up*, and
lifted me upward,
and *brought me* to heaven.
⁹ And *I went in* until *I drew near* to a wall built of hailstones;
And tongues of fire were encircling them all around;
And they began to frighten me.
¹⁰ And *I went into* the tongues of fire,
and *I drew near* to a great house built of hail stones;
And the walls of this house were like stone slabs;
And they were all of snow, and the floor was of snow. (1 En. 14.8–10)[34]

In this opening scene to the seer's journey to the heavenly throne room, the reader is given details about Enoch's phenomenal experience of movement through space. Frequently, apocalypses include descriptions that highlight the extended body of the seer as it interacts with the surrounding environment. Seers often report collapsing or falling on the ground during the moment of encounter with a divine being.[35]

2.2. Interoception

Interoception refers to an individual's awareness of his or her interior physiological state and is usually mediated through the skin or the viscera. These experiences include those that we experience through our bodies, like "temperature, pain, itch, tickle, sensual touch, muscular and visceral sensations, vasomotor flush, hunger, thirst."[36] For example, both extreme hot or cold temperatures are disliked or avoided. These physiological states are assessed by the self and inflected with a motivational or emotional meaning. Certain negative emotions like fear and disgust are associated with the viscera and have a strong biological basis and are therefore also

---

34. All quotations from 1 Enoch follow the translation from George W. E. Nickelsburg, *1 Enoch 1: A Commentary on the Book of 1 Enoch, Chapters 1–36; 81–108*, Hermeneia (Minneapolis: Fortress, 2001), 257.

35. This literary form is discussed by Loren T. Stuckenbruck in the context of what he calls the "refusal tradition" in which the veneration of angels was corrected. See Loren T. Stuckenbruck, *Angel Veneration and Christology: A Study in Early Judaism and in the Christology of the Apocalypse of John* (Tübingen: Mohr Siebeck, 1995).

36. A. D. Craig, "How Do You Feel? Interoception: The Sense of the Physiological Condition of the Body," *Nature Reviews Neuroscience* 3 (2002): 655.

considered interoceptive experiences.[37] Herein lies the Hebrew idioms for emotions that locate these experiences in various internal organs like the heart, liver, belly, or womb.[38] Reading about the interoceptive experiences of a seer in a first-person report can further layer aspects of realism and contribute to a reader's ability to infer consciousness for a figure like Enoch.

Enoch's report of the divine throne room is layered with both proprioceptive and interoceptive details that express the magnitude of the seer's fear as he enters into the new environment:

> [11]And the ceiling was like shooting stars and lightning flashes; and among them were fiery cherubim, and their heaven was water; [12]and a flaming fire encircled all their walls, and the doors blazed with fire. [13]*And I went into that house*—hot as fire and cold as snow; and no delight of life was in it. *Fear enveloped me, and trembling seized me*; [14]and *I was quaking and trembling, and I fell on my face*.... [24]And I had been until now on my face, prostrate and trembling, and the Lord called me with his mouth and said to me, "Come here, Enoch, and hear my word(s)." [25]And one of the holy ones came to me and raised me up and stood me (on my feet) and brought me up to the door. But I had my face bowed down. (1 En. 14.11–14, 24–25)

Enoch's entry into the heavenly throne room is described for the reader with multiple references to his interior bodily state and his heightened experience of fear, which is expressed in his "quaking and trembling." His proprioceptive experiences in the new environment are recounted as he moves forward into the house and include the details about his loss of balance as he collapses on his face. A little later, we read about how his body is configured when one of the angels lifts him up onto his feet—Enoch's head remains downward (1 En. 14.24–25). In this scene, Enoch also gives us interoceptive details when he describes the temperature of the heavenly space as "hot like fire, and cold as snow" (14.13). His emotional state, which

---

37. Anil K. Seth, "Interoceptive Inference, Emotion, and the Embodied Self," *Trends in Cognitive Sciences* 17 (2013): 565–73.

38. Mark S. Smith, "The Heart and Innards in Israelite Emotional Expressions: Notes from Anthropology and Psychobiology," *JBL* 117 (1998): 427–36. His opening example is from Lam 2:11: "My eyes are spent with weeping; *my belly* [מעי] *is in turmoil; my liver/bile is poured out on the ground* [נשפך לארץ כבדי] because of the destruction of my people, because infants and babes faint in the streets of the city."

is displayed in his "quaking and trembling" (14.14), expresses his visceral reaction to being in the new environment. The range of interoceptive experiences that are described when he enters into the throne room includes embodied sensations from deep within Enoch's viscera (trembling in fear) and from the contact of his skin with the heavenly space (temperature). The layering of the proprioceptive and interoceptive details assists a reader in conceptualizing Enoch as a character with consciousness and allows a reader to immerse him/herself in the narrative world of the apocalypse.

Enoch's phenomenal journey report of entry into the heavenly space replicates our own lived experiences of being in a new environment. Today television and other media allow for the possibility of viewing a reality from an optimal and disembodied vantage point as the camera zooms quickly in to see the expression on someone's face and then zooms out to a panoramic view of an entire city skyline in a moment's time. This differs significantly from our actual physical experience of entering a new environment where the activity of looking around integrates and involves the entire body; we crane our neck and move around or even closer to the item we wish to examine. The embodied experience of seeing includes the phenomenal experiences of both proprioceptive and interoceptive experiences, which Enoch's first-person report provides with some detail, yet this otherworldly space includes incongruous elements of flaming fire and extreme cold, and we are given an incomplete description of how exactly those elements fit together in the same space. References to the heavenly space are provided, which the reader must then extend and complete in his or her imagination.

Fear or other interoceptive states and their embodied expressions also accompany journeys to otherworldly realms. So too in the Jewish apocalypse known as 4 Ezra from the first century CE. Ezra is lying in bed, in anguish over the desolation of Zion, and tells us that "his spirit was greatly agitated" (3.2–3). The first vision ends with his report, "Then I woke up, and my body shuddered violently, and my soul was so troubled that it fainted" (5.14). Ezra's report of his dream vision includes emotions that mark his body with tremors.

In the case of the book of Daniel, the visionary reports various interoceptive experiences like fear, dismay, and trance states. In the midst of retelling the nighttime vision in 7:15, Daniel recounts his interoceptive experiences: "As for me, Daniel, my spirit was troubled within me, and the visions of my head terrified me" (אתכרית רוחי אנה דניאל בגוא נדנה וחזוי ראשי יבהלנני). Readers are also given interoceptive details of the seer's vasomotor flush: "As for me, Daniel, *my thoughts greatly terrified me*, and *the pallor* (*of my face*) *changed*; but I kept the matter in my mind" (אנה דניאל שגיא רעיוני יבהלנני וזיוי ישתנון עלי ומלתא בלבי נטרת; 7:28). Unlike the scenario in Dan 10:7–9 in which the people around Daniel can see that he has had a vision because he grows pale and faints, these references in chapter 7 describe interior emotional states that were not witnessed by anyone and have to be divulged during the process of retelling for the benefit of the reader.[39] These two interoceptive statements also include the reminder that these were certainly Daniel's experiences by emphatically stating, "*as for me, Daniel*" (אנה דניאל). The first-person voice allows the reader to access the prophet's interoceptive experiences of confusion, feelings of dismay, and palpable fear from the visions themselves (7:15, 28; cf. Dan 8:17–18, 27; 10:8). The experiences of Daniel are retold with a verisimilitude that suggests the vividness of actual lived experiences because they make explicit for the reader various interoceptive experiences typically had in lived experiences of terror and confusion. Both enactive reading and enactive perception speak to the ways that first-person referential descriptions of embodied experiences contribute qualities of vividness and solidity to the apocalypses from the Second Temple period.

Both interoceptive and proprioceptive experiences are described in detail in many apocalypses through the first-person voice.[40] In the case of our previous example of Daniel's vision of the four beasts, the vision is laced with the seer's repeated reminders of his eyewitness reporting. Daniel retells his visions to the reader in first-person voice, insisting on his firsthand testimony with the repetition of the phrase "I saw" (7:2, 4, 6, 7, 9, 11 [2x], 13). For the person who imaginatively reads this text, the repeated use of the first-person pronoun serves as a reminder that these are eyewitness reports of an otherworldly scene. These interoceptive reports in first-person voice can greatly facilitate how the vision might be experienced in

---

39. Other interoceptive reports include Dan 8:27, "So, I, Daniel, was overcome and lay sick for some days; then I arose and went about the king's business. But I was dismayed by the vision and did not understand it."

40. Loren T. Stuckenbruck, "Pseudepigraphy and First Person Discourse in the Dead Sea Documents: From the Aramaic Texts to Writings of the Yaḥad," in *The Dead Sea Scrolls and Contemporary Culture*, ed. Adolfo D. Roitman, Lawrence H. Schiffman, and Shani Tzoref (Leiden: Brill, 2011), 295–326; and Harkins, *Reading with an "I" to the Heavens*.

the body of a subsequent reader with an intensity that conveys a quality of presence.[41]

Emotional responses are a significant part of how a literary environment is experienced, and they can be far more compelling than a mere description of a building or landscape and the things found within it. In many instances, otherworldly realms are described only in piecemeal, and the reader must construct the larger world from these fragmentary descriptions in his or her imagination. These spaces and the events that take place in them elicit an emotional response from the individual who journeys there, even if those journeys take place in the fragmentary landscapes of a dream or a vision. The seer discloses a great deal about his emotional experiences of fear or worry and his introspective thinking within those spaces.[42] Both Enoch and Daniel emphasize visual experiences, but their apocalypses are also accompanied by other wide-ranging details about the seers' interoceptive and proprioceptive experiences of physicality and sen-

---

41. Tagliabue, "Embodied Reading of Epiphanies," 214. See also G. Gabrielle Starr, "Multisensory Imagery," in *Introduction to Cognitive Cultural Studies*, ed. Lisa Zunshine (Baltimore: Johns Hopkins University Press, 2010), 275–91, and Starr, *Feeling Beauty: The Neuroscience of Aesthetic Experience* (Cambridge: MIT Press, 2015). For a description of the enactive mental imaging of a scene, see the detailed description of breakfast in Hemingway's novel the *Garden of Eden* in which a wide range of sensory imagery achieves the state of experiencing the breakfast (taste, smell, touch, movement) in Anežka Kuzmičová, "Does It Matter Where You Read? Situating Narrative in Physical Environment," *Communication Theory* 26 (2016): 290–308. This kind of phenomenal experience is related to imitative and mirroring processing in the brain; see Elhanan Borenstein and Eytan Ruppin, "The Evolution of Imitation and Mirror Neurons in Adaptive Agents," *Cognitive Systems Research* 6 (2005): 229–42. Marie-Laure Ryan uses the term *mental simulation* to refer to this phenomenon in immersive reading in which the reader mirrors the emotional experiences or consciousness had by the characters in the text; see her "Text as World," 78–84.

42. This process of active reading is one in which kinesthetic language is processed by sensorimotor areas of the mind in such a way that the embodied mind experiences in part the action that is being described. We might think about these immersive narrative worlds as being marked by a high level of absorption—like a reader losing oneself in a book. Literary theorists who study the experiential effects of reading emotionally arousing fantasy literature note that language about the emotional experiences of the protagonists assist in deepening a reader's immersive experiences. In such studies, "immersion ratings were significantly higher for fear-inducing than for neutral passages." See Chun-Ting Hsu, Markus Conrad, and Arthur M. Jacobs, "Fiction Feelings in Harry Potter: Haemodynamic Response in the Mid-Cingulate Cortex Correlates with Immersive Reading Experience," *Neuroreport* 25 (2014): 1356.

sory perception within his or her environs. Apocalypses describe in detail the seer's emotional responses to the things that are seen and experienced and, of course, the things that the seer hears, smells, tastes, touches, and moves toward, around, or away from.

Attention to the embodied mind is also the occasion to remember that hearing and reading engage cognitive processes in complex ways to generate experiences of spatial perception that compare in intensity with firsthand bodily experiences. Here it is worth remembering too that the reader's body does not physically need to be in motion for the vivid perception of space or movement to take place through mediated experiences such as video gaming, viewing art, or reading. On this point, the work of cognitive science theorist Vittorio Gallese suggests that perhaps the physical body's immobilization while reading or hearing a text may actually allow for the greater intensification of the imagined body's active participation in a textualized scene. According to his hypothesis, immobility actually "liberates new simulative energies.... Our being still simultaneously enables us to fully deploy our simulative resources at the service of the immersive relationship with the fictional world, thus generating an even greater feeling of body. Being forced to inaction, we are more open to feelings and emotions."[43] Such studies speak to the different ways the mind may be intensely engaged but which may not be visibly apparent in the practitioner's face or body. These are also aspects of how we should consider the experience of passively hearing apocalypses being read aloud.

3. Immersive Reading and the Generation of Pseudepigrapha

Daniel was highly regarded shortly after its publication and generated many interpretations and rewritings in the form of Danielic legenda and other apocryphal traditions. At Qumran, a significant number of manuscript copies of the book of Daniel or scrolls mentioning Daniel have been identified. Eight biblical manuscripts of Daniel have been identified from Caves 1, 4, and 6 (1Q71; 1Q72; 4Q112–116; 6Q7), which correspond to the text found in all but one of the chapters of the MT

---

43. Vittorio Gallese, "Mirroring, a Liberated Embodied Simulation and Aesthetic Experience," in *Mirror Images: Reflections in Art and Medicine*, ed. Helen Hirsch and Alessandra Pace (Vienna: Verlag für moderne Kunst, 2017), 27–37.

edition of the book (Dan 12).[44] While it is not certain if all of these eight manuscripts represent entire copied scrolls, it does demonstrate that all chapters of what we know as the MT book of Daniel existed or were known in some form during the late Second Temple period. It does not mean, however, that there were eight complete scrolls of the book. Furthermore, it seems that 4Q116, which overlaps with the prayer in Dan 9:12–17, could very well be an excerpted text. Notably, there are as many as nine additional scrolls that contain texts that can be associated with Danielic traditions (4Q242–246; 4Q489; 4Q551–553).[45] A significant total of seventeen manuscripts of Daniel or Danielic traditions suggest that the story gained popularity shortly after the final editing of this book in 160s BCE. So too the additions to the Greek LXX editions known as the tale of Susanna and the Elders, Azariah's Prayer, and Bel and the Dragon.

Insofar as the book of Daniel purports to be a book of the experiences of a seer from the time of the exile, it and the related Danielic literature can be considered as pseudepigrapha. The visions can be loosely tethered to a legendary and enigmatic figure named Daniel, mentioned along with Noah and Job in Ezek 14:14–20, as an individual known for his righteousness and intercessory power. The name Daniel is also mentioned in Ezek 28:3 as a measure of wisdom and understanding. The literature associated with Daniel from the Second Temple period can be considered as pseudepigrapha anchored to this remarkable but completely obscure sage referenced twice in the book of Ezekiel. Texts that modern scholars would classify as pseudepigraphic use the language of prophecy to describe Daniel's experiences. In the case of Daniel, late Second Temple texts refer to Daniel as a prophet because his experiences were revelatory. These experiences, both interpreting dreams and the visions themselves, were constitutive experiences that defined him as a prophet. According to 4Q174 (1–3 II, 3–4), Daniel was known as a prophet (אש]ר כתוב בספר דניאל הנביא, "which was written in the book of Daniel the prophet"). So, too, Josephus uses the label of prophet in several instances to speak of Daniel (*A.J.* 9.267–269; 10.245–246, 249, 267–276).

---

44. Peter W. Flint, "The Daniel Tradition at Qumran," in *The Book of Daniel: Composition and Reception*, ed. John J. Collins and Peter W. Flint, vol. 2, VTSup 83.2 (Leiden: Brill, 2001), 329–67. The information here about the seventeen manuscripts depends on pp. 330–32.

45. Flint, "Daniel Tradition at Qumran," 331–32.

In the book of Daniel, the protagonist goes from being the interpreter of dreams (chs. 1–6) to being the one seeking interpretations of his own visions (chs. 7–12). In the apocalypse, the seer's experiences of dreams and visions are reported to the reader through scenarios that we might associate with the phenomenon of pseudepigraphy. For example, the visions in chapter 7 are described as being read from a written account of the night visions that Daniel had during the first year of King Belshazzar of Babylon in 7:1.[46] The opening of the apocalypse presumes a scenario in which Daniel is retelling an experience that has been written down. This nighttime dream report concludes in 7:28 with the words "here the account ends" (עד־כה סופא די־מלתא).[47] Henceforth, the book of Daniel shifts from third-person narration to first-person reporting, a characteristic feature of visionary texts. Even more remarkable is the way Daniel's visions came to generate further visionary texts. For example, the seven-headed monster with ten horns that rises out of the sea in Rev 13 is a conflation of the four beasts of Dan 7.

> [1]And I saw a beast rising out of the sea, having ten horns and seven heads; and on its horns were ten diadems, and on its heads were blasphemous names. [2]And the beast that I saw was like a leopard, its feet were like a bear's, and its mouth was like a lion's mouth. And the dragon gave it his power and his throne and great authority. [3]One of its heads seemed to have received a death-blow, but its mortal wound had been healed. In amazement the whole earth followed the beast. (Rev 13:1–3)

Why did the reading of Daniel's apocalypse lead to the generation of new writings?[48]

---

46. "In the first year of King Belshazzar of Babylon, Daniel had a dream and visions of his head as he lay in bed. Then he wrote down the dream. The beginning of the account" (7:1). This felicitous translation is suggested by Carol Newsom and it provides a more intelligible reading of the words than the other major options: "Then he wrote down the dream" (a translation of ראש מלין is omitted by NRSV); "Then he wrote the dream and told the sum of the matters" (JPS). See Carol A. Newsom, *Daniel* (Louisville: Westminster John Knox Press, 2014), 212.

47. "Here the account ends. As for me, Daniel, my thoughts greatly terrified me, and my face turned pale; but I kept the matter in my mind" (Dan 7:28; NRSV).

48. For an excellent discussion of the texts generated by the book of Daniel, see Lorenzo DiTommaso, *The Book of Daniel and the Apocryphal Daniel Literature*, SVTP 20 (Leiden: Brill, 2005).

Discussions of pseudepigraphy reflect the vast interest that scholars of the late twentieth century have had in the idea of authority and the expression of legitimacy during a postmodern era in which such issues have been increasingly problematized. Annette Reed has well described the long association that pseudepigraphy and fraudulent deception has had in scholarly circles in the modern period.[49] What have we gained by examining how visionary texts might have been read and experienced in antiquity? How did these texts come to generate further writings? The examination of the immersive qualities of apocalypses can help modern scholars to recognize how visions of otherworldly realia—monsters, angels, and throne rooms—were extremely compelling for ancient readers. The rumination generated by the suspenseful, surprising, and detailed descriptions of the seer's proprioceptive and interoceptive experiences in otherworldly spaces can lead to the further generation of writing as the reader extends and completes these scenes in their imagination. Thus, we might imagine that the reading of these visions participated in the generative writing of new texts and the production of new pseudepigrapha.

4. Conclusion

Spaces in apocalypses gain solidity by the proprioceptive and interoceptive experiences of the seer that take place in them. The first-person voice makes the seer's dramatic emotional responses to the things that he sees (Dan 7:15, 28; 8:17–18, 27; 10:7–9, 16–17) accessible to the reader. The vivid sensory language that is used to describe the experiences of the seer, either Daniel or Enoch, is detailed in such a way that a reader gains access to the interior and emotional states of the seer through the first-person voice. This integrative approach offers a rich way to conceptualize how reading apocalyptic visions could be understood to deeply engage the

---

49. Annette Yoshiko Reed, "Pseudepigraphy, Authorship, and Reception of 'the Bible' in Late Antiquity," in *The Reception and Interpretation of the Bible in Late Antiquity: Proceedings of the Montreal Colloquium in Honour of Charles Kannengiesser, 11–13 October 2006*, ed. Lorenzo DiTommaso and Lucian Turcescu, BAC 6 (Leiden: Brill, 2008), 467–69. Jason M. Silverman does well to state that pseudonymous attribution, understood as an authorizing strategy, could serve as a "non-judgmental corrective to earlier accusations of intent to fraud" yet would not on its own resolve all questions about a text's authority. See Jason M. Silverman, "Pseudepigraphy, Anonymity, and Auteur Theory," *Religion and the Arts* 15 (2011): 522.

reader and effect the reader by cultivating responses to the text that are both preparatory for moral formation and by giving the reader access to an experience of presence. In the case of the former, the cumulative reading of the book of Daniel, from the court tales to the visions, works to cultivate the emotional predispositions needed for courage and perseverance in the face of a hostile foreign regime.[50] In the case of the latter, the visions, like ancient Jewish apocalypses, draw in the reader and hearer and convey a quality of presence. The lasting power of Daniel may have very little to do with its historicity[51] and more to do with the narrative's ability to create compelling experiences for the reader. This effect of narrative is well described by Tanya Luhrmann as the creation of a special world, which she calls a *paracosm*.[52] Such imaginary spaces are so compelling that subsequent readers extend and continue the interactive narrative in such a way, I propose, that leads to the further generation of writings.[53]

The effect of these scenarios is to underscore the image of the seer ruminating over visionary experiences that have been written down—thereby scripting a scenario that could be reenacted by subsequent readers who might read these visions at a later time.[54] Michael Swartz does well

---

50. This emotional effect of reading Daniel is described well by Ari Mermelstein, "Constructing Fear and Pride in the Book of Daniel: The Profile of a Second Temple Emotional Community," *JSJ* 46 (2015): 449–83, who uses a social-constructivist understanding of emotion to consider how emotions are used in the formation of common values and beliefs (450).

51. The ability to immerse oneself in reading does not depend upon the text being historically true. According to Cain Todd ("Fictional Immersion: Attending Emotionally to Fiction," *Journal of Value Inquiry* [2012]: 449–65), humans have the natural capacity to suspend disbelief, even when the content is known to be fictional. Also Angela Kim Harkins, "The Pro-social Role of Grief in Ezra's Penitential Prayer," *BibInt* 24 (2016): 490–91; and Sarah Iles Johnston, "How Myths and Other Stories Help to Create and Sustain Beliefs," in *Religion: Narrating Religion*, ed. Sarah Iles Johnston (Farmington Hills, MI: MacMillan, 2017), 141–56; and Johnston, *The Story of Myth* (Cambridge: Harvard University Press, 2018).

52. Tanya M. Luhrmann, *How God Becomes Real: Kindling the Presence of Invisible Others* (Princeton: Princeton University Press, 2020).

53. This generative effect is the subject of my long-term research project, "Visions as Immersive Narratives."

54. While we speak here about the experience of reading the visions of Daniel, it is worthwhile to consider the general effect of reading the book in its entirety, from beginning to end, as it would have been experienced with a scroll apparatus that would not allow for random access of passages. What kind of effect is achieved from

to remind us that the process of reading is itself far more complex from an integrative perspective than most text-based scholars may be willing to keep in mind: "Indeed, the force of recitation needs to be taken quite seriously as a potent form of ritual behavior and as an example of the actualization of sacred space in time. Memorization, recitation and performance, we must remember, are physical acts, requiring intensive preparation, stamina, and physical prowess."[55] Swartz's comments highlight the various performative and embodied aspects of reading that I think are helpful for thinking about how we might imagine the literary scene of Daniel reporting the night visions to the first hearers. Reading and ruminating over past prophecies is an embodied experience that is joined to other ritual practices. In the case of Dan 9, fasting, sackcloth, and ashes intensify his experience of reading: "I turned my face to the Lord my God, to seek with prayer, supplication, in fasting, sackcloth, and ashes" (ואתנה את־פני אל־אדני האלהים לבקש תפלה ותחנונים בצום ושק ואפר; v. 3). The passage from Jer 25, which speaks of the duration of the exile as a seventy-year prophecy, could not easily be accessed with precision in a scroll of the prophet's writings, since the apparatus of a scroll does not allow for random access, and so we might imagine the seer reading and mulling over several of Jeremiah's written prophecies, including the poignant descriptions of rejection and passages of anguished laments, all of which are written in the first-person voice.[56] The scene that is depicted here is often identified as the classic example of revelatory exegesis.[57]

---

sequencing the court tales prior to the amazing visions in chapters 7 to 12? Perhaps one not unimportant effect from reading the court tales is the heightening of a reader's attentiveness to the visions that are described.

55. Michael D. Swartz, "Ritual about Myth about Ritual: Towards an Understanding of the Avodah in the Rabbinic Period," *The Journal of Jewish Thought and Philosophy* 6 (1997): 153. See, too, Ophir Münz-Manor, "Narrating Salvation: Verbal Sacrifices in Late Antique Liturgical Poetry," in *Jews, Christians, and the Roman Empire: The Poetics of Power in Late Antiquity*, ed. Annette Yoshiko Reed and Natalie Dohrmann (Philadelphia: University of Pennsylvania Press, 2013), 154–66, nn. 315–19.

56. For a discussion of how ritually induced states of grief can generate experiences of presence, see Harkins, "Ritual Mourning in Daniel's Interpretation," 14–32; and Harkins, "Function of Prayers of Ritual Mourning," 80–101.

57. Pierre Grelot, "Soixante-dix semaines d'années," *Bib* 50 (1969): 169–86; Michael Fishbane, *Biblical Interpretation in Ancient Israel* (Oxford: Clarendon, 1985), 482–89; Lester L. Grabbe, "'The End of the Desolations of Jerusalem': From Jeremiah's Seventy Years to Daniel's Seventy Weeks of Years," in *Early Jewish and Christian Exege-*

This study has examined the features of apocalypses that make them compelling, even to readers who stand far removed from the historical events that they describe. The lasting power of apocalypses lies in their ability to generate immersive experiences of otherworldly experiences for readers. The visions of otherworldly narrative realms that are seen only by the seer are reported with a firsthand vividness to subsequent readers. Visions are described with counterintuitive elements, and the strategic deployment of emotions through the element of surprise or suspense succeeds in slowing down the pace of reading and effectively increases the ongoing rumination over the events that are described. Features found in these apocalypses impact the reader creating a deeper and more empathic bond with the seer. Daniel's first-person report of his own emotional responses to the events (7:15, 28; 8:15–18, 27; 9:3–4; 10:2–9) could be understood to enscript emotions for a subsequent reader so that the imaginative reading of these visions could be said to generate a firsthand intensity. In such a scenario, the phenomenon of pseudepigraphy—that is, the generation of writings which then become attached to a known figure—could be considered as an effect experienced by a reader who has immersed him/herself in the narrative world of the apocalypse.

Bibliography

Andrews, Isolde. "Being Open to the Vision: A Study from Fourth Ezra." *Literature and Theology* 12 (1998): 231–41.

Applegate, John. "Jeremiah and the Seventy Years in the Hebrew Bible." Pages 91–110 in *The Book of Jeremiah and Its Reception—Le Livre de Jérémie et sa réception*. Edited by Adrian H. W. Curtis and Thomas Römer. BETL 128. Leuven: Leuven University Press; Peeters, 1997.

---

sis: *Studies in Memory of William Hugh Brownlee*, ed. Craig A. Evans and William F. Stinespring (Atlanta: Scholars Press, 1987), 67–72; Gerald H. Wilson, "The Prayer of Daniel 9: Reflection of Jeremiah 29," *JSOT* 48 (1990): 91–99; Antti Laato, "The Seventy Year Weeks in the Book of Daniel," *ZAW* 102 (1990): 212–23; John Applegate, "Jeremiah and the Seventy Years in the Hebrew Bible," in *The Book of Jeremiah and Its Reception—Le Livre de Jérémie et sa réception*, ed. Adrian H. W. Curtis and Thomas Römer, BETL 128 (Leuven: Leuven University Press; Peeters, 1997), 106–8; Alex Jassen, *Mediating the Divine: Prophecy and Revelation in the Dead Sea Scrolls and Second Temple Judaism* (Leiden: Brill, 2007), 214–30; and Harkins, "Function of Prayers of Ritual Mourning," 80–101.

Avrahami, Yael. *The Senses of Scripture: Sensory Experience in the Hebrew Bible*. New York: T&T Clark, 2012.

Borenstein, Elhanan, and Eytan Ruppin. "The Evolution of Imitation and Mirror Neurons in Adaptive Agents." *Cognitive Systems Research* 6 (2005): 229–42.

Boyer, Pascal. *The Naturalness of Religious Ideas: A Cognitive Theory of Religion*. Berkeley: University of California Press, 1994.

———. *Religion Explained: The Evolutionary Origins of Religious Thought*. New York: Basic Books, 2001.

Boyer, Pascal, and Charles Ramble. "Cognitive Templates for Religious Concepts: Cross-Cultural Evidence for Recall of Counter-Intuitive representations." *Cognitive Science* 25 (2001): 535–64.

Caracciolo, Marco. "Cognitive Literary Studies and the Status of Interpretation: An Attempt at Conceptual Mapping." *New Literary History* 47 (2016): 187–207.

———. *The Experientiality of Narrative: An Enactivist Approach*. Berlin: de Gruyter, 2014.

———. "Fictional Consciousnesses: A Reader's Manual." *Style* 46 (2012): 42–65.

———. "Ungrounding Fictional Worlds: An Enactivist Perspective on the 'Worldlikeness' of Fiction." Pages 113–31 in *Possible Worlds Theory and Contemporary Narratology*. Edited by Alice Bell and Marie-Laure Ryan. Lincoln: University of Nebraska Press, 2019.

Craig, A. D. "How Do You Feel? Interoception: The Sense of the Physiological Condition of the Body." *Nature Reviews Neuroscience* 3 (2002): 655–66.

Collins, John J. "The Heavenly Representative: The 'Son of Man' in the Similitudes of Enoch." Pages 111–33 in *Ideal Figures in Ancient Judaism*. Edited by George W. E. Nickelsburg and John J. Collins. SCS 12. Chico, CA: Scholars Press, 1980.

———. "Introduction: The Genre Apocalypse Reconsidered." Pages 1–20 in *Apocalypse, Prophecy, and Pseudepigraphy: On Jewish Apocalyptic Literature*. Edited by John J. Collins. Grand Rapids: Eerdmans, 2015.

DiTommaso, Lorenzo. *The Book of Daniel and the Apocryphal Daniel Literature*. SVTP 20. Leiden: Brill, 2005.

Easterlin, Nancy. *A Biocultural Approach to Literary Theory and Interpretation*. Baltimore: Johns Hopkins University Press, 2012.

———. "'Loving Ourselves Best of All': Ecocriticism and the Adapted Mind." *Mosaic* 37 (2004): 1–18.

Feldt, Laura. "Religious Narrative and the Literary Fantastic: Ambiguity and Uncertainty in Ex. 1–18." *Religion* 41 (2011): 251–83.

Fishbane, Michael. *Biblical Interpretation in Ancient Israel*. Oxford: Clarendon, 1985.

Flint, Peter W. "The Daniel Tradition at Qumran." Pages 329–67 in vol. 2 of *The Book of Daniel: Composition and Reception*. Edited by John J. Collins and Peter W. Flint. VTSup 83.2. Leiden: Brill, 2001.

Gallese, Vittorio. "Mirroring, a Liberated Embodied Simulation and Aesthetic Experience." Pages 27–37 in *Mirror Images: Reflections in Art and Medicine*. Edited by Helen Hirsch and Alessandra Pace. Vienna: Verlag für moderne Kunst, 2017.

Geertz, Armin W. "Religious Bodies, Minds and Places: A Cognitive Science of Religion Perspective." Pages 35–52 in *Spazi e luoghi sacri: Espressioni ed esperienze di vissuto religioso*. Edited by Laura Carnevale. Santo Spirito [Bari]: Edipuglia, 2017.

Grabbe, Lester L. "'The End of the Desolations of Jerusalem': From Jeremiah's Seventy Years to Daniel's Seventy Weeks of Years." Pages 67–72 in *Early Jewish and Christian Exegesis: Studies in Memory of William Hugh Brownlee*. Edited by Craig A. Evans and William F. Stinespring. Atlanta: Scholars Press, 1987.

Grelot, Pierre. "Soixante-dix semaines d'années." *Bib* 50 (1969): 169–86.

Harkins, Angela Kim. "The Emotional Re-experiencing of the Hortatory Narratives Found in the Admonition of the Damascus Document." *DSD* 22 (2015): 285–307.

———. "The Function of Prayers of Ritual Mourning in the Second Temple Period." Pages 80–101 in *Functions of Psalms and Prayers in the Late Second Temple Period*. Edited by Mika S. Pajunen and Jeremy Penner. BZAW 486. Berlin: de Gruyter, 2017.

———. "The Pro-social Role of Grief in Ezra's Penitential Prayer." *BibInt* 24 (2016): 466–91.

———. *Reading with an "I" to the Heavens: Looking at the Qumran Hodayot through the Lens of Visionary Traditions*. Ekstasis 3. Berlin: de Gruyter, 2012.

———. "Ritual Mourning in Daniel's Interpretation of Jeremiah's Prophecy." *The Journal of Cognitive Historiography* 2 (2015): 14–33.

Heffernan, Thomas J. *The Passion of Perpetua and Felicity*. Oxford: Oxford University Press, 2011.

Hellholm, David. "The Problem of Apocalyptic Genre." *Semeia* 36 (1986): 13–64.

Hsu, Chun-Ting, Markus Conrad, and Arthur M. Jacobs. "Fiction Feelings in Harry Potter: Haemodynamic Response in the Mid-Cingulate Cortex Correlates with Immersive Reading Experience." *Neuroreport* 25 (2014): 1356–61.

Jassen, Alex. *Mediating the Divine: Prophecy and Revelation in the Dead Sea Scrolls and Second Temple Judaism*. Leiden: Brill, 2007.

Johnston, Sarah Iles. "How Myths and Other Stories Help to Create and Sustain Beliefs." Pages 141–56 in *Religion: Narrating Religion*. Edited by Sarah Iles Johnston. Farmington Hills, MI: MacMillan, 2017.

———. *The Story of Myth*. Cambridge: Harvard University Press, 2018.

Kaplan, Stephen. "Environmental Preference in a Knowledge-Seeking, Knowledge-Using Organism." Pages 581–98 in *The Adapted Mind: Evolutionary Psychology and the Generation of Culture*. Edited by Jerome Barkow, Leda Cosmides, and John Tooby. New York: Oxford University Press, 1992.

Kosmin, Paul. *Time and Its Adversaries in the Seleucid Empire*. Cambridge: Harvard University Press, 2018.

Kukkonen, Karin, and Marco Caracciolo. "Introduction: What Is the 'Second Generation'?" *Style* 48 (2014): 261–74.

Kuzmičová, Anežka. "Does It Matter Where You Read? Situating Narrative in Physical Environment." *Communication Theory* 26 (2016): 290–308.

———. "Mental Imagery: A View from Embodied Cognition." *Style* 48 (2014): 275–93.

———. "Presence in the Reading of Literary Narrative: A Case for Motor Enactment." *Semiotica* 189 (2012): 23–48.

Laato, Antti. "The Seventy Year Weeks in the Book of Daniel." *ZAW* 102 (1990): 212–23.

Lachmann, Renata. *Erzählte Phantastik: Zu Phantasiegeschichte und Semantik phantastischer Texte*. Frankfurt am Main: Suhrkamp, 2002.

Love, Glen A. "Ecocriticism and Science: Toward Consilience?" *New Literary History* 30 (1999): 661–76.

Luhrmann, Tanya M. *How God Becomes Real: Kindling the Presence of Invisible Others*. Princeton: Princeton University Press, 2020.

Martin, Leonard L., and Abraham Tesser. "Clarifying Our Thoughts." Pages 189–208 in *Ruminative Thoughts*. Edited by Robert S. Wyer Jr. Advances in Social Cognition 9. Mahwah, NJ: Erlbaum, 1996.

McNamara, Patrick. *The Neuroscience of Religious Experience*. Cambridge: Cambridge University Press, 2009.

Merkur, Daniel. "The Visionary Practices of Jewish Apocalypticists." Pages 119–48 in *Essays in Honor of Paul Parin*. Edited by L. Bryce Boyer and Simon A. Gronick. The Psychoanalytic Study of Society 14. New York: Routledge, 1989.

Mermelstein, Ari. "Constructing Fear and Pride in the Book of Daniel: The Profile of a Second Temple Emotional Community." *JSJ* 46 (2015): 449–83.

Miall, David S. "Emotions and the Structuring of Narrative Responses." *Poetics Today* 32 (2011): 323–48.

Müller, Ulrich B. *Messias und Menschensohn in jüdischen Apokalypsen und in der Offenbarung des Johannes*. SNT 6. Gütersloh: Gütersloh Verlagshaus, 1972.

Münz-Manor, Ophir. "Narrating Salvation: Verbal Sacrifices in Late Antique Liturgical Poetry." Pages 154–66 in *Jews, Christians, and the Roman Empire: The Poetics of Power in Late Antiquity*. Edited by Annette Yoshiko Reed and Natalie Dohrmann. Philadelphia: University of Pennsylvania Press, 2013.

Närhi, Jani. "Beautiful Reflections: The Cognitive and Evolutionary Foundations of Paradise Representations." *MTSR* 20 (2008): 339–65.

Newsom, Carol A. *Daniel*. Louisville. Westminster John Knox, 2014.

Nickelsburg, George W. E. *1 Enoch 1: A Commentary on the Book of 1 Enoch, Chapters 1–36; 81–108*. Hermeneia. Minneapolis: Fortress, 2001.

Noë, Alva. *Action in Perception*. Cambridge: MIT Press, 2004.

Pyysiäinen, Ilkka, Marjaana Lindeman, and Timo Honkela. "Counterintuitiveness as the Hallmark of Religiosity." *Religion* 33 (2003): 341–55.

Reed, Annette Yoshiko. "Pseudepigraphy, Authorship, and Reception of 'the Bible' in Late Antiquity." Pages 467–90 in *The Reception and Interpretation of the Bible in Late Antiquity: Proceedings of the Montreal Colloquium in Honour of Charles Kannengiesser, 11–13 October 2006*. Edited by Lorenzo DiTommaso and Lucian Turcescu. BAC 6. Leiden: Brill, 2008.

Robinson, Jenefer. *Deeper than Reason: Emotion and Its Role in Literature, Music, and Art*. Oxford: Clarendon, 2007.

Ryan, Marie-Laure. "The Text as World: Theories of Immersion." Pages 61–84 in *Revisiting Immersion and Interactivity in Literature and Electronic Media*. Vol. 2 of *Narrative as Virtual Reality*. Baltimore: Johns Hopkins University Press, 2015.

Scarry, Elaine. "On Vivacity: The Difference between Daydreaming and Imagining-Under-Authorial-Instruction." *Representations* 52 (1995): 1–26.
Schwartz, Seth. *Imperialism and Jewish Society: 200 B.C.E. to 640 C.E.* Princeton: Princeton University Press, 2001.
Seth, Anil K. "Interoceptive Inference, Emotion, and the Embodied Self." *Trends in Cognitive Sciences* 17 (2013): 565–73.
Silverman, Jason M. "Pseudepigraphy, Anonymity, and Auteur Theory." *Religion and the Arts* 15 (2011): 520–55.
Sjöberg, Erik. *Der Menschensohn im äthiopischen Henochbuch*. ARSHLL 41. Lund: Lund University Press, 1946.
Smith, Mark S. "The Heart and Innards in Israelite Emotional Expressions: Notes from Anthropology and Psychobiology." *JBL* 117 (1998): 427–36.
Speer, Nicole K., Jeremy R. Reynolds, Khena M. Swallow, and Jeffrey M. Zacks. "Reading Stories Activates Neural Representations of Visual and Motor Experiences." *Psychological Science* 20 (2009): 289–99.
Starr, G. Gabrielle. *Feeling Beauty: The Neuroscience of Aesthetic Experience*. Cambridge: MIT Press, 2015.
———. "Multisensory Imagery," Pages 279–91 in *Introduction to Cognitive Cultural Studies*. Edited by Lisa Zunshine. Baltimore: Johns Hopkins University Press, 2010.
Stuckenbruck, Loren T. *Angel Veneration and Christology: A Study in Early Judaism and in the Christology of the Apocalypse of John*. Tübingen: Mohr Siebeck, 1995.
———. "Pseudepigraphy and First Person Discourse in the Dead Sea Documents: From the Aramaic Texts to Writings of the Yahad." Pages 295–326 in *The Dead Sea Scrolls and Contemporary Culture: Proceedings of the International Conference Held at the Israel Museum, Jerusalem (July 6–8, 2008)*. Edited by Adolfo Daniel Roitman, Lawrence H. Schiffman, and Shani Tzoref. STDJ 93. Leiden: Brill, 2011.
Swartz, Michael D. "Ritual about Myth about Ritual: Towards an Understanding of the Avodah in the Rabbinic Period." *The Journal of Jewish Thought and Philosophy* 6 (1997): 135–55.
Tagliabue, Aldo. "An Embodied Reading of Epiphanies in Aelius Aristides' Sacred Tales." *Ramus* 45 (2016): 213–30.
Todd, Cain. "Fictional Immersion: Attending Emotionally to Fiction." *Journal of Value Inquiry* (2012): 449–65.

VanderKam, James C. "Righteous One, Messiah, Chosen One, and Son of Man in 1 Enoch 37-71." Pages 169-91 in *Enoch and the Messiah Son of Man*. Edited by Gabriele Boccaccini. Grand Rapids: Eerdmans, 2007.

Wilson, Gerald H. "The Prayer of Daniel 9: Reflection of Jeremiah 29." *JSOT* 48 (1990): 91-99.

Zunshine, Lisa. ed. *Introduction to Cognitive Cultural Studies*. Baltimore: Johns Hopkins University Press, 2010.

Poor Subjects of the Hodayot: Apocalyptic Class Subjectivities in Practice

G. Anthony Keddie

A foundational assumption in scholarship on apocalypticism has been and remains that apocalyptic thinking is a response to oppression. If religion is what Karl Marx dubbed the "sigh of the oppressed creature,"[1] then apocalyptic religion is the last gasp of the utterly subjugated. This oppression narrative has dominated scholarship on the apocalypses as much as the Dead Sea Scrolls.[2] Whether the sect known from the scrolls produced texts that fit the genre apocalypse is debatable, but few would doubt that this sect was apocalyptic in orientation (i.e., special revelation, eschatology, dualism, and determinism are prominent across the sectarian texts).[3] Consistent with the oppression theory, scholars tend to describe this apocalyptic group as oppressed—as economically impoverished, culturally alienated, politically disenfranchised, and/or religiously marginalized.[4]

I would like to express my deep gratitude to R. Gillian Glass and Elisabeth Schrottner for providing thoughtful suggestions that improved this study.

1. Karl Marx, *Critique of Hegel's "Philosophy of Right,"* trans. Annette Jolin and Joseph O'Malley (Cambridge: Cambridge University Press, 1977), 131.

2. For a fuller critique of the oppression theory (with references), see my *Revelations of Ideology: Apocalyptic Class Politics in Early Roman Palestine*, JSJSup 189 (Leiden: Brill, 2018), 11–41.

3. John J. Collins, *Seers, Sibyls, and Sages in Hellenistic-Roman Judaism*, JSJSup 54 (Leiden: Brill, 1997), 261–85; and Collins, *Apocalypticism in the Dead Sea Scrolls* (London: Routledge, 1997). Cf. Jörg Frey and Michael Becker, eds., *Apokalyptik und Qumran*, Einblicke 10 (Paderborn: Bonifatius, 2007). See also the essays by Collins and Lange in the present volume.

4. E.g., Richard A. Horsley, *Revolt of the Scribes: Resistance and Apocalyptic Origins* (Minneapolis: Fortress, 2010), 123–42.

By focusing their analysis on sect(s) in opposition to wider society, scholars have often portrayed the Dead Sea sect as a collectivity of individuals who were more-or-less uniform in interests, power, and socioeconomic position. Eyal Regev thus cites communal property and aversion to wealth as proof of the introversionist and revolutionist *yaḥad*'s characteristic egalitarianism.[5] But it is now quite clear that the sect represented by some of the scrolls was internally less equal and externally more integrated into the wider society and economy than a rigid theory of sectarian alienation and reciprocity allows. Therefore, it is important to examine the ways that the apocalyptic discourse conveyed in some of the sectarian texts both legitimated authority structures within the sect and encouraged sociopolitical and economic views that shaped sectarians' practices inside and outside of the sect. This apocalyptic discourse should be viewed as an "argument that is intended to persuade" instead of an innocuous expression of shared beliefs and values.[6]

In this essay, I identify scholarship on subjectivities in the Dead Sea Scrolls as a fruitful avenue for reimagining apocalypticism. Building on studies of sectarian subjectivities, I begin by theorizing "apocalyptic class subjectivities" as a lens for deciphering the social functions of apocalyptic ideologies. Next, I apply this concept to apocalyptic class rhetoric in the Hodayot. Finally, I investigate the material culture of Qumran for traces of the apocalyptic class subjectivity advanced by the Hodayot.

1. Apocalyptic Class Subjectivities: Theoretical Considerations

Subjectivity is a category that is prevalent across the humanities and social sciences but has enjoyed surprisingly little currency in the study of Second

---

5. Regev describes the *yaḥad*, represented by the S tradition, as "relatively egalitarian" (this qualification acknowledges that the "*yaḥad* maintained a hierarchy of obedience based on religious merit"). The S sect (*yaḥad*), for Regev, is nevertheless far less hierarchical than the group represented by D; see Eyal Regev, *Sectarianism in Qumran: A Cross-Cultural Perspective*, RS 45 (Berlin: de Gruyter, 2007), 285–90, and cf. Regev, "Wealth and Sectarianism: Comparing Qumranic and Early Christian Social Approaches," in *Echoes from the Caves: Qumran and the New Testament*, ed. Florentino García Martínez, STDJ 85 (Leiden: Brill, 2009), 211–30. For a subtler approach to the different sectarian tensions in the scrolls, see Jutta Jokiranta, *Social Identity and Sectarianism in the Qumran Movement*, STDJ 105 (Leiden: Brill, 2013).

6. Stephen D. O'Leary, *Arguing the Apocalypse: A Theory of Millennial Rhetoric* (Oxford: Oxford University Press, 1994), 15.

Temple Judaism. It is a binary-collapsing category that occupies the nexus between history and consciousness, structure and agency, self and Other, real and symbolic, imagination and performance, and so on. The common thread in theories of subjectivity is that "the subject is always linked to something outside of it—an idea or principle or the society of other subjects.... One is always the subject *to* or *of* something."[7]

Two erudite books apply subjectivity theory to the Dead Sea Scrolls with much success: Carol Newsom's *The Self as Symbolic Space* (2004) and Angela Kim Harkins's *Reading with an "I" to the Heavens* (2012).[8] Newsom defines subjectivity as "the culturally specific ways in which the meaning of one's self is produced, experienced, and articulated."[9] Building on an Althusserian-Foucauldian theoretical trajectory, she focuses on the ways that a subject is always both an active participant in a discourse or ideology and also one who is subjected to a wider system of meaning.[10] Through close analysis of the Community Rule and Hodayot, she argues that these texts advance a common sectarian subjectivity that situates sectarian individuals in relation to other sectarians and outsiders. Harkins takes this approach a step further by emphasizing that subjectivity is embodied and performed, following poststructuralist theorists in particular.[11] Also focusing on the Hodayot, she contends that performative readings of these prayers predisposed subjects to have religious experiences. Like Newsom, she recognizes a social distinction in the Hodayot. For Newsom, the self-presentation of the persona of a leader (whether the Mebaqqer or Maskil) in certain prayers of the Hodayot normalizes his power.[12] For Harkins, however, the Hodayot not only generated a sectarian subjectivity that implied a leadership myth but showcased the religious experiences of an elite member of the community (the Maskil). This affirmed the Maskil's power as a religious virtuoso but could also serve as a catalyst for subjects' own religious experiences.[13]

---

7. Nick Mansfield, *Subjectivity: Theories of the Self from Freud to Haraway* (New York: New York University Press, 2000), 3 (italics original).

8. Carol A. Newsom, *The Self as Symbolic Space: Constructing Identity and Community at Qumran*, STDJ 52 (Leiden: Brill, 2004); and Angela Kim Harkins, *Reading with an "I" to the Heavens: Looking at the Qumran Hodayot through the Lens of Visionary Traditions*, Ekstasis 3 (Berlin: de Gruyter, 2012).

9. Newsom, *Self as Symbolic Space*, 192.

10. Newsom, *Self as Symbolic Space*, 13–14.

11. Harkins, *Reading with an "I" to the Heavens*, 56–67.

12. Newsom, *Self as Symbolic Space*, 287–346.

13. Harkins, *Reading with an "I" to the Heavens*, 8 and *passim*.

Both books recognize, but do not dwell on, the apocalyptic quality of these rhetorically formed subjectivities. Harkins, for instance, demonstrates that the Hodayot craft an ideal persona that resembles the visionary exemplars of Daniel and Enoch.[14] In her words, "the strong 'I' of the texts can be seen to construct a rhetorical persona of an imaginal body that progressively experiences transformation and ascent into the heavens."[15] In a somewhat different vein, Newsom presents discourse and subjectivity as categories for analyzing apocalypticism apart from genre. She speaks of "apocalyptic subjects" and "apocalyptic discourse."[16] Moreover, she divorces the apocalyptic "rhetoric of the margins" from theories of absolute and relative deprivation, asserting that "those who opt for a rhetoric of the margins ... may well have been persons who had various forms of social capital (education, most obviously), as well as material resources. Marginality should also not be equated with weakness."[17] Thus, in slightly different ways, both Newsom and Harkins have laid the groundwork for analyzing the ways that apocalyptic rhetoric shapes subjectivities.

Neither author, however, has given much attention to apocalyptic *class* subjectivities—that is, the ways that apocalyptic rhetoric advances dispositions about class relations, the structure of the economy, economic interactions with outsiders, and agency. "Class subjectivity" is a social-scientific analytical tool that has proven useful to scholars in diverse fields. The sociologist Beverly Skeggs, for instance, stresses that class is not simply a structural location in the relations of production or a status defined by life chances and cultural choices in relation to the market.[18] Instead, fol-

---

14. Harkins, *Reading with an "I" to the Heavens*, esp. 141–51; Harkins, "Reading the Qumran Hodayot in Light of the Traditions Associated with Enoch," *Hen* 32 (2010): 359–400; and Trine Bjørnung Hasselbalch, *Meaning and Context in the Thanksgiving Hymns: Linguistic and Rhetorical Perspectives on a Collection of Prayers from Qumran*, EJL 42 (Atlanta: SBL Press, 2015), 208–13.

15. Harkins, *Reading with an "I" to the Heavens*, 87.

16. Newsom, *Self as Symbolic Space*, 48–50; Newsom, "Apocalyptic Subjects: Social Construction of the Self in the Qumran Hodayot," *JSP* 12 (2001): 3–35.

17. Newsom, *Self as Symbolic Space*, 48. See also Newsom's discussion of genre blending in the Hodayot in "Pairing Research Questions and Theories of Genre: A Case Study of the Hodayot," *DSD* 17 (2010): 241–59, esp. 253–54.

18. Beverley Skeggs, *Class, Self, Culture* (London: Routledge, 2004). Unlike traditional Marxist notions of collective subjectivity, this approach emphasizes discursive construction, contestation, and individuation, and it does not depend on self-consciousness.

lowing Pierre Bourdieu,[19] it is a subjective set of dispositions shaped by rhetoric and practice. As such, class subjectivities may be analyzed among societies that lack the modern, Western, industrialist category of class by attending to the ways that subject formation implicates socioeconomic position—how an individual's relation to a broader social group is articulated in economic terms. Thus, Xiaowei Zang has found that minority ethnic identity is a primary basis for class subjectivities among Uyghurs in contemporary Ürümchi, China.[20] Additionally, Elmira Satybaldieva has shown that laborers in contemporary Kyrgyzstan draw on Soviet nostalgia and traditional and Islamic morality to generate subjectivities that delineate boundaries with outsiders engaged in post-Soviet neoliberal capitalism: the pious workers eschew wealth as a basis of morality.[21] Finally, Sean McCloud has advocated analysis of "class subjectivities" in religious studies as a way to probe the neglected intersections of class and religion in various contexts. In his own ethnographic work, he has examined the ways that American religious actors from the same economic level, regional context, and religious tradition sometimes generate quite different class subjectivities through bodily practices and discourse.[22]

In my recent book, I developed a model for applying these social-scientific insights to apocalyptic class politics in Second Temple Judaism.[23] According to this model, the elite and subelite scribes that produced nonsectarian apocalyptic texts advanced class subjectivities that situate them within the same class as their constituents. This class, which is given titles such as "the righteous," "the pious," "God's people," and "slaves of God," is cast as economically exploited by a wealthy and politically powerful

---

19. Pierre Bourdieu, *Distinction: A Social Critique of the Judgement of Taste* (London: Routledge, 1986).

20. Xiaowei Zang, "Socioeconomic Attainment, Cultural Tastes, and Ethnic Identity: Class Subjectivities among Uyghurs in Ürümchi," *Ethnic and Racial Studies* 39 (2016): 2169–86.

21. Elmira Satybaldieva, "Working Class Subjectivities and Neoliberalisation in Kyrgyzstan: Developing Alternative Moral Selves," *International Journal of Politics, Culture, and Society* 31 (2018): 31–47.

22. Sean McCloud, *Divine Hierarchies: Class in American Religion and Religious Studies* (Chapel Hill: University of North Carolina Press, 2007).

23. Keddie, *Revelations of Ideology*; cf. Keddie, "Poverty and Exploitation in the Psalms of Solomon: At the Intersection of Sapiential and Apocalyptic Discourses," in *The Psalms of Solomon: Texts, Contexts, and Intertexts*, ed. Patrick Pouchelle, G. Anthony Keddie, and Kenneth Atkinson, EJL 54 (Atlanta: SBL Press, 2021).

class. These texts generate apocalyptic class subjectivities that legitimate the social power of their authors by simultaneously revealing that certain opponents are an exploitative class and diminishing the agency of exploited individuals to change their socioeconomic situation. The class subjectivities these texts posit are distinctly apocalyptic because they rely on the trope of revelation to undergird their claim that certain opponents are evil exploiters and assert that only God's intervention can bring justice to the exploited. I based this model on the Psalms of Solomon, the Parables of Enoch, the Testament of Enoch, and the Sayings Source (Q), but I have not yet applied it directly to a sectarian text. In what follows, I build on Harkins's and Newsom's work on subject formation by using the Hodayot as a sectarian case study for this model of apocalyptic class subjectivities.

2. God's Poor Subjects and Belial's Wealthy Oppressors in the Hodayot

Since the relatively late publication of the full witnesses to the Hodayot (Thanksgiving Hymns) in 1999 and the DJD reconstruction of the text in 2009, many insightful studies have appeared.[24] However, I am not aware of any contribution that specifically addresses the role of class in apocalyptic discourse in this work, which is my intent here. Following scholarly consensus, I view the Hodayot as a sectarian work and focus my analysis on its most extensive witness, 1QH^a, reconstructed with recourse to other manuscripts (1QH^b, 4QH^{a-e}, 4QpapH^f). The 1QH^a manuscript dates to 30–1 BCE, but this work, or at least significant parts of it, were produced as much as a century earlier. For instance, the 4QH^b manuscript dates to the first quarter of the first century BCE and might indicate that the work cir-

---

24. Eileen M. Schuller, "Hodayot," in *Qumran Cave 4.XX. Poetical and Liturgical Texts, Part 2*, ed. Esther G. Chazon et al., DJD 29 (Oxford: Clarendon, 1999), 69–254; Hartmut Stegemann and Eileen M. Schuller, with translations by Carol A. Newsom, *Qumran Cave 1.III. 1QHodayot^a with Incorporation of 1QHodayot^b and 4QHodayot^{a-f}*, DJD 40 (Oxford: Clarendon, 2009). Schuller and Newsom published the DJD 40 edition in a more accessible form as *The Hodayot (Thanksgiving Psalms): A Study Edition of 1QH^a*, EJL 36 (Atlanta: Society of Biblical Literature, 2012). This latter edition is the source of transcriptions and translations of the Hodayot in this study, although I have slightly modified some translations. Except when other manuscripts are specified, citations refer to the reconstructed text of 1QH^a. For overviews of research, see Eileen M. Schuller and Lorenzo DiTommaso, "A Bibliography of the Hodayot, 1948–1996," *DSD* 4 (1997): 55–101; Schuller, "Recent Scholarship on the Hodayot 1993–2010," *CurBR* 10 (2011): 119–62.

culated at an earlier stage without 1QH[a] I–VIII.[25] While I focus on 1QH[a], then, I acknowledge that this collection of prayers may have existed in multiple forms that circulated prior to and at the same time as the form contained in 1QH[a].[26]

There has been much debate over whether the Hodayot should be viewed as a liturgical text that served as an authoritative script for worship. At certain points, the text presents itself as liturgical, for example, "[For the Instruc]tor, [th]anksgiving and prayer for prostrating oneself and supplicating continually at all times" (1QH[a] XX, 7).[27] At the same time, the Hodayot rarely use the first-person plural and also lack poetic devices that facilitate recitation.[28] Two recent articles have helpfully complicated this liturgical/public versus devotional/private dichotomy. Shem Miller has argued that the prayers betray a public setting of oral performance but do not need to be understood as the script for communal liturgical worship.[29] From a different angle, Christine Leroy has associated the Hodayot with perfective spiritual exercises akin to those of the Greco-Roman paideutic tradition. Viewing the prayers as didactic, she rightly notes that they could have been performed in both "devotional" and "liturgical" settings.[30] The prayers could have been performed across a spectrum of social settings, in every case contributing to the formation of subjects.

The apocalyptic rhetoric of the Hodayot generates subjects whose experience of revelation draws them into the divine presence. In this real-

---

25. Angela Kim Harkins, "A New Proposal for Thinking about 1QH[a] Sixty Years after Its Discovery," in *Qumran Cave 1 Revisited, Texts from Cave 1 Sixty Years after Their Discovery: Proceedings of the Sixth Meeting of the IOQS in Ljubljana*, ed. Daniel K. Falk et al., STDJ 91 (Leiden: Brill, 2010), 101–34, esp. 125–30.

26. See Schuller, "Hodayot," 74–75; Schuller, "Recent Scholarship," 134; and Angela Kim Harkins, "The Community Hymns Classification: A Proposal for Further Differentiation," *DSD* 15 (2008): 121–54. Note, however, that in areas of overlap, the surviving copies show that the text itself "is remarkably stable and consistent" (Schuller, "Recent Scholarship," 131).

27. Cf. 1QH[a] V, 12 and XIX, 7–8, 28–29. See Shem Miller, "The Role of Performance and the Performance of Role: Cultural Memory in the Hodayot," *JBL* 137 (2018): 365.

28. Bilhah Nitzan, *Qumran Prayer and Religious Poetry*, trans. Jonathan Chipman, STDJ 12 (Leiden: Brill, 1994), 348. Note, however, the plural imperatives in IX, 36–39 (Miller, "Role of Performance," 365).

29. Miller, "Role Performance." Cf. Newsom, "Pairing Research Questions," 250.

30. Christine Leroy, "Spiritual Exercises in the Hodayot? 1QH[a] as Perfective Trajectory," *JSJ* 48 (2017): 455–79.

ized eschatology, membership in the sect admits subjects into fellowship with the angels (VII, 12–20; XI, 19–24; XIV, 12–14; XIX, 13–17).[31] The prayers envision a final cosmic war in which the faithful are vindicated and the wicked are violently destroyed: "And then the sword of God will come quickly at the time of judgment. All the children of his truth will rouse themselves to extermin[ate] wickedness, and all the children of guilt will be no more" (XIV, 32–33).[32] As John J. Collins has noted, the prayers envision God's impending eschatological intervention but nevertheless emphasize continuity between subjects' transformed lives in the present and in the eschatological age.[33] As with the parable of the mustard seed in the Sayings Source (13:18–19), the change between the present and future ages is best described through botanical metaphors of growth and blossoming (XIV, 17–21).

Through the special revelation that the Hodayot prime them to hear (XIV, 6–7) and recite (XIV, 14), subjects enter into a holy council: "for you have brought [...] your secret counsel [סודכה] to all the people of your council, and in a common lot with the angels of the presence, without an intermediary [מליץ] between them" (XIV, 15–16). Hearing and reciting the Hodayot compresses the gap between humans and God, eliminating the need for an intermediary through the embodied performance of divine revelation. When one is in communion with the angels, there is no need for an *angelus interpres*![34] Notably, the text diminishes human agency in this experience of revelation, in keeping with its staunch determinism:[35]

---

31. For different perspectives on community with the angels, see Devorah Dimant, "Men as Angels: The Self-Image of the Qumran Community," in *Religion and Politics in the Ancient Near East*, ed. Adele Berlin, STJHC (Bethesda: University Press of Maryland, 1996), 93–103; and Esther G. Chazon, "Human and Angelic Prayer in Light of the Dead Sea Scrolls," in *Liturgical Perspectives: Prayer and Poetry in Light of the Dead Sea Scrolls*, ed. Esther G. Chazon, STDJ 48 (Leiden: Brill, 2003), 35–48.

32. Cf. 1 En. 90.19; 91.11–12; Q (Sayings Source) 22:28, 30.

33. John J. Collins, "Metaphor and Eschatology: Life beyond Death in the Hodayot," in *Is There a Text in This Cave? Studies in the Textuality of the Dead Sea Scrolls in Honour of George J. Brooke*, ed. Ariel Feldman, Charlotte Hempel, and Maria Cioată, STDJ 119 (Leiden: Brill, 2017), 420. Collins observes that the evidence from the Hodayot is inconclusive on bodily resurrection.

34. Cf. 1QH[a] XXVI, 36–39 (4QH[a] 7 II, 18–21): ואין מליץ ... דברנו לכה (ellipsis mine).

35. See further Armin Lange, *Weisheit und Prädestination: Weisheitliche Urordnung und Prädestination in den Textfunden von Qumran*, STDJ 18 (Leiden: Brill, 1995), 195–232; and Nicholas A. Meyer, *Adam's Dust and Adam's Glory in the Hodayot*

These things I know because of understanding that comes from you, for you have opened my ears to wondrous mysteries [כיא גליתה אוזני לרזי פלא]. Yet I am a vessel of clay and a thing kneaded with water, a foundation of shame and a well of impurity, a furnace of iniquity, a structure of sin, a spirit of error, and a perverted being, without understanding, and terrified by righteous judgments. (IX, 23; cf. 1QH[a] XIII, 13–14)

As instruction heard and recited, the Hodayot thus position hearers and readers as subjects of hidden knowledge that brings them into the divine presence precisely by rejecting human agency.

This apocalyptic ideology of revelation and determinism undergirds a class subjectivity as the poor. Subjects of the Hodayot repeatedly identify as poor, or with poverty, using a range of terms: אביון (adj.: "needy, oppressed"), ענו (adj.: "meek, humble, oppressed"), ענוה (n.: "humility"), עני (adj.: "poor, afflicted"; n.: "misery, affliction, distress"), רוש (v.: "to be poor/destitute").[36] As is the case with other Dead Sea Scrolls, and notably 4QInstruction, scholars have taken this language as either metaphorical/theological or literal/material.[37] If we approach this language as integral to

---

and the Letters of Paul: Rethinking Anthropogony and Theology, NovTSup 168 (Leiden: Brill, 2016), 18–94. On the minimization of human agency in apocalypticism, see Lorenzo DiTommaso, "The Apocalyptic Other," in *The "Other" in Second Temple Judaism: Essays in Honor of John J. Collins*, ed. Daniel C. Harlow et al. (Grand Rapids: Eerdmans, 2011), 221–46.

36. אביון: 1QH[a] II, 27; X, 34; XI, 26; XIII, 18, 20, 24; XXVI, 27 (4QH[a] 7 II, 8; 4QH[e] 2 7). ענו: 1QH[a] VI, 14; XIII, 23; XXIII, 15. ענוה: 1QH[a] IV, 34. עני: 1QH[a] VI, 15; IX, 38; X, 6 (4QpapH[f] 3 3); X, 36 (4QH[b] 3 3); XIII, 15, 16. רוש: 1QH[a] X, 36; XIII, 16, 22. Other terms imply poverty or marginalization in the text but not as directly as these, e.g., יתום, נגש, אשק, פתי. See Norbert Lohfink, *Lobgesänge der Armen: Studien zum Magnifikat, den Hodajot von Qumran und einigen späten Psalmen*, SBS 139 (Stuttgart: Katholisches Bibelwerk, 1990), 42; and Johannes Un-Sok Ro, *Poverty, Law, and Divine Justice in Persian and Hellenistic Judah*, AIL 32 (Atlanta: SBL Press, 2018), 189–95.

37. The following studies may be taken as representative of the more literal/material and more metaphorical/theological ends of the spectrum, respectively: Catherine M. Murphy, *Wealth in the Dead Sea Scrolls and in the Qumran Community*, STDJ 40 (Leiden: Brill, 2002); and Mark D. Mathews, *Riches, Poverty, and the Faithful: Perspectives on Wealth in the Second Temple Period and the Apocalypse of John*, SNTSMS 154 (Cambridge: Cambridge University Press, 2013). Regarding 4QInstruction, Matthew Goff has shown that this text recognizes different levels of poverty: Matthew Goff, *The Worldly and Heavenly Wisdom of 4QInstruction*, STDJ 50 (Leiden: Brill, 2003), 127–67. He has also observed thematic similarities that suggest that the nonsectar-

an apocalyptic class subjectivity, however, this distinction collapses: poor is both a spiritual and a socioeconomic state. As Johannes Un-sok Ro puts it, this language "emphasizes the suppliant's relationship to God."[38] Yet, as Catherine Murphy has argued, this "spiritual poverty" relies on an ancient socioeconomic theory of poverty that fits with, and relies on, the socioeconomic assumptions of other sectarian texts and has implications for subjects' socioeconomic practices.[39]

As poor individuals, subjects of the Hodayot are situated in a class defined not only in relation to God, but also in relation to a class of wealthy enemies.[40] The "us" and "them" of the Hodayot are the poor and the mighty. One passage, in particular, firmly establishes this relationship:

> I wait hopefully, for you yourself have formed the spi[rit of your servant, and according to] your [wil]l you have determined me. You have not put my support upon unjust gain nor in wealth [על בצע ובהון] [acquired by violence, nor ...] my [hea]rt, and a vessel of flesh you have not set up as my refuge. The strength of the mighty rests upon an abundance of luxuries [חיל גבורים על רוב עדנים], [and they delight in] abundance [רוב(ב)] of grain, wine, and oil. They pride themselves on property and acquisitions, [and they sprout like] a [fl]ourishing [tree] beside channels of water, putting forth foliage and producing abundant branches. Truly, you have chosen[them from all human]kind so that all might fatten themselves from the land. But to the children of your truth you have given insight °°°[...]°t everlasting, and according to their knowledge they are honored, one more than the other. And thus for the mortal being °[...in a m]an you have made his inheritance great through the knowledge of your truth. According to his knowledge y°b°[...f]or the soul of your servant abhors wealth and unjust gain [הון ובצע] and does not °°°°° in the affluence of luxuries [ברום עדנים]. Truly my heart rejoices in your covenant, and your truth delights my soul. (XVIII, 24–32)

---

ian 4QInstruction influenced the later, sectarian Hodayot: Goff, "Reading Wisdom at Qumran: 4QInstruction and the Hodayot," *DSD* 11 (2004): 263–88. A class subjectivity as poor is one potential point of influence, though I do not detect any of the economic gradations that are present in 4QInstruction.

38. Ro, *Poverty, Law, and Justice*, 199.
39. Murphy, *Wealth in the Dead Sea Scrolls*, 243–50.
40. Ro recognizes both characterizations but fails to substantiate the claim that "the evaluation as poor before God is placed above the evaluation as poor vis-à-vis one's adversaries" (*Poverty, Law, and Justice*, 209).

And I tremble when I hear of your judgments upon the mighty of
strength [גבורי כוח], and your case against the host of your holy ones in
the heavens ... (XVIII, 36–37)

As a descriptor for the exploitative class, "mighty" asserts a power differential of social and cosmic proportions. The negative usage of the term גבורים in 1QH[a] XVIII, 26, 36 (and X, 27) bears a striking resemblance to the "mighty" (Eth. ʿazizān/ḥayyālān) who are condemned in the Parables of Enoch for their economic exploitation of the "righteous" (Eth. ṣādeqān).[41] These mighty in the Parables are conflated with kings and landowners as part of a class that corresponds to the antediluvian giants (הגברים/ γίγαντες) of Gen 6:1–4 and the Book of the Watchers.[42] Harkins has noted that the גבר who is born in 1QH[a] XI, 10 might allude to traditions about the giants,[43] but I would suggest that such an allusion is even more likely when the term is used in the plural and in a clearly negative sense as in X, 27; XVIII, 26; and XVIII, 36.

The same language of a mighty class occurs in the Damascus Document in the context of Watchers traditions:

For mighty men of strength [גבורי חיל] stum[bled on account of them [i.e., thoughts of a guilty inclination], from ancient times until now. For having walked in the stubbornness of their hearts] the Watchers [עירי] of the [heavens fell (CD II, 17–18).

The following lines indicate that the sons of the Watchers, who are described as gigantic but not explicitly called גבורים, fell in the same way as the Watchers. Remarking about the use of גבורים to describe humans

---

41. Keddie, *Revelations of Ideology*, 149–62. Note also the titles חזק in 1QH[a] X, 37 and אדירים in 1QH[a] X, 37 and XIII, 9. This class is more often described as the "wicked" (רשע): 1QH[a] VI, 35; VII, 30; X, 12, 14, 26, 38; XII, 35, 39; XIII, 19; XV, 15; and XXV, 15 (4QH[b] 18 5). The Hodayot describe the poor as the righteous, casting them as the counterpart to the mighty/wicked, e.g., 1QH[a] XII, 39: כי אתה בראתה צדיק ורשע. Nickelsburg notes that ʿazizān in the Parables corresponds to Greek κραταιοί and Hebrew חזקים; see George W. E. Nickelsburg and James C. VanderKam, *1 Enoch 2: A Commentary on the Book of 1 Enoch; Chapters 37–82*, Hermeneia (Minneapolis: Fortress, 2012), 103.

42. The titles "the strong" (Eth. ṣenuʿān) and "the exalted" (Eth. leʿul) also appear to describe parts of this class.

43. Harkins, "Reading the Qumran Hodayot," 385–91.

but not the primordial giants, Samuel Thomas has suggested that this was a wordplay "employed in order to link those who continue to sin (viz., the opponents of the sect) with the demonic forces 'of old.'"[44] The *hodayah* similarly refers to the mighty class as גבורים and then proceeds to discuss God's judgment against angelic beings, although it does not use the term גבורים for them. The descriptor גבורי כוח in XVIII, 36 likely refers to angels, since it is used in apposition with "angels" in Ps 103:20 (מלאכיו גברי כח) and describes angels in 1QH[a] XVI, 12–13 and 4Q510 (4QShir[a]) 1 I, 2–3.[45] The Hodayot present the angels in XVIII, 36–37 negatively, as an object of fear, and it juxtaposes God's judgments against them with his case against "your holy ones in the heavens." It is difficult to understand the meaning of this lacunose section of the text, but for our purposes, it is significant that the title גבורים appears twice in the same *hodayah*—once for mighty oppressors and once for angels who have been judged in a terrifying manner. In this way, the text invites comparison between the mighty class and the antediluvian giants of Genesis much like the Parables, conflating sociopolitical and cosmic forces of evil.

This mighty class is thus the human counterpart to the Enochic Giants: they are agents of evil who have rebelled against God by using their might to exploit the poor (among other faults). Like the Enochic literature, the Hodayot associate these mighty oppressors and the nets, or traps, which they set for the righteous with the pit (שוחה, שחת), a site of eternal punishment that features prominently in Enochic cosmography.[46] It is important to note, however, that the Hodayot also use "mighty" positively to describe the poor as God's warriors (e.g., 1QH[a] VII, 18; XIII, 23).[47] The incomparable might of the poor comes, however, from God

---

44. Samuel Thomas, "Watchers Traditions in the Dead Sea Scrolls," in *The Watchers in Jewish and Christian Traditions*, ed. Angela Kim Harkins, Kelley Coblentz Bautch, and John C. Endres, S. J. (Minneapolis: Fortress, 2014), 145.

45. John Elwolde, "The Hodayot's Use of the Psalter: Text-Critical Contributions (Book 4: Pss 90–106)," in *The Scrolls and Biblical Traditions: Proceedings of the Seventh Meeting of the IOQS in Helsinki*, ed. George J. Brooke et al., STDJ 103 (Leiden: Brill, 2012), 78.

46. 1QH[a] X, 19, 23, 40; XI, 13 (4QH[b] 4 2), 17 (4QpapH[f] 5 5), 19, 20, 27, 28 (4QH[b] 5 1); XIII, 8; XVI, 30; XXI, 21 (4QH[b] 13 4); cf. 1 En. 18.6–11; 53.1–7. See Harkins, *Reading with an "I" to the Heavens*, 138–48.

47. The War Scroll similarly uses גבורים for both the oppressors and the army of the righteous and angels (e.g., 1QM XII, 7–18).

rather than wealth: "and for your might there is no price [ולגבורתכה אין מחיר]" (XVIII, 12).⁴⁸

This class of the mighty that will be destroyed at the impending judgment (e.g., 1QHª XIV, 32–38) fetishizes "unjust gain" (בצע) and "wealth" (הון).⁴⁹ The term בצע connotes exploitative practices of surplus accumulation and consumption much like "ill-gotten wealth" (Eth. *newāya ʿammaḍā*) in the Parables of Enoch (1 En. 63.10) and *mammon* (Heb. ממון; Aram. ממונא; Gk. μαμ[μ]ωνᾶς) in 1QMysteries (1 II, 5) and the Sayings Source (16:13).⁵⁰ The term הון bears similar connotations, while also invoking the tradition of the three nets of Belial—unchastity, wealth, and defilement of the sanctuary. The Hodayot frequently mention Belial and his nets that trap the poor, though the work does not articulate the precise formulation of three nets of Belial, a polemic designed on the basis of Isa 24:17 to malign the temple priests.⁵¹ Wealth is the primary net in view in the Hodayot and the work clarifies that the wealth of the mighty consists of property and acquisitions (מקנה וקנין) as well as an abundance of grain, wine, and oil. This implies land ownership and agricultural exploitation and positions the poor as the victims of the mighty's surplus-maximization. In 1QHª XIII, 12 and 29, this process is described as "robbery" (חתף). The enemies are cast, on the one hand, as venomous vipers, drawing on Ps 140:4 to condemn their deception as in the Psalms of Solomon (4:9) and Matthew (12:34; 23:33; cf. Q 3:7). They are described, on the other hand, as lions kept at bay by God (XIII, 8–18), echoing Ps 57:5 and Dan 6:17–24.⁵²

---

48. See also Murphy, *Wealth in the Dead Sea Scrolls*, 248; cf. 260–61 on מחיר in portraits of the wealthy in the Mysteries text.

49. On these terms, see Heinz-Josef Fabry and Ulrich Dahmen, eds., *Theologisches Wörterbuch zu den Qumrantexten*, vol. 1 (Stuttgart: Kohlhammer, 2011), 493–96, 758–62.

50. Mammon does not necessarily carry negative connotations (e.g., m. Ber. 9.5) but often does in the Second Temple period. Even CD XIV, 20 and 1QS VI, 2 portray wealth as a problem, even if it is not explicitly linked to exploitation.

51. 1QHª X, 23, 31; XI, 27; XII, 13; XIII, 10, 20; XIX, 11, 21 (4QHᵇ 13 4), 24 (4QHª 11 2). For the three nets, see CD VI, 14–17; 1QpHab VII, 3–IX, 7; and Pss. Sol. 8.10–12. See also Julie Hughes, *Scriptural Allusions and Exegesis in the Hodayot*, STDJ 59 (Leiden: Brill, 2006), 221–22.

52. Harkins, *Reading with an "I" to the Heavens*, 148–51; John Elwolde, "The Hodayot's Use of the Psalter: Text-Critical Contributions (Book 2: Pss 42–72)," in *The Dead Sea Scrolls in Context: Integrating the Dead Sea Scrolls in the Study of Ancient*

At the same time, the Hodayot reveal that the mighty's "unjust profit and wealth" is the foundation of their distinctive class culture. An abundance or affluence of luxuries characterizes this culture.[53] By using the term "luxury" (עדן), the text posits a contrast between the material luxuries of the mighty class and the revealed knowledge of the poor, which the text likens to dwelling in Eden.[54] Furthermore, the mighty class's עדנים refer to luxuries beyond the "abundance of grain, wine, and oil" listed separately and perhaps specifically to imported luxury items and foods. That at least one fraction of these wealthy enemies of the poor is accused of idolatry (1QH[a] XII, 16, 20) and speaking in an "alien tongue" (X, 21; XII, 17) supports this association by signifying the mighty's assimilation with foreigners. This fraction is called Seekers of Smooth Things (דורשי חלקות), a sobriquet based on Isa 30:9–11, which might refer to the Pharisees in other sectarian texts (esp. Pesher Nahum; 1QH[a] X, 17, 34; cf. XII, 8, 11).[55] The Hodayot liken this class fraction to a "congregation of Belial" that places nets to trap the poor. Through hypocrisy, deceit, and lying, this group "withholds the drink of knowledge from the thirsty" (XII, 12). Because this fraction of the "mighty" (X, 27) seeks to destroy the "soul of the poor one," the poor will bless God's name "far away from their assembly" (X, 32).

Altogether, then, the Hodayot portray the mighty (including the "Seekers of Smooth Things") as a class that is economically, culturally, and socially distinct from the poor. Here, the poor is an undifferentiated class that faces affliction caused by the mighty. Anthropologically, the work claims that all humans are subject to their evil inclination—that is, Belial acting as a counselor in their hearts (1QH[a] XIV, 24–25; XV, 6).[56] The poor, however, have been made privy to revealed knowledge that has shown them the corruption of this powerful class and turned them towards God's

---

Texts, Languages, and Cultures, ed. Armin Lange, Emanuel Tov, and Matthias Weigold, VTSup 140 (Leiden: Brill, 2011), 92.

53. The language of "affluence" corresponds to the description of part of the exploitative class in the Parables as "exalted" (Eth. le'ul).

54. The name "Eden" occurs in XIV, 19, but descriptions of Edenic abundance/prosperity recur in the work. See Meyer, *Adam's Dust*, 71–72; Matthew Goff, "Gardens of Knowledge: Teachers in Ben Sira, 4QInstruction, and the Hodayot," in *Pedagogy in Ancient Judaism and Early Christianity*, ed. Karina M. Hogan, Matthew Goff, and Emma Wasserman, EJL 41 (Atlanta: SBL Press, 2017), 181–86.

55. See Matthew A. Collins, *The Use of Sobriquets in the Qumran Dead Sea Scrolls*, LSTS 67 (London: T&T Clark, 2009), 101–5, 186–91.

56. Newsom, *Self as Symbolic Space*, 261–73.

truth. The Hodayot teach subjects that they have chosen truth instead of wealth (VI, 31; XII, 36), the way of the poor instead of the way of the mighty. This alignment has present and future implications. The poor have already been rescued by God, but their fate will be secured when the mighty are destroyed at judgment. Because the Hodayot focus mainly on the present, the prayers do not dwell on future material rewards. Instead, all that is stressed is that the mighty will be destroyed and cast into the Pit. The emphasis here is thus different than the pesher on Ps 37 (4Q171), for instance, where the "congregation of the poor" (עדת האביונים) endures the nets of Belial in the present but will soon experience an eschatological reversal in which they will come to "possess the land and enjoy peace in plenty" (1QH^a II, 9–11).[57]

The apocalyptic class subjectivity the Hodayot advance deploys this present-focused discourse of revelation to simultaneously delegitimate the mighty and legitimate the sect's leaders. Apocalyptic class rhetoric legitimates authorities by situating them in the same class (the poor) as their constituents, while still identifying them as having special access to salvation goods.[58] While controlling wealth and knowledge, these leaders are discursively construed as exemplary in their pious poverty.

The Hodayot position the Instructor (משכיל) within the poor class, but also legitimates his control over access to eschatological revelation.[59] Just before impugning the Seekers of Smooth Things for setting traps for the poor through deceptive interpretations, the Maskil's script legitimates his own authority:

> But you have made me a banner for the elect of righteousness and a mediator of knowledge in the wonderful mysteries [ומליץ דעת ברזי פלא]

---

57. Ro, *Poverty, Law, and Divine Justice*, 203–4.

58. On salvation goods as a form of religious capital that authorities compete to possess through discourses of legitimation and delegitimization, see Pierre Bourdieu, "Genèse et structure du champ religieux," *Revue française de sociologie* 12 (1971): 295–334.

59. Without positing a rigid distinction between the Community Hymns and Leader/Teacher Hymns in terms of form, authorship, and social settings, I acknowledge that certain parts of the work construct the persona of an ideal leader (following Newsom). This occurs not only in the Leader/Teacher Hymns (1QH^a IX, 1–XX, 6), but also elsewhere in the Hodayot (e.g., 1QH^a XX, 7–XXII, 39). For a lucid critique of the literary bifurcation of the Hodayot, see Hasselbalch, *Meaning and Context in the Thanksgiving Hymns*, 1–34.

in order to test [persons of] truth and to prove those who love moral discipline. And I have become an adversary to erring interpreters, and a conten[der] for all who see what is right. (1QHᵃ X, 15–17)

As Miller has demonstrated, the Community Rule attributes the understanding and mediation of the "wonderful mysteries" (רזי פלא) to the Maskil (1QS IX, 18).[60] Moreover, parts of the Hodayot (1QHᵃ VI, 28–33; VII, 21–25) are drawn from initiation oaths also presented in the Community Rule and thus reaffirm the power of the Maskil within the sect.[61] In one of these oaths, the speaker proclaims, "I will not exchange your truth for wealth" (VI, 31). According to the Community Rule, the Maskil bases his decisions about the rank of initiates on God's truth and judgments instead of wealth. The Maskil assumes divine agency as the basis of his own power.

Subjects of the Hodayot learn that the Maskil is the mediator of divinely revealed instruction such as that contained in these prayers. Despite this power differential, the Maskil's revelation indicates that he is among the poor who have been exploited by the mighty class. By accepting the Maskil's discipline, subjects will join the angelic host in preparing for the destruction of the mighty. These subjects identify with poverty that has a theological rationale, but it is also a socioeconomic position defined in relation to the mighty class. In the following section, I suggest that this apocalyptic class subjectivity had tangible social implications.

3. Apocalyptic Class Subjectivities in Practice

Subjectivities are not merely cognitive; they are generated in practice. The Hodayot and other sectarian texts form apocalyptic subjects that would identify with poverty. How was this poverty represented in practice? Although Qumran should be viewed as only one location of one community of the sect associated with the scrolls, the archaeological remains at the site evince precisely the paradox that texts like the Hodayot lead us to expect: a community that identified as poor and separatist but was not actually living below subsistence level or in isolation.[62] In what follows, I

---

60. Miller, "Role of Performance," 373–81; cf. Newsom, *Self as Symbolic Space*, 287–346.

61. Miller, "Role of Performance," 378–81.

62. Alison Schofield, *From Qumran to the Yaḥad: A New Paradigm of Textual*

briefly relate aspects of the apocalyptic class subjectivity expressed by the Hodayot to the material culture of Qumran.

3.1. "Far away from their assembly I will bless your name" (1QH^a X, 32)

Subjects of the Hodayot declare that they worship far away from the mighty class, and especially the Seekers of Smooth Things. This social separation is thus expressed in terms of class but also through apocalyptic metaphors: "But I became like one who enters a fortified city and finds refuge behind a high wall until deliverance (comes)" (XIV, 27–28). The compound at Qumran represented a site of separation for a sect that was probably much more widespread and integrated into society.[63] Some of the pottery and glass found at the site shows connections with Jericho and Jerusalem, for instance, while the documentary, inscriptional, and numismatic evidence from the caves and site attest commercial interactions, including with outsiders.[64] The Damascus Document and Community Rule do not forbid such interactions but do restrict them by putting the Mebaqqer in

---

Development for The Community Rule, STDJ 77 (Leiden: Brill, 2009); and John J. Collins, *Beyond the Qumran Community: The Sectarian Movement of the Dead Sea Scrolls* (Grand Rapids: Eerdmans, 2010). On economic stratification based on calculations of subsistence, see Walter Scheidel and Steven J. Friesen, "The Size of the Economy and the Distribution of Income in the Roman Empire," *JRS* 99 (2009): 69–91; and Keddie, *Revelations of Ideology*, 60–70. On the socioeconomic level of the Dead Sea sect as middling or better, see Albert I. Baumgarten, *The Flourishing of Jewish Sects in the Maccabean Era: An Interpretation*, JSJSup 55 (Leiden: Brill, 1997), 42–51.

63. Schofield, *From Qumran to the Yaḥad*, 268–71.

64. Schofield, *From Qumran to the Yaḥad*, 234–36, 260–61 (with further references); and Dennis J. Mizzi, "The Glass from Khirbet Qumran: What Does It Tell Us about the Qumran Community?," in *The Dead Sea Scrolls: Texts and Contexts*, ed. Charlotte Hempel, STDJ 90 (Leiden: Brill, 2010), 99–198, esp. 120. Documents: esp. 4Q345, 4Q359, 6Q29, with Murphy, *Wealth in the Dead Sea Scrolls*, 382–99. Inscriptions: André Lemaire, "Inscriptions du khirbeh, des grottes et de 'Aïn Feshkha," in *Khirbet Qumrân et 'Aïn Feshkha II*, ed. Jean-Baptiste Humbert and Jan Gunneweg, NTOA 2 (Gottingen: Vandenhoeck & Ruprecht, 2003), 341–88. Coins: Bruno Callegher, "The Coins of Khirbet Qumran from the Digs of Roland de Vaux: Returning to Henri Seyrig and Augustus Spijkerman," in *The Caves of Qumran: Proceedings of the International Conference, Lugano 2014*, ed. Marcello Fidanzio, STDJ 118 (Leiden: Brill, 2016), 221–37. It is also possible that the use of coffins suggests that bodies were transported from elsewhere; see Murphy, *Wealth in the Dead Sea Scrolls*, 338; and Schofield, *From Qumran to the Yaḥad*, 269.

charge of them.[65] As Alison Schofield explains, "Qumran served as a special place within the larger *Yaḥad* movement," likely serving special liturgical and legal purposes for members, who could experience the heightened purity of this site "permanently or on a temporary basis."[66] Subjects of the Hodayot at Qumran would recognize themselves as removed from the mighty class in a community realizing angelic life while awaiting the destruction of the mighty.

3.2. "They pride themselves on property and acquisitions" (1QH[a] XVIII, 27).

For subjects of the Hodayot and other sectarian texts, the attitude of the mighty class towards wealth is their reason for condemnation. Property is dangerous inasmuch as the pursuit of it leads one away from God's truth. But according to some of the scrolls, it was not strictly forbidden. The Damascus Document, for instance, acknowledges adherents who earn wages and own livestock, grain, wine, oil, and slaves (e.g., CD XI, 12; XII, 7–10). One might understand this as either ownership of private property or individual responsibility for property whose usufruct is owned by the community. According to the stricter stipulations of the Community Rule, initiates avoided the dangers of wealth by depositing most or all of their wealth into the communal fund, which was overseen by the leaders of the *yaḥad* (e.g., 1QS VII, 6–7, 24–25). This communal pooling of resources was more comprehensive than the communal funds of other types of associations and supported members' isolation from legal and economic institutions ruled by the mighty class.[67] The notorious "*yaḥad* ostracon" (KhQOstracon 1) discovered at Qumran arguably evinces this process, even though it does not include the term יחד, as some have claimed.[68] This lacunose deed recognizes a gift of property (land, a house, fig and olive trees, and a slave) exchanged in Jericho but apparently executed or at least kept as a record at Qumran. The recipient of this gift may have been the

---

65. Murphy, *Wealth in the Dead Sea Scrolls*, 45–61, 158–61.
66. Schofield, *From Qumran to the Yaḥad*, 271.
67. Yonder Moynihan Gillihan, *Civic Ideology, Organization, and Law in the Rule Scrolls: A Comparative Study of the Covenanters' Sect and Contemporary Voluntary Associations in Political Context*, STDJ 97 (Leiden: Brill, 2012), 400.
68. Murphy, *Wealth in the Dead Sea Scrolls*, 383–89, 529; and Schofield, *From Qumran to the Yaḥad*, 261–63.

Mebaqqer. If Émile Puech's reading is correct, the deed even uses this title.[69] This difficult document might thus illuminate how subjects from Jericho identifying as the poor would transmit their property to the sect's treasury and how the sect's administrative officials would document the exchange.

3.3. "The strength of the mighty rests upon an abundance of luxuries" (1QH[a] XVIII, 26).

Subjects of the Hodayot would eschew displays of luxury. Even though they identified as poor, subjects benefited from the community's aggregate wealth, which supported the compound, communal meals and other events and supplied the overhead needed to create more wealth (e.g., slaves, land, seed, tools). Despite being able to afford them, the poor at Qumran generally rejected luxury styles—for instance, frescoes, mosaic floors, and fancy fineware.[70] Subjects associated these imported styles with the assimilationist mighty class whose destruction they awaited.

3.4. "I clothed myself in darkness" (1QH[a] XIII, 33); "And I ate the bread of my sighs and my drink was endless tears" (1QH[a] XIII, 35–36)

For subjects of the Hodayot, those in the mighty class afflict and impoverish the poor. Three main sites of class difference—clothing, food, and drink—express this relationship. Because of the social and existential conflict caused by the mighty, subjects wear darkness, eat sighs, and drink tears. It is reasonable to expect that, in practice, this sentiment translated as a distinctive class culture for the poor. At Qumran, we catch glimpses of this class culture not only in the eschewal of luxury styles but also in dress, food, and burials. The garments discovered at Qumran were made of a fine white linen. These were not the ragged brown woolen garments of those actually living in destitution.[71] Nonetheless, for subjects, their

---

69. Émile Puech, "L'ostracon de Khirbet Qumrân (KHQ 1996/1) et une vente de terrain à Jéricho, témoin de l'occupation Essénienne à Qumrân," in *Flores Florentino: Dead Sea Scrolls and Other Early Jewish Studies in Honour of Florentino García Martínez*, ed. A. Hilhorst, Émile Puech, and Eibert J. C. Tigchelaar, JSJSup 122 (Leiden: Brill, 2007), 17.

70. Jodi Magness, *The Archaeology of Qumran and the Dead Sea Scrolls* (Grand Rapids: Eerdmans, 2002), 90–100, 202–6.

71. See Gregg Gardner, *The Origins of Organized Charity in Rabbinic Judaism* (Cambridge: Cambridge University Press, 2015), 52–53.

lack of dye and uniform use of linen (rather than wool, which was more common) signified a class distinction.[72] As Josephus observed, "Riches they despise, ... for they make a point of ... always being dressed in white" (Josephus, *B.J.* 2.122–123 [Thackeray]). Similarly, the tableware evidence suggests that communal meals were enjoyed with common tableware. This locally produced tableware signifies the rejection of the styles of the mighty class, yet the great quantity of it (enough for multiple courses per person) indicates a lack of want.[73] Moreover, animal bone deposits show that the sectarians were eating meat when most of the population could not afford it and the human osteological data further demonstrates that this community enjoyed a much fuller diet than those below subsistence level.[74] Finally, it deserves mention that the sectarians buried their dead in trench graves like the poorer strata of society, rather than in rock-cut tombs with ossuaries like elites and some middlers.[75]

The material culture from Qumran betrays a community that distinguished itself from the practices of the mighty class—that is, the elites associated with the city and temple of Jerusalem. In no way does the evidence from Qumran suggest that the community lived like those below subsistence level; on the contrary, they enjoyed a relatively comfortable lifestyle. Even still, subjects of the Hodayot construed this lifestyle as poverty, where poverty represents one side of a socioeconomic struggle between the poor and the mighty and one side of an apocalyptic struggle between God and Belial.

4. Conclusion

Whereas apocalypticism orients us towards the future, the critical examination of apocalyptic class subjectivities directs our analysis towards the

---

72. Orit Shamir and Naama Sukenik, "Qumran Textiles and the Garments of Qumran's Inhabitants," *DSD* 18 (2011): 206–25; and Magness, *Archaeology of Qumran*, 193–201.

73. Magness, *Archaeology of Qumran*, 73–79. The sect's leaders may have expressed their social power at various ways at communal meals (e.g., special seats, food, tableware). Nevertheless, one is struck by the uniformity of the tableware (Murphy, *Wealth in the Dead Sea Scrolls*, 319). Eyal Regev, "The Archaeology of Sectarianism: Ritual, Resistance and Hierarchy in Kh. Qumran," *RevQ* 24 (2009): 175–213, esp. 179–88.

74. Regev, "Archaeology of Sectarianism," 194; and Murphy, *Wealth in the Dead Sea Scrolls*, 333–43.

75. Magness, *Archaeology of Qumran*, 168–75.

present social implications of a group's apocalyptic discourse. The dynamic, constructed, and contested character of subjectivities commends caution in attributing apocalyptic texts that express the plight of the poor and oppressed to demographics that we would typically understand as poor and oppressed. At the same time, we should also be careful not to retreat towards interpreting apocalyptic poverty and oppression as merely metaphorical or theological. The evidence from comparative studies of class subjectivities suggests that religious discourse shaped social and economic practices and vice versa.

In this essay, I used the Hodayot as a case study to show how one sectarian text engages in apocalyptic discourse to categorize subjects as the poor victims of afflictions caused by a wealthy class of mighty enemies. Not only does this work advance a model of the class structure (poor versus mighty), but it also attributes cosmological and eschatological significance to it: the poor align with God and are recipients of salvific mysteries whereas the mighty are agents of Belial whose pursuit of wealth will achieve destruction. In the archaeological evidence from Qumran, we can detect some of the ways that subjects maintained this apocalyptic class distinction in practice within a particular sectarian space. Subjects who learned, fraternized, and worshiped at Qumran lived comfortably above subsistence but represented themselves in a way they construed as poor.

Sectarian distinctions in this case are also class distinctions: subjects of the Hodayot would have viewed themselves as a socially, culturally, and economically distinct class defined in relation to the mighty class. Although not all subjects of the Hodayot were equal in social power, they could all claim to be poor. This ideology enabled the sect's leaders to legitimate themselves as genuine representatives of their shared class interests while controlling all of the wealth.

If we expand our scope beyond Qumran and beyond the Hodayot, we should imagine that there were significant social and economic implications when apocalyptic class subjectivities like these materialized in nonsectarian spaces. The disdain for powerful elites encouraged by these texts is undercut by a severely pessimistic view of humans' potential to change their society or their position within it. At the same time, apocalyptic constructions of poverty might very well have obscured the plight of victims of structural poverty struggling for their subsistence, thereby discouraging the development of institutions to relieve poverty. Apocalyptic subjects might have lobbied against elites when given the chance, but they would not have actively pursued social transformation for themselves or others on the basis of these ideologies alone. Instead, the Hodayot exhort subjects with this special knowledge: "O you who are cru]shed by poverty, be patient" (1QH^a IX, 38).

Bibliography

Baumgarten, Albert I. *The Flourishing of Jewish Sects in the Maccabean Era: An Interpretation*. JSJSup 55. Leiden: Brill, 1997.

Bourdieu, Pierre. *Distinction: A Social Critique of the Judgement of Taste*. London: Routledge, 1986.

———. "Genèse et structure du champ religieux." *Revue française de sociologie* 12 (1971): 295–334.

Callegher, Bruno. "The Coins of Khirbet Qumran from the Digs of Roland de Vaux: Returning to Henri Seyrig and Augustus Spijkerman." Pages 221–37 in *The Caves of Qumran: Proceedings of the International Conference, Lugano 2014*. Edited by Marcello Fidanzio. STDJ 118. Leiden: Brill, 2016.

Chazon, Esther G. "Human and Angelic Prayer in Light of the Dead Sea Scrolls." Pages 35–48 in *Liturgical Perspectives: Prayer and Poetry in Light of the Dead Sea Scrolls; Proceedings of the Fifth International Symposium of the Orion Center for the Study of the Dead Sea Scrolls and Associated Literature*. Edited by Esther G. Chazon. STDJ 48. Leiden: Brill, 2003.

Collins, John J. *Apocalypticism in the Dead Sea Scrolls*. London: Routledge, 1997.

———. *Beyond the Qumran Community: The Sectarian Movement of the Dead Sea Scrolls*. Grand Rapids: Eerdmans, 2010.

———. "Metaphor and Eschatology: Life beyond Death in the Hodayot." Pages 407–22 in *Is There a Text in This Cave? Studies in the Textuality of the Dead Sea Scrolls in Honour of George J. Brooke*. Edited by Ariel Feldman, Charlotte Hempel, and Maria Cioată. STDJ 119. Leiden: Brill, 2017.

———. *Seers, Sibyls, and Sages in Hellenistic-Roman Judaism*. JSJSup 54. Leiden: Brill, 1997.

Collins, Matthew A. *The Use of Sobriquets in the Qumran Dead Sea Scrolls*. LSTS 67. London: T&T Clark, 2009.

Dimant, Devorah. "Men as Angels: The Self-Image of the Qumran Community." Pages 93–103 in *Religion and Politics in the Ancient Near East*.

Edited by Adele Berlin. STJHC. Bethesda: University Press of Maryland, 1996.

DiTommaso, Lorenzo. "The Apocalyptic Other." Pages 221–46 in *The "Other" in Second Temple Judaism: Essays in Honor of John J. Collins.* Edited by Daniel C. Harlow, Karina Martin Hogan, Matthew Goff, and Joel S. Kaminsky. Grand Rapids: Eerdmans, 2011.

Elwolde, John. "The Hodayot's Use of the Psalter: Text-Critical Contributions (Book 2: Pss 42–72)." Pages 79–100 in *The Dead Sea Scrolls in Context: Integrating the Dead Sea Scrolls in the Study of Ancient Texts, Languages, and Cultures.* Edited by Armin Lange, Emanuel Tov, and Matthias Weigold. VTSup 140. Leiden: Brill, 2011.

———. "The Hodayot's Use of the Psalter: Text-Critical Contributions (Book 4: Pss 90–106)." Pages 65–88 in *The Scrolls and Biblical Traditions: Proceedings of the Seventh Meeting of the IOQS in Helsinki.* Edited by George J. Brooke, Daniel K. Falk, Eibert J. C. Tigchelaar, and Molly M. Zahn. STDJ 103. Leiden: Brill, 2012.

Fabry, Heinz-Josef, and Ulrich Dahmen, eds. *Theologisches Wörterbuch zu den Qumrantexten,* Vol. 1. Stuttgart: Kohlhammer, 2011.

Frey, Jörg, and Michael Becker, eds. *Apokalyptik und Qumran.* Einblicke 10. Paderborn: Bonifatius, 2007.

Gardner, Gregg. *The Origins of Organized Charity in Rabbinic Judaism.* Cambridge: Cambridge University Press, 2015.

Gillihan, Yonder Moynihan. *Civic Ideology, Organization, and Law in the Rule Scrolls: A Comparative Study of the Covenanters' Sect and Contemporary Voluntary Associations in Political Context.* STDJ 97. Leiden: Brill, 2012.

Goff, Matthew. "Gardens of Knowledge: Teachers in Ben Sira, 4QInstruction, and the Hodayot." Pages 171–94 in *Pedagogy in Ancient Judaism and Early Christianity.* Edited by Karina M. Hogan, Matthew Goff, and Emma Wasserman. EJL 41. Atlanta: SBL Press, 2017.

———. "Reading Wisdom at Qumran: 4QInstruction and the Hodayot." *DSD* 11 (2004): 263–88.

———. *The Worldly and Heavenly Wisdom of 4QInstruction.* STDJ 50. Leiden: Brill, 2003.

Harkins, Angela Kim. "The Community Hymns Classification: A Proposal for Further Differentiation." *DSD* 15 (2008): 121–54.

———. "A New Proposal for Thinking about 1QH[a] Sixty Years after Its Discovery." Pages 101–34 in *Qumran Cave 1 Revisited, Texts from Cave 1 Sixty Years after Their Discovery: Proceedings of the Sixth Meeting of the*

IOQS in Ljubljana. Edited by Daniel K. Falk, Sarianna Metso, Donald W. Parry, and Eibert J. C. Tigchelaar. STDJ 91. Leiden: Brill, 2010.

———. "Reading the Qumran Hodayot in Light of the Traditions Associated with Enoch." *Hen* 32 (2010): 359–400.

———. *Reading with an "I" to the Heavens: Looking at the Qumran Hodayot through the Lens of Visionary Traditions*. Ekstasis 3. Berlin: de Gruyter, 2012.

Hasselbalch, Trine Bjørnung. *Meaning and Context in the Thanksgiving Hymns: Linguistic and Rhetorical Perspectives on a Collection of Prayers from Qumran*. EJL 42. Atlanta: SBL Press, 2015.

Horsley, Richard A. *Revolt of the Scribes: Resistance and Apocalyptic Origins*. Minneapolis, MN: Fortress, 2010.

Hughes, Julie. *Scriptural Allusions and Exegesis in the Hodayot*. STDJ 59. Leiden: Brill, 2006.

Jokiranta, Jutta. *Social Identity and Sectarianism in the Qumran Movement*. STDJ 105. Leiden: Brill, 2013.

Josephus. *The Jewish War, Books I–III*. Translated by H. St. J. Thackeray. LCL. London: Heinemann; Cambridge: Harvard University Press, 1956.

Keddie, G. Anthony. "Poverty and Exploitation in the Psalms of Solomon: At the Intersection of Sapiential and Apocalyptic Discourses." Pages 81–110 in *The Psalms of Solomon: Texts, Contexts, and Intertexts*. Edited by Patrick Pouchelle, G. Anthony Keddie, and Kenneth Atkinson. EJL 54. Atlanta: SBL Press, 2021.

———. *Revelations of Ideology: Apocalyptic Class Politics in Early Roman Palestine*. JSJSup 189. Leiden: Brill, 2018.

Lange, Armin. *Weisheit und Prädestination: Weisheitliche Urordnung und Prädestination in den Textfunden von Qumran*. STDJ 18. Leiden: Brill, 1995.

Lemaire, André. "Inscriptions du Khirbeh, des grottes et de 'Ain Feshkha." Pages 341–88 in *Khirbet Qumrân et 'Aïn Feshkha II*. Edited by Jean-Baptiste Humbert and Jan Gunneweg. NTOA 2. Gottingen: Vandenhoeck & Ruprecht, 2003.

Leroy, Christine. "Spiritual Exercises in the Hodayot? 1QH[a] as Perfective Trajectory." *JSJ* 48 (2017): 455–79.

Lohfink, Norbert. *Lobgesänge der Armen: Studien zum Magnifikat, den Hodajot von Qumran und einigen späten Psalmen*. SBS 139. Stuttgart: Katholisches Bibelwerk, 1990.

Magness, Jodi. *The Archaeology of Qumran and the Dead Sea Scrolls.* Grand Rapids: Eerdmans, 2002.
Mansfield, Nick. *Subjectivity: Theories of the Self from Freud to Haraway.* New York: New York University Press, 2000.
Marx, Karl. *Critique of Hegel's "Philosophy of Right."* Translated by Annette Jolin and Joseph O'Malley. Cambridge: Cambridge University Press, 1977.
Mathews, Mark D. *Riches, Poverty, and the Faithful: Perspectives on Wealth in the Second Temple Period and the Apocalypse of John.* SNTSMS 154. Cambridge: Cambridge University Press, 2013.
McCloud, Sean. *Divine Hierarchies: Class in American Religion and Religious Studies.* Chapel Hill: University of North Carolina Press, 2007.
Meyer, Nicholas A. *Adam's Dust and Adam's Glory in the Hodayot and the Letters of Paul: Rethinking Anthropogony and Theology.* NovTSup 168. Leiden: Brill, 2016.
Miller, Shem. "The Role of Performance and the Performance of Role: Cultural Memory in the Hodayot." *JBL* 137 (2018): 359–82.
Mizzi, Dennis J. "The Glass from Khirbet Qumran: What Does It Tell Us about the Qumran Community?" Pages 100–98 in *The Dead Sea Scrolls: Texts and Contexts.* Edited by Charlotte Hempel. STDJ 90. Leiden: Brill, 2010.
Murphy, Catherine M. *Wealth in the Dead Sea Scrolls and in the Qumran Community.* STDJ 40. Leiden: Brill, 2002.
Newsom, Carol A. "Apocalyptic Subjects: Social Construction of the Self in the Qumran Hodayot." *JSP* 12 (2001): 3–35.
———. "Pairing Research Questions and Theories of Genre: A Case Study of the Hodayot." *DSD* 17 (2010): 270–88.
———. *The Self as Symbolic Space: Constructing Identity and Community at Qumran.* STDJ 52. Leiden: Brill, 2004.
Nickelsburg, George W. E., and James C. VanderKam. *1 Enoch 2: A Commentary on the Book of 1 Enoch; Chapters 37–82.* Hermeneia. Minneapolis: Fortress, 2012.
Nitzan, Bilhah. *Qumran Prayer and Religious Poetry.* Translated by Jonathan Chipman. STDJ 12. Leiden: Brill, 1994.
O'Leary, Stephen D. *Arguing the Apocalypse: A Theory of Millennial Rhetoric.* Oxford: Oxford University Press, 1994.
Puech, Émile. "L'ostracon de Khirbet Qumrân (KHQ 1996/1) et une vente de terrain à Jéricho, témoin de l'occupation Essénienne à Qumrân." Pages 1–30 in *Flores Florentino: Dead Sea Scrolls and Other Early*

Jewish Studies in Honour of Florentino García Martínez. Edited by A. Hilhorst, Émile Puech, and Eibert J. C. Tigchelaar. JSJSup 122. Leiden: Brill, 2007.

Regev, Eyal. "The Archaeology of Sectarianism: Ritual, Resistance and Hierarchy in Kh. Qumran." *RevQ* 24 (2009): 175–213.

———. *Sectarianism in Qumran: A Cross-Cultural Perspective*. RS 45. Berlin: de Gruyter, 2007.

———. "Wealth and Sectarianism: Comparing Qumranic and Early Christian Social Approaches." Pages 211–30 in *Echoes from the Caves: Qumran and the New Testament*. Edited by Florentino García Martínez. STDJ 85. Leiden: Brill, 2009.

Ro, Johannes Un-Sok. *Poverty, Law, and Divine Justice in Persian and Hellenistic Judah*. AIL 32. Atlanta: SBL Press, 2018.

Satybaldieva, Elmira. "Working Class Subjectivities and Neoliberalisation in Kyrgyzstan: Developing Alternative Moral Selves." *International Journal of Politics, Culture, and Society* 31 (2018): 31–47.

Scheidel, Walter, and Steven J. Friesen. "The Size of the Economy and the Distribution of Income in the Roman Empire." *JRS* 99 (2009): 69–91.

Schofield, Alison. *From Qumran to the Yaḥad: A New Paradigm of Textual Development for The Community Rule*. STDJ 77. Leiden: Brill, 2009.

Schuller, Eileen M. "Hodayot." Pages 69–254 in *Qumran Cave 4.XX. Poetical and Liturgical Texts, Part 2*. Edited by Esther G. Chazon et al. DJD 29. Oxford: Clarendon, 1999.

———. "Recent Scholarship on the Hodayot 1993–2010." *CurBR* 10 (2011): 119–62.

Schuller, Eileen M., and Lorenzo DiTommaso, "A Bibliography of the Hodayot, 1948–1996." *DSD* 4 (1997): 55–101.

Schuller, Eileen M., and Carol A. Newsom. *The Hodayot (Thanksgiving Psalms): A Study Edition of 1QH^a*. EJL 36. Atlanta: Society of Biblical Literature, 2012.

Shamir, Orit, and Naama Sukenik. "Qumran Textiles and the Garments of Qumran's Inhabitants." *DSD* 18 (2011): 206–25.

Skeggs, Beverley. *Class, Self, Culture*. Transformations. London: Routledge, 2004.

Stegemann, Hartmut, and Eileen M. Schuller, with translations by Carol A. Newsom. *Qumran Cave 1.III. 1QHodayot^a with Incorporation of 1QHodayot^b and 4QHodayot^{a-f}*. DJD 40. Oxford: Clarendon, 2009.

Thomas, Samuel. "Watchers Traditions in the Dead Sea Scrolls." Pages 137–50 in *The Watchers in Jewish and Christian Traditions*. Edited by

Angela Kim Harkins, Kelley Coblentz Bautch, and John C. Endres, S. J. Minneapolis: Fortress, 2014.

Zang, Xiaowei. "Socioeconomic Attainment, Cultural Tastes, and Ethnic Identity: Class Subjectivities among Uyghurs in Ürümchi." *Ethnic and Racial Studies* 39 (2016): 2169–86.

The Changing Apocalypse: Apocalyptic Literature as a Provisional Genre in Early Rabbinic Judaism

Rebecca Scharbach Wollenberg

Over the course of the past century, we have come to something of a quiet scholarly consensus that rabbinic Judaism rejected apocalyptic literature in all its forms.[1] Late antique rabbinic literature as we have received it appears to include no explicit citations from the apocalyptic literature

---

I want to thank Michael E. Stone for originally suggesting this topic to me and for reading a previous draft of these thoughts more time ago than I would like to admit.

1. As Hindy Najman aptly summarizes the current state of affairs, "There are two assumptions that guide the study of apocalyptic literature. The first contends that apocalypticism arose in ancient Judaism when prophecy ended, around the second century BCE. The second asserts that apocalypticism exhausted itself or was suppressed within rabbinic Judaism but continued in Christianity"; see Hindy Najman, "Apocalypse in the History of Judaism: Continuities and Discontinuities," *AJS Perspectives* (2012): 13. When exactly this parting of the ways took place, of course, has been a matter of debate inasmuch as some researchers have attributed 2 Baruch and/or 4 Ezra to communities connected to the prehistory of rabbinic Judaism; see the discussion and literature cited in Robert Kirschner, "Apocalyptic and Rabbinic Responses to the Destruction of 70," *HTR* 78 (1985): 27. Most scholars, however, would concur with Lorenzo DiTommaso that a definitive parting of early rabbinic tradition and apocalyptic literature at least by the end of the Bar Kochba revolt in the early second century CE; see Lorenzo DiTommaso, "The Armenian *Seventh Vision of Daniel* and the Historical Apocalyptica of Late Antiquity," in *The Armenian Apocalyptic Tradition: A Comparative Perspective; Essays Presented in Honor of Professor Robert W. Thompson on His Eightieth Birthday*, ed. Kevork B. Bardakjian and Sergio La Porta, SVTP 25 (Leiden: Brill, 2014), 126–48; DiTommaso, "Il genere 'apocalisse' e 'apocalittico' nella tarda antichità," *Rivista di storia del cristianesimo* 17 (2020): 73–99. For a survey of classic explanations for this parting of the ways, see Anthony J. Saldarini, "Apocalyptic and Rabbinic Literature," *CBQ* 37 (1975): 348–58.

that we are familiar with from the Second Temple period and the early Common Era, including in large measure even the apocalyptic portions of the book of Daniel.[2] Certainly, such striking silence might be read as evidence of a universal rabbinic rejection of the apocalypse as a literary genre or even a rabbinic distaste for apocalyptic thought more broadly. I would like to propose, however, that classical rabbinic traditions are not nearly as innocent of references to apocalyptic literature as this portrait suggests. Rather, I would tentatively suggest that we have been able to find no hint of apocalyptic literature in early rabbinic tradition because we have been looking for the wrong sort of traces.

If we examine a representative sample of classical rabbinic literature on topics that are traditionally associated with apocalyptic thought and literature, we encounter: (1) a suggestive mélange of anonymous citations from literary materials with definite apocalyptic features; (2) descriptions of lost works that sound suspiciously like apocalyptic literature; and (3) rabbinic discussions that are structured around many of the formulas and themes that can be found in extant late antique apocalyptic literature. In other words, we do seem to find traces of an ongoing engagement with *some* form of apocalyptic literature in early rabbinic materials even though these materials do not cite the extant apocalyptic literature with which we are familiar.

What has made these traces difficult to discern is the utilitarian and provisional way in which these early rabbinic materials engage with their apocalyptic sources. Apocalyptic materials appear to have been valued in

---

2. As Louis Ginzberg put it in one of the seminal pieces establishing this position, "In the entire rabbinic literature of the first six centuries of the Common Era, there is not one quotation from the extant apocalyptic literature"; see Louis Ginzberg, "Some Observations on the Attitude of the Synagogue towards the Apocalyptic-Eschatological Writings," *JBL* 41 (1922): 119. Indeed, conceived in this way, the paucity of sources is so marked that Anthony J. Saldarini was able to collect in a single short article all of the indirect uses of imagery in early rabbinic literature that might be conceivably categorized as apocalyptic under the currently scholarly model, including broad generic categories such as "the world to come"; see Anthony J. Saldarini, "Uses of Apocalyptic in Mishnah and Tosefta," *CBQ* 39 (1979): 396–409. The most famous possible exception to this rule, of course, are the echoes of 2 Baruch and 4 Ezra woven together in one rabbinic tradition sometimes attributed to Pesiqta Rabbati 26. For more on the history of this case and its relationship to a contemporary lamentation of the liturgical poet Qillir, see Tzvi Novick, "Between First Century Apocalyptic and Seventh Century Liturgy: On *4 Ezra*, *2 Baruch* and Qillir," *JSJ* 44 (2013): 356–78.

this context not for their specific revelatory authority or definite predictive powers but as an almost secular source of knowledge about esoteric matters—a provisional form of informational literature that could be mined, revised, and judged in tandem with other evidence.[3]

1. The Historical Search for Rabbinic Apocalyptic: A Thought Experiment

I have no virtuoso technical arguments to demonstrate that we have been going about our search for rabbinic apocalyptic in the wrong way. Instead, I would ask readers to conduct a very simple thought experiment that I hope will awaken a glimmer of doubt. The classic technique for evaluating the rabbinic relationship to apocalyptic has been to scour the Talmuds and Midrash for references to the apocalyptic literature we are familiar with from the Second Temple period and late antiquity. This would seem at first glance to be a reasonable technique. After all, late antique Christian literature contains many references to extant apocalyptic literature.

But if we consider the matter for a moment, it is hardly surprising to find the apocalyptic literature we are familiar with quoted in early Christian literature, since a significant portion of the apocalyptic literature that survived beyond late antiquity was preserved by these same Christian authors, translators, and copyists. In other words, what we are seeing here is a feedback loop. Early Christian authors embraced the apocalyptic literature with which we are familiar because the apocalyptic literature with which we are familiar is the literature that these authors preserved.

When the Dead Sea Scrolls were discovered, of course, they significantly expanded our vision of what apocalyptic literature and thought looked like in the Second Temple period. The order in which these materials were edited and analyzed, moreover, may have created something of a

---

3. In proposing this model, I understand myself to be adapting the models of more complex and ambivalent structures of interaction proposed by Peter Schäfer and Ra'anan Boustan to describe the relationship of early rabbinic tradition with late antique Hekhalot literature and Merkavah mysticism; see Peter Schäfer, "From Cosmology to Theology: Rabbinic Appropriation of Apocalyptic Cosmology," in *Creation and Re-creation in Jewish Thought: Festschrift in Honor of Joseph Dan on the Occasion of His Seventieth Birthday*, ed. Rachel Elior and Peter Schäfer (Tübingen: Mohr Siebeck, 2005), 39–58; and Ra'anan Boustan, "Rabbinization and the Making of Early Jewish Mysticism," *JQR* 101 (2011): 482–501.

colloquial impression that the Jordan valley finds overlapped heavily with the apocalyptic literature and thought preserved by various early Christian communities—thereby further naturalizing those categories as the only form of late antique apocalyptic thought. It was only natural that scholars were eager to pounce on turn-of-the-millennium fragments of Enochic literature and were quick to identify materials as offshoots of a Danielic tradition. And yet, the cache ultimately offered up far more new examples of apocalyptic literature and thought (broadly conceived) than it did familiar works.[4] Qumran thus revealed a body of late antique apocalyptic material that overlapped with but was far from identical to that which had been preserved by early Christian authors.

The question, of course, is what this means in the search for rabbinic apocalyptic. The question of whether apocalyptic materials from Qumran find echoes in early rabbinic tradition has not by and large been explored, since a negative answer is generally presumed. The more urgent theoretical question for our purposes is whether the Qumran discoveries represent a final expansion of the available apocalyptic material from the period or whether they suggest that a more varied late antique apocalyptic tradition has been lost than has been recovered thus far. The latter would seem to be suggested by the barest practical facts, inasmuch as the Dead Sea Scrolls reflect two separate accidents of preservation. To begin with, these materials represent the portion of Second Temple literature that was considered worthy of conservation by the group of individuals that thought to store these works in remote caves in the Jordan valley salt flats. But they also represent the random selection of this literature that happened to survive centuries of degradation, looting, and other historical accidents. One cannot help but wonder, therefore, whether the rich apocalyptic veins in the Aramaic materials preserved at Qumran represents the tip of a larger Aramaic iceberg of late antique apocalyptic thought that has escaped us.

In other words, the question I would like to pose is this: Why do we suppose that the portion of late antique apocalyptic literature that has survived until modernity includes the apocalyptic literature that interested the rabbis? Indeed, I would maintain that the available evidence compels us to ask if there were at the very least a third body of late antique apoca-

---

4. Devorah Dimant, "Apocalyptic Texts at Qumran," in *The Community of the Renewed Covenant: The Notre Dame Symposium on the Dead Sea Scrolls*, ed. Eugene Ulrich and James C. VanderKam (Notre Dame: University of Notre Dame Press, 1994), 175–91.

lyptic literature that does not appear among the extant materials we currently possess. The question thus becomes: would we find that lost work quoted by the rabbis? I think that a close reading of the classical rabbinic sources suggests that we would.

Indeed, I would even go so far as to speculate that we have traces of such a literature among the extant literary evidence. That is, I would speculate that we can find no body of extant apocalyptic literature alluded to in classical rabbinic traditions because the apocalyptic works that the rabbis engaged with continued to be a living literature in classical rabbinic circles, with the result that late antique apocalypses were revised and adapted throughout the period until they became the medieval apocalyptic works that we call neo-Hebraic apocalypses and their original formulas were no longer easily recognizable in the final product.

2. Some Traces from a Chapter in Rabbinic Apocalyptic

I would like to explore the possibility that classical rabbinic traditions allude to lost versions of apocalyptic works by examining the smallest possible sample size, a few passages from a single talmudic tractate: the eleventh chapter of tractate Sanhedrin in the Babylonian Talmud, commonly known as Pereq Heleq.

Consider, for instance, the following story from b. Sanh. 97b. As I read it, this story describes an anonymous (and probably fictional) document bearing the unmistakable markers of a Second Temple apocalypse:

שלח ליה רב חנן בר תחליפא לרב יוסף מצאתי אדם אחד ובידו מגילה אחת כתובה אשורית ולשון קדש אמרתי לו זו מניין לך אמר לי לחיילות של רומי נשכרתי ובין גינזי רומי מצאתיה וכתוב בה לאחר ד' אלפים ומאתים ותשעים ואחד שנה לבריאתו של עולם יתום העולם מהן מלחמות תנינים מהן מלחמות גוג ומגוג ושאר ימות המשיח ואין הקב"ה מחדש את עולמו אלא לאחר שבעת אלפים שנה

Rabbi Chanan bar Tachlifa sent to Rabbi Yosef [saying]: "I found a certain man, and he possessed a certain scroll. Its writing was Aramaic square script and its language was Hebrew. I said to him, 'Where did you get this?' He said to me, 'I was a mercenary among the soldiers of Rome. And I found it in the storehouses of Rome.' In this [scroll] it is written, 'The world will end 4291 [7 x 613][5] years after the creation of the world. Then there will be the war of the sea monsters. Then the war of Gog and

---

5. For other possible readings of this number and the related literature, see

Magog. And the rest of [the time allotted to this world] will be the days of the messiah. And the Holy One, blessed be he, won't renew the world until 7,000 years [have passed]."[6]

So what does this story tell us about the rabbinic relationship to apocalyptic literature? I would suggest that this story demonstrates that, while it has proven impossible to discover explicit references to *extant* Second Temple apocalypses in classical rabbinic works, that category of literature as a whole was familiar to early rabbinic audiences and was even granted some measure of authority by classical rabbinic thinkers.

The document described here bears several key markers that define a significant portion of Second Temple apocalyptic literature. First, it is attributed to a source from pre-70 CE Palestine (by means of the claim that it was discovered in the Roman archives—suggesting that the document was taken as booty after the destruction of Jerusalem). Moreover, it is described as possessing a form resembling a biblical book. At least, it is described as meeting all of the formal requirements that the early rabbinic sages had laid out for the inscription of biblical books: inasmuch as it was composed in "the holy tongue," inscribed in the Aramaic square script necessary to render a book appropriate for pubic readings in the rabbinic imagination, and it was written on a *"megillah"*—a parchment scroll suitable for liturgical use. Finally, the contents of the scroll are said to consist of a periodization of the scope of human history, a calculation of the end of days in relation to that periodization, an account of the struggles that will precede the advent of the messianic age—first between the great sea monsters and then between Gog and Magog—and, finally, assurances that these times of struggle will be followed by a period of peace for the "remaining days of the messiah." It is difficult to identify a genre other than Second Temple apocalypse that would have united an ancient Palestinian text, resembling a biblical book, with both eschatological calculations and, what were from a rabbinic perspective, esoteric predictions regarding the nature of the end times.

Michael E. Stone, *Ancient Judaism: New Visions and Views* (Grand Rapids: Eerdmans, 2011), 72–73.

6. Unless otherwise noted, the Aramaic and Hebrew text provided is from the Vilna edition, checked against variant manuscript traditions as needed, and all translations are my own.

More important for our purposes, the aforementioned description was evidently not meaningful to the author of the tradition alone. On the contrary, this portrait was almost certainly formulated to correspond to a widely recognized literary typology. That is, while it is conceivable that R. Hanan b. Tahlifa might actually have encountered an apocalypse written in square script on a parchment scroll, it is exceedingly unlikely that a Roman conscript was actually allowed to root through the storehouses of Rome and remove such a document. Thus, it is evident that at least a portion of this depiction was fabricated to conform to a recognized literary type. I would argue further, if more tentatively, that the type continued to be recognized well into the talmudic period. It would be difficult to explain the preservation of an otherwise theologically challenging textual history in any other way. One need only review the reactions of later rabbinic commentators to this passage to see that, without a cultural memory of Second Temple apocalypses, the description on b. Sanh. 97b is at best meaningless and at worst disturbing since it implies the existence of lost works with the trappings of canonical texts. Finally, it is imperative to note that the use of such an identification to lend authority to a particular eschatological calculation demonstrates that this type of apocalyptic literature had achieved some degree of authority in some rabbinic circles and was understood to contain a certain amount of authentic knowledge concerning eschatological matters.

The aforementioned narrative on b. Sanh. 97b establishes that Pereq Heleq contains at least one openly acknowledged allusion to the generic category of narrative apocalypse. Other passages in the tractate appear to contain excerpts from lost Jewish literature that resembled in many respects the extant apocalyptic literature that has been preserved from earlier and later periods. Let us consider, for instance, the lengthy interview between R. Joshua b. Levi, Elijah, and the messiah on b. Sanh. 98a, which I would argue could be read as an excerpt or precis of an apocalyptic work:

ר' יהושע בן לוי אשכח לאליהו דהוי קיימי אפיתחא דמערתא דרבי שמעון בן יוחאי אמר ליה אתינא לעלמא דאתי אמר ליה אם ירצה אדון הזה אמר רבי יהושע בן לוי שנים ראיתי וקול ג' שמעתי אמר ליה אימת אתי משיח אמר ליה זיל שייליה לדידיה והיכא יתיב אפיתחא דרומי[7] ומאי סימניה יתיב ביני עניי סובלי חלאים וכולן שרו ואסירי בחד זימנא איהו שרי חד ואסיר חד אמר דילמא מבעינא דלא איעכב

---

7. Transcription amended here in keeping with the Yad HaRav Herzog and Firenze, Biblioteca Nazionale Centrale, 2.1.8–9 manuscripts.

אזל לגביה אמר ליה שלום עליך רבי ומורי אמר ליה שלום עליך בר ליואי א"ל
לאימת אתי מר א"ל היום אתא לגבי אליהו א"ל מאי אמר לך א"ל שלום עליך בר
ליואי א"ל אבטחך לך ולאבוך לעלמא דאתי א"ל שקורי קא שקר בי דאמר לי היום
אתינא ולא אתא א"ל הכי אמר לך היום אם בקולו תשמעו

R. Joshua b. Levi encountered Elijah, who was standing at the opening of the burial cave of R. Shimon b. Yochai. [R. Joshua b. Levi] said to him, "Will I reach the World to Come?" [Elijah] said to him, "If this Master [R. Shimon b. Yochai][8] wills it." R. Joshua b. Levi said, "I saw two but I heard the voice of three." [R. Joshua b. Levi] said to him, "When will the messiah come?" [Elijah] said to him, "Go ask him [the messiah]!" [R. Joshua asked] "And where does he sit?" [Elijah answered], "At the opening [gate] of Rome." [R. Joshua b. Levi asked], "And what are his signs?" [Elijah answered], "He sits amidst the poor suffering from sicknesses and while the rest of them loosen and tie all [their bandages] at once, he unties ones and reties one [at a time]. For he said, 'I should not be delayed [this way] if there is need for me.'" [R. Joshua b. Levi] went to [the messiah]. [R. Joshua b. Levi said to the messiah], "Peace be upon you my master and teacher." [The messiah said to R. Joshua b. Levi], "Peace be upon you Son of Levi." He said to him, "When will you come, Sir?" He said to him, "Today." [R. Joshua b. Levi] came to Elijah. [Elijah] said to him, "What did he say to you?" He said, "'Peace be upon you, Son of Levi.'" [Elijah] said to him, "He was promising you and your father the World to Come." [R. Joshua b. Levi] said, "[But] he told me a lie since he said he would come today and he didn't come." [Elijah] said to him, "[He meant] 'today, if you will listen to his voice' (Ps 95:7)."

I quote this brief narrative in full here so that the reader can discern for herself whether this passage also strikes her as an excerpt or echo of an apocalyptic work. If pressed to identify what precisely leads me to identify this as part of an apocalyptic tradition in the absence of detailed eschatological predictions, I would point to the following technical features—matching them up for our purposes with John J. Collins's list of common genre elements. Thus, for instance, the tale begins with an account of the disposition of the recipient: R. Joshua b. Levi begins his journey of discovery while visiting the tomb of R. Shimon bar Yochai, an individual famous

---

8. Although Rashi famously interpreted this statement (ad loc.) as a reference to the Shekhinah, the simple meaning of the phrase would appear to be a reference to the grave of the mystical hero at whose grave Elijah was waiting when R. Joshua b. Levi discovered him.

for his knowledge of eschatological secrets and the hidden realms.[9] It continues with the epiphany of Elijah to R. Joshua b. Levi and a dialogue between mediator and recipient in which R. Joshua b. Levi questions Elijah concerning both personal salvation and the eschatological salvation of Israel.[10] Finally, this brief excerpt concludes with what might be best described as a variation on an apocalyptic journey to otherworldly regions in which R. Joshua b. Levi is transported to Rome (a geographical location that had begun to take on mythical proportions in the eschatological speculations of Israel during this period) to meet the messiah (a mythical figure who, though human, was thought to possess the supernatural powers of an otherworldly being).[11] Here again, then, we find Pereq Heleq drawing on a source that sounds suspiciously like apocalyptic literature.

If the dialogue between R. Joshua b. Levi and Elijah in b. Sanh. 98a is indeed more or less exactly drawn from a contemporary apocalypse (and, indeed, Israel Lévi once proposed that this passage represents a quotation from a lost version of Sepher Zerubbabel),[12] then this passage also adds to our understanding of the rabbinic relationship to a form of apocalyptic literature in two ways. On the most mundane level, the use of anonymous citation in this instance offers an explanation for why other citations have been hard to find. How exactly does one recognize an anonymous excerpt from an apocalyptic work in cases in which the relevant iteration of that work has not survived to the contemporary period and even the general outlines of the shape that the genre took in that particular time and place has not yet been established? More importantly for our purposes, perhaps, the use of anonymous citation also suggests that the rabbinic editors valued these works not as inspired writings as such but as works that incidentally preserved an independent body of esoteric knowledge and sacred history.

The notion that the rabbinic editors of this material engaged with some sort of apocalyptic literature as a provisionally enlightening but con-

---

9. John J. Collins, "Introduction: Towards the Morphology of a Genre," *Semeia* 14 (1979): 6, §3.2. As Israel Lévi puts it: by the beginning of the Muslim era, R. Shimon bar Yochai played "the same role" in the neo-Hebraic apocalyptic tradition as "Daniel, Enoch, Ezra, and Moses [played] in the earlier [apocalyptic] literature"; see Israel Lévi, "Apocalypses dans le Talmud," *RÉJ* 1 (1880): 112 (my translation).

10. See Collins, "Introduction," 6–7: epiphany: §1.1.2; dialogue: §1.2.2; personal salvation: §9.2; eschatological salvation: §9.

11. See Collins, "Introduction," 7: journey to otherworldly regions: §10.1; meeting the messiah: §10.2.

12. Lévi, "Apocalypses dans le Talmud," 108–14.

tingent genre is supported by other allusions to possibly apocalyptic works in the eleventh chapter of tractate Sanhedrin. The exact nature of the phrase "tanna debe Eliyahu" as it is used in the Babylonian Talmud, and the relationship (if any) of this phrase to the tenth century midrashic work by that name, has, of course, been hotly debated. However, the citations of this phrase at the end of tractate Sanhedrin certainly do not foreclose the possibility that they refer to some sort of apocalyptic work by that name. For the only direct citation attributed to Debe Eliyahu in this chapter (b. Sanh. 92a) could certainly represent part of an apocalyptic pesher form reinterpreting the book of Isaiah as a unified eschatological text:

תנא דבי אליהו צדיקים שעתיד הקדוש ברוך הוא להחיותן אינן חוזרין לעפרן שנאמר והיה הנשאר בציון והנותר בירושלים קדוש יאמר לו כל הכתוב לחיים בירושלים מה קדוש לעולם קיים אף הם לעולם קיימין

According to the School of Elijah, righteous people who the Holy One, blessed be he, will bring back to life in the future are not returned to dust, as it is written, "It will be that the remnant in Zion and the remainder in Jerusalem will be called holy to him, all those written for life in Jerusalem" (Isa 4:3). What does "holy" mean? Existing forever. So they will also exist forever.

Although whether such a work would have included a continuous pesher-style treatment is unclear since the eleventh chapter in tractate Sanhedrin also is punctuated with a series of rich descriptions of Elijan revelations that would fit well with an apocalyptic work that traced its origins to late antique revelations of the long-dead prophet Elijah. In an interesting (and frankly amusing) twist on what a rabbinic apocalyptic revelation might look like, for instance, b. Sanh. 113a–b records R. Yose of Sepphoris arguing with his prophetic revelatory guide:

דרש ר' יוסי בצפורי אבא אליהו קפדן הוה רגיל למיתי גביה איכסי' מיניה תלתא יומי ולא אתא כי אתא א"ל אמאי לא אתא מר א"ל קפדן קרית לי א"ל הא דקמן דקא קפיד מר

R. Yose of Sepphoris expounded: "Our Father Elijah is a hot-tempered one." Though Elijah made a habit of appearing [to R. Yose], he hid himself [from him] for three days and didn't come. [R. Yose said] "Why didn't you come, Master?" [Elijah replied] "[Because] you called me hot-tempered." [R. Yose retorted] "What just happened shows Master is hot-tempered."

Moreover, the summary that is offered of the work's overarching eschatological predictions (b. Sanh. 97a) could easily be understood as a synopsis of an apocalyptic timeline:

תנא דבי אליהו ששת אלפים שנה הוי עלמא שני אלפים תוהו שני אלפים תורה
שני אלפים ימות המשיח

> According to the School of Elijah, the world will exist six thousand years. Two thousand years of chaos, two thousand years of Torah, two thousand years of messianic age.

How these various materials might have fit together into a single work or genre of writing is not entirely clear. However, I would note that if the material referred to in these citations did represent some sort of a late antique apocalyptic precursor to the medieval work we know as Tanna debe Eliyahu, two interesting observations emerge concerning the Talmud's relationship with apocalyptic materials in this case. First, it is interesting to note that here, as in the case of the scroll from Rome we considered above, the rabbinic editor openly cites his apocalyptic source, suggesting that such works were not illicit but approved sources of speculative knowledge. Second, this citation of Debe Eliyahu's mythical time is followed by a telling rejoinder on b. Sanh. 97b:

בעונותינו שרבו יצאו מהם מה שיצאו

> But because of our sins, which multiplied, a certain amount has been taken from the [Messianic age].

Or as Rav Ashi remarks on a similar exchange that immediately follows:

הכי א"ל עד הכא לא תיסתכי ליה מכאן ואילך איסתכי ליה

> This is what [Elijah] said to [R. Yehuda]: Up until this point, don't look for it, but from this point onwards, look for it.

In other words, the chapter marks these particular predictions as simultaneously true on some fundamental level and yet potentially unreliable as a source of practical knowledge, since the greater streams of mythical time are contingent structures that can be changed in some measure by human behavior.

Although this suggestion remains the merest speculation at this point, I would also contend that the overarching structure and form of Pereq Heleq supports this vision of classical rabbinic engagement with apocalyptic thought and literature. Where virtually all of the other material in the two Talmuds is structured as a linguistic, practical, or legal analysis of the mishnaic text, Pereq Heleq is structured as an anthology of discrete Tannaitic and early Amoraic statements on a series of non-mishnaic topics. The arrangement is not haphazard, however, but represents a linear progression of topics. Which compels us to ask: if this series of topics was not inspired directly by the Mishnah, what did inspire this arrangement? Or to put another way, what genre logic structures this chapter if not that of the Mishnah? I would like to suggest that the genre which inspired this deviation from the typical talmudic pattern was a form of apocalyptic literature.

Certainly, each of the topics treated in Pereq Heleq is also prominent in the extant genres of apocalyptic literature with which we are familiar. In the interest of space, I will cite only a very small selection here. The chapter opens, for instance, with a series of verbal contests in which the rabbis best a series of clever gentiles in debates about esoteric matters (b. Sanh. 91a–92a). R. Meir outdoes Cleopatra. R. Ammi triumphs over a sectarian (*min*). R. Joshua b. Hananiah silences the Romans. Each victory thus reveals not only the superior understanding of the particular sage involved in the contest but also of the ascendancy in understanding of Israel as a community over outsiders to the tradition.[13] To my mind, this lengthy series of universal debates in which the rabbis prove themselves to be the wisest of the wise evokes the sapiential themes in apocalypses such as 1 Enoch and the Second Temple Daniel literature.[14] More importantly,

---

13. Indeed, it seems that at least one editor understood the unifying purpose of this section to be the demonstration of this superiority and not the exposition of eschatological and related themes. We see, for instance, that the only three deviations from the topics of protology and eschatology in this section each involve a clever triumph of rabbinic figures over outsiders to the community in a verbal contest (b. Sanh. 91a).

14. For a list of sources on sapiential themes in early Jewish apocalypses, see Torleif Elgvin, "Wisdom with and without Apocalyptic," in *Sapiential, Liturgical, and Poetical Texts from Qumran: Proceedings of the Third Meeting of the International Organization for Qumran Studies, Oslo 1998; Published in Memory of Maurice Baillet*, ed. Daniel K. Falk, Florentino García Martínez, and Eileen M. Schuller, STDJ 35 (Leiden: Brill, 1999), 18–19.

perhaps, these wisdom tropes seem to serve a similar literary function in both sets of literature. In other words, the tropes convey the prestige of extraordinary wisdom concerning hidden matters in general upon the figures who will reveal esoteric knowledge concerning the timing of the end and the nature of redemption in particular—as an indirect means of validating their unverifiable claims concerning the future.

Along similar lines, I would suggest that the extensive exploration of the more perplexing facets of biblical history we encounter in the pages that follow (b. Sanh. 92a–96b) parallels a particular use of revealed history in both apocalyptic literature in which the destructions of the first and second temple is a major theme (such as 2 Baruch) and in the neo-Hebraic apocalypses such as Ma'aseh Daniel. In some cases, the historical events described in the rabbinic material derive their esoteric import from a messianic connection. For example, b. Sanh. 94a reveals the otherworldly logic behind Hezekiah's rejection as the messiah. In other cases, the event in question is a miracle, the form of which particularly perplexed the rabbinic expounders. A considerable portion of b. Sanh. 93a, for instance, is devoted to clarifying how Joshua the High Priest might simultaneously be worthy to miraculously survive a journey into Nebuchadnezzar's fiery furnace and yet at the same time emerge with his garments singed—a sign of sin. Many of the events treated in the first half of Pereq Heleq—like those discussed in extant historical apocalypses—concern moments in the history of Israel in which God's plan appeared particularly inscrutable to early rabbinic thinkers. As in the historical apocalypses mentioned above, moreover, the primary function of these talmudic examinations of historical events does not appear to be either homiletic or explanatory in any systematic sense. Rather the goal of these expositions appears to be to demonstrate an intimate and privileged knowledge of the secrets of history on the part of the rabbinic expounders, according to a logic in which privileged knowledge concerning difficult or esoteric aspects of Israel's history is treated as a necessary precursor to receiving knowledge about future events.

Once this groundwork has been laid establishing the rabbis and their guides as uniquely knowledgeable transmitters of esoteric wisdom, the tractate finally turns to symbolic divisions of history in the calculation of the timing of the end on folios 97a–97b. Even in its formal structures, Pereq Heleq thus appears to draw on certain genre conventions from apocalyptic literature without being guided by them, once again utilizing apocalyptic materials without granting them any sort of unique primacy of knowledge and reflecting apocalyptic genre conventions without (re-)producing apocalyptic literature.

3. The Notion of Provisional Literature in Rabbinic Thought

If Pereq Heleq is a telling sample, then it seems possible that early rabbinic thinkers did engage with apocalyptic literature and thought. Perhaps the traces of this engagement have remained somewhat obscure because these rabbinic thinkers did not treat apocalyptic materials as inspired sacred writings but as a form of informational literature to be appreciated for its use value rather than its claims to religious authority. As predictions failed or contradicted one another, they could be revised, evaluated, or merged with other forms of esoteric knowledge. The result was that whatever apocalyptic materials passed through rabbinic hands changed and grew until their extant forms (in the neo-Hebraic apocalypses, for instance) were no longer recognizable in the traces that they left in early rabbinic literature.

Such a provisional attitude toward apocalyptic writings would certainly be in keeping with rabbinic notions concerning two contrasting modes of engaging with written text, which we see expounded (among other places) in the Palestinian Talmud's commentary on tractate Sanhedrin (y. Sanh. 10:1):[15]

רבי עקיבה אומר אף הקורא בספרים החיצונים. כגון ספרי בן סירא וסיפרי בן לענה אבל סיפרי המירם וכל ספרים שנכתבו מיכן והילך הקורא בהן כקורא באיגרת מאי טעמא ויותר מהמה בני היזהר וגו' להגיון ניתנו ליגיעה לא ניתנו.

> R. Aqiva says "[The World to Come is forfeited] likewise by one who read-recites the 'outside books,' such as the books of Ben Sira or the books of Ben La'ana. But regarding the books of Homerus[16] and all the books that were written from that point on, one who reads from them is like one who reads a letter." Where is this [distinction] indicated

---

15. Compare m. Sanh. 10:1; b. Sanh. 100b; and Qoh 12:12.

16. On the terminology that I have translated "Books of Homerus," compare m. Yad. 4:6 and Midr. Ps. 1:12. Concerning the highly debated meaning of this term, see George A. Kohut, "Talmudic Miscellanies I: Sifre Homeros, Books of Entertainment," *JQR* 3 (1891): 546–48; and Saul Lieberman, *Hellenism in Jewish Palestine* (New York: Jewish Theological Seminary of America, 1962), 106–7. For an interesting confirmation of the reading of this term as Homer, see Daniel Sperber, *Greek in Talmudic Palestine* (Ramat Gan: Bar Ilan University Press, 2012), 136–37.

in Scripture? [In the verse,] "Beyond these, my son, be careful [of the making of many books there is no end and much study [להג] is much wearying [יגעת] of the flesh]" (Eccl 12:12). [Which means that] they were given for reading in a murmur [הגיון][17] but not for wearying labor [יגיעה].

The meaning of this passage has been much debated. However, I would propose the following reading: the formulator of this passage understood some pseudepigraphic works composed at the end of the biblical period to be stylistic imitations of the canonical biblical books, including inasmuch as—like canonical biblical works—they were composed to be compatible with a ritual liturgical reading practice based heavily on oral memorization and recitation. As the Babylonian Talmud describes this compositional practice in relation to the biblical book of Esther, "The Book of Esther was given to be ritually read-recited [לקרות]" (b. Meg. 7a). According to y. Sanh. 10:1, it would be particularly tempting to memorize and recite these imitative works from memory just as one did with canonical biblical books. And yet, to do so would inappropriately blur the line between these later imitations and authorized biblical works by engaging with these outside works in the same mode as one engaged with canonical biblical literature—that is, as a formula worth laboriously committing to memory so that it might shape one's perceptions of, and responses to, the challenges of daily life. For as we see in the reading practices of other early Mediterranean communities, a significant ethical distinction was sometimes made in such milieus between those written works that were scrupulously preserved and internalized through memorization and written works that were consumed by means of more casual informational reading.[18]

---

17. "Reading in a murmur" would seem to represent the translation that accounts best for the bifurcated use of the term הגיון as alternately "thinking" and "pronouncing" in the context of this passage (and, indeed, classical rabbinic literature more generally). Other suggested translations have included: "casual reading" (Jacob Schacter, *Judaism's Encounter with Other Cultures: Rejection or Integration?* [New York: Jason Aronson, 1997], 22); "recitation [or: reading lessons]" (Catherine Hezser, *Literacy in Jewish Palestine*, TSAJ 81 [Tübingen: Mohr Siebeck, 2001], 71); and "talk about" (Lawrence H. Schiffman, *Texts and Traditions: A Source Reader for the Study of Second Temple and Rabbinic Judaism* [Hoboken: Ktav Publishing, 1998], 307).

18. In a study that would seem to increase the plausibility of this reading, Elizabeth Asmis has observed a similar hierarchy of laboriously memorized canonical literature and casual informational reading in other ancient Mediterranean educational systems, first and foremost in Epicurean educational theory but also in more "tradi-

According to this reading of y. Sanh. 10:1, other genres of postbiblical writing did not pose such a threat since they had been composed for (or as our text puts it using the rabbinic idiom, "they were given for" (y. Meg. 4:11; y. Moed Qatan 2:3; and y. Sotah 5:3) a very different type of reading—a more cursory informational reading in which one might pronounce the words under one's breath in a murmur as one deciphered the written text but would not invest the labor necessary to commit the literary text firmly to memory as an oral formula. Thus, even if one were to intone such a text aloud, it would not resemble the rabbinic practice of liturgical ritual recitation reading but would be identifiable as a form of casual informational reading that happens to be performed aloud—as when one reads a letter to its intended recipient.[19] Such texts, like the forms of apocalyptic writing envisioned in this chapter, would thus represent a more casual and contingent genre of written material, engaged with pleasure but with a certain casualness at the edges of the rabbinic literary canon.

4. Summary

On the strength of such the small selection of examples cited here, I would ask us to consider the possibility that classical rabbinic authorities did not

---

tional [Greek] education" based on the memorization of Homer. As she puts it: "Children were required to memorize large sections of Homeric and other poetry. This foundation remained with them in adult life.... Epicurean memorization takes the place of this core of knowledge [in Epicurean circles]. It takes the place of 'myth' along with all other established beliefs. The Epicurean may indeed become highly familiar with the false beliefs of others. So long as he does not derive more trouble from this pursuit than pleasure, there is no harm in it. What allows him to escape harm is that he has previously fortified himself with the [memorized] doctrines of Epicurus." See Elizabeth Asmis, "Basic Education in Epicureanism," in *Education in Greek and Roman Antiquity*, ed. Yun Lee Too (Leiden: Brill, 2001), 222. However, the understanding that some Greek literature was indeed incompatible with the practice of committing core literature to memory seems to be hinted at in Epicurus's *Letter to Pythocles*. As Asmis reads the first paragraph of the letter, Pythocles has written to Epicurus to complain that Epicurus's available writings on astronomical phenomena are not conducive to the memorization that is appropriate to core beliefs and requests that he compose a work on the topic more appropriate for memorization (221).

19. In the rabbinic imagination, reading a letter aloud apparently had a recognizably stilted quality. As we learn in y. Ber. 4:4, for instance: "R. Eliezer says, 'one who fixes his prayers, his praying is not an entreaty'.... R. Abahu said in the name of R. Eliezer, '[Which is to say,] just so long as you don't recite them as one reads a letter.'"

reject apocalyptic literature but rather engaged with such materials slightly differently, perhaps, than many of the late antique thinkers we have associated with apocalyptic literature to date. That is, this very small sampling of the available material opens up the possibility that the formulators of the eleventh chapter of tractate Sanhedrin engaged with apocalyptic literature and thought of it as an informative but contingent (and thus potentially unreliable) source of esoteric knowledge to be consumed, revised, and replaced along with other sources of information about the hidden workings of the world.

Bibliography

Asmis, Elizabeth. "Basic Education in Epicureanism." Pages 209–39 in *Education in Greek and Roman Antiquity*. Edited by Yun Lee Too. Leiden: Brill, 2001.

Boustan, Raʿanan. "Rabbinization and the Making of Early Jewish Mysticism." *JQR* 101 (2011): 482–501.

Collins, John J. "Introduction: Towards the Morphology of a Genre." *Semeia* 14 (1979): 1–20.

Dimant, Devorah. "Apocalyptic Texts at Qumran." Pages 175–91 in *The Community of the Renewed Covenant: The Notre Dame Symposium on the Dead Sea Scrolls*. Edited by Eugene Ulrich and James C. VanderKam. Notre Dame: University of Notre Dame Press, 1994.

DiTommaso, Lorenzo. "The Armenian *Seventh Vision of Daniel* and the Historical Apocalyptica of Late Antiquity." Pages 126–48 in *The Armenian Apocalyptic Tradition: A Comparative Perspective; Essays Presented in Honor of Professor Robert W. Thompson on His Eightieth Birthday*. Edited by Kevork B. Bardakjian and Sergio La Porta. SVTP 25. Leiden: Brill, 2014.

———. "Il genere 'apocalisse' e 'apocalittico' nella tarda antichità." *Rivista di storia del cristianesimo* 17 (2020): 73–99.

Elgvin, Torleif. "Wisdom with and without Apocalyptic." Pages 13–38 in *Sapiential, Liturgical, and Poetical Texts from Qumran: Proceedings of the Third Meeting of the International Organization for Qumran Studies, Oslo 1998; Published in Memory of Maurice Baillet*. Edited by Daniel K. Falk, Florentino García Martínez, and Eileen M. Schuller. STDJ 35. Leiden: Brill, 1999.

Ginzberg, Louis. "Some Observations on the Attitude of the Synagogue towards the Apocalyptic-Eschatological Writings." *JBL* 41 (1922): 115–36.
Hezser, Catherine. *Literacy in Jewish Palestine*. TSAJ 81. Tübingen: Mohr Siebeck, 2001.
Kirschner, Robert. "Apocalyptic and Rabbinic Responses to the Destruction of 70." *HTR* 78 (1985): 27–46.
Kohut, George A. "Talmudic Miscellanies I: Sifre Homeros, Books of Entertainment." *JQR* 3 (1891): 546–48.
Lévi, Israel. "Apocalypses dans le Talmud." *REJ* 1 (1880): 108–14.
Lieberman, Saul. *Hellenism in Jewish Palestine*. New York: Jewish Theological Seminary of America, 1962.
Najman, Hindy. "Apocalypse in the History of Judaism: Continuities and Discontinuities." *AJS Perspectives* (2012): 13–16.
Novick, Tzvi. "Between First Century Apocalyptic and Seventh Century Liturgy: On *4 Ezra*, *2 Baruch* and Qillir." *JSJ* 44 (2013): 356–78.
Saldarini, Anthony J. "Apocalyptic and Rabbinic Literature." *CBQ* 37 (1975): 348–58.
———. "Uses of Apocalyptic in Mishnah and Tosefta." *CBQ* 39 (1979): 396–409.
Schacter, Jacob. *Judaism's Encounter with Other Cultures: Rejection or Integration?* New York: Jason Aronson, 1997.
Schäfer, Peter. "From Cosmology to Theology: Rabbinic Appropriation of Apocalyptic Cosmology." Pages 39–58 in *Creation and Re-creation in Jewish Thought: Festschrift in Honor of Joseph Dan on the Occasion of His Seventieth Birthday*. Edited by Rachel Elior and Peter Schäfer. Tübingen: Mohr Siebeck, 2005.
Schiffman, Lawrence H. *Texts and Traditions: A Source Reader for the Study of Second Temple and Rabbinic Judaism*. Hoboken: Ktav Publishing, 1998.
Sperber, Daniel. *Greek in Talmudic Palestine*. Ramat Gan: Bar Ilan University Press, 2012.
Stone, Michael E. *Ancient Judaism: New Visions and Views*. Grand Rapids: Eerdmans, 2011.

Part 3
The Jewish Apocalyptic Tradition and Early Christianity

Divine Kingdom: Between the Songs of the Sabbath Sacrifice and the Synoptic Gospels

Giovanni B. Bazzana

There is little question that the discovery and subsequent publication of the Qumran documents have had a truly revolutionizing influence on New Testament studies. This is obviously felt more directly in some subsectors of the field than in others (for instance, far more in the study of the historical Jesus than in the analysis of Paul's letters).[1] However, it is undeniable that the overall picture of the early Christ movement has been massively impacted by this spate of publication of new primary sources. Even against such an encouraging backdrop though, not all the Qumran documents have been given the same attention, often because the publication of these materials has proceeded with ebbs and flows, not always privileging their respective importance for the historical reconstruction of Second Temple Judaism.[2]

In particular, it is clear that the research at the intersection between New Testament studies and Dead Sea Scrolls has been focused for the most part on issues of law observance and purity. These are certainly important themes, but the main goal of this contribution will be to shed some light also on other aspects of the Qumranic materials in their relationship with the history of the earliest Jesus movement. This is a very broad nexus of themes and historical problems. Thus, the main focus will be restricted to

---

1. To confirm this, it suffices to look at the sheer number of references to the Dead Sea Scrolls in the massive, four-volume *Handbook for the Study of the Historical Jesus*, ed. Tom Holmén and Stanley E. Porter (Leiden: Brill, 2011), 3569–75.

2. Again, to confirm this point, it suffices to note that, in Holmén and Porter's *Handbook for the Study of the Historical Jesus*, almost half of the references are from the documents from Cave 1, which were published first.

an element that has great importance for our understanding of the earliest Jesus movement but remains largely and puzzlingly understudied. This essay will argue that the theme of God's kingdom might be more adequately illuminated through the examination of some Dead Sea texts whose potential contribution has not been exploited in full yet. This treatment is intended as a further exemplification of the importance that the Qumran scrolls can have for New Testament studies and of how much work remains to be done at their intersection with the New Testament.

The first section of this contribution will be devoted to a brief description of an important Qumran document, the Songs of the Sabbath Sacrifice, in juxtaposition to a long-standing problem in New Testament studies, the origin and significance of the phrase "kingdom of God." The Qumranic text will be introduced, and then I will look at its significance for our understanding of the occurrences of kingdom of God, with a specific focus on the three Synoptic Gospels. The second section of this essay will consider in more detail an image related to the kingdom of God (entering into it) that occurs often in some of the earliest materials and thus has been the object of heated theological discussions. In the third and last section, I will reconsider the political and historical significance of the kingdom imagery by paying particular attention to the ways in which the notion of agency is evoked and deployed in relationship to the kingdom imagery.

1. The Kingdom of God and the Songs of the Sabbath Sacrifice

The "kingdom of God" (βασιλεία τοῦ θεοῦ) is almost universally considered an element that belonged to the original preaching of the historical Jesus.[3] Even though scholarly opinions on everything related to the histor-

---

3. The traditional translation of the Greek *basileia* with "kingdom" has been rightly criticized because the semantic domain evoked by *basileia* (even within the gospels, whose use of the phrase is quite differentiated, as we will see below) is much broader than the one carried by "kingdom" for a modern reader. Alternative proposals are "rule" or "empire," which have merits and carry significant theological weight but ultimately fall under the same sorts of problems. Elsewhere, I have resorted to employ the transliteration *basileia*, which seems the most adequate solution, but here I will use also the more traditional "kingdom" for the sake of clarity; for a more thorough discussion of this issue, see Giovanni B. Bazzana, *Kingdom of Bureaucracy: The Political Theology of Village Scribes in the Sayings Gospel Q*, BETL 274 (Leuven: Peeters, 2015), 19–22.

ical Jesus are rarely in agreement, this is one case in which the abundance and the diversity of the evidence are so great that dissension is inevitable. However, this is only the beginning of a much more complex conversation. While scholars can be quite sure that the historical Jesus spoke about the kingdom of God and that this notion was central to his message, it is a completely different affair to establish what he meant when he used the phrase and how it shaped the overall structure of his teaching. The main stumbling block is that, despite its repeated occurrences in the traditions on Jesus, nowhere can one find an explanation of what kingdom of God means. It is as if the authors who assembled these materials could take for granted that their audiences knew already what speaking of a kingdom of God meant. An immediate conclusion would be to expect to find that reflected in the Jewish literature of the Second Temple period. But here also the situation appears immediately and surprisingly much more complicated. While the entire Jewish scriptures are full of references to God as king in a way that can make this notion a taken-for-granted one in the Second Temple period, the state of affairs is quite different as far as the abstract kingdom is concerned. To a certain extent, one encounters in this case a pattern of the evidence that is almost the polar opposite in the gospel materials compared to other Jewish texts belonging to the Second Temple period. On the one hand, in most contemporary Jewish documents God is often referred to as a king, while his kingdom is often not mentioned. On the other hand, Jesus and his early followers and believers have recourse to the language of divine kingdom quite often, while the proclamation of God as king (while by no means absent: one may only think about the Apocalypse of John) is much rarer in comparison.

The historical and theological problem is further complicated by the fact that gospel materials seem to employ the phrase kingdom of God in a host of diverse and only partially consistent ways. It goes without saying that the very recourse to a term such as the Greek *basileia* must have elicited in hearers and readers a number of political associations. But it is also obvious that this very political imagery could then be directed in many and not immediately coherent directions. So, for example, Jesus can speak about "entering" (Mark 10:15 and parallels) or "inheriting" the "kingdom of God" (Matt 25:31–46): these uses are quite understandable if the kingdom is understood—in analogy with a meaning that is still current—as "sovereignty" (which can be inherited) over a "territory" (in which one can then enter). But other gospel passages seem to work out of a very different understanding of what *basileia* is. So, for example, one encounters verses in which the kingdom has "reached out" to people in connection with Jesus's exorcisms (Matt 12:28 // Luke 11:20) or the kingdom is exhorted to "come" as in the Lord's Prayer. Even without considering the many parables ascribed to Jesus and in which the kingdom of God is compared with a most diverse array of characters and situations, it is clear already that the common-sense understanding of kingdom as "territory subject to a monarchic sovereign" is patently insufficient.[4]

As noted above, scholars have already lamented the lack—in the gospel materials—of a definition for the kingdom of God as well as the apparent absence of valid antecedents in the Jewish literature of the Second Temple period. A few years ago, Roy Harrisville observed that the entire structure of the evidence in this case puzzlingly resembles a pyramid "stood on its apex."[5] Indeed, the scanty occurrences of the concept in contemporary Jewish literature hardly explain the significant spread and diversity of its appearance in the writings belonging to the early Christ movement. In fact, there are relatively significant occurrences of the phrase kingdom of God both in the canonical Hebrew Bible (notably in Ps 145, one of the latest in the collection) as well as in the pseudepigraphical works (again, a notable occurrence is the so-called Testament of Moses). John Collins reviewed these materials a few decades ago in a survey article that remains a seminal contribution, but even he had to admit that these texts could only be of limited usefulness to understand the development of the concept in the writings of the earliest Christ movement.[6] Naturally, as I have argued more extensively elsewhere, part of this puzzling historical conundrum depends on the fact that scholars have been reluctant to recognize that the notion of kingdom of God in the gospels is influenced by the kingship-discourse spread through all the eastern Mediterranean by Hellenistic monarchies.[7] That being said, however, it remains difficult to understand how such notions might have left their traces in the earli-

---

4. See a clear and brief discussion of this diverse evidence in Volker Gäckle, *Das Reich Gottes im Neuen Testament: Auslegungen—Anfragen—Alternativen*, BTS 176 (Göttingen: Vandenhoeck & Ruprecht, 2018), 35–133, even though this author's conclusions are somewhat biased by a theological presupposition, as one will see in the latter section of this essay.

5. Roy A. Harrisville, "In Search of the Meaning of the 'Reign of God,'" *Int* 47 (1993): 140–51.

6. John J. Collins, "The Kingdom of God in the Apocrypha and Pseudepigrapha," in *Seers, Sibyls, and Sages in Hellenistic-Roman Judaism* (Leiden: Brill, 1997), 99–114.

7. Bazzana, *Kingdom of Bureaucracy*, 213–26.

est Christ traditions (and arguably even in the preaching of the historical Jesus) without appearing also in other contemporary Jewish writings. To find an answer, an important step is obviously a thorough investigation of the Qumran scrolls, which are notably absent from Collins's survey.

The reason for this absence is obviously that—at the moment of the publication of the survey—the published scrolls did not contain almost any mention of a kingdom of God. In that sense, the Qumran evidence did not seem to diverge in any significant way from the pattern evident in the remaining literature of the Second Temple period. But newer texts have been published after the appearance of Collins's article, and at least a couple of them do offer important evidence that can be fruitfully compared with the materials from the gospels.[8]

As noted at the beginning, the present analysis will focus on the so-called Songs of the Sabbath Sacrifice, a collection of Hebrew liturgical poems in which the phrase kingdom of God (מלכות in the Hebrew) occurs quite frequently and meaningfully in a relatively short space. The fact that the Songs have received scant critical attention compared to other scrolls may be due in part to the fact that they had to be put together by assembling and reordering the fragments of several manuscripts found at Qumran and at Masada. The credit for such a painstaking feat of philological prowess goes to Carol Newsom, who has provided the critical edition that will be taken as reference point here, alongside a series of illuminating scholarly analyses.[9] Besides the eight manuscripts from Cave 4 (4Q400–407), the Songs appear also on a scroll from Cave 11 (11Q17), while some additional fragments have surfaced at Masada as well. Thus, the cumulative evidence seems to indicate that the text enjoyed a good deal of favor within the Qumran group and in all likelihood also outside of it.

---

8. Another text that could be considered for analysis here is 4Q246, the Aramaic Son of God document that has generated much discussion, but not so much on account of its mention of the divine and eschatological kingdom. The text might have a bearing on the interpretation of some New Testament passages (notably the announcement to Mary in Luke 1), but it is less relevant for the present discussion. See the fine and comprehensive treatment in Michael Segal, "Who Is the 'Son of God' in 4Q246? An Overlooked Example of Biblical Interpretation," *DSD* 21 (2014): 289–312.

9. Carol A. Newsom, *Songs of the Sabbath Sacrifice: A Critical Edition*, HSS 27 (Atlanta, GA: Scholars Press, 1985). The text and translation of the Songs will be taken from James H. Charlesworth and Carol A. Newsom, eds., *Angelic Liturgy: Songs of the Sabbath Sacrifice*, vol. 4B of *The Dead Sea Scrolls: Hebrew, Aramaic, and Greek Texts with English Translations* (Tübingen: Mohr Siebeck, 1999).

As with many other Dead Sea Scrolls, it is debated whether the Songs were composed originally by the sectarians or whether they adopted it. In this respect, the copy of the Songs found in Masada plays an important role. Some have suggested that some refugees from Qumran brought a copy of the Songs to the last stronghold of the Jewish resistance to Roman invasion. But this is an unlikely scenario, and it appears far more reasonable to conclude from the pattern of preservation of the Songs that this text was known and used also outside the group linked to Qumran in the first century CE. This is also Newsom's conclusion, and she has bolstered it with a series of insightful observations on the language employed in the Songs. Indeed, the poetic Hebrew of the hymns does show several features that are far from good matches for the language normally used in the documents that are ascribed to the sectarians with some reasonable measure of confidence. For instance, the Songs often employ the term אלהים to designate God. Such a designation occurs in a similar way in some very early parts of the Hebrew Bible, but it is definitely extremely rare at Qumran.[10] On these grounds, Newsom suggests that in all likelihood the Songs were composed independently from and earlier than the establishment of the Qumran group. Afterwards, they were introduced among the sectarians, and again the pattern of preservation all but indicates that they enjoyed quite a good deal of success in that context. Such a conclusion, hypothetical as it may be, is significant for the purposes of the present treatment, since it establishes that the Songs, while beloved at Qumran, could certainly be known also elsewhere, so that its theological and linguistic makeup can be profitably compared with the materials included in the Synoptic Gospels.

The Songs of the Sabbath Sacrifice are a collection of thirteen hymns, and each of them is designed to be recited on a Sabbath in a cycle. Accordingly, each hymn is prefaced by a line in which the *maśkil* is tasked with initiating the recitation of the first hymn on the fourth day of the first month, the second hymn on the eleventh day of the first month, and so on for thirteen weeks.[11] The fact that the Sabbath falls on the fourth day

---

10. Carol A. Newsom, "'Sectually Explicit' Literature from Qumran," in *The Hebrew Bible and Its Interpreters*, ed. William H. Propp, Baruch Halpern, and David Noel Freedman (Winona Lake, IN: Eisenbrauns, 1990), 179–85.

11. On the figure of the *maśkil* at Qumran, see Carol A. Newsom, "The Sage in the Literature of Qumran: The Function of the *Maskil*," in *The Sage in Israel and the Ancient Near East*, ed. John G. Gammie and Leo G. Perdue (Winona Lake, IN: Eisenbrauns, 1990), 373–82.

of the month indicates that the Songs presuppose the use of a solar calendar, in which the year begins on a Wednesday. It has been suggested that there might have been other three cycles of Sabbath hymns to cover the remaining three quarters of a full year, but no trace of these compositions have surfaced at Qumran or anywhere else. Thus, it is reasonable to think that this cycle might have been put together expressly with the purpose of structuring from a liturgical point of view the thirteen weeks leading from the beginning of the year to roughly the celebration of Shavuot, as argued in a lengthy and important article by Judith Newman.[12]

The contents of the hymns and their changing literary style indicate quite clearly that the collection is structured in three smaller subsections. Hymns 1–5 present the angels and describe their roles as priests in the heavenly sanctuary and conveyors of the divine mysteries. Hymns 6–8 describe the climax of the angelic liturgy, which had been introduced before, with the invitation to praise the power and glory of God in accordance with the respective locations of the angels within the heavenly ranks. Finally, hymns 9–13 describe in great detail the architectural structure of the heavenly sanctuary (which participates in the liturgical act of praising God) culminating in a sacrifice and the presentation of the priesthood assigned to the angels. Such a tripartite structure has a clear climax—as noted before—in the central subsection. Indeed, hymn 7 is clearly longer and more elaborate than the rest, while hymns 6 and 8 have a transparently mirror-like organization that seems to provide a frame for hymn 7. A structure centered around hymn 7 would also be consistent with the importance assigned to number 7 in a collection of hymns designed for recitation on the occasion of the Sabbath. That being said though, the final subsection of the Songs should not be taken as pure filling out needed in order to get to number thirteen. Several scholars have, in fact, pointed out that the concluding hymns do fulfill a purpose, in particular by leading the readers (and arguably reciters) of the Songs into the heavenly sanctuary and at same time elevating the role of the priesthood in a crucial mediating and brokering role. In sum, it can be said that the Songs have a two-pronged structure, culminating both with hymns 7 and 13.[13]

---

12. Judith H. Newman, "Priestly Prophets at Qumran: Summoning Sinai through the Songs of the Sabbath Sacrifice," in *The Significance of Sinai: Traditions about Sinai and Divine Revelation in Judaism and Christianity*, ed. George J. Brooke, Hindy Najman, and Loren T. Stuckenbruck (Leiden: Brill, 2008), 29–72.

13. See the literature quoted in Newman, "Priestly Prophets at Qumran," 38–39.

Both the contents and the linguistic characteristics of the Songs have immediately inspired scholars of early Judaism to identify this text as a precursor of the mystical trends that will be later codified in the Hekhalot literature.[14] In many ways, this is an appropriate observation, even though a lot of confusion is introduced in the matter by the difficulty of defining what can be designated as mysticism, as noted recently by David Hamidovic. The matter of categorization, however, is less central for the present concerns than the recognition—shared by almost all the scholars who have worked on the Songs—that the hymns invite human participation in the liturgical activity that they describe. As in several other Qumran documents, here too it seems that the human members of the liturgical community are united with the angels.[15]

The following pages will attempt to read the recurring theme of the kingdom of God in the Songs in light of this liturgical and mystical context with an eye to the significance that such a reading might have for a more adequate understanding of the idea of a kingdom of God in the gospel materials.

2. The Songs and Kingdom

As observed at the very beginning of the present essay, the Songs of the Sabbath Sacrifice stand out among the other Jewish literature of the Second Temple period because they contain a significant number of occurrences

---

14. See, e.g., the reexamination of the seminal discussions of Lawrence Schiffman and James Davila in the contributions of Ra'anan Abusch, "Sevenfold Hymns in the *Songs of the Sabbath Sacrifice* and the Hekhalot Literature: Formalism, Hierarchy, and the Limits of Human Participation," in *The Dead Sea Scrolls as Background to Postbiblical Judaism and Early Christianity*, ed. James R. Davila, STDJ 46 (Leiden: Brill, 2003), 220–47; and David Hamidović, "La contribution des *Cantiques de l'holocauste du Sabbat* à l'étude de la pensée mystique juive au tournant de l'ère chrétienne," in *La mystique théorétique et théurgique dans l'antiquité gréco-romaine*, ed. Simon Claude Mimouni and Madeline Scopello (Brepols: Turnhout, 2016), 303–19.

15. See, e.g., Joseph Angel, *Otherworldly and Eschatological Priesthood in the Dead Sea Scrolls*, STDJ 86 (Leiden: Brill, 2010). Crispin H. T. Fletcher-Louis, "Heavenly Ascent or Incarnational Presence? A Revisionist Reading of the *Songs of the Sabbath Sacrifice*," in *Society of Biblical Literature 1998 Seminar Papers*, SBLSP 37 (Atlanta: Society of Biblical Literature, 1998), 367–99, has suggested that the human members of the liturgical community actually *became* angels, but this has remained a minority opinion.

of the phrase kingdom of God.[16] This observation has been already made and then put to work in connection with the kingdom of God in the gospels by Anna Maria Schwemer in a very detailed analysis that was published in 1991.[17] Schwemer has already noted that the Songs employ the terminology of God's *malkut* with two different nuances, which, however, are deeply intertwined in their respective occurrences within the series of thirteen hymns. On the one hand, the first two and the final two poems—focused as they are on the ritual activities within the heavenly temple—include several mentions of the kingdom that indicate a specific space, often identified with the heavenly sanctuary. For instance, in the surviving section of the second hymn, God is directly praised in this way: "For you are honored among [...] the most godlike divine beings [...] to the chiefs of the dominion [...] the heavens of your glorious kingdom" (17–18).[18] Again, a similar theme—focused on the angelic praise for God—is taken up towards the end of hymn 13: "These are the chiefs of those wondrously arrayed for service, the chiefs of the kingdom of kingdoms, holy ones of the king of holiness in all the heights of the sanctuaries of his glorious kingdom" (21–23).[19]

On the other hand, the hymns collected in the center of the sequence seem to refer to a different nuance for the Hebrew *malkut*. In this case, the referent seems to be more an abstract notion of royal sovereignty. For instance, in hymn 6 the divine response to the blessing of God pronounced by the seventh order of the chief princes has this content: "He will bless all [...] those who praise his glorious kingdom [...] forever, with seven wondrous words for eternal peace" (57–58).[20] In cases such as this, it is quite clear that the current English translation "kingdom" is particularly awkward because it hardly grasps the abstract nuance of *malkut* (an abstract nuance that is present in the Greek *basileia* as

---

16. See the instances listed in Newsom, *Songs of the Sabbath Sacrifice*, 426.

17. Anna Maria Schwemer, "Gott als König und seine Königsherrschaft in den Sabbatliedern aus Qumran," in *Königsherrschaft Gottes und himmlischer Kult im Judentum, Urchristentum, und in der hellenistischen Welt*, ed. Martin Hengel and Anna Maria Schwemer, WUNT 55 (Tübingen: Mohr Siebeck, 1991), 46–118.

18. Charlesworth and Newsom, *Angelic Liturgy*, 144 (שמי מלכות כבודכה); Newsom translates *malkut* alternatively as "realm" (as in this case) or "kingship" (as in the immediately following 2.19), but I have normalized all instances as "kingdom" as a means to show the ambivalence of the Hebrew term.

19. Charlesworth and Newsom, *Angelic Liturgy*, 188 (מקדשי מלכות כבודו).

20. Charlesworth and Newsom, *Angelic Liturgy*, 158.

well). It should be emphasized that in distinguishing these two nuances of kingdom of God in the Songs, one cannot conclude that they are mutually exclusive (as if, for instance, the spatial meaning constituted a more superficial version of the abstract sovereignty understood as carrying a more mystical nuance). Appropriately, Schwemer has not only observed the coexistence of the two above-mentioned nuances, but she has also pointed out that they come together and are intertwined in hymn 7.[21] Since the latter constitutes the structural peak of the entire composition (as we have seen above), one is led to conclude that the two nuances are actually combined on an equal footing in the Songs. One will come back later on the more abstract nuance of *malkut* and its relationship with the gospel materials. For the time being, it is worth adding a few more reflections developing Schwemer's thoughts on the ambivalent nature of the kingdom of God in the Songs and more specifically on its spatial understanding.

A long-standing debate among scholars dealing with the kingdom of God in the early Jesus movement concerns whether the historical Jesus in his preaching understood the kingdom as something that had to be expected in the future—more or less consistently with other Jewish apocalyptic expectations of the Second Temple period—or if he envisaged the kingdom as already present in his activities of healing and exorcizing. It is well known that the gospels contain materials that can be marshaled to support either hypothesis.[22] On the one hand, most references to the kingdom are in contexts that presuppose—implicitly or explicitly—an apocalyptic expectation. (It will suffice to name, for instance, the mention of the *basileia* in the Lord's Prayer at Matt 6:10 // Luke 11:2 or the prophecy about drinking new wine in the kingdom of God in Mark 14:25.) On the other hand, there are a few, but important sayings that can only be interpreted as indicating the kingdom as already present (as in the famous reference to Jesus performing exorcisms with the "finger/spirit of God" in Matt 12:28 // Luke 10:20 or the much-discussed verse Luke 17:21, in which ἐντὸς ὑμῶν can be translated to mean that the *basileia* is either "within" or "amid" Jesus's interlocutors).

---

21. Schwemer, "Gott als König," 116.
22. To indicate the sheer magnitude of the historical and theological debate, Meier, in his detailed discussion of this topic in the second volume of his magnum opus on the historical Jesus, devotes exactly 108 pages to the future *basileia* and 108 to the present one; see John P. Meier, *A Marginal Jew: Rethinking the Historical Jesus*, (New York: Doubleday, 1994).

The issue is largely mired in the more general methodological *empasse* that haunts the quest for the historical Jesus. However, in the specific case of the future or present kingdom, the state of affairs is rendered all the more complicated by the ideological weight that has been associated with an oversimplified temporal alternative. On the one hand, in the context of the North American debate in particular, the conclusion that Jesus announced a present *basileia* (or, said in other terms, a realized eschatology) has become a hallmark of liberal Christianity at least since the controversial interventions of the Jesus Seminar in the 1980s.[23] In a mirror-like fashion, most conservative scholars have consistently pushed for a more apocalyptic Jesus, often seeing in that historiographical construction a means to assure that their historical Jesus would remain more Jewish than the Jesus of their theological opponents.[24] On the other hand, and to make the waters even murkier, it must be noted that scholarship from other geographical and cultural areas has been operating in an almost opposite direction. For large sectors of the academic world in Europe and South America, for instance, and under the influence of various forms of liberationist theologies, the more left-leaning scholarship tends to associate eschatological and apocalyptic expectations with the representation of a socially engaged or even radical Jesus.[25]

That being said, this ponderous debate has been settled in the most recent scholarly writing on the kingdom of God through a mainstream recognition that it is in all likelihood impossible to pinpoint definitively whether Jesus preached a future or a present *basileia*.[26] Already Schwemer had noted that the Songs at a minimum do confirm such a conclusion by offering a parallel treatment of divine *malkut* in which future and present

---

23. This position is represented most clearly and influentially in the seminal works of John D. Crossan, *The Historical Jesus: The Life of a Mediterranean Jewish Peasant* (San Francisco: Harper, 1991).

24. For an overview of this particular use of Schweitzer's thoroughgoing apocalyptic Jesus, see John S. Kloppenborg, "As One Unknown, without a Name? Co-opting the Historical Jesus," in *Apocalypticism, Anti-Semitism, and the Historical Jesus: Subtexts in Criticism*, ed. John S. Kloppenborg and John W. Marshall, JSNTSup 275 (London: T&T Clark International, 2005), 1–23.

25. See, for instance, the essays collected in Michael Welker and Francis Schüssler Fiorenza, eds., *Politische Theologie: Neuere Geschichte und Potenziale* (Neukirchen: Neukirchener Verlag, 2011).

26. One can consider as representative of a consensus, for instance, the recent conclusions reached in Gäckle, *Das Reich Gottes im Neuen Testament*, 129–33, but also Meier, *Marginal Jew*, 450–54.

perspectives are combined without running a great risk of logical contradiction. On the one hand, the Songs, like many other Jewish texts of the Second Temple period, envisage the *malkut* as something that will be established definitively in the eschatological future. On the other hand, the same liturgical texts present the same *malkut* as something already accessible, even though clearly only for those humans who know and can recite the hymns.[27]

To Schwemer's observations, one must add an important corollary. The Songs do indeed offer a significant parallel, which indirectly confirms the conclusions reached by New Testament scholarship on God's *basileia*. Moreover, one must emphasize quite strongly that the copresence of present and future perspectives both in the Songs and the Synoptic Gospels is not the product of unsystematic thought or of lack of adequate reflection, as it is often suggested.

In fact, much of the critical discomfort with this overlap between regimes of temporality is due to a modern ontological bias. Biblical criticism operates within a paradigm of temporality that is a product of post-Enlightenment European thought and presupposes a linear and irreversible flow of time. By definition, within this regime, present and future cannot overlap. But it is worth considering whether using such a paradigm can actually enable one to provide an adequate account of the temporality presupposed by the Songs and by the Synoptic Gospels. In recent years, anthropologists and philosophers have offered very compelling descriptions of alternative regimes of temporality, showing that one can identify them both in non-Western cultures as well as in the historical record of the West itself.[28] It seems that accounting for such a paradigmatic difference is crucial in order to achieve a better understanding of the apparently contradictory temporality of the kingdom of God in the texts considered here. Far from revealing a superficially reflected inconsistency, the Songs as well as the Synoptic Gospels were, in fact, operating within a regime of temporality in which—for some specific cases—present and future could coincide. It goes without saying that a similar situation obtained also for a good number of the other apocalyptic writings belonging to the Second Temple period.

---

27. Schwemer, "Gott als König," 117.

28. See, for instance, the work of Charles Stewart, "Historicity and Anthropology," *Annual Review of Anthropology* 45 (2016): 79–94; and Stewart, *Dreaming and Historical Consciousness in Island Greece* (Cambridge: Harvard University Press, 2012).

3. Entering the Kingdom

The Songs can be helpful to solving some other puzzles concerning the *basileia* of God that have not been taken into specific consideration by Schwemer. A much-discussed topic in regard to the kingdom in the Synoptic Gospels is the often-used expression "entering in the kingdom" (εἰσελθεῖν εἰς τὴν βασιλείαν).[29] More than a century ago Gustaf Dalman argued that the Greek *basileia* could not be translated as "kingdom" or "realm."[30] According to Dalman, the Semitic *malkut* that stood behind the Greek could not have the passive meaning that one associates with a territorial kingdom but could only be active, indicating the saving action of God entering human history. Dalman's suggestion is flawed in important methodological ways that will be taken up again in the next section of this essay. However, his analysis generated a series of alternative proposals for the translation of *basileia*, including various options such as "sovereignty," "rule," or "kingly power" that have been mentioned above.

While many exegetes have embraced Dalman's ideas, an important stumbling block for a very active understanding of God's kingdom have always been those Synoptic passages in which Jesus speaks about entering in it. At first sight, it seems that this phrase can only designate a place, a territorial kingdom, to which it is very difficult to ascribe any agency. As in the case of the temporality of the kingdom (examined above), this exegetical problem too is compounded by significant theological issues that elevate the stakes of the debate. An active *basileia* is very easy to associate with the idea of God's irresistible intervention in human history, but again the same is not as true for the passive version of the kingdom. Indeed, several of the Synoptic passages that speak about entering the kingdom connect the expression to something that the disciples of Jesus are expected to do in order to obtain access to it. Thus, for example, in Mark 9:47 they

---

29. The occurrences are quite widespread throughout the entire three books (a good indicator that the origins of the phrase should be considered quite early): Mark 9:47; Mark 10:15 // Matt 18:3 // Luke 18:17; Mark 10:23–25 // Matt 19:23–24 // Luke 18:24–25; Matt 5:20; 7:21; 21:31; 23:13.

30. Gustaf Dalman, *Die Worte Jesu, mit Berücksichtigung des nachkanonischen jüdischen Schrifttums und der aramäischen Sprache*, 2nd ed. (Leipzig: Henrichs, 1930), 77. It goes without saying that Dalman was reacting not against the English phrases but against the German *Reich* in the context of the political situation of his time; for this, see Ludger Schenke, "Die Botschaft vom kommenden 'Reich Gottes,'" in *Jesus von Nazaret—Spuren und Konturen* (Stuttgart: Kohlhammer, 2004), 106–47.

are gruesomely exhorted to tear out even one of their eyes if that body part can hinder their access into the *basileia*, or in Matt 5:20 their righteousness must exceed that of the Pharisees in order for them to gain admittance. Particularly if the *basileia* is taken as a symbol of definitive salvation (as it is often done in the very gospels) such passive connotations might introduce in the mix an unwelcome measure of human synergism.

Thus, several exegetes have attempted to rescue the phrase "entering into the kingdom" from such a passivity, even though their conclusions appear less then convincing.[31] In this case (as in many other aspects of the discussion), scholars have too often forgotten that the imagination of the *basileia* in the early Jesus movement might have been shaped by the royal propaganda of the time as much as by the materials included in the Jewish scriptures. In this specific case, it is quite likely that the idea of an eschatological entry of God into the *basileia* with his disciples was influenced less by rather vague scriptural antecedents than by the Seleucid practice of crowning an heir to the throne when he entered for the first time the kingdom from abroad.[32] That being said, this is not the place to discuss further how Hellenistic royal ideology might have shaped the understanding of *basileia* in the early Jesus movement.

On the contrary, attention should be paid again to the Songs and their potential contribution to the historical and theological debates. On that account, there is little doubt that the hymns from Qumran and Masada attest clearly that entering into a divine *malkut* could well be understood in very concrete terms in the Second Temple period. Above, a couple of passages were mentioned in which the *malkut* of God is unequivocally identified with a heavenly sanctuary. It goes without saying that one is not dealing here with any type of direct influence of the *Songs* on the Synoptic imagination of the kingdom. The *malkut* of the Songs is clearly a sanctuary, and there is no trace in the Synoptic traditions that the *basileia* of God

---

31. For instance, Joel Marcus, "Entering into the Kingly Power of God," *JBL* 107 (1988): 663–75, develops a subtle argument to the effect that the phrase should be understood as meaning "an incorporation of the disciple into God's powerful invasion of this world" (674), but the scriptural parallels that he marshals to support his hypothesis do not appear sufficient.

32. The Seleucid practice—together with its ideological connection to the specific Seleucid understanding of royal sovereignty as always on the move—is well described by Paul J. Kosmin, *The Land of the Elephant Kings: Space, Territory, and Ideology in the Seleucid Empire* (Cambridge: Harvard University Press, 2014), 129–41.

had analogous temple features (even though other very early traditions belonging to the Jesus movement do indeed describe the kingdom with priestly traits).[33] The present comparison can only make sense in terms of a shared discourse about *malkut* and, in particular, about divine *malkut*. In this perspective, the Songs show that *malkut* and *basileia* could be understood as physical spaces (be they sanctuaries or territorial realms) into which one could indeed enter.[34]

What then about the important theological issue of divine and human passivity in obtaining access to the *malkut*? On this account, again similarly to the issue of temporality discussed above, it is important to emphasize that the Songs invite one to look at the situation differently than as a rather static binary. One of the most striking traits of the Songs is that, besides exhorting heavenly beings to give praise to God, this liturgical activity is extended to include even the architectural elements of the heavenly sanctuary. In hymns 9 to 12, one witnesses a kind of climax of praise that progressively involves the more external architectural elements of the sanctuary to reach eventually its innermost recesses. Thus, the liturgical recitation starts from the mentions of "the engravings of living godlike beings" in 9.14–16 and of the "veils of the wondrous inner rooms" in 10.6–8.[35] All these elements effectively "take life" to join in the praising of God that culminates in hymn 12 when the overall movement reaches the most internal chamber and the "chariots" (מרכבה) in 12.6. This section of the

---

33. The case in point is obviously provided by the Apocalypse of John, whose similarities with the Songs have been noted already by many scholars; see Håkan Ulfgard, "The Songs of the Sabbath Sacrifice and the Heavenly Scene of the Book of Revelation," in *Northern Lights on the Dead Sea Scrolls*, ed. Anders K. Petersen et al., STDJ 80 (Leiden: Brill, 2009), 251–66.

34. This should not be read immediately as spiritualization or, combined with a heavily teleological frame, as prefiguring the replacement of the Jerusalem temple in Judaism and the Christ movement after 70 CE; on this, see the balanced reflection in Beate Ego, "Der Gottesdienst der Engel—Von den biblischen Psalmen zur jüdischen Mystik: Traditionskritische Überlegungen zu den Sabbatopferliedern von Qumran," *TLZ* 140 (2015): 886–901.

35. The presence of (perhaps) anthropomorphic figurations is surprising at first sight, but several commentators have noted that it indicates that the heavenly sanctuary was imagined on the basis of the scriptural antecedents in 1 Kgs 6:29 and Ezek 41:15–26 (see Newsom, *Songs of the Sabbath Sacrifice*, 282–83). The reference to "veils of the wondrous inner rooms" is a multiplied reference to the *parokhet* ("veil") located at the entrance of the *debir* ("inner room"), for which see Exod 26:31–35.

collection in particular is the one that has fueled more than anything else the scholarly interest in connecting the Songs with later developments of Jewish mysticism. For the purposes of the present discussion, however, it is worth highlighting that by animating and including even architectural features in the praising activity of the hymns, the Songs perform a sort of ontological blurring of the lines that should otherwise separate superhuman beings, humans, and material objects.[36]

However one may judge the origin of this peculiar feature of the Songs, it is clear that it complicates quite a bit the attribution of agency with respect to the *malkut*, even when the latter is understood as a physical space. One will come back to this crucial issue again in the following section of the paper. For the time being, it is worth observing that the ontology of the Songs does not match very well the contemporary theological discussion sketched above. It disturbs the concern of New Testament exegetes that entering the *basileia* might depict a scenario in which the divine world is too passive and humans are too active. In fact, this very framing of the problem is predicated on a binary that is entangled by modern ontological constraints. As for the case of linear time above, also the understanding of agency as something that belongs only to human (or superhuman) beings is a modern presupposition and is currently called into question by several philosophers and anthropologists.[37] In this perspective, the witness of the Songs forces us to reconsider the very terms of the theological and historical conversation in light of the fact that even a space or a building can be considered active within a specific ontological paradigm. Thus, one can come to revise also the conceptualization of the agency of the kingdom of God and of human participation in its establishment.

---

36. Interestingly, a similar element is present also in some descriptions of the apocalyptic kingdom produced by the early Christ movement; thus, for example, a good parallel is provided once more by the Apocalypse of John, in which disciples are promised to become "columns in the temple of God" (3:12) and the "twelve apostles of the Lamb" seems to become the foundations of the wall of the new Jerusalem (21:14).

37. See the intervention of Benjamin Alberti, "Archaeologies of Ontology," *Annual Review of Anthropology* 45 (2016): 163–79; and the seminal book by Eduardo Kohn, *How Forests Think: Toward an Anthropology beyond the Human* (Berkeley: University of California Press, 2013).

4. The Sovereignty of God and Its Activity

As noted before, the occurrences of *malkut* in the Songs seem to vindicate Dalman's urge to understanding the Synoptic *basileia* in light of the Semitic usage of comparable phrases. However, it is important to keep in mind that Dalman's hypothesis needs recalibration and revision in at least two important respects.

First, one does not need to invoke a Semitic layer beneath *basileia* in the Synoptic Gospels in order to demonstrate that the Greek cannot mean merely a territorial kingdom. *Basileia* was commonly used to indicate also the more abstract sovereignty understood as a royal prerogative. In fact, an examination of Hellenistic literary and documentary materials shows quite easily that the Greek *basileia* already carries both the nuances, which are also found in the *malkut* of the Songs.[38] This is one of many cases in which there is no need to trace a Semitic background for the Greek that was presumably spoken or written by the early Christ followers. On the contrary, cases like this suggest that the Aramaic and Hebrew of the Second Temple period were often participating in more general linguistic phenomena common to *koine* Greek as well in the context of the eastern Mediterranean.

Second, it is not as clear as maintained by Dalman and his followers that speaking of *basileia* or *malkut* of God as sovereignty or rule attributes all agency to God (and thus eliminates the theological risk of human synergism). For one thing, it is not immediately evident whether the Greek genitive τοῦ θεοῦ ("of God") should be taken as subjective or objective. For instance, a very ambiguous case is offered by the beatitude of Matt 5:3 // Luke 6:20 (Μακάριοι οἱ πτωχοὶ ὅτι ὑμετέρα ἐστὶν ἡ βασιλεία τοῦ θεοῦ). It is equally possible exegetically to wonder whether the *basileia* belongs to God and is for the poor or if it belongs to the poor and the genitive only describes its divine character.[39]

The problem is crucial for the issue of agency at stake here and it is further compounded by the observation that, while the Synoptic Gospels contain very few proclamations of God as king (something that, on the contrary, is quite common in other Jewish scriptures), the *basileia* seems to have quite a bit of agency and even actually do things on same occasions.

---

38. See Bazzana, *Kingdom of Bureaucracy*, 165–212, in particular employing Egyptian documentary papyri.
39. See the discussion in Bazzana, *Kingdom of Bureaucracy*, 278–79.

It will suffice to point at the very first words that Mark puts on the mouth of Jesus in 1:15 (// Matt 4:17) to the effect that "the kingdom of God has come near" as an exhortation for humans to respond with a quick action of repentance.[40] Another much-discussed saying of Jesus is attested in Matt 12:28 // Luke 11:20.[41] There the *basileia* seems to have actually already reached out to the audiences of the prophet from Nazareth.

Does it make any sense to attribute agency to the abstract *basileia* or *malkut*? Both the Songs and the Synoptic Gospels seem to lead in that direction. To this, traditional scholarship has replied by stating that speaking about the sovereignty of God in these terms was nothing more than speaking metaphorically about the agency of God. However, we have seen above that such a solution makes sense only on the basis of some modern and western ontological presuppositions that might not have applied to other cultures and to other times. In fact, there are plenty of indications showing that ancient people might have considered the abstract *basileia* as well as *malkut* in terms that were ontologically quite different from what we moderns might expect.

Elsewhere, I have shown that, for instance, documentary papyri bear witness to a situation in which *basileia* (understood as sovereignty) acts on its own most of the time in contexts in which it is a question of the welfare of subject populations, in particular in times of crisis.[42] Likewise, several of the Synoptic references to the *basileia* focus on its activity in bringing relief to situations of poverty (Matt 5:3 // Luke 6:20), illness (Luke 10:9), hunger (Matt 8:11 // Luke 13:28–29), or the already mentioned demonic possession. Such a configuration is a reflection of ancient models of political theology, common to the ancient Near East and the Hellenistic kingdoms, in which sovereigns were legitimized because they were entrusted with protecting their subjects from enemies, famines, and ultimately any other sort of crisis. In the troubled centuries stretching from the fifth BCE to the definitive Roman conquest of the eastern Mediterranean, one

---

40. "The time is fulfilled and the kingdom of God has come near [ἤγγικεν]"; the ambiguous verb ἤγγικεν has been the subject of much discussion in the debate on the temporality of the *basileia*, for which see the previous section of this article and the analysis in Meier, *Marginal Jew*, 430–35, who translates as "has drawn near."

41. "But if it is by the finger ["spirit" in Matthew] of God that I cast out the demons, then the kingdom of God has come to you."

42. See, for instance, Bazzana, *Kingdom of Bureaucracy*, 208–10, for the case of coming or reaching of the *basileia* in the above-mentioned Matt 12:28 // Luke 11:20.

can observe a trajectory in which traditional monarchs are progressively weakened and their position in the theological political scheme is slowly occupied by native elites. Thanks to the papyrological record, this can be seen in Egypt quite distinctly in a progression through the Persian and Greek conquests. Traditionally, Egyptians associated pharaonic sovereignty with the ideal *ma'at*. During the Hellenistic period, one can witness a process through which *ma'at* (like *basileia*) is progressively personified and detached from the figures of Ptolemaic monarchs who have replaced the native pharaohs. The resulting autonomous *basileia* can be deployed by native elites—mostly the priesthood in Egypt—to advocate, in political-theological terms, for themselves the right to confer legitimacy on kings or queens.[43] In all likelihood, a similar transformation might have taken place in the land of Israel as well at the turn of the eras when the Herodian dynasty offered a particularly weak model of native Jewish kingship. In this perspective, it is not surprising to observe that the occurrences of an autonomous *basileia* of God are more frequent in documents, such as the Synoptic Gospels, which depend on traditions formed in that time period and under the impulse of circles of subelite intellectuals.[44]

Interestingly, the Songs are, as noted above, one of the few documents of the Second Temple period that shares with the Synoptics a comparable use of the abstract, divine *malkut*. In the case of the Songs as well, the *Sitz im Leben* of the composition can be located within circles of elites or subelites, in this case of a markedly priestly character.[45] Consistently with a pattern that defines the literary products of priestly as well as secular bureaucratic elites, also the Songs have a fondness for imagining the divine world in terms of hierarchical and orderly organization. Even a cursory reading of the Songs reveals plenty of interlocking patterns, beginning with the very headings of each hymn that prescribes its chronological and liturgical rhythm of use. But the passion for hierarchic organization reaches a climax in hymns 6 and 8 (which bookend the crucial hymn 7). In hymn

---

43. For a good analysis of this historical trajectory, see Janet H. Johnson, "The Demotic Chronicle as a Statement of a Theory of Kingship," *JSSEA* 13 (1983): 61–72.

44. For the last point, see Bazzana, *Kingdom of Bureaucracy*, passim; and Sarah E. Rollens, *Framing Social Criticism in the Jesus Movement: The Ideological Project in the Sayings Gospel Q*, WUNT 2/374 (Tübingen: Mohr Siebeck, 2014).

45. This point holds true whether one considers the Songs a product of the priestly group connected to Qumran or, as it seems more likely, one thinks that the hymns originated elsewhere and became very popular among the Qumranites later on.

6, seven orders of "chief princes" (נשיאי רוש) are described as offering in succession seven times seven praises each to God. In an almost mirror-like fashion, in hymn 8 the same pattern of seven is repeated for the seven orders of "deputy princes" (נשיאי משני).

In keeping with the function performed by earthly bureaucracies, the complex articulation of this heavenly hierarchy has also an important role to play in mediating divine power to the human realm. Newman has highlighted this aspect of the Songs' ideological structure quite well in her study of the ways in which the hymns can be read as a conduit of revelation. For instance, in hymn 8.9–10, the sevenfold praise to God is introduced as the "offering of tongues" (תרומת לשוניהם) of the angelic princes. In the immediately following lines, such an offering is associated with "seven mysteries of knowledge in the wondrous mystery of the seven territories of the holiest holiness." Newman insightfully suggests that these "mysteries of knowledge" (רזי דעת), albeit never explicitly illustrated in hymn 8, are likely to be "connected closely with the revelatory description of the purposeful divine will" in hymn 7.[46] Thus, the angels constitute a sort of chain of communication that delivers the divine mystery to humans. Appropriately, Newman notes an additional connection with the first hymns, in which humans are still in focus. In the first section of the Songs, a great emphasis is put on the role of priests in mediating knowledge and teaching (1.17–18): "[…] knowledge among the priests of the inner sanctum. And from their mouths teachings (concerning) all holy things (together) with the precepts […]."

As noted above, it is clear that the Synoptic portrayal of the dynamics encountered in God's *basileia*, while similar to the ones attributed to the *malkut* in the Songs, is not perfectly identical. For one thing, the Synoptic materials do not present the same priestly characterization. This is a difference that is understandable when one considers that the language of *basileia* in the Jesus movement was probably developed within groups of royal administrators, not in priestly circles. That being said, the functioning of the discourse of *basileia*/*malkut* in these texts is interestingly analogous. Like their angelic and priestly counterparts in the Songs, the disciples in the Synoptics have an important role in mediating revelation and thus power from the divine kingdom to humans. The most telling example is obviously the much-discussed

---

46. Newman, "Priestly Prophets at Qumran," 49.

saying that Mark places between the narration of the parable of the sower and its allegorical explanation in 4:11: "To you has been given the mystery of the kingdom of God, but for those outside, everything comes in parables."[47] The Greek μυστήριον in Mark is clearly connected to the occurrences of the Hebrew רז that one encounters in several other Qumran documents and, as just seen above, in the Songs in particular.[48] A similar pattern seems to hold true for the mediating function of the disciples (in Mark, literally "those around Jesus" over against "those outside") in comparison to the one played by priestly angels and human priests in the Songs. Other Synoptic materials point in the same direction. For instance, the promise, which possibly stood at the end of the Sayings Gospel Q, to the disciples that they are going to be installed as figures of authority over the tribes of Israel in the kingdom (Matt 19:28 // Luke 22:28–30).[49]

Finally, an important formal feature of the Songs has also significant theological political implications. As noted again by Newman, the language employed in the hymns can be compared to a form of "disciplined glossolalia."[50] Indeed, the content of the praise spoken by the angels is almost never put on the page throughout the entire thirteen hymns. On the contrary, what one reads (and was probably recited by the ancient users of the Songs) is a human description of the angelic praise. This feature, together with the peculiar style of the hymns, confers on the entire composition a remarkable air of indirectness and obscurity. In part, this is comparable—following Newman's suggestion—to the function of glos-

---

47. The parallels in Matt 13:11 // Luke 8:10 have the plural "mysteries" instead of the singular as in Mark.

48. See the good discussions in Adela Yarbro Collins, *Mark: A Commentary* (Minneapolis: Fortress, 2007), 248–49; and Joel Marcus, "Mark 4:10–12 and Markan Epistemology," *JBL* 103 (1984): 557–74.

49. For a more detailed reading of this passage, see Giovanni B. Bazzana, "Q 22:28–30: Judgment or Governance in the Sayings Gospel Q?," in *Q in Context I: The Separation between the Just and the Unjust in Early Judaism and in the Sayings Source*, ed. Markus Tiwald, BBB 172 (Göttingen: Vandenhoeck & Ruprecht, 2015), 169–83.

50. Newman, "Priestly Prophets at Qumran," 49. The inspiration for this might come to Newman from the identification of the glossolalia of 1 Cor 12–14 with angelic tongues, for which see John C. Poirer, *The Tongues of Angels: The Concept of Angelic Languages in Classical Jewish and Christian Texts*, WUNT 2/287 (Tübingen: Mohr Siebeck, 2010).

solalia also in other religious contexts: obscure and unintelligible speech is authorized as holy and divine.[51]

In a recent contribution, Eric Reymond has pointed out that the very linguistic obscurity of the Songs serves the purpose of highlighting the absolute transcendence of God's power. Humans can speak of or even praise God only indirectly, because he is ultimately above them and their linguistic capability.[52] However, Reymond's observation tells only part of this important story. While God is indeed above all praise and glorification on the part of humans and (one can safely say) angels, it seems that in fact God needs human and angelic glorification in order to constitute (one could say, in political-theological terms, legitimize) his glory. It is a circular pattern to which Schwemer had already drawn attention in her seminal exploration of the Songs. For instance, at the very beginning of hymn 7.2, one encounters the following exhortation: "Let the Holy Ones of the godlike beings sanctify[53] the king of glory who sanctifies by his holiness all his Holy Ones."

This circular model of political theology is quite different from the autocratic one that has been the object of the classic debate between Carl Schmitt and Erik Peterson. In more recent times, Giorgio Agamben has brought attention to this alternative scheme, which he designates as "economic" political theology.[54] According to Agamben, the circular model is suitable for preserving God's transcendence (by depicting him as an idle sovereign, not embroiled in earthly affairs) and, at the same time, God's authority (by building it through the glorification of beings, angels and

---

51. See, for instance, Kristina Wirtz, "'Where Obscurity Is a Virtue': The Mystique of Unintelligibility in Santería Ritual," *Language & Communication* 25 (2005): 351–75.

52. Eric D. Reymond, "Poetry of the Heavenly Other: Angelic Praise in the *Songs of the Sabbath Sacrifice*," in *The "Other" in Second Temple Judaism: Essays in Honor of John J. Collins*, ed. Daniel C. Harlow et al. (Grand Rapids: Eerdmans, 2011), 368–80. Reymond analyzes 6.61, which he translates as "blessed be the Lord, king of all, who is above all blessing and praise."

53. The manuscript 4Q403 has here יקדילו, which is generally taken as a scribal mistake. Against Schwemer (who corrects the verb as יקדישו, as done here), Charlesworth and Newsom (*Angelic Liturgy*, 50), following a suggestion of Puech, correct as יגדילו ("magnify"). But this is certainly a *lectio facilior* as it eliminates the theological problem of having angels who are exhorted to make God "holy."

54. Giorgio Agamben, *Il regno e le Gloria: Per una genealogia teologica dell'economia e del governo* (Turin: Bollati Boringhieri, 2009).

special humans, who are ultimately dependent on God). It goes without saying that such a model is also quite fitting for advancing the ideological and sociopolitical interests of subelites acting within or in competition with monarchic regimes. In this perspective, it cannot be surprising that such a model can be traced also in the background of the Songs as well as the Synoptic Gospels, since these materials are the literary products of priestly and administrative subelites.

5. Conclusion

The present essay analyzed an example of the potential contribution that the study of the Dead Sea scrolls can offer to New Testament research. The Songs of the Sabbath Sacrifice are an especially important document, because they are one of the few Jewish texts of the Second Temple period that contain a significant number of references to God's kingdom (*malkut*). As such, they lend themselves quite well to a comparison with the Synoptic Gospels and the concept of God's *basileia*. The analysis of the Songs reveals that their understanding of divine *malkut* is quite similar to the one encountered in the Synoptics, in its apparent temporal and spatial contradiction. Such a contradiction can only be resolved by accepting that the Songs and the Synoptics worked with regimes of temporality and ontology that were markedly different from those hegemonic in western modernity. Once they are looked at against such a different background, both the Songs and the Synoptics formulate their imagination of a divine kingdom in a way that is consistent with the ideological and sociopolitical situation of priestly and administrative subelites at a time of crisis for native autonomies facing imperial expansion.

Bibliography

Abusch, Ra'anan. "Sevenfold Hymns in the *Songs of the Sabbath Sacrifice* and the Hekhalot Literature: Formalism, Hierarchy, and the Limits of Human Participation." Pages 220–47 in *The Dead Sea Scrolls as Background to Postbiblical Judaism and Early Christianity*. Edited by James R. Davila. STDJ 46. Leiden: Brill, 2003.
Agamben, Giorgio. *Il regno e le Gloria: Per una genealogia teologica dell'economia e del governo*. Turin: Bollati Boringhieri, 2009.
Alberti, Benjamin. "Archaeologies of Ontology." *Annual Review of Anthropology* 45 (2016): 163–79.

Angel, Joseph. *Otherworldly and Eschatological Priesthood in the Dead Sea Scrolls.* STDJ 86. Leiden: Brill, 2010.

Bazzana, Giovanni B. *Kingdom of Bureaucracy: The Political Theology of Village Scribes in the Sayings Gospel Q.* BETL 274. Leuven: Peeters, 2015.

———. "Q 22:28–30: Judgment or Governance in the Sayings Gospel Q?" Pages 169–83 in *Q in Context I: The Separation between the Just and the Unjust in Early Judaism and in the Sayings Source.* BBB 172. Edited by Markus Tiwald. Göttingen: Vandenhoeck & Ruprecht, 2015.

Charlesworth, James H., and Carol A. Newsom, eds. *Angelic Liturgy: Songs of the Sabbath Sacrifice.* Vol. 4B of *The Dead Sea Scrolls: Hebrew, Aramaic, and Greek Texts with English Translations.* Tübingen: Mohr Siebeck, 1999.

Collins, John J. "The Kingdom of God in the Apocrypha and Pseudepigrapha." Pages 99–114 in *Seers, Sibyls, and Sages in Hellenistic-Roman Judaism.* Edited by John J. Collins. Leiden: Brill, 1997.

Crossan, John D. *The Historical Jesus: The Life of a Mediterranean Jewish Peasant.* San Francisco: Harper, 1991.

Dalman, Gustaf. *Die Worte Jesu, mit Berücksichtigung des nachkanonischen jüdischen Schrifttums und der aramäischen Sprache.* 2nd ed. Leipzig: Henrichs, 1930.

Ego, Beate. "Der Gottesdienst der Engel—Von den biblischen Psalmen zur jüdischen Mystik: Traditionskritische Überlegungen zu den Sabbatopferliedern von Qumran." *TLZ* 140 (2015): 886–901.

Fletcher-Louis, Crispin H. T. "Heavenly Ascent or Incarnational Presence? A Revisionist Reading of the *Songs of the Sabbath Sacrifice.*" Pages 367–99 in *Society of Biblical Literature 1998 Seminar Papers.* SBLSP 37. Atlanta: Society of Biblical Literature, 1998.

Gäckle, Volker. *Das Reich Gottes im Neuen Testament: Auslegungen—Anfragen—Alternativen.* BThS 176. Göttingen: Vandenhoeck & Ruprecht, 2018.

Hamidović, David. "La contribution des *Cantiques de l'holocauste du Sabbat* à l'étude de la pensée mystique juive au tournant de l'ère chrétienne." Pages 303–19 in *La mystique théorétique et théurgique dans l'antiquité gréco-romaine.* Edited by Simon Claude Mimouni and Madeline Scopello. Brepols: Turnhout, 2016.

Harrisville, Roy A. "In Search of the Meaning of the 'Reign of God.'" *Int* 47 (1993): 140–51.

Holmén, Tom, and Stanley E. Porter, eds. *Handbook for the Study of the Historical Jesus*. 4 vols. Leiden: Brill, 2011.

Johnson, Janet H. "The Demotic Chronicle as a Statement of a Theory of Kingship." *JSSEA* 13 (1983): 61–72.

Kloppenborg, John S. "As One Unknown, without a Name? Co-opting the Historical Jesus." Pages 1–23 in *Apocalypticism, Anti-Semitism, and the Historical Jesus: Subtexts in Criticism*. JSNTSup 275. Edited by John S. Kloppenborg and John W. Marshall. London: T&T Clark International, 2005.

Kohn, Eduardo. *How Forests Think: Toward an Anthropology beyond the Human*. Berkeley: University of California Press, 2013.

Kosmin, Paul J. *The Land of the Elephant Kings: Space, Territory, and Ideology in the Seleucid Empire*. Cambridge: Harvard University Press, 2014.

Marcus, Joel. "Entering into the Kingly Power of God." *JBL* 107 (1988): 663–75.

———. "Mark 4:10–12 and Markan Epistemology." *JBL* 103 (1984): 557–74.

Meier, John P. *A Marginal Jew: Rethinking the Historical Jesus*. New York: Doubleday, 1994.

Newman, Judith H. "Priestly Prophets at Qumran: Summoning Sinai through the Songs of the Sabbath Sacrifice." Pages 29–72 in *The Significance of Sinai: Traditions about Sinai and Divine Revelation in Judaism and Christianity*. Edited by George J. Brooke, Hindy Najman, and Loren T. Stuckenbruck. Leiden: Brill, 2008.

Newsom, Carol A. "The Sage in the Literature of Qumran: The Function of the *Maskil*." Pages 373–82 in *The Sage in Israel and the Ancient Near East*. Edited by John G. Gammie and Leo G. Perdue. Winona Lake, IN: Eisenbrauns, 1990.

———. "'Sectually Explicit' Literature from Qumran." Pages 167–87 in *The Hebrew Bible and Its Interpreters*. Edited by William H. Propp, Baruch Halpern, and David Noel Freedman. Winona Lake, IN: Eisenbrauns, 1990.

———. *Songs of the Sabbath Sacrifice: A Critical Edition*. HSS 27. Atlanta: Scholars Press, 1985.

Poirer, John C. *The Tongues of Angels: The Concept of Angelic Languages in Classical Jewish and Christian Texts*. WUNT 2/287. Tübingen: Mohr Siebeck, 2010.

Reymond, Eric D. "Poetry of the Heavenly Other: Angelic Praise in the *Songs of the Sabbath Sacrifice*." Pages 368–80 in *The "Other" in Second*

Temple Judaism: Essays in Honor of John J. Collins. Edited by Daniel C. Harlow, Karina Martin Hogan, Matthew Goff, and Joel S. Kaminsky. Grand Rapids: Eerdmans, 2011.

Rollens, Sarah E. *Framing Social Criticism in the Jesus Movement: The Ideological Project in the Sayings Gospel Q*. WUNT 2/374. Tübingen: Mohr Siebeck, 2014.

Schenke, Ludger. "Die Botschaft vom kommenden 'Reich Gottes.'" Pages 106–47 in *Jesus von Nazaret—Spuren und Konturen*. Stuttgart: Kohlhammer, 2004.

Schwemer, Anna Maria. "Gott als König und seine Königsherrschaft in den Sabbatliedern aus Qumran." Pages 46–118 in *Königsherrschaft Gottes und himmlischer Kult im Judentum, Urchristentum, und in der hellenistischen Welt*. Edited by Martin Hengel and Anna Maria Schwemer. WUNT 55. Tübingen: Mohr Siebeck, 1991.

Segal, Michael. "Who Is the 'Son of God' in 4Q246? An Overlooked Example of Biblical Interpretation." *DSD* 21 (2014): 289–312.

Stewart, Charles. *Dreaming and Historical Consciousness in Island Greece*. Cambridge: Harvard University Press, 2012.

———. "Historicity and Anthropology." *Annual Review of Anthropology* 45 (2016): 79–94.

Ulfgard, Håkan. "The Songs of the Sabbath Sacrifice and the Heavenly Scene of the Book of Revelation." Pages 251–66 in *Northern Lights on the Dead Sea Scrolls*. Edited by Anders Klostergaard Petersen et al. STDJ 80. Leiden: Brill, 2009.

Welker, Michael, and Francis Schüssler Fiorenza, eds. *Politische Theologie: Neuere Geschichte und Potenziale*. Neukirchen: Neukirchener Verlag, 2011.

Wirtz, Kristina. "'Where Obscurity Is a Virtue': The Mystique of Unintelligibility in Santería Ritual." *Language & Communication* 25 (2005): 351–75.

Yarbro Collins, Adela. *Mark: A Commentary*. Minneapolis: Fortress, 2007.

Aramaica Qumranica Apocalyptica and the Book of Revelation

Garrick V. Allen

It seems obvious that the book of Revelation and the Aramaic texts from Qumran make for a mutually illuminating set of *comparanda*. Revelation's close connections to Aramaic apocalyptic traditions known before the discovery of the scrolls suggest as much, especially works like Dan 2–7.[1] Revelation also shares a number of conceptual resources with works discovered among the Scrolls, including a focus on eschatology, heavenly journeys, allusions to the patriarchs, a New Jerusalem, and vision reports. Moreover, Revelation's mode of composition and continual string of allusions to Jewish scripture locates it securely within the Jewish textual culture of the late Second Temple period.[2] The author of the book of Revelation shares many of the compositional habits of the *yaḥad* and their literature, as well as an apocalyptic worldview. Despite these similarities, most critical attention toward the relationship between the New Testament and the

---

1. See especially the vision of the "one like a son of man" (Rev 1:7, 13–20), elements of the throne room scene (Rev 4–5), the beast vision (Rev 13), and the interpretation of the beast with seven heads and the whore (Rev 17:7–18). Cf. also Gregory K. Beale, *The Use of Daniel in Jewish Apocalyptic Literature and in the Revelation of St. John* (Lanham: University of America Press, 1984), which instigated the cottage industry of "Old Testament in the New Testament" studies. Beale argues that the use of Daniel in Revelation is the structuring principle for interpreting Revelation. This now seems a simplistic conclusion in light of the complexities of John's scriptural reuse, but he is correct to note that Danielic traditions are central to Revelation's linguistic substance.

2. I have advanced this argument elsewhere in detail: Garrick V. Allen, *The Book of Revelation and Early Jewish Textual Culture* (Cambridge: Cambridge University Press, 2017), but without engaging the Aramaic apocalyptic texts from Qumran in any detail.

Scrolls has focused on the *yaḥad's* relationship to the earliest Jesus movement, shared thematic parallels with the gospels, Johannine literature, and Paul's letters, and the ways that both the New Testament and the Scrolls are witnesses to early interpretations of Jewish scripture.[3] Surprisingly, the relationship between Revelation and the Qumran Aramaic apocalyptica remains to be adequately interrogated.[4]

This sustained comparison between the Aramaic apocalyptic texts and the New Testament Apocalypse brings Revelation into the broader discourse on apocalyptic and apocalypses in early Judaism, a discourse to which it is often only an oblique partner. Because of ongoing discussion regarding Revelation's place within the genre apocalypse and the largely inward facing interrogation of the Aramaic texts in Qumran studies,[5] its relationship to the Aramaic apocalyptica has been overlooked. Despite the literary and thematic differences between these works, they share a view about the way the cosmos functions and the place of God's people within this world, even if the morphologies of this worldview are multiform.

---

3. E.g., James H. Charlesworth, ed., *John and Qumran* (London: Geoffrey Chapman, 1972); Mary L. Coloe and Tom Thatcher, eds., *John, Qumran, and the Dead Sea Scrolls: Sixty Years of Discovery and Debate*, EJL 32 (Atlanta: Society of Biblical Literature, 2011); Jean-Sébastien Rey, ed., *The Dead Sea Scrolls and Pauline Literature*, STDJ 102 (Leiden: Brill, 2014); Serge Ruzer, *Mapping the New Testament: Early Christian Writings as a Witness to Jewish Biblical Exegesis* (Leiden: Brill, 2007).

4. On the question of whether the Qumran Aramaic material represents a corpus, see the survey of opinions in Andrew B. Perrin, *The Dynamics of Dream-Vision Revelation in the Aramaic Dead Sea Scrolls*, JAJSup 19 (Göttingen: Vandenhoeck & Ruprecht, 2015), 23–38, and his "prospectus" of Aramaic dream-vision texts on pp. 41–89; and Florentino García Martínez, "Aramaica qumranica apocalyptica?," in *Aramaica Qumranica: Proceedings of the Conference on the Aramaic Texts from Qumran in Aix-en-Provence 30 June–2 July 2008*, ed. Katell Berthelot and Daniel Stökl Ben Ezra, STDJ 94 (Leiden: Brill, 2010), 435–48. I adopt the term *apocalyptica* to describe these texts because, while most of these traditions are not apocalypses in an obvious generic sense, they reflect the broader matrix of early Jewish apocalypticism and share certain features with the genre apocalypse.

5. Take, for example, the questions posed by the editors of the *Aramaica Qumranica* volume: (1) What is the relationship of the Aramaic texts to other Aramaic texts outside Qumran and the Hebrew traditions within the Scrolls? (2) What are the origins of these traditions? (3) What was their function within the Qumran library? See Katell Berthelot, "Response," in Berthelot and Stökl Ben Ezra, *Aramaica Qumranica*, 448–49. Appropriate as these questions are, this approach, paradigmatic of most forms of enquiry, is entirely focused on the Aramaic traditions' relationship to other Aramaic and Hebrew literature, not the New Testament or broader literary or cultural currents.

One of the reasons that this comparison has not yet been undertaken is an overemphasis on the genre apocalypse as the key point of interest between these traditions. Indeed, the Qumran Aramaic traditions do shed light on the genre and Revelation's tenuous place within this network of ancient Jewish and Christian works, but their relationship need not center on this question. For example, in his seminal 1999 article "Qumran and the Book of Revelation," David Aune mentions a number of Aramaic apocalyptica in relationship to Revelation (Aramaic Levi Document [4Q213-214], 4Q246, 4Q552-553, New Jerusalem, 4QVisions of Amram [4Q543-548]), but he is primarily interested in whether or not the Qumran texts can be classified as apocalypses.[6] However, as is well-known, texts that reflect apocalyptic worldviews do not always take the form of formal apocalypses in terms of genre, and the interplay between Revelation and these traditions speaks to other areas of critical concern beyond the question of genre.[7]

The lack of attention to Aramaic texts specifically is especially surprising in light of the quantity of studies that examined the connections between Revelation and Qumran text more broadly. Explorations of Revelation's relationship to sectarian rules, liturgical texts, rewritten scriptural texts, and exegetical traditions at Qumran have been undertaken, in addition to analysis of shared thematic correspondences on temple imagery and priesthood and examinations of Revelation's relationship to 1 Enoch and other early Jewish apocalypses preserved in secondary or tertiary languages.[8] Despite this breadth of research, Aramaic apocalyptica have not

---

6. Repr. as David Aune, "Qumran and the Book of Revelation," in *Apocalypticism, Prophecy, and Magic in Early Christianity* (Tübingen: Mohr Siebeck, 2006), 79-98, see esp., 80-85. Aune goes on to explore the relationship between a number of other Qumran texts and New Jerusalem (focusing largely on New Jerusalem, ritual purity [in conversation with 11QTemple], and eschatological war, engaging mainly with 1QM).

7. Cf. Lorenzo DiTommaso, "Apocalypticism and the Aramaic Texts from Qumran," in Berthelot and Stökl Ben Ezra, *Aramaica Qumranica*, 451-75; and Devorah Dimant, "Apocalyptic Texts at Qumran," in *The Community of the Renewed Covenant: The Notre Dame Symposium on the Dead Sea Scrolls*, ed. Eugene Ulrich and James C. VanderKam (Notre Dame: Notre Dame University Press, 1994), 175-91: "even if not every Aramaic text constitutes a real apocalypse, all are relevant to the discussion of apocalyptic literature" (180).

8. E.g., Adela Yarbro Collins, "The Book of Revelation," in *The Origins of Apocalypticism in Judaism and Christianity*, vol. 1 of *The Encyclopedia of Apocalypticism*, ed. John J. Collins (New York: Continuum, 1998), 392-93; Richard Bauckham, "The

yet been explored in an equally rigorous way. The analysis that follows does not posit direct literary relationships between Revelation and these traditions but seeks to understand how these traditions are mutually illuminating and how they enhance understanding of the way these traditions witness to the larger matrix of late Second Temple apocalypticism. These comparisons enlighten issues that remain at the center of critical discourse on Revelation in particular, including the flexibility of scriptural interpretation in apocalyptic texts, the broad network of literary references embedded in Revelation, and its genre. As test cases, I examine the Visions of Amram (4Q543-548) and the Son of God text (4Q246).

1. Visions of Amram (4Q543-548?)

Visions of Amram, preserved in at least five manuscript copies, is a literary work with a complex generic makeup that purports to be a written report of a visionary experience.[9] It takes the form of a deathbed testament (cf. 1. En. 83.1-2; 4QLevi[a] ar 1 I, 1-4; T. Reu. 1.1-3; T. Sim. 1.1-2; etc.), following

---

Apocalypse as a Christian War Scroll," in *The Climax of Prophecy: Studies on the Book of Revelation* (Edinburgh: T&T Clark, 1993), 210-37; James R. Davila, *Liturgical Works*, ECDSS (Grand Rapids: Eerdmans, 2000), 83-167, in his commentary on the Songs of Sabbath Sacrifice; Håkan Ulfgard, "The Songs of Sabbath Sacrifice and the Heavenly Scene of the Book of Revelation," in *Northern Lights on the Dead Sea Scrolls*, ed. Anders Klostergaard Petersen et al., STDJ 80 (Leiden: Brill, 2009), 251-66; Marco Jauhiainen, "Revelation and Rewritten Prophecies," in *Rewritten Bible Reconsidered*, ed. Antti Laato and J. van Ruiten (Winona Lake, IN: Eisenbrauns, 2008), 177-97; George J. Brooke, *The Dead Sea Scrolls and the New Testament* (Minneapolis: Fortress, 2005), 86-89 (on 4Q385 and Rev 4); Benjamin Wold, "Revelation's Plague Septets: New Exodus and Exile," in *Echoes from the Caves: Qumran and the New Testament*, ed. Florentino García Martínez, STDJ 85 (Leiden: Brill, 2009), 279-97; Torleif Elgvin, "Priests on Earth as in Heaven: Jewish Light on the Book of Revelation," in García Martínez, *Echoes from the Caves*, 257-78; and David Aune, "The Apocalypse of John and Palestinian Jewish Apocalyptic," *Neot* 40 (2006): 1-33.

9. Cf. Józef T. Milik, "4Q Visions de 'Amram et une citation d'Origen," *RB* 79 (1972): 77-97; Milik, "Milkî-sedeq et Milkî-reša' dans les anciens écrits juifs et chrétiens," *JJS* 23 (1972): 95-144; Émile Puech, *Qumrân Grotte 4.XXII: Textes araméens, première partie, 4Q529-549*, DJD 31 (Oxford: Clarendon, 2001), 283-405; and Andrew Perrin, "Another Look at Dualism in 4QVisions of Amram," *Hen* 36 (2014): 106-17. I follow the fragment and line citations in Florentino García Martínez and Eibert J. C. Tigchelaar, eds., *The Dead Sea Scrolls Study Edition* (Leiden: Brill, 1999), which differs in some cases from Puech's DJD edition.

the marriage of Amram's daughter Miriam and brother Uzziel. Amram, the grandson of Levi (Exod 6:20; Num 26:59), reports to his children information about his past as part of a dualistic dream-vision.[10] The testament has significance for his immediate heirs and their offspring. Amram relays that he was separated from his family in Egypt for forty-one years (4Q544 1 3-8; cf. Jub. 46-47) when the border between Egypt and Canaan was closed during a war when Amram was building the tombs of his fathers in Canaan.[11] Although separated from his family, he refused to take another wife (4Q544 1 8-9) and had a vision in a dream (בחזוי חזוה די חלמא; 4Q544 1 10; cf. 4Q543 4, 6; 4Q544 1 10-14; 4Q545 1 II; 4Q546 2). The core of the vision, as far as it can be reconstructed, is a debate between two angelic figures arguing over Amram. One figure has a "dreadful appearance like pestilence" (חזוה דחיל מוותן), with clothing "colored and obscured by darkness" (ומלבושה צבענין וחשיך חשוך); cf. T. Abr. 17.12-16 and Zech 3:1-5).[12] The other is described as smiling (חעכין), but the extant description of this Watcher is more fragmentary. The characterization of the angels as either light or dark corresponds to the text's view of humanity, who are either "sons of light/truth" or "sons of darkness/lie" (4Q548 1 II-2, 16; cf. 1QM I, 1; 4Q177 12-13 I; 4Q280), giving the vision an eschatological dimension, especially if one considers 4Q548 to be a witness to the Visions of Amram.

More immediately, Amram's choice between the angels represents the choice between a legitimate and a corrupt priesthood, and his choice of the more appealing angel (and other hints at the importance of endogamy) supports the legitimacy of his own priestly line.[13] The two angels quarrel

---

10. Cf. Jörg Frey, "On the Origins of the Genre of the 'Literary Testament': Farewell Discourses in the Qumran Library and Their Relevance for the History of the Genre," in Berthelot and Stökl Ben Ezra, *Aramaica Qumranica*, 345-70.

11. On this portion of the text, see Liora Goldman, "The Burial of the Fathers in the *Visions of Amram* from Qumran," in *Rewriting and Interpreting the Hebrew Bible: The Biblical Patriarchs in the Light of the Dead Sea Scrolls*, ed. Devorah Dimant and Reinhard G. Kratz, BZAW 439 (Berlin: de Gruyter, 2013), 231-49.

12. Cf. Klaus Berger, "Der Streit des guten und des bösen Engels um die Seele: Beobachtungen zu 4Q Amr^b und Judas 9," *JSJ* 4 (1973): 1-18; translations from García Martínez and Tigchelaar, *The Dead Sea Scrolls Study Edition*.

13. E.g., Miriam's marriage to her uncle and Amram's refusal to take another wife during his separation from Jochebed. Cf. Aramaic Levi Document (4Q213a 3-4); Tob 3:15; 1 En. 106.13; perhaps also Testament of Qahat (4Q542 3 II, 12). See discussion in Devorah Dimant, "Tobit and Qumran Aramaic Texts," in *Is There a Text in this Cave?*, ed. Ariel Feldman, Charlotte Hempel, and Maria Cioată, STDJ 119 (Leiden:

over the seer. Amram asks them, "who are you that you have received control and rule over me?" The angels reply that they rule over all the sons of Adam and that Amram can choose to whose rule he must submit (4Q544 1 10; cf. the Seventy Shepherds of 1 En. 89.59).[14] After apparently choosing the less ominous figure, likely Melchizedek, the smiling angel turns interpreter, providing more information on his imposing counterpart: he is Malki-resha (מלכי רשע, 4Q544 2 3; cf. 4Q280 2) who "rules over all darkness" (4Q544 2 5), while the other rules "over all that is bright" (4Q544 2 6; 3 1).[15]

The narrative flow of the work is not entirely clear and the vision only partially preserved, but it appears that Amram interprets the significance of his vision for his children. Amram tells one of his children, perhaps Moses, that "you will be God, and angel of God you will be called" (אל תהוה ומלאך אל תתקרה, 4Q543 3 1; cf. 2 Sam 19:27 where the king is described as "like the angel of God") and a judge (דין; 4Q543 3 2; cf. 4Q545 3 3; Exod 2:14; 18:13). Another of his children, perhaps Aaron, is referred to as one chosen as "eternal priest" (לכהן עלמין; יתבחר 4Q545 3 6), connecting the text to Melchizedek traditions (e.g., Gen 14:19 [כהן לאל עליון]; Ps 110:3 [אתה כהן לעולם]; Heb 5:6; 6:20; 11Q13). The episode concludes with Amram noting his response to the vision: "and I awoke from the sleep of my eyes and I wrote the vision" (4Q547 9 8).

As a pre-Mosaic patriarchal seer who views a symbolic angelic dispute, the overlap between the Visions of Amram and Revelation is initially rather minimal. Revelation's pseudepigraphy—if it is indeed pseudepigraphic—does not appeal to a figure of the ancient past, and, although its narrative engages the cosmological forces of good and evil, the balance of power between good and evil is uneven.[16] Revelation is visionary

---

Brill, 2017), 391–99. Cf. Blake Alan Jurgens, "Reassessing the Dream-Vision of the *Vision of Amram* (4Q543–547)," *JSP* 24 (2014): 3–42; and Goldman, "Burial of the Fathers," 239–41.

14. Perrin, "Another Look at Dualism," 110–11, argues that reconstruction 4Q544 1 12 has led to an over-emphasis on what he calls "free choice" dualism. But see Liora Goldman, "Dualism in the *Visions of Amram*," *RevQ* 24 (2010): 421–32, who points to Deuteronomistic models of choice as parallels (e.g., Deut 30:15, 19).

15. Cf. Florentino García Martínez, "4Q'Amram b i 14: ¿Melki-resha' o Melisedeq?," *RevQ* 12 (1985): 111–14.

16. Jörg Frey, "Das Corpus Johanneum und die Apokalypse des Johannes: Die Johanneslegende, die Probleme der johanneischen Verfasserschaft und die Frage der Pseudonymität der Apokalypse," in *Poetik und Intertextualität der Johannesapokalypse*,

in orientation like the Visions of Amram but contains no dream-visions and lacks the testamentary aspect central to the Visions of Amram's narrative framework. John's visions occur "in the spirit on the Lord's day" (Rev 1:10), and its narrative frame is prophetic and epistolary, containing multiple governing voices. Revelation's visions are also expressly eschatological in that they disclose the present precarious state of the cosmos and foretell in multiple ways the catastrophic events that immediately precede the appearance of the New Jerusalem and the end. In contrast, the Visions of Amram's vision—at least as far as it is extant—emphasizes the legitimacy of Levi's priestly line through the actions of his grandson, even though this too has cosmic consequences.

Despite the lack of direct literary connections and other differences, the Visions of Amram does illuminate several issues pertaining to Revelation. First, the complexities of the Visions of Amram's self-description in its *incipit* enlighten the intricacies of Revelation's own self-presentation and the question of genre. Preserved in two copies, the incipit of the Visions of Amram is "copy of the writing of the words of the vision of Amram, son of Qahat, son of Levi" (פרשגן כתב מלי חזות עמרם בר קהת בר לוי; 4Q543 1a–c 1; 4Q545 1 I, 1). In addition to legitimating Amram's credentials,[17] this construct chain describes the perceived qualities of the literary artefact. (1) This manuscript is a copy (פרשגן), signifying knowledge of its transmission; (2) it is a writing or literary work (כתב) that (3) contains the words or exposition of a vision (מלי חזות) that (4) Amram experienced. The *incipit* reveals a chain of composition, from (pseudepigraphic) visionary experience to interpretation to literary work to copies in circulation. The Visions of Amram retains a high level of self-awareness as a transmitted report of a visionary experience.[18]

---

ed. Stefan Alkier et al., WUNT 346 (Tübingen: Mohr Siebeck, 2015), 71–133, and Lorenzo DiTommaso, "Pseudonymity and the Revelation of John," in *Revealed Wisdom: Studies in Apocalyptic in Honour of Christopher Rowland*, ed. John F. Ashton, AJEC 88 (Leiden: Brill, 2014), 305–15.

17. Cf. Henryk Drawnel, "The Initial Narrative of the *Visions of Amram* and its Literary Characteristics," *RevQ* 24 (2010): 517–54; Andrew B. Perrin, "Capturing the Voices of Pseudepigraphic Personae: On the Form and Function of Incipits in the Aramaic Dead Sea Scrolls," *DSD* 20 (2013): 110.

18. This feature is prevalent in a number of the Aramaic works from Qumran, especially those dealing with pre-Sinaitic patriarchs that are testamentary in nature (at least in some parts of their texts), e.g., Testament of Qahat, Aramaic Levi Document, Genesis Apocryphon, and parts of 1 Enoch. See Devorah Dimant, "Themes

Revelation's *incipit* (Rev 1:1–2) functions similarly, even though we do not see a fully developed view of Revelation as something to be transmitted until 22:18–19.[19] The first three words, "Revelation of Jesus Christ" (Ἀποκάλυψις Ἰησοῦ Χριστοῦ), reveal the primary subject of the material that follows. The work emphasizes consequences of Jesus's ongoing action in the world, unveiling the cosmic realities behind the quotidian political and economic machinations of life in the empire. Following Revelation's *incipit* is a chain of transmission: God shows this revelation to his servants by sending his angel to John, who then witnesses (ἐμαρτύρησεν) to what it is he sees (ὅσα εἶδεν; Rev 1:1–2). Revelation presents itself as a message from God to his people, mediated through angels and a prophet. After experiencing a vision of Jesus walking among seven lampstands (Rev 1:12–16), the seer is commanded by Jesus to "write what you have seen, what is and what will take place after these things" (γράψον οὖν ἃ εἶδες καὶ ἃ εἰσὶν καὶ ἃ μέλλει γενέσθαι μετὰ ταῦτα; 1:19). Unlike the Visions of Amram, Revelation is not an interpretation of the vision but a purported verbatim account of the vision itself. John does not take on the mantle of mantic interpreter but of scribal transcriptionist.

Like the Visions of Amram, Revelation presents itself as a written account of visions, visions that are prophetic in nature (Rev 1:3; 10:11; 22:7, 10, 18–19) and that testify to the plans of God in the world.[20] Revelation is a "testimony of Jesus" (1:2, 9; 12:17; 19:10; 20:4), something to be transmitted and copied.[21] But the way that the Visions of Amram justifies the legitimacy of its visionary content—connecting the seer as a midpoint

---

and Genres in the Aramaic Texts from Qumran," in Berthelot and Stökl Ben Ezra, *Aramaica Qumranica*, 15–43, esp. 36.

19. The consensus view is that the opening words of the Apocalypse functioned as its title antiquity. For a fuller appraisal of the forms of the title appended to Revelation in later tradition, cf. Garrick V. Allen, "Paratexts and the Reception History of the Apocalypse," *JTS* 70 (2019): 600–32.

20. Cf. 4Q547 9 8: "I wrote the vision" (חזוא כתבת).

21. On the potential generic significance of the phrase ἡ μαρτυρίαν Ἰησοῦ for Revelation, see Sarah Underwood Dixon, "'The Testimony of Jesus' in Light of Internal Self-References in the Book of Daniel and *1 Enoch*," in *The Book of Revelation: Currents in British Research on the Apocalypse*, ed. Garrick V. Allen, Ian Paul, and Simon Patrick Woodman, WUNT 2/411 (Tübingen: Mohr Siebeck, 2015), 81–93; and Sean Michael Ryan, "'The Testimony of Jesus' and 'the Testimony of Enoch': An *Emic* Approach to the Genre of the Apocalypse," in Allen, Paul, and Woodman, *Book of Revelation*, 95–113.

between the progenitor of Israel's priesthood (Levi) and the key figures of the exodus generation (Moses, Aaron, Miriam)—appears quaint compared to Revelation's authorization strategy. The message of the Apocalypse is legitimated not by appeal to venerable figures of the past, although they make appearances,[22] but by direct appeal to God and his messiah who are worshiped together by all creation (Rev 1:1; 5:6-14). Cosmic antagonists and heavenly conflict populate both works (e.g., Rev 12:7-9), but the Apocalypse's seer exercises no agency in the conflict.

While both texts make use of the dualism of good and evil and the choices they offer, evil is deceptive in the apocalypse; beasts speak like dragons but look like lambs (Rev 13:11). Evil does not necessarily appear pestilent or dark (although a swarm of militant locusts may qualify as pestilent, Rev 9:7-11). Revelation acknowledges that the boundaries between good and evil are ambiguous and appearances deceiving. Revelation's view of evil and cosmic antagonists subverts the choice apparently offered to the seer in the Visions of Amram. There is no efficacious choice because the outcome of the conflict is already decided.

Even if we follow Andrew Perrin's suggestion that the Visions of Amram does not necessarily offer a sort of "free choice" dualism,[23] the Visions of Amram's presentation of angelic personifications of good and evil vying for control of individual humans differs from Revelation. For Revelation, the forces of evil, real, active, and even attractive as they may be, are entirely subordinate to heavenly actions instigated by God, the lamb, or angels. For example, the sounding of the fifth trumpet (Rev 9:1) precipitates the falling of a star (or angel, 9:11) to earth that is given the keys to the abyss. Out of the open abyss come smoke, fire, and fearsome locusts who are allowed to torture humanity for five months (9:5, 10).

Although formidable and grotesque, the appearance of the locusts and their angelic commander's ability to set them upon the earth is the result of the divinely instigated machinations of the heavenly court. The angel had no authority, he is given the keys by some unacknowledged

---

22. Moses (15:3), David (3:7; 5:5; 22:16), the twelve tribes (7:4-8; 21:12-14), and less reputable figures like Jezebel (2:20), Balaam, and Balak (2:14).

23. Perrin, "Another Look at Dualism." But see 4QInstruction (e.g., 4Q417 2 II // 4Q418 9-11), where the choice between good and evil corresponds to one's righteousness or unrighteousness based on their observations of the world, and Goldman, "Dualism in the *Visions of Amram*." Choice is a particular theme in wisdom and more sapiential forms of the apocalyptic tradition, 4QInstruction being a prime example.

(divine) agent; he does not take them. There is no direct report of the locust's activity. This is due in part to the presentation of this vision as a future event, but it also reflects the author's perspective on evil: it may appear menacing, but it is ultimately powerless. The impotence of evil is also reflected in the repetition of the length of time of their torturing—five months. The bounding of their activity reflects their subordination to the larger plan and activity of God moving toward the New Jerusalem. A hint of this movement is seen at the end of the cycle of the trumpets in 11:19 when the temple of God is opened in heaven and the seer beholds the ark of the covenant. Despite appearances, the conflict between good and evil in Revelation does not take place on a level playing field; the conquering of the lamb through his death (Rev 5:9), paralleled by the repetitious refrain to the seven churches to conquer, has already decided the outcome of this longstanding cosmic conflict.

Both the Visions of Amram and Revelation share a particular set of apocalyptic features: heavenly conflict, angelic interpreters, cosmic dualism, visions that span temporal and cosmological planes, attempts to legitimate revelations. Nonetheless, reading the Visions of Amram and Revelation side by side emphasizes the ways in which Revelation subverts apocalyptic traditions by minimizing the seer's interpretive agency. John presents himself as a mere scribe, copying what he sees, which legitimates further the authority of his message as a divine revelation. The incipit of the Visions of Amram and its self-presentation also clarifies some of Revelation's literary complexity. Both works are presented as one instantiation of a written report of a visionary experience by a prophetic or priestly figure, making for complicated layers of communication and conduits of authority. This blending of visionary, literary, and scribal activity leads to the blurring of generic boundaries and formal variation as part of the essential substance of apocalyptic. Both texts share an apocalyptic worldview in which the division between the earthly and heavenly is porous, a world where angelic beings play pivotal roles in the lives of humans and the fate of the humankind, but the cosmic struggle in Revelation has already been decided irrespective of the seer's actions in response to his vision.

2. 4Q246 (Apocryphon of Daniel ar)

The second text that illuminates Revelation's relationship to Aramaic apocalyptica is 4Q246 (4QApocryphe de Daniel ar), the so-called Son of God text. The manuscript, dated by Émile Puech to the end of the first century BCE, preserves two partially conserved columns of nine lines.[24] The right half of the first column is lost, but the second column is well preserved.[25] From what remains, the text depicts an eschatological vision related to Dan 7. In column I, an unnamed figure falls before a throne and speaks to a king (מל[כא, I, 2) about coming tribulation and bloodshed (I, 4–5), the menacing action of the military forces of Assyria and Egypt (I, 6), and the servitude of some nation or force to a conqueror, perhaps the figure called the Great One (רב[א, I, 9). The incomplete nature of the column leaves much to be desired, but its thrust is clear: an eschatological vision is being narrated to a king, a vision that includes warfare, strife, and a messianic (or pseudo-messianic) figure, not unlike the throne room scene in Dan 7:1–14 (cf. 2:31–45).

Column II continues to describe this figure, calling him "son of God" (ברה די אל) and "son of the Most High" (בר עליון, II, 1). The rule of this figure and his line (the text moves to third person plural in II, 2) leads to oppression and continued strife. But when the people of God arise, the sword will be put away (II, 4). An eternal kingdom of truth and peace will reign, and the peoples of the earth will pay homage to God/his people (II, 7). His/their dominion will be eternal (II, 5, 9).[26]

4Q246 preserves four main sections: (1) a narrative framework, placing the text in the context of a throne room scene (I, 1–3); (2) a note on successive kingdoms, describing the destructive actions of Assyria and Egypt (I, 4–6), probably referring to the Seleucids and Ptolemies; (3) an extended section on (a) final kingdom(s) led by a figure known as "Son of God" and "Son of the Most High" (I, 7–II, 3); and (4) a description of a future eschatological and everlasting kingdom.[27] This narrative pattern is similar to Dan 7. Both texts discuss successive kingdoms that perpetrate evil on the world, the final of which is excessively menacing and destructive (Dan 7:2–8, 16–27). The final king in each text is symbolically described, either

---

24. Émile Puech, "246. 4QApocryphe de Daniel ar," in *Qumrân Grotte 4.XXII*, 166.

25. For competing transcriptions and material analysis, see Edward M. Cook, "4Q246," *BBR* 5 (1995): 43–66; Puech, "4Q246," 167–70; Reinhard G. Kratz, "Son of God and Son of Man: 4Q246 in the Light of the Book of Daniel," in *Son of God: Divine Sonship in Jewish and Christian Antiquity*, ed. Garrick V. Allen et al. (University Park: Penn State University Press, 2019), 9–27; and Joseph A. Fitzmyer, "4Q246: The 'Son of God' Document from Qumran," *Bib* 74 (1993): 155–57.

26. The abruptness of the end of the text suggests that it likely continued on from this point.

27. Cf. Kratz, "Son of God and Son of Man."

as the arrogant horn with human eyes (Dan 7:8) or ironically as "Son of God" and "Son of the Most High" (4Q246 II, 1), although the identification of the "Son of God" as a negative figure in 4Q246 is controversial. The judgment of these figures takes place before thrones (כרסיה/כרסיא), and eternal dominion is handed over to God's representative, be it the "one like a human" (כבר אנש, Dan 7:13) or the "people of God" (עם אל, 4Q246 II, 4).

Much of the discussion of 4Q246 has revolved around the identity of the eschatological figure in column II and his title on line 1 as it relates to New Testament descriptions of Jesus (cf. Luke 1:32–35): is the "Son of God" and "Son of the Most High" a positive figure; an eschatological antagonist, either a heavenly representative of the fourth kingdom or the king himself (like Antiochus IV Epiphanes), who sarcastically takes on exalted titles; or an angelic figure?[28] I lean toward the view that the "son of God" in II, 1 is a negative figure, the king or representative of the final kingdom before the eschatological period.[29] This question is central to the

---

28. For the evaluation as a positive figure, see, e.g., John J. Collins, *Daniel: A Commentary on the Book of Daniel*, Hermeneia (Minneapolis: Fortress, 1993), 77–78, 190; Fitzmyer, "4Q246," 153–74; Émile Puech, "Le fils de Dieu, le fils du Très-Haut, messie roi en 4Q246," in *Le jugement dans l'un et l'autre Testament*, ed. Eberhard Bons (Paris: Cerf, 2006), 271–84; Puech, "Le volume XXXVII des *Discoveries in the Judaean Desert* et les manuscrits araméens de lot Starcky," in Berthelot and Stökl Ben Ezra, *Aramaica Qumranica*, 48–49; John J. Collins, *The Scepter and the Star: Messianism in Light of the Dead Sea Scrolls*, 2nd ed. (Grand Rapids: Eerdmans, 2010); George J. Brooke, "Kingship and Messianism in the Dead Sea Scrolls," in *King and Messiah in Israel and the Ancient Near East*, ed. John Day, LHBOTS 270 (London: T&T Clark, 2013), 445–49, and further nuanced in Brooke, "Son of God, Sons of God, and Election in the Dead Sea Scrolls," in Allen, *Son of God*, 28–40; and Nathan C. Johnson, "Romans 1:3-4: Beyond Antithetical Parallelism," *JBL* 136 (2017): 473–76. For the evaluation as an eschatological antagonist, see, e.g., David Flusser, "The Hubris of the Antichrist in a Fragment from Qumran," *Immanuel* 10 (1980): 31–37; and Cook, "4Q246," 43–66. Annette Steudel, "The Eternal Reign of the People of God: Collective Expectations in Qumran Texts (4Q246 and 1QM)," *RevQ* 17 (1996): 507–25, argues that this figure is Antiochus IV Epiphanes. For the evaluation as an angelic figure, see Florentino García Martínez, *Qumran and Apocalyptic*, STDJ 9 (Leiden: Brill, 1992), 162–73. Cf. the overview of perspectives in Michael Segal, "Who Is the 'Son of God' in 4Q246? An Overlooked Example of Early Biblical Interpretation," *DSD* 21 (2014): 302–5, who argues for a negative figure, based in part on the in-depth linguistic analysis of the Aramaic t-stem in Noam Mizrahi, "The Aramaic 'Son of God' Scroll from Qumran (4Q246): Exegetical Problems in Linguistic Perspective" [Hebrew] (MA thesis, Hebrew University of Jerusalem, 2001).

29. See in particular the arguments in Kratz, "Son of God and Son of Man."

interpretation of 4Q246 and germane to the complex of eschatological *dramatis personae* in Revelation, especially since Jesus is also called "Son of God" in Revelation.[30] More interesting, however, is the shared reliance on Danielic language in Revelation and 4Q246 since the wording of Danielic texts is constitutive of their basic literary composition.[31] 4Q246 is not the only text at Qumran that reuses, interprets, or expands on Daniel, but, as Michael Segal and Reinhard G. Kratz have shown in their recent debate regarding the identity of the pseudo-messianic figure in the text, the wording of Daniel is essential to the text's basic structure and argumentation.[32]

Consider Rev 11 as an example, a passage that describes the prophetic activity of the two witnesses (11:1–14) and the consequences of the seventh trumpet (11:15–19). After the seer is commanded to measure the temple of God, the altar, and those who worship there (11:1–2), the topic shifts: "And I will give [δώσω] my two witnesses and they will prophesy 1,260 days clothed in sackcloth" (cf. Rev 12:6, 14). This first-person speech by an anonymous governing voice is closely connected to Dan 7:25, where the "holy ones of the Most High" (קדישי עליונין, cf. 4Q246 II, 1: בר עליון) "will be given over into his hand" (ויתיהבון בידה, cf. Dan 2:38), referring to the fourth beast (Dan 7:23). The use of the passive form of יהב in Dan 7:25 signals divine action, not unlike the giving (ἐδόθησαν) of two great eagle wings to the woman fleeing the dragon in Rev 12:14 (cf. 4Q530 7 II, 4–6). The use of forms of δίδωμι and יהב in texts where God is the unacknowledged actor creates an initial connection, a connection strengthened further by the eschatological context of both passages. The two witnesses in Revelation appear between the sixth and seventh trumpet, and the fourth beast's actions immediately proceed the sitting of the divine court in judgement (Dan 7:27). Moreover, both texts limit the activity of the figures that are given authority. Dan 7:25 limits the authority of the beast for "a time, two times, and half a time" (עד עדן ועדנין ופלג עדן), which Rev 11:3 inter-

---

30. On divine sonship traditions in Revelation, which are primarily collocated around allusions to Ps 2, see Garrick V. Allen, "Son of God in the Book of Revelation and Apocalyptic Literature," in Allen, *Son of God*, 53–71.

31. Cf. Beale, *Use of Daniel in Jewish Apocalyptic Literature*, 154–270.

32. Segal, "Who Is the 'Son of God,'" 289–312; Kratz, "Son of God and Son of Man." For other examples of texts that expand Daniel, see Prayer of Nabonidus (4Q242); Pseudo-Daniel (4Q243–245); Four Kingdoms (4Q552–553/553a?) and other explicit examples of interpretation (Dan 9:25 in 11Q13 II, 18; Dan 11:32 in 4Q174 1–3 II, 3–4a). See Dimant, "Themes and Genres," 39; and García Martínez, *Qumran and Apocalyptic*, 137–61.

prets in terms of years: 1,260 days roughly corresponds to 42 months—the time of the trampling of the outer courts in 11:2—or three and a half years.

Although the symbolic limiting of time is not present in 4Q246, the idiom of giving into the hand is present.[33] Following the future arising of the people of God (II, 4), a period is instigated that is defined by an eternal kingdom (II, 5), the putting away of the sword (II, 6), and the obeisance of all provinces to God (II, 7). In this period the great God "will wage war for them [i.e., his people], He will give the peoples [i.e., not God's people] into their hand [i.e., God's people]" (ינתן בידה). This text inverts the situation described by Dan 7:25 where the holy ones are handed over into the power of a menacing force immediately prior to that force's final judgement. In contrast, 4Q246 describes a situation in which all other peoples are given into the hands of the עם אל by God, immediately before the eternal rule of God and/or his people commences (שלטן עלם, II, 9).

This focus on everlasting rule and eternal kingdoms is another commonality of these three traditions. In Dan 7:14, the one like a son of man is given dominion, all peoples, nations, and tongues serve him, and "his dominion is an everlasting dominion [שלטנה שלטן עלם] that shall not pass away." Similar language is used in Dan 7:27, which describes the giving of the kingdom to the holy ones of the Most High, using a parallel phrase "their kingdom will be an everlasting kingdom" (מלכותה מלכות עלם). Both of these phrases describing the eternality of this eschatological kingdom reappear verbatim in 4Q246: מלכותה מלכות עלם (II, 5) and שלטנה שלטן עלם (II, 9). These near quotations, in combination with the fact that the people of God are given authority over all peoples (II, 8), indicate that the eschatological scenario in 4Q246 is a further development of Daniel's vision. Instead of being handed over to an eschatological adversary, the people of God take a more dominant role in subduing their opponents before the end.

Revelation 11 also further develops the scenario of Dan 7, but in a christological direction. In Rev 11:15, the final trumpet is sounded by the seventh angel, whereupon a voice from heaven is heard to say: "the kingdom of the world has become the kingdom of our Lord and his Messiah [τοῦ χριστοῦ αὐτοῦ], and he will reign forever and ever." This passage, too, has connections with Dan 7:14 and 7:27. Revelation 11:15 conflates the son of man, who is given a kingdom in Dan 7:14, with Christ, who rules

---

33. Cf. Kratz, "Son of God and Son of Man."

with God when the kingdom of the world reverts to its proper ruler after the final trumpet. Like the rule of the son of man and holy ones of the Most High in Dan 7:14 and 7:27, Christ's rule will be eternal (note the third-person singular βασιλεύσει).

The narratives of both Rev 11 and 4Q246 are indebted to interpretations of Dan 7, among other traditions (e.g., Ezek 37:5, 10 and Rev 11:11 and the concrete connections between 4Q246 and Aramaic court tales in Dan 2–6),[34] but they interpreted the oft ambiguous narrative and its characterization in different ways. Revelation 11 focuses on the boundedness of the penultimate stage before the eschaton, limiting the prophecy of the two witnesses to correspond to the time of the trampling of the outer courts of the temple, a reframing of the "time, two times, and half a time" that the fourth beast has dominion over the holy ones of the Most High (Dan 7:25). For Revelation, the period of the beast's rule corresponds to the trampling of the temple (Rev 11:2), but it is not without prophetic resistance in the form of two witnesses (11:7–9).

Revelation also emphasizes the fact that the dominion, glory, kingship in Dan 7:14 is transferred to the one like a son of man. Revelation 11:15 identifies this figure with Christ, using a singular verb to describe his eternal kingdom (cf. 5:10, 13; 22:5). Instead of being given a kingdom by the Ancient of Days as in Dan 7:13–14, the kingdom of the world reverts to the rightful ownership of "our Lord and his Christ" (Rev 11:15) without mention of agency.

4Q246 takes its engagement with Dan 7 in another direction, emphasizing the role of the people of God in the eschatological scenario at the expense of a messianic figure.[35] Although it describes some strife and successive kingdoms (I, 4–II, 3), it is their opponents who are given into the hands of God's people (II, 8), instead of the holy ones of the Most High who are under the authority of the fourth beast (Dan 7:25). The deep engagement with Dan 7 preserved in these two texts, coupled with their different interpretations, demonstrate the importance and ambiguity of Daniel's vision of the Ancient of Days and one like a son of man in early Jewish apocalyptic discourse.

---

34. E.g., 4Q246 I, 1–2 and Dan 5:20; 4Q246 I, 2 and Dan 3:13 (רגז); and 4Q246 II, 7 and Dan 2:46 (סגד), among others. Cf. Kratz, "Son of God and Son of Man."

35. This is especially true if one views the "Son of God" and "Son of the Most High" in 4Q246 II, 1 as a negative eschatological antagonist as opposed to a Jewish king or messianic figure.

3. Concluding Thoughts

This comparison between the book of Revelation, the Visions of Amram, and 4Q246 illustrates the literary and ideological flexibility of apocalyptic traditions in the late Second Temple period. Broadly speaking these texts share a number of obvious features—visions, angelic intermediaries, cosmic or eschatological antagonists, an expectation of the coming vindication and rule of God and his people—but their messages and goals differ. The Visions of Amram uses the testamentary report of a dualistic vision to support endogamy and a particular view of priestly lineage; Revelation uses a complex of visions to argue that Christ is the king of the world and that Roman imperial power is misleading; 4Q246 interprets Danielic traditions, emphasizing an impending reversal in the fortunes of God's people. Comparing Revelation to Aramaic traditions, even in this selective way, highlights the subtleties of interpretation that are central to the production of apocalyptic literature, especially since the composition of these texts are intimately connected to Jewish scriptural traditions and engaged with the political situations that define their contexts of production. Apocalyptic symbolism and literary forms are pluriform in their application and argumentation.

Another point to highlight is that engaging Aramaic apocalyptica is essential for interpreting the book of Revelation, especially since a significant quantity of recent research has focused on the Aramaic corpus, but with only selective reference to non-Aramaic traditions. For example, in his 2006 monograph *An Apocalypse for the Church and for the World*, Ronald Herms explores the dynamics of universal and particular language relating to the eschatological makeup of God's people in Revelation.[36] Herms compares Revelation's incongruous depictions of the composition of humanity in the age to come—for example, the notice that the kings of the earth are destroyed by the sword and gorged upon by birds (Rev 19:20–21), paired with the subsequent depiction of the New Jerusalem to which the kings of the earth bring tribute (21:24)—to the deployment of similar language in a series of Jewish apocalypses, primarily 4 Ezra, the Similitudes of Enoch, and the Animal Apocalypse.

---

36. Ronald Herms, *An Apocalypse for the Church and for the World: The Narrative Function of Universal Language in the Book of Revelation*, BZNW 143 (Berlin: de Gruyter, 2006).

Although portions of Tobit and the Enochic Dream Visions are also transmitted among the material from Qumran,[37] apocalyptic traditions and apocalypses in the Scrolls play little role in his analysis. Herms is right that the eschatological vision and social attitudes of the *yaḥad* do not comport themselves to universal language, particularly the Cave 1 sectarian documents,[38] but he does not engage in a substantive way with Aramaic apocalyptica unknown before the discovery of the Scrolls. The question of universality and eschatology is relevant for a number of these traditions, like 4Q246, where linguistic ambiguity in the final section of the text creates a situation where it is not simple to disentangle or map the relationship between the עם אל (II, 4) from the עממין (II, 8).

This observation is not to fault Herms since his selection of *comparanda* is germane to his primary question. But what is interesting in reading Herms's book more than a decade after its publication is how glaring this lack of engagement with apocalyptic traditions in the Scrolls now appears at the outset. His book emphasizes how much broader the conceptual network of scholarship has become when it comes to the book of Revelation. There has never been a lack of interest in the relationship between the Scrolls and Revelation, but this relationship continues to require further exploration as perspectives on the Scrolls develop.

The final point to take from this analysis relates to the question of genre. The genre of the book of Revelation and its relationship to other apocalypses continues to be an area of concern, even though this line of enquiry often focuses on the poles of apocalypse and prophecy and rarely engages the Qumran corpus in a substantive way, focusing instead on other Jewish apocalypses.[39] Discussion of the generic relationship between Revelation and other apocalypses have stalled, in part because studies continue, for obvious reasons, to emphasize Revelation's connections to Daniel, 1 Enoch, Jubilees, 4 Ezra, 2 Baruch, and the like.[40]

---

37. 4Q196–200; 4Q204 4; 4Q205 2; 4Q206 5; 4Q207.
38. Herms, *Apocalypse for the Church and for the World*, 52–61.
39. See a number of articles in Allen, Paul, and Woodman, eds., *Book of Revelation*, especially Dixon, "Testimony of Jesus," 81–93; Ryan, "Testimony of Jesus," 95–113, and Michelle Fletcher, "Apocalypse Noir: How Revelation Defined and Defied a Genre," 115–34.
40. E.g. Ulrich B. Müller, *Messias und Menschensohn in jüdischen Apokalypsen und in der Offenbarung des Johannes*, SNT 6 (Gütersloh: Gütersloh Verlagshaus, 1972); and Pierre-Maurice Bogaert, "Les apocalypses contemporaines de Baruch, d'Esdras et

This vector of research has led to a situation where Revelation's place among the apocalypses is perceived as tenuous.[41] It is simultaneously central to the concept and resistant to type cast, even if most scholars admit that its relationship to other Jewish apocalypses is an essential part of its literary substance.[42] The question of Revelation's genre lacked a consensus answer for some time in the twentieth century, although a synthesis is beginning to develop. For example, in the Leuven conference volume on Revelation and New Testament apocalyptic from 1979, multiple contributions directly address genre. Ugo Vanni, for example, asks, "Is the Apocalypse an apocalyptic book?" and notes that "the reality of the simultaneity of apocalyptic and prophecy within the Apocalypse constitutes a serious problem that has not yet been completely resolved" (my trans.).[43] The case has little changed in this regard, due in large part to the conflicting ways Revelation refers to itself, including apocalypse (1:1), prophecy (1:3; 10:11; 22:7, 10, 18–19), and testimony of Jesus (1:2, 9; 12:17; 19:10; 20:4), an issue of self-presentation located also in the Visions of Amram.

The Leuven Colloquium again focused on Revelation in 2015. John J. Collins's article in its proceedings represents, for the most part, the current

---

de Jean," in *L'Apocalypse johannique et l'apocalyptique dans le Nouveau Testament*, ed. Jan Lambrecht, BETL 53 (Leuven: Leuven University Press, 1980), 47–68.

41. Although it was included in Adela Yarbro Collins, "The Early Christian Apocalypses," in *Apocalypse: The Morphology of a Genre*, Semeia 14 (1979): 61–121, it is treated as a tenuous entity due to its lack of pseudonymous attribution, absence of historical survey, and preservation of other literary forms (prophetic and epistolary forms). The most full-throated critique of Revelation as an apocalypse is Frederick David Mazzaferri, *The Genre of the Book of Revelation from a Source-Critical Perspective*, BZNW 54 (Berlin: de Gruyter, 1989), especially his lengthy penultimate chapter (259–378).

42. E.g., see Martin Karrer, *Johannesoffenbarung (Offb. 1,1–5,14)*, EKK 24.1 (Göttingen: Vandenhoeck & Ruprecht, 2017), 90, who argues that "ancient revelatory literature constitutes the framework for the Apocalypse" (my trans.), even if prophecy, the letter form, and apocalyptic imagery contribute also to understanding the book.

43. Ugo Vanni, "L'Apocalypse johannique: État de la question," in Lambrecht, *L'Apocalypse johannique et l'apocalyptique*, 27. Vanni remains reticent to sever Revelation's relationship with apocalypses/apocalyptic altogether (p. 28). Cf. Kallas, "Apocalypse," 69–80; and Bruno Corsani, "L'apocalisse di Giovanni: Scritto apocalittico, o profetico?," *BeOr* 17 (1975): 253–68. Note that asking if Revelation is an apocalyptic book is different than asking if it is apocalypse, although I am not sure that Vanni would have intuited too great a difference, especially since John J. Collins, ed., *Apocalypse: The Morphology of a Genre*, Semeia 14 (1979) had only recently been published.

majority opinion. He argues that, although Revelation lacks some standard characteristics of apocalypses like historical reviews and pseudonymity, and although it contains characteristics of prophetic literature like oracular material (1:7–8, 17–20; 13:9–10; 18:21–24; 21:5–8; 22:7, 12–14), "this by no means excludes its being simultaneously an apocalypse."[44] For Collins, "the dominant genre, the one that shapes the work as a whole, is the apocalypse," even though Revelation is also prophetic and epistolary.[45]

Other more innovative attempts have been made to understand Revelation's relationship to the genre apocalypse beyond appeals to the now-classic schema produced by Collins and his collaborators. Gregory Linton has argued that perceptions of genre are an exercise in intertextuality and that the intertextual relationships between texts undermine generic identification.[46] The dialectic of genre and intertextuality leads Linton to contend that the Apocalypse "overruns its boundaries" in the quantity of

---

44. John J. Collins, "Revelation as Apocalypse," in *New Perspectives on the Book of Revelation*, ed. Adela Yarbro Collins, BETL 291 (Leuven: Peeters, 2017), 42. Cf. also Elizabeth Schüssler Fiorenza, "*Apokalypsis* and *Propheteia*: The Book of Revelation in the Context of Early Christian Prophecy," in Lambrecht, *L'Apocalypse johannique et l'apocalyptique*, 105–28; and Craig R. Koester, *Revelation*, AYB 38A (New Haven: Yale University Press, 2014), 104–9, who sees prophecy and apocalypse working hand in hand in Revelation. A more emic approach is adopted by Karrer, *Johannesoffenbarung*, 85–86, who points out that late antique commentators referred to the Apocalypse by a number of terms absent in modern scholarship, like "mystical work" (πραγμετεία μυστικωτάτη; Oecumenius), a "vision" (ὀπτασία; Arethas of Caesarea), or a "prophetic sign" (προφηθευτέντα; Andrew of Caesarea).

45. Collins, "Revelation as Apocalypse," 43. See also Franz Tóth, "Erträge und Tendenzen in der gegenwärtigen Forschung zur Johannesapokalypse," in *Die Johannesapokalypse: Kontexte—Konzepte—Rezeption*, ed. Jörg Frey, James A. Kelhoffer, and Franz Tóth, WUNT 287 (Tübingen: Mohr Siebeck, 2012), 10–11: "References to apocalyptic literature and prophecy, like the formal elements of letters, are no longer evaluated as mutually exclusive alternatives but as integral components of the work, with the Johannine Apocalypse being increasing qualified as a prophetic book" (my trans.).

46. Gregory L. Linton, "Reading the Apocalypse as Apocalypse: The Limits of Genre," in *The Reality of Apocalypse: Rhetoric and Politics in the Book of Revelation*, ed. David L. Barr, SymS 39 (Atlanta: Society of Biblical Literature, 2006), 9–41: "To specify the genre of a text is to clarify and delineate the text's intertextual relations with other texts" (9). See also the interesting suggestion of Michelle Fletcher, *Reading Revelation as Pastiche: Imitating the Past*, LNTS 571 (London: T&T Clark, 2017), 182–213. She uses the development of the film noir—film neonoir genre as a parallel test case to emphasise the diachronic developments of genre construction.

literary relationships that the work engenders.[47] Revelation is in this sense a work defined by its complex literary interrelationships: allusions and literary reuse are central to the mode of Revelation's composition and, as a corollary, to its generic makeup. This is a point that has not been previously considered when it comes to thinking about Revelation's genre, but the idea is suggestive when compared to the relentless allusions and outright borrowing from Daniel witnessed in 4Q246. If generic insatiability is something that defines both Revelation and Aramaic apocalyptica at Qumran,[48] then perhaps considering their shared reliance upon antecedent scriptural traditions will continue to enlighten their interrelationships.

Bibliography

Allen, Garrick V. *The Book of Revelation and Early Jewish Textual Culture*. Cambridge: Cambridge University Press, 2017.

———. "Paratexts and the Reception History of the Apocalypse." *JTS* 70 (2019): 600–32.

———. "Son of God in the Book of Revelation and Apocalyptic Literature." Pages 53–71 in *Son of God: Divine Sonship in Jewish and Christian Antiquity*. Edited by Garrick V. Allen, Kai Akagi, Paul Sloan, and Madhavi Nevader. University Park: Penn State University Press, 2019.

Aune, David. "The Apocalypse of John and Palestinian Jewish Apocalyptic." *Neot* 40 (2006): 1–33.

———. "Qumran and the Book of Revelation." Pages 79–98 in *Apocalypticism, Prophecy, and Magic in Early Christianity*. Edited by Peter W. Flint and James C. VanderKam. Tübingen: Mohr Siebeck, 2006.

Bauckham, Richard. "The Apocalypse as a Christian War Scroll." Pages 210–37 in *The Climax of Prophecy: Studies on the Book of Revelation*. Edinburgh: T&T Clark, 1993.

Beale, Gregory K. *The Use of Daniel in Jewish Apocalyptic Literature and in the Revelation of St. John*. Lanham: University of America Press, 1984.

Berger, Klaus. "Der Streit des guten und des bösen Engels um die Seele: Beobachtungen zu 4Q Amr^b und Judas 9." *JSJ* 4 (1973): 1–18.

Berthelot, Katell. "Response." Pages 448–49 in *Aramaica Qumranica: Proceedings of the Conference on the Aramaic Texts from Qumran in*

---

47. Linton, "Reading the Apocalypse," 10.
48. Cf. DiTommaso, "Apocalypticism and the Aramaic Texts from Qumran," 457.

Aix-en-Provence 30 June–2 July 2008. Edited by Katell Berthelot and Daniel Stökl Ben Ezra. STDJ 94. Leiden: Brill, 2010.
Bogaert, Pierre-Maurice. "Les apocalypses contemporaines de Baruch, d'Esdras et de Jean." Pages 47–68 in *L'Apocalypse johannique et l'apocalyptique dans le Noveau Testament*. Edited by Jan Lambrecht. BETL 53. Leuven: Leuven University Press, 1980.
Brooke, George J. *The Dead Sea Scrolls and the New Testament*. Minneapolis: Fortress, 2005.
———. "Kingship and Messianism in the Dead Sea Scrolls." Pages 434–55 in *King and Messiah in Israel and the Ancient Near East*. Edited by John Day. LHOTS 270. London: T&T Clark, 2013.
———. "Son of Gog, Sons of God, and Election in the Dead Sea Scrolls." Pages 28–40 in *Son of God: Divine Sonship in Jewish and Christian Antiquity*. Edited by Garrick V. Allen, Kai Akagi, Paul Sloan, and Madhavi Nevader. University Park: Penn State University Press, 2019.
Charlesworth, James H., ed. *John and Qumran*. London: Geoffrey Chapman, 1972.
Collins, John J., ed. *Apocalypse: The Morphology of a Genre*. Semeia 14 (1979).
———. *Daniel: A Commentary on the Book of Daniel*. Hermeneia. Minneapolis: Fortress, 1993.
———. "Revelation as Apocalypse." Pages 33–48 in *New Perspectives on the Book of Revelation*. Edited by Adela Yarbro Collins. BETL 291. Leuven: Peeters, 2017.
———. *The Scepter and the Star: Messianism in Light of the Dead Sea Scrolls*. 2nd ed. Grand Rapids: Eerdmans, 2010.
Coloe, Mary L., and Tom Thatcher, eds. *John, Qumran, and the Dead Sea Scrolls: Sixty Years of Discovery and Debate*. EJL 32. Atlanta: Society of Biblical Literature, 2011.
Cook, Edward M. "4Q246." *BBR* 5 (1995): 43–66.
Corsani, Bruno. "L'apocalisse di Giovanni: Scritto apocalittico, o profectico?" *BeO* 17 (1975): 253–68.
Davila, James R. *Liturgical Works*. ECDSS. Grand Rapids: Eerdmans, 2000.
Dimant, Devorah. "Apocalyptic Texts at Qumran." Pages 175–91 in *The Community of the Renewed Covenant: The Notre Dame Symposium on the Dead Sea Scrolls*. Edited by Eugene Ulrich and James C. VanderKam. Notre Dame: University of Notre Dame Press, 1994.
———. "Themes and Genres in the Aramaic Texts from Qumran." Pages 15–45 in *Aramaica Qumranica: Proceedings of the Conference on the*

Aramaic Texts from Qumran in Aix-en-Provence 30 June–2 July 2008. Edited by Katell Berthelot and Daniel Stökl Ben Ezra. STDJ 94. Leiden: Brill, 2010.

———. "Tobit and Qumran Aramaic Texts." Pages 385–406 in *Is There a Text in This Cave? Studies in the Textuality of the Dead Sea Scrolls in Honour of George J. Brooke*. Edited by Ariel Feldman, Charlotte Hempel, and Maria Cioată. STDJ 119. Leiden: Brill, 2017.

DiTommaso, Lorenzo. "Apocalypticism and the Aramaic Texts from Qumran." Pages 451–79 in *Aramaica Qumranica: Proceedings of the Conference on the Aramaic Texts from Qumran in Aix-en-Provence 30 June–2 July 2008*. Edited by Katell Berthelot and Daniel Stökl Ben Ezra. STDJ 94. Leiden: Brill, 2010.

———. "Pseudonymity and the Revelation of John." Pages 305–15 in *Revealed Wisdom: Studies in Apocalyptic in Honour of Christopher Rowland*. Edited by John F. Ashton. AJEC 88. Leiden: Brill, 2014.

Dixon, Sarah Underwood. "'The Testimony of Jesus' in Light of Internal Self-References in the Book of Daniel and *1 Enoch*." Pages 81–93 in *The Book of Revelation: Currents in British Research on the Apocalypse*. Edited by Garrick V. Allen, Ian Paul, and Simon Patrick Woodman. WUNT 2/411. Tübingen: Mohr Siebeck, 2015.

Drawnel, Henryk. "The Initial Narrative of the *Visions of Amram* and Its Literary Characteristics." *RevQ* 24 (2010): 517–54.

Elgvin, Torleif. "Priests on Earth as in Heaven: Jewish Light on the Book of Revelation." Pages 257–78 in *Echoes from the Caves: Qumran and the New Testament*. STDJ 85. Edited by Florentino García Martínez. Leiden: Brill, 2009.

Fitzmyer, Joseph A. "4Q246: The 'Son of God' Document from Qumran." *Bib* 74 (1993): 153–74.

Fletcher, Michelle. "Apocalypse Noir: How Revelation Defines and Defied a Genre." Pages 115–34 in *The Book of Revelation: Currents in British Research on the Apocalypse*. Edited by Garrick V. Allen, Ian Paul, and Simon Patrick Woodman. WUNT 2/411. Tübingen: Mohr Siebeck, 2015.

———. *Reading Revelation as Pastiche: Imitating the Past*. LNTS 571. London: T&T Clark, 2017.

Flusser, David. "The Hubris of the Antichrist in a Fragment from Qumran." *Immanuel* 10 (1980): 31–37.

Frey, Jörg. "Das Corpus Johanneum und die Apokalypse des Johannes: Die Johanneslegende, die Probleme der johanneischen Verfasserschaft und die Frage der Pseudonymität der Apokalypse." Pages 71–133 in *Poetik und Intertextualität der Johannesapokalypse*. Edited by Stefan Alkier, Thomas Hieke, Tobias Nicklas, and Michael Sommer. WUNT 346. Tübingen: Mohr Siebeck, 2015.

———. "On the Origins of the Genre of the 'Literary Testament': Farewell Discourses in the Qumran Library and Their Relevance for the History of the Genre." Pages 345–72 in *Aramaica Qumranica: Proceedings of the Conference on the Aramaic Texts from Qumran in Aix-en-Provence 30 June–2 July 2008*. Edited by Katell Berthelot and Daniel Stökl Ben Ezra. STDJ 94. Leiden: Brill, 2010.

García Martínez, Florentino. "4Q'Amram b I 14: ¿Melki-resha' o Melisedeq?" *RevQ* 12 (1985): 111–14.

———. "Aramaica qumranica apocalyptica?" Pages 435–48 in *Aramaica Qumranica: Proceedings of the Conference on the Aramaic Texts from Qumran in Aix-en-Provence 30 June–2 July 2008*. Edited by Katell Berthelot and Daniel Stökl Ben Ezra. STDJ 94. Leiden: Brill, 2010.

———. *Qumran and Apocalyptic*. STDJ 9. Leiden: Brill, 1992.

García Martínez, Florentino, and Eibert J. C. Tigchelaar. *The Dead Sea Scrolls Study Edition*. 2 vols. Leiden: Brill, 1997.

Goldman, Liora. "The Burial of the Fathers in the *Visions of Amram* from Qumran." Pages 231–49 in *Rewriting and Interpreting the Hebrew Bible: The Biblical Patriarchs in the Light of the Dead Sea Scrolls*. Edited by Devorah Dimant and Reinhard G. Kratz. BZAW 439. Berlin: de Gruyter, 2013.

———. "Dualism in the *Visions of Amram*." *RevQ* 24 (2010): 421–32.

Herms, Ronald. *An Apocalypse for the Church and for the World: The Narrative Function of Universal Language in the Book of Revelation*. BZNW 143. Berlin: de Gruyter, 2006.

Jauhiainen, Marco. "Revelation and Rewritten Prophecies." Pages 177–97 in *Rewritten Bible Reconsidered*. Edited by Antti Laato and J. van Ruiten. Winona Lake: Eisenbrauns, 2008.

Johnson, Nathan C. "Romans 1:3–4: Beyond Antithetical Parallelism." *JBL* 136 (2017): 467–90.

Jurgens, Blake Alan. "Reassessing the Dream-Vision of the *Vision of Amram* (4Q543–547)." *JSP* 24 (2014): 3–42.

Kallas, James. "The Apocalypse—An Apocalyptic Book?" *JBL* 76 (1968): 69–80.

Karrer, Martin. *Johannesoffenbarung (Offb. 1,1–5,14)*. EKKNT 24.1. Göttingen: Vandenhoeck & Ruprecht, 2017.

Koester, Craig R. *Revelation*. AYB 38A. New Haven: Yale University Press, 2014.

Kratz, Reinhard G. "Son of God and Son of Man: 4Q246 in the Light of the Book of Daniel." Pages 9–27 in *Son of God: Divine Sonship in Jewish and Christian Antiquity*. Edited by Garrick V. Allen, Kai Akagi, Paul Sloan, and Madhavi Nevader. University Park: Penn State University Press, 2019.

Linton, Gregory L. "Reading the Apocalypse as Apocalypse: The Limits of Genre." Pages 9–41 in *The Reality of Apocalypse: Rhetoric and Politics in the Book of Revelation*. Edited by David L. Barr. SymS 39. Atlanta: Society of Biblical Literature, 2006.

Mazzaferri, Frederick David. *The Genre of the Book of Revelation from a Source-Critical Perspective*. BZNW 54. Berlin: de Gruyter, 1989.

Milik, Józef T. "4Q Visions de 'Amram et une citation d'Origen." *RB* 79 (1972): 77–97.

———. "Milkî-ṣedeq et Milkî-reša' dans les anciens écrits juifs et chrétiens." *JJS* 23 (1972): 95–144.

Mizrahi, Noam. "The Aramaic 'Son of God' Scroll from Qumran (4Q246): Exegetical Problems in Linguistic Perspective" [Hebrew]. MA thesis. Hebrew University of Jerusalem, 2001.

Müller, Ulrich B. *Messias und Menschensohn in jüdischen Apokalypsen und in der Offenbarung des Johannes*. SNT 6. Gütersloh: Gütersloh Verlagshaus, 1972.

Perrin, Andrew B. "Another Look at Dualism in 4QVisions of Amram." *Hen* 36 (2014): 106–17.

———. "Capturing the Voices of Pseudepigraphic Personae: On the Form and Function of Incipits in the Aramaic Dead Sea Scrolls." *DSD* 20 (2013): 98–123.

———. *The Dynamics of Dream-Vision Revelation in the Aramaic Dead Sea Scrolls*. JAJSup 19. Göttingen: Vandenhoeck & Ruprecht, 2015.

Puech, Émile. *Qumrân Grotte 4.XXII: Textes araméens, première partie, 4Q529–549*. DJD 31. Oxford: Clarendon, 2001.

———. "Le fils de Dieu, le fils du Très-Haut, messie roi en 4Q246." Pages 271–84 in *Le jugement dans l'un et l'autre Testament*. Edited by Eberhard Bons. Paris: Cerf, 2006.

———. "Le volume XXVII des *Discoveries in the Judean Desert* et les manuscrits araméens de lot Starcky." Pages 47–61 in *Aramaica Qumranica: Proceedings of the Conference on the Aramaic Texts from Qumran at*

Aix-en-Provence, 30 June–2 July 2008. Edited by Katell Berthelot and Daniel Stökl Ben Ezra. STDJ 94. Leiden: Brill, 2010.

Rey, Jean-Sébastien, ed. *The Dead Sea Scrolls and Pauline Literature*. STDJ 102. Leiden: Brill, 2014.

Ruzer, Serge. *Mapping the New Testament: Early Christian Writings as a Witness to Jewish Biblical Exegesis*. Leiden: Brill, 2007.

Ryan, Sean Michael. "'The Testimony of Jesus' and 'the Testimony of Enoch': An *Emic* Approach to the Genre of the Apocalypse." Pages 95–113 in *The Book of Revelation: Currents in British Research on the Apocalypse*. Edited by Garrick V. Allen, Ian Paul, and Simon Patrick Woodman. WUNT 2/411. Tübingen: Mohr Siebeck, 2015.

Schüssler Fiorenza, Elisabeth. "*Apokalypsis* and *Propheteia*: The Book of Revelation in the Context of Early Christian Prophecy." Pages 105–38 in *L'Apocalypse johannique et l'apocalyptique dans le Noveau Testament*. Edited by Jan Lambrecht. BETL 53. Leuven: Leuven University Press, 1980.

Segal, Michael. "Who Is the 'Son of God' in 4Q246? An Overlooked Example of Biblical Interpretation." *DSD* 21 (2014): 289–312.

Steudel, Annette. "The Eternal Reign of the People of God: Collective Expectations in Qumran Texts (4Q246 and 1QM)." *RevQ* 17 (1996): 507–25.

Tóth, Franz. "Erträge und Tendenzen in der gegenwärtigen Forschung zur Johannesapokalypse." Pages 1–30 in *Die Johannesapokalypse: Kontexte-Konzepte-Rezeption*. Edited by Jörg Frey, James A. Kelhoffer, and Franz Tóth. WUNT 287. Tübingen: Mohr Siebeck, 2012.

Ulfgard, Håkan. "The Songs of the Sabbath Sacrifice and the Heavenly Scene of the Book of Revelation." Pages 251–66 in *Northern Lights on the Dead Sea Scrolls*. Edited by Anders Klostergaard Petersen et al. STDJ 80. Leiden: Brill, 2009.

Vanni, Ugo. "L'Apocalypse johannique: État de la question." Pages 21–46 in *L'Apocalypse johannique et l'apocalyptique dans le Noveau Testament*. Edited by Jan Lambrecht. BETL 53. Leuven: Leuven University Press, 1980.

Wold, Benjamin. "Revelation's Plague Septets: New Exodus and Exile." Pages 279–97 in *Echoes from the Caves: Qumran and the New Testament*. Edited by Florentino García Martínez. STDJ 85. Leiden: Brill, 2009.

Yarbro Collins, Adela. "The Book of Revelation." Pages 384–414 in *The Origins of Apocalypticism in Judaism and Christianity*. Vol. 1 of *The*

Encyclopedia of Apocalypticism. Edited by John J. Collins. New York: Continuum, 1998.

———. "The Early Christian Apocalypses." *Semeia* 14 (1979): 61–121.

Heavenly Ascent Revisited

Martha Himmelfarb

The dominant understanding today of the development of Jewish and Christian apocalypses involving heavenly ascent has its roots in the 1970s. In 1976 Józef T. Milik published the fragments from the Dead Sea Scrolls of the Aramaic works behind four of the units of the Ethiopic 1 Enoch.[1] The publication brought increased scholarly attention to all of these works, including the one most important for our purposes, the Book of the Watchers, with its two revelatory journeys: an ascent to heaven and a tour of the ends of the earth. In 1979 the journal *Semeia* published a volume entitled *Apocalypse: The Morphology of a Genre*, under the editorship of John J. Collins, consisting of papers by members of a group of the Society of Biblical Literature devoted to the subject.[2] While their project was part of a larger discussion of the relevance of genre for the study of ancient Jewish and Christian literature, the category of genre seemed particularly useful for the study of the apocalypses since it provided greater clarity about a problem peculiar to them. On the one hand, the expectation of a cataclysmic end of the world—*apocalyptic* as usually understood—is not restricted to texts usually designated as apocalypses; on the other hand, not all apocalypses are apocalyptic in the sense just noted. The *Semeia* 14 volume addressed the second aspect of the problem: the existence of apocalypses that are not very apocalyptic. Its master paradigm divided ancient apocalypses into two subgenres, one with otherworldly journeys, the other, without; its charts made it clear that apocalypses with otherworldly journeys are more concerned with heavenly secrets and the

---

1. Józef T. Milik, *The Books of Enoch: Aramaic Fragments from Qumrân Cave 4*, with the collaboration of Matthew Black (Oxford: Clarendon, 1976).

2. John J. Collins, ed., *Apocalypse: The Morphology of a Genre*, *Semeia* 14 (1979).

fate of souls after death than with collective eschatology.[3] The timing of the publication of *Semeia* 14 meant that many of its readers were already primed by the Aramaic fragments of the Book of the Watchers to be receptive to a way of thinking about apocalypses that gave more attention to otherworldly journeys.

Recent discussion continues to be appreciative of the volume's pioneering contribution, although some scholars have come to prefer other modes of understanding genre, notably prototype theory, which argues that human beings identify categories not by consulting a list of characteristics like that of the *Semeia* definition but by comparing new or less obvious cases to a prototype.[4] But despite the undoubted contributions attention to genre have made to our understanding of apocalyptic literature, looking back, it seems to me that the interest in genre in the years following the publication of the Aramaic fragments had some unfortunate effects. Genre inevitably implies continuity, and the assumption of continuity made it harder for scholars to see the distinctiveness of the Book of the Watchers relative to later ascent apocalypses and to consider the implications of the gap of centuries that separated later ascent apocalypses from the Book of the Watchers—and I am one of those scholars. Furthermore, in the years since *Semeia* 14, it has become clear that the Scrolls contain a significant number of fragmentary Aramaic works from the last centuries before the Common Era that provide an important context for understanding the Book of the Watchers, a context that was not available to the *Semeia* authors or students of the Book of the Watchers in the late 1970s.[5]

Here I would like to sketch a picture of the development of the later ascent apocalypses and their relationship to the Book of the Watchers that is considerably different from the one I offered in my 1993 book *Ascent to Heaven in Jewish and Christian Apocalypses*.[6] The new picture takes account

---

3. John J. Collins, "Introduction: Towards the Morphology of a Genre," *Semeia* 14 (1979): 1–20.

4. See, e.g., Carol A. Newsom, "Spying out the Land: A Report from Genology," in *Seeking Out the Wisdom of the Ancients: Essays Offered to Honor Michael V. Fox on the Occasion of His Sixty-Fifth Birthday*, ed. Ronald L. Troxel, Kelvin G. Friebel, and Dennis Robert Magary (Winona Lake, IN: Eisenbrauns, 2005), 437–50; and the essays in Hindy Najman and Mladen Popović, eds., *Rethinking Genre: Essays in Honor of John J. Collins, DSD* 17 (2010).

5. See also the essay by Matthew Goff in the present volume.

6. Martha Himmelfarb, *Ascent to Heaven in Jewish and Christian Apocalypses* (New York: Oxford University Press, 1993).

of discontinuity as well as continuity, and it is more cautious about the likelihood of historical connections among the ascent apocalypses as a group and more reticent about claiming that later apocalypses should be understood as manipulating conventions of the genre to achieve their effects. I begin by considering the evidence for visionary journeys by other heroes in Aramaic works found among the Scrolls that are roughly contemporary with the Book of the Watchers. Next I discuss the second century BCE reception of the Book of the Watchers. Finally, I attempt a reconsideration of the ascent apocalypses from the early centuries of this era.

1. Otherworldly Journeys in Early Aramaic Works

1.1. Ascent

After Enoch draws up a petition on behalf of the fallen watchers (1 En. 13.4–7), the Book of the Watchers recounts his ascent to heaven in a dream (13.8–14.2). This is the earliest extant narrative of heavenly ascent as opposed to a mere notice in Jewish literature. In the dream, winds carry Enoch to heaven, where he enters God's residence, which is depicted as a temple; appropriately terrified and trembling, he progresses through its chambers to stand before the divine throne (14.8–25). Enoch's ability to enter the heavenly temple is an indication that he is worthy to be among the angels, a point the Book of the Watchers makes in other ways as well (15.1, chaps. 17–36).[7]

Andrew Perrin has recently argued that the importance of dream visions for their message serves to define a corpus of more than twenty Aramaic works found in the Tanakh or among the Scrolls, some very fragmentary.[8] The fact that the ascent of the Book of the Watchers takes place in a dream makes it part of the corpus, as, in Perrin's view, are the other works considered in this section: the Aramaic Levi Document, the New Jerusalem text, and the Astronomical Book; for the last, the fragments offer no evidence of a dream vision, but they contain other elements that connect to the corpus.[9] Some of the works from the corpus, such as the New Jerusalem text, are undoubtedly apocalypses by the *Semeia* definition, and

---

7. Himmelfarb, *Ascent to Heaven*, 9–28.
8. Andrew B. Perrin, *The Dynamics of Dream-Vision Revelation in the Aramaic Dead Sea Scrolls*, JAJSup 19 (Göttingen: Vandenhoeck & Ruprecht, 2015), esp. ch. 1.
9. Perrin, *Dynamics of Dream-Vision Revelation*, 44–46, 160–61.

others share some features with the genre.[10] But by showing the Book of the Watchers' connections to a significant number of roughly contemporary Aramaic works, Perrin calls attention to the ways in which the Book of the Watchers differs from the later ascent apocalypses.

Apart from the Book of the Watchers, the only other Jewish work from before the Maccabean Revolt that contains an ascent is the Aramaic Levi Document, only partially preserved in Aramaic manuscripts from the Scrolls and the Cairo Genizah and in two passages from a Greek translation.[11] Recent scholarship has suggested dates ranging from the fourth to the late second century BCE, the likely date of the earliest manuscript. I am inclined to follow those who place the Aramaic Levi Document in the third or early second century BCE, that is, roughly contemporary with the Book of the Watchers.[12]

The text of the Aramaic Levi Document is frustratingly fragmentary at the point at which Levi's ascent to heaven takes place: "Then I was shown a vision … in the vision of visions. And I saw heaven … below me, high until it reached heaven … to me the gates of heaven, and one angel" (4Q213a 2 15-18).[13] But despite the lacunae, the phrase "below me" makes it virtually certain that the vision in question involves Levi's presence in heaven. After a break of perhaps several columns, seven angels tell Levi that they have exalted him and given him "the anointing of eternal peace." This passage presumably represents the end of the vision or of a second vision.[14]

---

10. Lorenzo DiTommaso, *The Dead Sea* New Jerusalem *Text: Contents and Contexts*, TSAJ 110 (Tübingen: Mohr Siebeck, 2005), 110. For Perrin's thoughts on the implications of his work for the apocalypse as a genre, *Dynamics of Dream-Vision Revelation*, 238-46.

11. Jonas C. Greenfield, Michael E. Stone, and Esther Eshel, *The Aramaic Levi Document: Edition, Translation, Commentary*, SVTP 19 (Leiden: Brill, 2004), 1-6.

12. Greenfield, Stone, and Eshel, *Aramaic Levi Document*, 19-20.

13. The translation is mine. I have consulted Robert A. Kugler, *From Patriarch to Priest: The Levi-Priestly Tradition from* Aramaic Levi *to* Testament of Levi, EJL 9 (Atlanta: Scholars Press, 1996), 78; Greenfield, Stone, and Eshel, *Aramaic Levi Document*, 67, and Henryk Drawnel, *An Aramaic Wisdom Text from Qumran: A New Interpretation of the Levi Document*, JSJSup 86 (Leiden: Brill, 2004), 104. The main issue is whether to translate *shemaya'* as heaven or heavens; the form is plural, but it is the standard term for the sky. I have chosen to use "heaven" throughout in keeping with my understanding that the Aramaic Levi Document's cosmology involves only a single heaven.

14. I bracket the problem of the plural visions that Levi claims to have seen and their implications for our understanding of the text. The debate is based to a

There is nothing in the Aramaic Levi Document to suggest that it knew the Book of the Watchers or in the Book of the Watchers to suggest that it knew the Aramaic Levi Document. But the use of numbers to identify months in the Aramaic Levi Document indicates use of the solar calendar associated with Enoch in the Astronomical Book, which makes it likely that the Aramaic Levi Document comes from the same milieu as the Astronomical Book and the Book of the Watchers.[15] It probably served as a source for the book of Jubilees, as the Book of the Watchers did.[16]

1.2. Revelatory Journeys on Earth[17]

Immediately following his ascent in the Book of the Watchers, Enoch travels to the ends of the earth in the company of angelic guides, who show him sights inaccessible to ordinary human beings, including the place of punishment of the watchers, the chambers in which souls await judgment after death, the garden of Eden, and various natural phenomena (1 En. 17–36). The tour is punctuated by Enoch's questions to his guides and their answers. This section makes up more than half of the Book of the Watchers measured by chapters, and it is composed of multiple sources. The first unit of the tour is the earliest (chs. 17–19); it is brief and somewhat obscure. A second source reworks and expands the first (chs. 20–32).

---

considerable extent on assumptions about the nature of the relationship between the Aramaic Levi Document and the Testament of Levi, which contains two visions. See Kugler, *From Patriarch to Priest*, 28–33, and also Greenfield, Stone, and Eshel, *Aramaic Levi Document*, 13–16.

15. Stone, and Eshel, *Aramaic Levi Document*, 20–22.

16. For the view that Jubilees made use of the Aramaic Levi Document, see Michael E. Stone, "Enoch, Aramaic Levi and Sectarian Origins," *JSJ* 19 (1988): 159 n. 2 and 170; and Cana Werman, "Levi and Levites in the Second Temple Period," *DSD* 4 (1997): 220–21. This opinion is not universally shared, however. See Kugler, *From Patriarch to Priest*, 146–55, for the views of others who favor a common source and his arguments in favor of that view, and James C. VanderKam, "Isaac's Blessing of Levi and His Descendants in *Jubilees* 31," in *The Provo International Conference on the Dead Sea Scrolls: Technological Innovations, New Texts, and Reformulated Issues*, ed. Donald W. Parry and Eugene Ulrich, STDJ 30 (Leiden: Brill, 1999), 513–18.

17. This essay was completed in 2019. I regret that I was unable to take account of Eshbal Ratzon, "A Sectarian Background for 1 Enoch 22," in *On Using Sources in Graeco-Roman, Jewish and Early Christian Literature*, ed. Joseph Verheyden et al., BETL 327 (Leuven: Peeters, 2022), esp. 175–81, which has important implications for this section.

The distinctive content and style of the concluding chapters of the tour (chs. 33–36) suggest that they come from a third source.

Apart from the Book of the Watchers, the clearest instance of a revelatory tour on earth in the early Aramaic literature appears in the New Jerusalem text, preserved in seven manuscripts from the Scrolls, all unfortunately quite fragmentary. The earliest of the manuscripts dates to the first half of the first century BCE, but the scholarly consensus places the work itself in the late third or early second century, which would make it roughly contemporary with the Book of the Watchers.[18] Most of the surviving material from the text consists of a tour of the eschatological Jerusalem guided by an angel who takes measurements as he goes. In the course of the tour, the visionary sees sacrifices taking place in the temple. The text also includes a passage that appears to be an eschatological prophecy with a four-kingdom schema. The name of the visionary is not preserved, nor does any indication survive of the setting in which the visionary tour takes place.

There are important differences between the tour of the New Jerusalem text and the tour to the ends of the earth in the Book of the Watchers. One is the apparent silence of the angelic guide through most of the tour of the New Jerusalem in contrast to the important role of angelic explanations in the tour to the ends of the earth—apparent because the text is only partially preserved but reasonably certain. It is not until the visionary arrives at the new temple that the angelic guide speaks and reads to him (11Q18 15 4; 19 3). Unfortunately, the text is extremely fragmentary here, making it difficult to draw conclusions about the significance of the introduction of speech.

Another difference has to do with the status of the sights the visionaries see. The sights Enoch sees during his tour are presented as current reality from Enoch's point of view. This point is made explicit when the travelers arrive at the cursed valley and the angel explains that, at the last judgment, it will serve as the place of punishment for the wicked (1 En. 27). The eschatological Jerusalem of the New Jerusalem text, in contrast, cannot represent present reality no matter who the visionary is. If the patriarch Jacob is the visionary, as Eibert Tigchelaar argues, even the earthly Jerusalem is in the future from the visionary's point of view.[19] Furthermore, the

---

18. See, e.g., DiTommaso, *The Dead Sea New Jerusalem Text*, 191–94; and Perrin, *Dynamics of Dream-Vision Revelation*, 58–59, esp. n. 47.

19. Eibert J. C. Tigchelaar, "The Imaginal Context and the Visionary of the Ara-

New Jerusalem tour is clearly modeled on the tour of the future temple in Ezek 40–43, which is also a tour of a future rather than a present structure.

The New Jerusalem text, then, provides more evidence for the importance of the book of Ezekiel and, in particular, its concluding chapters for the literature of the Second Temple period, and it demonstrates that the Book of the Watchers was not alone in taking up the idea of a tour of earthly sites in angelic company. But it is also noteworthy that while the subject matter of the New Jerusalem tour appears to be restricted to topics that appear in Ezekiel's tour, the Book of the Watchers makes use of the form pioneered by Ezekiel to address topics dictated by the narrative of the descent of the watchers.

Finally, I turn to the Astronomical Book, which may well be the earliest of the extant Enochic works, earlier even than the Book of the Watchers.[20] Like the Aramaic of the Book of the Watchers, the Astronomical Book survives only in fragments, but in contrast to the situation for the Book of the Watchers, where the surviving Aramaic generally matches the Ethiopic quite well, the Astronomical Book shows significant differences from the Book of the Luminaries (1 En. 72–82), the corresponding portion of the Ethiopic 1 Enoch.[21] The detailed account of the movements of the moon through heavenly gates in the Astronomical Book indicates an Aramaic work far longer than the Book of the Luminaries and of a somewhat different character.[22] In the absence of any significant evidence for its Greek form, it is impossible to reconstruct the development of the work.[23] It should also be noted that neither Enoch's name nor Methuselah's

---

maic New Jerusalem," in *Flores Florentino: Dead Sea Scrolls and Other Early Jewish Studies in Honour of Florentino García Martínez*, ed. A. Hilhorst, Émile Puech, and Eibert J. C. Tigchelaar, JSJSup 122 (Leiden: Brill, 2007), 260–68. For other opinions, see Perrin, *Dynamics of Dream-Vision Revelation*, 60–61 n. 50.

20. For discussion of the date and issues in dating, see James C. VanderKam in George W. E. Nickelsburg and James C. VanderKam, *1 Enoch 2: A Commentary on the Book of 1 Enoch; Chapters 37–82*, Hermeneia (Minneapolis: Fortress, 2012), 339–45.

21. Nickelsburg and VanderKam, *1 Enoch 2*, 355, for the use of the different titles to distinguish the Aramaic and Ethiopic.

22. Nickelsburg and VanderKam, *1 Enoch 2*, 351–57, for a discussion of the evidence. There is now a significant body of scholarly literature on the relationship between the works.

23. Nickelsburg and VanderKam, *1 Enoch 2*, 345–50, for discussion of the possible Greek evidence.

appears in the surviving Aramaic fragments, although it seems reasonable to assume that they were once found there.[24]

Despite the complexities, the Astronomical Book is undoubtedly relevant to the discussion of the development of heavenly ascent and tours of earth. In the Book of the Luminaries, the account of the paths of moon and sun through the gates of heaven is presented as a revelation to Enoch by the angel Uriel (1 En. 72.1). Uriel is said to show Enoch heavenly phenomena, and Enoch is said to see them.[25] To readers accustomed to the idea of Enoch's ascent, this language suggests that Enoch receives Uriel's words from a vantage point in heaven even in the absence of any mention of ascent or of Enoch and Uriel's travels through heaven. It must be noted, however, that the objects of some of the seeing and showing are laws, presumably not physical entities.

The verb *show* also appears in the Astronomical Book, as the speaker shows information to his son or pupil and is himself shown calculations by an unnamed figure (4Q209 25 3 and 26 7).[26] Comparison to the Book of the

---

24. See esp. 4Q209 23 2 and 26 6.

25. Seeing and showing: 1 En. 72.1 ("Uriel ... showed me"), 72.3 ("I saw six gates"), 73.1 ("I saw a second law"), 74.1 ("Another course and law I saw for it"), 74.2 ("Uriel ... showed me ... their positions I wrote down as he showed me"), 74.9 ("I saw their positions"), 75.3 ("Uriel ... showed me the sign, the seasons, the year, and the days"), 75.4 ("Uriel showed me twelve gates"), 75.8 ("I saw chariots"), 76.1 ("I saw twelve gates"), 76.14 ("I have shown to you everything, my son Methuselah"), 78.10 ("Uriel showed me another law"), 79.1 ("Now my son I have shown you everything"), and 79.6 ("the appearance and the likeness of each luminary that Uriel ... showed me"). I omit 1 En. 80–82 from consideration here because they have a somewhat different character and may have been later additions. All translations of 1 Enoch come from George W. E. Nickelsburg, *1 Enoch 1: A Commentary on the Book of 1 Enoch, Chapters 1–36; 81–108*, Hermeneia (Minneapolis: Fortress, 2001) and Nickelsburg and VanderKam, *1 Enoch 2*. For the language of showing as drawn from the instructions for the building of the tabernacle in Exodus, see Seth L. Sanders, "'I Was Shown Another Calculation' (אחזית חשבון אחרן): The Language of Knowledge in Aramaic Enoch and Priestly Hebrew," in *Ancient Jewish Sciences and the History of Knowledge in Second Temple Literature*, ed. Jonathan Ben-Dov and Seth L. Sanders (New York: New York University Press, 2014), 69–101.

26. I restrict myself to words actually attested as opposed to restored: 4Q209 23 2 ("Their complete explanation [I] have sh[own to you, my son Methuselah]"); 25 3 ("I was shown another [cal]culation for it"); and 26 6–7 ("And now, I am showing to you, my son *vacat* ... a calculation he sho[w]ed [me"). Translation from Eibert J. C. Tigchelaar and Florentino García Martínez, "209. 4QAstronomical Enoch[b] ar," in *Qumran*

Luminaries would suggest that the figure is the angel Uriel, but no indication of his identity survives in the fragments. Furthermore, in contrast to the Book of the Luminaries, where Uriel shows and Enoch sees astronomical and other natural phenomena as well as laws, in the surviving fragments of the Astronomical Book the speaker is shown only calculations, not astronomical phenomena. By themselves, then, the fragments of the Astronomical Book provide no reason to think that its speaker learned the knowledge he is communicating in heaven. Indeed, Henryk Drawnel argues that the showing and seeing not only of the Astronomical Book but of the Book of the Luminaries as well should be understood not as elements of a tour but rather as the interchange between teacher and student: the teacher shows or explains a calculation, and the student sees or understands the calculation.[27]

In addition to its account of the motion of heavenly phenomena, the Book of the Luminaries offers a short description of the four quarters of the earth (1 En. 77.1–3) followed by Enoch's first-person report of seeing mountains from which the snow comes, rivers, and islands (77.4–8).[28] Enough of the Astronomical Book is preserved to show that it, too, included a brief account of the quarters of the earth followed by mountains and snow (4Q209 23 and 4Q210 1 II 2a+b+c); although no verb of seeing is preserved in the Aramaic, the editors restore it on the basis of the Ethiopic.[29] A report of seeing natural phenomena might suggest a tour, and the mountains of the passage as well as mention of the Garden of Righteousness (1 En. 77.3; only partially preserved but nonetheless clear in 4Q209 23 9), recall the tour to the ends of the earth in the Book of the Watchers. But neither the Book of the Luminaries nor the fragments of the Astronomical Book contain any hints of motion on the part of the speaker, and here too Drawnel insists that the proper context for understanding the passage in the Astronomical Book and perhaps even the Book of the Luminaries is didactic: a teacher instructing a student as the student looks

---

Cave 4.XXVI: Cryptic Texts and Miscellanea, Part 1, ed. Stephen J. Pfann et al., DJD 36 (Oxford: Clarendon, 2000), 104–31.

27. Henryk Drawnel, *The Aramaic Astronomical Book (4Q208–4Q211) from Qumran: Text, Translation, and Commentary* (Oxford: Clarendon, 2011), 36–37.

28. 1 En. 77.4 ("I saw seven lofty mountains"), 77.5 ("I saw seven rivers"), and 77.8 ("I saw seven large islands"). The translations are from Nickelsburg and VanderKam, *1 Enoch 2*.

29. They also restore it once where it is lacking in the Ethiopic in 4Q209 23 8 (Tigchelaar and García Martínez, "209. 4QAstronomical Enoch^b ar," 159, and see 161, comments to line 8). Drawnel objects (*Aramaic Astronomical Book*, 192, note to line 8).

at a map incised on a tablet.[30] The suggestion is appealing although the evidence for such maps, to judge by Drawnel's notes, is more limited than one would wish.[31]

Drawnel goes on to suggest that "the literary genre of a heavenly journey probably developed from the kind of didactic literature attested in the *AAB* [Astronomical Book], because Enoch's travels in *1 Enoch* 17–19 and 20–36 have uncontestable points of contact with the *AAB*."[32] The points of contact are indeed notable, and it may well be that the tour form of the Book of the Watchers is indebted to the conventions of didactic literature to which Drawnel points. But it is also clearly indebted to Ezek 40–48 for its verbs of motion and to the tradition of interpretation of dreams and visions attested in biblical literature for the formal features of the angels' explanations of the sights Enoch sees.[33] Furthermore, the New Jerusalem text demonstrates the existence very early of a tour without the elements shared by the Book of the Watchers and the Astronomical Book.

2. The Early Reception of the Book of the Watchers

The Book of Dreams (1 En. 83–90), the Apocalypse of Weeks (1 En. 91, 93), the Book of Giants, and Jubilees can all be placed in the second century BCE with considerable confidence even if there is some disagreement about precisely where in that century each of them belongs.[34] All show sig-

---

30. Drawnel, *Aramaic Astronomical Book*, 37–38.

31. Drawnel, *Aramaic Astronomical Book*, 37, refers to BagM. Beih. 2 no. 98 (n. 132) and Late Babylonian tablet BM 92687 (n. 133); both are in Wayne Horowitz, *Mesopotamian Cosmic Geography* (Winona Lake, IN: Eisenbrauns, 1998), 193–207 and 20–42, respectively.

32. Drawnel, *Aramaic Astronomical Book*, 37.

33. Martha Himmelfarb, *Tours of Hell: An Apocalyptic Form in Jewish and Christian Literature* (Philadelphia: University of Pennsylvania Press, 1983), 50–60.

34. Book of Dreams: Nickelsburg, *1 Enoch 1*, 360–61, with the possibility of a late third-century date, which would presumably require a slightly earlier date for the Book of the Watchers. Apocalypse of Weeks: Nickelsburg, *1 Enoch 1*, 440–41. Book of the Giants: Loren T. Stuckenbruck, *The Book of Giants from Qumran: Text, Translation, Commentary*, TSAJ 63 (Tübingen: Mohr Siebeck, 1997), 31; Émile Puech, *Qumrân Grotte 4.XXII. Textes araméens, première partie: 4Q529–549*, DJD 31 (Oxford: Clarendon, 2001), 14. Jubilees: James C. VanderKam, *Jubilees: A Commentary on the Book of Jubilees, Chapters 1–21*, Hermeneia (Minneapolis: Fortress, 2018), 31–38.

nificant points of contact with the Book of the Watchers. All depict Enoch as an authoritative visionary; indeed, the Apocalypse of Weeks and the Book of Dreams attribute their revelations to him. The Book of Giants (4Q203 8 4 and 4Q530 2 II, 14, 21-22), and Jubilees (4.17-23) refer to or describe Enoch as a scribe, and this role is implicit in the Book of Dreams (1 En. 83.2).

The story of the descent of the watchers also figures prominently in three of the works. It is central to the Book of Giants, in which the protagonists are the offspring of the watchers and their human wives. The Animal Apocalypse of the Book of Dreams includes the story in its review of history with all the actors given animal form (1 En. 86-88).[35] Jubilees offers a version of the story more in keeping with its attitude toward the divine/human divide (Jub. 4.15; 5.1-18).[36] The Apocalypse of Weeks' description of the second week, which includes Enoch's time on earth and the flood—"deceit and violence will spring up" (1 En. 93.4)—does not refer to the story but fits well with it, and the absence of explicit reference needs to be seen in the context of the extreme brevity of all the descriptions of events in the work.[37]

Apart from the Book of Giants, all of the works make mention of or allude to Enoch's sojourn in heaven and his interaction with angels. The introduction to the Apocalypse of Weeks ascribes the revelation that follows to Enoch's "vision of heaven … the words of the watchers and holy ones … and … the heavenly tablets" (93.2).[38] In the Animal Apocalypse, Enoch watches the vision unfold from "a high place" to which he is taken by three angels (1 En. 87.3); from that spot he sees a "tower high above the earth." Jubilees reports that Enoch spent six jubilees with the angels, who showed him "everything on earth and in the heavens" (4.21).[39] Yet none

---

35. The Animal Apocalypse depicts the descent of only a single angelic leader (1 En. 86.1-3) rather than the two of the Book of the Watchers. See Nickelsburg, *1 Enoch 1*, 372.

36. VanderKam, *Jubilees*, 248-49, 290-91.

37. For relation to the story of the watchers, Loren T. Stuckenbruck, *1 Enoch 91-108*, CETL (Berlin: de Gruyter, 2007), 91.

38. The heavenly tablets recur in the story of the birth of Noah together with "the mysteries of the Lord that the holy ones have revealed and shown me" (1 En. 106.19; 4Q204 5 II, 26-27).

39. Trans. VanderKam, *Jubilees*. VanderKam argues that Jubilees intends its "six jubilees of years" to equal 294 years (6 x 49), not the 300 of Gen 5:22 (*Jubilees*, 256-57).

of the texts shows an interest in the process of ascent or the details of the vision of the heavenly throne room.

The impact of the tour to the ends of the earth on these three works is also quite limited. The only aspect of Jubilees' brief account of Enoch's career that might point to it is his residence in the garden of Eden; the calendrical revelation it attributes to Enoch likely alludes to the Astronomical Book.[40] I cannot discern any evidence of the tour's impact on the Apocalypse of Weeks, which is not surprising given its length, or on the Book of Dreams.

The surviving fragments of the Book of Giants do not mention Enoch's time in heaven or his travels with the angels, but they describe the flight of the giant Mahaway across the great wilderness that lies beyond the inhabited world to consult Enoch about the ominous dreams of Ohayah and Hahyah (4Q530 7 II, 4–6). Matthew Goff has argued persuasively that the geography of the flight indicates that the Book of Giants, like Jubilees, understands Enoch to reside in the garden of Eden.[41] Goff also suggests that this picture is shared by the Genesis Apocryphon and the story of Noah's birth (1 En. 106–7), both roughly contemporary with or perhaps slightly later than the works already considered, in their accounts of Methuselah's journey to consult Enoch on behalf of Lamech, Methuselah's son and thus Enoch's grandson, who fears that the marvelous characteristics of the baby Noah mean that he was fathered not by Lamech but by a watcher (1 En. 106.1–18, Gen. Apoc. II, 21–V, 27).[42]

If Mahaway's flight retraces at least a portion of Enoch's tour to the ends of the earth, we learn from another fragment of ascent by a giant: "I, O[hayah], went up into h[eaven] " (4Q531 46). These are the only words the fragment preserves so it impossible to know whether the ascent was described in any detail, either at this point by the speaker or perhaps earlier in the text as part of the third-person narration.

---

40. VanderKam, *Jubilees*, 257.

41. Matthew Goff, "Where's Enoch? The Mythic Geography of the Qumran *Book of Giants*," in *Sibyls, Scriptures, and Scrolls: John Collins at Seventy*, ed. Joel Baden, Hindy Najman, and Eibert J. C. Tigchelaar, JSJSup 175 (Leiden: Brill, 2017), 1:472–88.

42. Goff, "Where's Enoch?," 487–88. Neither work names the garden of Eden, but the story of the birth of Noah locates Enoch's dwelling at "the ends of the earth" (1 En. 106.8), while the Genesis Apocryphon places it at "the end [sing.] of the earth" (Gen. Apoc. II, 23 according to Daniel Machiela, *The Dead Sea Genesis Apocryphon: A New Text and Translation with Introduction and Special Treatment of Columns 13–17*, STDJ 79 [Leiden: Brill, 2009], 37).

In addition, Ohayah's dream (4Q530 2 II+6+7 I+8+9+10+11+12[?], 15–20) attests ongoing interest in the divine throne room, with points of contact with Dan 7 as well as 1 En. 14. The similarities among the three throne visions probably reflect shared traditions adapted for the purposes of each work rather than direct dependence of one on another.[43] Indeed, it is noteworthy that despite its deep debt to the Book of the Watchers, the Book of Giants describes its throne room not as a temple as in 1 En. 14 but as a royal court as in Dan 7.[44]

In summary, for the four texts just discussed, the fact of Enoch's ascent to heaven described in the Book of the Watchers contributes to his authority, as does his acquaintance with angels, which in Watchers is primarily a result of the tour to the ends of the earth. Yet of the four works, only the Book of Giants displays an interest in the content of the vision Enoch sees in the course of his ascent, and only the Book of Giants describes journeys undertaken by other beings, although its fragmentary state unfortunately makes it difficult to discern the significance of the fact that the journeys are undertaken by monstrous antiheroes rather than an extraordinarily pious human being.[45] Nor is it clear how Ohayah's ascent relates to the descent of God on his throne made explicit in Ohayah's dream (4Q530 2 II+6+7 I+8+9+10+11+12[?], 16).

Finally, one further Aramaic text from the second century BCE relevant to the question of interest in Enoch's ascent and tour to the ends of the earth is the Words of Michael.[46] Only a very small portion of the

---

43. For a recent discussion, Amanda M. Davis Bledsoe, "Throne Theophanies, Dream Visions, and Righteous (?) Seers: Daniel, the *Book of Giants*, and *1 Enoch* Reconsidered," in *Ancient Tales of Giants from Qumran and Turfan: Contexts, Traditions, and Influences*, ed. Matthew Goff, Loren T. Stuckenbruck, and Enrico Morano, WUNT 360 (Tübingen: Mohr Siebeck, 2016), 81–96, and see references there at 81 n. 2 and 82 n. 3.

44. Ryan E. Stokes, "The Throne Visions of Daniel 7, *1 Enoch* 14, and the Qumran *Book of Giants* (4Q530): An Analysis of Their Literary Relationship," *DSD* 15 (2008): 340–58. Bledsoe, "Throne Theophanies," 83–89, is critical of Stokes's claims for the dependence of the vision in the Book of the Watchers on a source close to the vision of Dan 7, but Stokes's observations about the similarities and differences of specific features of the visions of Daniel and the Book of the Watchers retain their force even if one prefers a different understanding of the relationship of the visions.

45. On the implications of attributing prophetic dreams to "culpable giant[s]," see Bledsoe, "Throne Theophanies," 95–96 (quotation, 96).

46. Perrin, *Dynamics of Dream-Vision Revelation*, 51–52. See also David

work survives, though in two or three manuscripts. It begins with the angel Michael's description of a tour of the earth: "The words of the writing that Michael spoke to the angels.... He said, I found there troops of fire ... nine mountains, two to the east ... south.... There I saw the angel Gabriel ... And I showed him his vision" (4Q529 1 1-5).[47] The identity of the word "him" to whom the vision is shown is unfortunately lost, but the summary of the content of the tour shows some similarities to the first source in the tour to the ends of the earth in the Book of the Watchers (1 En. 17-19).[48] That source includes both fire and mountains, although there, as in the Astronomical Book (4Q210 1 II, 20) and the Book of the Luminaries (1 En. 77.4), the mountains number seven rather than nine. The possibility of a report on Enoch's tour to the ends of the earth, or even a part of it, from the point of view of one of the angelic participants is extremely tantalizing.

The authority attributed to Enoch in the texts just discussed clearly derives in significant part from his ascent and tour to the ends of the earth and the opportunities they provided for learning heavenly secrets and conversing with angels. The Animal Apocalypse places Enoch above the earth for much of its revelation, and the Book of Giants, the story of Noah's birth (1 En. 106-107), and the Genesis Apocryphon report journeys by others to consult Enoch in his dwelling place beyond the world of human beings. The Book of Giants also apparently included an ascent by a giant. But nobody in the second century BCE (as far as we can tell given the fragmentary state of some of the works) develops the form of ascent or earthly revelatory journey, and apart from the Book of Giants, none of these texts makes a description of the divine throne room or the hidden parts of the earth the content of or the setting for revelation.

To put it a little differently, for all the impact the Book of the Watchers had on them, none of the works just discussed is placed by the *Semeia* 14 volume in the category of apocalypse with an otherworldly journey.

Hamidović, "La transtextualité dans le *livre de Michel* (4Q529; 6Q23): Une étude du répertoire des motifs littéraires apocalyptiques sur Hénoch, Daniel et les *Jubilés*," *Sem* 55 (2013): 117-37.

47. I have made a few changes to the translation of Florentino García Martínez and Eibert J. C. Tigchelaar, *The Dead Sea Scrolls Study Edition* (Leiden: Brill, 1997-1998), 2:1061.

48. Perrin, *Dynamics of Dream-Vision Revelation*, 51, for the identification with Enoch.

The same would surely have been true even for those works that were not available to the authors of the *Semeia* volume. The period on either side of the turn of the third to the second century BCE saw the composition not only of the Book of the Watchers but of the Aramaic Levi Document with its ascent and the New Jerusalem text with its earthly revelatory tour; the tour of the earth attested in the Astronomical Book may be even older. But until the turn of the era, we have no evidence for further development of the form of ascent, while the revelatory tour of earth never experiences a revival.[49]

3. Ascent Apocalypses from the Turn of the Era and Later

Around the turn of the era, two centuries after the composition of the Book of the Watchers, Jews and Christians began to compose apocalypses in which ascent to heaven plays a central role: the Parables of Enoch (1 En. 37–71), 2 Enoch, 3 Baruch, the Apocalypse of Abraham, the Testament of Levi (chs. 2–5), the Ascension of Isaiah, and the Apocalypse of Zephaniah. Other works could certainly be included in the discussion. The visionary of the Revelation of John, for example, spends much of his time in heaven, although the ascent is mentioned rather than described. The Apocalypse of Peter and Apocalypse of Paul with their tours of hell and paradise are also relevant, especially because two of the apocalypses to be discussed show significant points of contact with the Apocalypse of Paul. In the interests of

---

49. The only later instance I know is the brief tour toward the beginning of Sefer Eliyyahu (the Book of Elijah), a late antique Hebrew apocalyptic work written in response to the wars between the Persian and Byzantine Empires during the first decades of the seventh century. The tour is reminiscent of Enoch's tour, but there is no evidence of direct dependence; see Martha Himmelfarb, "*Sefer Eliyyahu*: Jewish Eschatology and Christian Jerusalem," in *Shaping the Middle East: Jews, Christians, and Muslims in an Age of Transition, 400–800 C.E.*, ed. Kenneth G. Holum and Hayim Lapin (Bethesda: University Press of Maryland, 2011), 227–28. James Davila, "Heavenly Ascents in the Qumran Scrolls," in *The Dead Sea Scrolls after Fifty Years: A Comprehensive Assessment*, ed. Peter W. Flint and James C. VanderKam (Leiden: Brill, 1999), 2:461–85, claims a considerable body of texts involving ascent among the Scrolls. But many of the texts in question picture communion with the angels of an individual or the community without a description of the process of ascent. These texts certainly share an understanding of the boundaries between humanity and the angels as permeable with the Book of the Watchers and many of the apocalypses to be discussed below, but they do not provide evidence for ascent in the sense I use the term.

keeping the task more manageable, I have chosen to restrict myself to the apocalypses I studied in *Ascent to Heaven*. All the works I discuss figure as apocalypses involving otherworldly journeys in the *Semeia* volume, the Ascension of Isaiah in the chapter on Christian apocalypses, the others in the chapter on Jewish apocalypses. The only work the *Semeia* 14 volume treats as a Jewish apocalypse involving otherworldly journey that I did not include in *Ascent to Heaven* is the Testament of Abraham, on the grounds that it is not an apocalypse but "a didactic but entertaining story"; for the same reason, I do not treat it here.[50]

Greek is the dominant language of composition for the ascent apocalypses; only the Parables and the Apocalypse of Abraham are usually understood to have been composed in a language other than Greek. But only the Testament of Levi and 3 Baruch are preserved in Greek, and the Greek of 3 Baruch is often seen as a later form of the work than the Slavonic, which is thought to preserve the Greek original better. So too, although all but one of the apocalypses are regarded as Jewish works by the *Semeia* volume and some likely are, all reach us as transmitted by Christians and only because Christians transmitted them.[51]

I shall argue that the ascent apocalypses do not constitute a corpus in the sense that they are closely related to each other. Indeed, there are not many instances in which one apocalypse can be shown to have knowledge of another. Given their independence from each other, any effort to account for the emergence of ascent as an important mode of revelation in apocalyptic texts two centuries after the Book of the Watchers must reckon with the likelihood that no single explanation will apply to all of them. Still, one development that undoubtedly played an important role in encouraging the composition of heavenly ascents after a gap of centuries was the emergence of a new cosmology that allowed for the replacement of the single heaven of the Book of the Watchers with seven heavens.[52] It is important to remember, however, that this new cosmology

---

50. George W. E. Nickelsburg, *Jewish Literature between the Bible and the Mishnah*, 2nd ed. (Minneapolis: Fortress, 2005), 322. For my reasons for omitting the Testament of Abraham, see *Ascent to Heaven*, 8. Unlike John Collins ("The Jewish Apocalypses," *Semeia* 14 [1979]: 42), I am skeptical about its early Jewish provenance. Note also James R. Davila, *The Provenance of the Pseudepigrapha: Jewish, Christian, or Other?* (Leiden: Brill, 2005), 199–207, who is skeptical as well.

51. All of these points will be discussed in greater detail below.

52. On this cosmology and its sources, Adela Yarbro Collins, "The Seven Heavens

never drives out the old so that the picture of a single heaven continues to appear in Jewish and Christian works, including the Parables of Enoch and the Apocalypse of Zephaniah among the ascent apocalypses and the book of Revelation.

3.1. The Parables of Enoch

The consensus dating places the Parables around the turn of the era;[53] the only other ascent apocalypse that can plausibly be placed before the destruction of the temple is 2 Enoch. But the purported historical allusions on which the dating of the Parables is based are by no means certain.[54] Nor, in my view, are the parallels in the Apocalypse of Peter or a supposed reference by Celsus in Origen's *Contra Celsum* (5.52-55) compelling.[55] Furthermore, unlike the other units of 1 Enoch, the Parables is not attested in Aramaic or Greek; indeed, it is impossible to be certain that the original language was Aramaic or that a Greek translation ever existed.[56] In other words, despite the consensus, the grounds for dating the Parables to the turn of the era are quite shaky. For our purposes, I would emphasize that the Parables shows few points of contact with the other ascent apocalypses. Thus, even if it could be shown more convincingly to date to the turn of the era, its significance for understanding the emergence and development of the other ascent apocalypses would be limited.

George Nickelsburg describes the Parables as "a revision" of the Book of the Watchers, and it would certainly be difficult to make sense of the Parables without knowledge of the Book of the Watchers.[57] The Parables begins with a notice of Enoch's ascent to the divine throne

---

in Jewish and Christian Apocalypses," in *Death, Ecstasy, and Other Worldly Journeys*, ed. John J. Collins and Michael Fishbane (Albany: SUNY Press, 1995), 59-93.

53. Nickelsburg and VanderKam, *1 Enoch 2*, 58-63.

54. As Ted M. Erho argues in a series of articles: "The Ahistorical Nature of *1 Enoch* 56:5-8 and Its Ramifications upon the *Opinio Communis* on the Dating of the *Similitudes of Enoch*," *JSJ* 40 (2009): 23-54; "Internal Dating Methodologies and the Problem Posed by the *Similitudes of Enoch*," *JSP* 20 (2010): 83-103; and "Historical-Allusional Dating and the Similitudes of Enoch," *JBL* 130 (2011): 493-511.

55. Nickelsburg in Nickelsburg and VanderKam, *1 Enoch 2*, 76-78.

56. Nickelsburg and VanderKam, *1 Enoch 2*, 31-34, on the possibility of a Hebrew original.

57. Nickelsburg and VanderKam, *1 Enoch 2*, 55-57 (quotation, 55).

room (1 En. 39.3). Heaven is the scene of elaborate liturgical activity (1 En. 39–40). The righteous dead pray on behalf of humanity (39.5), and Enoch joins the angelic praise (39.9–12). Enoch's tour of heaven in the Parables is clearly modeled on the tour to the ends of the earth in the Book of the Watchers, with an angelic guide who explains some of the sights Enoch sees, sometimes in response to his questions, although the Parables hardly mentions directions.[58] Like the Book of the Watchers, the Parables also gives some attention to cosmological phenomena.[59]

The concluding chapters of the Parables offer two more reports of ascent, both apparently intended to represent Enoch's disappearance at the end of his earthly career. The first report (1 En. 70.2) is as brief as the notice at the beginning of the work. The second (1 En. 71) is longer and includes elements clearly drawn from the ascent in the Book of the Watchers (1 En. 14), such as a house of hailstones and flame (1 En. 71.5–6), that do not appear anywhere else in the work. This ascent contains the identification of Enoch as the son of man he has seen in the course of the preceding visions (71.14), an identification that comes as a surprise to a first-time reader. Nickelsburg argues that the presence of the elements from the Book of the Watchers that appear nowhere else in the Parables shows that this section was not part of the original form of the Parables.[60]

The Parables as we have it, then, contains two sources that understand heavenly ascent as central to Enoch's revelation. Yet the dominant concern of the Parables is eschatological judgment, a theme far less central to the Book of the Watchers. The judgment, in which both wicked oppressors and righteous victims receive their due, is to be presided over by a heavenly figure designated as "chosen one," "righteous one," "anointed one," and "son of man."[61] The last designation suggests that the description in Dan 7 of the figure who receives dominion from the

---

58. For discussion and references to the relevant passages, see Nickelsburg and VanderKam, *1 Enoch 2*, 22–23. I note two instances of directions: "West" (1 En. 52.1); "And I looked and turned to another part of the earth" (54.1), presumably from a heavenly vantage point, since Enoch is never said to have descended to earth.

59. Himmelfarb, *Ascent to Heaven*, 80–82.

60. Nickelsburg and VanderKam, *1 Enoch 2*, 330–32.

61. Nickelsburg and VanderKam, *1 Enoch 2*, 44–45.

Ancient of Days—"one like a son of man"—has become a title. Indeed, one way to make sense of the form and content of the Parables is to understand it as an adaptation of the Book of the Watchers intended to correct what it perceived as the earlier work's insufficient attention to the last judgment.

3.2. 2 Enoch

The scholarly consensus treats 2 Enoch as a Jewish work, probably from Egypt, written before the destruction of the temple.[62] But just as the Parables is not attested until the Ethiopic manuscripts, 2 Enoch is first attested in Slavonic manuscripts from the fourteenth century, without any citations or allusions to demonstrate its existence in antiquity. Even the Coptic fragments recently identified as belonging to 2 Enoch would not place the work before the eighth century, although they would strengthen the case for Egyptian provenance and provide early evidence for the short recension of the work.[63] If, however, the case below for 3 Baruch's use of the ascent of 2 Enoch is persuasive, even the fourth-century CE date I would assign 3 Baruch, which is late compared to the turn of the first to the second century of the majority view, would guarantee that at least the ascent of 2 Enoch was written in antiquity.

Like the Parables, 2 Enoch is deeply indebted to the Book of the Watchers, but in contrast to the Parables, it is structured by its seven-heaven schema.[64] Its ascent reconfigures the sights of the ascent and journey to the

---

62. For a helpful recent discussion of provenance, see Christfried Böttrich, "The 'Book of the Secrets of Enoch' (2 En): Between Jewish Origin and Christian Transmission; An Overview," in *New Perspectives on 2 Enoch: No Longer Slavonic Only*, ed. Andrei A. Orlov and Gabriele Boccaccini, StJud 4 (Leiden: Brill, 2012), 37–67.

63. For the fragments, Joost L. Hagen, "No Longer 'Slavonic' Only: 2 Enoch Attested in Coptic from Nubia," in Orlov and Boccaccini, *New Perspectives on 2 Enoch*, 7–34. Hagen dates the fragments to the eighth to tenth century on paleographic grounds (15). For an assessment of the significance of the fragments that highlights the importance of the early attestation of the short recension together with criticism of Hagen's arguments for their identification with 2 Enoch, Christfried Böttrich, "The Angel of Tartarus and the Supposed Coptic Fragments of 2 Enoch," *EC* 4 (2013): 509–21.

64. The long recension includes ten heavens (2 En. 21.6–22.1). Heavens eight through ten are widely viewed as a later addition to the work. See, e.g., Böttrich, "Book of the Secrets," 45 n. 48.

ends of the earth of the Book of the Watchers, using the new cosmology to organize them. The first and third heavens of 2 Enoch (chs. 3–6, 8–10) contain sights related to the tour to the ends of the earth in the Book of the Watchers.[65] From the third heaven up (chs. 8–21), angels offer praise, an adaptation of the Book of the Watchers' picture of heaven as temple. Second Enoch also displays its loyalty to the Book of the Watchers by placing the punishment of the fallen watchers in the second heaven (ch. 7), despite the fact that the story of the descent of the watchers otherwise plays no role in the book. In the fifth heaven, the watchers who remained in heaven mourn their sinful brethren (ch. 18).

One of the most remarkable features of 2 Enoch is its description of Enoch's transformation into a glorious angel:

> Michael extracted me from my clothes. He anointed me with the delightful oil; and the appearance of that oil is greater than the greatest light, its ointment is like sweet dew, and its fragrance like myrrh; and its shining is like the sun. And I gazed at all of myself, and I had become like one of the glorious ones, and there was no observable difference. (22.9–10)[66]

The mode of the transformation in 2 Enoch, anointing with oil, is surely intended to evoke priestly consecration, just as Enoch's glorious appearance evokes the glorious garments in which the high priest is clothed.[67] But even as 2 Enoch goes well beyond the Book of the Watchers' picture of Enoch as a human being welcome in the divine sphere, it draws on the Book of the Watchers' picture of heaven as temple, which implies not only that angels are priests but also that Enoch enjoys priestly status because he is able to traverse the heavenly temple in safety.

To be sure, not all aspects of the ascent in 2 Enoch reflect the influence of the Book of the Watchers. Perhaps most striking, the revelation about cosmogony that constitutes the climax of the ascent (chs. 24–33) has no parallel in the Book of the Watchers. But the author of the ascent must have known the Book of the Watchers and known it well. If, as most scholars believe, the original language of 2 Enoch was Greek and Egypt

---

65. References to 2 Enoch are from F. I. Andersen, "2 (Slavonic Apocalypse of) Enoch," *OTP* 1:91–221, with translation on facing pages of manuscripts representing the long and short recensions.

66. I quote the short manuscript, but the text of the long is very close.

67. Himmelfarb, *Ascent to Heaven*, 40–41.

was the place of composition, the author likely made use of the Greek translation of the Book of the Watchers rather than the Aramaic original. Although the only manuscript of the Book of the Watchers in Greek comes from fifth or sixth century Egypt, there are good grounds for placing that translation before the turn of the era.[68] If so, the Greek translation of the Book of the Watchers became available at about the time the seven-heaven cosmology was becoming popular. The combination of access to the Book of the Watchers and the new cosmology provided at least one reader with the inspiration to imagine ascent in light of contemporary cosmological assumptions.

3.3. 3 Baruch

As already noted, 3 Baruch is preserved in both Greek and Slavonic. While Greek was surely the original language, the Slavonic appears to preserve an earlier form of the work than the Greek that has come down to us.[69] Both versions contain clearly Christian elements, but the elements differ, suggesting that they were added in the course of transmission, and most scholars continue to read 3 Baruch as a Jewish work from the diaspora written in response to the destruction of the second temple.[70] Against this view, I have argued that 3 Baruch should be understood as a Christian

---

68. The Codex Panapolitanus contains almost all of the text known from the Ethiopic. For the date of the codex, see Nickelsburg, *1 Enoch 1*, 12. The Aramaic fragments from the Scrolls make it possible to study the techniques used by the translators of the Book of the Watchers into Greek, and they appear to be similar to those of the translators of LXX Daniel, which is usually dated to the turn of the second to first century BCE. See James Barr, "Aramaic-Greek Notes on the Book of Enoch (I)," *JSS* 23 (1978): 184–98; Barr, "Aramaic-Greek Notes on the Book of Enoch (II)," *JSS* 24 (1979): 179–92; and Erik W. Larson, "The Translation of Enoch: From Aramaic into Greek" (PhD diss., New York University, 1995), 203 and 345. The quotation from the Book of the Watchers in the New Testament Letter of Jude (14–15) shows that the translation was available in the first century CE, and patristic works attest its continued circulation from the second century into late antiquity. See Nickelsburg, *1 Enoch 1*, 86–95.

69. See, e.g., Harry E. Gaylord Jr., "3 (Greek Apocalypse of) Baruch," *OTP* 1: 655; and Alexander Kulik, *3 Baruch: Greek-Slavonic Apocalypse of Baruch*, CEJL (Berlin: de Gruyter, 2010), 13–14.

70. Christian elements: Gaylord, "3 Baruch," 656; and Kulik, *3 Baruch*, 19–24. For discussion of recent scholarship, see Martha Himmelfarb, "*3 Baruch* Revisited: Jewish or Christian Composition, and Why It Matters," *ZAC* 20 (2016): 41–62, esp. 46–53.

work from the same milieu as the Apocalypse of Paul, a tour of paradise and hell from Egypt with a strong monastic flavor, written toward the end of the fourth century CE, with which 3 Baruch shares some important features.[71] I will touch on some of the arguments below.

The structure of the ascent in 3 Baruch is very similar to that of 2 Enoch: the visionary enters each heaven in the company of an angelic guide (3 Baruch) or guides (2 Enoch), who explain the sights they encounter. There are similarities in content as well. Like 2 Enoch, 3 Baruch understands the highest heavens as a temple. While Baruch does not go beyond the fifth heaven, the archangel Michael's ascent from the fifth heaven in order to offer the prayers of humanity to God (3 Bar. 11–16) indicates that there are heavens above the fifth—presumably two—in which liturgical activity takes place.[72]

Another similarity to 2 Enoch is the sight of the personified sun and moon in 3 Baruch's third heaven (3 Bar. 6–9), which recall the personified sun and moon in the fourth heaven of 2 Enoch (2 En. 11–17). The focus of 3 Baruch's narrative of the sun's travels is a remarkable bird, unique to 3 Baruch, which accompanies the sun to protect the earth from its rays, but in both 2 Enoch and 3 Baruch the sun is male and the moon female, and in both works the sun and moon travel in chariots. Both texts also describe the sun as wearing a crown, but 3 Baruch alone reports that the crown must be cleansed every night after becoming defiled by the sins the sun sees on earth (3 Bar. 8.4–5). This point is of particular interest because according to the Apocalypse of Paul, the sun often complains to God about the sins it must witness (Apoc. Paul 4).

At other points 3 Baruch appears to be critical of 2 Enoch. Second Enoch makes the second heaven the place of punishment of the watchers (2 En. 7). Third Baruch eliminates the watchers and instead places the builders of the Tower of Babel in the first heaven (ch. 2) and the planners of the tower in the second heaven (ch. 3); both builders and planners have

---

71. Himmelfarb, "*3 Baruch* Revisited," 57–59, on the relationship of 3 Baruch to the Apocalypse of Paul. For a fourth-century date for the Apocalypse of Paul, see Pierluigi Piovanelli, "Les origines de l'*Apocalypse de Paul* reconsidérées," *Apocrypha* 4 (1993): 25–64; and Kirsti B. Copeland, "Mapping the Apocalypse of Paul: Geography, Genre and History" (PhD diss., Princeton University, 2000).

72. Richard Bauckham, "Early Jewish Visions of Hell," *JTS* 41 (1990): 373–74, argues that 3 Baruch originally contained a description of seven heavens. I am no longer persuaded by the arguments as I was in *Ascent to Heaven*, 90–91.

taken on hybrid animal form. A preference for the story of the Tower of Babel over the story of the watchers might reflect the belief that humanity alone is to blame for evil in the world and that the divine sphere is in no way implicated.[73] Of course, 2 Enoch never actually tells the story of the descent of the watchers, so 3 Baruch would have had to know it from elsewhere to understand its implications, perhaps from the Book of the Watchers itself, which we know to have been in available in Egypt both before and after 3 Baruch's likely date.

The understanding that I have just suggested of the replacement of the watchers with the builders and planners of the tower is complicated by the presence in 3 Baruch's third heaven of a vine identified as the tree of knowledge. The tree of knowledge inevitably calls to mind Genesis's story of Adam and Eve's disobedience, which would support the understanding just suggested. But according to Baruch's angelic guide, it is the devil who was responsible for planting the vine in the garden of Eden (3 Bar. 4.6–17 [Slavonic]; 4.8–17 [Greek]). In this passage, then, 3 Baruch embraces a view of angelic complicity in human evil, though by means of a different narrative from that of the Enoch tradition. Some scholars suggest that the passage about the vine is an interpolation, which would mean that the original form of the work did indeed reject the idea of angelic responsibility for human sin.[74]

Third Baruch also rejects the view found in the Book of the Watchers, 2 Enoch, and, as we shall see, other ascent apocalypses, that pious visionaries can achieve equality with the angels. Baruch never undergoes a transformation, and he continues to address his angelic guide as "lord" throughout the work. In the Ascension of Isaiah, to be discussed next, Isaiah's angelic guide rejects the title (8.5). So too, toward the end of the book of Revelation, John's angelic interlocutor twice insists that they are fellow servants (19:10, 22:8–9). Baruch's failure to ascend higher than the fifth heaven and thus to enter the heavenly temple should also be understood

---

73. Bauckham, "Early Jewish Visions of Hell," 372; and Himmelfarb, *Ascent to Heaven*, 91–93. As is evident from the discussion here, I am now convinced that there exists a relationship between 2 Enoch and 3 Baruch.

74. See Kulik, *3 Baruch*, 192–223, for discussion, commentary, and references. Kulik sees the passage as "an intrusion" but not necessarily an interpolation (192). He is also committed to reading it in Jewish terms. For discussion of the range of the parallels he amasses, Himmelfarb, "*3 Baruch* Revisited," 54.

as reflecting his continued inferiority to the angels, an important point of connection with the Apocalypse of Paul.[75]

If I am correct that 3 Baruch is a Christian work of the fourth century, the chronological gap between 2 Enoch and 3 Baruch is as great as or greater than the gap between the Book of the Watchers and 2 Enoch. Still, it appears that in both cases the gaps were bridged by textual knowledge. Second Enoch adapts and reworks the Book of the Watchers, and 3 Baruch adapts, criticizes, and revises 2 Enoch.

3.4. The Ascension of Isaiah

The Ascension of Isaiah consists of two parts, an account of Isaiah's martyrdom (chs. 1–5) and an account of an ascent that takes place sometime before the martyrdom (chs. 6–11). While the Ethiopic version and one Latin manuscript transmit the entire work, the Slavonic version and a now lost Latin manuscript transmit only the ascent.[76] There is a wide range of views about the relationship between the two sections, but fortunately for our purposes, that question is not crucial to the discussion here.[77] The only surviving Greek witness is a papyrus fragment of a portion of the martyrdom, but there is nonetheless widespread agreement that the original language of the ascent was Greek. The culmination of the ascent is a vision of the descent of Christ, so there can be no doubt that the ascent is a Christian work. It is usually dated to the later first or early second century and often located in Syria.[78]

The ascent describes Isaiah's progress through the seven heavens in the company of an angelic guide. The contents of the six lower heavens are very similar to each other. Each heaven has a throne in the center, occupied by the most glorious angel of the particular heaven (the first heaven lacks an enthroned angel [Ascen. Isa. 7.14–15]), and angels to the left and

---

75. For the Apocalypse of Paul's unwillingness to grant human beings angelic status, see Martha Himmelfarb, "The Experience of the Visionary and Genre in the Ascension of Isaiah 6–11 and the Apocalypse of Paul," *Semeia* 36 (1986): 104–6.

76. Michael A. Knibb, "Martyrdom and Ascension of Isaiah," *OTP* 2:144–45.

77. For a discussion of selected recent scholarship on the Ascension of Isaiah, see Jonathan Knight, "The *Ascension of Isaiah*: A New(er) Interpretation," in *The Ascension of Isaiah*, ed. Jan N. Bremmer, Thomas R. Karmann, and Tobias Nicklas (Leuven: Peeters, 2016), 47–51, as well as the other essays in this volume, which offer a variety of opinions on this question and others discussed here.

78. Thus Knight, "*Ascension of Isaiah*," 70.

right sing praises. As he ascends, Isaiah notes the increasing glory of each successive heaven (e.g., 7.20). In the second heaven, Isaiah attempts to worship the angel seated on the throne, but his angelic guide warns him to wait until the seventh heaven where the appropriate recipient of worship will be found (7.21). Not only should angels not be worshipped, the angelic guide tells Isaiah, but Isaiah himself is superior to the angels: "Your throne, your garments, and your crown ... are set above all these heavens and their angels" (7.22).[79] Indeed, in the third heaven, Isaiah notices that he is undergoing a transformation (7.25), and when he reaches the sixth heaven, his angelic guide, as noted above, tells him not to call him "lord": "I am not your lord but your companion" (8.5).

As Isaiah is about to enter the seventh heaven, the angel in charge of the sixth heaven calls out: "How far may anyone go up who lives among aliens?" (Ascen. Isa. 9.1). But Christ responds: "The holy Isaiah is permitted to come up here, for here is his garment" (9.2). This is the only instance of such a challenge in the ascent apocalypses, but it fits well with the picture of heaven as temple implicit in the liturgical activity Isaiah encounters in each heaven since access to much of the earthly temple is restricted to priests: "The alien [זר] who approaches shall die" (Num 1:51; 3:10, 38; 18:7).[80] The picture of the heavens in Isaiah's ascent is significantly different from that in Christ's descent, but the hostility Isaiah encounters during his ascent prepares the reader for the picture of the descent, in which Christ disguises himself from the fifth heaven down by taking the form of the angels of the heaven in which he finds himself so as not to be recognized and from the third heaven down must provide a password to the angelic gatekeepers (Ascen. Isa. 10.19-31).

When Isaiah arrives in the seventh heaven, he finds not only angels but the righteous dead "stripped of the garments of the flesh ... in their garments of the world above ... like angels, standing there in great glory" (Ascen. Isa. 9.9). They will not receive their thrones and crowns, however, until Christ's ascent after the crucifixion (9.10-18). Isaiah himself becomes "like an angel" and joins the angels in offering praise (9.30-31), but, like the angels, he cannot look upon the Great Glory for long (9.37).

---

79. All translations of the Ascension of Isaiah are taken from Robert H. Charles, revised by J. M. T. Barton, "The Ascension of Isaiah," in *The Apocryphal Old Testament*, ed. H. F. D. Sparks (Oxford: Clarendon, 1984), 775-812.

80. See Johann Maier, "Das Gefährdungsmotiv bei der Himmelsreise in der jüdischen Apokalyptik und 'Gnosis,'" *Kairos* 5 (1963): 18-40.

The righteous dead thus clearly occupy a place in the heavenly hierarchy more exalted than that of the angels, for they are able to "gaz[e] intently upon the Glory" (9.38). The angelic guide's assurance that Isaiah ranks higher than the angels apparently applies only after death.

The Ascension of Isaiah, then, shares some important features of structure and content with 2 Enoch and 3 Baruch, but it also differs in significant ways. Like 2 Enoch and 3 Baruch, it provides its hero with an angelic guide who answers the visionary's questions as he accompanies him through the heavens. It too embraces a seven-heaven cosmology and a picture of heaven as temple, but it differs from 2 Enoch and 3 Baruch in depicting each of the heavens below the seventh in quite similar terms. Furthermore, while Isaiah's garments and the garments of the righteous dead recall Enoch's investiture in 2 Enoch, there are important differences. One might argue that the fact that the righteous dead are superior to the angels, who are more or less by definition the priests of the heavenly temple, implies that the righteous dead are also priests and that their garments should thus be understood in priestly terms. But the Ascension of Isaiah does nothing to make such a connection.

There is nothing in the Ascension of Isaiah that suggests knowledge of earlier ascent apocalypses. Indeed, there were not many such works, especially if I am correct about the date of 3 Baruch. It is certainly possible that the author of the Ascension of Isaiah knew the Book of the Watchers even though it leaves no clear mark on his work. If so, it would have provided him with a model for a tour involving questions and answers, though its tour took place on earth. Yet it is also possible that with the seven-heaven cosmology widely known, the author of the Ascension of Isaiah arrived at a work with significant parallels to 2 Enoch and 3 Baruch without benefit of any literary links. The concern for Christ's descent and ascent evident in the work would provide a motive for describing the ascent of the prophet whose prophecies were of most interest to early Christians.

3.5. The Apocalypse of Abraham

The Apocalypse of Abraham is preserved only in Slavonic, with the earliest manuscript dating to the fourteenth century, but despite some undoubtedly Christian elements and other elements difficult to explain as Jewish, most scholars understand it as a Jewish work composed in Hebrew sometime not long after 70 CE; the date is based on the description of the destruction of a temple in its vision of history (Apoc. Abr. 27.5).[81] The work begins with an account of Abraham's discovery of monotheism as he helps his father with his business of selling idols (chs. 1–7). Once Abraham has rejected idols, God reveals himself and calls to Abraham (chs. 8–9). The ascent follows (chs. 10–19). It culminates in a vision of history that Abraham sees as he stands before the divine throne before returning to earth (chs. 20–31).

The Apocalypse of Abraham shares a seven-heaven cosmology with 2 Enoch, 3 Baruch, and the Ascension of Isaiah, but the process of ascent it describes is significantly different from theirs. Rather than progressing through the heavens one by one, Abraham ascends straight to the seventh heaven. There is therefore neither the opportunity nor the need to describe the contents of the lower heavens. Once Abraham has arrived in the seventh heaven, he looks down and sees the sixth and fifth heavens (Apoc. Abr. 19.6–9), and their contents are briefly noted. The focus of his downward gaze, however, is not the lower heavens but the earth (ch. 21).

The means by which Abraham ascends in the Apocalypse of Abraham is also unparalleled in the ascent apocalypses or any other texts I know. The setting for the ascent is a scene based on the covenant between the pieces of Gen 15. Abraham and his angelic guide depart from the edge of the flames of the furnace of Gen 15 and ascend on the wings of the two birds of the sacrifice (Apoc. Abr. 15.3–4). As they ascend, Abraham sees a terrifying fire with human beings in it, perhaps to be understood as hell (15.7–16.2).[82] In response to Abraham's fear and distress, his angelic guide teaches him a song of praise to protect him on the journey. Upon arriving in the seventh heaven, Abraham discovers that the song is being sung by the angels of the divine throne, including the four living creatures. The throne is described in terms that recall Ezek 1 (Apoc. Abr. 18.3, 12–13),

---

81. On the date, Alexander Kulik, *Retroverting Slavonic Pseudepigrapha: Toward the Original of the Apocalypse of Abraham* (Atlanta: Society of Biblical Literature, 2014), 2–3, and for arguments in favor of a Hebrew original, 61–76. Michael Sommer, "Ein Text aus Palästina? Gedanken zur einleitungswissenschaftlichen Verortung der Apokalypse des Abraham," *JSJ* 47 (2016): 236–56, argues that the Apocalypse of Abraham comes from the diaspora rather than Palestine, as is usually claimed. If so, the most likely language of composition would be Greek. But Sommer does not address the question of the original language.

82. See the notes in R. Rubinkiewicz, "Apocalypse of Abraham," *OTP* 1:696 n. f to ch. 15.

but in contrast to Ezekiel, the Apocalypse of Abraham does not offer a description of God or even note that he is seated on the throne, a point to which I shall return shortly.[83] Abraham also hears the recitation of the heavenly trishagion (18.14).[84] Altogether, there can be no doubt that the seventh heaven is to be understood as a temple, a picture that fits well with Abraham's ascent from the midst of a sacrifice.

In 2 Enoch, as we saw, Enoch's transformation into a glorious angel is described in terms that recall high priestly anointing. In the Ascension of Isaiah, garments, though without explicit priestly indicators, mark the transformation of the righteous dead to a status above that of the angels, though if heaven is understood as a temple, any garment that allows its wearer to join the angels could be understood as priestly. In the Apocalypse of Abraham, Abraham is promised the garment that had once belonged to Azazel, the wicked angel who attempts to prevent the sacrifice of the covenant between the pieces (chs. 13–14; garment, 13.14); he does not receive it in the course of the work, however. Furthermore, Abraham's angelic guide is not an ordinary angel, but rather Yahoel, the angel who bears the name of the Lord. Although he has a griffin's body (Apoc. Abr. 11.2), other aspects of his marvelous appearance recall Ezekiel's description of the enthroned glory and Daniel's description of the Ancient of Days (Apoc. Abr. 11.2–3; Ezek 1:27–28; Dan 7:9), while the headdress, garment, and staff are surely intended to mark him as high priest.[85]

The Apocalypse of Abraham, then, shares some central features with the other ascent apocalypses, but it also differs in significant ways. One of those ways is the absence of a description of God enthroned noted above; the only other apocalypse that avoids such a description is 3 Baruch. Andrei Orlov has recently argued that the Apocalypse of Abraham's avoidance of the vision of God is an aspect of its "aural mysticism," which involves a polemic against anthropomorphism. The argument for polemi-

---

83. For the contrast to Ezekiel, see Christopher Rowland, *The Open Heaven: A Study of Apocalyptic in Judaism and Early Christianity* (New York: Crossroad, 1982), 86–87. This point is developed by Andrei A. Orlov, *Heavenly Priesthood in the* Apocalypse of Abraham (Cambridge: Cambridge University Press, 2013), 45–72, who emphasizes the importance of sound and hearing for the Apocalypse of Abraham.

84. See the translation of Kulik, *Retroverting Slavonic Pseudepigrapha*, 24; and Rubinkiewicz, "Apocalypse of Abraham," 698 n. l to ch. 18.

85. Griffin: Kulik, *Retroverting Slavonic Pseudepigrapha*, 83; and Orlov, *Heavenly Priesthood*, 66–68. High priest: Himmelfarb, *Ascent to Heaven*, 62; and Orlov, *Heavenly Priesthood*, 96.

cal intent relies in part on the assumption that the authors of the Apocalypse of Abraham purposely deviated from the details of other apocalyptic accounts of the heavens.[86]

Many of Orlov's insights are compelling. The case for the Apocalypse of Abraham's avoidance of aspects of the throne visions of Ezekiel is very strong; there can be no doubt that the Apocalypse of Abraham knew the work. But there is no similar evidence in the Apocalypse of Abraham for knowledge of the Book of the Watchers, the Parables of Enoch, or 2 Enoch, the only ascent apocalypses likely to have been available to authors writing not long after the destruction of the second temple. It is, of course, possible that the authors of the Apocalypse of Abraham absorbed the picture found in one or more of those apocalypses without leaving any clear indications in their work. But it is also possible, and perhaps probable, that the differences between the Apocalypse of Abraham and the other apocalypses reflect independent development.

3.6. The Testament of Levi 2–5

The Testament of Levi forms part of the Greek Testaments of the Twelve Patriarchs, a Christian work of the second century CE that made extensive use of Jewish traditions.[87] The Testament of Levi is a special case within the testaments, however, since it is a reworking of an earlier text, the Aramaic Levi Document discussed above. The presence of an ascent in the Testament of Levi thus does not necessarily indicate any particular interest in ascent on the part of the author of the testaments. Rather, it was required by the work on which he drew. The ascent of Aramaic Levi has not survived, but comparison of the Testament of Levi to the surviving portions

---

86. The arguments throughout Orlov, *Heavenly Priesthood*, 45–72, rely on this assumption. I cannot discuss here Orlov's assumptions about knowledge of Jewish mystical traditions attested only later. For "aural mysticism," Orlov, *Heavenly Priesthood*, 61. My use of the plural "authors" follows Orlov.

87. Marinus de Jonge argued for this position for half a century. See, especially, "The Pre-Mosaic Servants of God in the Testaments of the Twelve Patriarchs and in the Writings of Justin and Irenaeus," *VC* 39 (1985): 157–70; and "Defining the Major Issues in the Study of the *Testaments of the Twelve Patriarchs*," in *Pseudepigrapha of the Old Testament as Part of Christian Literature: The Case of the Testaments of the Twelve Patriarchs and the Greek Life of Adam and Eve*, SVTP 18 (Leiden: Brill, 2003), 71–82, to the best of my knowledge his last statement on the subject.

of Aramaic Levi shows both the extent of its debt and the thorough-going character of the revision.[88]

The author of the Testaments of the Twelve Patriarchs may well have known Aramaic, but since he wrote the testaments in Greek, it seems likely that he would have made use of the Greek translation of the Aramaic Levi Document for his project. That translation has been lost except for two passages that survive as additions to the Testament of Levi in the eleventh-century manuscript *e* (Athos, Koutloumous 39) of the Testaments of the Twelve Patriarchs. There are unfortunately no citations to guarantee an earlier date for the translation.[89] Use by the author of the Testaments of the Twelve Patriarchs would mean that it was available in the second century of this era. The translation was apparently not of great interest to Christians, or at least not for very long, as demonstrated by their failure to transmit it and the absence of daughter translations. This fact provides some support for the view that the translation was made by Jews and thus likely predated the composition of the Testaments of the Twelve Patriarchs.

Whatever the role of the Greek translation of the Aramaic Levi Document in the composition of the Testament of Levi, there can be no doubt about the importance of the availability of the seven-heaven schema that also provided the framework for 2 Enoch's reworking of the Book of the Watchers. But the structure of the Testament of Levi's ascent is far less straightforward than that of 2 Enoch. To begin, while it suggests that Levi will reach the seventh heaven (T. Lev. 2.9–10), it does not actually report his progress beyond the second heaven (2.6–8). The lack of progress is emphasized by the fact that the angelic guide's description of the contents of the heavens takes place in one long speech rather than heaven by heaven, with the four highest heavens described in reverse order (ch. 3). Eventually the angel opens the "gates of heaven" to allow Levi to see God seated on his throne of glory (5.1). The singular "heaven" is surprising after the account of the seven

---

88. On the Testament of Levi's relationship to the Aramaic Levi Document, Marinus de Jonge, "Levi in the Aramaic Levi Document and the Testament of Levi," in *Pseudepigrapha of the Old Testament*, 124–40. De Jonge characterizes the Christian author's activity as "at the same time conservative and drastic" (139–40).

89. The passages discussed by Johannes Tromp, "Two References to a Levi Document in an Epistle of Ammonas," *NovT* 39 (1997): 235–47, are intriguing but do not constitute such evidence.

heavens, and Marinus de Jonge suggests that is a relic of the picture of the Aramaic, although the Aramaic word for heaven is, of course, a plural form. But it is by no means clear that Levi actually ascends to the seventh heaven; perhaps with the gates open, he sees the sight from afar.[90]

As in 2 Enoch, the higher heavens in the Testament of Levi are described in terms that suggest that they are a temple. The angels of the fourth heaven offer praise (3.8). The significance of the activity of the angels of the fifth heaven, bearing answers to the angels of the Presence (3.7), is less obvious, but it likely involves mediating between human beings and the upper reaches of heaven.[91] The sixth heaven is the scene of sacrifice, "a pleasant odor, a reasonable and bloodless offering" (3.5-6); the phrase "reasonable and bloodless offering" appears in other Christian sources, sometimes of the Eucharist.[92] The seventh heaven, where God dwells, is called both "the holy temple" (5.1) and the "holy of holies" (3.5).

But despite the fact that its hero is the ancestor of the priesthood, the Testament of Levi offers nothing like 2 Enoch's description of Enoch's transformation via anointing in the course of Levi's ascent. The absence of transformation fits well with a picture in which Levi never actually reaches the seventh heaven. Not long after the ascent, however, the Testament of Levi describes a second vision in which seven angels consecrate Levi as priest. It is impossible to be certain how to understand the separation of Levi's heavenly ascent and consecration in the Testament of Levi. In the Aramaic Levi Document, one of the fragments makes it clear that Jacob consecrated his son, but this act does not preclude earlier consecration by angels in the lost ascent or in a second vision that the Aramaic document may have contained.[93]

Altogether, there is no reason to understand the ascent in the Testament of Levi as indebted to any earlier ascent apart from the lost ascent

---

90. For discussion of the complexities of the picture of the heavens in the Testament of Levi, see Marinus de Jonge, "Notes on Testament of Levi II–VII," in *Studies on the Testaments of the Twelve Patriarchs: Text and Interpretation*, ed. Marinus de Jonge, SVTP 3 (Leiden: Brill, 1975), 252–56 and 259; on the singular "heaven," 253.

91. See Harm W. Hollander and Marinus de Jonge, *The Testaments of the Twelve Patriarchs: A Commentary*, SVTP 8 (Leiden: Brill, 1985), 138–39.

92. Trans. Hollander and de Jonge, *Testaments of the Twelve Patriarchs*, 136, on "reasonable and bloodless sacrifice," 138.

93. The lacunae in the text make certainty impossible, but see, e.g., Greenfield, Stone, and Eshel, *Aramaic Levi Document*, 138 to 4.4 and 146 to 4.13.

of the Aramaic Levi Document. Its points of contact with 2 Enoch, 3 Baruch, and the Ascension of Isaiah are very broad: a seven-heaven cosmology, an angelic guide, and a picture of heaven or rather the highest heavens as a temple. The author of the Testaments of the Twelve Patriarchs need not have read or even been aware of 2 Enoch or any other ascent apocalypse available in the second century CE to have written the ascent he composed.

3.7. The Apocalypse of Zephaniah

I use this title for a partially preserved work from an Akhmimic manuscript from the end of the fourth century. The name of the visionary is not preserved, and some scholars reasonably prefer to refer to the work as the Anonymous Apocalypse. But the points of contact with a fragment of an apocalypse from a Sahidic manuscript of the early fifth century in which the name Zephaniah appears have led other scholars to conclude that the two manuscripts attest the same work.[94] Years ago, I argued on the basis of the single heaven that the Apocalypse of Zephaniah was Jewish and relatively early.[95] It now seems to me more likely that the single heaven reflects the focus on the reward and punishment of souls after death, especially in light of its relationship to the Apocalypse of Paul, for which the Apocalypse of Zephaniah was a source and which also describes a single heaven as the place of reward for good souls, though it labels it the third heaven.[96] As I have already indicated, the current scholarly consensus dates the Apocalypse of Paul to the late fourth century rather than to the second century; thus, a work used by the Apocalypse of Paul need be no earlier than the middle of the fourth century.

The dating has some bearing on the question of whether the Apocalypse of Zephaniah is of Jewish or Christian provenance. There can be no doubt that in its present form it is Christian, since as far as we know Jews never used Coptic. But it is widely agreed that the Coptic is a translation of a Greek original, and the work does not contain the kind of clearly Christian elements that appear in the Ascension of Isaiah, the Testament

---

94. K. H. Kuhn, "The Apocalypse of Elijah," in *The Apocryphal Old Testament*, ed. H. F. D. Sparks (Oxford: Clarendon, 1984), 753–55, and "The Apocalypse of Zephaniah and an Anonymous Apocalypse," in Sparks, *Apocryphal Old Testament*, 915–18.

95. Himmelfarb, *Tours of Hell*, 13–16 and 151–53.

96. Himmelfarb, *Tours of Hell*, 147–51.

of Levi, and even 3 Baruch. It does, however, contain some lines that could be understood as echoes of New Testament passages, and it uses the term "catechumen."[97] An earlier date would make the case for Jewish composition more powerful. But if use by the Apocalypse of Paul no longer assures a date before the middle of the fourth century, Christian composition should be the default assumption.

The Apocalypse of Zephaniah is unusual not only in its picture of a single heaven but also in its protagonist's identity. He is not a living hero of the past but a dead soul, pious but not without flaws. The flaws do not perhaps preclude identification with the prophet Zephaniah, but it would be a little surprising if the identification is intended. The work recounts Zephaniah's experience as he leaves the body. He is at first accompanied by an angelic guide, whom he questions as he sees the punishment of the wicked. The guide disappears as Zephaniah enters a beautiful city but reappears at the end of the surviving portion of the manuscript as Zephaniah sees more punishments. The beautiful city soon becomes threatening, and Zephaniah misperceives a fiery sea as a sea of water. He is then rescued by an angel and attempts to worship him, only to discover that the angel is the accuser. Despite his various *faux pas*, he is rescued by the glorious angel Eremiel, and after a reading of his sins and presumably his good deeds (now lost), he is taken by boat to paradise and given an angelic garment that permits him to join the angels in prayer. But he remains inferior to the great angel with whom the patriarchs residing in paradise converse "like a friend with friends."[98]

The Apocalypse of Zephaniah shares some elements with other ascent apocalypses, such as the angelic guide and the garment that allows him to join the angels. But its single-heaven cosmology and its focus on reward and punishment to the exclusion of other concerns sets it apart from the other works considered, and there is no evidence for its use or knowledge of other ascent apocalypses.

---

97. For possible Christian elements, see discussion and references in Himmelfarb, *Tours of Hell*, 15–16; and O. S. Wintermute, "Apocalypse of Zephaniah," *OTP* 1:501, 515 n. b to 10.10 (catechumen).

98. Trans. Kuhn, "Apocalypse of Zephaniah," 924 (3.10 in Kuhn's numbering; there is, unfortunately, no standard system of chapters and verse for the text).

4. Conclusions

Let me conclude by pointing to some of the implications of this attempt at a more historical approach to the development of the ascent apocalypses. Attention to genre has enabled many important advances in the study of apocalyptic literature. But it has also led us to overlook some important questions regarding the relationship between the Book of the Watchers and the later ascent apocalypses and the relationship of the later ascents to each other. The point of departure for my dissatisfaction with the picture I once embraced is the observation that, despite the impact of the Book of the Watchers in the second century, it is not until late in the first century BCE or even early in the first century CE that the first ascent apocalypses appear. That is, in the century or so following its composition, the Book of the Watchers made Enoch a figure of great authority, or at least confirmed him as such, and inspired the composition of apocalypses focused on history and the eschaton. Yet it took two centuries from the composition of the Book of the Watchers until another ascent apocalypse was produced. This two-century gap serves to underline the differences between the Book of the Watchers and the later texts, notably its single heaven in contrast to the seven-heaven schema that dominates the later works, and its connections to the Aramaic literature of the early Hellenistic period.

Despite the gap, the Parables of Enoch and 2 Enoch are deeply indebted to the Book of the Watchers. Remarkably, in light of the assumptions built into the idea of a subgenre of apocalypses with otherworldly journeys, the only other literary debt of one ascent apocalypse to another is that of 3 Baruch to 2 Enoch. Apart from these cases, there is no clear evidence for knowledge of one text considered above by another, and so we need to account not for the development of the subgenre out of the Book of the Watchers but rather for the independent composition of works with similar forms in the service of related concerns, though always with distinctive differences.

One important factor in the emergence of the ascent apocalypses around the turn of the era was undoubtedly the new popularity of the idea of seven heavens among Jews and Christians. Such a cosmology offered new opportunities for organizing earthly and celestial phenomena and for depicting the relationship between the human and the divine sphere. Second Enoch is the first of the ascent apocalypses to adopt this cosmology. It uses the multiple heavens as a repository for phenomena of both the ascent and tour to the ends of the earth of the Book of the Watchers. Second Enoch was likely written in Greek in Egypt and probably could not have been written without the availability of the Greek translation of the Book of the Watchers. Yet the translation seems unlikely to be the impetus for its composition since it likely took place a century or more before the turn of the era.

Angelic guides play a role in all the ascent apocalypses, and in many of them the guides engage in dialogue with the visionary. But the author of an ascent apocalypse need not have known the Book of the Watchers or other ascent apocalypses to arrive at the figure of the guide. Possible models appear in works likely to have been widely available by the turn of the era, such as the angel who measures the future temple in Ezek 40–43 and the interpreting angels of Zech 1–8 and the book of Daniel. For someone who embraced a picture of seven heavens, it clearly did not require a textual model to assign an angel the role of tour guide.

Many of the ascent apocalypses reflect an understanding of the boundaries between humanity and the divine sphere as permeable. Such a view is already on display in the Book of the Watchers, but the ascent apocalypses take it considerably farther. In my earlier study of the ascent apocalypses, I tried to suggest reasons why such a picture would be attractive to Jews in the Second Temple period.[99] Here I want to suggest the possibility that the Christian provenance of several of the works may have been a factor in motivating the composition of ascents. Christian authorship of the Ascension of Isaiah is uncontroversial, and I also understand the Testament of Levi, 3 Baruch, and the Apocalypse of Zephaniah (in descending order of confidence) as Christian works. One might have thought that ascent to heaven would have lost its appeal for Christians since Christ's ascent presumably trumped the others and perhaps even made them unnecessary, or one might have expected anxiety about depicting anyone but Christ ascending to heaven. But for some Christians it appears that the ascent of worthies of the past provided a pattern that Christ could follow and bring to fruition.[100] Their ascent also offered an opportunity for prophecy of the coming of Christ and for revelation about a subject of great interest to early Christians: the fate of souls after death, the central concern of the

---

99. Himmelfarb, *Ascent to Heaven*, 69–71.

100. For the heroes of the invented apocalypses of the Mani Codex as predecessors to Mani, John C. Reeves, *Heralds of That Good Realm: Syro-Mesopotamian Gnosis and Jewish Traditions* (Leiden: Brill, 1996); and David Frankfurter, "Apocalypses Real and Alleged in the Mani Codex," *Numen* 44 (1997): 60–73.

Apocalypse of Zephaniah and a prominent topic in the Ascension of Isaiah and 3 Baruch.

The picture I have sketched is messier than the picture implied by the *Semeia* 14 volume. The publication of the New Jerusalem text in the decades since the *Semeia* volume and scholarly attention to the Aramaic Levi Document and the Astronomical Book provide a richer context for the Book of the Watchers. But for the later ascent apocalypses my picture perhaps takes away more than it gives. It certainly requires us to rethink the significance of the variety of pictures of ascent and to move away from the very appealing picture of conscious manipulation of conventions by authors and for audiences acquainted with multiple apocalyptic ascents. It is my hope, however, that it will contribute to a deeper and more historically informed understanding of ascent apocalypses and of the significance of ascent to heaven for ancient Jews and Christians.

Bibliography

Andersen, F. I. "2 (Slavonic Apocalypse of) Enoch." *OTP* 1:91–221.

Barr, James. "Aramaic-Greek Notes on the Book of Enoch (I)." *JSS* 23 (1978): 184–98.

———. "Aramaic-Greek Notes on the Book of Enoch (II)." *JSS* 24 (1979): 179–92.

Bauckham, Richard. "Early Jewish Visions of Hell." *JTS* 41 (1990): 355–85.

Bledsoe, Amanda M. Davis. "Throne Theophanies, Dream Visions, and Righteous (?) Seers: Daniel, the *Book of Giants*, and *1 Enoch* Reconsidered." Pages 81–96 in *Ancient Tales of Giants from Qumran and Turfan: Contexts, Traditions, and Influences*. Edited by Matthew Goff, Loren T. Stuckenbruck, and Enrico Morano. WUNT 360. Tübingen: Mohr Siebeck, 2016.

Böttrich, Christfried. "The Angel of Tartarus and the Supposed Coptic Fragments of 2 Enoch." *EC* 4 (2013): 509–21.

———. "The 'Book of the Secrets of Enoch' (2 En): Between Jewish Origin and Christian Transmission; An Overview." Pages 37–67 in *New Perspectives on 2 Enoch: No Longer Slavonic Only*. Edited by Andrei A. Orlov and Gabriele Boccaccini. StJud 4. Leiden: Brill, 2012.

Charles, Robert H., revised by J. M. T. Barton. "The Ascension of Isaiah." Pages 775–812 in *The Apocryphal Old Testament*. Edited by H. F. D. Sparks. Oxford: Clarendon, 1984.

Collins, John J., ed. *Apocalypse: The Morphology of a Genre. Semeia* 14 (1979).
———. "Introduction: Towards the Morphology of a Genre." *Semeia* 14 (1979): 1–20.
———. "The Jewish Apocalypses." *Semeia* 14 (1979): 21–60.
Copeland, Kirsti B. "Mapping the Apocalypse of Paul: Geography, Genre and History." PhD diss., Princeton University, 2000.
Davila, James. "Heavenly Ascents in the Qumran Scrolls." Pages 461–85 in vol. 2 of *The Dead Sea Scrolls after Fifty Years*. Edited by Peter W. Flint and James C. VanderKam. Leiden: Brill, 1999.
———. *The Provenance of the Pseudepigrapha: Jewish, Christian, or Other?* Leiden: Brill, 2005.
DiTommaso, Lorenzo. *The Dead Sea New Jerusalem Text: Contents and Contexts*. TSAJ 110. Tübingen: Mohr Siebeck, 2005.
Drawnel, Henryk. *The Aramaic Astronomical Book (4Q208–4Q211) from Qumran: Text, Translation, and Commentary*. Oxford: Clarendon, 2011.
———. *An Aramaic Wisdom Text from Qumran: A New Interpretation of the Levi Document*. JSJSup 86. Leiden: Brill, 2004.
Erho, Ted M. "The Ahistorical Nature of *1 Enoch* 56:5–8 and Its Ramifications upon the *Opinio Communis* on the Dating of the *Similitudes of Enoch*." *JSJ* 40 (2009): 23–54.
———. "Historical-Allusional Dating and the Similitudes of Enoch." *JBL* 130 (2011): 493–511.
———. "Internal Dating Methodologies and the Problem Posed by the *Similitudes of Enoch*." *JSP* 20 (2010): 83–103.
Frankfurter, David. "Apocalypses Real and Alleged in the Mani Codex." *Numen* 44 (1997): 60–73.
García Martínez, Florentino, and Eibert J. C. Tigchelaar. *The Dead Sea Scrolls Study Edition*. 2 vols. Leiden: Brill, 1997–1998.
Gaylord, Harry E., Jr. "3 (Greek Apocalypse of) Baruch." *OTP* 1:653–79.
Goff, Matthew. "Where's Enoch? The Mythic Geography of the Qumran *Book of Giants*." Pages 472–88 in vol. 1 of *Sibyls, Scriptures, and Scrolls: John Collins at Seventy*. Edited by Joel Baden, Hindy Najman, and Eibert J. C. Tigchelaar. JSJSup 175.1. Leiden: Brill, 2017.
Greenfield, Jonas C., Michael E. Stone, and Esther Eshel. *The Aramaic Levi Document: Edition, Translation Commentary*. SVTP 19. Leiden: Brill, 2004.

Hagen, Joost L. "No Longer 'Slavonic' Only: 2 Enoch Attested in Coptic from Nubia." Pages 7–34 in *New Perspectives on 2 Enoch: No Longer Slavonic Only*. Edited by Andrei A. Orlov and Gabriele Boccaccini. StJud 4. Leiden: Brill, 2012.

Hamidović, David. "La transtextualité dans le *livre de Michel* (4Q529; 6Q23): Une étude du répertoire des motifs littéraires apocalyptiques sur Hénoch, Daniel et les *Jubilés*." *Sem* 55 (2013): 117–37.

Himmelfarb, Martha. "*3 Baruch* Revisited: Jewish or Christian Composition, and Why It Matters." *ZAC* 20 (2016): 41–62.

———. *Ascent to Heaven in Jewish and Christian Apocalypses*. New York: Oxford University Press, 1993.

———. "The Experience of the Visionary and Genre in the Ascension of Isaiah 6–11 and the Apocalypse of Paul." *Semeia* 36 (1986): 97–111.

———. "*Sefer Eliyyahu*: Jewish Eschatology and Christian Jerusalem." Pages 223–38 in *Shaping the Middle East: Jews, Christians, and Muslims in an Age of Transition, 400–800 C.E.* Edited by Kenneth G. Holum and Hayim Lapin. Bethesda: University Press of Maryland, 2011.

———. *Tours of Hell: An Apocalyptic Form in Jewish and Christian Literature*. Philadelphia: University of Pennsylvania Press, 1983.

Hollander, Harm W., and Marinus de Jonge. *The Testaments of the Twelve Patriarchs: A Commentary*. SVTP 8. Leiden: Brill, 1985.

Horowitz, Wayne. *Mesopotamian Cosmic Geography*. Winona Lake, IN: Eisenbrauns, 1998.

Jonge, Marinus de. "Defining the Major Issues in the Study of the *Testaments of the Twelve Patriarchs*." Pages 71–82 in *Pseudepigrapha of the Old Testament as Part of Christian Literature: The Case of the Testaments of the Twelve Patriarchs and the Greek Life of Adam and Eve*. SVTP 18. Leiden: Brill, 2003.

———. "Levi in the Aramaic Levi Document and the Testament of Levi." Pages 121–40 in *Pseudepigrapha of the Old Testament as Part of Christian Literature: The Case of the Testaments of the Twelve Patriarchs and the Greek Life of Adam and Eve*. SVTP 18. Leiden: Brill, 2003.

———. "Notes on Testament of Levi II–VII." Pages 247–60 in *Studies on the Testaments of the Twelve Patriarchs: Text and Interpretation*. Edited by Marinus de Jonge. SVTP 3. Leiden: Brill, 1975.

———. "The Pre-Mosaic Servants of God in the Testaments of the Twelve Patriarchs and in the Writings of Justin and Irenaeus." *VC* 39 (1985): 157–70.

Knibb, Michael A. "Martyrdom and Ascension of Isaiah." *OTP* 2:143–76.

Knight, Jonathan. "The *Ascension of Isaiah*: A New(er) Interpretation." Pages 47–51 in *The Ascension of Isaiah*. Edited by Jan N. Bremmer, Thomas R. Karmann, and Tobias Nicklas. Leuven: Peeters, 2016.

Kugler, Robert A. *From Patriarch to Priest: The Levi-Priestly Tradition from Aramaic Levi to Testament of Levi*. EJL 9. Atlanta: Scholars Press, 1996.

Kuhn, K. H. "The Apocalypse of Elijah." Pages 753–73 in *The Apocryphal Old Testament*. Edited by H. F. D. Sparks. Oxford: Clarendon, 1984.

———. "The Apocalypse of Zephaniah." Pages 915–25 in *The Apocryphal Old Testament*. Edited by H. F. D. Sparks. Oxford: Clarendon, 1984.

Kulik, Alexander. *3 Baruch: Greek-Slavonic Apocalypse of Baruch*. CEJL. Berlin: de Gruyter, 2010.

———. *Retroverting Slavonic Pseudepigrapha: Toward the Original of the Apocalypse of Abraham*. Atlanta: Society of Biblical Literature, 2014.

Larson, Erik W. "The Translation of Enoch: From Aramaic into Greek." PhD diss., New York University, 1995.

Machiela, Daniel. *The Dead Sea Genesis Apocryphon: A New Text and Translation with Introduction and Special Treatment of Columns 13–17*. STDJ 79. Leiden: Brill, 2009.

Maier, Johann. "Das Gefährdungsmotiv bei der Himmelsreise in der jüdischen Apokalyptik und 'Gnosis.'" *Kairos* 5 (1963): 18–40.

Milik, Jósef T. *The Books of Enoch: Aramaic Fragments of Qumrân Cave 4*. With the collaboration of Matthew Black. Oxford: Clarendon, 1976.

Najman, Hindy, and Mladen Popović, eds. *Rethinking Genre: Essays in Honor of John J. Collins*. DSD 17 (2010).

Newsom, Carol A. "Spying out the Land: A Report from Genology." Pages 437–50 in *Seeking Out the Wisdom of the Ancients: Essays Offered to Honor Michael V. Fox on the Occasion of His Sixty-Fifth Birthday*. Edited by Ronald L. Troxel, Kelvin G. Friebel, and Dennis Robert Magary. Winona Lake, IN: Eisenbrauns, 2005.

Nickelsburg, George W. E. *1 Enoch 1: A Commentary on the Book of 1 Enoch, Chapters 1–36; 81–108*. Hermeneia. Minneapolis: Fortress, 2001.

———. *Jewish Literature between the Bible and the Mishnah*. 2nd ed. Minneapolis: Fortress, 2005.

Nickelsburg, George W. E., and James C. VanderKam. *1 Enoch 2: A Commentary on the Book of 1 Enoch; Chapters 37–82*. Hermeneia. Minneapolis: Fortress, 2012.

Orlov, Andrei A. *Heavenly Priesthood in the* Apocalypse of Abraham. Cambridge: Cambridge University Press, 2013.

Perrin, Andrew B. *The Dynamics of Dream-Vision Revelation in the Aramaic Dead Sea Scrolls.* JAJSup 19. Göttingen: Vandenhoeck & Ruprecht, 2015.

Piovanelli, Pierluigi. "Les origines de l'*Apocalypse de Paul* reconsidérées." *Apocrypha* 4 (1993): 25–64.

Puech, Émile, ed. *Qumrân Grotte 4.XXII. Textes araméens, première partie: 4Q529–549.* DJD 31. Oxford: Clarendon, 2001.

Ratzon, Eshbal. "A Sectarian Background for 1 Enoch 22." Pages 171–97 in *On Using Sources in Graeco-Roman, Jewish and Early Christian Literature.* Edited by Joseph Verheyden et al. BETL 327. Leuven: Peeters, 2022.

Reeves, John C. *Heralds of That Good Realm: Syro-Mesopotamian Gnosis and Jewish Traditions.* Leiden: Brill, 1996.

Rowland, Christopher. *The Open Heaven: A Study of Apocalyptic in Judaism and Early Christianity.* New York: Crossroad, 1982.

Rubinkiewicz, R. "Apocalypse of Abraham." *OTP* 1:681–705.

Sanders, Seth L. "'I Was Shown Another Calculation' (אחזית חשבון אחרן): The Language of Knowledge in Aramaic Enoch and Priestly Hebrew." Pages 69–101 in *Ancient Jewish Sciences and the History of Knowledge in Second Temple Literature.* Edited by Jonathan Ben-Dov and Seth L. Sanders. New York: New York University Press, 2014.

Sommer, Michael. "Ein Text aus Palästina? Gedanken zur einleitungswissenschaftlichen Verortung der Apokalypse des Abraham." *JSJ* 47 (2016): 236–56.

Stokes, Ryan E. "The Throne Visions of Daniel 7, *1 Enoch* 14, and the Qumran *Book of Giants* (4Q530): An Analysis of Their Literary Relationship." *DSD* 15 (2008): 340–58.

Stone, Michael E. "Enoch, Aramaic Levi and Sectarian Origins." *JSJ* 19 (1988): 159–70.

Stuckenbruck, Loren T. *1 Enoch 91–108.* CEJL. Berlin: de Gruyter, 2007.

———. *The Book of Giants from Qumran: Text, Translation, Commentary.* TSAJ 63. Tübingen: Mohr Siebeck, 1997.

Tigchelaar, Eibert J. C. "The Imaginal Context and the Visionary of the Aramaic New Jerusalem." Pages 260–68 in *Flores Florentino: Dead Sea Scrolls and Other Early Jewish Studies in Honour of Florentino García Martínez.* Edited by A. Hilhorst, Émile Puech, and Eibert J. C. Tigchelaar. JSJSup 122. Leiden: Brill, 2007.

Tigchelaar, Eibert J. C., and Florentino García Martínez. "209. 4QAstronomical Enoch[b] ar." Pages 104–31 in *Qumran Cave 4.XXVI: Cryptic*

Texts and Miscellanea, Part 1. Edited by Stephen J. Pfann et al. DJD 36. Oxford: Clarendon, 2000.

Tromp, Johannes. "Two References to a Levi Document in an Epistle of Ammonas." *NovT* 39 (1997): 235–47.

VanderKam, James C. "Isaac's Blessing of Levi and His Descendants in *Jubilees* 31." Pages 513–18 in *The Provo International Conference on the Dead Sea Scrolls: Technological Innovations, New Texts, and Reformulated Issues*. Edited by Donald W. Parry and Eugene Ulrich. STDJ 30. Leiden: Brill, 1999.

———. *Jubilees: A Commentary on the Book of Jubilees, Chapters 1–21*. Hermeneia. Minneapolis: Fortress, 2018.

Werman, Cana. "Levi and Levites in the Second Temple Period." *DSD* 4 (1997): 211–25.

Wintermute, O. S. "Apocalypse of Zephaniah." *OTP* 1:497–515.

Yarbro Collins, Adela. "The Seven Heavens in Jewish and Christian Apocalypses." Pages 59–93 in *Death, Ecstasy, and Other Worldly Journeys*. Edited by John J. Collins and Michael Fishbane. Albany: SUNY Press, 1995.

Apocalypses and Apocalyptic Literature in the Early Church: Apocalypse and Apocalyptic as Rhizome

Harry O. Maier

This essay considers some of the sites of apocalyptic production, including their relation to Jewish apocalyptic in early Christianity, in the early church through to the start of the Byzantine period, through an analysis of early Christian apocalyptic as an irreducible and creative hybrid cultural phenomenon.[1] I use the phrase *sites of apocalyptic production* to describe

---

1. The phrase *the early church* and the terms *Jewish* and *Judaism* are not intended to simplify an irreducibly complex period of origins; they are used broadly to refer to phenomena from the second to fifth century. There is no attempt to be encyclopedic as such a discussion, which, were it even possible, would stretch into hundreds of pages. My chief aim is to take up illustrative examples and uses of apocalypse and apocalyptic in the period that stretches roughly from the middle of the second century through to the fifth century. There are a variety of general studies, surveys, and collections of essays by experts, none of which systematically relate Jewish and Christian apocalyptic with one another across the period of the second to fifth century, but which are nevertheless useful for broad treatments. The most important include: Christopher Rowland, *The Open Heaven: A Study of Apocalyptic in Judaism and Early Christianity* (New York: Crossroad, 1982); Adela Yarbro Collins, ed., *Early Christian Apocalypticism: Genre and Social Setting*, Semeia 36 (1986); Brian E. Daley, *The Hope of the Early Church: A Handbook of Patristic Eschatology* (Cambridge: Cambridge University Press, 1991); David Frankfurter, *Elijah in Upper Egypt: The Apocalypse of Elijah and Early Egyptian Christianity* (Minneapolis: Fortress, 1993); James C. VanderKam and William Adler, eds., *The Jewish Apocalyptic Heritage in Early Christianity*, CRINT 3.4 (Assen: Van Gorcum; Minneapolis: Fortress, 1996); Brian E. Daley, "Apocalypticism in Early Christian Theology," in *Apocalypticism in Western History and Culture*, vol. 2 of *The Encyclopedia of Apocalypticism*, ed. Bernard McGinn (New York: Continuum, 1999), 3–48; Charles E. Hill, *Regnum Caelorum: Patterns of Millennial Thought in Early Christianity*, 2nd ed. (Grand Rapids: Eerdmans, 2001); Jerry L. Walls, ed., *The Oxford Handbook of Eschatology* (Oxford: Oxford University Press, 2008); Renato Uglione, ed., *"Millennium"—L'attesa della fine nei primi secoli cristiani: Atti delle 3. Giornate Patristiche Torinesi; Turin 23-24 ottobre 2000* (Turin: CELID, 2000); Robert J. Daly,

complex processes and forms of cultural creation and transmission incapable of easy summary or taxonomic description. While broad definitions, typological categorization, and taxonomies of kinds of apocalyptic literature furnish useful heuristic tools for analysis and comparison in many instances of apocalyptic literature of the period, they can overlook the more complicated interrelations and influences of apocalyptic texts.

The two definitions of *apocalypse* and *apocalyptic* by John J. Collins and Christopher Rowland, respectively, which are useful in fixing attention on a particular body of literature conforming to their set parameters, lose their utility as one moves farther afield.[2] For example, while Collins's and Rowland's treatments work well for the study of a host of Christian apocalypses as well as a host of Jewish apocalypses and other intertestamental and later literature, they offer less insight (because their interests are not focused there) on the adoption, appropriation, textual

---

ed., *Apocalyptic Thought in Early Christianity* (Grand Rapids: Baker Academic, 2009); Catherine Wessinger, ed., *The Oxford Handbook of Millennialism* (Oxford: Oxford University Press, 2011); and John J. Collins, ed., *The Oxford Handbook of Apocalyptic Literature* (Oxford: Oxford University Press, 2014); as well as the review essays by Lorenzo DiTommaso, "Apocalypses and Apocalypticism in Antiquity, Part I," *CurBR* 5 (2007): 235–86; and DiTommaso, "Apocalypses and Apocalypticism in Antiquity, Part II," *CurBR* 5 (2007): 367–432.

2. Thus John J. Collins, "Introduction: Towards the Morphology of a Genre," *Semeia* 14 (1979): 9: "'Apocalypse' is a genre of revelatory literature with a narrative framework, in which a revelation is mediated by an otherworldly being to a human recipient, disclosing a transcendent reality which is both temporal, insofar as it envisages eschatological salvation, and spatial insofar as it involves another, supernatural world" with a distinction between the "historical type" that concern themselves with the end of the world and that concerned with "otherworldly journeys" or visionary tours to the heavens or nether regions. "Apocalyptic eschatology" refers to the eschatology found in apocalypses and centers on postmortem judgment, so John J. Collins, "Apocalyptic Eschatology in the Ancient World," in Walls, *Oxford Handbook of Eschatology*, 46–47. Alternatively, Rowland, *Open Heaven*, uses the terms more broadly to "concentrate on the theme of direct communication of the heavenly mysteries in all their diversity. With such an understanding one can attempt to do justice to all the elements of the apocalyptic literature" (14). In both understandings, Adela Yarbro Collins states, in a programmatic essay that considers second-century apocalypses with the help of John J. Collins's typology, the literary function of the genre is "intended to interpret present, earthly circumstances in light of the supernatural world and of the future, and to influence both the understanding and the behavior of the audience by means of divine authority" ("Introduction: Early Christian Apocalypticism," *Semeia* 36 [1986], 7).

transcription, translation, and motives of interpolation of Jewish apocalypses and apocalyptic materials by later redactors.[3] We may speak, in this broader sense, of a vast set of writings that Christianize earlier Jewish apocalypses, that draw on earlier Jewish traditions, motifs, or figures such as in the Enoch traditions or two-ways ethical codes that suggest a common heritage or reworked received apocalyptic.[4] Other apocalypses, such as 4 Ezra and 2 Baruch, as well as the Apocalypse of Elijah in its Christian redaction, helped to shape belief in a literal messianic reign on earth, which translated into Christian chiliasm among many early Christians.[5] In another appropriation of apocalyptic for Christian purposes, David Frankfurter analyses the role of fourth-century Egyptian anchorites who drew on earlier Jewish apocalyptic writings to develop what he describes as "a kind of 'institutionalized' Christian apocalypticism" that had the effect of "effectively transforming apocalypticism into an indigenous system of discourse for the definition of authority and

---

3. For application to Christian second-century apocalypses, see Adela Yarbro Collins, "The Early Christian Apocalypses," *Semeia* 14 (1979): 61–121 as well as the essays in Yarbro Collins, *Early Christian Apocalypticism*. In "Early Christian Apocalypses," Yarbro Collins demonstrates the usefulness of the definition (see 104–5 for a table of the literature treated) in the treatment of the book of Revelation; Apocalypse of Peter; Apocalypse of Paul; Apocalypse of Elijah; Apocalypse of Thomas; Ascen. Isa. 6–11; Sib. Or. 1–2, 7, 8; the Shepherd of Hermas; Did. 16, Testament of the Lord; Testament of Adam. T. Isaac 2–3, 5–6; T. Jacob 1–3, 5–6; the Book of Elchasai; 5 Ezra 2.42–48; 6 Ezra; Questions of Bartholomew; the Mysteries of Saint John the Apostle and the Holy Virgin; The Apocalypse of the Virgin Mary; the Apocalypse of Esdras; the Apocalypse of James, the Brother of the Lord; Book of the Resurrection of Jesus Christ by Bartholomew the Apostle 8b–14a, 17b–19b; Apocalypse of Sedrach; Jacob's Ladder; and the Story of Zosimus. This is an extensive literature that will not be taken up here. My interest is rather in other instances of apocalypse and apocalyptic production as well as their settings and purposes.

4. The two-ways traditions that are represented by 1QS III, 13–IV, 26; T. Ash. 1.3–5; Barn. 18–20, Herm. Mand. 6.1–2; and Did. 1–6, bookended by an apocalyptic set of exhortations to be watchful at this the end of the age in ch. 16, represent a development of Jewish tradition, altered for new purposes, and are at home in apocalyptic where they refer to the influence of two powers, angels, or spirits, or where they are represented as heavenly revelations; for a general overview, Kurt Niederwimmer, *The Didache*, Hermeneia, trans. Linda M. Maloney (Philadelphia: Fortress, 1998), 59–63. For popular movements, see the discussion of chiliasm below.

5. For Jewish sources of Christian millennialism, Hill, *Regnum Caelorum*, 45–67.

power."[6] Treatment of early apocalyptic in the early church requires a more expansive perspective than the ones that can be used to define and interpret a discrete body of texts. The more widely one increases the scope of apocalypse and apocalyptic in nascent and then imperially sanctioned Christianity, the more complicated the terms become.

In short, to borrow a concept from Gilles Deleuze and Félix Guatari, early Christian apocalypse and apocalyptic literature is rhizomatic.[7] Like a rhizome, it reveals a complex root structure, whose tendrils move often just beneath the surface of ancient culture, which, when they break through, can be seen in variegated forms, hybrids, expressions, and historical situations. Liturgy, for example, furnished important *Sitze im Leben* for apocalyptic production. The obvious setting was the homily, where apocalyptic could be drawn upon for various ends; John Chrysostom championed the homiletical use of apocalyptic visions of hell as a means to secure Christian obedience.[8] In his *Hom. Matt.* 43.7, for example, he invites his listeners to "imagine how great the mockery, how great the condemnation" of those in hell. Meghan Henning insightfully links Chrysostom's preaching application to the genre of tours of hell apocalyptic as a means of moral persuasion and formation, including gender performativity.[9] In the fifth-century Christian West,

---

6. David Frankfurter, "The Legacy of Jewish Apocalypses in Early Christianity: Regional Trajectories," in VanderKam and Adler, *Jewish Apocalyptic Heritage in Early Christianity*, 185.

7. The term, appropriated by Gilles Deleuze and Félix Guatarri (*A Thousand Plateaus: Capitalism and Schizophrenia*, trans. Brian Massumi [Minneapolis: University of Minnesota Press, 1987], 3–25), is drawn from botany to describe plants that reproduce by sending out shoots from interconnected root systems that break the surface of the soil as new plants. As the root system grows and spreads, it generates other root systems and develops complex constellations of growth and generation.

8. For a review of the role of apocalyptic tours of hell in Christian paideia, see Meghan Henning, *Educating Early Christians through the Rhetoric of Hell: 'Weeping and Gnashing of Teeth' as Paideia in Matthew and the Early Church*, WUNT 2/382 (Tübingen: Mohr Siebeck, 2014), 218–20.

9. Henning, *Educating Early Christians*, 174-232; also Henning, "Lacerated Lips and Lush Landscapes: Constructing This-Worldly Theological Identities in the Otherworld," in *The Other Side: Apocryphal Perspectives on Ancient Christian 'Orthodoxies'*, ed. Tobias Nicklas et al., NTOA 117 (Göttingen: Vandenhoeck & Ruprecht, 2017), 99–116; for otherworldly tours and this-worldly gender construction, see Henning, "Weeping and Bad Hair: The Bodily Suffering of Early Christian Hell as a Threat to Masculinity," in *Phallacies: Historical Intersections of Disability and Masculinity*, ed.

Salvian of Marseilles, in his sermons against avarice, deploys ekphrastic accounts of hell's torments and the paradise's delights to motivate his listeners to replace greed with charity.[10] In the seventh century, Romanos the Melodist produced a series of first-person hymns for liturgical use. One of them is *On the Second Coming*, the autobiographical account of a conscience-stricken sinner responding to the prophecy of the last judgment, whose ending models penitential prayer for mercy for its worshiping listeners.[11] The hymn formed part of the Byzantine liturgy as part of the start of the penitential season before Lent. Georgia Frank detects the influence of tours of hell apocalypses on liturgical celebrations of the Easter Vigil and baptismal rites in the Eastern church.[12] Differing sites giving rise to hybridized apocalyptic production for new life situations abound in the early Christianity.

A further example of apocalyptic as rhizomatic can be seen in what we may call the "manuscript production habit" of early Christianity, through which writers adapted earlier apocalyptic traditions often originating in Jewish texts, thereby creating an unfolding history of apocalypse effects mediated and transformed by Christian scribes into new manuscripts designed for different purposes.[13] Jewish apocalypses, for example, were read and used by Christians, but they were also altered, improvised, and even cannibalized to reflect new uses and needs, such as, for example, in public reading at worship in the form of lectionaries with portions from different apocalypses set alongside each other for reading at particular liturgical festivals.[14] Other times, as manuscript

---

Kathleen M. Brian and James W. Trents (Oxford: Oxford University Press, 2017), 282–300.

10. For example, *To the Church* 2.10; 3.18.

11. Derek Krueger, *Liturgical Subjects: Christian Ritual, Biblical Narrative, and the Formation of the Self in Byzantium* (Philadelphia: University of Pennsylvania Press, 2014), 33–36, for its liturgical use in the formation of the self.

12. Georgia Frank, "Christ's Descent to the Underworld in Ancient Ritual and Legend," in Daly, *Apocalyptic Thought in Early Christianity*, 211–26.

13. Hugo Lundhaug and Liv Ingeborg Lied, "Studying Snapshots: On Manuscript Culture, Textual Fluidity, and New Philology," in *Snapshots of Evolving Traditions: Jewish and Christian Manuscript Culture, Textual Fluidity, and New Philology*, ed. Hugo Lundhaug and Liv Ingeborg Lied, TUGAL 175 (Berlin: de Gruyter, 2017), 1–19.

14. See, for example, the discussion of variants of 4 Ezra and 2 Baruch in various textual transmissions by Liv Ingeborg Lied and Matthew Monger, "Look to the East: New and Forgotten Sources of 4 Ezra," in *The Embroidered Bible: Studies in Biblical*

traditions indicate, it is clear that Jewish apocalypses coexisted as part of a storehouse of literary production, used alongside expressly Christian material. For example, the Apocalypse of Zephaniah, which was originally in Greek and reflects little if any expressly Christian redaction, is partially preserved only in two manuscripts, one Akhmimic and the other Sahidic, from the Egyptian White Monastery of Shenuda near Sohag, reflecting its availability in a monastic setting.[15] In another kind of apocalypse manuscript production, the Nag Hammadi apocalyptic literature found in Codex V (The Apocalypse of Paul, The First and Second Apocalypse of James, The Apocalypse of Adam, and The Apocalypse of Peter) has been compellingly linked, together with the rest of the codices, with Egyptian, perhaps Pachomian, monastic practices and suggests a use of their contents for ascetical devotion, whatever their esoteric, gnostic origins and authorial intentions. "Those who read these books may well have been more interested in, for example, their allegorical interpretations of Scripture, and what they had to teach about demons, bodily passions, ascesis, prayer, visions, and heavenly ascents, the experience of the soul, and soteriological issues related to baptism, the Eucharist, and resurrection."[16] The collection of apocalypses brought together by a scribe into a single volume, prefaced by Eugnostos the Blessed, an account of the order of the cosmos, is marked by scribal colophons bringing them into a unity and each reflecting differing

---

Apocrypha and Pseudepigrapha in Honour of Michael E. Stone, ed. Lorenzo DiTommaso, Matthias Henze, and William Adler, SVTP 26 (Leiden: Brill, 2018), 639–52. Lied argues that the manuscript tradition of 2 Baruch "witnesses to the complex set use and engagement with texts and works and with works and autonomously circulating excerpts, that defy our categorization of what a text 'really is' or 'once was.'" Liv Ingeborg Lied, "Transmission and Transformation of 2 Baruch: Challenges to Editors (The Rest Is Commentary, Yale, 28 April 2013)" (unpublished paper; https://tinyurl.com/SBLPress3551b), 11.

15. For the manuscript tradition, see O. S. Wintermute, "Apocalypse of Zephaniah: A New Translation and Introduction," OTP 1:499.

16. Hugo Lundhaug and Lance Jenott, *The Monastic Origins of the Nag Hammadi Codices*, STAC 97 (Tübingen: Mohr Siebeck, 2015); see also Emiliano Fiori, "Death and Judgment in the Apocalypse of Paul: Old Imagery and Monastic Reinvention," ZAC 20 (2016): 92–108. Nicola Denzey Lewis and Justine Ariel Blount, "Rethinking the Origins of the Nag Hammadi Codices," JBL 133 (2014): 412–19, argue alternatively that the texts were possibly grave artifacts used by literati to signify their wealth as well as a kind of *vademecum* for the afterlife and hence represent a different use of apocalyptic far removed from the intentions of original authors.

beliefs and cosmologies and religious traditions—pagan, Christian, and Jewish—which may indicate a practice of inter-textual reading and uses for private devotion and practices. Still again, material related to Enoch, as a complex of literary documents, concepts, and historical figure reveals itself in multiple situations, often under thinly veiled disguise, captured in new historical situations, manifested in various literary forms, and produced, alongside other Christian apocalypses, in monastic codices.[17] Finally, we may draw attention to the Jewish-Christian apocalypse, the Shepherd of Hermas, one of the most widely read writings of the early church. The many fragments that constitute its noncontinuous manuscript tradition attest a variety of uses of the text—prayer, liturgical use, and doctrinal applications—thus indicating the reproduction and utilization of an apocalyptic text in a diversity of manuscripts produced for applications that extended far beyond the intentions of its author and original setting.[18]

Jewish apocalypses and apocalyptic literature exhibited a lively history of effects in the early church. The Enochic literature exerted a wide influence, as the New Testament Letter of Jude 14–16 already attests. In Barn. 16.3–6, the author adapts the Apocalypse of Weeks (1 En. 93.1–10; 91.11–17) in his forecasting of the deliverance "the sheep of his [God's] pasture" and a rebuilt temple "when the week is ended" (16.5, 6), the

---

17. For the uses of 1 Enoch, Enochic motifs, and Enoch as figure adapted for Christian uses in early Christian tradition, see James C. VanderKam, "1 Enoch, Enochic Motifs, and Enoch in Early Christian Literature," in VanderKam and Adler, *Jewish Apocalyptic Heritage in Early Christianity*, 33–101; and Annette Yoshiko Reed, *Fallen Angels and the History of Judaism and Christianity: The Reception of Enochic Literature* (Cambridge: Cambridge University Press, 2005). George W. E. Nickelsburg, "Two Enochic Manuscripts: Unstudied Evidence for Egyptian Christianity," in *Of Scribes and Scrolls: Studies on the Hebrew Bible, Intertestamental Judaism, and Christian Origins presented to John Strugnell on the Occasion of his Sixtieth Birthday*, ed. Harold W. Attridge, John J. Collins, and Thomas H. Tobin (Lanham, MD: University Press of America, 1990), 251–60, draws attention to the extracts from the Gospel of Peter, the Apocalypse of Peter, and the Book of the Watchers in Greek, in the sixth-century Codex Panopolitanus, from Akhmim in Egypt.

18. P. Mich. Inv. 6427 was included in a prayer, Bodl. MS Gr. Liturgy c.3 (P)[223], is part of the Deir-Bala'izah Papyrus, a liturgical text, while P. Oxy. 1.5 arguably cites Hermas as an authority on prophetic and apocalyptic issues. For discussion of these fragments and their *Sitze im Leben*, see Dan Batovici, *The Reception of the Shepherd of Hermas in Late Antiquity* (Piscataway, NJ: Gorgias, 2021), 72–80. I am grateful to Batovici for allowing me access to his manuscript.

latter of which echoes the Aramaic expectation of a new temple in 4QEn^g 1 IV, 17-18 and the former of which is probably based on a conglomerate of Enoch passages.[19] His conceptualization of history as six thousand years with a final seventh thousand-year period of Sabbath rest on earth also may reflect the influence of 2 En. 33.1-3.[20] Analogous to Enoch literature are the Daniel apocalyptica. Lorenzo DiTommaso identifies twenty-seven of them, composed between the fourth and seventeenth century, seventeen of which were created between the fourth and ninth century, known in Syriac, Armenian, Slavonic, Persian, Arabic, Greek, and Hebrew translations.[21] The figure of Daniel is productive of manuscripts that contain the traces of its source text but that take on a life of their own under new historical and cultural circumstances in which a text or a motif or the figure himself becomes a site of apocalyptic production. Daniel also proved productive of apocalyptically inspired material in other ways, specifically in commentary and in assessments of the best interpretation of the statement of seventy weeks in Dan 9:24-27, which "are decreed for your people, and your holy city" (v. 24) and included reference to "an anointed one" being cut off "after … sixty-two weeks" (v. 26) and his making " a strong covenant with many for one week, and for half of the week" to "make sacrifice and offering cease," replaced with "an abomination that desolates, until the decreed end is poured upon the desolator." Outside of the New Testament, from at least Hippolytus on, largely in commentary but also in church history and Christian chronicles, the passage invited a good deal of exposition and prediction, complete with precise identifications of the year when the seventieth week

---

19. Jósef T. Milik, *The Books of Enoch: Aramaic Fragments of Qumrân Cave 4*, with the collaboration of Matthew Black (Oxford: Oxford University Press, 1976), 47; VanderKam, "1 Enoch, Enochic Motifs, and Enoch," 40; and Eric Rowe, "The Enochic Library of the Author of the Epistle of Barnabas," in *"Non-canonical" Religious Texts in Early Judaism and Early Christianity*, ed. Lee Martin McDonald and James H. Charlesworth (London: T&T Clark, 2012), 88-102. For evidence of other Barnabas borrowing from other Jewish apocalyptic preserved at Qumran, namely, the Apocryphon of Ezekiel, in 12.1 and 4.3, see Menachem Kister, "Barnabas 12.1, 4.3 and 4Q Second Ezekiel," *RB* 97 (1990): 63-67.

20. Jean Danielou, "La typologie millenariste de la semaine dans le Christianisme primitive," *VC* 2 (1948): 6-7.

21. Lorenzo DiTommaso, *The Book of Daniel and Apocryphal Daniel Literature*, SVTP 20 (Leiden: Brill, 2005), 96-97, table 1; and DiTommaso, "The Apocryphal Daniel Apocalypses: Works, Manuscripts, and Overview," *ETL* 94 (2018): 275-316.

would end.[22] One discovers an analogous site of Christian production in 4 Ezra.[23]

As attention to scribal activities would indicate and borrowing and nativizing apocalyptic materials in new literary settings attests, it is clear that no single social theory can account for the production of apocalyptic in the early church. It is often theorized that apocalypticism, namely, social movements in which apocalyptic expectations are central, are to be accounted for by reference to deprivation, (perceived) persecution, marginalization, and social turmoil and can be seen to reflect a pessimistic historical worldview.[24] There is good evidence for this theory of generation in the early church. Cyprian the bishop of Carthage, faced with persecution in the church and an epidemic of disease in the empire, confirms that the end of the world was at hand.[25] Eusebius refers to a Christian

---

22. For discussion of the scheme in Clement of Alexandria, Hippolytus, Julius Africanus, Eusebius of Caesarea, Apollinaris of Laodicea, and Jerome, see William Adler, "The Apocalyptic Survey of History Adapted by Christians: Daniel's Prophecy of 70 Weeks," in VanderKam and Adler, *Jewish Apocalyptic Heritage in Early Christianity*, 201–38; also the survey of Paula Fredriksen, "Apocalypse and Redemption in Early Christianity: From John of Patmos to Augustine of Hippo," *VC* 45 (1991): 151–83; as well as Hippolytus, *Comm. Dan.* 4.35; Julius Africanus, *Chron.* 6.130-38 (*ANF*); Jerome, *Comm. Dan.* 9.23; and Eusebius, *Dem. Ev.* 8.2, *Hist. eccl.* 1.6.11, and *Ecl. proph.* 3.45-46. The influence of the six thousand-year intervals corresponding to the six days of creation, which works together with the seventy-week scheme,

23. Fourth Ezra represents another complex case of translation and adaptation of a preexisting Jewish text; see Theodore A. Bergren, "Christian Influence on the Transmission History of 4, 5, and 6 Ezra," in VanderKam and Adler, *Jewish Apocalyptic Heritage in Early Christianity*, 102–28.

24. Paul D. Hanson, *The Dawn of Apocalyptic: The Historical and Sociological Roots of Jewish Apocalyptic Eschatology*, rev. ed. (Philadelphia: Fortress, 1979), 25–31; Philipp Vielhauer, introduction to *Writings Related to the Apostles; Apocalypses and Related Subjects*, vol. 2 of *New Testament Apocrypha*, ed. Edgar Hennecke and William Schneemelcher, trans. R. McLean Wilson (Philadelphia: Westminster, 1965), 589; and Anathea Portier-Young, *Apocalypse against Empire: Theologies of Resistance in Early Judaism* (Grand Rapids: Eerdmans, 2011), 3–48. For a discussion of the history of linking deprivation and suffering with apocalyptic and millennialism, see Stephen L. Cook, *Prophecy and Apocalypticism: The Postexilic Social Setting* (Minneapolis: Fortress, 1995), 1–45, together with historical examples where millennialism is not associated with deprivation.

25. Cyprian, *Demetr.* 5, where he interprets famine, death, and disease and "the human race … wasted by desolation" as the fulfillment of prophecy that "evils should be multiplied in the last times" due to failure to worship the true God. Cyprian goes

historian named Jude, who "discoursing on the seventy weeks of Daniel extends his chronology down to the tenth year of Severus." On the basis of calculations as well as "the agitation of persecution," Jude taught "that the appearance of the Antichrist, so much in the mouths of men, was now fully at hand" (Eusebius, *Hist. eccl.* 6.7). The Nero redivivus legend found in the second-century Sibylline Oracles (3.63–74; 5.25–35, 93–110, 214–227, 361–385), the belief that Nero had either not died or that he was in a kind of hot storage awaiting the right time to rise from hell to persecute the church as antichrist, blending of the antichrist of 1 John 2:18 and the wounded head of the beast of Rev 13:3, remained throughout antiquity all the way to the end of the Reformation a popular belief fueled by bad times or poor government.[26] Sulpicius Severus, for example, champions millennialism in *Dial.* 2.14 when he records a conversation with Martin of Tours (316–397) in which Martin, reflecting anxieties about threats of incursions across the northern imperial frontier, told him that Nero redivivus, the antichrist, having been conceived by an evil spirit, had been born and had achieved boyhood and that he would receive power upon reaching manhood.[27] Augustine for his part was "astonished at the great presumption of those who venture such guesses" (*Civ.* 20.19).[28] Earlier in the fourth century, Lactantius similarly described "some persons of extravagant imagination" (probably referring to the third-century poet

---

on to cite a series of Old Testament texts in support of his expectation of a swift end to the world on account of divine wrath against the ungodly (*Demetr.* 6–7). In *Ep.* 55, he exhorts the persecuted to martyrdom with the help of a variety of New Testament texts predicting the coming of persecution and tribulation (2–4), including the account of martyrdom brought by the antichrist, equated with the Beast of Rev 13 (7). The suffering of the fiery furnace of Dan 3:16–18 and the Maccabean brothers and their mother furnish Cyprian with a pattern for discipleship (6). In *Ep.* 58.7 he interprets the persecution of Valerian as the antichrist: "Antichrist comes, but Christ is coming after him."

26. Harry O. Maier, "Nero in Jewish and Christian Tradition from the First Century to the Reformation," in *A Companion to the Neronian Age*, ed. Emma Buckley and Martin T. Dinter, Blackwell Companions to the Ancient World (Oxford: Wiley-Blackwell, 2013), 385–405.

27. For a discussion of Sulpicius Severus and widespread apocalyptic expectation, see S. Prete, "Sulpico Severo e il millenarismo," *Convivium* 26 (1958): 394–404.

28. For a discussion of early Christian detractors of such popular expectations, usually associated with millennial expectations, Richard Landes, "Lest the Millennium Be Fulfilled: Apocalyptic Expectations and the Pattern of Western Chronography 100–800 CE," in *The Use and Abuse of Eschatology in the Middle Ages*, ed. Werner Verbeke and D. Verhelst (Leuven: Leuven University Press, 1988), 137–211.

Commodian and his contemporary, the commentator on Revelation, Victorinus of Pettau) who believed that Nero would return "from the uttermost boundaries of earth" and conceived of him as "forerunner of the Antichrist" (*Mort.* 2). Then, as now, thoughtful exegesis could not limit those armed with chapter and verse to speculate about the date of the end of the world. Lactantius nevertheless interpreted the injustices of his archnemesis, the persecuting emperor Diocletian, with the help of Daniel passages, furnishing an excellent example of the use of apocalyptic as a means of engaging oppressive imperial realities. Later writers, depending on the emperor, reached for apocalyptic to decry imperial regimes as fulfillment of end-time expectations.[29]

Pessimism and apocalyptic are only one half of the story, however. As Robert Daly has stated,

> in early Christianity apocalyptic ideas were not heavily dominated by negative and terrifying ideas of a terrible fearsome event. Quite the contrary! By the end of the second century the early Christian writers were interpreting the Apocalypse as pointing not toward some awe-inspiring future event, but to the challenges of contemporary life in the church.[30]

Augustine is an excellent example. As we will see, he championed a reading of biblical apocalyptic that acknowledged its future predictions while rendering it applicable to spiritual practices in everyday daily life. The literature associated with revelatory tours of heaven and hell shows a kind of persuasion not deployed to chronicle an imminent second coming of Jesus but to secure awareness of the pressing inevitability of death and the consequences for sin. "Hell frightens usefully," observed John Chrysostom on

---

29. The pro-Nicene Hilary of Poitiers pilloried the semi-Arian Constantius II as the antichrist (*Against the Emperor Constantius* 5). In Opus Imperfectum in Matthaeum 49, an Arian commentary on Matt 24, the author targets the pro-Nicene Constantine, Theodosius I, particularly their control of the churches in Jerusalem, as the army of the antichrist and the desolating sacrilege of Matt 24:15; the commentator expects an imminent advent of the antichrist as part of the half week of tribulation foretold in Dan 7:25, 9:26–27, and 12:7 and Rev 11:2–3, 12:6, 14, and 13:5. For Arians and Donatists and others using apocalyptic motifs to criticize their imperial opponents, see Jesse A. Hoover, *The Donatist Church in an Apocalyptic Age* (Oxford: Oxford University Press, 2018), 65–115.

30. Robert J. Daly, preface, in Daly, *Apocalyptic Thought in Early Christianity*, 13.

the teaching of hell and apocalyptic judgment as a useful means of securing contrition for sin (*Paenit.* 7).[31]

The final complicating feature of apocalypse and apocalyptic in the early church is its ability to transmogrify into multiple forms of literature. Under the general heading apocalyptic from the second century, there are a variety of types of literature that we can include: chiliasm or belief in a thousand year reign of Christ on earth before the second judgment; tours of heaven and hell; commentaries on Daniel and Revelation as well as apocalyptic sections of the canon; treatises of various kinds that deploy apocalyptic or are dedicated to the exposition of apocalyptic topics found in the Bible; handbooks for interpreting John's apocalypse; visions and oracles; martyrologies; poetry; testaments of various biblical figures; letters; monastic apocalypses and monastic biographies and desert Christian apophthegmata; dialogues; and so-called gnostic writings. Further, we should take into account cases where harmonies and syntheses of apocalyptic texts are created from texts found in a developing canon, of which Augustine's *Civ.* 20 is perhaps the most magnificent example. Nor can we ignore the generation of Christian iconography dedicated to visual representations of apocalyptic texts in scripture and tradition.[32] This represents an explosion of material that cannot be easily summarized but which bears the imprint or influence of apocalyptic thought.

1. Chiliasm and Its Multiple Applications

Chiliasm, the belief that following the second coming of Christ and the last judgment there would be a thousand-year rule of Christ and his believers on earth, was a widely but by no means universally held belief of the nascent church.[33] Charles Hill identifies the chief features of Christian chiliasm as "the luxuriant superabundance of earth's produce, the animal world's mutual reconciliation and peaceful submission to mankind, increased human longevity, a rebuilt Jerusalem, the servitude of the

---

31. Cited by Henning, *Educating Early Christians*, 219.

32. For an account with images, see John Herrmann and Annewies van den Hoek, "Apocalyptic Themes in Monumental and Minor Art of Early Christianity," in Daly, *Apocalyptic Thought in Early Christianity*, 33–80.

33. Hill, *Regnum Caelorum*, 75–208, for an extensive discussion of the chief second and third-century nonchiliastic authors.

nations, and the return of the ten tribes."³⁴ He traces belief in a future earthly millennium and an intermediate state for the dead in the underworld to a broad range of Jewish apocalyptic influences, most importantly to 2 Baruch and 4 Ezra, two writings that developed protochiliastic themes found earlier Second Temple apocrypha and pseudepigrapha.³⁵

For our purposes here, most notable in Hill's patient detective work of the presence of chiliasm in and its influence on nascent Christian thought and life is that millennialism recurs in a variety of kinds of literature and social contexts that include polemic, apologetic, and commentary. We see polemical use in the second-century bishop of Lugdunum Irenaeus's refutation of Valentinian denial of the resurrection of the body and spiritualizing interpretation of biblical texts. *Against Heresies* furnishes an extended account of chiliastic expectation that by the time of writing had already become an established tradition, influenced in particular by Jewish notions of a creation made up of seven thousand-year-long periods, the last one being an earthly millennium.³⁶ Irenaeus champions belief in a physical, literal, worldwide thousand-year reign of Christ in a restored Jerusalem as the antidote to the gnostic spiritualizing exegesis and the belief that the creation is evil. He asserts the continuity of the incarnation and physical redemption with the creation story by reading history as an unfolding of weeks, with the antichrist coming at the close of the six thousandth year (*Haer.* 5.23.2; 24.1–28.4). In 5.35.1–36.3, he harmonizes prophetic passages from the Hebrew Bible together with apocalyptic predictions found in Daniel, the gospels, Paul's letters, and the book of Revelation to produce an account of a thousand-year reign of Christ in a restored Jerusalem with a rebuilt temple, again with a view to championing the physical world. In keeping with a central theme of his refutation against heresy, he defends

---

34. Hill, *Regnum Caelorum*, 237–38; also James D. Tabor, "Ancient Jewish and Early Christian Millennialism," in *The Oxford Handbook of Millennialism*, ed. Catherine Wessinger (Oxford: Oxford University Press, 2011), 252–66; and Clementina Mazzucco, "Il millenarismo alle origini del cristianesimo (secc. II–III)," in Uglione, *"Millennium,"* 145–82.

35. Hill, *Regnum Caelorum*, 45–68; see also Martin Erdmann, *The Millennial Controversy in the Early Church* (Eugene, OR: Wipf & Stock, 2005), 107–34.

36. Specifically, 4 Ezra 7.26–44 and 2 En. 33.1–3. The longer chief recension of 2 Enoch refers to a final, eighth unending thousand-year period: "the eighth thousand is the end, neither years nor months nor weeks nor days." For the numerology in the preexisting tradition and its presence in the early church, see Danielou, "La typologie," 1–16.

his teaching as originating in the public teaching of Jesus and the apostles, passed on publicly, and preserved through a succession of teachers. Thus, a critical plank of support for his belief is the teaching he heard from Papias (5.33.4), who, Irenaeus reports, passed on, via John, Jesus's teaching concerning a superabundant future. Papias's account bears such close resemblance to 2 Bar. 19.5–7 that literary influence cannot be excluded. Taken together, the trajectory from 2 Baruch, through Papias's sources to Papias and thence to Irenaeus indicates the existence of an apocalyptic tradition of received teachings the bishop polemically deploys in *Against Heresies*.

Irenaeus's contemporary, the North African polemicist and apologist Tertullian, also deployed chiliastic belief strategically.[37] He believed that the "antichrist was now close at hand" and that a violent end to the world was imminent (*Fug.* 12; *Apol.* 32). In his treatise *Against Marcion* (3.24), he opposes Marcionite dualism through belief in a literal thousand years of Christ, shored up by a report he has received of the appearance of a vision before the Roman army of a vision of a city suspended in the sky every day for forty days. Tertullian points to this vision as fulfillment of a Montantist prophecy—another form of second-century Christian chiliasm—that before the end a vision of heavenly Jerusalem would appear.[38] As with other apologists, apocalyptic belief also served Tertullian to defend Christian belief and to assault its detractors.[39] For example, against those who deny the resurrection of the body as nonsensical, he outlines belief in a punishment of reward of the departed as souls before the resurrection of

---

37. For an account of the scattered references in Tertullian to the end of the world and the last judgment, see Jaroslav Pelikan, "The Eschatology of Tertullian," *CH* 21 (1952): 108–22.

38. Montanism as chiliastic, the predominant view of earlier twentieth-century scholarship, has been challenged with the view that Montanus was focused on eschatology informed by visions, a view promoted by William Tabbernee, "Revelation 21 and the Montanist 'New Jerusalem,'" *ABR* 37 (1989): 52–60; also Hill, *Regnum Caelorum*, 143–59, with full literature. The discovery of Pepouza, however, by Tabbernee and Peter Lampe in archaeological expeditions from 1998–2000, where the Montanists expected the New Jerusalem of Rev 21 to descend, has led to a reassessment of the eschatological interpretation and the view that they were indeed millennialists; William Tabbernee, "Portals of the Montanist New Jerusalem: The Discovery of Pepouza and Tymion," *JECS* 11 (2003): 87–93.

39. For a review of apocalyptic in second-century apologists, Enrico dal Covolo, "Escatologia e apocalittica nei primi secoli cristiani: Il Regno di Dio e la sua attesta negli Apologisti greci del II secolo," *Salesianum* 62 (2000): 625–43.

the general resurrection at the last judgment. Tertullian depicts Hades as a chamber with two regions for the departed, one for the good and other the bad, awaiting the last judgment (*An.* 55–58), from which, at different intervals during the millennium, determined by their relative rewards, those in the good place will rise to eternal life (*An.* 56). He instructs his readers that even before this there are torments and rewards relative to those who sinned before death and to those who did not, even as there will be fuller punishment and reward to come after the resurrection of the dead (*On the Res.* 17; 35; *An.* 58). In these interpretations, Tertullian is guided in part by his interpretation of the apocalyptic references to judgment in Matthew (for example Matt 5:26, 10:28, 22:13; 25:30, 46 in *Res.* 35), passages that were also, in part, inspiration for the apocalyptic tours of heaven and hell in roughly contemporary apocalypses.[40]

Lactantius (250–325), also a North African Christian apologist and polemicist, concludes his defense of Christianity and polemic against pagan belief with a discussion of the end of the Roman Empire (*Inst.* 7.14–26) in which he chronicles the advent of a thousand-year reign of God in a renewed world (7.24). He weaves the belief that human history lasts six thousand years (7.14.2–4), with a final thousand-year period of rest with an exegesis of Daniel and Revelation in which he cloaks Diocletian as the fourth beast of Dan 7:23–25 (*Inst.* 7.16.3–4) and the emperor and Galerius as the two beasts of Rev 13:11–17 (*Inst.* 7.17.2–6).[41] Lactantius represents the thousand-year reign of Christ as the triumph over the Roman Empire and uses Daniel and Revelation to read imperial events around him and to denounce the reign of Rome.

In another polemical context, this time anti-Jewish, Justin Martyr similarly outlines chiliastic apocalyptic teaching in his *Dialogue with Trypho*, in which he describes Christian teaching of a thousand-year earthly reign of Christ from a rebuilt Jerusalem, where Christians will dwell. Justin shows that John's Revelation harmonizes with prophetic promises con-

---

40. Henning, *Educating Early Christians*, 138–73. Henning also notes the important influence of Greek and Latin as well as Jewish sources (43–107), a point also emphasized by Jan Bremmer, "Descents to Hell and Ascents to Heaven in Apocalyptic Literature," in Collins, *Oxford Handbook of Apocalyptic Literature*, 340–57 (with an extensive bibliography), with a view to Greek and Latin tour literature, which he argues exerted an important influence on the Jewish and Christian accounts.

41. Elizabeth DePalma Digeser, *The Making of a Christian Empire: Lactantius and Rome* (New York: Cornell University Press, 2000), 19, 150.

cerning Jerusalem, even as he warns the Jew Trypho against listening to false teachings from false Christians who deny a coming earthly millennium and teach that when Christians die, they go immediately to heaven (*Dial.* 80–81).

The fourth-century Latin Christian poet Commodian, in his *Carmen apologeticum*, similarly uses apocalyptic for the purposes of anti-Jewish polemic.[42] He dedicates the bulk of his poem to a chronicle of Israel's disobedience and persecution of the prophet and concludes with a vivid chiliastic prediction of the end of the age. He deploys an elaborate version of the Nero redivivus legend as part of an elaborate apocalyptic timetable in which Jews and the returned tyrant join together to persecute the church before God vanquishes them and then establishes a thousand-year reign with the saints on earth (ll. 785–1053). In his *Instructions*, Commodian uses apocalyptic for a different end. Again, there is a description of a coming thousand-year reign of Christ amid passages that describe a coming apocalyptic battle and torment of punishment (*Inst.* 2.1–4). The poems, however, take on a wider view, in as much as they are embedded in a series of refutations of pagan beliefs as well as admonitions against the wicked and exhortations to believers to pursue a life of virtue and good works in the church. He uses chiliastic teaching and speculation to exhort and admonish believers.

The *Commentary on the Book of Revelation* by Victorinus of Pettau, probably written circa 260 CE shortly after the persecution led by the emperor Valerian, represents both the earliest commentary on Revelation we possess as well as a chiliastic account of Jesus's coming rule. Victorinus uses allegorical exegesis to affirm John's Revelation as both an account of what is future, but also of what is true of the church in the present. He echoes earlier tradition in which each day of creation is a thousand-year period and interprets the sixth day as the millennium of Rev 19 (*Comm.* 20.1–3).[43] The thousand years are not literal

---

42. For broader discussion of the Latin poetry of Commodian's Christian contemporaries, see Daley, *Hope of the Early Church*, 156–64.

43. This was a schema that not all who interpreted the seven days as periods of thousand years shared. Hippolytus in his *Commentary on Daniel* (4.23–34), for example, which like Victorinus uses commentary on an apocalypse to form Christian belief in a more ethical and doctrinal form, adopts the cosmic-week theory, while embracing a chiliastic expectation of an earthly millennium and interregnum of Christ; see Hill, *Regnum Caelorum*, 161–65.

years but represent nevertheless a literal future period, which Victorinus numerologically interprets as a time when the church, freed from Satan's temptation, unites obedience to the Decalogue (the number 10) with virginity (the number 100), that is pure in body and mind (*Comm.* 20.6). Thus, allegory and numerology allow Victorinus to interpret the Apocalypse as both a prophecy of things to come and a revelation of what is true theologically of the church from its inception. Apocalyptic becomes a tool for instruction concerning the end of history as well as in Christian faith and the life of obedience inaugurated in baptism (e.g., *Comm.* 4.6–10).

Yet another chiliast was the fourth-century Methodius of Olympus, who developed a scheme partially motivated by his opposition to the spiritualizing interpretations of Origen (see below). Like Origen, he rejected a physical view of a millennium established somewhere on earth, but he promoted the idea that there would be a literal thousand-year reign of rest without harvest, eating, drinking, or procreation, corresponding to the first Sabbath after creation (*Symp.* 9.1). The thousand years, the seventh millennium, takes place "on the first day of resurrection, which is the day of judgment" on which Methodius will "celebrate with Christ the millennium of rest" (*Symp.* 9.5). Methodius's contemporary, Quintus Julius Hilarianus, in 397 CE took a more literal and traditional view in his assessment that the world would end 101 years later with the completion of six thousand years, when Satan would be defeated with the Second Coming after which there would be a thousand-year reign of the saints before the final battle (*On the Progress of Time* 17–18).

As this literary evidence indicates, chiliastic thinking was a widespread phenomenon in the early church, with its roots in Jewish tradition, whether mediated through the book of Revelation or through other Jewish documents, and was used for various purposes. It also was championed in less literate, popular contexts. Eusebius chronicles the opposition of Dionysius, the second-century bishop of Alexandria, to popular millennialism taught by Nepos, the local bishop of Arsinoë in the Faiyum Oasis, and Coracion, an otherwise unknown figure from the same region (*Hist. eccl.* 7.24.1–9). As David Frankfurter has argued, alongside the book of Revelation, there were other literary sources for this Egyptian movement, attested by the circulation of a variety of millennial-leaning texts such as the Shepherd of Hermas, Apocalypse of Peter, Enochic literature, and a Christian redaction of the Apocalypse of Elijah, as well as monastic liturgical texts. Frankfurter links the popularity of North African millennialism to agricultural, economic, political and social disintegration, a seedbed for many apocalyptic movements.[44]

2. The End without End

As we have seen, chiliasm had its detractors, as had those who ventured to predict too accurately the current state of affairs with reference to the end. Dionysius favored an allegorical reading of Revelation as a means of appropriating apocalyptic for the church's use. Others, in a nonpolemical vein, also interpreted biblical apocalyptic in a nonchiliastic direction. Hippolytus in *Comm. Dan.* 4.23.3 deployed the scheme of a six-thousand-year creation, which we have seen finds its origins in Jewish apocalyptic. He calculated the birth of Jesus at 5,500 years after the creation of Adam, thereby allotting another five hundred years before the final Sabbath, which he regarded as unending, and thus ruling out any notion of an imminent end or a literal millennium. He did not, however, interpret this in a chiliastic sense; the seventh day is an unending age.[45] Jerome and Ambrose (who, on account of the political calamities of the late fourth century, believed the end of the world was near) read biblical apocalyptic for what it might teach about an individual's confrontation with death or about ascetical self-control.[46] Eusebius of Caesarea did not accept the six thousand-year scheme, and while he believed that there would be an end of time and second judgment, he engaged in realized eschatological teaching by interpreting Constantine's rule as an anticipation of the eternal kingdom.[47] Augustine was arguably the most sophisticated reader of biblical apocalyptic of his age. He

---

44. Frankfurter, *Elijah in Upper Egypt*, 241–78.

45. For the place of Hippolytus's scheme and the use of a six thousand-year chronology in the early church, see Landes, "Lest the Millennium Be Fulfilled," 137–211; for his nonchiliastic application, Hill, *Regnum Caelorum*, 160–69; and for his tropological and ecclesiological reading of Revelation, see Bernard McGinn, "Turning Points in Early Christian Apocalypse Exegesis," in Daly, *Apocalyptic Thought in Early Christianity*, 93.

46. For the eschatology of Ambrose and Jerome, who focus on the last judgment and the afterlife and reject millennialism, see Daley, *Hope of the Early Church*, 97–104.

47. For Eusebius's political eschatology, see Harry O. Maier, "Dominion from Sea to Sea: Eusebius of Caesarea, Constantine the Great, and the Exegesis of Empire," in *The Calling of the Nations: Exegesis, Ethnography, and Empire in a Biblical-Historic Present*, ed. Mark Vessey et al. (Toronto: University of Toronto Press, 2011), 149–75.

drew on the Rules of Tyconius, a handbook written by the Donatist North African Christian who resisted the literalistic apocalyptic interpretation of his rigorist community by furnishing an exegetical set of guidelines for interpreting the metaphors and symbols of Revelation prophetically and typologically.[48] In part, Tyconius was motivated to resist literal interpretations of the Apocalypse fueling millennialism and circulating amongst militant apocalypticists circulating in his own Donatist church.[49] Augustine used Tyconius's rules to read New Testament apocalyptic both intercanonically and figuratively, without abandoning a futurist eschatology. At the conclusion of the *City of God*, Augustine, who resisted a literal application of the book of Revelation or other apocalyptic texts to his present context, expounds a reading of Revelation to imagine "the end without end" (22.30) of the coming age.[50] But this end, for Augustine, can already be seen, even if only in a glass darkly; biblical apocalyptic for the Augustine of the *City of God* is a revelation of what is to come *and* of the usually invisible battle of Christians on earth with the flesh, sin, and the devil. Biblical apocalyptic is a disclosure of life between the past age of the full disclosure of God's work in history as recorded in the canon and a timetable of an as yet indeterminate future, the signs of whose arrival one may provisionally adduce from the correct sequencing of New Testament apocalyptic texts.

In his *Catechetical Oration* 15, Augustine's earlier contemporary, Cyril of Jerusalem (313–386), similarly offered a harmony of New Testament apocalyptic scriptures to chronicle the coming end as part of instruction preparing catechumens for baptism and Christian life. Hippolytus's *Treatise on Christ and Antichrist* is perhaps an earlier similar catechetical teaching; he addresses his harmonization of apocalyptic New Testament texts together with Daniel to "my beloved brother Theophilus, to be thoroughly informed on those topics which I put summarily before you" (1).[51]

---

48. For Donatism and apocalyptic, see Hoover, *Donatist Church in an Apocalyptic Age*, 161–81, for Tyconius's alternative.

49. Fredriksen, "Apocalypse and Redemption in Early Christianity," 157–60.

50. For Augustine against the backdrop of applications of eschatology and apocalyptic to the Constantinian order, see Robert A. Markus, *Saeculum: History and Society in the Theology of Augustine* (Cambridge: Cambridge University Press, 1970).

51. For catechesis, see J. A. Cerrato, *Hippolytus between East and West: The Commentaries and the Provenance of the Corpus*, OTM (New York: Oxford University Press, 2002), 154–59.

Tyconius and Augustine offered one way to make sense of New Testament apocalyptic in a more prophetic and typological manner. Origen of Alexandria, like Augustine, did not reject a historical and prophetic understanding of apocalyptic texts, but, like Dionysius his fellow Alexandrian, he offered another avenue of their interpretation with the help of allegory, translating their passages into moral and spiritual interpretations of theological and cosmological truths. For Origen, there is a natural and narrative explanation for simple believers and a deeper meaning for advanced Christians. In this interpretation, passages that refer to the second coming of Christ refer to his spiritual coming in the souls of those who prepare for his advent through contemplation and ascetical preparation. Origen interprets apocalyptic passages literally and then supplements his reading with allegorical interpretations. In his *Comm. Matt.* 32–60, he moves beyond a simple literal reading of the apocalypse of Matt 24:3–44 and other New Testament apocalyptic texts for those with deeper understanding, as descriptions of Christian maturity. The antichrist, for example, is a symbol for all false doctrine and improper ethical teaching (33); the plagues are the assaults of heretics (38); famine is the Christian's hunger for the deeper truths hidden in scripture (37). For Origen, the uses of apocalyptic for spiritual diagnosis are part of his larger account of the drama of creation as restoration and growth in unity with God, which continues in the life to come, and, in some passages, includes a purgative or remedial punishment of the soul after death for those who had not wholly purified their lives while in the body through contemplation, in the hope of a universal salvation.[52] The Cappadocians, Basil, Gregory Nazianzus, and Gregory of Nyssa, continue Origen's tradition—either expressly, implicitly, or by way of correction of Origen—of translating apocalyptic into eschatological categories.[53] Gregory of Nyssa represents the most thoroughgoing translation, with affirmation of an end to sin and evil and a universal salvation in the fulfillment of Paul's eschatological timetable which "God will be all in all" (1 Cor 15:28), the central theme of his treatise *On the Soul and the Resurrection* (e.g., 7). Punishment after death is again purgative and remedial; the Christian life entails a preparation for the life to come through

---

52. For Origen's diverse accounts of hell as remedial and his views of the afterlife, see Daley, *Hope of the Early Church*, 55–59; for universal salvation, note *Hom. Lev.* 7.2 and *Comm. Jo.* 1.16.91.

53. For a general overview with bibliography, see Daley, *Hope of the Early Church*, 81–88.

an ascetical discipline of separating the soul from the bodily desires (*Virg.* 14, 31–32) as part of the exercise of a life of contemplation and the goal of becoming like God as possible (*Catech. Disc.* 5), a growth that will have no end.

In the authors cited above, to use prevalent scholarly categories, apocalyptic is transformed into a futurist as well as realized eschatological framework. Hebrew Bible and New Testament apocalyptic texts are harmonized to create a timetable of the order of events to unfold at the conclusion of the world, often understood as the end of six thousand years. In the meantime, they are conceived as revelations of the current spiritual life, its struggles with temptation, and its hope for the world to come. There is, however, another important way apocalyptic played a central role in the early church, in monastic contexts and in mystical-theological paradigms. The literature associated with desert Christianity, for example, is filled with references to monks seeing the heavens opened or to being transported heavenward to behold divine realities.[54] These are nonsystematic anecdotal and biographical accounts that reflect a larger tradition.

It is in the mystical theology of ascetical theologians like Gregory of Nyssa that one finds the fullest disclosure of apocalyptic theology, in accounts of the soul's vision of God through ascent. In these traditions, there is an attempt to recover the image of God in oneself through ascetical devotion and practice. Alexander Golitzin and April DeConick, in separate studies, insightfully speak of an interiorized or personal apocalypse in their accounts of mystical theology amongst Jews and Christians in the period under consideration here.[55] Ann Conway-Jones, for example, has shown ways in which themes in the Jewish heavenly ascent literature found in texts such as the Book of the Watchers (1 En. 14), Songs of Sabbath Sacrifice, the Similitudes of Enoch (1 En. 37–41), 2 En. 1–20, 3 Baruch, Ascen. Isa. 6–11, and T. Levi 2.5–5.2 and 8.1–19 parallel Greg-

---

54. For example, sayings 6; 7; 27; 29; 33; 48, as enumerated in John Worley, trans., *The Book of the Elders, The Sayings of the Desert Fathers: The Systematic Collection*, CSS 240 (Collegeville: Liturgical Press, 2012).

55. Alexander Golitzin, "Heavenly Mysteries: Themes from Apocalyptic Literature in the Macarian Homilies and Selected Other Fourth-Century Ascetical Writers," in Daly, *Apocalyptic Thought in Early Christianity*, 187; and April D. DeConick, "What Is Early Jewish and Christian Mysticism?," in *Paradise Now: Essays on Early Jewish and Christian Mysticism*, ed. April D. DeConick, SymS 11 (Atlanta: Society of Biblical Literature, 2006), 18.

ory of Nyssa's account of the soul's ascent and vision of the heavenly tabernacle of Exod 25–28 and Ezek 1 in his *Life of Moses* and the tabernacle imagery of 2.170–201.[56] In this sense, apocalypse refers to the revelation of heavenly mysteries received through a heavenly journey. In Gregory's treatise, Moses's ascent to Mount Sinai where he beholds the tabernacle is an account of the soul's eternal journey to God, which is simultaneously an ever-deeper journey into divine mystical doctrine and into the soul's true self as the likeness of God. The mind leaves the world of the senses and understanding behind to gain access to "the invisible and incomprehensible" and enters a reality where "seeing … consists in not seeing" and a "luminous darkness" (*Mos.* 2.163). Gregory's contemporary, the eastern monastic writer associated with the *Fifty Spiritual Homilies*, offers an analogous model of ascent and revelation and reflects the influence of *merkabah* mysticism. The Macarian homilist in this text celebrates Ezekiel's chariot, ascent, and vision of the heavenly throne room (Ezek 1:1–28) as an account of a vision of the "mystery of the soul that is going to receive its Lord and become his throne of glory." The soul, he states, "which has been illumined by the beauty of the ineffable glory after having prepared itself for him as a throne and dwelling-place, becomes all light, and all face, and all eye (*Hom.* 2.1.2). This passage is typical of the homilist's repeated references to the soul as the throne room of God and the *kabod* of Lord as internal.[57] Preparation refers to ascetical disciplines and illumination speaks to a journey that is both upward to God and inward to the soul's true likeness, the Son after whose image and likeness it has been created. "With Christ," Macarius states, "everything is within" (*Hom.* 3.8.1). In *Hom.* 2.1.2, he likens the four living creatures that carry the chariot heavenward as a type of the will, conscience, intellect and the power to love, the four governing faculties of the soul.

3. A Seat at the Arena

A widespread form of apocalyptic in the early church, adapted from both Jewish apocalyptic as well as Greek and Latin sources, took the form of

---

56. Ann Conway-Jones, *Gregory of Nyssa's Doctrine of the Celestial Tabernacle in Its Jewish and Christian Contexts* (Oxford: Oxford University Press, 2014).

57. Andrei Orlov and Alexander Golitzin, "'Many Lamps Are Lighted from the One': Paradigms of the Transformational Vision in Macarian Homilies," *VC* 55 (2001): 281–98.

vividly described tours of heaven and hell in which a seer is transported to the heaven or a place of punishment to receive graphic depictions and interpretations, often through an *angelus interpres*, of reward and punishment. The rich variety of these texts reflects complex literary relationships, evidence of several layers of redaction, and influence of Jewish texts on Christian ones and vice versa.[58] These tours of heaven and hell emerged as a genre of literature in the early church, with roots that go back to Jewish apocalyptic. First Enoch 17–36, a section of the Book of the Watchers, describes two tours of Enoch, one of the earth (17–19) and the other of the cosmos (20–36). The Apocalypse of Zephaniah and portions of 4 Ezra represent other Jewish examples of tour apocalypses. Martha Himmelfarb has shown the way these texts comprise a genre of apocalyptic literature especially popular throughout late antiquity, as testified by the multiple translations and redactions of the Apocalypse of Paul and the works it, together with the Apocalypse of Peter, inspired, through the Byzantine period, the Middle Ages, and the Renaissance, the most famous of which is Dante's *Divine Comedy*.[59] In another vein, Meghan Henning considers the influence of New Testament apocalyptic, specifically references in Matthew's Gospel to being cast out and suffering weeping and gnashing of teeth in Matt 13:41–43 and 25:41–46, or Paul's ascent to a third heaven in 2 Cor 12 as inspiration for this tour literature.[60] The apocalypse comes in vivid descriptions, especially of the torments of hell, a device that was rhetorically powerful, as Henning demonstrates in her discussion of these texts as a means of the promotion of Christian paideia.

These writings deploy vivid speech or *ekphrasis* as a form of rhetorical persuasion by helping audiences to imagine along with the narrator what is being disclosed and to awaken emotions connected with graphic depictions. The strategy proved to be a useful one in the application of apocalyptic to other situations. Tertullian, in his treatise, *On the Shows*, descries Christian attendance at the arena and the theater. At the conclu-

---

58. Martha Himmelfarb, *Tours of Hell: An Apocalyptic Form in Jewish and Christian Literature* (Philadelphia: University of Philadelphia Press, 1983); more recently, Bremmer, "Descents to Hell," 340–57.

59. Martha Himmelfarb, *The Apocalypse: A Brief History* (Oxford: Wiley-Blackwell, 2010), 103–4.

60. Henning, *Educating Early Christians*, 218–20, for the influence of Matthew's Gospel on the Apocalypse of Peter and of Matthew and Paul's letters on the Apocalypse of Paul.

sion, he puts on his own show for his audience, by offering them a vivid tour of the last judgment. He invites his audience to imagine the spectacles that will be on display on Judgment Day when "this old world and all its generation shall be consumed in one fire" (33). He goes on to list the cast of characters lit on fire at the grand finale, emperors, magistrates, philosophers, poets, actors, charioteers, athletes, and those who abused Christ at his crucifixion. The imagination of these things brings "greater joy than circus, theatre, amphitheater or any stadium."

On the heavenly side, the third-century Martyrdom of Perpetua and Felicitas, although not a tour apocalypse, can be considered here with reference to another set of divinely given vivid visions (1.3; 2.3–4; 3.2; 4.1–3) that contain apocalyptic elements and that resemble tour-like scenarios. In 1.3, fulfilling a promise to her brother to ask for a vision of heaven, Perpetua receives a vision in which she climbs a ladder fastened with implements, reaching to heaven, under which is a crouching dragon. She ascends the top and sees a great garden, a large white-haired man dressed like a shepherd, milking sheep, and surrounded by "many thousand white-robed ones." In 2.3–4, Perpetua receives a vision in which, after praying for her predeceased brother Dinocrates, she sees him "going out from a gloomy place, where there were also several others, and he was parched and very thirsty, with a filthy countenance and pallid color, and the [cancerous] wound on his face which he had when he died." Perpetua prays for him further and receives another vision in which gloom is replaced by light, and Dinocrates now "with a clean body and well clad was finding refreshment," has his wound healed and slakes his thirst at pool and then goes "to play joyously, after the manner of children." In the second (4.1–3), Perpetua's and Felicitas's imprisoned companion, Saturus, relates a vision in which four angels bear him and Perpetua to a heavenly garden; they see companions previously martyred and are led to a wall made of light with a gate that leads into the throne room described with motifs drawn from Rev 4 and 5. The hortatory purpose of the apocalyptic vision becomes clear when Saturus reports that the bishop Optatus and the teacher-presbyter Aspasius are denied entrance through the gate because of their quarrelsomeness and an angel instructs Optatus to rebuke his flock for its faction. Three of the visions attest the spiritual power of the martyrs and confessors; Perpetua's brother instructs her that because of her imprisonment for her faith she is "in a position of great dignity" and that she may ask for a vision; prayer transports Dinocrates from a dirty, gloomy, sickly, and thirsty postmortem existence to a clean, bright, healed and refreshing one; Saturus' vision aims to end ecclesial faction.

4. The Generative Apocalyptic Imagination

Taken together, the preceding discussion indicates that, in the period under consideration here, the terms *apocalypse* and *apocalyptic* describe a variety of phenomena that, like combinative DNA, joined together in processes of creative production.[61] This makes apocalypse and apocalyptic in the early church impossible to summarize or to codify. The terms reveal creative application of received traditions and generation of new ones for different settings, audiences, and purposes, mediated through a variety of forms. Apocalyptic was used to imagine the future, whether on earth, in heaven, or under the earth. It could be marshaled as a guide for interpreting and forming the spiritual life. Apocalyptic in the early church generated ways of imagining the end of history in the sense of both its temporal conclusion sense and its teleological purpose, whether conceived broadly as global account, or individually as interior one. Apocalypse and apocalyptic furnished a boundless means to generate new understandings of time and space in the varied contexts where early Christianity developed.

Bibliography

Adler, William. "The Apocalyptic Survey of History Adapted by Christians: Daniel's Prophecy of 70 Weeks." Pages 201–38 in *The Jewish Apocalyptic Heritage in Early Christianity*. Edited by James C. VanderKam and William Adler. CRINT 3.4. Assen: Van Gorcum; Minneapolis: Fortress, 1996.

Batovici, Dan. *The Reception of the Shepherd of Hermas in Late Antiquity*. Piscataway, NJ: Gorgias, 2021.

Bergren, Theodore A. "Christian Influence on the Transmission History of 4, 5, and 6 Ezra." Pages 102–28 in *The Jewish Apocalyptic Heritage in Early Christianity*. Edited by James C. VanderKam and William Adler. CRINT 3.4. Assen: Van Gorcum; Minneapolis: Fortress, 1996.

---

61. On the recombinative creation of postbiblical apocalyptic texts from older works and fragments of works, see DiTommaso, "Apocryphal Daniel Apocalypses."

Bremmer, Jan. "Descents to Hell and Ascents to Heaven in Apocalyptic Literature." Pages 340–57 in *The Oxford Handbook of Apocalyptic Literature*. Edited by John J. Collins. New York: Oxford University Press, 2014.

Cerrato, J. A. *Hippolytus between East and West: The Commentaries and the Provenance of the Corpus*. OTM. New York: Oxford University Press, 2002.

Collins, John J. "Apocalyptic Eschatology in the Ancient World." Pages 40–55 in *The Oxford Handbook of Eschatology*. Edited by Jerry L. Walls. Oxford: Oxford University Press, 2010.

———. "Introduction: Towards the Morphology of a Genre." *Semeia* 14 (1979): 1–20.

———, ed. *The Oxford Handbook of Apocalyptic Literature*. New York: Oxford University Press, 2014.

Conway-Jones, Ann. *Gregory of Nyssa's Doctrine of the Celestial Tabernacle in Its Jewish and Christian Contexts*. Oxford: Oxford University Press, 2014.

Cook, Stephen L. *Prophecy and Apocalypticism: The Postexilic Social Setting*. Minneapolis: Fortress, 1995.

Covolo, Enrico dal. "Escatologia e apocalittica nei primi secoli cristiani: Il Regno di Dio e la sua attesta negli Apologisti greci del II secolo." *Salesianum* 62 (2000): 625–43.

Daley, Brian E. "Apocalypticism in Early Christian Theology." Pages 3–48 in *Apocalypticism in Western History and Culture*. Vol. 2 of *The Encyclopedia of Apocalypticism*. Edited by Bernard McGinn. New York: Continuum, 1999.

———. *The Hope of the Early Church: A Handbook of Patristic Eschatology*. Cambridge: Cambridge University Press, 1991.

Daly, Robert J., ed. *Apocalyptic Thought in Early Christianity*. Grand Rapids: Baker Academic, 2009.

———. Preface in *Apocalyptic Thought in Early Christianity*. Edited by Robert J. Daly. Grand Rapids: Baker Academic, 2009.

Danielou, Jean. "La typologie millenariste de la semaine dans le Christianisme primitive." *VC* 2 (1948): 1–16.

DeConick, April D. "What Is Early Jewish and Christian Mysticism?" Pages 1–24 in *Paradise Now: Essays on Early Jewish and Christian Mysticism*. Edited by April D. DeConick. SymS 11. Atlanta: Society of Biblical Literature, 2006.

Deleuze, Gilles, and Félix Guatari. *A Thousand Plateaus: Capitalism and Schizophrenia*. Translated by Brian Massumi. Minneapolis: University of Minnesota Press, 1987.
Digeser, Elizabeth DePalma. *The Making of a Christian Empire: Lactantius and Rome*. New York: Cornell University Press, 2000.
DiTommaso, Lorenzo. "Apocalypses and Apocalypticism in Antiquity, Part I." *CurBR* 5 (2007): 235–86.
———. "Apocalypses and Apocalypticism in Antiquity, Part II." *CurBR* 5 (2007): 367–432.
———. *The Book of Daniel and Apocryphal Daniel Literature*. SVTP 20. Leiden: Brill, 2005.
———. "The Apocryphal Daniel Apocalypses: Works, Manuscripts, and Overview." *ETL* 94 (2018): 275–316.
Erdmann, Martin. *The Millennial Controversy in the Early Church*. Eugene, OR: Wipf & Stock, 2005.
Fiori, Emiliano. "Death and Judgment in the Apocalypse of Paul: Old Imagery and Monastic Reinvention." *ZAC* 20 (2016): 92–108.
Frank, Georgia. "Christ's Descent to the Underworld in Ancient Ritual and Legend." Pages 211–26 in *Apocalyptic Thought in Early Christianity*. Edited by Robert J. Daly. Grand Rapids: Baker Academic, 2009.
Frankfurter, David. *Elijah in Upper Egypt: The Apocalypse of Elijah and Early Egyptian Christianity*. Minneapolis: Fortress, 1993.
———. "The Legacy of Jewish Apocalypses in Early Christianity: Regional Trajectories." Pages 129–200 in *The Jewish Apocalyptic Heritage in Early Christianity*. Edited by James C. VanderKam and William Adler. CRINT 3.4. Assen: Van Gorcum; Minneapolis: Fortress, 1996.
Fredriksen, Paula. "Apocalypse and Redemption in Early Christianity: From John of Patmos to Augustine of Hippo." *VC* 45 (1991): 151–83.
Golitzin, Alexander. "Heavenly Mysteries: Themes from Apocalyptic Literature in the Macarian Homilies and Selected Other Fourth-Century Ascetical Writers." Pages 174–92 in *Apocalyptic Thought in Early Christianity*. Edited by Robert J. Daly. Grand Rapids: Baker Academic, 2009.
Hanson, Paul D. *The Dawn of Apocalyptic: The Historical and Sociological Roots of Jewish Apocalyptic Eschatology*. Rev. ed. Philadelphia: Fortress, 1979.
Henning, Meghan. *Educating Early Christians through the Rhetoric of Hell: 'Weeping and Gnashing of Teeth' as Paideia in Matthew and the Early Church*. WUNT 2/382. Tübingen: Mohr Siebeck 2014.

———. "Lacerated Lips and Lush Landscapes: Constructing This-Worldly Theological Identities in the Otherworld." Pages 99–116 in *The Other Side: Apocryphal Perspectives on Ancient Christian 'Orthodoxies'*. Edited by Tobias Nicklas, Candida R. Moss, C. M. Tuckett, and Joseph Verheyden. NTOA 117. Göttingen: Vandenhoeck & Ruprecht, 2017.

———. "Weeping and Bad Hair: The Bodily Suffering of Early Christian Hell as a Threat to Masculinity." Pages 282–300 in *Phallacies: Historical Intersections of Disability and Masculinity*. Edited by Kathleen M. Brian and James W. Trents. Oxford: Oxford University Press, 2017.

Herrmann, John, and Annewies van den Hoek. "Apocalyptic Themes in Monumental and Minor Art of Early Christianity." Pages 33–80 in *Apocalyptic Thought in Early Christianity*. Edited by Robert J. Daly. Grand Rapids: Baker Academic, 2009.

Hill, Charles E. *Regnum Caelorum: Patterns of Millennial Thought in Early Christianity*. 2nd ed. Grand Rapids: Eerdmans, 2001.

Himmelfarb, Martha. *The Apocalypse: A Brief History*. Oxford: Wiley-Blackwell, 2010.

———. *Tours of Hell: An Apocalyptic Form in Jewish and Christian Literature*. Philadelphia: University of Philadelphia Press, 1983.

Hoover, Jesse A. *The Donatist Church in an Apocalyptic Age*. Oxford: Oxford University Press, 2018.

Kister, Menachem. "Barnabas 12.1, 4.3 and 4Q Second Ezekiel." *RB* 97 (1990): 63–67.

Krueger, Derek. *Liturgical Subjects: Christian Ritual, Biblical Narrative, and the Formation of the Self in Byzantium*. Philadelphia: University of Pennsylvania Press, 2014.

Landes, Richard. "Lest the Millennium Be Fulfilled: Apocalyptic Expectations and the Pattern of Western Chronography 100–800 CE." Pages 137–211 in *The Use and Abuse of Eschatology in the Middle Ages*. Edited by Werner Verbeke and D. Verhelst. Leuven: Leuven University Press, 1988.

Lewis, Nicola Denzey, and Justine Ariel Blount. "Rethinking the Origins of the Nag Hammadi Codices." *JBL* 133 (2014): 399–419.

Lied, Liv Ingeborg. "Transmission and Transformation of 2 Baruch: Challenges to Editors (The Rest Is Commentary, Yale, 28 April 2013)." Unpublished paper. https://tinyurl.com/SBLPress3551b.

Lied, Liv Ingeborg, and Matthew Monger. "Look to the East: New and Forgotten Sources of 4 Ezra." Pages 639–52 in *The Embroidered Bible: Studies in Biblical Apocrypha and Pseudepigrapha in Honour of Michael E.*

Stone. Edited by Lorenzo DiTommaso, Matthias Henze, and William Adler. SVTP 26. Leiden: Brill, 2018.

Lundhaug, Hugo, and Lance Jenott. *The Monastic Origins of the Nag Hammadi Codices*. STAC 97. Tübingen: Mohr Siebeck, 2015.

Lundhaug, Hugo, and Liv Ingeborg Lied. "Studying Snapshots: On Manuscript Culture, Textual Fluidity, and New Philology." Pages 1–19 in *Snapshots of Evolving Traditions: Jewish and Christian Manuscript Culture, Textual Fluidity, and New Philology*. Edited by Hugo Lundhaug and Liv Ingeborg Lied. TUGAL 175. Berlin: de Gruyter, 2017.

Maier, Harry O. "Dominion from Sea to Sea: Eusebius of Caesarea, Constantine the Great, and the Exegesis of Empire." Pages 149–75 in *The Calling of the Nations: Exegesis, Ethnography, and Empire in a Biblical-Historic Present*. Edited by Mark Vessey, Sharon Betcher, Robert A. Daum, and Harry O. Maier. Toronto: University of Toronto Press, 2011.

———. "Nero in Jewish and Christian Tradition from the First Century to the Reformation." Pages 385–405 in *A Companion to the Neronian Age*. Edited by Emma Buckley and Martin T. Dinter. Blackwell Companions to the Ancient World. Oxford: Wiley-Blackwell, 2013.

Markus, Robert A. *Saeculum: History and Society in the Theology of Augustine*. Cambridge: Cambridge University Press, 1970.

Mazzucco, Clementina. "Il millenarismo alle origini del cristianesimo (secc. II–III)." Pages 145–82 in *"Millennium"—l'attesa della fine nei primi secoli cristiani: Atti delle 3. Giornate Patristiche Torinesi; Turin 23–24 ottobre 2000*. Edited by Renato Uglione. Turin: CELID, 2000.

McGinn, Bernard. "Turning Points in Early Christian Apocalypse Exegesis." Pages 81–105 in *Apocalyptic Thought in Early Christianity*. Edited by Robert J. Daly. Grand Rapids: Baker Academic, 2009.

Milik, Jósef T. *The Books of Enoch: Aramaic Fragments of Qumrân Cave 4*. With the collaboration of Matthew Black. Oxford: Clarendon, 1976.

Nickelsburg, George W. E. "Two Enochic Manuscripts: Unstudied Evidence for Egyptian Christianity." Pages 251–60 in *Of Scribes and Scrolls: Studies on the Hebrew Bible, Intertestamental Judaism, and Christian Origins presented to John Strugnell on the Occasion of His Sixtieth Birthday*. Edited by Harold W. Attridge, John J. Collins, and Thomas H. Tobin. Lanham, MD: University Press of America, 1990.

Niederwimmer, Kurt. *The Didache*. Hermeneia. Translated by Linda M. Maloney. Philadelphia: Fortress, 1998.

Orlov, Andrei, and Alexander Golitzin. "'Many Lamps Are Lighted from the One': Paradigms of the Transformational Vision in Macarian Homilies." *VC* 55 (2001): 281–98.
Pelikan, Jaroslav. "The Eschatology of Tertullian." *CH* 21 (1952): 108–22.
Portier-Young, Anathea. *Apocalypse against Empire: Theologies of Resistance in Early Judaism*. Grand Rapids: Eerdmans, 2011.
Prete, S. "Sulpico Severo e il millenarismo." *Convivium* 26 (1958): 394–404.
Reed, Annette Yoshiko. *Fallen Angels and the History of Judaism and Christianity: The Reception of Enochic Literature*. Cambridge: Cambridge University Press, 2005.
Rowe, Eric. "The Enochic Library of the Author of the Epistle of Barnabas." Pages 88–102 in *"Non-canonical" Religious Texts in Early Judaism and Early Christianity*. Edited by Lee Martin McDonald and James H. Charlesworth. London: T&T Clark, 2012.
Rowland, Christopher. *The Open Heaven: A Study of Apocalyptic in Judaism and Early Christianity*. New York: Crossroad, 1982.
Tabbernee, William. "Portals of the Montanist New Jerusalem: The Discovery of Pepouza and Tymion." *JECS* 11 (2003): 87–93.
———. "Revelation 21 and the Montanist 'New Jerusalem.'" *ABR* 37 (1989): 52–60.
Tabor, James D. "Ancient Jewish and Early Christian Millennialism." Pages 252–66 in *The Oxford Handbook of Millennialism*. Edited by Catherine Wessinger. Oxford: Oxford University Press, 2011.
Uglione, Renato, ed. *"Millennium"—L'attesa della fine nei primi secoli cristiani: Atti delle 3. Giornate Patristiche Torinesi; Turin 23–24 ottobre 2000*. Turin: CELID, 2000.
VanderKam, James C. "1 Enoch, Enochic Motifs, and Enoch in Early Christian Literature." Pages 33–101 in *The Jewish Apocalyptic Heritage in Early Christianity*. Edited by James C. VanderKam and William Adler. CRINT 3.4. Assen: Van Gorcum; Minneapolis: Fortress, 1996.
VanderKam, James C., and William Adler, eds. *The Jewish Apocalyptic Heritage in Early Christianity*. CRINT 3.4. Assen: Van Gorcum; Minneapolis: Fortress, 1996.
Vielhauer, Philipp. Introduction to *Writings Related to the Apostles; Apocalypses and Related Subjects*. Vol. 2 of *New Testament Apocrypha*. Edited by Edgar Hennecke and William Schneemelcher. Translated by R. McLean Wilson. Philadelphia: Westminster, 1965.
Walls, Jerry L., ed. *The Oxford Handbook of Eschatology*. Oxford: Oxford University Press, 2008.

Wessinger, Catherine, ed. *The Oxford Handbook of Millennialism*. Oxford: Oxford University Press, 2011.
Wintermute, O. S. "Apocalypse of Zephaniah." *OTP* 1:497–515.
Worley, John. *The Book of the Elders, The Sayings of the Desert Fathers: The Systematic Collection*. CSS 240. Collegeville: Liturgical Press, 2012.
Yarbro Collins, Adela. "The Early Christian Apocalypses." *Semeia* 14 (1979): 61–121.
———, ed. *Early Christian Apocalypticism: Genre and Social Setting. Semeia* 36 (1986).
———. "Introduction: Early Christian Apocalypticism." *Semeia* 36 (1986): 1–12.

The Importance of the Gnostic Apocalypses from Nag Hammadi for the Study of Early Jewish Mysticism

Dylan M. Burns

The ancient body of thought known today as Gnosticism—characterized by a distinction between the creator-deity and the true God, who shares a divine nature with an elect humanity that in turn is superior to the world and its maker—is of primary importance for our understanding of the earliest development of Christianity.[1] Its relationship with Judaism, and particularly the history of Jewish mysticism, is no longer a subject of dispute as much a nearly moribund topic.[2] Yet scholarship on ancient Judaism—

Given the interdisciplinary nature of this volume, I have focused on larger questions regarding the agenda of the study of Gnosticism and Jewish mysticism, rather than minutiae; nonetheless, I hope that the approach taken here proves to be a productive one. This paper was presented in various forms: at the University of Copenhagen (May 2015), at the Eighth Enoch Seminar at Gazzada (June 2015), and at the Zentrum für jüdische Kulturgeschichte, in Salzburg (December 2018). For comments and criticisms I am indebted to the audiences of each of these talks, especially Daniel Boyarin, Lorenzo DiTommaso, and Susanna Plietzsch, as well as Jeremy Brown. I eschew here the question of the relationship between ancient gnostic literary traditions and the (relatively) later kabbalistic literature, as discussed by Moshe Idel, *Kabbalah: New Perspectives* (New Haven: Yale University Press, 1988), esp. 112-55. The topic absolutely merits new investigation, and it is a hope of the present study to contribute to such an endeavor.

1. These are the primary characteristics of the works associated with the gnostic school of thought known to Irenaeus (*Haer.* 1.29-30) and Porphyry (*Vit. Plot.* 16). See David Brakke, *The Gnostics: Myth, Ritual, and Diversity in Early Christianity* (Cambridge: Harvard University Press, 2010); Dylan M. Burns, "Providence, Creation, and Gnosticism according to the Gnostics," *JECS* 24 (2016): 55-79.

2. *Mysticism* is a difficult term which continues to undergo scrutiny and revision by scholars. For the purposes of the present study, which is more concerned with sources that have been termed mystical in scholarship rather than the etic construct mysti-

ranging from rabbinic literature to the Dead Sea Scrolls, pseudepigrapha, and medieval mystical texts—has experienced a renaissance in recent decades, having transformed the terrain upon which the boundaries between and Gnosticism and Judaism were once divined by scholarship. In the present contribution, I hope to suggest how gnostic studies might digest these developments, allowing us to address, in fresh and new terms, the relationship of Gnosticism—particularly the Sethian apocalypses unearthed at Nag Hammadi in 1945—to Jewish mystical traditions and practices. Conversely, our gnostic evidence, principally the Sethian works from Nag Hammadi, provides us with valuable insight into the reception and transformation of Jewish mystical traditions during the second to fifth centuries CE, a period in which our evidence regarding these traditions is scarce indeed. The gnostic apocalypses thus may be of tremendous use in formulating new approaches to current problems regarding the evolution and contours of both our gnostic and Jewish sources.

1. Gnosticism, Judaism, and Jewish Mysticism Revisited

It is strange that gnosticism has more or less disappeared from research into the history of ancient Jewish mysticism (and vice versa), since it spent

---

cism, it is helpful to appropriate the term and its attendant cognates to describe these sources insofar as they push "toward the transcendent and toward that which exceeds the human, whether framed experientially or linguistically"—see Louise Nelstrop, "Mysticism," in *Vocabulary for the Study of Religion*, ed. Robert A. Segal and Kocku von Stuckrad (Brill Online, 2016). On debate about the term *mysticism* vis-à-vis *Jewish mysticism*, see esp. Eliot Wolfson, *Through a Speculum That Shines: Vision and Imagination in Medieval Jewish Mysticism* (Princeton: Princeton University Press, 1994), 50–73; Peter Schäfer, *The Origins of Jewish Mysticism* (Tübingen: Mohr Siebeck, 2009), 1–20; and Christoph Markschies, *Gottes Körper: Jüdische, christliche und pagane Gottesvorstellungen in der Antike* (München: Beck, 2016), 190–94. On the term *mysticism* more generally, the account of Bernard McGinn remains useful: *The Foundations of Mysticism: Origins to the Fifth Century* (New York: Crossroad, 1991), xiii–xx, 265–343. A contributing factor to the situation is the skepticism regarding the category Gnosticism fashionable in the previous generation of Nag Hammadi scholarship, following from the work of Michael A. Williams, *Rethinking "Gnosticism": Arguments for Dismantling a Dubious Category* (Princeton: Princeton University Press, 1995); and Karen L. King, *What Is Gnosticism?* (Cambridge: Harvard University Press, 2003). On reading sources once regarded as gnostic simply as Christian (and thus insulated from Judaism), see, for instance, Karen L. King, review of *The Gnostics*, by David Brakke, *HR* 52 (2013): 294–301; cf. also below, n. 12.

well over a century on the docket following the tremendous influence of Heinrich Graetz's *Gnostizismus und Judentum* (1846).[3] What happened? In short, the enterprise of putting ancient Jewish and gnostic sources in conversation with one another became tied up in the elusive search for the origins of Gnosticism in Judaism. This search proceeded—and failed—in three arenas, which are worth briefly reviewing since the fallout roughly demarcates the borders presently existing between the study of Gnosticism and that of ancient Jewish mysticism—and implicitly, our means for transgressing them.

The first is rabbinic evidence about Jewish mysticism, particularly regarding the character of Elisha ben Abuya, who appears in our rabbinic sources as a kind of mystical, intellectual rebel, who, torn by the problem of evil, rejects halakah in favor of licentiousness and Greek *paideia*.[4] Most famously, the Babylonian Talmud features him in its commentary on the legend of the four sages who ascend to paradise, wherein "Aḥer"—ben Abuya's nickname (Heb. for "other")—sees Metatron sitting and writing the merits of Israel. Knowing that angels are not allowed to sit, he is shocked and wonders (incredulously), "perhaps—God forfend!—there are two divinities!" "Permission was [then] given to him to strike out the merits of Aḥer. A Bath Kol went forth and said: Return, ye backsliding children—except Aḥer" (Hag. 15a).[5] Scholars have long drawn a connection

---

3. Helpful discussions of Graetz's work and influence and subsequent forays into the relationship between Gnosticism and Judaism can be found in Birger A. Pearson, "Friedländer Revisited: Alexandrian Judaism and Gnostic Origin," in *Gnosticism, Judaism, and Egyptian Christianity*, ed. Birger A. Pearson (Minneapolis: Fortress, 1990), 10–28; Gerald Luttikhuizen, "Monism and Dualism in Jewish-Mystical and Gnostic Ascent Texts," in *Flores Florentino: Dead Sea Scrolls and Other Early Jewish Studies in Honour of Florentino García Martínez*, ed. Anthony Hilhorst, Émile Puech, and Eibert J. C. Tigchelaar, JSJSup 122 (Leiden: Brill, 2007), 749–52; Annette Yoshiko Reed, "Rethinking (Jewish-)Christian Evidence," in *Hekhalot Literature in Context: Between Byzantium and Babylonia*, ed. Raʿanan S. Boustan, Martha Himmelfarb, and Peter Schäfer (Tübingen: Mohr Siebeck, 2013), 349–64; and Jan Lahe, *Gnosis und Judentum: Alttestamentliche und jüdische Motive in der gnostischen Literatur und das Ursprungsproblem der Gnosis*, NHMS 75 (Leiden: Brill, 2012), 99–157.

4. For a survey and discussion of the sources about ben Abuyah, see Alon Goshen-Gottstein, *The Sinner and the Amnesiac: The Rabbinic Invention of Elisha ben Abuyah and Eleazar ben Arach*, Contraversions (Stanford, CA: Stanford University Press, 2000), as well as the following notes regarding the *Pardes* narrative.

5. Trans. in Isidore Epstein, ed., *The Babylonian Talmud: Hagiga* (London: Soncino, 1935–1952). This account is also related in 3 En. 16.2 (cf. Peter Schäfer, ed.,

between ben Abuyah's Otherness, mysticism, antinomianism, and ostensible speculations about there being "two powers in heaven" and took him as evidence of pre-Christian, Jewish Gnosticism, a line of reasoning we still find today in some secondary literature.[6] Yet such a reading of the evidence is unpersuasive; the Babylonian Talmud is a highly redacted text of late antiquity (and thus a difficult witness of developments of the first century CE), while the whole phrasing of an orthodox Rabbinism that opposed ben Abuya likely blankets diversity in ancient Jewish culture, instead replicating the terms of early Christian heresiography.[7]

Synopse zur Hekhalot-Literatur [Tübingen: Mohr Siebeck, 1981], §20); Hekhalot Zutarti (Schäfer, *Synopse*, §§338–39, 344–46, 348, G7); and Merkabah Rabbah (Schäfer, *Synopse*, §§671–73). For critical discussion of the various recensions of these passages and their background in ancient Jewish literature, see Nathanael Deutsch, *Guardians of the Gate: Angelic Vice-Regency in Late Antiquity*, BSJS 22 (Leiden: Brill, 1999), 48–75; Schäfer, *Origins of Jewish Mysticism*, 193–94 and 231–42; Daniel Boyarin, "Beyond Judaisms: Meṭaṭron and the Divine Polymorphy of Ancient Judaism," *JSJ* 41 (2010): 345–56; and Andrei A. Orlov, "Two Powers in Heaven … Manifested," in *Wisdom Poured Out Like Water: Studies on Jewish and Christian Antiquity in Honor of Gabriele Boccaccini*, ed. J. Harold Ellens et al., DCLS 38 (Berlin: de Gruyter, 2018), 351–64.

6. For earlier *Forschungsgeschichte* on the "two powers controversy," see Alan F. Segal, *Two Powers in Heaven: Early Rabbinic Reports about Christianity and Judaism*, SJLA 25 (Leiden: Brill, 1977), 8–14. More recent studies (which have little to say regarding gnostic sources) include Alon Goshen-Gottstein, "Jewish-Christian Relations and Rabbinic Literature—Shifting Scholarly and Relational Paradigms: The Case of Two Powers," in *Interaction between Judaism and Christianity in History, Religion, Art, and Literature*, ed. Marcel Poorthuis, Joshua Schwartz, and Joseph Aaron Turner, JCP 17 (Leiden: Brill, 2008), 15–44, esp. 30–40; Boyarin, "Beyond Judaisms"; and Orlov, "Two Powers in Heaven," 351 n. 1. Segal acknowledged the evidence about ben Abuya to be highly redacted but nonetheless considered it indicative of interaction between gnostic and *merkabah* traditions in Tannaitic circles (*Two Powers in Heaven*, 60–67, 150–51). Others have regarded ben Abuya to be a historical personage and "gnostic heretic" (Pearson, "Friedländer Revisited," 24: "it can hardly be doubted any longer that Elisha ben Abuya [Aḥer] was a Gnostic heretic," who, dissatisfied with Judaism, "turned to Gnosticism" and "proselytized" on its behalf); see also Guy S. Stroumsa, "Aḥer: A Gnostic," in *The Rediscovery of Gnosticism: Proceedings of the International Conference on Gnosticism*, ed. Bentley Layton, NBS 41 (Leiden: Brill, 1981), 2:816.

7. Ithamar Gruenwald, "Aspects of the Jewish-Gnostic Controversy," in Layton, *Rediscovery of Gnosticism*, 2:713–23, esp. 721; Shaye J. D. Cohen, Review of *Two Powers in Heaven*, by Alan Segal, *AJSR* 10 (1985): 114–17. Boyarin emphasizes that Segal's analysis views the two-powers heresy as an intrusion on Judaism, rather than an integral, ancient current within developing Judaism ("Beyond Judaisms," 327–28). Less persuasive is Adiel Schremer's claim that one could read the rabbinic evidence

Meanwhile, the 1945 discovery of a cache of thirteen Coptic papyrus manuscripts near the city of Nag Hammadi (Upper Egypt) revolutionized the study of Gnosticism, for these ancient books seem to contain many works whose contents resemble the teachings of the gnostic school of thought mentioned by Irenaeus, Porphyry, and others. Scholars widely recognized that many of the Nag Hammadi texts recall *midrashim*, extensions of and commentaries on famous biblical stories, gnostic retellings of the creation of Adam, his fall with Eve from the garden of Eden, Noah and the flood, God's statement that he is jealous, and much else.[8]

Did Gnosticism then arise from Hellenized exegesis of problematic passages in the Hebrew Bible, producing the famous gnostic view of the Jewish God as foolish, if not arrogant and cruel?[9] Our earliest testimonies about gnostic teachers such as Satornilus or Basilides intimate that they were Christians in some sense, and every surviving gnostic manuscript from antiquity appears to be a Christian product (including those containing midrashic works from Nag Hammadi).[10] Our inability to extract

---

about two powers as not pertaining to the development of gnostic or even Christian ideas at all but an "existential response to despair" following Jewish military defeats at Roman hands ("Midrash, Theology, and History: Two Powers in Heaven Revisited," *JSJ* 39 [2007]: 23–54). Schremer's argument, if valid, furnishes rabbinic evidence undergirding the old thesis that Gnosticism arose as "an existential response to despair" following Jewish military defeats at Roman hands (see below), which would in turn mean that the two-powers controversy *does* constitute evidence pertinent to the development of Gnosticism!

8. Classic examples include but are not limited to Apocryphon of John (NHC II 1 par.), the Nature of the Rulers (NHC II 4), and Apocalypse of Adam (NHC V 5). On these and other texts from Nag Hammadi as *midrashim*, see e.g., Birger A. Pearson, "Jewish Haggadic Traditions in *The Testimony of Truth* from Nag Hammadi (CG IX,3)," in Pearson, *Gnosticism, Judaism, and Egyptian Christianity*, 457–70. For exhaustive analysis, see Lahe, *Gnosis und Judentum*, 191–356.

9. An old thesis; for a recent rehearsal, see Volker Henning Drecoll, "Martin Hengel and the Origins of Gnosticism," in *Gnosticism, Platonism, and the Late Ancient World: Essays in Honour of John D. Turner*, ed. Kevin Corrigan and Tuomas Rasimus, NHMS 82 (Leiden: Brill, 2013), 139–65, esp. 161–63. It is difficult to draw a line between this phrasing and Pearson's contention that "although much of the detail of Friedländer's argument is open to question, he has been vindicated in his basic contention, that Gnosticism is a pre-Christian phenomenon that developed on Jewish soil" ("Friedländer Revisited," 28).

10. On the manufacture of our Coptic gnostic sources by Egyptian Christians, see Hugo Lundhaug and Lance Jenott, *The Monastic Origins of the Nag Hammadi Codices* (Tübingen: Mohr Siebeck, 2015), focusing on the "monastic hypothesis." On the

evidence about Gnosticism from emergent Christianity—even if we deign to conflate the two—mitigates the famous hypothesis that such anti-Jewish exegesis of Scripture must have been the product of disenfranchised, educated Alexandrian Jewry, devastated by the failures of the cataclysmic Jewish Wars (68–70 CE) and the Jewish rebellion against Trajan (115–117).[11] The question of the Jewish origins of Gnosticism is commonly regarded as closed, for good reason.[12]

Gershom Scholem (1897–1982), meanwhile, attempted to sketch out a history of Jewish literature detailing visionary encounters with the Godhead and assigned Gnosticism a central role in this history (even if he ultimately regarded it as "metaphysical anti-Semitism").[13] Recognizing that Kabbalistic literature must have emerged from a wider spectrum of ancient and early medieval Jewish mystical texts—chiefly inspired by Ezekiel's vision of the celestial throne-chariot (Heb. *merkabah*)—his chief interest lay in the early medieval *hekhalot* ("palaces") literature. Scholem saw the ornate Jewish "throne-world" of the *hekhalot* treatises as resembling gnostic descriptions of heaven as a *plērōma* (Grk. "fullness") inhabited by various aeons, potencies, and archons.[14] For him, the ascent of the rabbis past dangerous obstacles in the heavenly palaces derived from

---

Christian character of even early evidence about Gnosticism, see Alistair H. B. Logan, *Gnostic Truth and Christian Heresy: A Study in the History of Gnosticism* (Edinburgh: T&T Clark, 1996).

11. The famous thesis of Robert M. Grant, *Gnosticism and Early Christianity* (San Francisco: Harper Torchbooks, 1959), 27–38, followed widely (as discussed in Lahe, *Gnosis und Judentum*, 111–13, 121–22).

12. For relevant recent scholarship on this topic, see Dylan Burns and Matthew Goff, eds., *The Dead Sea Scrolls and the Nag Hammadi Codices*, NHMS 103 (Leiden: Brill, 2022).

13. On Scholem's exploration of so-called Jewish Gnosticism in the context of German Jewish and Christian philosophy of his day, see Benjamin Lazier, *God Interrupted: Heresy and the European Imagination between the World Wars* (Princeton: Princeton University Press, 2008), 146–60; still useful is the discussion of Wolfson, *Through a Speculum That Shines*, 75–76. On Scholem's interpretation of Gnosticism as "metaphysical anti-Semitism" (a quip issued to Jonas), see Steven M. Wasserstrom, *Religion after Religion: Gershom Scholem, Mircea Eliade and Henry Corbin at Eranos* (Princeton: Princeton University Press, 2008), 190. For use of the term, see, e.g., Joel Fineman, "Gnosis and the Piety of Metaphor: The *Gospel of Truth*," in Layton, *Rediscovery of Gnosticism*, 2:309.

14. Gershom Scholem, *Major Trends in Jewish Mysticism* (New York: Schocken, 1995), 44.

The Importance of the Gnostic Apocalypses from Nag Hammadi 509

gnostic accounts of ascent past demonic archons.[15] The spells used by the rabbis to navigate these obstacles consist of foreign words (so-called *nomina barbara*), which Scholem saw as identical to the semi-intelligible incantations in our gnostic evidence.[16] He considered the Shiʿur Qomah literature—speculation on the shape and magnitude of God's body—to be influenced by the "mystical anthropomorphism" of gnostic thinkers.[17] Scholem believed that Elisha ben Abuya was a gnostic.[18] For him, then, gnostic texts provided evidence for a Hellenized "Jewish Gnosticism" that could be reconstructed from gnostic, rabbinic, and *hekhalot* sources.[19]

There are reasons to disagree with Scholem: the comparisons are primitive and, in many cases, forced.[20] Moreover, Scholem wrote without much knowledge of the Nag Hammadi texts and so worked with a considerably different set of data than we employ today. Finally, he paid little attention to Jewish apocalyptic literature.[21] So, while approaches similar to Scholem's live on in pockets of scholarship, his perspective has more or less disappeared from the study of Jewish mysticism and taken Gnosti-

---

15. Scholem, *Major Trends in Jewish Mysticism*, 49–54.
16. Gershom Scholem, *Jewish Gnosticism, Merkabah Mysticism, and Talmudic Tradition* (New York: JTS, 1960), 32–33.
17. Scholem, *Jewish Gnosticism*, 38–42; Scholem, *Major Trends in Jewish Mysticism*, 65. For recent discussions of the Shiʿur Qomah literature, see Schäfer, *Origins of Jewish Mysticism*, 306–15; and Markschies, *Gottes Körper*, 202–23.
18. Scholem, *Jewish Gnosticism*, 14–19.
19. Scholem, *Jewish Gnosticism*, 10, 34–35.
20. For instance, Scholem referred to Irenaeus's account of Marcus's description of the correspondence between Aletheia's body parts and the letters of the Greek alphabet as evidence for the circulation of Shiʿur Qomah traditions in second-century Gnosticism; see his *On the Mystical Shape of the Godhead: Basic Concepts in the Kabbalah* (New York: Schocken, 1997), 25–30, regarding Irenaeus, *Haer.* 1.14. Schäfer rightly points out that the parallels are superficial, since the letters are not names and Aletheia is neither a giant nor God (*Origins of Jewish Mysticism*, 311–13; see also Markschies, *Gottes Körper*, 234–38). Observing that "originally it was heavenly figures in the Jewish tradition, mainly angels, to whom outsize dimensions were attributed," Schäfer asks, "could it be that, once the vast size of the angels was adopted by the Christians (and, worse, these angels became divine figures), the Jewish tradition came to insist that only God himself has gigantic dimensions?" (315).
21. I.e., works written using the genre of apocalypse, wherein a supernatural mediator transmits heavenly knowledge, whether of the future or of cosmic secrets, to a seer or prophet, which is passed on in written form, often with the authority of an authoritative pseudonym (thus John J. Collins, "Introduction: Towards the Morphology of a Genre," *Semeia* 14 [1979]: 1–20).

cism along with it.[22] Thus Peter Schäfer's survey of 2010, entitled *The Origins of Jewish Mysticism*, does not treat Gnosticism at all. And why should it? After all, our rabbinic evidence tells us nothing about Gnosticism, our extant gnostic sources command us to read them as productions of Christian contexts, and Scholem's "Jewish Gnosticism" is today regarded as a serious misnomer.

Rather, the study of early Jewish mysticism today is consumed with different questions, largely arising from the treatment of new data, which may be broken down into three groups: the pseudepigrapha and apocalypses (and, more widely, apocalypticism, however construed); the Dead Sea Scrolls discovered at Qumran; and finally, the publication, translation, and interpretation of the *hekhalot* texts themselves. Students of early Jewish mysticism are then largely concerned with the problem of how to weave all this material together: for instance, what is the relationship in these texts between magical-theurgical practices (i.e., the controlling of angels) and visionary practices (i.e., joining angels in heaven before God in the *unio liturgica*)?[23] To what extent do these texts present evidence for Jewish mystical practice at all—or are they simply literary artifacts?[24] What are the implications of the Qumran find, if any, for our understanding of

---

22. This is a legacy of Gilles Quispel, who argued that an ancient, pre-Christian, Jewish Gnosticism could be reconstructed from the Hermetica, *hekhalot* literature, the pseudo-Clementines, and Samaritan sources, in addition to our patristic and Coptic evidence about Gnosticism; see, e.g., Gilles Quispel, "Christliche Gnosis, jüdische Gnosis, hermetische Gnosis," in *Gnostica, Judaica, Catholica: Collected Essays of Gilles Quispel*, ed. J. van Oort, NHMS 55 (Leiden: Brill, 2008), 3–36, esp. 17–19, regarding the Jewish origins of Gnosticism *apud* Scholem.

23. On this tension, see e.g., Peter Schäfer, *The Hidden and Manifest God: Some Major Themes in Early Jewish Mysticism* (Syracuse: State University of New York Press, 1992), 143, 150–57, esp. 151; James R. Davila, *Hekhalot Literature in Translation: Major Texts of Merkavah Mysticism*, JJTPSup 20 (Leiden: Brill, 2013), 8–9; Markschies, *Gottes Körper*, 221; and further below.

24. An extensive debate with many participants; for *Forschungsgeschichte*, see, e.g., Wolfson, *Through a Speculum That Shines*, 121–24; Vita Daphna Arbel, *Beholders of Divine Secrets: Mysticism and Myth in the Hekhalot and Merkavah Literature* (Albany: State University of New York Press, 2003), 12–14; April D. DeConick, "What Is Early Jewish and Christian Mysticism?," in *Paradise Now: Essays on Early Jewish and Christian Mysticism*, ed. April D. DeConick, SymS 11 (Atlanta: Society of Biblical Literature, 2006), 1–26, esp. 5–8; Ra'anan S. Boustan, "The Study of Heikhalot Literature: Between Mystical Experience and Textual Artifact," *CurBR* 6 (2007): 130–60, esp. 143–47; and Davila, *Hekhalot Literature in Translation*, 9–13.

the *hekhalot* literature and Jewish mysticism in general?[25] And where does apocalyptic literature fit into the mix?[26]

A central difficulty is the state of the evidence, despite its relative abundance—for between the angelic liturgies of Qumran and the *hekhalot* literature we have a more or less millennium-long gap in our data (extending from the Hellenistic period through the end of late antiquity) for developments in Jewish mysticism.[27] The bulk of our ancient Jewish apocalyptic texts, as well as our rabbinic evidence, roughly falls into this gap, but while the apocalypses furnish valuable evidence on a case-by-case basis, they are too diverse in origin, content, and transmission to constitute a coherent corpus that one could compare against the Qumran and *hekhalot* corpora. Meanwhile, our rabbinic evidence about Jewish mystical *practices* is slim indeed.[28]

2. Gnostic Apocalypses, Sethian Apocalypses

This is where our Coptic gnostic evidence steps in. Here, we have a corpus of texts that we can date to the fourth–fifth centuries CE in Roman Egypt but in some cases are translations of works we know to have circulated in the second and third centuries throughout the Roman Empire. Significantly, the predominant genre of these works is apocalypse—about half of them, in total.[29] Yet for the reasons outlined above, this body of texts has

---

25. Discussed further below.

26. The focus of Ithamar Gruenwald, *Apocalyptic and Merkavah Mysticism*, AJEC 90 (Leiden: Brill, 2014), esp. 68–110, and Martha Himmelfarb, *Ascents to Heaven in Jewish and Christian Apocalypses* (New York: Oxford University Press, 1993); see also Andrei Orlov, *From Apocalypticism to Merkavah Mysticism: Studies in the Slavonic Pseudepigrapha*, JSJSup 114 (Leiden: Brill, 2007), esp. 103–6.

27. Recognized by Reed, "Rethinking (Jewish-)Christian Evidence," 354.

28. Schäfer has argued that "the rabbis were preoccupied with the *exegesis* of certain passages perceived as dangerous, and not with ecstatic experiences" (*Origins of Jewish Mysticism*, 350, emphasis original; see also 350–52), but cf. Wolfson's reminder that exegesis and experience are not so easily demarcated from one another (*Through a Speculum*, 121–24). One need not take either side in this debate to recognize the value of an additional body of *Vergleichsmaterial* preserving a great deal of relevant evidence that antedates the earliest *hekhalot* manuscripts.

29. This figure assumes one regards revelation-dialogues without a heavenly journey under the heading of apocalypse, so Harold W. Attridge, "Valentinian and Sethian Apocalyptic Traditions," *JECS* 8 (2000): 208–9; see Dylan M. Burns, "The Gnostic Apocalypses," in *The Cambridge Companion to Apocalyptic Literature*, ed. Colin McAllister (Cambridge: Cambridge University Press, 2020), 59–78.

received little attention from specialists in ancient Judaism and especially Jewish mysticism, although a few scholars have flagged passages in gnostic literature that seem to describe speculation about the *merkabah*.[30]

Nonetheless, a particular set of gnostic apocalypses constitutes valuable evidence for our understanding of the history of Jewish mysticism. These apocalypses belong to a branch of gnostic literature called "Sethian," chiefly due to its focus on the figure of Seth as revealer and savior.[31] Within this group of Sethian apocalypses, Zostrianos (NHC VIII 1), Marsanes (NHC X 1), and Allogenes (NHC XI 3) stand out as particularly exotic. They are apocalypses of the cosmological stripe of Ethiopic or Slavonic Enoch, describing the heavenly journey and acquisition of cosmic secrets of the revealer-savior figures after whom the treatises are named.[32] However, they are also replete with the jargon of Neoplatonism, the later form of Platonic philosophy that was assumed by intellectual antagonists of

---

30. Philip S. Alexander, "Comparing Merkavah Mysticism and Gnosticism: An Essay in Method," *JJS* 35 (1984): 1–18, esp. 2 n. 2, following Gruenwald, "Aspects of the Jewish-Gnostic Controversy?" regarding Nature of the Rulers (NHC II 95.26–32; Orig. World NHC II 104.35–105.30). Descriptions of the *merkabah* are also to be found in fragments of the Valentinian Theodotus (Clement of Alexandria, *Exc.* 37–39 [Sagnard], per Scholem, *Jewish Gnosticism*, 34–35) and the Sethian Egyptian Gospel NHC IV 51.2-3 = NHC III 49.14, per C. R. A. Morray-Jones, "Transformational Mysticism in the Apocalyptic-Merkabah Tradition," *JJS* 43 (1992): 28–29, on the title "Domedōn Doxomedōn"; better, see NHC IV 53.3–54.20 = NHC III 43.8–44.13.

31. The seminal studies remain Hans-Martin Schenke, "Das sethianische System nach Nag-Hammadi-Handschriften," in *Studia Coptica*, ed. Peter Nagel, BBA 45 (Berlin: Akademie, 1974), 165–73; and Schenke, "Phenomenon and Significance of Gnostic Sethianism," in Layton, *Rediscovery of Gnosticism*, 2:588–616. Frederick Wisse rightfully points out that Schenke's recognition of a coherent body of mythologoumena and ideas spread throughout the Nag Hammadi texts does not necessarily constitute the existence of a Sethian social group; see "Stalking Those Elusive Sethians," in Layton, *Rediscovery of Gnosticism*, 2:563–76. Even so, scholars generally agree that the set of Sethian characteristics identified by Schenke constitutes a more or less coherent group; see, e.g., Michael A. Williams, "Sethianism," in *A Companion to Second-Century "Heretics"*, ed. Antti Marjanen and Petri Luomanen, VCSup 76 (Leiden: Brill, 2005), 33–34, 36. For criticism of the category (resulting in a trimmed Sethian corpus set next to a smaller Ophite corpus), see Tuomas Rasimus, *Paradise Reconsidered in Gnostic Mythmaking: Rethinking Sethianism in Light of the Ophite Evidence*, NHMS 68 (Leiden: Brill, 2009).

32. Per Collins, "Introduction," 9.

Christianity such as Porphyry, disciple of the great philosopher Plotinus.[33] Porphyry tells us that

> There were in his [Plotinus's] time many others, Christians, in particular heretics who had set out from the ancient philosophy, men belonging to the schools of Adelphius and Aculinus—who possessed many works of Alexander the Libyan and Philocomus and Demostratus of Lydia, and who produced revelations of Zoroaster and Zostrianos and Nicotheus and Allogenes and Messos and others of this sort who deceived many, just as they had been deceived, actually alleging that Plato really had not penetrated to the depth of intelligible substance. Wherefore, Plotinus often attacked their position in his seminars, and wrote the book which we have entitled *Against the Gnostics*. (Porphery, *Vit. Plot.* 16)[34]

Against the Gnostics (*Enn.* 2.9 [33]) is extant today.[35] Since works with titles identical to several of those mentioned by Porphyry have been unearthed in Coptic translation at Nag Hammadi, we possess versions of gnostic apocalypses that caused a fuss among Platonic philosophers in Ploti-

---

33. The relationship of these works to contemporary Platonism is an ongoing enterprise pioneered by John D. Turner in many publications, but esp. his *Sethian Gnosticism and the Platonic Tradition*, BCNH Études 6 (Québec: Université Laval; Leuven: Peeters, 2001). More recently, see Tuomas Rasimus, "Porphyry and the Gnostics: Reassessing Pierre Hadot's Thesis in Light of the Second- and Third-Century Sethian Treatises," in *Plato's "Parmenides" and Its Heritage*, ed. John Douglas Turner and Kevin Corrigan, WGRWSup 2–3 (Atlanta: Society of Biblical Literature, 2010), 2:81–110; Jean-Marc Narbonne, *Plotinus in Dialogue with the Gnostics*, SPNPT 11 (Leiden: Brill, 2011); Dylan M. Burns, *Apocalypse of the Alien God: Platonism and the Exile of Sethian Gnosticism*, Divinations (Philadelphia: University of Pennsylvania Press, 2014); and Zeke Mazur, *The Platonizing Sethian Gnostic Background of Plotinus' Mysticism*, NHMS 98 (Leiden: Brill, 2020).

34. Translation mine. On this passage, see inter alii Paul-Hubert Poirier and Thomas Schmidt, "Chrétiens, hérétiques et gnostiques chez porphyre: Quelques precisions sur la *Vie de Plotin* 16.1–9," *Académie des Inscriptions et Belles Lettres: Comptes rendus des séances de l'année 2010. Avril-juin*, ed. P. de Boccard (Paris: CRAI, 2010), 913–42; and Burns, *Apocalypse of the Alien God*, 161–63.

35. For commentary on *Enn.* 2.9, see Paul Kalligas, "Plotinus against the Gnostics," *Hermathena* 169 (2000): 115–28; Nicola Spanu, *Plotinus, 'Ennead' II 9 [33] 'Against the Gnostics': A Commentary*, StPatrSup 1 (Leuven: Peeters, 2012); Burns, *Apocalypse of the Alien God*, 32–47; and Sebastian R. P. Gertz, *Plotinus. Ennead II.9: Against the Gnostics; Translation with an Introduction and Commentary* (Las Vegas: Parmenides, 2017).

nus's seminar in Rome in 263 CE *and* an extant polemic written against their Christian gnostic readers—probably the most specific information we possess about the who, what, where, and when of *any* extant ancient apocalyptic text.

When we read the Coptic Zostrianos and Allogenes—and the two other treatises from Nag Hammadi that closely resemble them, Marsanes and the Three Steles of Seth (NHC VII 5)—the reason these Platonizing Sethian treatises circulated in an ancient postgraduate philosophy seminar is clear, given their use of technical language drawn from advanced, later Greek metaphysics. What scholarship is just beginning to ascertain, however, is that these works also are deeply indebted to Jewish mystical traditions we know from other ancient apocalypses, as well as the Qumran literature.[36] The most cogent example of this indebtedness is their interest in the angelification of the seer, particularly in the context of liturgical passages that appear to describe participation in the angelic glorification of the Godhead itself.[37]

3. Angelification in Sethian Literature

Two passages in the Sethian corpus mention this angelification explicitly. The first is from a revelatory work entitled First Thought in Three Forms, in which the narrator describes the transformation of a baptismal initiate at the hands of angelic figures:

> I delivered him unto the enrobers, Iammon, Elassō, Amēnai, and they [clothed] him with a robe, from the robes of light; and I delivered him unto the baptizers—they baptized him, Mikheus, Mikhar, Mnēsinous—and they immersed him in the fountain of the [Water] of Life. And I delivered him unto those who enthrone—Bariēl, Nouthan, Sabēnai—

---

36. Foundational research on the question was conducted by Madeline Scopello, "The Apocalypse of Zostrianos (Nag Hammadi VIII.1) and the Book of the Secrets of Enoch," *VC* 34 (1980): 376–85; Scopello, "Un rite idéal d'intronisation dans trois textes gnostiques de Nag Hammadi," in *Nag Hammadi and Gnosis: Papers Read at the First International Congress of Coptology (Cairo, December 1976)*, ed. R. McLachlan Wilson, NHS 14 (Leiden: Brill, 1978), 91–95; and Scopello, "Youel et Barbélo dans le Traité de l'Allogène," in *Colloque international sur les textes de Nag Hammadi, Québec 22–25 août 1978*, ed. Bernard Barc, BCNH Études 1 (Québec: Presses de l'université Laval; Leuven: Peeters, 1981), 374–82.

37. The following section recapitulates material I have treated elsewhere in more detail (Burns, *Apocalypse of the Alien God*, 122–30).

they gave him a throne from the throne of glory. And I delivered him unto those who glorify—Ariōm, Ēlien, Phariēl—they glorified him with the glory of the fatherhood. And [then those who snatch up] raptured— Kamaliēl [. .] . —anan, Samblō—servants of great luminaries, holy. They took him to the luminous place of his fatherhood, and [he received] the Five Seals, through [the] light of the Mother: Prōtennoia. And it was given to him to partake [in the mystery] of knowledge. (Three Forms NHC XIII 48*.15-34)[38]

Mikheus, Samblo, and their cohort are angelic baptizers that appear on multiple occasions in the Sethian corpus; the initiate, who joins them here in baptism, enrobement, enthronement, and so forth, thus joins the company of angels who give glory to God.

The Platonizing ascent apocalypse Zostrianos also features these celestial baptizers, as it describes the ascent of its eponymous seer into heaven:

And I was baptized in the [name of] the divine Self-Begotten One, by the powers that exist [upon the] living water: Michar and [Micheus], and I was purified by [the] great Barpharanges. And they [glorified] me, writing me into glory. [I was] sealed by [them], those who exist upon the powers—[Michar], Micheus—with Seldao and [Elenos], and Zogenethlos. And I [became] a [god]-seeing angel. (Zost. NHC VIII 6.7-18)[39]

Other stages of angelificaiton are reported in the text; the keyword in all these passages, however, is "glory" (Copt. *eoou*). In First Thought, the baptizers and baptized join one another in "giving glory" (*ti eoou*) while in Zostrianos, various passages discuss beings called "glories" (*heneoou*) who appear to be closely associated with angels (if not angels themselves; Zost. NHC VIII 46.15-30, 48.21-23). The name of a principal revelator-angel in Zostrianos and Allogenes is Youel, glossed as "she who belongs to the glories, the male, virgin glory."[40] The glories anoint Zostrianos, further divin-

---

38. My translation of the Coptic text in Paul-Hubert Poirier, ed. and trans., *La pensée première à la triple forme*, BCNH Textes 32 (Québec: Presses de l'université Laval; Leuven: Peeters, 2006).

39. My translation of the Coptic text in Catherine Barry et al., eds. and trans., *Zostrien*, BCNH Textes 24 (Leuven: Peeters, 2000).

40. See Zost. NHC VIII 53.13-14, 54.15-17, 62.11-12, 63.9-10, 125.13.17; Allogenes NHC XI 50.18-19, 52.13-14, 55.17-18, 55.32-34, 57.24-25. Youel's name (if not personage) likely derives from the same traditions that give us the angel Jahoel (Apoc. Abr. 10-11); see Madeline Scopello, "Portraits d'anges à Nag Hammadi," in

izing him after his baptisms (*Zost.* [NHC VIII 1.[63].20–22]). Eventually, he becomes elect, is crowned, and effectively acts as a revelatory angel *for the angels*:

> They set [me] down, and left. And Apophantēs, with Aphropais the virgin-light, came to me, and he brought me down to the Primary Manifestation—great, male, perfect intellect. And I saw all of them, in the form in which they exist: as one. And I united with them all, blessing the aeon of the Hidden One, the virgin Barbelo, and the Invisible Spirit. I become completely perfect, received power, was written into glory, and was sealed. I received a perfect crown there. I came to the perfect individuals, and they all made inquiries of me. They listened to the enormities of knowledge (I had to offer), rejoicing all the while and [receiving] power. (Zost. NHC VIII 129.1–22)

Many other Sethian works detail a similar dynamic of glorification, self-glorification, and transformation in the context of participation in the celestial liturgy, even if they do not explicitly say that human beings are transformed into angels. A particularly important example is to be found in the Three Steles of Seth (another one of those Platonizing works), a liturgical work where the speaker is often in the first-person plural, describing the group-activity of glorifying the deity as the central soteriological act:

> With what shall we bless you? We cannot—but we give thanks, since we are inferior to you, for you granted us (to see you), as He who is superior, to glorify you to the extent that we are able. We bless you, for we have been saved for all the time that we glorify you! Because of this do we glorify you: so that we might be saved, completely, eternally. We bless you, for we are able. We have been saved, because you, you wished at all times for all of us to do this. (Steles Seth NHC VII 126.17–32)[41]

Acts du huitième congrès international d'études coptes: Paris, 28 juin–3 juillet 2004, ed. N. Bosson and Anne Boud'hors, OLA 163, 2 vols. (Leuven: Peeters, 2007), 2:886. On Jaohel's similarities to Metatron, see Scholem, *Jewish Gnosticism*, 51; Scholem, *Major Trends in Jewish Mysticism*, 68; and Deutsch, *Guardians of the Gate*, 35–36.

41. My translation of the Coptic text given by James M. Robinson and James E. Goehring, "The Three Steles of Seth," in *Nag Hammadi Codex VII*, ed. Birger A. Pearson, NHS 30 (Leiden: Brill, 1996), 371–421.

Some kind of noetic ascent is implied in the text, as it is broken down in to three hymns (per the literary conceit of three steles), each addressed to a progressively more abstract and thus superior entity. (The above passage is addressed to the highest god, The One.) This dynamic of glorification, transformation, and salvation, practiced alongside other ascending glorifying beings, clearly derives from a greater body of well-known Jewish apocalyptic traditions that liken humans to angels insofar as they join these celestial beings in glorifying God in heaven—particularly in works that describe the transformation of a seer or the righteous to an angel as one joins the celestial liturgy.[42] In some of these cases, as in Zostrianos, the angelified seer is not just an angel but a being *superior to angels*.[43]

How does the presence of these Jewish traditions regarding angelification in gnostic apocalypses help us understand problems in Jewish mysticism, namely, the relationship between magical practices and visionary practices, the question of practice versus literary artifact, the importance of the Dead Sea Scrolls, and the role of apocalyptic literature? Let us tackle each question in turn.

4. Magic, Ascent, and Theurgy

As we saw earlier, there is a certain tension in the *hekhalot* corpus between practices that seem to elevate the seer on the journey to heaven and those that are concerned with controlling angels, particularly to obtain mastery of torah (the so-called Sar Torah praxes). Symptomatic of the confusion arising from this tension is the widespread use of the term *theurgy* in the scholarly literature to describe all manner of practices, whether they result in the adjuration of a celestial being or in some kind of interaction with celestial beings.[44] Scholarship on the Sethian treatises also toyed with using

---

42. Classic examples include 2 En. 22.8–10 and T. Levi 8.4. See further Scopello, "Un rite idéal"; Morray-Jones, "Transformational Mysticism," 22–23; and John D. Turner, "Baptismal Vision, Angelification, and Mystical Union in Sethian Literature," in *Beyond the Gnostic Gospels: Studies Building on the Work of Elaine Pagels*, ed. Eduard Iricinschi et al., STAC 82 (Tübingen: Mohr Siebeck, 2013), 210–11.

43. 2 Bar. 51.10–13; Ascen. Isa. 8.13–16, 9.1–6, and esp. 9.27–30.

44. For the use of the term *theurgy* to describe the adjuration and mastery of heavenly beings in *hekhalot* literature, see e.g., Schäfer, *Hidden and Manifest God*, 143–44, 150; Wolfson, *Through a Speculum That Shines*, 114 and passim; Crispin H. T. Fletcher-Louis, *All the Glory of Adam: Liturgical Anthropology in the Dead Sea Scrolls*,

theurgy to describe many of their practices, presumably because these Platonizing works derive from the mid-third to early fourth-century Platonist circles to which belonged Iamblichus of Chalcis, who systematized a body of cultic practices into what he called theurgy (*theourgia*, "divine work"): rituals designed to elevate the soul of the practitioner to the heaven.[45] A close look at the practices mentioned in the Sethian apocalypses shows that they operate on entirely different presuppositions than those of Iamblichus about the relationship of human beings to the divine in ritual, and so the use of the term theurgy for them is a misnomer. The same can be said of the *hekhalot* works, recognition of which could help us frame the issue of the variety of practices in them in a more productive way.

Indeed, a marked feature of the Sethian literature is widespread use of (pseudo-)Greek *nomina barbara* not superficially unlike what we find in the Jewish ascent literature, as, for example, in Allogenes:

STDJ 42 (Leiden: Brill, 2002), 320; Philip S. Alexander, *Mystical Texts: Songs of the Sabbath Sacrifice and Related Manuscripts*, LSTS 61 (London: T&T Clark, 2006), 25, 116–16; James R. Davila, "Ritual in the Hekhalot Literature," in *Practicing Gnosis: Ritual, Magic, Theurgy and Liturgy in Nag Hammadi, Manichaean and Other Ancient Literature; Essays in Honor of Birger A. Pearson*, ed. April D. DeConick, Gregory Shaw, and John D. Turner, NHMS 85 (Leiden: Brill, 2013), 457, 464; and Markschies, *Gottes Körper*, 221–22. Others use the term *theurgy* to describe the use of *nomina barbara*; see Johann Maier, "Das Gefährdungsmotiv bei der Himmelsreise in der jüdischen Apokalyptik und 'Gnosis,'" *Kairos* 5 (1963): 29; and Gruenwald, *Apocalyptic and Merkavah Mysticism*, 104. The term also sometimes seems to be used interchangeably with *magic*; so Scholem, *Jewish Gnosticism*, 75–92; Gruenwald, *Apocalyptic and Merkavah Mysticism*, 265; and Martha Himmelfarb, "Heavenly Ascent and the Relationship of the Apocalypses and the Hekhalot Literature," *HUCA* 59 (1988): 86. For *theurgy* as simply referring to practices that elicit encounters with heavenly beings (whether on earth or in heaven), see Alexander, *Mystical Texts*, 126. Covering virtually all these themes is Idel, *Kabbalah: New Perspectives*, 156–99.

45. On the theurgic character of the Platonizing Sethian literature (and esp. Marsanes), see Birger A. Pearson, "Introduction: Marsanes," in *Nag Hammadi Codices IX and X*, ed. Birger A. Pearson, NHS 15 (Leiden: Brill, 1981), 249–50, followed widely, e.g., by John D. Turner, "Introduction: Marsanes," in *Marsanès*, ed. and trans. Wolf-Peter Funk, Paul-Hubert Poirier, and John D. Turner, BCNH Textes 27 (Québec: Presses de l'université Laval; Leuven: Peeters, 2000), 20, 81, 231–34. The classic discussion of Iamblichaean theurgy remains Gregory Shaw, *Theurgy and the Soul: The Neoplatonism of Iamblichus* (University Park: Pennsylvania University Press, 1995); but see also Ilinca Tanaseanu-Döbler, *Theurgy in Late Antiquity: The Invention of a Ritual Tradition*, BERG 1 (Göttingen: Vandenhoek & Ruprecht, 2013), 95–135.

You are great, Armēdōn! You are perfect, Epiphaneus! And in accordance with the activity that is yours, the second power and the Mentality, from which derives Blessedness: Autoēr, Bēritheus, Ērigenaōr, Ōrimenaios, Aramen, Alphleges, Ēlēlioupheus, Lalameus, Yetheus, Noētheus! You (sg.) are great. (Allogenes NHC XI 53.11–21)

Speculation on the hidden mysteries of the Greek alphabet, meanwhile, is a central topic to the Platonizing Sethian apocalypse Marsanes, where different syllables are said to be useful in naming angels (and so in gaining power over them), as in a passage that remarks that "the rest are different: $\alpha\beta\epsilon\beta\eta\beta\iota\beta o\beta$, in order that you might [gather] them, and *be distinguished from the angels;* and effects shall be produced" (Marsanes NHC X 32*.1–6).[46] Read together with Zostrianos, it appears that, as in the *hekhalot* texts, some Sethian apocalypses presume that human beings can not only dwell among angelic beings but even wield power over them, by virtue of the height reached in ascent.

As much seems to be presumed by a passage in the Untitled Treatise in the Bruce Codex about the prophets Marsanes and Nicotheus:

> The powers of all the great aeons have worshiped the power that is in Marsanes, saying, "who is this one that has seen these things before his very face, so that for his sake did he manifest in this way?" Nicotheus said about him: "he saw him, for he is that one." He said, "the Father exists, transcending every perfect being." He has revealed the triple-powered, perfect, invisible one. Every single perfect human being saw him; they spoke about him, glorifying him, each in his own way.[47]

As Howard Jackson has argued, the passage explains how the seers Marsanes and Nicotheus have obtained visions of the "Only-Begotten (God)" (*monogenēs*), been transmogrified, acquired power that angels worship (*auouōšet ... enci ndynamis*), and engaged in "glorifying" (*euti eoou*) the deity, presumably by passing on their knowledge to the elect (in the apoca-

---

46. My translation of the Coptic text of Funk, Poirier, and Turner, *Marsanès*.

47. My translation of the Coptic text given in Carl Schmidt, ed., *The Books of Jeu and the Untitled Treatise in the Bruce Codex*, rev. and trans. Violet MacDermot, NHS 13 (Leiden: Brill, 1978), 235.14–23. My translation and interpretation of the passage follow Howard Jackson, "The Seer Nikotheos and His Lost Apocalypse in the Light of Sethian Apocalypses from Nag Hammadi and the Apocalypse of Elchasai," *NovT* 32 (1990): 261.

lypses bearing their names).[48] This dynamic of ascent, vision, and transformation into a supra-angelic being also seems to be presupposed in the work Marsanes:

> For it is I who have [apprehended] that which truly exists, [whether] individually or [universally]. According to category, [I have learned] that they exist from the [beginning, in the] entire universe, as eternal: namely, everything that has come into being, whether without substance or by means of substance, those who are unbegotten and the divine aeons, together with the angels and the souls which are without guile, and the psychic [garments], which resemble [the] simple (things). (Marsanes NHC X 4.24–5.9)[49]

The perspective of the Sethian apocalypses about the possibility of obtaining supra-angelic status is mutually exclusive with the terms and very purpose devised by Iamblichus in his construction of a theurgic system of ritual. He believed that when human souls descend into bodies, they descend entirely into bodies—and so into matter; therefore, they require the aid of material objects imbued with divinity in order to escape matter.[50] However, he emphasizes that the theurgist's mastery of these objects does not mean that the theurgist has power over the divine, for human beings and their corporeal tools occupy a relatively diminished place in the hierarchy of heavenly beings. Rather, the proper arrangement of bodies in ritual permits an irruption of the divine that elevates the human soul, which never itself possesses power over angels, demons, or gods.[51] Con-

---

48. "Marsanes" is, of course, the title of one of the Platonizing treatises from Nag Hammadi (NHC X 1), while an Apocalypse of Nicotheus was among the works Porphyry says the Christian gnostics circulated in Plotinus's seminar (*Vit. Plot.* 16).

49. My translation of the Coptic text of Funk, Poirier, and Turner, *Marsanès*; see also Turner, "Introduction: *Marsanes*," 139.

50. Plotinus and Porphyry, meanwhile, believed that the soul does not descend entirely into bodies but remains, on some level, in heaven, engaged in contemplation of the forms; therefore, contemplation alone will draw the descended part of the soul back up to the undescended soul, obviating any need for rituals dealing with bodies (see e.g., Iamblichus, *An.* 6–7 and commentary *ad loc.*; Damascius, *Comm. Phaedr.* 105; Shaw, *Theurgy and the Soul*, 61–69).

51. Iamblichus's logic derives in large part from his debate with his elder contemporary Porphyry, who in his *Letter to Anebo* charged that rituals have no place in the philosopher's life; rather, the presupposition of various rituals (such as intercessionary prayer, healing spells, divination, etc.) to have power over heavenly beings

fronted with a Marsanes or Zostrianos "worshiped" by "the powers," Iamblichus would have decried these prophets as would-be sorcerers (*goētes*), not theurgists (*theourgoi*).

He probably would have also said as much regarding the sages populating the *hekhalot* literature, although the corpus presents a diversity of explanations of what the relationship between human and divine beings looks like. Sometimes, the seer is capable of binding and controlling angels (a goetic claim, in Iamblichaean terms).[52] Sar Torah emphasizes the necessity of divine intervention, for it is God who chooses to bestow complete knowledge of torah—a model much closer to the grace that Iamblichus insists is at work in theurgic operations.[53] (On the other hand, the same macroform features angelic protestations to God's choice to render humans superior to angels—exactly what would bother a Neoplatonist.)[54] In any case, it is clear that the matter was approached by the writers and redactors of the *hekhalot* corpus without much (more likely: any) regard for the strictures of Neoplatonic theurgy and its rigid hierarchies.

Driving a wedge between adjuration and ascent in the *hekhalot* texts does us no favors in helping us understand these works; nor does use of the term theurgy in a second-order sense to describe certain of these practices.[55] Rather, as in the Sethian gnostic literature, the ability of a sage to

---

is the provenance of the vulgar sorcerer (*goēs*); for recent discussions of Porphyry's arguments, see Tanaseanu-Döbler, *Theurgy in Late Antiquity*, 74–83. By agreeing with Porphyry on the presupposition that human beings cannot exert control over superhuman beings, Iamblichus thus changes the terms of the argument, successfully differentiating the work of the *theourgos* from the fallible conjurer (thus e.g., *Myst.* 2.11; see further Tanaseanu-Döbler, *Theurgy in Late Antiquity*, 108–10).

52. For explicit remarks on the seer's ostensible mastery of the bound angel, see, for example, Hekhalot Zutarti (Schäfer, *Synopse*, §§419–21), Maʿaseh Mekabah (Schäfer, *Synopse*, §573), Merkabah Rabbah (Schäfer, *Synopse*, §686), and Sar Panim (Schäfer, *Synopse*, §623/G1).

53. Schäfer, *Synopse*, §§282–91; and Schäfer, *Hidden and Manifest God*, 49–53.

54. Schäfer, *Synopse*, §§291–94.

55. Cf., for instance, the wide use of the term by Idel in, e.g., *Kabbalah: New Perspectives*, 156–99. Tanaseanu-Döbler is not bothered in principle by use of the term theurgy in the study of kabbalah: "keeping the distinction between object level and meta-level clear, 'theurgy' can then be abstracted from its specific context of origin to be used as a scholarly tool as defined by the researcher" (*Theurgy in Late Antiquity*, 15). This is, of course, true for any term but begs the question whether usage of said term on the second-order "meta-level" is particularly clear—and in the case of theurgy in the context of Jewish mysticism, it is not. In any case, what is needed is an archaeol-

control angels appears to come from the same place as his ability to join them and even gain elevated status over them in heaven. Both the Sethian gnostic and *hekhalot* corpora describe a diversity of practices and goals, but this diversity rests on a foundation constituted by an anthropological perspective about the potential of certain human beings to overcome celestial obstacles and obtain some kind of divine status (relative to angels, at least).[56] The latter fact seems to have been more interesting than the former to those who produced and used this literature; maybe it should be for us, too.

5. Ritual Practice or Literary Cliché?

More difficult is the question of whether Jewish mystical texts describe things people actually *did*—for example, singing hymns, going into trances, and having visions of God's throne—or whether they were written and consumed as purely literary artifacts, preserving legends about rabbinic heroes for the sake of culture. Here, too, the Sethian gnostic material provides us fresh data, particularly in the liturgical text called the Three Steles of Seth, discussed above. Comprised of three hymns to three successively exalted deities, this work remarkably uses the first-person plural:

> Emoyniar, Nibareu, Kandephoros, Aphredon, Dephaneus, you who are Armedon to me, the giver of power, Thalanatheus, Antitheus! You who exist within yourself, and who are before yourself! And after you, nothing has come into activity. With what shall we bless you? We cannot—but we give thanks, since we are inferior to you, for you granted us (to see

---

ogy of the use of the term to the field. This archaeology would likely lead us back into the world of early modern European Christian kabbalah (as Annette Yoshiko Reed has related to me, in conversation). In the twentieth-century scholarly context, it is also worth recalling Scholem's friendship with the pioneer of the modern study of ancient theurgy, Hans Lewy, inaugurated in 1935, upon Scholem's arrival in Jerusalem and founding, together with Lewy and the great Coptologist Hans J. Polotsky, of the *pilegesh* ("concubine") group. See further Steven M. Wasserstrom, "Concubines and Puppies: Philologies of Esotericism in Jerusalem between the World Wars," in *Adaptations and Innovations: Studies on the Interaction between Jewish and Islamic Thought and Literature from the Early Middle Ages to the Late Twentieth Century; Dedicated to Professor Joel L. Kraemer*, ed. Y. Tzvi Langermann and Jossi Stern, Collection de la Revue des Études juives (Leuven: Peeters, 2007), 381–413.

56. See also the remarks of Wolfson, *Through a Speculum That Shines*, 115–17.

you), as He who is superior, to glorify you to the extent that we are able. (Steles Seth NHC VII 126.9–23)[57]

Together with the occasional use of paraenetic language throughout the Sethian apocalypses, it is difficult for me to imagine that these texts did not arise from some kind of communal milieu that engaged in meditative and hymnic practices that, their authors believed, brought them into communion with the angels.[58] This should not surprise us. Christian literature going back to the apostle Paul abounds with individuals and groups who likened themselves to angels or claimed to enjoy their company.[59] The presence of literary allusions and clichés in the Sethian literature, then, does not *preclude* the reality of a lived practice behind them. Can we say the same of the *hekhalot* texts?

The evidence should also give us pause when we consider Martha Himmelfarb's famous postulate of a shift in early Jewish ascent literature, from the accounts of "passive" raptures we find in the apocalypses to the prescriptions for "active" practice on the part of the seers portrayed in the *hekhalot* works.[60] We could apply no such binary to the Sethian apocalypses: on the one hand, the apocalyptic literary frame of these works presents revelation and rapture as passive events which simply happen to the seer, while on the other hand, it is most reasonable to suppose that these works were intended to be used, for the reasons outlined above. Moreover, the Sethian corpus furnishes the example of Marsanes, which seems to describe a variety of cultic practices, ranging from alphabet-mysticism to astrology and some sort of ritual involving carved objects; these passages are fragmentary, but their descriptions are probably not rhetorical.[61]

---

57. My translation of the Coptic text of Robinson and Goehring.
58. Paraenetic passages in the Platonizing Sethian texts include Marsanes NHC X 26*.12–17, 27*.21–23, 39*.18–41*.8; Zost. NHC VIII 130.16–132.5.
59. For a fine survey of these traditions, see Harold W. Attridge, "On Becoming an Angel: Rival Baptismal Theologies at Colossae," in *Religious Propaganda and Missionary Competition in the New Testament World: Essays Honoring Dieter Georgi*, ed. Lukas Bormann, Kelly Del Tredici, and Angela Standhartinger, NovTSup 74 (Leiden: Brill, 1994), 481–98.
60. Himmelfarb, "Heavenly Ascent"; Himmelfarb, *Ascent to Heaven*, 113; and widely followed, e.g., by Michael D. Swartz, "The Dead Sea Scrolls and Later Jewish Magic and Mysticism," *DSD* 8 (2001): 190; cf. Davila, *Hekhalot Literature in Translation*, 15–16.
61. Marsanes NHC X 35*.1–6: "[… and the] waters, and the [images of the]

Finally, we are presented with a slice of external evidence by Plotinus, who states that his gnostic opponents claim to be superior to the stellar deities, "because, they say, it is possible for them to exit (the cosmos) when they die, while this is not possible for those who eternally adorn heaven" (*Enn.* 2.9.18.36–37).[62] This means that the gnostics known to Plotinus and Porphyry, readers of the ascent apocalypses Zostrianos and Allogenes, took seriously these texts' descriptions of the makeup of the heavenly world to be experienced following the release of death.[63]

6. Qumran and the *Unio Liturgica*

The problem of lived practice versus literary cliché brings us back to Qumran, where similar questions have been raised concerning language about angelification in the Dead Sea Scrolls. A tenuous consensus among scholars exists that the authors of the Sabbath Songs and other works extant at Qumran must have believed themselves to possess some kind

---

wax shapes, [and] emerald images. As for the rest, I will teach you about them—this (treatise) is (about) [the] production [of] names." My translation of the Coptic text of Funk, Poirier, and Turner, *Marsanès*. Even more lacunous is the discussion of astrology on pp. 41–42 of the manuscript.

62. All translations of *Enn.* 2.9 in the following notes are my own, from the text of Plotinus, *Ennead II*, ed. and trans. Arthur H. Armstrong, LCL 441 (Cambridge: Harvard University Press, 1966).

63. Rightly Michael A. Williams, "Did Plotinus' 'Friends' Still Go to Church? Communal Rituals and Ascent Apocalypses," in DeConick, Shaw, and Turner, *Practicing Gnosis*, 510. Williams notes further (504) that Plotinus's remarks at *Enn.* 2.9.12.6–9 about the "one or two, who, with great difficulty and then just barely, are moved out of this world, and then, scarcely having recalled anything, state what they have seen" may refer to his (gnostic) friends who have obtained experiences of visionary ascent. As Gertz recognizes (*Plotinus*, 231–32), however, the context of 12.6–9 is Plotinus's own polemic against gnostic tales of the imperfect demiurge, whose dysfunctional creative power ostensibly operates by virtue of its memory of an "image" of the heavenly realities (12.1–5). To illustrate his point, Plotinus alludes in 12.6–9 to the difficulty faced even by people who have achieved a vision of the forms (and thus overcome some of the forgetfulness that is concomitant with worldly birth) to explain their vision, much less create a model of it; how then, he asks, could this mere "material reflection" of a heavenly being—the gnostic demiurge—"not only remember these things and take a real conception of <that celestial> world, but also learn from whence it came?" (12.9–12).

of special status regarding the angels and their liturgy.[64] I have argued elsewhere that the evidence from Nag Hammadi and Qumran is mutually illuminating, indicating that the readers of the Sethian works also likely regarded themselves as capable of dwelling with the angels.[65] I will not belabor this point further here.

However, it is worth commenting on the preference of some to contrast this *unio liturgica*—wherein humans celebrate God along with the angels—with the so-called *unio mystica* developed in Neoplatonism and favored in medieval Abrahamic religions, wherein humans claim experiences of union with God (angels aside).[66] The Sethian evidence exhibits the limitations of this distinction, insofar as the Platonizing texts could be representative of either side of the binary. Allogenes harmonizes doxologies to be uttered along with the angels with discourses on negative theology whose very reading likely constituted a mystical practice—*Lesemysterium*.[67] The third Stele of Seth begins by proclaiming the achievement of visionary union with the God of the Platonists: "We rejoice! We rejoice! We rejoice! We have seen! We have seen! We have seen that one

---

64. E.g., Carol Newsom, *Songs of the Sabbath Sacrifice: A Critical Edition*, HSS 27 (Atlanta: Scholars Press, 1985), 16–19; more recently, Alexander, *Mystical Texts*, 45–47, 54; Peter Schäfer, "Communion with the Angels: Qumran and the Origins of Jewish Mysticism," in *Wege mystischer Gotteserfahrung: Judentum, Christentum, und Islam*, ed. Peter Schäfer and Elisabeth Müller-Luckner, Schriften des Historischen Kollegs, Kolloquien 65 (München: Oldenbourg, 2006), 37–66, esp. 47, 56–59; and Schäfer, *Origins of Jewish Mysticism*, 132–46; cf. Fletcher-Louis, *All the Glory of Adam*.

65. Burns, *Apocalypse of the Alien God*, 130–32. See also Burns and Goff, *The Dead Sea Scrolls and the Nag Hammadi Codices*.

66. Eliot Wolfson, "Mysticism and the Poetic-Liturgical Compositions from Qumran: A Response to Bilhah Nitzan," *JQR* 85 (1994): 185–202, esp. 186–87; similarly, Swartz, "Dead Sea Scrolls," 187–88; Alexander, *Mystical Texts*, 105; Schäfer, *Hidden and Manifest God*, 165; Schäfer, *Origins of Jewish Mysticism*, 19–20, 349–50; Luttikhuizen, "Monism and Dualism," 762–63, 772; and Turner, "Baptismal Vision," 211. Cf. also the somewhat dissenting remarks of Markschies, *Gottes Körper*, 221–22.

67. Dylan Burns, "Apophatic Strategies in *Allogenes* (NHC XI,3)," *HTR* 103 (2010): 161–79. Cf. for instance the *Lesemysterium* of *Gos. Truth* (NHC I 3; XII 2) with its affinities to Neoplatonic and postmodern reading-strategies, as discussed by Fineman, "Gnosis and the Piety of Metaphor," and Eliot Wolfson, "Inscribed in the Book of the Living: *Gospel of Truth* and Jewish Christology," *JJS* 38 (2007): 234–71, esp. 253–55. The Gospel of Truth presents us with reading strategies for the *unio mystica*, but the element of *unio liturgica*, so emphatic in the Sethian texts under examination here, is subdued if not absent.

who is truly pre-existent, truly existing, for he is the first one, eternal" (Steles Seth NHC VII 124.17–21). Finally, in Zostrianos, the eponymous seer, having been transformed into an angel several times over and participated in numerous doxologies during his heavenly journey, is made privy to a revelation on the nature of the Godhead which shares a source with (or itself constitutes the source of) Marius Victorinus's speculations in *Adversus Arium*, in turn strongly resembling the mystical theology of the anonymous Turin Commentary on Plato's *Parmenides*.[68] To be sure, Eliot Wolfson is right that accounts of angelification and descriptions of practices for achieving union with God are two different things, but our Sethian sources envisioned them as complementary, rather than mutually exclusive.[69] What does this tell us?[70]

In any case, our Sethian evidence shows that interest in Jewish traditions about the *unio liturgica* persisted into late ancient gnostic circles and is probably the tip of the iceberg of such speculations, which must have also circulated among Jews in the first centuries of our era. *Unio liturgica* traditions prior to the *hekhalot* literature thus extended far beyond Qumran and constitute no isolated prologue in the history of Jewish mysticism but a long chapter, that continued to develop in a variety of Jewish and Christian contexts contexts throughout late antiquity.

---

68. Michel Tardieu, "Recherches sur la formation de l'Apocalypse de Zostrien et les sources de Marius Victorinus." *ResOr* 9 (1996): 7–114. The most recent *Forschungsbericht* on this complex of evidence is John D. Turner, "The Anonymous *Parmenides* Commentary, Marius Victorinus, and the Sethian Platonizing Apocalypses: State of the Question," in *Gnose et Manichéisme: Entre les oasis d'Égypte et la route de la soie; Hommage à Jean-Daniel Dubois*, ed. Anna van den Kerchove and L. Gabriela Soares Santoprete, BEHER 176 (Turnhout: Brepols, 2017), 93–126.

69. One could even say the same of our ancient Neoplatonic evidence itself, since the possibility of union with the supreme principle was under debate (thus e.g., Iamblichus, *An.* 50, discussed in Shaw, *Theurgy and the Soul*, 114–15).

70. Luttikhuizen, "Monism and Dualism," 772, thinks it tells us the following: the *yordē merkavah* "must nevertheless must have been aware of the ontologically infinite distance between God and his creature, whereas gnostics started from the conviction that the innermost core of their being … originated from, and was consubstantial with, the metacosmic unknowable God." While I do not disagree with any of this per se, I wonder if it is the whole story.

7. Conclusion

Reviving the question of the relationship between Gnosticism and Judaism and putting sources labeled gnostic and Jewish in conversation with one another are productive enterprises. We need not search for the origins of Gnosticism or Jewish mysticism in order to better diagnose the deep currents of Jewish thought, imagery, and terminology in certain gnostic sources and to, in turn, use these gnostic sources to help clarify some of the problems in our Jewish sources. Furthermore, abandoning the language of origins does not mean that we abandon the language of development. All of these traditions about angelification, ascent, and apocalypses were common lore in Hellenistic Judaism. Different groups drew on this heritage in different ways as they splintered and evolved in late antiquity, which explains the broad but significant parallels between diverse groups indebted to Jewish traditions, such as the authors of Sethian works—as detailed here—and other (anti-)baptismal movements, such as Manichaeism, Elchasaism, or Mandaeanism, which, like Sethianism, occupy the borderlines between and beyond Judaism and Christianity.[71] As primary interpreters of this stratum, contemporary with the redaction of apocalyptic and rabbinic traditions, Sethian gnostic writings literature then merit a sizable place not only in histories of apocalyptic literature, but also of the development of Jewish mysticism.

That is only a particular cut of extant gnostic literature relevant to this development: I have not discussed the Gospel of Philip's treatment of the heavenly temple,[72] the dimensions of the demiurge in the Bruce Codex,[73]

---

71. Wolfson rightly saw past the "Jewish-Christian divide" in his assessment of the social identity behind the author of the Gospel of Truth ("Inscribed in the Book of the Living," 337).

72. See recently Matthew Twigg, "Esoteric Discourse and the Jerusalem Temple in the *Gospel of Philip*," Aries 15 (2015): 47–80.

73. My translation of the Coptic given in Schmidt, *Books of Jeu*, 226.18–227.21: "The second place came into being, being called 'demiurge,' and 'father,' and 'word,' and 'source,' and 'intellect,' and 'human being,' and 'eternal,' and 'infinite.' This is the column, this is the overseer, and this is the father (of) the universe, and this is the one upon whose head the aeons are a crown, casting out rays of light. The outline of his face is the unknowability in the outer universes, which seek his face at all times, wishing to know it; for his word extends to them, and they desire to see him, and the light of his eyes penetrates the places of the outer fullness. And the word that comes from his mouth penetrates whatever is above and below, and the hair of his head is (equal

the methodological issues posed by the still-living category of "jüdische Gnosis,"[74] the common milieu of late ancient magic so influential on both the Nag Hammadi and *hekhalot* corpora,[75] or the principal issues in comparing gnostic and Jewish theophanies.[76] There is much work to do. We live in exciting times.

---

to) the number of the secret worlds, and the inner boundary of his face is something equal to the image of the aeons. The hairs of his face are (equal to) the number of the outer worlds. And the expanse of his hands is the manifestation of the cross. The expanse of the cross is the ennead which is on the right side and those on the left. The stem of the cross is the ungraspable human being. This is the father. This is the fountain that silently bubbles. It is this one who is sought after in every place. And this is the father from whom the monad came, like a luminous spark." General parallels of the description of God's body in the Untitled Treatise to the Shi'ur Qomah literature have been drawn already by David Brakke, "The Body as/at the Boundary of Gnosis," *JECS* 17 (2009): 208–9. Markschies also recalls this treatise in his discussion of gnostic speculations about the divine body but focuses rather on the usage of the Platonizing terminology of depth (*Gottes Körper*, 239–40).

74. On which see Klaus Herrmann, "Jüdische Gnosis? Dualismus und 'gnostische' Motive in der frühen jüdischen Mystik," in *Zugänge zur Gnosis: Akten zur Tagung der Patristischen Arbeitsgemeinschaft vom 02.–05.01.2011 in Berlin-Spandau*, ed. Christoph Markschies and J. van Oort, PtSt 12 (Leuven: Peeters, 2013), 43–90.

75. See e.g., Gruenwald, *Apocalyptic and Merkavah Mysticism*, 264–89, but esp. Reimund Leicht, "Gnostic Myth in Jewish Garb: Niriyah (Norea), Noah's Bride," *JJS* 51 (2000): 133–40.

76. In gnostic texts, we almost never hear about angels or the heaven in general as made of fire (exceptions: Clement of Alexandria, *Exc.* 37–39; Nat. Rulers NHC II 95.9–10; Marsanes NHC X 64*.1–5, a passage too fragmentary to be of much use), while in our material from Qumran, the Jewish pseudepigrapha, and the *hekhalot* literature, fire is ubiquitous. Plotinus's gnostic opponents claim that the demiurge first makes everything out of fire (*Enn.* 2.9.11.28–29, 12.12–21), a notion Plotinus finds absurd (see further Gertz, *Plotinus*, 232–33). In any case, it is striking how little interest gnostic apocalypses show in the fiery nature of the celestial world, given their welcoming attitude to other imagery common to apocalyptic literature, e.g., the crowns worn by heavenly beings, for which see Dylan M. Burns, "Sethian Crowns, Sethian Martyrs? Jewish Apocalyptic and Christian Martyrology in a Gnostic Literary Tradition," *Numen* 61 (2014): 552–68. Gnostic literature appears to prefer a more abstract visual metaphor, light. Cf. the emphasis on visual (heretical) vs. audial, aniconic (positive) theophanic metaphors in our primary sources about the two powers controversy as discussed in Orlov, "Two Powers in Heaven"; cf. Wolfson, who recommends caution before the distinction (*Through a Speculum That Shines*, 49–50).

Bibliography

Alexander, Philip S. "Comparing Merkavah Mysticism and Gnosticism: An Essay in Method." *JJS* 35 (1984): 1–18.

———. *Mystical Texts: Songs of the Sabbath Sacrifice and Related Manuscripts.* LSTS 61. London: T&T Clark International, 2006.

Arbel, Vita Daphna. *Beholders of Divine Secrets: Mysticism and Myth in the Hekhalot and Merkavah Literature.* Albany: State University of New York Press, 2003.

Attridge, Harold W. "On Becoming an Angel: Rival Baptismal Theologies at Colossae." Pages 481–98 in *Religious Propaganda and Missionary Competition in the New Testament World: Essays Honoring Dieter Georgi.* Edited by Lukas Bormann, Kelly Del Tredici, and Angela Standhartinger. NovTSup 74. Leiden: Brill, 1994.

———. "Valentinian and Sethian Apocalyptic Traditions." *JECS* 8 (2000): 173–211.

Barry, Catherine, Wolf-Peter Funk, Paul-Hubert Poirier, and John D. Turner, eds. and trans. *Zostrien.* BCNH Textes 24. Leuven: Peeters, 2000.

Boustan, Ra'anan S. "The Study of Heikhalot Literature: Between Mystical Experience and Textual Artifact." *CurBR* 6 (2007): 130–60.

Boyarin, Daniel. "Beyond Judaisms: Meṭaṭron and the Divine Polymorphy of Ancient Judaism." *JSJ* 41 (2010): 323–65.

Brakke, David. "The Body as/at the Boundary of Gnosis." *JECS* 17 (2009): 195–214.

———. *The Gnostics: Myth, Ritual, and Diversity in Early Christianity.* Cambridge: Harvard University Press, 2010.

Burns, Dylan M. *Apocalypse of the Alien God: Platonism and the Exile of Sethian Gnosticism.* Divinations. Philadelphia: University of Pennsylvania Press, 2014.

———. "Apophatic Strategies in *Allogenes* (NHC XI,3)." *HTR* 103 (2010): 161–79.

———. "The Gnostic Apocalypses." Pages 59–78 in *The Cambridge Companion to Apocalyptic Literature.* Edited by Colin McAllister. Cambridge: Cambridge University Press, 2020.

———. "Providence, Creation, and Gnosticism according to the Gnostics." *JECS* 24 (2016): 55–79.

———. "Sethian Crowns, Sethian Martyrs? Jewish Apocalyptic and Christian Martyrology in a Gnostic Literary Tradition." *Numen* 61 (2014): 552–68.

Burns, Dylan, and Matthew Goff, eds. *The Dead Sea Scrolls and the Nag Hammadi Codices*. NHMS 103. Leiden: Brill, 2022.

Clement of Alexandria. *Extraits de Théodote*. Edited and translated by François Sagnard. SC 23. Paris: Éditions du Cerf, 1948.

Cohen, Shaye J. D. Review of *Two Powers in Heaven*, by Alan Segal. *AJSR* 10 (1985): 114–17.

Collins, John J. "Introduction: Towards the Morphology of a Genre." *Semeia* 14 (1979): 1–20.

Davila, James R. *Hekhalot Literature in Translation: Major Texts of Merkavah Mysticism*. JJTPSup 20. Leiden: Brill, 2013.

———. "Ritual in the Hekhalot Literature." Pages 449–66 in *Practicing Gnosis: Ritual, Magic, Theurgy and Liturgy in Nag Hammadi, Manichaean and Other Ancient Literature; Essays in Honor of Birger A. Pearson*. Edited by April D. DeConick, Gregory Shaw, and John D. Turner. NHMS 85. Leiden: Brill, 2013.

DeConick, April D. "What Is Early Jewish and Christian Mysticism?" Pages 1–24 in *Paradise Now: Essays on Early Jewish and Christian Mysticism*. Edited by April D. DeConick. SymS 11. Atlanta: Society of Biblical Literature, 2006.

Deutsch, Nathanael. *Guardians of the Gate: Angelic Vice-Regency in Late Antiquity*. BSJS 22. Leiden: Brill, 1999.

Drecoll, Volker Henning. "Martin Hengel and the Origins of Gnosticism." Pages 139–65 in *Gnosticism, Platonism, and the Late Ancient World: Essays in Honour of John D. Turner*. Edited by Kevin Corrigan and Tuomas Rasimus. NHMS 82. Leiden: Brill, 2013.

Epstein, Isidore, ed. *The Babylonian Talmud. Hagiga*. London: Soncino, 1935–1952.

Fineman, Joel. "Gnosis and the Piety of Metaphor: The *Gospel of Truth*." Pages 289–318 in *The Rediscovery of Gnosticism: Proceedings of the International Conference on Gnosticism*. Edited by Bentley Layton. NBS 41. 2 vols. Leiden: Brill, 1981.

Fletcher-Louis, Crispin H. T. *All the Glory of Adam: Liturgical Anthropology in the Dead Sea Scrolls*. STDJ 42. Leiden: Brill, 2002.

Funk, Wolf-Peter, Paul-Hubert Poirier, and John D. Turner, eds. and trans. *Marsanès*. BCNH Textes 27. Québec: Presses de l'université Laval. Leuven: Peeters, 2000.

Gertz, Sebastian R.P. *Plotinus. Ennead II.9: Against the Gnostics; Translation with an Introduction and Commentary.* Las Vegas: Parmenides, 2017.

Robinson, James M., and James E. Goehring. "The Three Steles of Seth." Pages 371–421 in *Nag Hammadi Codex VII*. Edited by Birger A. Pearson. NHS 30. Leiden: Brill, 1996.

Goshen-Gottstein, Alon. "Jewish-Christian Relations and Rabbinic Literature—Shifting Scholarly and Relational Paradigms: The Case of Two Powers." Pages 15–44 in *Interaction between Judaism and Christianity in History, Religion, Art, and Literature*. Edited by Marcel Poorthuis, Joshua Schwartz, and Joseph Aaron Turner. JCP 17. Leiden: Brill, 2008.

———. *The Sinner and the Amnesiac: The Rabbinic Invention of Elisha ben Abuyah and Eleazar ben Arach*. Contraversions. Stanford, CA: Stanford University Press, 2000.

Grant, Robert M. *Gnosticism and Early Christianity*. San Francisco: Harper Torchbooks, 1959.

Gruenwald, Ithamar. *Apocalyptic and Merkavah Mysticism*. AJEC 90. Leiden: Brill, 2014.

———. "Aspects of the Jewish-Gnostic Controversy." Pages 713–23 in in *The Rediscovery of Gnosticism: Proceedings of the International Conference on Gnosticism*. Edited by Bentley Layton. NBS 41. 2 vols. Leiden: Brill, 1981.

Herrmann, Klaus. "Jüdische Gnosis? Dualismus und 'gnostische' Motive in der frühen jüdischen Mystik." Pages 43–90 in *Zugänge zur Gnosis: Akten zur Tagung der Patristischen Arbeitsgemeinschaft vom 02.–05.01.2011 in Berlin-Spandau*. Edited by Christoph Markschies and J. van Oort. PtSt 12. Leuven: Peeters, 2013.

Himmelfarb, Martha. *Ascent to Heaven in Jewish and Christian Apocalypses*. New York: Oxford University Press, 1993.

———. "Heavenly Ascent and the Relationship of the Apocalypses and the Hekhalot Literature." *HUCA* 59 (1988): 73–100.

Idel, Moshe. *Kabbalah: New Perspectives*. New Haven: Yale University Press, 1988.

Jackson, Howard. "The Seer Nikotheos and His Lost Apocalypse in the Light of Sethian Apocalypses from Nag Hammadi and the Apocalypse of Elchasai." *NovT* 32 (1990): 250–77.

Kalligas, Paul. "Plotinus against the Gnostics." *Hermathena* 169 (2000): 115–28.

King, Karen L. *What Is Gnosticism?* Cambridge: Harvard University Press, 2003.

———. Review of *The Gnostics*, by David Brakke. *HR* 52 (2013): 294–301.

Lahe, Jaan. *Gnosis und Judentum: Alttestamentliche und jüdische Motive in der gnostischen Literatur und das Ursprungsproblem der Gnosis.* NHMS 75. Leiden: Brill, 2012.

Lazier, Benjamin. *God Interrupted: Heresy and the European Imagination between the World Wars.* Princeton: Princeton University Press, 2008.

Leicht, Reimund. "Gnostic Myth in Jewish Garb: Niriyah (Norea), Noah's Bride." *JJS* 51 (2000): 133–40.

Logan, Alistair H. B. *Gnostic Truth and Christian Heresy: A Study in the History of Gnosticism.* Edinburgh: T&T Clark, 1996.

Lundhaug, Hugo, and Lance Jenott. *The Monastic Origins of the Nag Hammadi Codices.* Tübingen: Mohr Siebeck, 2015.

Luttikhuizen, Gerard P. "Monism and Dualism in Jewish-Mystical and Gnostic Ascent Texts." Pages 749–75 in *Flores Florentino: Dead Sea Scrolls and Other Early Jewish Studies in Honour of Florentino García Martínez.* Edited by A. Hilhorst, Émile Puech, and Eibert J. C. Tigchelaar. JSJSup 122. Leiden: Brill, 2007.

Maier, Johann. "Das Gefährdungsmotiv bei der Himmelsreise in der jüdischen Apokalyptik und 'Gnosis.'" *Kairos* 5 (1963): 18–40.

Markschies, Christoph. *Gottes Körper: Jüdische, christliche und pagane Gottesvorstellungen in der Antike.* München: Beck, 2016.

Mazur, Zeke. *The Platonizing Sethian Gnostic Background of Plotinus' Mysticism.* NHMS 98. Leiden: Brill, 2020.

McGinn, Bernard. *The Foundations of Mysticism: Origins to the Fifth Century.* New York: Crossroad, 1991.

Morray-Jones, C. R. A. "Transformational Mysticism in the Apocalyptic-Merkabah Tradition." *JJS* 43 (1992): 1–31.

Narbonne, Jean-Marc. *Plotinus in Dialogue with the Gnostics.* SPNPT 11. Leiden: Brill, 2011.

Nelstrop, Louise. "Mysticism." In *Vocabulary for the Study of Religion.* Edited by Robert A. Segal and Kocku von Stuckrad. Brill Online, 2016.

Newsom, Carol A. *Songs of the Sabbath Sacrifice: A Critical Edition.* HSS 27. Atlanta: Scholars Press, 1985.

Orlov, Andrei. *From Apocalypticism to Merkavah Mysticism: Studies in the Slavonic Pseudepigrapha.* JSJSup 114. Leiden: Brill, 2007.

———. "Two Powers in Heaven … Manifested." Pages 351–64 in *Wisdom Poured Out Like Water: Studies on Jewish and Christian Antiquity in*

Honor of Gabriele Boccaccini. Edited by J. Harold Ellens et al. DCLS 38. Berlin: de Gruyter, 2018.

Pearson, Birger A. "Friedländer Revisited: Alexandrian Judaism and Gnostic Origins." Pages 10–28 in *Gnosticism, Judaism, and Egyptian Christianity*. Edited by Birger A. Pearson. Studies in Antiquity and Christianity. Minneapolis: Fortress, 1990.

———. "Introduction: *Marsanes*." Pages 229–50 in *Nag Hammadi Codices IX and X*. Edited by Birger A. Pearson. NHS 15. Leiden: Brill, 1981.

———. "Jewish Haggadic Traditions in *The Testimony of Truth* From Nag Hammadi (CG IX,3)." Pages 39–51 in *Gnosticism, Judaism, and Egyptian Christianity*. Edited by Birger A. Pearson. Studies in Antiquity and Christianity. Minneapolis: Fortress, 1990.

Plotinus. *Ennead II*. Edited and translated by Arthur H. Armstrong. LCL 441. Cambridge: Harvard University Press, 1966.

Poirier, Paul-Hubert, ed. and trans. *La pensée première à la triple forme*. BCNH Textes 32. Québec: Presses de l'université Laval. Leuven: Peeters, 2006.

Poirier, Paul-Hubert, and Thomas Schmidt. "Chrétiens, hérétiques et gnostiques chez porphyre: Quelques precisions sur la *Vie de Plotin* 16.1–9." Pages 913–42 in *Académie des Inscriptions et Belles Lettres: Comptes rendus des séances de l'année 2010. Avril-juin*. Edited by P. de Boccard. Paris: CRAI, 2010.

Quispel, Gilles. "Christliche Gnosis, jüdische Gnosis, hermetische Gnosis." Pages 3–36 in *Gnostica, Judaica, Catholica: Collected Essays of Gilles Quispel*. Edited by J. van Oort. NHMS 55. Leiden: Brill, 2008.

Rasimus, Tuomas. *Paradise Reconsidered in Gnostic Mythmaking: Rethinking Sethianism in Light of the Ophite Evidence*. NHMS 68. Leiden: Brill, 2009.

———. "Porphyry and the Gnostics: Reassessing Pierre Hadot's Thesis in Light of the Second- and Third-Century Sethian Treatises." Pages 81–110 in vol. 2 of *Plato's "Parmenides" and Its Heritage*. Edited by John Douglas Turner and Kevin Corrigan. 2 vols. WGRWSup 2–3. Atlanta: Society of Biblical Literature, 2010.

Reed, Annette Yoshiko. "Rethinking (Jewish-)Christian Evidence for Jewish Mysticism." Pages 349–77 in *Hekhalot Literature in Context: Between Byzantium and Babylonia*. Edited by Raʿanan S. Boustan, Martha Himmelfarb, and Peter Schäfer. TSAJ 153. Tübingen: Mohr Siebeck, 2013.

Schäfer, Peter. "Communion with the Angels: Qumran and the Origins of Jewish Mysticism." Pages 37–66 in *Wege mystischer Gotteserfahrung: Judentum, Christentum, und Islam*. Edited by Peter Schäfer and Elisabeth Müller-Luckner. Schriften des Historischen Kollegs, Kolloquien 65. München: Oldenbourg, 2006.

———. *The Hidden and Manifest God: Some Major Themes in Early Jewish Mysticism*. SUNY Series in Judaica: Hermeneutics, Mysticism, and Religion. Syracuse: State University of New York Press, 1992.

———. *The Origins of Jewish Mysticism*. Tübingen: Mohr Siebeck, 2009.

———, ed. *Synopse zur Hekhalot-Literatur*. Tübingen: Mohr Siebeck, 1981.

Schenke, Hans-Martin. "The Phenomenon and Significance of Gnostic Sethianism." Pages 588–616 in *The Rediscovery of Gnosticism: Proceedings of the International Conference on Gnosticism*. Edited by Bentley Layton. Translated by Bentley Layton. NBS 41. 2 vols. Leiden: Brill, 1981.

———. "Das sethianische System nach Nag-Hammadi-Handschriften." Pages 165–73 in *Studia Coptica*. Edited by Peter Nagel. BBA 45. Berlin: Akademie, 1974.

Schmidt, Carl, ed. *The Books of Jeu and the Untitled Treatise in the Bruce Codex*. Revised and translated by Violet MacDermot. NHS 13. Leiden: Brill, 1978.

Scholem, Gershom. *Jewish Gnosticism, Merkabah Mysticism, and Talmudic Tradition*. New York: JTS, 1960.

———. *Major Trends in Jewish Mysticism*. London: Thames & Hudson, 1955.

———. *On the Mystical Shape of the Godhead: Basic Concepts in the Kabbalah*. New York: Schocken, 1997.

Scopello, Madeline. "The Apocalypse of Zostrianos (Nag Hammadi VIII.1) and the Book of the Secrets of Enoch." *VC* 34 (1980): 376–85.

———. "Un rite idéal d'intronisation dans trois textes gnostiques de Nag Hammadi." Pages 91–95 in *Nag Hammadi and Gnosis: Papers Read at the First International Congress of Coptology (Cairo, December 1976)*. Edited by R. McLachlan Wilson. NHS 14. Leiden: Brill, 1978.

———. "Portraits d'anges à Nag Hammadi." Pages 879–92 in vol. 2 of *Acts du huitième congrès international d'études coptes: Paris, 28 juin–3 juillet 2004*. Edited by N. Bosson and Anne Boud'hors. OLA 163. 2 vols. Leuven: Peeters, 2007.

———. "Youel et Barbélo dans le Traité de l'Allogène." Pages 374–82 in *Colloque international sur les textes de Nag Hammadi, Québec 22–25 août 1978*. Edited by Bernard Barc. BCNH Études 1. Québec: Presses de l'université Laval. Leuven: Peeters, 1981.

Schremer, Adiel. "Midrash, Theology, and History: Two Powers in Heaven Revisited." *JSJ* 39 (2007): 1–25.

Segal, Alan F. *Two Powers in Heaven: Early Rabbinic Reports about Christianity and Judaism*. SJLA 25. Leiden: Brill, 1977.

Shaw, Gregory. *Theurgy and the Soul: The Neoplatonism of Iamblichus*. University Park: Pennsylvania University Press, 1995.

Spanu, Nicola. *Plotinus, 'Ennead' II 9 [33] 'Against the Gnostics': A Commentary*. StPatrSup 1. Leuven: Peeters, 2012.

Stroumsa, Guy G. "Aher: A Gnostic." Pages 808–18 in *The Rediscovery of Gnosticism: Proceedings of the International Conference on Gnosticism*. Edited by Bentley Layton. NBS 41. 2 vols. Leiden: Brill, 1981.

Swartz, Michael D. "The Dead Sea Scrolls and Later Jewish Magic and Mysticism." *DSD* 8 (2001): 183–93.

Tanaseanu-Döbler, Ilinca. *Theurgy in Late Antiquity: The Invention of a Ritual Tradition*. BERG 1. Göttingen: Vandenhoek & Ruprecht, 2013.

Tardieu, Michel. "Recherches sur la formation de l'Apocalypse de Zostrien et les sources de Marius Victorinus." *ResOr* 9 (1996): 7–114.

Turner, John D. "The Anonymous *Parmenides* Commentary, Marius Victorinus, and the Sethian Platonizing Apocalypses: State of the Question." Pages 93–126 in *Gnose et Manichéisme: Entre les oasis d'Égypte et la route de la soie; Hommage à Jean-Daniel Dubois*. Edited by Anna van den Kerchove and L. Gabriela Soares Santoprete. BEHER 176. Turnhout: Brepols, 2017.

———. "Baptismal Vision, Angelification, and Mystical Union in Sethian Literature." Pages 204–16 in *Beyond the Gnostic Gospels: Studies Building on the Work of Elaine Pagels*. Edited by Eduard Iricinschi, Lance Jenott, Nicola Denzey Lewis, and Philippa Townsend. STAC 82. Tübingen: Mohr Siebeck, 2013.

———. "Introduction: *Marsanes*." Pages 1–248 in *Marsanès*. Edited and translated by Wolf-Peter Funk, Paul-Hubert Poirier, and John D. Turner. BCNH Textes 27. Québec: Presses de l'université Laval. Leuven: Peeters, 2000.

———. *Sethian Gnosticism and the Platonic Tradition*. BCNH Études 6. Québec: Université Laval. Leuven: Peeters, 2001.

Twigg, Matthew. "Esoteric Discourse and the Jerusalem Temple in the Gospel of Philip." *Aries* 15 (2015): 47–80.

Wasserstrom, Steven M. "Concubines and Puppies: Philologies of Esotericism in Jerusalem between the World Wars." Pages 381–413 in *Adaptations and Innovations: Studies on the Interaction between Jewish and Islamic Thought and Literature from the Early Middle Ages to the Late Twentieth Century; Dedicated to Professor Joel L. Kraemer*. Edited by Y. Tzvi Langermann and Jossi Stern. Collection de la Revue des Études juives. Leuven: Peeters, 2007.

———. *Religion after Religion: Gershom Scholem, Mircea Eliade and Henry Corbin at Eranos*. Princeton: Princeton University Press, 2008.

Williams, Michael Allen. "Did Plotinus' 'Friends' Still Go to Church? Communal Rituals and Ascent Apocalypses." Pages 495–522 in *Practicing Gnosis: Ritual, Magic, Theurgy and Liturgy in Nag Hammadi, Manichaean and Other Ancient Literature; Essays in Honor of Birger A. Pearson*. Edited by April D. DeConick, Gregory Shaw, and John D. Turner. NHMS 85. Leiden: Brill, 2013.

———. *Rethinking "Gnosticism": Arguments for Dismantling a Dubious Category*. Princeton: Princeton University Press, 1995.

———. "Sethianism." Pages 32–63 in *A Companion to Second-Century 'Heretics'*. Edited by Antti Marjanen and Petri Luomanen. VCSup 76. Leiden: Brill, 2005.

Wisse, Frederick. "Stalking Those Elusive Sethians." Pages 563–76 in *The Rediscovery of Gnosticism: Proceedings of the International Conference on Gnosticism*. Edited by Bentley Layton. NBS 41. 2 vols. Leiden: Brill, 1981.

Wolfson, Eliot. "Inscribed in the Book of the Living: *Gospel of Truth* and Jewish Christology." *JJS* 38 (2007): 234–71.

———. "Mysticism and the Poetic-Liturgical Compositions from Qumran: A Response to Bilhah Nitzan." *JQR* 85 (1994): 185–202.

———. *Through a Speculum That Shines: Vision and Imagination in Medieval Jewish Mysticism*. Princeton: Princeton University Press, 1994.

Contributors

Garrick V. Allen, Senior Lecturer in New Testament Studies at the University of Glasgow

Giovanni B. Bazzana, Professor of New Testament at Harvard Divinity School

Stefan Beyerle, Professor of Hebrew Bible at Greifswald University

Dylan M. Burns, Assistant Professor in the History of Western Esotericism in Late Antiquity at the Universiteit van Amsterdam

John J. Collins, Holmes Professor of Old Testament Emeritus, Yale University

Devorah Dimant, Professor Emerita, University of Haifa

Lorenzo DiTommaso, Professor of Religions and Cultures at Concordia University Montréal

Frances Flannery, Professor of Religion, Department of Philosophy and Religion, James Madison University

Matthew Goff, Professor of Religion in the Department of Religion at Florida State University

Angela Kim Harkins, Professor, Boston College School of Theology and Ministry

Martha Himmelfarb, William H. Danforth Professor of Religion Emerita, Princeton University

G. Anthony Keddie, Associate Professor, Fellow of the Ronald Nelson Smith Chair in Classics and Christian Origins, Department of Religious Studies, University of Texas at Austin

Armin Lange, Professor for Second Temple Judaism at the University of Vienna, Institute for Jewish Studies

Harry O. Maier, Professor of New Testament and Early Christian Studies, Vancouver School of Theology; Fellow, The Max Weber Center for Advanced Cultural and Social Studies at the University of Erfurt

Andrew B. Perrin, Associate Vice President, Research at Athabasca University

Christopher Rowland, Dean Ireland Professor of the Exegesis of Holy Scripture at the University of Oxford, 1991–2014

Alex Samely, Professor of Jewish Thought in the Department of Religions and Theology at the University of Manchester, and codirector of the University's Centre for Jewish Studies

Jason M. Silverman, University Researcher in the Centre of Excellence in Ancient Near Eastern Empires in the Faculty of Theology at the University of Helsinki

Rebecca Scharbach Wollenberg, Assistant Professor of Judaic Studies at the University of Michigan

Ancient Sources Index

Hebrew Bible/Old Testament		26:58–59	212
		26:59	407
Genesis	3, 22, 214, 340		
5:21–24	146, 153, 178	Deuteronomy	
5:22	439	10:17	154
6:1–4	339	18:9–22	123
11:32	210	26:5	211
12	220	28:15	154
12:4–5	210	28:15–69	154
14:19	408	29:29	73
15	455	30:11–14	73
31	211	32:17	247
31:47	211		
41	88	Judges	
41:32	88	8:26	210
Exodus	101, 153, 258, 279, 436	1 Kings	
1–18	303, 324	6:29	391
2:14	408	8:47	154
6:18–20	212		
6:20	407	2 Kings	
18:13	408	14:25	150
25–28	492	19:16	154
26:31–35	391		
33:20	153	2 Chronicles	
		6:37	154
Leviticus			
26:14–39	154	Ezra	209
		4:7–6:18	207
Numbers		7:12–26	207
1:51	453	9:7	154
3:10	453		
3:19	212	Nehemiah	
3:38	453	1:5	154
18:7	453	9	258

Nehemiah (cont.)

9:33	154
9:34	154

Esther

Job

28:25	137

Psalms

2	415
18:7	150
22:26	150
30:4	150
31:7	150
31:23	150
37	343
40:3	150
42–72	341, 351
42:8	150
57:5	341
69:2–3	150
90–106	340, 351
95:7	364
103:20	340
106	14
106:37	247
106:40	247, 249
106:41	248–49
110:3	408
116:17–18	150
130:1	150
140:4	341
145	380

Ecclesiastes 151

12:12	370–71

Isaiah 71, 149, 266

4:3	366
6	77
6:1	77, 153
6:5	77
30:9–11	342
37:17	154
40–55	149, 258
40:12–13	137
60	265
65	265

Jeremiah 146–47, 149, 299

16:15	154
23:3	154
23:8	154
25	321
25:11–12	154
29	322, 328
32(39):20–21	154
32(39):37	154

Lamentations

2:11	312

Ezekiel 69, 71, 146, 149, 456–57

1	51, 62–63, 79, 455, 492
1–3	294
1:1–28	492
1:16	153
1:26–28	153
1:27–28	456
1:28–2:2	153
14:14	147, 153
14:14–20	317
14:20	147, 153
28:3	147, 153, 317
37	51
37:5	417
37:10	417
38–39	51
40–43	435, 463
40–48	48, 102, 265, 438
41:15–26	391
43:1–5	51

Daniel 2, 9, 13–14, 16, 29, 37–38, 43–44, 54–55, 65–66, 71, 85–86, 90, 95, 112, 115, 144, 146–47, 157, 160–61, 187, 209, 233–35, 237–38, 251, 253–56, 264, 278, 316, 320, 322–26, 332, 358, 410, 419, 422–24, 426, 463, 482–83, 497

1–6	318	8	46, 52, 99
2	40–41, 46, 49, 52, 102	8–12	88, 132
2–6	417	8:15	304
2–7	403	8:15–18	322
2:26	241	8:17–18	314, 319
2:31–45	413	8:27	287, 289, 314, 319, 322
2:38	415	9	99–100, 120, 299, 306, 321
2:46	417	9:2	154
3–6	210	9:3–4	322
3:13	417	9:4	154
3:16–18	480	9:4b–19	99
5	46, 88	9:5	154
5:13	241	9:6	154
5:20	417	9:7	154
6:17–24	341	9:8	154
6:19	287	9:10	154
6:20	241	9:11	154, 247
7	10, 17–19, 22–23, 40–41, 46, 49, 52, 99, 102, 131, 133, 201, 300, 302–4, 417, 440, 446	9:12–17	317
		9:14	154
		9:15	154
7–8	153	9:18	154
7–12	14, 44, 47, 93, 99, 118, 318, 321	9:24–27	478
7:1	210, 285–86, 292, 318	9:25	415
7:1–14	413	9:26	135, 478
7:2	291, 314	9:26–27	481
7:2–8	413	10–12	99
7:4	303–4, 314	10:2–9	322
7:6	298, 314	10:7–9	314, 319
7:7	314	10:8	314
7:8	305, 414	10:16–17	319
7:9	314, 456	11	42–44
7:9–10	133, 304	11:32	415
7:9–14	99	11:39	99
7:11	304, 314	11:43	99
7:13	314, 414	12	317
7:13–14	417	12:2	251
7:14	416–17	12:6	135
7:15	313–14, 319, 322	12:7	43, 481
7:16	298		
7:16–17	413	Hosea	149
7:17	303	13:7–8	303
7:23	415		
7:25	415–17, 481	Joel	149
7:27	415–17	2:13	150
7:28	314, 318–19, 322	2:14	150

Amos	71, 149	Sirach (Ben Sira)	152, 162, 196, 342, 351, 370
Obadiah	149	18:4–6	73
		20:30	73
Jonah	11, 149	48:22	78
2:2–10	150	48:25	78
2:13	150		
2:14	150	Susanna	317
3:9	150		
4:2	150	Tobit	131, 136–37, 139–41, 211, 226, 229, 243, 254, 407, 419, 424
Micah	149	3:15	407
Nahum	149	Wisdom of Solomon	151
Habakkuk	149	The Dead Sea Scrolls	
Zephaniah	146–47, 149	1QpHab (1QPesher Habakkuk)	121, 125
		II, 2	74
Haggai	149	V, 7–8	136
		VII, 1–5	73
Zechariah	71, 149	VII, 3–IX, 7	341
1–6	294	VII, 4–5	121
1–8	463	VII, 10–12	121
1:8	282	VII, 13	136
3	270, 280	VIII, 1–3	121
3:1–5	407	X, 9–XI, 2	121
Malachi	149	1Q20 (1QGenesis Apocryphon)	3, 41, 57, 201, 212, 409, 440, 442
Deuterocanonical Books		II–XI	211–12
		II, 21–V, 27	440
Bel and the Dragon	317	II, 23	440
		XII, 26–XV, 35	41
Judith		XIII–XVII	41, 57, 440, 467
8:26	210		
		Book of Giants	12, 35, 93, 123, 201, 212, 215, 227, 286, 295, 438–39, 464–65
1 Maccabees	216		
2 Maccabees	216	1Q26 (1QInstruction)	152
Prayer of Azariah	317	1Q27 (1QMysteries)	152
		1 II, 5	341

Ancient Sources Index

1QS (1QCommunity Rule)   3, 50, 115, 120, 138, 234, 248, 251, 254, 267–69, 273, 277, 331, 344–46, 354
II, 26–III, 6	120
III, 13–IV, 26	15, 50, 120, 152, 258, 266–67, 272, 274, 277–78, 473
III, 15	267
III, 15–16	272
III, 18–20	268
III, 20–25	268
III, 21–24	268
III, 25–26	272
IV, 2–6	268
IV, 2–14	268
IV, 6–8	268
IV, 9–11	268
IV, 11–14	268
IV, 15–17	268
IV, 18	268
IV, 18–26	268
IV, 20–23	268
IV, 20–26	268
V–VI	152
VI, 1–6	120
VI, 2	341
VII, 6–7	346
VII, 24–25	346
VIII, 4–8	120
IX, 12–14	137–38
IX, 18	344
IX, 26–X, 8	136
X, 1, 5	135
XI, 5–9	73
XI, 7–9	116

1Q28b (1QRule of the Congregation)
V, 21–23	116

Hodayot   3, 10, 20, 72, 74, 92, 95–96, 115–16, 123–25, 310, 329–32, 334, 338–43, 345–46, 349–54

1QH^a (1QHodayot^a)   95, 127, 334–35, 351–52, 354
I–VIII	335
II, 9–11	343
II, 27	337
IV, 34	337
V, 12	335
V, 26	136
VI, 14–15	337
VI, 28–33	344
VI, 31	343–44
VI, 35	339
VII, 12–20	336
VII, 18	340
VII, 21–25	344
VII, 30	339
IX, 1–XX, 6	343
IX, 23	337
IX, 26	136
IX, 38	337, 350
X, 6	337
X, 12	339
X, 13	74
X, 14	339
X, 15–17	343–44
X, 17	342
X, 19	340
X, 21	342
X, 23	340–41
X, 26	339
X, 27	339, 342
X, 31	341
X, 32	342, 345
X, 34	337, 342
X, 36	337
X, 37	339
X, 38	339
X, 40	340
XI	116
XI, 10	339
XI, 13	340
XI, 17	340
XI, 19–23	96
XI, 19–24	335
XI, 20–23	115
XI, 26	337
XI, 27	341
XII, 6–XIII, 6	116

1QH^a (cont.)

XII, 8	342	XVI, 30	340
XII, 11	342	XVIII, 12	341
XII, 12	342	XVIII, 24–32	338
XII, 13	341	XVIII, 26	339, 347
XII, 16	342	XVIII, 27	346
XII, 17	342	XVIII, 35	116
XII, 20	342	XVIII, 36	340
XII, 27–28	74	XVIII, 36–37	339–40
XII, 35	339	XIX, 7–8	335
XII, 36	343	XIX, 10–14	116
XII, 39	339	XIX, 11	341
XIII, 7–8	122	XIX, 13–16	116
XIII, 8	340	XIX, 13–17	336
XIII, 8–18	341	XIX, 21	341
XIII, 9	339	XIX, 24	341
XIII, 10	341	XIX, 28–29	335
XIII, 11–15	122	XX, 7	335
XIII, 12	341	XX, 7–XXII, 39	343
XIII, 13–14	337	XX, 8–14	136
XIII, 15–16	337	XX, 11	135–36
XIII, 18	337	XXI, 16	136
XIII, 19	339	XXI, 21	340
XIII, 20	337, 341	XXII, 9	136
XIII, 22	337	XXII, 15	337
XIII, 23	337, 340	XXV, 15	339
XIII, 24	337	XXVI, 27	337
XIII, 29	341	XXVI, 36–39	336
XIII, 33	347		
XIII, 35–36	347	1QH^b (1QHodayot^b)	116, 334, 354
XIV, 6–7	336		
XIV, 12–14	336	1Q32 (1QNew Jerusalem)	12, 48, 50,
XIV, 14	336	115, 147	
XIV, 15–16	336		
XIV, 17–21	336	1QM (1QWar Scroll)	3, 50, 111, 117,
XIV, 19	342	120–21, 125, 414, 427	
XIV, 24–25	342	I, 1	407
XIV, 27–28	345	III, 2	251
XIV, 32–33	336	IV, 10–11	251
XIV, 32–37	116	X, 8–11	120–21
XIV, 32–38	341	X, 15	135–36
XV, 6	342	XII, 7–18	340
XV, 15	339		
XV, 26–27	74	1Q33 (1QWar Scroll)	121, 125
XVI, 12–13	340	1Q71 (1QDaniel^a)	316

Ancient Sources Index

1Q72 (1QDaniel[b])	316	4Q196 (4QTobit[a] ar)	
		17 I, 5	243
2Q18 (2QBen Sira)	152	18 1	243
2Q24 (2QNew Jerusalem)	12, 48, 101, 115, 147	4Q201 (4QEnoch[a] ar)	9, 29, 93, 108, 146, 201, 226
3Q7 (3QTestament of Judah [?])	149	4Q202 (4QEnoch[b] ar)	9, 29, 93, 108, 146, 201, 226
4Q112–116 (4QDaniel[a–e])	316	4Q203 (4QBook of Giants[a])	
4Q114 (4QDaniel[c])	2	8 3	212
		8 4	439
4Q116 (4QDaniel[e])	2	4Q204 (4QEnoch[c] ar)	9, 17, 29, 93, 108, 153, 201, 226, 281, 291–92
4Q160 (4QVision of Samuel)		1 I–XIII	146
1 3	282	1 VI, 10	292
		4	146, 419
4Q166 (4QHosea Pesher[a])		4 7–8	251
I, 12	136	5 II, 26–27	439
4Q169 (4QNahum Pesher)	342	4Q205 (4QEnoch[d] ar)	9, 29, 93, 108, 201, 226
4Q171 (4QPsalms Pesher[a])	343	1 XI–XII	146
		2	419
4Q174 (Florilegium)		2 I–III	146
1–3 II, 3–4	317, 415	2 I, 25	213
4Q177 (4QCatena[a])		4Q206 (4QEnoch[e] ar)	9, 29, 93, 108, 201, 226
12–13 I	407	1 XX–XXII	146
4Q180 (4QAges of Creation A)	136, 140–41	1 XXVI–XXVIII	146
1 1–4	135	4 I–III	146
		4 II, 13	213
4Q181 (4QAges of Creation B)	136, 140–41	5	419
		4Q207 (4QEnoch[f] ar)	9, 29, 93, 108, 201, 226, 419
4Q184 (4QWiles of the Wicked Woman) 152		4	146
4Q185 (4QSapiential Work)	152	4Q208 (4QAstronomical Enoch[a] ar)	214, 227
4Q196–200 (Qumran Tobit)	211, 419		

4Q208–4Q211 (Aramaic Astronomical Book)   10, 12–13, 25, 48, 90, 92–95, 101, 108, 146, 201, 213–14, 216, 219, 221–24, 226, 431, 433, 435–38, 440, 443, 464–65

4Q209 (4QAstronomical Enoch[b] ar)
214, 227, 436–37, 468
2 3	437
2 3 9	437
2 5 3	436
2 6 6–7	436

4Q210 (4QAstronomical Enoch[c] ar)
| 1 II 2a+b+c | 437 |
| 1 II, 20 | 442 |

4Q212 (4QEnoch[g] ar) 9, 29, 93, 108, 201, 226
1 I, 1–II, 21	146
1 III, 25	213
1 IV, 17–18	478
1 V, 17	213
1 V, 20	213
1 V, 22	213

ALD (Aramaic Levi Document)   3, 6, 25, 49–50, 52, 57, 59, 161, 201–2, 226, 409, 431–33, 443, 457–60, 464–68
| 11–61 (Drawnel) | 214 |
| 32a–47 (Drawnel) | 214 |

4Q213 (4QAramaicLevi[a])   405
| 1 I, 1–4 | 406 |

4Q213a (4QAramaicLevi[b])
2 14–18	133–34, 405
2 15–18	49, 432
3–4	407
3 15	213

4Q213b (4QAramaicLevi[c])   405

4Q214 (4QAramaicLevi[d])   405

4Q217 (4QpapJubilees[b])
| 2 1 | 136 |

4Q228 (Text with a Citation of Jubilees)
| 1 I, 2 | 136 |

4Q242 (4QPrayer of Nabonidus ar)
13, 36, 46, 58, 233, 236, 239, 241, 246, 250, 255, 317, 415

4Q243–245 (4QPseudo-Daniel[a–c] ar)
13–14, 35–37, 42, 52–53, 55, 115, 132, 233–37, 239–41, 243–47, 249–53, 317, 415

4Q243 (4QPseudo-Daniel[a] ar)   46, 132, 147, 234–35, 238–41, 243–44, 249–53
1	238
1 2	241–44, 248
2	237–38
3	238
6	46, 238
12 1	239
13	46, 237, 246–47
13 2	246–47
13 3	239
14 2	239
16 1	239
20 2	239
21 2	238–39
24	239, 249–50
24 1–2	250
24 5	250
25	239
28	237

4Q244 (4QPseudo-Daniel[b] ar)   46, 132, 147, 234–35, 238–41, 247–53
1	237, 246
1–4	238
5 II, 5	243
12	46, 237, 246–47
12 1	246
12 3	246
13 1	246

Ancient Sources Index

4Q245 (4QPseudo-Daniel^c ar)	46–47,	VI, 14–17	341
132, 147, 234–40, 251, 256		XI, 12	346
1 I	237	XII, 7–10	346
2	46, 240	XII, 20–21	138
2 3	251	XII, 23	136
2 4–5	251	XIV, 20	341
		XV, 7	136
4Q246 (4QApocryphon of Daniel ar)		XVI, 3	
3, 10, 13, 23, 37, 40, 52, 111, 115, 123,		136	
132, 381, 402, 405–6, 412–19, 422–24,			
426–27		4Q266 (4QDamascus Document^a)	
I, 1–2	417	2 II, 11	251
I, 1–3	413	11 19	136
I, 2	413, 417		
I, 4–5	413	4Q269 (4QDamascus Document^d)	
I, 6	413	8 II, 5	136
I, 4–II, 3	417		
I, 7–II, 3	413	4Q270 (4QDamascus Document^e)	
I, 9	413	7 II, 13	136
II	414, 417		
II, 1	414–15	4Q271 (4QDamascus Document^f)	
II, 1–2	40, 413	2 12	136
II, 4	251, 413–14, 416, 419		
II, 5	413, 416	4Q275 (4QCommunal Ceremony)	
II, 6	416	1 I, 2	251
II, 7	413, 416–17		
II, 8	416–17, 419	4Q280 (4QCurses)	407
II, 9	413, 416	2	408
4Q248 (4QHistorical Text A)	42–43,	4Q298 (4QCryptic A: Words of the	
54–55, 146–47		Maskil to All Sons of Dawn)	137,
9–10	43	141, 152	
4Q257 (4QCommunity Rule^c)	152	4Q299 (4QMysteries^a)	152
CD (Cairo Damascus Document)		4Q300 (4QMysteries^b)	152
2, 115, 121, 238, 245, 248–49, 251–52,			
300, 339, 345–46, 354		4Q301 (4QMysteries^c?)	152
I, 5–6	248		
I, 9	251	4Q302 (4QpapAdmonitory Parable)	152
II, 11	251		
II, 13	251	4Q303 (4QMeditation on Creation A)	
II, 17–18	339	152	
VI, 10	136		
VI, 14	136		

4Q305 (4QMeditation on Creation C) 152

4Q320 (4QCalendrical Document A) 138

4Q345 (4QDeed A ar or heb) 345

4Q359 (4QpapDeed C ar or heb) 345

Apocryphon of Jeremiah 38, 51–52, 55, 132, 134

4Q383 (4QApocryphon of Jeremiah C) 44, 59, 147

4Q384 (4QApocryphon of Jeremiah B?) 35, 44, 147

Pseudo-Ezekiel 51–52, 115, 134, 478, 498

4Q385 (4QPseudo-Ezekiel^a) 35, 37, 44, 51, 115, 282
   2+3   51
   3a–c 3   251
   4   51
   6   51

4Q385a (4QApocryphon of Jeremiah C^a) 35, 37, 44, 147
   17 II, 2–3   45
   18 I, 2   134

4Q385b (4QPseudo-Ezekiel^c) 35, 37, 42, 44, 51

4Q386 (4QPseudo-Ezekiel^b) 35, 37, 44, 51, 115
   1 I   51

4Q387 (4QPseudo-Moses^b) 35, 37, 44, 147
   2 II, 3–4   134
   3 9   134

4Q387a (4QApocryphon of Jeremiah D) 35, 37, 44, 147

4Q388 (4QPseudo-Ezekiel^d) 35, 37, 44, 51, 115
   7   51

4Q388a (4QPseudo-Moses^c) 35, 37, 44, 147

4Q389 (4QPseudo-Moses^d) 35, 37, 44, 147

4Q389a (4QApocryphon of Moses^e) 35, 37, 44, 147

4Q390 (4QApocryphon of Jeremiah E) 37, 44–45, 56, 147
   1 7   134

4Q391 (4QPseudo-Ezekiel^e) 44

4QHalakhic Letter (4QMMT) 74, 120, 122, 248
   C 21   120

Songs of the Sabbath Sacrifice 21, 35, 50, 117, 135, 377–78, 381–84, 388–89, 391–92, 395–402, 406, 427, 491, 525, 529

4Q400–407 (4QSongs of the Sabbath Sacrifice^{a-h}) 381

4Q403 (4QSongs of the Sabbath Sacrifice^d) 398

4Q411 (4QSapiential Hymn) 152

4Q412 (4QSapiential–Didactic Work A) 152

4Q413 (4QComposition concerning Divine Providence) 152

Ancient Sources Index   549

4QInstruction	3, 72, 74, 337–38, 342, 351, 411	1 8 5	339
4Q415 (4QInstruction[a])	152	4Q431 (4QHodayot[e]) 2 7	337
4Q416 (4QInstruction[b])	152, 317	4Q432 (4QHodayot[f])	334
		3 3	337
4Q417 (4QInstruction[c])	152	5 5	340
1 I, 11–13	74		
2 II	411	4Q473 (4QThe Two Ways)	152
4Q418 (4QInstruction[d])		4Q484 (4QTestament of Judah)	149
9–11	411		
81 + 81a 12	251	4Q489 (4QApocalypse ar)	317
126 II, 3	137		
127 5–6	137	4Q491–497 (4QWar Scroll[a–g])	121, 125
4Q418a (4QInstruction[e])	152	4Q491 (4QWar Scroll[a])	
		19 4	251
4Q418c (4QInstruction[f?])	152	4Q496 (4QWar Scroll[f])	
4Q423 (4QInstruction[g])	152	8 9	251
4Q424 (4QInstruction-like Composition B)	152	4Q504 (4QWords of the Luminaries[a]) 1–2 II, 12	251
4Q425 (4QSapiential-Didactic Work B) 152		4Q510 (4QShirot[a]) 1 I, 2–3	340
4Q426 (4QSapiential-Hymnic Work A) 152		4Q521 (4QMessianic Apocalypse) 115	50,
4Q427–432 (4QHodayot[a–f]) 334, 354	116, 127,	4Q525 (4QBeatitudes)	152
		4Q529–549	210, 286, 295, 426, 438
4Q427 (4QHodayot[a])		4Q529 (4QWords of Michael ar)	36–38,
2 11	341	42, 47, 52, 58, 146–47, 441–42, 466	
7 II, 8	337	1 1–5	442
7 II, 18–21	336	9–10	47
11 2	341		
4Q428 (4QHodayot[b])	334	4Q530 (4QBook of Giants[b] ar) 281, 286, 295, 441	17, 133,
3 3	337		
4 2	340	2 II	11, 133
13 4	340–41	2 II, 1	213

4Q530 (*cont.*)
- 2 II, 3 — 286
- 2 II, 4 — 286–87
- 2 II, 6–7 — 288, 441
- 2 II, 9–10 — 288
- 2 II, 12 — 288
- 2 II, 14 — 439
- 2 II, 15–20 — 441
- 2 II, 16 — 288, 441
- 2 II, 16–20 — 133
- 2 II, 20 — 288–89
- 2 II, 21–22 — 439
- 7 II, 4–6 — 415, 440

4Q531 (4QBook of Giants[c] ar)
- 22 9 — 289
- 4 6 — 440

4Q534 (4QNoah[a] ar) — 37

4Q535 (4QNoah[b] ar) — 37

4Q536 (4QNoah[c] ar) — 37, 210

4Q537 (4QApocryphon of Jacob ar) 148

4Q538 (4QApocryphon of Judah ar) 149

4Q540 (4QApocryphon of Levi[a] ar) 37, 149

4Q541 (4QApocryphon of Levi[b] ar) 37, 149
- 9 I, 7 — 251

4Q542 (4QTestament of Qahat ar) 212, 409
- 3 II, 12 — 407

Visions of Amram 35–38, 50–52, 57–58, 115, 123, 201–2, 212, 230, 406, 408–12, 418, 420, 424–26

4Q543 (4QVisions of Amram[a] ar) 23, 115, 149, 212, 405–6, 408, 425
- 1a–c 1 — 212, 409
- 3 1 — 408
- 4 6 — 407

4Q544 (4QVisions of Amram[b] ar) 17, 23, 115, 149, 212, 281, 289, 405–6, 408, 422, 425
- 1 10 — 290–91, 408
- 1 3–8 — 407
- 1 8–9 — 407
- 1 10 — 407
- 1 10–14 — 407
- 1 12 — 408
- 2 3 — 408
- 2 5 — 408
- 2 6 — 408
- 3 1 — 408

4Q545 (4QVisions of Amram[c] ar) 23, 115, 149, 212, 405–6, 408, 425
- 1 I, 1 — 409
- 1 II — 407
- 3 3 — 408
- 3 6 — 408

4Q546 (4QVisions of Amram[d] ar) 23, 115, 149, 212, 405–6, 408, 425
- 2 — 407

4Q547 (4QVisions of Amram[e] ar) 23, 115, 149, 212, 405–6, 408, 425
- 9 8 — 408, 410

4Q548 (4QVisions of Amram[f] ar) 23, 115, 149, 212, 405–7
- 1 II–2, 16 — 407

4Q549 (4QVisions of Amram[g?] ar) 149, 212

4Q550 (4QJews in the Persian Court ar) 36, 210

Ancient Sources Index

4Q551 (4QDaniel-Suzanna? ar)   317

4Q552 (4QFour Kingdoms[a] ar)   12–13, 36–37, 40–41, 52, 111, 123, 132, 147, 317, 405, 415

4Q553 (4QFour Kingdoms[b] ar)   12–13, 36–37, 40–41, 52, 111, 123, 132, 147, 317, 405, 415

New Jerusalem   6, 10, 12, 15, 25, 35–38, 48–49, 52, 56–57, 59, 66, 99, 101–2, 108, 111, 115, 123, 147, 258, 265–66, 276, 278, 403, 405, 409, 411–12, 418, 431–32, 434–35, 438, 443, 464–65, 468

4Q554 (4QNew Jerusalem[a] ar) 12, 17, 48, 101, 115, 147
   2 III, 22   49

4Q555 (4QNew Jerusalem[b] ar)   12, 48, 101, 115, 147

5Q15 (5QNew Jerusalem ar) 12, 48, 101, 115, 147

6Q7 (6QDaniel)   316

6Q23 (6QWords of Michael?)   146–47, 442, 466

6Q29 (6QpapCursive unclassified frag.) 345

11Q10 (11QTargum of Job)
   38 3–4   243

11Q13 (11QMelchizedek)   408
   II, 18   415

11Q17 (Songs of the Sabbath Sacrifice) 381

11Q18 (11QNew Jerusalem ar)   12, 48, 57, 101, 115, 147
   15 4   434
   19 3   434

11Q19 (11QTemple Scroll)   3, 191, 195, 265, 405

New Testament

Matthew   474, 497
4:17   394
5:3   393–94
5:20   389
5:26   485
6:10   386, 390
7:21   389
8:11   394
10:28   485
12:28   380, 386, 394
12:34   341
13:11   397
13:41–43   493
18:3   389
19:23–24   389
19:28   397
21:31   389
22:13   485
23:13   389
23:33   341
24:3–44   490
24:15   481
25:30   485
25:31–46   379
25:41–46   493
25:46   485

Mark
1:15   394
4:10–12   397, 401
4:11   397
9:47   389
10:15   379, 389
10:23–25   389
14:25   386

Luke (includes references to Q)	381	7:6	76
1:32–35	414	7:8	76
3:7	341	7:10	76
6:20	393–94	7:12	76
8:10	397	9:1–23	76
10:9	394	11:1	76
10:20	386	11:2	76
11:2	386	11:33	76
11:20	380, 394	12–14	397
13:18–19	336	13:2	75
13:28–29	394	14:37	76
16:13	341	15:28	490
17:21	386	15:51	75
18:17	389	16:1	76
18:24–25	389		
22:28	336	2 Corinthians	
22:28–30	397, 400	2:16	76
22:30	336	3–4	76
		3:14	69
John	62, 80–83, 109, 423	3:18	69
1:17	76, 78	6:14–7:1	76
1:18	77	12	493
1:51	77	12:2–4	75
5:39	77		
6:46	77	Ephesians	62, 82
12:41	77	Colossians	
12:49–50	77	2:3	77
14:8	77		
14:9	77–78	Hebrews	
		5:6	408
Romans		6:20	408
1:3–4	414, 425		
11:25	75	1 Peter	
16:25	75	1:11–12	77
1 Corinthians		1 John	
2:1	75–76	2:18	480
2:6	76		
2:7	75	Jude	
2:10	69, 74–75	9	407, 422
3:16	76	14–15	449
4:1	75–76	14–16	477
4:16	76		
5:12	294		
6:19	76		

Revelation	18, 19, 23, 28–30, 61, 67, 74, 79, 81, 85, 99, 103, 107–9, 113, 118, 144, 156, 157, 326, 337, 353, 379, 391, 402, 404–6, 408, 419–20, 422–24, 426–27, 443, 445		11:2–3		481
			11:3		415
			11:7–9		417
			11:11		417
			11:15		416–17
1:1	90, 104, 411, 420, 483, 487–88		11:15–19		415
1:1–2		410	11:19		412
1:1–5:14		420, 425	12:6		415, 481
1:2		410, 420	12:7–9		411
1:3		410, 420	12:14		415, 481
1:7		403	12:17		410, 420
1:7–8		421	13		303, 403
1:9		410, 420	13:1–3		318
1:10		409	13:3		480
1:12–16		410	13:5		481
1:13–20		403	13:9–10		421
1:17–20		421	13:11		411
1:19		410	13:11–17		485
2–3		104	15:1–16:21		305
2:14		411	15:3		411
2:20		411	17:1–9		104
3:7		411	17:7		71
3:12		392	17:7–18		403
4		494	17:9–14		63
4–5		403	18:3		104
4–22		22	18:21–24		421
4:5		63	19		486
5		494	19:10		410, 420, 451
5:5		411	19:20–21		418
5:6–14		411	20:4		410, 420
5:9		412	21		484, 500
5:10		417	21–22		265
5:13		417	21:5–8		421
6:1–8:5		305	21:12–14		411
7:4–8		411	21:14		392
8:6–9:21		305	21:24		418
9:1		411	21:25		266
9:5		411	22:5		266, 417
9:7–11		411	22:7		410, 420–21
9:10		411	22:8–9		451
9:11		411	22:10		410, 420
10:11		410, 420	22:12–14		421
11:1–2		415	22:16		411
11:1–14		415	22:18–19		410, 420
11:2		416–17			

Other Ancient Jewish Texts

Ahiqar 208, 211

Apocalypse of Abraham 65, 90, 103, 443–44, 454, 457, 467–68
1–7	455
8–9	455
10–11	515
10–19	455
11.2	456
11.2–3	456
13–14	456
15.3–4	455
15.7–16.2	455
18.3	455
18.12–13	455
18.14	456
19.6–9	455
20–31	455
21	455
27.5	455

Apocalypse of Zephaniah 90, 118, 147, 443, 445, 460–61, 463–64, 467, 469, 476, 493, 501

Apocryphon of Ezekiel 150

Artapanus (*apud* Eusebius, *Praeparatio Evangelica*)
9.27.4–5	219
9.27.6	219

Ascension of Isaiah 1, 66, 443–44, 455, 460, 463–64
1–5	452
2.7–11	78
3.6–10	78
6–11	452, 473, 491
7.14–15	452
7.20	453
7.21	453
7.22	453
7.25	453
8.5	451, 453
8.13–16	517
9.1	453
9.1–16	517
9.2	453
9.9	453
9.10–18	453
9.27–30	517
9.30–31	453
9.37	453
9.38	454
10.19–31	453
13–14	456
13.14	456

2 Baruch 22, 65, 86, 90, 103, 108, 118, 132, 137, 139–40, 187, 294, 299, 357–58, 369, 374, 419, 423, 473, 475–76, 483–84, 498
4	265
19.5–7	484
36.1	291
51.10–13	517

3 Baruch 24, 90, 118, 443–44, 447, 449, 452, 454–56, 460–67, 491
2	450
3	450
4.6–17 (Slavonic)	451
4.8–17 (Greek)	451
6–9	450
8.4–5	450
11–16	450

Book of Biblical Antiquities (Liber antiquitatum biblicarum)
9.10	291

1 Enoch 2, 8–9, 11, 37–38, 46, 64–65, 67, 72, 74, 112, 115, 117, 123, 157–58, 160–63, 165–66, 169–73, 177, 188–91, 235, 238, 265, 286, 327, 332, 368, 405, 409–10, 419, 429
1–5	94

1–36 (The Book of Watchers) 10, 12–

Ancient Sources Index

14, 17, 22, 24, 48–49, 90, 92–94, 97, 109, 132, 146, 150, 180, 201, 214–16, 220, 229, 245, 276, 291, 294, 310–11, 326, 339, 430–33, 435–36, 440, 442–43, 446–49, 452, 457–58, 462–64, 467		14.7	184
		14.8	133
		14.8–10	311
		14.8–25	180, 431
		14.8–16.4	93
		14.10–15.1	153
1.1	180	14.11–14	312
1.1–2a	182	14.13	312
1.2	183	14.14	313
1.2b–9	180	14.18	153
1.2b–5.9	180	14.18–20	153
2.1	186	14.18–23	133
2.1–5.3	180	14.19	153
5.3	186	14.21	153
5.4	180	14.24–25	312
5.5–9	180	15.1	431
5.6–7	94	15.6–10	186
6–11	139	15.9–16.1	139
6.1–8	179	17–19	433, 438, 442, 493
6.1–12.2	179–82	17–36	94, 102, 180, 431, 433, 493
7	216	18	94
7.1–6	179	18.1–5	186
8.1–4	179	18.6–11	340
8.3	223	19.1	139, 186
9.1–11	179	20	94
10.1–22	179	20–32	433
10.11–15	94	20–36	438, 493
10.17–19	180	21	94
11.1–2	179	22	94, 433
12–16	139	24.5–6	180
12.1–2	179	27	434
12.3	179	27.1–4	94
13.4–7	431	27.2–4	180
13.7	291	32.3–6	94
13.7–8	291	33	221
13.7–10	93	33–36	94, 434
13.8	292	33.1–3	223
13.8–14.2	431	33.4	184
14	77, 292, 441, 446, 491	37–41	491
14–16	133	37–71 (Similitudes of Enoch)	24, 90, 92, 95, 146, 164, 264, 305, 328, 334, 339–40, 418, 443–45, 457, 462
14.1	184		
14.1–2	133, 292		
14.1–7	93	37–82	93, 110, 339, 353, 435, 467
14.2	183, 282, 293	37.1	182, 306
14.4–7	180	38.1–39.1	180

1 Enoch (cont.)

39.1–2	182	60.6	180
39.2	184	60.11–23	180
39.3	446	61.3–5	180
39.4–7	180	61.8–12	180
39.5	446	62.3–6	180
39.9–12	446	62.8–63.11	180
39.11	185	63.1–12	96
40.1–7	180	63.10	341
41.3	186	65.1–2	182
41.3–44	180	65.1–67.3	96
41.5	186	65.2b–69.25	179–80
42.1–3	164	65.7–8	180
45.2–6	180	65.11–12	180
45.3–6	180	66.1–2	180
46	96	67.1–13	180
46.1	180	68.1	184
46.4–47.2	180	69.2–15	180
47.3	184	69.8	184
47.3–48.1	180	69.13–22	187
48.2–10	96	69.16–21	180
48.4–5	180	69.25	180
48.8–10	180	69.26–105.2	180
49.4	180	69.27b–29	180
49.1–3	180	70.1–2	182
50.1–5	96	70–71	306
50.1–51.5	180	70.2	446
50.1–51.5b	96	71	446
52.1–9	180	71.1–17	180
53.1–2a	180	71.5–6	446
53.1–7	340	71.14	305–6, 446
53.2b–10	180	72–82 (Astronomical Book)	10, 12–13, 25, 48, 90, 92–95, 101, 110, 132, 146, 150, 180, 201, 203, 213–14, 216, 219–21, 223–24, 431, 433, 435, 438, 440, 464
54.1–56.8	180		
54.7–55.2	96		
55.3–56.8	180		
56.5–8	264, 276, 445, 465	72.1	95, 184, 436
57.2	186	72.1–78.17	186
58.2	180	72.2–79.6	180
58.2–6	180	72.3	436
59.12	186	73.1	436
59.13–15	186	74.1	436
60.1	186	74.2	436
60.1–2	180	74.9	436
60.1–25	96	75.3	436
60.4	186	75.4	436

Ancient Sources Index 557

75.8	436	85.3	291
76.1	436	86–88	439
76.14	436	86.1–3	439
77.1–3	437	86.6	139
77.3	437	87.3	439
77.4	437, 442	89.51–58	100
77.4–8	437	89.59	408
77.5	437	89.59–90.25	139
77.8	437	89.62–63	184
78.10	436	89.68–71	184
79.1	436	89.76	184
79.6	436	90.14	184
80–82	436	90.17	184
80.2–7	186	90.19	336
80.2–8	180	90.20	184
81.1–2	184	91–108 (Epistle of Enoch)	164, 178, 182, 196, 439, 468
81–108	93, 109, 216, 229, 291, 294, 311, 326, 436, 467	91.2	181
81.2	184	91.2–3a	181–82
81.4	184	91.3–4	181
81.5	178	91.5–10	181
81.7–9	180	91.11	186
82.1	184	91.11–12	336
82.2–5	180	91.11–17	181
82.2–8	95	91.12–17	147
82.4	180	91.18–92.2	181
82.6–12	180	92.1	184
82.9–20	186	92.1a	182
82.13–20	180	92.2	185
83.1–2	406	93.1	182, 184
83–90 (Book of Dreams)	120, 131, 180, 438–40	93.1–10 + 91.11–17 (Apocalypse of Weeks)	42, 90, 95, 131–32, 438–40, 477
83–91	146	93.2	184, 439
83.1–90.38	180	93.3	184
83.2	439	93.3a	182
83.3	291	93.4	439
83.3–5	186	93.4–10	181
83.5	186	93.11–14	181
83.7	186	94.1–5	181
83.11	186	95.2	181
84.2a	182	96	181
85.1–89.8	100	97.1–100.11	181
85–90 (Animal Apocalypse)	40, 90, 95, 99–100, 102, 132, 180, 213, 418, 439, 442	98.7	181
		100.6	184

1 Enoch (cont.)

101.1	181
102.2	186
102.2–3	181
102.4–104.9	181
103.2	184
103.7	184
104.10	184
104.10–105.2	181
104.12	184
105.1b	181
105.2b	181
106–107	181, 440, 442
106.1a	178
106.1–18	440
106.1–107.1	181
106.8–107.3	181
106.8	178, 440
106.13	407
106.13–15	139
106.19	184
107.3	182
108.1	182, 184
108.2	181
108.2–15	181–82
108.3	181, 184
108.6–9	181
108.10	184
108.11–15	181
108.15	184

2 Enoch 8, 47, 90, 92, 265, 443, 445, 450, 452, 454–60, 462, 464, 514, 534

1–20	491
3–6	448
7	448, 450
8–10	448
8–21	448
11–17	450
18	448
21.6–22.1	447
22.8–10	517
22.9–10	448
24–33	448
33.1–3	478, 483

3 Enoch	158, 194
16.2	505

4 Ezra (2 Esdras 3–14)   22, 30, 51, 65–66, 85–86, 90, 99–100, 107–8, 110, 118, 132, 139–40, 165, 187, 283, 294–95, 299, 322, 357–58, 374, 418–19, 473, 475, 479, 493, 495, 498

3.2–3	313
3.3	289
3.3–27	103
3.3–5.20	289
4.1–12	103
4.37–38	137
5.14	283, 287, 289, 313
5.21–6.34	289
5.33–40	103
6.13	287
6.35–9.25	289
6.38–53	103
6.55–59	103
7	265
7.1	287
7.26–44	483
7.75–101	103
7.102–115	103
8.19–36	306
9.26	16
10	265
10.29	289
10.32–36	289
10.36	289
11.1	282
13.1	291

5 Ezra (2 Esdras 1)	
2.42–48	473, 479, 495

6 Ezra (2 Esdras 2)	473, 479, 495

Josephus, *Jewish Antiquities*

1.154–169	217, 230
9.267–269	317
10.245–246	317
10.249	317

Ancient Sources Index

10.267–276	317	Sibylline Oracles	43, 99
		1–2	473
Josephus, *Jewish War*		3.8–45	102
1–3	352	3.63–74	480
2.122–123	348	3.762–766	102
		4.6–24	102
Jubilees	37–38, 55, 65, 74, 90, 99, 100–	4.24–39	102
	101, 109, 112, 115, 160–62, 192, 195,	5	265
	220, 235, 265, 419, 440	5.25–35	480
1	132, 134	5.93–110	480
1–21	2, 30, 100, 110, 290, 295, 438,	5.214–227	480
	469	5.361–385	480
1.11	247	7	473
1.29	101	8	473
4.10	290	8.17–36	102
4.15	439	8.359–428	102
4.17–19	219		
4.17–23	439	Testament of Abraham	90, 148, 444
4.21	439	17.12–16	407
5.1–18	439		
5.13	101	Testament of Adam	473
6.32–38	101		
12.25	211	Testament of Isaac	
23	101, 118, 132, 134	2–3	473
23.8–31	146	5–6	473
23.21	120		
29.5–9	211	Testament of Jacob	
31	433, 469	1–3	473
46–47	407	5–6	473
50.6	182		
		Testament of Job	149
Ladder of Jacob	294, 473		
3.2–3	283	Testament of Moses	149, 380
Psalms of Solomon	333–34	Early Christian Texts	
4.9	341		
8.10–12	341	Allogenes (NHC XI 3)	512, 514, 518,
			525, 529, 534
Pseudo-Eupolemus (*apud* Eusebius, *Prae-*		XI 50.18–19	515
paratio Evangelica)		XI 52.13–14	515
9.17.8	220	XI 53.11–21	519
		XI 55.17–18	515
Sentences of Pseudo-Phocylides	151	XI 55.32–34	515
		XI 57.24–25	515

Ancient Sources Index

Ammonas, *Epistle*	458, 469	Barnabas	500
		4.3	478, 498
Andrew of Caesarea	421	12.1	478, 498
		16.3–6	477
Apocalypse of Adam (NHC V 5)	476, 507	16.5	477
		16.6	477
		18–20	473
Apocalypse of Elijah	460, 467, 471, 473, 487, 497		
		Book of Elchasai	473, 519, 531
Apocalypse of Esdras	473	Book of the Resurrection of Jesus Christ by Bartholomew the Apostle	
(First) Apocalypse of James (NHC V 3)	473, 476	8b–14a	473
		17b–19b	473
(Second) Apocalypse of James (NHC V 4)	476	Books of Jeu (Bruce Codex)	519, 527, 534
Apocalypse of Paul	24, 90, 92, 97, 107–9, 443, 450, 452, 460–61, 465–66, 468, 473, 476, 493, 497	Chronicon ad annum Christi 1234 pertinens	290, 294
		Clement of Alexandria, *Excerpta ex Theodoto*	530
4	450		
17	98	37–39	528
Apocalypse of Peter	24, 90, 92, 97–98, 107, 109, 443, 445, 473, 476, 477, 487, 493	Commodian, *Carmen apologeticum*	
		785–1053	486
		Commondian, *Instructiones*	
Apocalypse of Pseudo-Methodius	97	2.1–4	486
Apocalypse of Sedrach	473	Cyprian, *Ad Demetrianum*	
		5	479
Apocalypse of the Virgin Mary	473	6–7	480
Apocalypse of Thomas	473	Cyprian, *Epistles*	
		55.2–4	480
Apocryphon of John (NHC II 1)	507	55.7	480
		58.7	480
Arethas of Caesarea	421		
		Cyril of Jerusalem, *Catechetical Oration*	
Augustine, *De civitate Dei*		15	489
20	482		
20.19	480	Didache	499
22.30	489	1–6	473
		16	473

Eusebius, *Demonstratio evangelica*
   8.2   479

Eusebius, *Eclogae propheticae*
   3.45–46   479

Eusebius, *Historia ecclesiastica*
   1.6.11   479
   6.7   480
   7.24.1–9   487

Eusebius, *Praeparatio evangelica*
   9.17.8   220
   9.27.4–5   219
   9.27.6   219

Gospel of Peter   477

Gospel of Philip   527, 535

Gospel of Truth (NHC I 3; XII 2)   508, 525, 527, 530, 536

Gregory of Nyssa, *Catechetical Discourse*
   5   491

Gregory of Nyssa, *De virginitate*
   14   491
   31–32   491

Gregory of Nyssa, *De vita Moses*
   2.163   492
   2.170–201   492

Gregory of Nyssa, *On the Soul and the Resurrection*
   7   490

Hilary of Poitiers, *Against the Emperor Constantius*
   5   481

Hippolytus, *Commentary on Daniel*
   4.23–34   486
   4.23.3   488
   4.35   479

Hippolytus, *Treatise on Christ and Antichrist*
   1   489

Irenaeus, *Adversus haereses*
   1.14   509
   1.29–30   503
   5.23.2   483
   5.33.4   484
   5.35.1–36.3   483
   24.1–28.4   483

Jerome, *Commentary on Daniel*
   9.23   479

John Chrysostom, *De paenitentia*
   7   482

John Chrysostom, *Homily on Matthew*
   43.7   474

Julius Africanus, *Chronographia*
   6.130–38   479

Justin Martyr, *Dialogue with Trypho*   485
   80–81   486

Lactantius, *De mortibus persecutorum*
   2   481

Lactantius, *Divinarum institutionum*
   7.14–26   485
   7.14.2–4   484
   7.16.3–4   485
   7.17.2–6   485
   7.24   485

Life of Adam and Eve   457, 566

Lives of the Prophets   150

Ancient Sources Index

Marsanes (NHC X 1) 512, 514, 518, 533, 535
- X 4.24–5.9 — 520
- X 26*.12–17 — 523
- X 27*.21–23 — 523
- X 32*.1–6 — 519
- X 35*.1–6 — 523
- X 39*.18–41.8 — 523
- X 64*.1–5 — 528

Methodius of Olympus, *Symposium*
- 9.1 — 487
- 9.5 — 487

Mysteries of Saint John the Apostle and the Holy Virgin — 473

Nature of the Rulers (NHC II 4) — 507
- II 95.9–10 — 528

Oecumenius — 421

Opus Imperfectum in Matthaeum
- 49 — 481

Origen, *Commentarium in evangelium Matthaei*
- 32–60 — 490
- 33 — 490
- 37 — 490
- 38 — 490

Origen, *Commentarii in evangelium Joannis*
- 1.16.91 — 490

Origen, *Contra Celsum*
- 5.52–55 — 445

Origen, *Homiliae in Leviticum*
- 7.2 — 490

The Passion of Perpetua and Felicity 324
- 1.3 — 494
- 2.3–4 — 494
- 3.2 — 494
- 4 — 310
- 4.1–3 — 494
- 11.3 — 310

Pseudo-Macarius, *Fifty Spiritual Homilies* — 491, 497, 500
- 2.1.2 — 492
- 3.8.1 — 492

Questions of Bartholomew — 473

Quintus Julius Hilarianus, *On the Progress of Time*
- 17–18 — 487

Romanos the Melodist, *On the Second Coming* — 475

Salvian of Marseilles, *To the Church*
- 2.10 — 475
- 3.18 — 475

Sayings of the Desert Fathers — 501
- 6 — 491
- 7 — 491
- 27 — 491
- 29 — 491
- 33 — 491
- 48 — 491

Sethian Egyptian Gospel (NHC IV 2)
- IV 51.2–3 — 512
- IV 53.3–54.20 — 512

Seventh Vision of Daniel — 357, 373

Shepherd of Hermas — 477, 487, 495
- 6.1–2 — 473

Sulpicius Severus, *Dialogues*
- 2.14 — 480

Story of Zosimus — 473

Syncellus	217	3.5–6	459
		3.7	459
Syriac World Chronicle	290	3.8	459
		5.1	458–59
Tertullian, *Against Marcion*		8.1–19	491
3.24	484	8.4	517
Tertullian, *Apologeticus*		Testament of Reuben	
32	484	1.1–3	406
Tertullian, *De anima*		Testament of Simeon	
55–58	485	1.1–2	403
56	485		
58	485	Testimony of Truth (NHC IX,3) 507, 533	
Tertullian, *De fuga in persecutione*		Three Forms of First Thought (NHC XIII	
12	484	1)	27, 533
		XIII 48*.15–34	515
Tertullian, *De resurrection carnis*			
17	485	Three Steles of Seth (NHC VII 5)	514,
35	485	522, 525, 531	
		VII 124.17–21	526
Tertullian, *On the Shows*	493	VII 126.9–23	523
33	494	VII 126.17–32	516
Testament of the Lord	473	Tyconius, *The Book of Rules*	489
Testaments of the Twelve Patriarchs	50,	Untitled Work (Bruce Codex)	519
57, 149, 156, 457–60, 466			
		Victorinus, *Commentary on the Book of*	
Testament of Asher		*Revelation*	
1.3–5	473	4.6–10	487
		20.1–3	486
Testament of Judah		20.6	487
23.1	247		
		Zostrianos (NHC VIII 1) 513, 514, 517,	
Testament of Levi 432–33, 444, 463, 467		526, 529, 534, 535	
2	50	VIII 1.[63].20–22	516
2–5	90, 443, 457	VIII 6.7–18	515
2–7	459, 466	VIII 46.15–30	515
2.5–5.2	491	VIII 48.21–23	515
2.6–8	458	VIII 53.13–14	515
2.9–10	458	VIII 54.15–17	515
3	50, 458	VIII 62.11–12	515
3.5	459	VIII 63.9–10	515

Zostrianos (cont.)
- VIII 125.13.17 — 515
- VIII 129.1–22 — 516
- VIII 130.16–132.5 — 523

Rabbinic and Other Jewish Texts

b. Hagigah
- 13a — 73
- 15a — 505

b. Megillah
- 7a — 371

b. Sanhedrin
- 38b — 212
- 90a–113b (Pereq Heleq) — 21, 368, 370, 373
- 91a–92a — 368
- 92a — 366
- 92a–96b — 369
- 93a — 369
- 94a — 369
- 97a — 367
- 97a–97b — 369
- 97b — 361, 363, 367
- 98a — 363, 365
- 100b — 370
- 113a–b — 366

Hekhalot Zutarti — 506, 521

Ma'aseh Daniel — 369

Ma'aseh Merkabah — 521

Merkabah Rabbah — 506, 521

Midrash on Psalms
- 1:12 — 370

m. Berakot
- 9:5 — 341

m. Hagigah
- 2:1 — 76

m. Sanhedrin
- 10:1 — 370

m. Yadayim
- 4:6 — 370

Pesiqta Rabbati
- 26 — 358

Pirqei deRabbi Eliezer — 192, 194

Qillir — 358, 374

Sar Panim — 521

Sefer Eliyyahu — 443, 466

Sefer Yetsirah — 191, 192

Sefer Zerubbabel — 365

Tanna debe Eliyahu — 367

Targum Neofiti on Deut 32:17 — 247

y. Berakot
- 4.4 — 372

y. Megillah
- 4:11 — 372

y. Moed Qatan
- 2:3 — 372

y. Sanhedrin
- 10:1 — 370–72

y. Sotah
- 5:3 — 372

Ancient Sources Index

Classical Greek and Latin Texts

Aelius Aristides, *Sacred Tales*   309

Berossus (*apud* Eusebius and Syncellus)
   217–18

Cicero, *De divinatione*
   1.19   218

Charaemon
   2   218

Damascius, *Commentary on the Phaedrus*
   105   520

Diodorus Siculus, *Bibliotheca Historica*
   1.16.1   218
   1.28.1–3   219
   1.81.6   218

Epicurus, *Letter to Pythocles*   372

Gaius Marius Victorinus, *Adversus Arium*   526

Herodotus, *Histories*
   4.87   207

Homer, *Iliad*   169

Iamblichus, *De anima*
   6–7   520
   50   526

Iamblichus, *De mysteriis Aegyptiorum*
   2.11   521

Manetho (*apud* Eusebius and Syncellus)
   217

Philo of Byblos   217

Plutarch, *Isis and Osiris*
   369e   267–68, 271
   370a   268
   370b–c   268
   370b   268

Plotinus, *Enneads*
   2.9 [33]   513, 524, 531, 533, 535
   2.9.11.28–29   528
   2.9.12.1–5   524
   2.9.12.6–9   524
   2.9.12.9–12   524
   2.9.12.12–21   528
   2.9.18.36–37   524

Porphyry, *Letter to Anebo*   520

Porphyry, *Vita Plotini*
   16   503, 513, 520, 533

Theopompus (*apud* Plutarch, *Isis and Osiris*)   267–68

Thucydides, *History of the Peloponnesian War*   207

Turin Commentary on Plato's *Parmenides*
   526, 535

Virgil, *Aeneid*   161

Other Texts

Assur Ostracon (KAI 233)   205, 226

Ashoka Edict (Kandahar; KAI 279)   205

Ashoka Edict (Taxila; KAI 273)   205

Avesta   257, 275

Barates   205

Cuneiform Tablets
   BagM. Beih. 2 no. 98   438
   BM 92687   438

Dante, *Divine Comedy*   493

Deir-Bala'izah Papyrus   477

Demotic Chronicle   395, 401

Enūma Anu Enlil   214

Gilgamesh   48, 215, 227
   2.32–34 (Old Babylonian)   284

Khirbet Ostracon 1   346–47, 353

Mani Codex   463, 465

Maresha Bowls
   A   209, 226
   B   209, 226

Oxyrhynchus Papyri
   1.5   477

Tel Dan (KAI 310)   222

Tel Fekheriye (KAI 309)   204

Underworld Vision of an Assyrian Crown Prince   285

Vidēvdāt   265

Modern Authors Index

Abegg, Martin G.   43, 59, 247–48, 256
Abrams, Meyer Howard   159, 196
Abusch, Ra'anan   384, 399
Adler, William   471, 474, 476–77, 479, 495, 497, 499, 500
Agamben, Giorgio   398–99
Agostini, Domenico   258, 275
Akagi, Kai   422–23, 426
Alberti, Benjamin   392, 399
Alexander, Philip S.   91, 106, 145, 156, 175–76, 191, 195, 216, 224, 268, 275, 512, 518, 525, 529
Alkier, Stefan   409, 425
Allen, Garrick V.   23, 92, 107, 403, 410, 413–15, 419, 422–24, 426–27
Althaus, Paul   113
Andersen, F. I.   448, 464
Anderson, Jeff S.   167, 192
Andrews, Isolde   306, 322
Angel, Joseph   384, 400
Angulo, Giancarlo   199
Anquetil-Duperron, Abraham-Hyacinthe   257, 275
Applegate, John   322
Arbel, Vita Daphna   510, 529
Arcari, Luca   7, 28
Ariel, Chanan   135, 140
Armstrong, Arthur H.   524, 533
Ashton, John F.   22, 29, 72–77, 80, 409, 424
Asmis, Elizabeth   371–73
Atkinson, Kenneth   333, 352
Attridge, Derek   168, 193
Attridge, Harold W.   477, 499, 511, 523, 529

Aune, David A.   7, 28, 405–6, 422
Avrahami, Yael   308, 323
Baden, Joel   118, 127, 267, 278, 440, 465
Baek, Kyung S.   44, 55
Baillet, Maurice   368, 373
Barc, Bernard   514, 535
Bardakjian, Kevork B.   357, 373
Barkow, Jerome   307, 325
Barr, David L.   7, 30, 421, 426
Barr, James   130, 140, 264, 269, 275, 449, 464
Barrera, Julio Trebolle C.   44, 56
Barry, Catherine   515, 529
Barton, J. M. T.   453, 464
Barton, Stephen C.   75, 81
Batovici, Dan   477, 495
Bauckham, Richard   97, 107, 405, 422, 450–51, 464
Baumgarten, Albert I.   345, 350
Baumgarten, Joseph M.   248, 255
Baynes, Leslie   184, 192
Bazzana, Giovanni B.   21, 378, 380, 393–95, 397, 400
Beale, Gregory K.   403, 415, 422
Beard, Mary   205, 224
Becker, Michael   38, 56, 329, 351
Bell, Alice   301, 323
Ben-Dov, Jonathan   138, 140, 199, 203–5, 210–15, 222–24, 248, 253, 436, 468
Ben Zvi, Ehud   261, 275
Benjamin, Walter   54
Bentley, G. E., Jr.   68, 80
Berger, Klaus   407, 422
Bergren, Theodore A.   91, 107, 479, 495

Modern Authors Index

Berlin, Adele 336, 351
Bernasconi, Rocco 175–76, 191–92, 195
Bernstein, Moshe J. 248, 255
Berthelot, Katell 12, 29, 36–37, 56–57, 148, 155, 200, 204, 208, 210, 225–27, 404–5, 407, 410, 414, 422–25, 427
Betcher, Sharon 499
Bevan, Anthony Ashley 43, 54
Beyer, Klaus 199, 204–5, 208, 225, 236–37, 239–40, 246–47, 253
Beyerle, Stefan 115–16, 119–20, 124
Bidawid, R. J. 289, 291, 294
Bilde, Per 26, 28, 88, 107
Black, Matthew 9, 30, 35, 58, 93, 109, 201, 229, 233, 253, 286, 294, 429, 467, 478, 499
Blake, William 69, 80
Bledsoe, Amanda M. Davis 441, 464
Blount, Justine Ariel 476, 498
Boccaccini, Gabriele 2, 30, 92–93, 103, 108, 110, 115, 126, 161–62, 164, 166–67, 171, 192, 194–95, 201, 228, 305, 328, 447, 464, 466, 506, 533
Boccard, P. de 513, 533
Bockmuehl, Marcus 91, 107
Bogaert, Pierre-Maurice 419, 423
Böklen, Ernst 265, 276
Bonacossi, Daniele Morandi 228
Bons, Eberhard 414, 426
Borenstein, Elhanan 315, 323
Bormann, Lukas 523, 529
Bosson, N. 516, 534
Böttrich, Christfried 447, 464
Boud'hors, Anne 516, 534
Bourdieu, Pierre 333, 343, 350
Boustan, Raʿanan 359, 373, 505, 510, 529, 533
Bowersock, Glen W. 268, 276
Bowker, John W. 62, 80
Boyarin, Daniel 503, 506, 529
Boyce, Mary 271–72, 276
Boyd, James W. 271, 276
Boyer, L. Bryce 299, 326
Boyer, Pascal 302, 323
Brakke, David 503–4, 528–29, 532

Bremmer, Jan N. 97, 107, 109, 242, 254, 452, 467, 485, 493, 496
Brian, Kathleen M. 475, 498
Briggs, Charles A. 285
Brooke, George J. 43, 46, 49, 54–55, 59, 116, 124, 212, 230, 235, 253, 336, 340, 350–51, 383, 401, 406, 414, 423–24
Broshi, Magen 42–43, 54
Brown, Francis 285
Brown, Jeremy 503
Brownlee, William Hugh 322, 324
Bruce, Frederick F. 233, 253
Buckley, Emma 480, 499
Bundvad, Mette 12, 28, 203, 228, 252, 254
Burkitt, Crawford 8, 117, 127–28
Burns, Dylan M. 26–28, 503, 508, 511, 513–14, 525, 528–30
Callegher, Bruno 345, 350
Caracciolo, Marco 17, 301, 307, 309, 323, 325
Carey, Greg 88, 92, 107
Carmignac, Jean 35, 53, 55, 88, 107, 129, 140,
Carnevale, Laura 308, 324
Carozzi, Claude 97, 107
Carr, David M. 165, 192
Carruthers, Mary 64, 80
Cerrato, J. A. 489, 496
Chabot, J. B. 290, 294
Charles, Robert H. 8, 28, 183, 192, 453, 464
Charlesworth, James H. 121, 125–26, 130, 138, 140–41, 234, 255, 381, 385, 398, 400, 404, 423, 478, 500
Chazon, Esther G. 137, 141, 164, 193, 334, 336, 350, 354
Chipman, Jonathan 335, 353
Cioată, Maria 116, 124, 212, 230, 336, 350, 407, 424
Clements, Ruth 137, 141
Coblentz Bautch, Kelley N. 340, 355
Cohen, Shaye J. D. 506, 530
Cohn, Norman 19, 28, 86, 107
Coleridge, Samuel Taylor 68–70, 80

Modern Authors Index

Collins, John J.   2–7, 10, 14–15, 18, 25–30, 35–37, 40, 42–43, 46–47, 52–53, 55–58, 66, 80, 87–90, 93, 96, 101–2, 105, 107–8, 110–20, 122–25, 127, 129–30, 132–33, 140, 144, 148, 155, 157–59, 164–66, 168, 172, 178, 188, 190, 193–94, 199, 201, 225, 229, 234–35, 237–39, 241, 243, 246–47, 250–51, 253–56, 264, 267, 273, 276–78, 297, 306, 317, 323–24, 329, 336–37, 345, 350–51, 364–65, 373, 380–81, 398, 400, 402, 405, 414, 420–21, 423, 428, 429–30, 440, 444–45, 465, 467, 469, 472, 477, 485, 496, 499, 509, 512, 530
Collins, Matthew A.   342, 350
Coloe, Mary L.   73, 80, 404, 423
Conrad, Markus   315, 325
Conway-Jones, Ann   491–92, 496
Cook, Edward M.   43, 59, 200, 213, 225, 246–48, 253, 256, 413–14, 423
Cook, Stephen L.   479, 496
Copeland, Kristi B.   97, 107, 450, 465
Corbin, Henry   508, 536
Cordoni, Constanza   170, 195
Corrigan, Kevin   507, 513, 530, 533
Corsani, Bruno   420, 423
Cosmides, Leda   307, 325
Covolo, Enrico dal   484, 496
Craig, A. D.   311, 323
Crawford, Sidnie White   5, 29, 42, 58, 111–12, 115, 117, 125, 127–28, 199, 229, 252, 254
Crenshaw, James L.   261, 276
Crosby, Donald A.   271, 276
Cross, Frank Moore   8, 30, 64, 82–83, 85, 110, 114, 124, 129, 140, 167, 196,
Crossan, John D.   387, 400
Crown, Alan D.   243, 253
Cuddon, John Anthony   159, 193
Curtis, Adrian H. W.   322
Czachesz, István   97, 107, 109
Dahmen, Ulrich   341, 351
Dalman, Gustaf   389, 393, 400
Daley, Brian E.   471, 486, 488, 490, 496

Daly, Robert J.   471, 475, 481–82, 488, 491, 496–99
Daly-Denton, Margaret   264–65, 278
Dan, Joseph   359, 374
Danielou, Jean   478, 483, 496
Daum, Robert A.   499
Davies, James P.   92, 107
Davies, Philip R.   151, 156
Davies, W. D.   87, 110, 263, 279
Davila, James R.   384, 399, 406, 423, 443–44, 465, 510, 518, 523, 530
Davis, C. J. Patrick   44, 55
Davis, Kipp   44–45, 56
Day, John   414, 423
DeConick, April   491, 496, 510, 518, 524, 530, 536
Dedering, S.   291, 294
Delcor, Mathias   242, 255
Deleuze, Gilles   25, 474, 497
Del Tredici, Kelly   523, 529
Derrida, Jacques   168–69, 193
Deutsch, Nathanael   506, 516, 530
Dietrich, Manfried   206, 225
Digeser, Elizabeth DePalma   485, 497
Dijkstra, Jitse H. F.   242, 254
Dillery, John D.   217, 225
Dillmann, August   67, 80
Dimant, Devorah   6, 10–11, 36–37, 44–45, 51, 56, 117, 125, 131, 135–37, 139–41, 177, 193, 200–2, 204, 210, 225, 336, 350, 360, 373, 405, 407, 409, 415, 423, 425
Dinter, Martin T.   480, 499
DiTommaso, Lorenzo   3, 9, 18, 22–25, 28–29, 36, 48–49, 56, 87, 99, 101, 103–04, 106, 108, 111–12, 115, 118–19, 125, 131, 141, 161, 193, 237–38, 251, 253, 265, 276, 318–19, 323, 326, 334, 337, 351, 354, 357, 373, 405, 409, 422, 424, 432, 434, 465, 472, 476, 478, 495, 497, 499, 503
Dixon, Sarah Underwood   410, 419, 424
Dodd, Charles Harold   116, 125
Dohrmann, Natalie   321, 326
Doubinsky, Claude   145, 155

Drawnel, Henryk 9, 29, 93–94, 108, 201, 206–7, 214, 226, 409, 424, 432, 437–38, 465
Drecoll, Volker Henning 507, 530
Driver, Samuel R. 285
Dubois, Jean-Daniel 526, 535
Duhaime, Jean 45, 55, 121, 125
Duke, Dennis 214, 227
Dušek, Jan 207, 209, 226
Easterlin, Nancy 302, 307, 323
Ego, Beate 391, 400
Eisenman, Robert 236, 240, 256
Eliade, Mircea 508, 536
Elgvin, Torleif 368, 373, 406, 424
Eliav, Yaron Z. 259, 278
Elior, Rachel 359, 374
Elledge, Casey 94, 96, 108
Ellens, J. Harold 506, 533
Ellis, E. Earle 233, 253
Elwolde, John 340–41, 351
Endres, S. J., John C. 340, 355
Engberg-Pedersen, Troels 217, 224
Epstein, Isidore 505, 530
Erdmann, Martin 483, 497
Erho, Ted M. 264, 276, 445, 465
Eshel, Esther 42–43, 49, 54, 57, 209, 226, 432–33, 459, 465
Esler, Philip F. 270, 276
Evans, Craig A. 322, 324
Fabry, Heinz-Josef 341, 351
Fales, Frederick Mario 205–7, 226, 228
Falk, Daniel K. 41, 57, 335, 351–52, 368, 373
Fassberg, Steven E. 208, 210, 226
Feldman, Ariel 116, 124, 212, 230, 336, 350, 407, 424
Feldt, Laura 303–4, 324
Ferber, Michael 68, 80
Fidanzio, Marcello 345, 350
Fineman, Joel 508, 525, 530
Finkelstein, Louis 263, 279
Fiori, Emiliano 98, 108, 476, 497
Firby, Nora Kathleen 257, 276
Fishbane, Michael 114, 125, 321, 324, 445, 469

Fitzmyer, Joseph A. 208, 211, 226, 236, 239, 246, 254, 413–14, 424
Fitzpatrick-McKinley, Anne 265, 269, 276, 278
Flannery[-Dailey], Frances 6, 17, 53, 56, 62, 80, 281–83, 285, 289, 290, 293, 294
Fletcher, Michelle 90, 108, 419, 421, 424
Fletcher-Louis, Crispin H. T. 92, 108, 384, 400, 517, 525, 530
Flexsenhar, Michael 18, 28, 104, 108
Flint, Peter W. 2, 29, 37, 44, 46, 55, 114, 124, 213, 225, 234–35, 237–39, 241, 243, 246–47, 250–51, 253–55, 317, 324, 422, 443, 465
Flusser, David 414, 424
Folmer, Margaretha L. 204, 227
Fowler, Alastair 168, 193
Fox, Michael V. 5, 30, 52, 58, 113, 126, 168, 194, 430, 467
Frank, Georgia 475, 497
Frankfurter, David 463, 465, 471, 473–74, 487–88, 497
Fredriksen, Paula 479, 489, 497
Freedman, David Noel 242, 255, 382, 401
Frey, Jörg 38, 45, 49–51, 56, 115, 124, 148, 155, 267, 276, 329, 351, 407–8, 421, 424, 427
Freyne, Seán 264, 278
Friebel, Kelvin G. 5, 30, 52, 58, 113, 126, 194, 430, 467
Friesen, Steven J. 18, 104, 108, 345, 354
Frow, John 160, 193
Frye, Richard N. 264, 276
Funk, Wolf-Peter 518–20, 524, 529–30, 535
Gäckle, Volker 380, 387, 400
Gadamer, Hans-Georg 79, 81
Gallese, Vittorio 316, 324
Gammie, John G. 382, 401
García Martínez, Florentino 12, 29, 36–37, 43, 48–49, 55–57, 59, 73–74, 81, 200, 202, 225, 227, 236, 240, 242, 246–48, 254–55, 267, 276, 286–89, 294, 330, 347, 354, 368, 373, 404,

García Martínez, Florentino (cont.) 406–8, 414–15, 424–25, 427, 435–37, 442, 465, 468, 505, 532
Gardner, Gregg 347, 351
Gardner, Iain 96, 109
Gaylord, Harry E., Jr. 449, 465
Geertz, Armin W. 308, 324
Genette, Gérard 144–45, 155, 160, 168, 193
Gertz, Sebastian R. P. 513, 524, 528, 531
Gillihan, Yonder Moynihan 346, 351
Ginzberg, Louis 358, 374
Giorgi, Dieter 523, 529
Glass, R. Gillian 329
Godrej, Pheroza J. 258, 279
Goehring, James E. 516, 523, 531
Goff, Matthew 5, 13, 29, 38, 111, 125, 130, 214–15, 218, 227, 286, 295, 337–38, 342, 351, 402, 430, 440–41, 464–65, 508, 525, 530
Goldman, Liora 50, 57, 407–8, 411, 425
Golitzin, Alexander 491–92, 497, 500
Goodman, Martin 191, 195
Goshen-Gottstein, Alon 505–6, 531
Gosling, Frank A. 119, 125
Grabbe, Lester L. 115, 126, 167, 194, 201, 228, 321, 324
Grant, Robert M. 508, 531
Grassi, Giulia Francesca 206, 226
Graetz, Heinrich 505
Greenfield, Jonas C. 49, 57, 59, 209, 227, 432–33, 459, 465
Grelot, Pierre 321, 324
Gronick, Simon A. 299, 326
Griggs, Earl Leslie 68, 80
Gruenwald, Ithamar 178, 194, 506, 511–12, 518, 528, 531
Guattari, Félix 25, 474, 497
Gunkel, Hermann 18, 30
Gunneweg, Jan 345, 352
Gurtner, Daniel M. 122, 126
Gzella, Holger 204–8, 213, 227, 270, 276
Hadot, Pierre 513, 533
Hagen, Joost L. 447, 466
Halperin, David 63, 81

Halpern, Baruch 242, 255, 382, 401
Hamidović, David 384, 400, 441–42, 466
Hanneken, Todd 90, 109
Hanson, John S. 285, 294
Hanson, Paul D. 65, 81, 167, 194, 479, 497
Harding, Anthony J. 69, 81
Harkins, Angela Kim 6, 17–18, 122, 125, 299–300, 309, 314, 320–22, 324, 331–32, 335, 339–41, 351, 355
Harlow, Daniel C. 337, 351, 398, 402
Harrington, Daniel J. 236, 239, 246, 254
Harrisville, Roy A. 380, 400
Hartman, Louis F. 115, 125
Hasselbalch, Trine Bjørnung 123, 125, 332, 343, 352
Haubold, Johannes 217, 227
Hayward, Robert 175–76, 191, 195
Hefferman, Thomas J. 310, 324
Heger, Paul 267, 269, 272, 277
Hellholm, David 9, 29, 35, 53, 55, 58, 65–66, 81, 88, 107, 119, 127, 129, 142, 297, 324
Hemingway, Ernest 315
Hempel, Charlotte 116, 124, 212, 230, 234, 251, 254, 267, 277, 336, 345, 350, 353, 407, 424
Hendel, Ronald 211, 227
Hengel, Martin 68, 81, 265, 278, 385, 402, 507, 530
Hennecke, Edgar 68, 83, 479, 500
Henning, Meghan 98, 109, 474, 482, 485, 493, 497
Henze, Matthias 103, 108, 476, 499
Hermes, Ronald 418–19, 425
Herrmann, John 482, 498
Herrmann, Klaus 528, 531
Hezser, Catherine 371, 374
Hieke, Thomas 425
Hilhorst, Anthony 37, 48, 56, 59, 97, 109, 200, 225, 347, 354, 435, 468, 505, 532
Hill, Charles E. 471, 473, 482–84, 486, 488, 498
Himmelfarb, Martha 6, 24–25, 29, 430–31, 438, 443, 446, 448–52, 456,

Himmelfarb, Martha (cont.)
460–61, 463, 466, 493, 498, 505, 511, 518, 523, 531, 533
Hinnells, John R. 260, 277
Hirsch, Helen 316, 324
Hjelde, Sigurd 113, 125
Hobsbawm, Eric 19, 29
Hoeck, Annewies van den 482, 498
Hogan, Karina Martin 342, 351, 402
Hollander, Harm W. 459, 466
Holmén, Tom 92, 109, 377, 401
Holum, Kenneth G. 443, 466
Honkela, Timo 302, 326
Hoover, Jesse A. 481, 489, 498
Horbury, William 87, 110
Horgan, Mauyra P. 121, 125
Horowitz, Wayne 438, 466
Horsley, Richard A. 329, 352
Horst, Pieter van der 218, 227
Hsu, Chun-Ting 315, 325
Hübner, Ulrich 270, 276
Hughes, Julie 341, 352
Hultgård, Anders 266, 278
Humbert, Jean-Baptiste 345, 352
Hume, David 172, 194
Hyde, Thomas 257, 277
Ibba, Giovanni 161, 192
Idel, Moshe 503, 518, 521, 531
Iricinschi, Eduard 517, 535
Jackson, Howard 519, 531
Jackson, Virginia 160, 193
Jacobs, Arthur M. 315, 325
Janzen, David 258, 277
Jassen, Alex P. 121–22, 126, 322, 325
Jauhiainen, Marco 406, 425
Jenott, Lance 476, 499, 507, 532, 535
Jensen, Jeppe Sinding 261, 280
Jeppesen, Knud 26, 28, 89, 107
Johnson, Janet H. 395, 401
Johnson, Nathan C. 414, 425
Johnston, Sarah Iles 320, 325
Jokiranta, Jutta 257, 273, 277, 330, 352
Jolin, Annette 329, 353
Jong, Albert de 264, 267, 271, 277
Jonge, Marinus de 50, 57, 457–59, 466

Jurgens, Blake 199, 408, 425
Jursa, Michael 206, 227
Kallas, James 420, 425
Kaminsky, Joel S. 351, 402
Kampen, John 248, 255
Kanagaraj, Jey 77, 81
Kannengiesser, Charles 319, 326
Kaplan, Stephen 307, 325
Kalligas, Paul 513, 531
Karmann, Thomas R. 452, 467
Karrer, Martin 420–21, 425
Kautsky, John H. 261, 277
Kautzsch, Emil 8, 29
Keddie, Anthony 18, 20, 28, 104, 108, 333, 339, 345, 352
Keim, Katharina E. 192, 194
Kelhoffer, James A. 421, 427
Kerchove, Anna van den 526, 535
Khan, Geoffrey 205, 228
Kiel, Yishai 258, 277
King, Karen 504, 532
Kirschner, Robert 357, 374
Kister, Menahem 137–38, 141, 478, 498
Kloner, Amos 209, 226
Kloppenborg, John S. 387, 401
Knibb, Michael A. 117, 126, 170, 184, 194, 452, 466
Knight, Jonathan 452, 467
Knight, Mark 79, 81
Kobelski, Paul J. 50, 57
Koester, Craig R. 104, 109, 421, 426
Kohn, Eduardo 392, 401
Kohut, George A. 370, 374
Koller, Aaron 209, 213, 228
Korzybski, Alfred 87, 109
Kosmin, Paul 297, 325, 390, 401
Kraemer, Joel L. 522, 536
Kratz, Reinhard G. 407, 413–17, 425–26
Kroesen, Justin 242, 254
Krueger, Derek 475, 498
Kugler, Robert A. 115, 127, 149, 156, 235, 256, 432–33, 467
Kuhn, Heinz-Wolfgang 116, 126
Kuhn, K. H. 460–61, 467
Kuhrt, Amélie 264, 279

Modern Authors Index

Kuiper, Yme 242, 254
Kukkonen, Karin 307, 309, 325
Kulik, Alexander 85, 90, 109, 119, 126, 449, 451, 455–56, 467
Kuzmičová, Anežka 17, 298, 309–10, 315, 325
Kvanvig, Helge S. 214–15, 228
Laato, Antti 322, 325, 406, 425
Lachmann, Renata 303, 325
Lahe, Jan 505, 507–8, 532
Lambrecht, Jan 420–21, 423, 427
Lampe, Peter 484
Landes, Richard 480, 488, 498
Lanfranchi, Giovanni B. 207, 227–28
Lange, Armin 6, 11, 38–40, 42, 47–48, 50–51, 57, 143, 145–46, 148–50, 153, 156, 166, 194, 210, 228, 245, 247, 254, 329, 336, 342, 351–52
Langer, Gerhard 170, 195
Langermann, Y. Tzvi 522, 536
Lapin, Hayim 443, 466
La Porta, Sergio 357, 373
Larson, Erik W. 449, 467
Laurence, Richard 67, 81
Layton, Bentley 506, 508, 512, 530–31, 534–36
Lazier, Benjamin 508, 532
Lemaire, André 345, 352
Leicht, Reimund 528, 532
Lemke, Werner E. 8, 30, 64, 83, 85, 110, 196
Lenzi, Alan 261, 275
Leopold, Anita M. 260, 280
Lerberghe Karel van 206, 229
Lerner, Jeffrey D. 264, 277
Leroy, Christine 335, 352
Lévi, Israel 365, 374
Leuchter, Mark 270, 277
Lewin, Jane E. 145, 156, 160, 193
Lewis, Nicola Denzey 476, 498, 535
Lewy, Hans 522
Lieb, Michael 79, 81
Lieberman, Saul 370, 374
Lied, Liv Ingeborg 475–76, 498–99
Lieu, Samuel Nan-Chiang 96–97, 109

Light, Timothy 260–61, 277
Lim, Timothy H. 264, 273, 277
Lindeman, Marjaana 302, 326
Linton, Gregory L. 7, 30, 421–22, 426
Logan, Alistair H. B. 508, 532
Lohfink, Norbert 337, 352
Longenecker, Bruce W. 75, 81
Looijer, Gwynned de 267, 272, 277
Love, Glen A. 307, 325
Lücke, Friedrich 65, 81, 144, 156
Luhrmann, Tanya M. 320, 325
Lundhaug, Hugo 475–76, 499, 507, 532
Luomanen, Petri 512, 536
Luttikhuizen, Gerald 505, 525–26, 532
Luukko, Mikko 206, 228
Luz, Ulrich 75, 81
Macaskill, Grant 68, 81
MacDermot, Violet 519, 534
Machiela, Daniel A. 41–42, 57, 115, 122, 126, 199–203, 209, 212–13, 228, 243, 252, 254, 440, 467
Magary, Dennis Robert 5, 30, 52, 58, 113, 126, 194, 430, 467
Magen, Yitzhak 209, 229
Magness, Jodi 347–48, 353
Maier, Johann 453, 467, 518, 532
Maier, Harry O. 25–26, 480, 488, 499
Maloney, Linda M. 473, 499
Mansfield, Nick 331, 353
Marchand, Suzanne L. 257, 278
Marcus, Joel 390, 397, 401
Marjanen, Antti 512, 536
Markus, Robert A. 489, 499
Markschies, Christoph 112, 126, 504, 509–10, 518, 525, 528, 531–32
Marlow, Hilary 3, 29, 106, 108
Marshall, John W. 387, 401
Martin, James D. 151, 156
Martin, Leonard L. 299, 325
Marwick, Arthur 161, 194
Marx, Karl 329, 353
Massumi, Brian 474, 497
Mathews, Mark D. 337, 353
Mattila, Raija 206, 228
Mason, Eric F. 37, 55

Mazur, Zeke 513, 532
Mazzaferri, Frederick David 420, 426
Mazzucco, Clementina 483, 499
McAllister, Colin 24, 26, 28–29, 511, 529
McCants, William F. 217, 229
McCloud, Sean 333, 353
McDonald, Lee Martin 478, 500
McGinn, Bernard 20, 30, 72, 81, 471, 488, 496, 499, 504, 532
McLay, Timothy 191, 195
McNamara, Patrick 299, 325
Meier, John P. 386–87, 394, 401
Merkur, Daniel 299, 326
Mermelstein, Ari 320, 326
Mertens, Alfred 236, 254
Metso, Sarianna 215, 230, 352
Meyer, Anthony 247–48, 254
Meyer, Nicholas A. 336, 342, 353
Meyer, Rudolf 236, 255
Miall, David S. 309, 326
Milik, Józef T. 9, 30, 35, 43–44, 46, 58, 93, 109, 201, 213, 229, 236, 239, 241, 243, 246, 250, 255, 286–87, 292, 294, 406, 426, 429, 467, 478, 499
Miller, Patrick D. 8, 30, 64, 83, 85, 110, 196
Miller, Shem 335, 344, 353
Mimouni, Simon Claude 191–92, 384, 400
Mistree, Firoza Punthakey 258, 279
Mittmann, Siegfried 265, 278
Mittmann-Richert, Ulrike 38–39, 42, 47–48, 50–51, 57, 143, 146, 148–49, 156
Misgav, Haggai 209, 229
Mizrahi, Noam 414, 426
Mizzi, Dennis J. 345, 353
Momigliano, Arnaldo 207, 229
Monger, Matthew 475, 498
Montaner, Luis Vega 44, 56
Morano, Enrico 286, 295, 441, 464
Moore, Carey A. 211, 229
Morray-Jones, Christopher R. A. 62–63, 82, 512, 517, 532
Moss, Candida R. 498

Moyer, Ian S. 269, 278
Müller, Ulrich B. 306, 326, 419, 426
Müller-Luckner, Elisabeth 525, 534
Muntz, Charles 219, 229
Münz-Manor, Ophir 321, 326
Muraoka, Takamitsu 200, 229
Murphy, Catherine M. 337–38, 341, 345–46, 348, 353
Murphy, Frederick James 112, 126
Nagel, Peter 512, 534
Najman, Hindy 52, 54, 58, 118, 127, 215, 230, 267, 278, 357, 374, 383, 401, 430, 440, 465, 467
Napiorkowska, Lidia 205, 228
Narbonne, Jean-Marc 513, 532
Närhi, Jani 301, 326
Naveh, Joseph 207–8, 229
Nelson, Robert S. 282, 295
Nelstrop, Louise 504, 532
Newman, Channa 145, 155
Newman, Judith H. 383, 396–97, 401
Neujahr, Matthew 206, 214–15, 229
Neusner, Jacob 264, 268, 278
Newsom, Carol A. 5, 7, 30, 52, 58, 113, 116, 118, 122, 126–27, 138, 141, 162, 168, 187, 190, 194, 242, 251, 255, 318, 326, 331–32, 334–35, 342–44, 353–54, 381–82, 385, 391, 398, 400–1, 430, 467, 525, 532
Nevader, Madhavi 422–23, 426
Nickelsburg, George W. E. 64, 81, 93–94, 97, 100, 109–10, 119, 121, 126, 178, 184, 194, 216, 229, 291–92, 294, 306, 311, 323, 326, 339, 353, 435–39, 444–46, 449, 467, 477, 499
Nicklas, Tobias 131, 141, 425, 452, 467, 474, 498
Nidditch, Peter H. 172, 194
Niederwimmer, Kurt 473, 499
Nielsen, Kirsten 26, 28, 89, 107
Niehr, Herbert 270, 276
Niskanen, Paul 264, 278
Nissinen, Martti 257
Nitzan, Bilhah 335, 353, 525, 536
Noë, Alva 301, 326

Modern Authors Index

Noort, Edward 43, 55
Norich, Anita 259, 278
Novick, Tzvi 358, 374
Odeberg, Hugo 62, 82
Oegema, Gerbern S. 106, 108, 111, 125
O'Leary, Stephen D. 330, 353
O'Malley, Joseph 329, 353
Oort, J. van 510, 528, 531, 533
Oppenheim, Leo 39, 58, 281–84, 294
Orlov, Andrei 92, 108, 447, 456–57, 464, 466–67, 492, 500, 506, 511, 528, 532
Overman, J. Andrew 264–65, 278
Pace, Alessandra 316, 324
Pagels, Elaine 517, 535
Pajunen, Mika S. 300, 324
Pappi, Cinzia 228
Parin, Paul 299, 326
Parpola, Simo 206, 228
Parry, Donald W. 248, 255, 352, 433, 469
Paul, Ian 406, 419, 424, 427
Paul, Shalom 209, 227
Pearce, L. E. 206, 229
Pearson, Birger A. 505–7, 516, 518, 530–31, 533, 536
Pelikan, Jaroslav 484, 500
Penner, Jeremy 54, 58, 300, 324
Penner, Ken M. 117, 126
Pennington, A. 283, 294
Perdue, Leo G. 382, 401
Perrin, Andrew B. 12, 14, 30, 39, 40, 42, 49–50, 53, 58, 199–202, 229, 239, 255, 285, 295, 404, 406, 408–9, 411, 426, 431–32, 434–35, 441–42, 468
Petersen, Anders Klostergaard 391, 402, 406, 427
Peterson, Erik 398
Pfann, Stephen J. 42, 54, 437, 469
Philonenko, Marc 265–66, 278
Pillinger, Renate 145, 156
Pinnick, Avital 227
Piovanelli, Pierluigi 97, 109, 450, 468
Plietzsch, Susanna 503
Plöger, Otto 65, 82
Poirer, John C. 397, 401

Poirier, Paul-Hubert 513, 515, 518–20, 524, 529–30, 533, 535
Pollmann, Karla 3, 29, 106, 108
Polotsky, Hans J. 522
Ponchia, Simonetta 228
Poorthuis, Marcel 506, 531
Porten, Bezalel 209, 230, 269, 278
Popović, Mladen 52, 58, 199, 212, 215, 229, 231, 245, 256, 258, 267, 278–79, 430, 467
Porter, Stanley E. 92, 109, 377, 401
Portier-Young, Anathea 210, 216, 230, 479, 500
Pouchelle, Patrick 333, 352
Preston, Claire E. 159, 193
Prete, S. 480, 500
Prins, Yopie 160, 193
Propp, William H. 242, 255, 382, 401
Puech, Émile 37, 47–48, 50, 58–59, 116–17, 126, 200, 209–10, 225–26, 230, 286–88, 290, 295, 347, 353–54, 398, 406, 412–14, 426, 435, 438, 468, 505, 532
Puig i Tàrrech, Armand 131, 141
Pyysiäinen, Ilkka 302, 326
Qimron, Elisha 135, 138, 140–41
Quispel, Gilles 510, 533
Ramble, Charles 302, 323
Raphael, Rebecca 118–19, 127
Rasimus, Tuomas 507, 512–13, 530, 533
Ratzon, Eshbal 433, 468
Reed, Annette Yoshiko 10, 30, 158, 166, 181, 192, 194, 203, 212, 215–18, 220, 223, 230, 319, 321, 326, 477, 500, 505, 511, 522, 533
Reeves, John C. 463, 468
Regev, Eyal 330, 348, 354
Reiner, Erica 270, 280
Rey, Jean-Sébastien 404, 427
Reymond, Eric 398, 401
Reynolds, Benjamin E. 75, 82, 87, 91, 109–10
Reynolds, Bennie H. 6, 11, 38–42, 44–47, 58, 112, 127, 143, 156
Reynolds, Jeremy R. 327

Ro, Johannes Un-Sok 337–38, 343, 354
Roark, Kyle 216, 230
Robinson, James M. 516, 523, 531
Robinson, Jenefer 309, 326
Rochberg[-Halton], Francesca 185, 195, 270, 280
Rodgers, Zuleika 264, 278
Roitman, Adolfo Daniel 212, 231, 248, 253, 314, 327
Rollens, Sarah E. 395, 402
Rollinger, Robert 227
Römer, Thomas 322
Ronell, Avital 168, 193
Rosendal, Bent 26, 28, 89, 107
Rowe, Eric 478, 500
Rowland, Christopher 7–10, 22, 25, 27, 29–30, 62, 68, 75, 77, 82–83, 87, 89–92, 110, 409, 424, 456, 468, 471–72, 500
Rubin, Benjamin B. 265, 279
Rubinkiewicz, R. 455–56, 468
Rudman, S. 65, 82
Ruiten, J. van 406, 425
Ruppin, Eytan 315, 323
Rupschus, Nicole 114, 127
Ruzer, Serge 404, 427
Ryan, Marie-Laure 298, 301, 315, 323, 326
Ryan, Sean Michael 410, 419, 427
Saldarini, Anthony J. 357–58, 374
Samely, Alexander 170, 175–76, 178, 182, 191, 195
Sanders, Seth L. 204, 206–7, 214–15, 221–22, 230, 261, 270, 278, 285, 295, 436, 468
Santoprete, L. Gabriela Soares 526, 535
Satlow, Michael L. 259, 278
Satybaldieva, Elmira 333, 354
Scarry, Elaine 302, 327
Schacter, Jacob 371, 374
Schäfer, Peter 63, 82, 359, 374, 504–6, 509–11, 517, 521, 525, 533–34
Schattner-Rieser, Ursula 200, 230
Schechter, Solomon 2
Scheidel, Walter 345, 354
Schenke, Hans–Martin 512, 534
Schenke, Ludger 389, 402
Schiffman, Lawrence H. 49, 57, 200, 212, 231, 248, 253, 314, 327, 371, 374, 384
Schlude, Jason M. 265, 278–79
Schmid, Konrad 258, 279
Schmidt, Carl 519, 527, 534
Schmidt, Johann M. 67, 82
Schmidt, Thomas 513, 533
Schmitt, Carl 398
Schneemelcher, Wilhelm 68, 83, 86, 110, 479, 500
Schniedewind, William M. 201, 209, 230
Schofield, Alison 344–46, 354
Scholem, Gershom 62–63, 78, 82, 508–10, 512, 516, 518, 522, 534, 536
Schoonover, Myles 258, 279
Schremer, Adiel 506–7, 535
Schröter, Jens 131, 141
Schrottner, Elisabeth 329
Schuller, Eileen 116, 122, 127, 215, 230, 334–35, 354, 368, 373
Schulte, Lucas L. 258, 279
Schüssler Fiorenza, Elizabeth 421, 427
Schüssler Fiorenza, Francis 387, 402
Schwartz, Joshua 506, 531
Schwartz, Seth 297, 327
Schweitzer, Albert 62, 387
Schwemer, Anna Maria 265, 278, 385–89, 398, 402
Scopello, Madeleine 191–92, 384, 400, 514–15, 517, 534
Segal, Alan F. 75, 82, 506, 530, 535
Segal, Michael 101, 110, 381, 402, 414–15, 427
Segal, Robert A. 504, 532
Selby-Bigge, Lewis Amherst 172, 194
Seth, Anil K. 312, 327
Seyrig, Henri 345, 350
Shaffer, Elinor S. 70, 82
Shaked, Shaul 207–8, 229, 258, 263, 271, 279
Shamir, Orit 348, 354
Shantz, Colleen 75, 82

Modern Authors Index

Shaw, Gregory   518, 520, 524, 526, 530, 535–36
Sherwin-White, Susan   264, 279
Shrimpton, Gordon S.   268, 279
Shupak, Nili   137, 142
Siegismund, Kasper   12, 28, 203, 228, 252, 254
Sigvartsen, Jan A.   94, 97, 110
Silverman, Jason   15, 258–61, 263, 265–66, 268, 270–71, 274–75, 279–80, 319, 327
Sjöberg, Erik   306, 327
Skeggs, Beverley   332, 354
Skehan, Patrick   242, 255
Skinner, Quentin   171–72, 177, 196
Sloan, Paul   422–23, 426
Smith, Jonathan Z.   87, 110
Smith, Mark S.   312, 327
Sokoloff, Michael   213, 230
Sommer, Michael   425, 455, 468
Spanu, Nicola   513, 535
Sparks, H. F. D.   283, 294, 453, 460, 464, 467
Speer, Nicole K.   310, 327
Sperber, Daniel   370, 374
Spijkerman, Augustus   345, 350
Standhartinger, Angela   523, 529
Stanton, Graham N.   75, 81
Starr, G. Gabrielle   315, 327
Steele, John M.   227
Stegemann, Hartmut   35, 58, 116, 119, 122, 127, 129, 142, 242, 255, 334, 354
Stern, Jossi   522, 536
Steudel, Annette   414, 427
Stewart, Charles   388, 402
Stinespring, William F.   322, 324
Stokes, Ryan E.   133, 142, 441, 468
Stökl, Jonathan   261, 275
Stökl Ben Ezra, Daniel   2, 12, 29, 36–37, 56–57, 120, 127, 148, 155, 200, 204, 208, 210, 225–27, 404–5, 407, 410, 414, 423–25, 427
Stolper, Matthew W.   269–70, 280
Stone, Michael E.   8, 10, 22, 30, 49, 57, 59, 64–65, 68, 82, 85–86, 91, 103, 107,
Stone, Michael E. (cont.)
    110, 114, 127, 148, 155, 164, 167, 193, 196, 201, 227, 230, 283, 289, 295, 357, 362, 374, 432–33, 459, 465, 468, 476, 498–99
Strootman, Rolf   274, 280
Stroumsa, Guy S.   506, 535
Strugnell, John   35, 477, 499
Stuckenbruck, Loren T.   2, 30, 75, 82, 87, 91, 93, 109–10, 117, 127, 163–64, 178–79, 182, 196, 212, 230, 234, 247, 255, 286–87, 295, 311, 314, 327, 383, 401, 438–39, 441, 464, 468
Stuckrad, von Kocku   504, 532
Sturdy, John   87, 110
Sugandhi, Namita   205, 231
Sukenik, Naama   348, 354
Sulimani, Iris   218, 231
Svärd, Saana   206, 228, 257
Swallow, Khena M.   327
Swartz, Michael D.   320–21, 327, 523, 525, 535
Sweeney, Marvin A.   113, 127
Tabbernee, William   484, 500
Tabor, James D.   483, 500
Tagliabue, Aldo   308–9, 315, 327
Tanaseanu-Döbler, Ilinca   518, 521, 535
Tardieu, Michel   526, 535
Teeter, Andrew   245, 255
Tesser, Abraham   299, 325
Thackeray, H. St. J.   348, 352
Thatcher, Tom   73, 80, 404, 423
Thomas, Samuel   340, 354
Thompson, Robert   357, 373
Thraede, Klaus   217, 231
Thrupp, Sylvia L.   19, 30
Tigchelaar, Eibert J. C.   37, 44, 48, 57, 59, 73–74, 81, 118, 127, 137, 142, 199–200, 225, 231, 236, 245–47, 254–55, 267, 278, 286–89, 294, 347, 351–52, 354, 406–7, 425, 434–37, 440, 442, 465, 468, 505, 532
Tisserant, Eugène   290, 295
Tiwald, Markus   397, 400

Modern Authors Index

Tobin, Thomas H. 477, 499
Todd, Cain 320, 327
Tomson, Peter J. 76, 83
Too, Yun Lee 372–73
Tooby, John 307, 325
Toorn, Karel van der 261, 280
Tóth, Franz 421, 427
Townsend, Philippa 535
Tov, Emanuel 38, 57, 143, 156, 210, 228, 242, 244, 256, 342, 351
Trents, James W. 475, 498
Trever, John C. 233, 256
Tromp, Johannes 458, 469
Trotter, Jonathan R. 133, 142
Troxel, Ronald L. 5, 30, 52, 58, 113, 126, 168, 194, 430, 467
Tsfania, Levana 209, 229
Tuckett, C. M. 498
Turcescu, Lucian 319, 326
Turner, John Douglas 507, 513, 517–20, 524–26, 529–30, 533, 535–36
Turner, Joseph Aaron 506, 531
Twigg, Matthew 527, 535
Tzoref, Shani 212, 231, 248, 253, 314, 327
Uglione, Renato 471, 483, 499, 500
Ulfgard, Håkan 391, 402, 406, 427
Ulrich, Eugene 36, 56, 117, 126, 360, 373, 405, 423, 433, 469
Vandenberghe, Marijn 258, 279
VanderKam, James C. 2, 30, 36–37, 55–56, 93, 95, 97, 100–1, 110, 114–15, 117, 124, 126–27, 151, 156, 167, 178, 184, 194, 196, 213, 225, 235, 251–53, 256, 290, 295, 305–6, 328, 339, 353, 360, 373, 405, 422–23, 433, 435–40, 443, 445–46, 465, 467, 469, 471, 474, 477–79, 495, 497, 500
Van Noorden, Helen 3, 29, 106, 108
Vanni, Ugo 420, 427
Verbeke, Werner 480, 498
Verbrugghe, Gerald P. 218, 231
Verhelst, D. 480, 498
Verheyden, Joseph 433, 468, 498
Vermes, Géza 268, 275

Versluys, Miguel John 274, 280
Vessey, Mark 488, 499
Vielhauer, Philipp 68, 83, 86, 110, 479, 500
Villiers, Pieter G. R. de 18, 30
Voet, Gabriela 206, 229
Vroom, Hendrik M. 260, 280
Wacholder, Ben Zion 43, 59, 200, 231
Waerzeggers, Caroline 258, 279
Walls, Jerry L. 471–72, 496, 500
Wassén, Cecilia 5, 29, 42, 58, 111–12, 115, 117, 120, 125, 127–28, 199, 229, 252, 254
Wasserman, Emma 342, 351
Wasserstrom, Steven M. 508, 522, 536
Webb, Robert L. 167, 196
Weigold, Matthias 153, 156, 210, 228, 245, 247, 254, 342, 351
Weiss, Johannes 62
Welker, Michael 387, 402
Werman, Cana 138, 142, 433, 469
Wessinger, Catherine 472, 483, 500–1
Whalley, George 70, 80
Whitters, Mark 258, 280
Wickersham, John M. 218, 231
Widengren, Geo 264, 266, 278, 280
Wilcox, Max E. 233, 253
Williams, Catrin H. 77, 83, 92, 110
Williams, Michael A. 504, 512, 524, 536
Wills, Lawrence M. 151, 156, 162, 196
Wilson, Gerald H. 322, 328
Wilson, R. McL. 68, 83, 479, 500, 514, 534
Winston, David 266, 280
Winter, Irene J. 282, 284, 295
Wintermude, O. S. 461, 469, 476, 501
Wirtz, Kristina 398, 402
Wise, Michael O. 43, 59, 236, 240, 247–48, 256
Wisse, Frederick 512, 536
Wittgenstein, Ludwig 118, 168
Wold, Benjamin 406, 427
Wolfson, Eliot 504, 508, 510–11, 517, 522, 525–28, 536
Wolter, Michael 123, 128

Woodman, Simon Patrick   410, 419, 424, 427
Worley, John   491, 501
Woude, A. S. van der   48, 57
Wright, Benjamin G., III   151, 156, 161–62, 196
Wright, G. Ernest   8, 30, 64, 82, 85, 110, 167, 196
Wyer, Robert S., Jr.   299, 325
Xeravits, Géza G.   117, 128, 267, 277
Yadin, Yigael   200, 231
Yarbro Collins, Adela   4, 31, 50, 59, 158, 192, 397, 402, 405, 420–21, 423, 427, 444, 469, 471–73, 501
Yardeni, Ada   209, 230, 269, 278
Yuditsky, Alexey (Eliyahu)   135, 140
Zacks, Jeffrey M.   327
Zahn, Molly M.   145, 156, 351
Zang, Xiaowei   333, 355
Zenger, Erich   149, 156
Zunshine, Lisa   307, 315, 327–28
Zurawski, Jason   115, 126, 201, 228

Printed in the USA
CPSIA information can be obtained
at www.ICGtesting.com
JSHW021935181223
53907JS00010B/10